P9-APW-237

THE

CHALLENGE

OF

PSYCHOLOGY

THE
CHALLENGE
OF
PSYCHOLOGY

edited by

RICHARD GREENBAUM

John Jay College of Criminal Justice
City University of New York

and

HARVEY A. TILKER

San Diego State College

Prentice-Hall, Inc., Englewood Cliffs, New Jersey

ISBN: 0-13-125120-1

Library of Congress Catalog Card Number: 79-149977

Printed in the United States of America

10 9 8 7 6 5 4 3 2 1

Prentice-Hall International, Inc., *London*
Prentice-Hall of Australia, Pty. Ltd., *Sydney*
Prentice-Hall of Canada, Ltd., *Toronto*
Prentice-Hall of India Private Limited, *New Delhi*
Prentice-Hall of Japan, Inc., *Tokyo*

ELLEN SILVER

for caring

and

DICK ROE

for encouragement

PREFACE

No being in nature is more curious than man. From the time when rational thought first emerged in the course of pre-history men have continued to wonder about themselves: their origins, their feelings, their behavior, their very nature. While such speculations can be found in the most ancient writings of virtually every cultural tradition it was not until the fourth century B.C. in Athens that the philosopher, Aristotle, laid the foundations of formal psychology in his treatise *On the Soul*. The word "psychology" (which Aristotle himself did not use) derives from the Greek *psykhe,* meaning "soul" or "spirit" and *logos,* meaning (among other things) "word," "writing," "proposition," or even "thought." Since the fourth century B.C., however, the meaning of "psychology" and the things done in its name have ramified far beyond the furthest imaginings of the Classical Greeks.

Through most of Western history since Aristotle's time psychology was treated as a branch of philosophy and, until relatively recently, those who have written systematically about human nature have accounted themselves primarily philosophers. Their work, stimulating and insightful as much of it was (and still remains) was based almost exclusively on deductive reasoning and personal experience. In a few cases—Saint Augustine of Hippo (354–430), René Descartes (1595–1650) and William James (1842–1910) are famous examples—it was grounded in a close examination of the individual's subjective consciousness, a technique known as introspection. It was only after the middle of the nineteenth century that psychologists, inspired by the advances in the natural sciences won through controlled observation and deliberate experimentation, began to break free of the deductive, philosophical approach and to move toward an inductive and experimental inquiry into actual behavior. But while a model drawn from the natural sciences now dominates the work of most American psychologists, European psychology, especially in its clinical variant, continues to be influenced by philosophical movements such as phenomenology and existentialism. Whether or not the natural sciences—particularly physics—presents the most appropriate or fruitful model for psychology to emulate continues to be a matter of debate within the ranks of psychologists themselves.

Psychology as a science is thus largely a product of the twentieth century Western, especially the American, mind and nowhere else does it enjoy the popularity and influence it has attained in contemporary America. Some writers, such as Ernest Havemann, have maintained that ours is the "Age of Psychology," but if this is perhaps too facile a characterization (the craze for "cocktail party psychoanalyzing" seems to have subsided) it is nonetheless true that preoccupation with psychology and the seeking from it of answers to the problems and even to the meaning of life is stronger and more pervasive in America than elsewhere. Such extreme demands are surely unrealistic (albeit sometimes encouraged by overzealous psychologists themselves) and those who press them risk overlooking or undervaluing the more limited contributions that psychology can make both to human self-understanding and to social policy. Yet, as we contemplate the growing interdependence among people in industrial societies, the anxiety and confusion consequent on rapid technological and social change, and the ever greater destructive potential of behavioral aberrations, the insistent demands on psychology for enlightenment and guidance are at least understandable.

What makes the study of psychology at once so fascinating and so important is precisely that it does not deal with ethically neutral or socially irrelevant sub-atomic particles, schools of flatworms, or colonies of white rats but with the perceptions, the emotions, the motives and, ultimately, the behavior of individual human beings in all their mental and moral complexity. Narcissistic though it may be, little so captivates man's imagination as the study of himself, a study that now appears more essential than ever.

The aim of investigating the complexities of human behavior is to be able to formulate valid general propositions (or "laws") describing the relationship among relevant independent and dependent variables, how and under what conditions they interrelate and, at least in a proximate sense, why they are so related. On the foundation of such knowledge "we" hope that we will be able to predict behavior more accurately and, as a corollary, to control it more effectively. Yet, the very possibility of consciously controlling human behavior (through psychological or other means) raises the most serious ethical and political questions regarding who is to use such power and for what purposes. In the laudable quest for increased scientific understanding and given the immense prestige of "science" in the contemporary world it is easy to lose sight of those ethical and political questions. While some of the authors represented in this collection are cognizant of them others are not. Without attempting to propagandize for any particular set of values or any special point of view regarding the uses of scientific knowledge we feel strongly that students of psychology, whether or not they proceed any further than an introduction to the field, should be made aware of the ethical and political implications of psychology's findings and of the likelihood that, in their role as citizens, they will be called upon to make moral decisions regarding the use of those findings.

Given the aims of psychology and the widespread attention it already commands, a book such as this would ordinarily require no special justification. But, as there is already a plethora of such anthologies vying for the attention (and the money) of both instructors and students it may be appropriate to answer the question: "Why still another?"

We have, in the first instance, *not* tried to provide a comprehensive overview of *all* the problems, approaches, theories, and important findings in contemporary psychology. Such an enterprise is more appropriately left to a textbook, many of which have undertaken it—with varying results. Rather, these readings represent our conviction that the ultimate vindication of psychology is what it can contribute to the understanding of *human* life, the illumination and amelioration (if not the solution) of *human* problems. Psychology, in other words, must focus its attention on the study of *human* behavior.

Our emphases on the social, clinical, and even applied aspects of the field follow logically from this conviction and we have included accounts of experimental work only when it has clear and significant implications for human behavior and human concerns. Psychology has developed primarily as an academic discipline pursuing disinterested knowledge and so, in large part, it remains. But it is more than *just* an academic discipline and its knowledge is potentially far too important to be confined within an academic cloister. That knowledge must be made relevant to life-as-it-is-lived lest its pursuit degenerate into little more than a narcotizing self-indulgence. There can be no virginal science unsullied by the demands and desires of everyday life— surely the history of the past few decades should have taught us that—and what can be said of science in general is all the more true in the case of social or behavioral science.

We believe that the readings we have collected in this volume both reflect and sustain our conception of the field; we further believe that they are intrinsically interesting and will effectively engage the interest and stimulate the curiosity of those coming to psychology for the first time. Only out of such involvement can insight emerge and learning take place. Because dullness is a sin both deadly and unnecessary we have tried to choose selections that are absorbing and well-written; because humor and lightheartedness are not incompatible with effective learning we have occasionally turned to the ancient modes of satire and parody to make a cogent point or to puncture pretentious pomposity.

For understandable historical and cultural reasons American psychology, over the past half century, has concerned itself less and less with the phenomenon of "consciousness" (or subjective experience) and more and more with the observation and analysis of "behavior." "Behavior"—what the observer of an acting organism can see, record, and measure—often under closely controlled laboratory conditions and with the aid of sensitive instruments—alone seems to meet the requirements for scientific data: to be unambiguous, publicly verifiable, and free (or almost free) of the dreaded taint of subjectivity.

This approach has led to much valuable work (some examples of which are reprinted below), yet we should be aware that behavior as such, especially when isolated from its usual occasion and meaningful context, is by no means unambiguous in its import, that there exists a realm of phenomenological "experience" to which "behavior" is an inadequate index. Superficially identical behaviors may have radically different meanings to different actors even under the very same conditions. No introduction to psychology can be held adequate that does not at least make clear the real distinction between "behavior" and "experience" or "consciousness" (see selection 4 below, among others) and the need to understand behavior subjectively, from the viewpoint of the *actor,* not of the observer nor of the statistician. Because the realm of subjective experience has for millennia been the province of poets and novelists we have included a number of literary selections that try to convey to the reader something of the texture and feel of those realities that lie behind some of the categories both of "normal" life and of psychopathology.

Finally, we are convinced that if the study of psychology is to have meaning to the student it must be relevant (to use that now much overworked word) to the ongoing concerns of his own life as he lives it. Partly for this reason we have dealt, in this book, with such currently controversial topics as the effects of psychedelic drugs on consciousness and behavior and the role of "instinct," more particularly the "instinct" of aggression, in human behavior. We hope that all these readings will raise questions in the minds of students, questions about their feelings, their motives, their actions, and their world, questions which they might otherwise never have asked so clearly, if at all. For the essence of education is less the answering of questions than their asking, less the shutting of doors than their opening. We trust that confrontation with the challenging and disconcerting realities that often lie beyond those opening doors will prove a healthy and, in the best sense, an educating experience.

R. G.

New York, N. Y.

ACKNOWLEDGMENTS

By now it is a threadbare platitude that no book is the work solely of him whose name it bears. But platitude or no it is true and all the more so of an anthology such as this. We are acutely sensible of what we owe to others and we wish, most importantly, to thank all those publishers and authors, museums and collectors, who have generously allowed us to reprint and reproduce the materials contained in this volume.

We wish further to thank all those colleagues who commented, some anonymously and some not, on the original idea for this anthology and who constructively criticized it in the various stages of its development, most especially Dr. Walter Mink of Macalester College. We are grateful for all their many comments and suggestions, even for those we ultimately rejected.

The senior editor, in particular, wishes to thank DeDe Newman for her careful typing of the manuscripts of the section introductions and Stephen Calvert and Andria M. Barzilay for their efficient handling of the tedious but essential permissions correspondence.

Finally, but certainly not of the least importance, we want to thank our editors—Edward Lugenbeel and Helen S. Harris—and the staff of Prentice-Hall for their assistance and encouragement and their painstaking attention to all the myriad details that were involved in producing this book. Indeed, "What a piece of work is a book!"

R. G.
H. A. T.

CONTENTS

PART I

PSYCHOLOGY AS AN INTELLECTUAL ENTERPRISE   1

1. Unity in Psychology, *Geoffrey Leytham*, 7

2. Why Organisms Behave, *B. F. Skinner*, 11

3. Persons and Experience, *R. D. Laing*, 19

4. Two Models of Man, *William D. Hitt*, 23

PART II

THE BEHAVING-EXPERIENCING ORGANISM   33

5. How the Machine Called the Brain Feels and Thinks, *Dean E. Wooldridge*, 36

6. The Happiest Creatures on Earth? *Ruth and Edward Brecher*, 41

7. The Mammal and His Environment, *D. O. Hebb*, 47

8. In Quest of Dreaming, *Frederick Snyder*, 53

PART III

GROWTH AND DEVELOPMENT OF THE ORGANISM   61

9. The Nature of Love, *Harry Harlow*, 66

10. The Wild Boy of Aveyron, *Jean-Marc-Gaspard Itard*, 75

11. Why Some 3-Year Old's Get A's—And Some Get C's, *Maya Pines*, 78

12. My Oedipus Complex, *Frank O'Connor*, 87

13. The Children of the Dream: Their Mold and Ours,
Bruno Bettelheim, 93

PART IV
LEARNING   101

14. Operant Behavior, *B. F. Skinner,* 105

15. Learning Theory, *James V. McConnell,* 109

16. The Misbehavior of Organisms, *Keller and Marian Breland,* 116

17. The Chemistry of Learning, *David Krech,* 120

18. What Do We Know About Learning? *Goodwin Watson,* 125

19. The Ultimate Teaching Machine, *R. J. Heathorn,* 129

PART V
PERCEPTION AND ITS VICISSITUDES   133

20. The Involuntary Bet, *William H. Ittelson,* 137

21. Perceptual Changes in Sensory Deprivation: Suggestions for a Cognitive
Theory, *Sanford J. Freedman,* 141

22. Verbal Stereotypes and Racial Prejudice, *Daniel Katz and
Kenneth W. Braly,* 145

23. They Saw A Game: A Case Study, *Albert Hastorf
and Hadley Cantril,* 151

24. They Split My Personality *or* 'I Go Off My Rocker,'
Harry Asher, 157

PART VI
LANGUAGE AND COMMUNICATION   165

25. Science and Linguistics, *Benjamin Lee Whorf,* 168

26. How To Read Body Language, *Flora Davis,* 175

27. Toward A Theory of Non-Verbal Communication, *Jurgen
Ruesch and Weldon Kees,* 182

28. What Is Being Communicated? *An Exercise in Non-Verbal
Communication,* 186

PART VII
THE MOTIVATION OF BEHAVIOR   193

29. Motivation Reconsidered: The Concept of Competence,
Robert W. White, 198

A. Sex and Its Varieties   209

30. Human Sexual Behavior in Perspective, *Clellan S. Ford and Frank A. Beach,* 209

31. Immediate Situational Factors in Human Sexual Response, *Paul H. Gebhard,* 216

32. What Is Normal? *Wardell Pomeroy,* 219

33. The Adjustment of the Male Overt Homosexual, *Evelyn Hooker,* 223

B. Is Man A Killer By Nature?   235

34. The Nature and Functions of Aggression, *Konrad Lorenz,* 236

35. Is Aggression An Instinct? *Anthony Storr,* 241

36. War Is Not in Our Genes, *Sally Carrighar,* 246

37. Biology and Human Aggression, *J. P. Scott,* 253

PART VIII
PSYCHOLOGICAL TESTING: WHAT AND HOW?   261

38. Negro-White Differences in Intelligence Test Performance: A New Look at an Old Problem, *Otto Klineberg,* 267

39. Psychometric Scientism, *Banesh Hoffmann,* 273

40. The Human Uses of Personality Tests: A Dissenting View, *Victor R. Lovell,* 281

PART IX
PERSONALITY AND THE SELF   295

41. The Psychic Apparatus, *Sigmund Freud,* 301

42. The Marketing Orientation, *Erich Fromm,* 305

43. The Self *Gordon W. Allport,* 309

44. The Alienated Self, *Kenneth Keniston,* 316

45. The Outsider, *Albert Camus,* 323

46. Toward A Psychology of Health, *A. H. Maslow,* 325

PART X
THE BREAKDOWN OF BEHAVIOR: PROBLEMS IN LIVING   331

47. The Myth of Mental Illness, *Thomas S. Szasz,* 336

48. The Gambler, *Fyodor Dostoyevsky,* 342

49. Ward No. 6, *Anton Chekhov*, 349

50. The Death of Ivan Ilyich, *Lëv Tolstoy*, 352

PART XI
TO MAKE MEN WHOLE AGAIN : THE TASK OF THERAPY   *363*

51. The Psychotherapeutic Experience, *R. D. Laing*, 371

52. Alternatives to Analysis, *Ernest Havemann*, 375

53. Mental Health's Third Revolution, *Nicholas Hobbs*, 386

PART XII
DRUGS AND DRUG USE: DAMNATION OR SALVATION?   *397*

54. Ours Is The Addicted Society, *Leslie Farber*, 404

55. Heads and Seekers: Drugs on Campus, Counter-Cultures and American Society, *Kenneth Keniston*, 410

56. How to Change Behavior, *Timothy Leary*, 423

57. Mescaline, LSD, Psilocybin and Personality Change, *Sanford M. Unger*, 431

PART XIII
PSYCHOLOGY IN THE WIDER WORLD   *441*

58. Effects of Group Pressure Upon the Modification and Distortion of Judgments, *S. E. Asch*, 448

59. If Hitler Asked You to Electrocute A Stranger, Would You? *Philip Meyer*, 457

60. The Psychology of Toleration, *J. C. Flugel*, 465

61. The Mob and The Ghost, *Lillian Smith*, 469

62. The Anatomy of Violence, *Hans Toch*, 474

63. Psychological Alternatives to War, *Morton Deutsch*, 479

64. The Psychological Effects of the Draft, *American Friends Service Committee*, 490

65. Behavior Control and Social Responsibility, *Leonard Krasner*, 498

THE

CHALLENGE

OF

PSYCHOLOGY

PART I

PSYCHOLOGY

AS

AN INTELLECTUAL ENTERPRISE

What exactly is psychology? The question seems deceptively simple but in fact it is far easier to talk about what psychologists *do* than to define what psychology *is*. Is psychology a science; if so, what sort of science; or is it more akin to an art? Should the primary aim of psychologists be to discover truth in the abstract or to solve specific problems? These issues, like many others in contemporary psychology, are in dispute even among psychologists themselves.

There are today some 30,000 people in the United States who call themselves psychologists. Many of them, perhaps more than half, teach in colleges and universities and do academic research but many are self-employed as therapists and consultants or do applied work in government, industry, advertising, and the communications media. While it is impossible to explore all these activities in depth it will be useful, by way of introduction to the field, to discuss briefly the most important competing intellectual and practical orientations within contemporary psychology.

Historically, the deepest and most significant division in American psychology—a division that even today shows but few signs of reconciliation—has been between those who call themselves "experimentalists" (sometimes "behaviorists") and those who call themselves "clinicians" although, since the 1950s, a third group calling themselves "humanistic" psychologists has further divided the field. The causes of this division as well as its persistence can be traced to the differing origins of the various branches of psychology, differing conceptions of the goals of psychology, and differing models of what constitutes a science.

Experimental psychology as it developed in late nineteenth-century Europe under the leadership of men such as Gustav Fechner and Wilhelm Wundt was influenced primarily by the experimental methods of the natural sciences and took as its goal the discovery of facts and relationships ("truth") and the formulation of those facts and relationships into universally valid "laws." Given this goal, itself derived from natural sciences such as physics and chemistry, experimental psychologists have concerned themselves overwhelmingly with the observation and analysis of "behavior." Because behavior can be produced by external stimuli, observed, recorded, measured, and often manipulated it lends itself to quantification, which, from the point of view of the experimentalists, is a prerequisite to the formulation of accurate laws and a defining characteristic of science. This attitude is a very old one: As far back as the mid-seventeenth century Descartes asserted that science has nothing to do with "Whatever depends on experience alone." Because of ethical, economic, and other practical considerations, most experimental research has been done on lower animals (especially white rats) rather than on human subjects, thus raising the question of how much light the results of such research can cast on problems of human behavior. To this question we will return later

Clinical psychology, on the other hand, developed somewhat later than the experimental variety (Freud published his first clinical papers in 1895 while Wundt had established the first experimental laboratory at Leipzig in 1879) and under the influence of medical psychiatry and neurology rather than physics and chemistry. Freud himself was a neurologist by training and most of the early psychoanalysts came to that specialty by way of medicine. (Today all psychiatrists and most psychoanalysts are M.D.'s, while the clinical psychologist or psychotherapist usually has a Ph.D. in clinical or social psychology.) The founders of clinical psychology were more interested in helping seriously disturbed and unhappy people than in discovering abstract truth or formulating general laws of human behavior. Such generalizations or theories as they did develop (such as Freud's) were the result of work with patients (combined, no doubt, with a fondness for theorizing) rather than of controlled laboratory experiments. Unlike the experimentalists, clinicians have tended to accept as "real" (at least in its consequences) an entire realm of feelings and subjective experience or consciousness not available to direct observation or measurement by others. While a clinician has the advantage of dealing with whole people rather than with isolated fragments of behavior he necessarily sacrifices the precision of the experimentalist, the latter's ability to control all or most of the variables that affect the outcome of his experiments. Additionally, the clinician risks the distortion of his observations and interpretations through the interference of his own personality and its necessarily idiosyncratic responses. On the whole, however, clinicians have been less concerned with their status as scientists than have experimentalists. As we will see in Part XI the movement called behavior therapy, which has blossomed since 1960, represents an attempt—the only significant one thus far—to apply the findings and techniques of experimental psychology to the solution of human "problems in living."

The humanistic orientation, the last of the major divisions within contemporary American psychology, developed in the 1950s as a reaction against both the behaviorist and the classical psychoanalytic approaches. Humanistic psychology retains the latter's focus on the person but rejects its emphasis on psychopathology and the darker, more destructive aspects of human personality in favor of stressing the autonomy of the individual and his potentialities for growth, creativity, responsibility, becoming, "self-actualization," and "peak experiences." More philosophic in its outlook than the other orientations, humanistic psychology has been influenced both by contemporary European existential philosophy and existential psychoanalysis. Professor Maslow's selection in Part IX well represents the humanistic point of view (Maslow was one of the founders of the movement) while Robert White's views on motivation (Selection 29) are consistent with the humanistic orientation. Humanistic psychologists are still a numerically small group within American psychology but their influence is already apparent in the Human Potential Movement and in many of the newer forms of psychotherapy.

We can also look at psychology in terms of a division between "pure" and "applied" orientations, a distinction which overlaps that between experimentalists and clinicians without being identical with it. The pure psychologist (usually an experimentalist) is interested primarily in the discovery of knowledge regarding human behavior—its causes, interrelations and consequences—for its own sake, while the applied psychologist is interested primarily in how existing knowledge can be used to solve problems facing individuals, organizations, or even entire societies. From the standpoint of this distinction most clinicians and virtually all psychologists working for government, industry, and business are applied practitioners. To the degree that the solving of problems involves changing or manipulating the behavior of individuals the ethical and political dilemmas of scientific knowledge and its uses, to which we alluded in the Preface, are most acute for the applied psychologist. The recent emergence of the behavior therapy movement into prominence (see Part XI) suggests, however, that the distinction between experimentalists (the pure) and clinicians (the applied) may shortly have to be abandoned.

Cutting across the categories we have already discussed and applicable within each of them is the distinction between a developmental and an interactive (or transactional) point of view. This distinction refers to whether a psychologist believes that whatever behavior or experience he is examining has a history in terms of which it must be comprehended or whether he believes it can be understood solely as a function of whatever constellation of factors was operating at the time of or immediately preceding the behavior in question. Adherence to one or the other of these points of view can have important effects on a psychologist's practical work; it underlies, for example, some of the most important differences between psychoanalytic and behavior therapies (see Part XI).

But is psychology a science? If we consider the great prestige of science and of scientists in the contemporary world and the tangible rewards that accrue to the latter it is not surprising that those who study human behavior, most notably psychologists and sociologists, have been anxious to draw the mantle of science (whether they call it "social" or "behavioral") over their own work. Much energy has been spent in arguing whether behavioral science is "really" scientific but the answer to that question necessarily rests on how one defines "science." As we suggested above, many of the differences between the work and the self-images of experimentalists and clinicians can be traced to the differing goals and models of science that inform their work.

If one considers science to be defined by a given set of techniques, as dealing only with precisely measurable quantities, and as leading necessarily to the formulation of laws from which highly specific and accurate predictions can be made then, of all the branches of psychology, only the experimental can lay legitimate claim to being truly scientific. Yet, all too often, the experimentalist's precision and predictive accuracy are purchased at the price of substantive triviality, albeit such a result is not inherent in the experimental method as such.

If, on the other hand, one believes that science is not so much a set of results as a set of attitudes and procedures that seeks ever more precise answers to ever more precise questions, that subjects all hypotheses to the test of fact, that considers all answers provisional and none final, that adapts its methods to the nature of its material, and that asks for no more precise answers than the problems before it demand, then all branches of psychology, rigorously pursued, may have equal claim to the dignity of science. Which is not to deny that one branch of the field may have progressed further along the path to its goal than others. From this perspective the controversy over whether or not psychology is "really" a science is a sterile and misleading one, a fight over words and labels, not over substance. The ultimate significance of psychology will lie not in whether or not it is a "science," but in whether psychologists will be able to find adequate and sufficient answers to the questions they themselves ask and that are asked of them by others.

In the first selection of the book Geoffrey Leytham of the University of Liverpool, England reviews some of the high points in the comparatively short history of psychology, experimental and clinical, human and animal. He notes that contemporary psychologists are far more interested in techniques and applications than in all-encompassing theories and he further suggests that a new synthesis based on the model of the "individual" may now be in the making.

In the second selection B.F. Skinner of Harvard University presents a classic statement of the behaviorist or positivist position. Science, he believes, must be concerned with the causes of human behavior and, after analyzing the concept of causality, he concludes that causes must be external to the acting organism (a basic postulate of what is known as psychophysics). To be scientifically usable data must be observable (by instruments if not necessarily by unaided human sense organs) and measurable; Skinner then reviews the major sources of such data. The conception of science undergirding his discussion is, as mentioned above, derived ultimately from the philosophy of Descartes and the methods that have proved so fruitful in physics and chemistry. Whether such methods will be comparably fruitful in psychology still remains, in the absence of a general theory of human behavior, to be determined.

In sharp contrast to Skinner's position is that of Ronald Laing, a British clinician with extensive experience in the treatment of schizophrenics and other seriously disturbed persons. From a humanistic and philosophic point of view Laing argues for a science of *persons* and challenges the traditional dichotomy between behavior and experience (or consciousness). Experience may be defined as the meaning attributed by the acting organism itself to stimuli (both internal and external) and to overt behavior. For Laing, there are only different modalities of experience, all of which center in and on the person, while behavior itself may be seen as a function of experience. Laing's chief interest lies in the "interbehavior" or "interexperience" between living, acting individuals and he makes a clear distinction between natural and behavioral science. If science is, as he claims, "a form of knowledge adequate to its subject," the reader might ask himself whether Laing's or Skinner's position holds the greater promise for the future development of psychology. The answer to this question cannot itself be a scientific one because it will depend ultimately on a nonrational value choice of what psychology's goals "ought" to be.

Finally, William Hitt of the Battelle Memorial Institute characterizes the fundamental conflict within American psychology as that between behaviorism and phenomenology (or existential psychology). Each of these philosophical positions connotes a particular model of man's essence as well as appropriate methods of studying it. Hitt presents the two models in terms of ten important philosophical and methodological contrasts. He maintains that each model apprehends part of the truth about man, that the two have divergent implications for practical action and public policy, and that the utility of each may vary depending on the problem under study. But he concludes that no single model can exhaust all the reality that is man, a conclusion that suggests Sophokles' assertion in *Antigone* (ca. 440 B.C.) that "Many are the world's wonders/But none more wondrous than man."

1. UNITY IN PSYCHOLOGY

Geoffrey Leytham

What has been the most important contribution to psychology in the last ten years? I have asked this question of several of my colleagues, and have had a wide range of replies. I would like to mention two which demonstrate clearly how difficult it is to think of psychology as a single subject. On the one hand, there was a British psychiatrist. He voted for the introduction of drugs in the treatment of mental illness as the biggest recent advance in psychological medicine. An American professor of psychology was much more hesitant in answering. He finally opted for the technique for measuring the pressure applied to a lever by a rat in a Skinner-box, which is a small cage named after its American constructor, Professor Skinner of Harvard University, in which the hungry animal has to learn to press a bar to obtain a pellet of food. How hard the rat presses is obviously of interest in these experiments.

I would agree that the question I asked was an unfair one. Nobody can assess the worth of a contribution so soon after it has been made. We realize now that Mendel's experiments into the heredity of peas in the eighteen-seventies formed the basis of the new science of genetics, which only came into being after 1900 when Mendel's work was rediscovered. A particular contribution to any science can only be assessed against the backdrop of history, when it can be put into perspective. I would like here to consider the history of psychology and the point I think it has now reached in its development as a science; and then to suggest a framework within which fresh contributions can be related and assessed.

PROGRESS OF A SCIENCE

The history of psychology is comparatively short, when it is considered in terms of the long past that led to its emergence as a separate science. I cannot hope to give a full survey of even such a brief history, and so I will make a quick selection of dates and events to indicate what seem to me to be the main trends. As Dingle has pointed out, the logical progress of a science is not the same as its historical development; the logical progress is like an ascending straight line, about which historical development oscillates, wandering from side to side. The points on the straight line where the curve crosses it are usually new syntheses or generative ideas, which act as a new higher-level thesis, and induce their opposites or antitheses. These proliferate to the next peak of the curve, and masses of facts are accumulated. At this stage the ideas lose their force, and a stress on techniques guides research. The two lines now converge, and a new synthesis appears as the historical curve once more crosses the line of logical progression.

Let us apply these notions now to the development and growth of psychology. Its long past need not concern us here: men have always been interested in each other as well as in the universe around them, and theories about the nature of man have been as plentiful as those about the nature of the cosmos. If we take 1860 as the starting point of our curve we shall not be too far out: several things happened around that time which not only led to the emergence of psychology as a science but very much influenced its subsequent development—and, I may say, the influence is still very much alive.

Philosophy and physiology are usually regarded as the parents of psychology, and we can see them starting to come together in the work of the British philosopher Bain. The first part of his two-volume treatise was published in 1855. It was called *The Senses and the Intellect,* and the second instalment appeared in 1859 under the title *The Emotions and the Will.* Bain's work was based largely on the philosophy of associationism, but it also included references to the work then being done in physiology. But the problems of psychology —especially if it were to be empirically based and not just speculative—were rather different from those of physiology. The biggest problem was how to measure mental events. Fittingly enough, the answer came from a one-time professor of physics at Leipzig, Fechner by name, as he lay philosophizing on his bed on the morning of October 22, 1850. Fechner was more interested in philosophy than physics at that time, and he was searching for a scientific foundation for his view that consciousness was in everything as well as in everybody. He hit upon a way of relating mental events, or sensations, with physical events, or environmental stimuli, and wrote these methods up in the *Elements of Psychophysics,* which was published in 1860. Unfortunately for Fechner, his philosophy was almost ignored; but fortunately for psychology, his psychophysical methods were taken up. Without them, Wundt could hardly have founded the first psychological laboratory, less than twenty years later, at Leipzig. So the science of psychology was—officially— born on the Continent by the founding of Wundt's laboratory, but its growth in Britain and America was profoundly influenced by the publication in 1859 of Charles Darwin's *The Origin of Species.*

MEDICAL AND EDUCATIONAL DEVELOPMENTS

Wundt's laboratory was for the study of the generalized, normal, adult, human mind, but what about individual differences? In the light of evolutionary theory this became an important problem, as only the fittest survived. And what about animals? What about the abnormal, adult, human mind, and the normal child's mind? Questions like these led to the development of medical and educational psychology. Before long certain psychologists

were objecting to 'minds' of any sort: psychology had already lost its 'soul'; soon it was to be out of its 'mind' also.

We can take the initial point as which the historical curve crosses the logical line at about 1886. The first laboratory had then been going for seven years, and the independence of the new science was fittingly marked by an article on psychology in the ninth edition of the *Encyclopaedia Britannica.* In the previous edition, psychology had been included under metaphysics, but now it rated a section to itself. The author was James Ward, then lecturer in philosophy at Cambridge, and although he paid tribute to Wundt and the physiologists, his approach was primarily philosophical. While it is true that Wundt was influenced by the British philosophical traditions of associationism and empiricism, the research in his laboratory drew its inspiration from Fechner, and from the sensory physiologists such as Helmholtz. Subjects taking part in Wundt's experiments were specially trained to analyse their own introspections into their component parts. In this way they studied the structure of the mind or states of consciousness. Wundt conceived of the mind as a mass of identifiable sensations—an approach which came to be known as 'structuralism', and which provided the necessary thesis to stimulate the rapid growth of the infant science.

PSYCHIATRIC CLASSIFICATION

The various antitheses which arose as a protest against different aspects of this foundation school swept psychology into a creative phase. Before leaving the Leipzig laboratory, we should note one other development: the coming together of medical and experimental psychology through the work of Kraepelin, a psychiatrist and one of Wundt's students. Kraepelin was the first person to introduce some order into psychiatric classification. Ever since the end of the eighteenth century, when the idea of demonic possession went out of fashion and the mentally ill were literally relieved of their chains, the problem which had engrossed psychiatrists had been the cataloguing of all the different forms of insanity—or psychosis as we would now call it. Kraepelin's study of the different sensory and motor responses of his patients did much to clarify the picture. He established two of the better known categories—manic-depression and *dementia praecox**—but he listed several other varieties as well.

By this time, the idea of the association of mind and brain was well established. It was the logical descendant of Hippocrates' four humours and the correlation of constitution with temperament, and it has led in turn to the more modern forms of physical treatment, be they electrical, surgical, or pharmacological. But Kraepelin had not these techniques at his disposal, so, although he could diagnose more effectively, he could not prescribe any new treatment. It was Sigmund Freud who provided a more positive approach to psychotherapy. Freud and Kraepelin were exact contemporaries, but in comparing their work we must keep in mind two important and related points: one, that Kraepelin was mainly concerned with psychotics and Freud with neurotics; and the other, that Kraepelin was immersed in the tradition of psychiatry, while Freud took his departure from neurology.

FREUD'S APPRENTICESHIP

It was in Charcot's famous neurological clinic in Paris, where hysterical patients were treated by hypnosis, that Freud served his apprenticeship. He set up private practice in Vienna in 1886, and later abandoned hypnosis in favour of free association in the treatment of neurotic patients. The publication of *The Interpretation of Dreams* in 1900 brought the psycho-analytical method to the notice of others, and Freud gathered disciples—Adler and Jung among them.

The historical curve was rising fast. It turned during the nineteen-tens when schools of psychology were in full flood. First Adler and then Jung broke away from Freud, to form their own groups of 'individual' and 'analytical' psychology; Binet in Paris had introduced intelligence tests for the assessment of individual children; Spearman in London was working on the mathematical approach to ability, using Galton's correlation techniques; McDougall had written a purposive social psychology based on instincts; Watson in America had dismissed the structuralist

---

* Literally "early dementia (madness)," now generally referred to as "schizophrenia." (Eds.) See Part X.

methods and launched his 'behaviourism'. James had supported 'functionalism' which stressed what the mind did rather than what it was composed of; and in Germany the 'Gestalt' movement under the leadership of Wertheimer was arguing that what we perceive is a patterned whole, and is more than the sum of sensations—may, in fact, be different from them. Psychology had come a long way in twenty-five years, but there were now so many antitheses to structuralism, that it was difficult to know what it all added up to, and the various proponents were so busy forwarding their own case that few had the time or inclination to step back and look at the whole—not even the Gestaltists.

But there were one or two who tried to synthesize some of these different approaches, and to formulate new theses. If we regard ourselves as back on course again in the nineteen-thirties, it will be largely due to the work of people such as Tolman, at the University of California. Tolman fused behaviourism and Gestalt, and showed that rather than having the worst of two worlds—the philosophical and physiological—it was possible to have the best of one psychological world. He did this by taking philosophical concepts such as 'purpose' and identifying them with behaviour, such as the persistent seeking of a goal by a rat in a maze. Another thesis was put forward by Bartlett at Cambridge. In his classic book called *Remembering,* he showed that memory did not necessarily lead to a mere reproduction of the original, but was a dynamic process involving change. Or there was the work of Murray and his colleagues in their clinic at Harvard. They had been testing psycho-analytical concepts by assessing the personalities of several students over a period of time. Their findings were published in 1938 in a book called *Explorations in Personality.*

TECHNIQUES RATHER THAN THEORIES

But nowadays theories have lost their force and techniques have taken their place. The psychiatrist's drugs and the psychologist's Skinner-box reflect the contemporary mood. There has been a tremendous expansion in applied psychology. The war brought psychiatrists and clinical psychologists together as never before, and the work of Eysenck in this* country is one example of its effects. It has also led to the introduction into clinics of methods devised in psychological laboratories. Behaviour therapy joins the psychiatrist's physical treatments and the analyst's psychological methods. In spite of some outward appearances of conflicts, there are definite trends towards unity in psychology, and many of the blanks are now being filled in. Human development is now being considered at all age levels. Instead of confining themselves to children and adolescents, psychologists are now publishing such things as the recent studies of mature people. These have thrown much light on the process of psychological growth—and they would earn my vote as the most significant work of the last ten years. Clinical concepts are being brought into the laboratory, and words such as 'love,' previously unheard of in academic psychological circles, are now acceptable as the basis for research. We have definitely turned the corner, and if our interpretation of the history of psychology has any predictive value, we should be crossing the line again some time in the nineteen-seventies.

But how can this new synthesis be brought about when so many different and apparently unrelated approaches are still actively pursued? It seems to me that what psychology lacks is a comprehensive conceptual framework, a whole or a unit of study. Physics has its atoms, chemistry its molecules, biology its cells, sociology its groups, and anthropology its societies, but so far there has been no agreed unit for the science of psychology. The most obvious possibility is the individual. The organism is too biological, and the person excludes animals. But if a model of the individual is to serve our purpose it will have to cover the whole range of behaviour, from the lowliest animal to the most developed and mature human being. In other words, it must comprehend all the subject-matter of the various schools and approaches that I have mentioned: animals, children, neurotics, psychotics, normal adults, and mature people, with reference to their learning, thinking, perception, emotions, motivation, and so on.

A MODEL OF THE INDIVIDUAL

I would like to propose a model of the individual, which could satisfy these requirements.

* That is, England. (Eds.)

Its basic structure can be visualized by imagining four concentric circles with a large dot at the centre. This central dot I shall call the nucleus, and the four circles are levels of awareness, developing outwards from the nucleus—the physical, emotional, mental, and intuitive levels. The ego, the perceptual world of immediate experience, can function on any one of these levels of awareness, and so we can symbolize it as another dot travelling in and out of the circular structure. The particular level it operates on at any one time will depend, among other things, upon the stage of development reached by the individual and upon the environmental forces which are acting on the nucleus. The nucleus is both a transformer and a relay station: it transforms all the incoming stimuli from the environment —information on bodily processes, group activities, physical situation, and so on—and relays them to the ego. The ego has choice— that is, we observe it selecting from alternatives—and it can send messages to the nucleus, which are then transformed into action or response. I use the word 'choice' there because the 'will' used by early psychologists has too many philosophical overtones, and the rather mechanistic determinism of 'motivation' does not do justice to the facts.

This model represents dynamic relationships, and so terms such as 'memory' and 'the unconscious' are avoided. Such phenomena would be expressed in terms of the relative availability of material to the ego, as measured by comparative thresholds of arousal.

The model is, of course, a theoretical abstraction, and the proper concern of the research worker or pure scientist, but the laws derived from it can be applied with suitable modifications to particular people in particular situations. The applied psychologists and psychiatrists can also help to improve the model by indicating further aspects of behaviour which it ought to cover.

Will this sort of co-operation ever come to pass? As I have mentioned, psychology is already tending in this direction. For instance, an international symposium on psychotropic drugs was held recently in Milan, and the participants were from the universities, hospitals, and clinics of fourteen different nations. It comes as no surprise to learn that more than one paper read at that conference dealt with the influence of drugs on the lever-pressing activity of rats in a Skinner-box.

2. WHY ORGANISMS BEHAVE

B. F. Skinner

The terms "cause" and "effect" are no longer widely used in science. They have been associated with so many theories of the structure and operation of the universe that they mean more than scientists want to say. The terms which replace them, however, refer to the same factual core. A "cause" becomes a "change in an independent variable" and an "effect" a "change in a dependent variable." The old "cause-and-effect connection" becomes a "functional relation." The new terms do not suggest *how* a cause causes its effect; they merely assert that different events tend to occur together in a certain order. This is important, but it is not crucial. There is no particular danger in using "cause" and "effect" in an informal discussion if we are always ready to substitute their more exact counterparts.

We are concerned, then, with the causes of human behavior. We want to know why men behave as they do. Any condition or event which can be shown to have an effect upon behavior must be taken into account. By discovering and analyzing these causes we can predict behavior; to the extent that we can manipulate them, we can control behavior.

There is a curious inconsistency in the zeal with which the doctrine of personal freedom has been defended, because men have always been fascinated by the search for causes. The spontaneity of human behavior is apparently no more challenging than its "why and wherefore." So strong is the urge to explain behavior that men have been led to anticipate legitimate scientific inquiry and to construct

highly implausible theories of causation. This practice is not unusual in the history of science. The study of any subject begins in the realm of superstition. The fanciful explanation precedes the valid. Astronomy began as astrology; chemistry as alchemy. The field of behavior has had, and still has, its astrologers and alchemists. A long history of prescientific explanation furnishes us with a fantastic array of causes which have no function other than to supply spurious answers to questions which must otherwise go unanswered in the early stages of a science.

SOME POPULAR "CAUSES" OF BEHAVIOR

Any conspicuous event which coincides with human behavior is likely to be seized upon as a cause. The position of the planets at the birth of the individual is an example. Usually astrologers do not try to predict specific actions from such causes, but when they tell us that a man will be impetuous, careless, or thoughtful, we must suppose that specific actions are assumed to be affected. Numerology finds a different set of causes—for example, in the numbers which compose the street address of the individual or in the number of letters in his name. Millions of people turn to these spurious causes every year in their desperate need to understand human behavior and to deal with it effectively.

The predictions of astrologers, numerologists, and the like are usually so vague that they cannot be confirmed or disproved properly. Failures are easily overlooked, while an occasional chance hit is dramatic enough to maintain the behavior of the devotee in considerable strength. Certain valid relations which resemble such superstitions offer spurious support. For example, some characteristics of behavior can be traced to the season in which a man is born (though not to the position of the planets at his birth), as well as to climatic conditions due in part to the position of the earth in the solar system or to events in the sun. Effects of this sort, when properly validated, must not be overlooked. They do not, of course, justify astrology.

Another common practice is to explain behavior in terms of the structure of the individual. The proportions of the body, the shape of the head, the color of the eyes, skin, or hair, the marks on the palms of the hands, and the features of the face have all been said to determine what a man will do. The "jovial fat man," Cassius with his "lean and hungry look," and thousands of other characters or types thoroughly embedded in our language affect our practices in dealing with human behavior. A specific act may never he predicted from physique, but different types of personality imply predispositions to behave in different ways, so that specific acts are presumed to be affected. This practice resembles the mistake we all make when we expect someone who looks like an old acquaintance to behave like him also. When a "type" is once established, it survives in everyday use because the predictions which are made with it, like those of astrology, are vague, and occasional hits may be startling. Spurious support is also offered by many valid relations between behavior and body type. Studies of the physiques of men and women predisposed to different sorts of disorders have from time to time held the attention of students of behavior. The most recent classification of body structure—the somatotyping of W. H. Sheldon—has already been applied to the prediction of temperament and of various forms of delinquency. Valid relations between behavior and body type must, of course, be taken into account in a science of behavior, but these should not be confused with the relations invoked in the uncritical practice of the layman.

Even when a correlation between behavior and body structure is demonstrated, it is not always clear which is the cause of which. Even if it could be shown by proper statistical methods that fat men are especially likely to be jolly, it still would not follow that the physique causes the temperament. Fat people are at a disadvantage in many ways, and they may develop jolly behavior as a special competitive technique. Jolly people may grow fat because they are free of the emotional disturbances which drive other people to overwork or to neglect their diet or their health. Fat people may be jolly because they have been successful in satisfying their needs through excessive eating. Where the feature of physique can be modified, then, we must ask whether the behavior or the feature comes first.

When we find, or think we have found, that conspicuous physical features explain part of a man's behavior, it is tempting to suppose that inconspicuous features explain other parts. This is implied in the assertion that a man shows certain behavior because he was "born that way." To object to this is not to argue that behavior is never determined by hereditary factors. Behavior requires a behaving organism which is the product of a genetic process. Gross differences in the behavior of different species show that the genetic constitution, whether observed in the body structure of the individual or inferred from a genetic history, is important. But the doctrine of "being born that way" has little to do with demonstrated facts. It is usually an appeal to ignorance. "Heredity," as the layman uses the term, is a fictional explanation of the behavior attributed to it.

Even when it can be shown that some aspect of behavior is due to season of birth, gross body type, or genetic constitution, the fact is of limited use. It may help us in predicting behavior, but it is of little value in an experimental analysis or in practical control because such a condition cannot be manipulated after the individual has been conceived. The most that can be said is that the knowledge of the genetic factor may enable us to make better use of other causes. If we know that an individual has certain inherent limitations, we may use our techniques of control more intelligently, but we cannot alter the genetic factor.

The practical deficiencies of programs involving causes of this sort may explain some of the vehemence with which they are commonly debated. Many people study human behavior because they want to do something about it—they want to make men happier, more efficient and productive, less aggressive, and so on. To these people, inherited determiners—as epitomized in various "racial types"—appear to be insurmountable barriers, since they leave no course of action but the slow and doubtful program of eugenics. The evidence for genetic traits is therefore closely scrutinized, and any indication that it is weak or inconsistent is received with enthusiasm. But the practical issue must not be allowed to interfere in determining the extent to which behavioral dispositions are inherited. The matter is not so crucial as is often supposed, for we shall see that there are other types of causes available for those who want quicker results.

INNER "CAUSES"

Every science has at some time or other looked for causes of action inside the things it has studied. Sometimes the practice has proved useful, sometimes it has not. There is nothing wrong with an inner explanation as such, but events which are located inside a system are likely to be difficult to observe. For this reason we are encouraged to assign properties to them without justification. Worse still, we can invent causes of this sort without fear of contradiction. The motion of a rolling stone was once attributed to its *vis viva.** The chemical properties of bodies were thought to be derived from the *principles* or *essences* of which they were composed. Combustion was explained by the *phlogiston* inside the combustible object. Wounds healed and bodies grew well because of a *vis medicatrix.†* It has been especially tempting to attribute the behavior of a living organism to the behavior of an inner agent, as the following examples may suggest.

NEURAL CAUSES

The layman uses the nervous system as a ready explanation of behavior. The English language contains hundreds of expressions which imply such a causal relationship. At the end of a long trial we read that the jury shows signs of *brain fag,* that the *nerves* of the accused are *on edge,* that the wife of the accused is on the verge of a *nervous breakdown,* and that his lawyer is generally thought to have lacked the *brains* needed to stand up to the prosecution. Obviously, no direct observations have been made of the nervous systems of any of these people. Their "brains" and "nerves" have been invented on the spur of

* Life force. (Eds.)
† Healing force. (Eds.)

the moment to lend substance to what might otherwise seem a superficial account of their behavior.

The sciences of neurology and physiology have not divested themselves entirely of a similar practice. Since techniques for observing the electrial and chemical processes in nervous tissue had not yet been developed, early information about the nervous system was limited to its gross anatomy. Neural processes could only be inferred from the behavior which was said to result from them. Such inferences were legitimate enough as scientific theories, but they could not justifiably be used to explain the very behavior upon which they were based. The hypotheses of the early physiologist may have been sounder than those of the layman, but until independent evidence could be obtained, they were no more satisfactory as explanations of behavior. Direct information about many of the chemical and electrical processes in the nervous system is now available. Statements about the nervous system are no longer necessarily inferential or fictional. But there is still a measure of circularity in much physiological explanation, even in the writings of specialists. In World War I a familiar disorder was called "shell shock." Disturbances in behavior were explained by arguing that violent explosions had damaged the structure of the nervous system, though no direct evidence of such damage was available. In World War II the same disorder was classified as "neuropsychiatric." The prefix seems to show a continuing unwillingness to abandon explanations in terms of hypothetical neural damage.

Eventually a science of the nervous system based upon direct observation rather than inference will describe the neural states and events which immediately precede instances of behavior. We shall know the precise neurological conditions which immediately precede, say, the response. "No, thank you." These events in turn will be found to be preceded by other neurological events, and these in turn by others. This series will lead us back to events outside the nervous system and, eventually, outside the organism. In the chapters which follow we shall consider external events of this sort in some detail. We shall then be better able to evaluate the place of neurological explanations of behavior. However, we may note here that we do not have and may never have this sort of neurological information at the moment it is needed in order to predict a specific instance of behavior. It is even more unlikely that we shall be able to alter the nervous system directly in order to set up the antecedent conditions of a particular instance. The causes to be sought in the nervous system are, therefore, of limited usefulness in the prediction and control of specific behavior.

PSYCHIC INNER CAUSES

An even more common practice is to explain behavior in terms of an inner agent which lacks physical dimensions and is called "mental" or "psychic." The purest form of the psychic explanation is seen in the animism of primitive peoples. From the immobility of the body after death it is inferred that a spirit responsible for movement has departed. The *enthusiastic* person is, as the etymology of the word implies, energized by a "god within." It is only a modest refinement to attribute every feature of the behavior of the physical organism to a corresponding feature of the "mind" or of some inner "personality." The inner man is regarded as driving the body very much as the man at the steering wheel drives a car. The inner man wills an action, the outer executes it. The inner loses his appetite, the outer stops eating. The inner man wants and the outer gets. The inner has the impulse which the outer obeys.

It is not the layman alone who resorts to these practices, for many reputable psychologists use a similar dualistic system of explanation. The inner man is sometimes personified clearly, as when delinquent behavior is attributed to a "disordered personality," or he may be dealt with in fragments, as when behavior is attributed to mental processes, faculties and traits. Since the inner man does not occupy space, he may be multiplied at will. It has been argued that a single physical organism is controlled by several psychic agents and that its behavior is the resultant of their several wills. The Freudian concepts of the ego, superego, and id are often used in this way. They are frequently regarded as nonsubstantial creatures, often in violent conflict, whose defeats or victories lead to the adjusted or maladjusted behavior of the physical organism in which they reside.

Direct observation of the mind comparable with the observation of the nervous system has not proved feasible. It is true that many people believe that they observe their "mental states" just as the physiologist observes neural events, but another interpretation of what they observe is possible. Introspective psychology no longer pretends to supply direct information about events which are the causal antecedents, rather than the mere accompaniments, of behavior. It defines its "subjective" events in ways which strip them of any usefulness in a causal analysis. The events appealed to in early mentalistic explanations of behavior have remained beyond the reach of observation. Freud insisted upon this by emphasizing the role of the unconscious—a frank recognition that important mental processes are not directly observable. The Freudian literature supplies many examples of behavior from which unconscious wishes, impulses, instincts, and emotions are inferred. Unconscious thought-processes have also been used to explain intellectual achievements. Though the mathematician may feel that he knows "how he thinks," he is often unable to give a coherent account of the mental processes leading to the solution of a specific problem. But any mental event which is unconscious is necessarily inferential, and the explanation is therefore not based upon independent observations of a valid cause.

The fictional nature of this form of inner cause is shown by the case with which the mental process is discovered to have just the properties needed to account for the behavior. When a professor turns up in the wrong classroom or gives the wrong lecture, it is because his *mind* is, at least for the moment, *absent*. If he forgets to give a reading assignment, it is because it has slipped his *mind* (a hint from the class may *remind* him of it). He begins to tell an old joke but pauses for a moment, and it is evident to everyone that he is trying to make up his *mind* whether or not he has already used the joke that term. His lectures grow more tedious with the years, and questions from the class confuse him more and more, because his *mind* is failing. What he says is often disorganized because his *ideas* are confused. He is occasionally unnecessarily emphatic because of the force of his *ideas*. When he repeats himself, it is because he has an *idée fixe*; and when he repeats what others have said, it is because he borrows his *ideas*. Upon occasion there is nothing in what he says because he lacks *ideas*. In all this it is obvious that the mind and the ideas, together with their special characteristics, are being invented on the spot to provide spurious explanations. A science of behavior can hope to gain very little from so cavalier a practice. Since mental or psychic events are asserted to lack the dimensions of physical science, we have an additional reason for rejecting them.

CONCEPTUAL INNER CAUSES

The commonest inner causes have no specific dimensions at all, either neurological or psychic. When we say that a man eats *because* he is hungry, smokes a great deal *because* he has the tobacco habit, fights *because* of the instinct of pugnacity, behaves brilliantly *because* of his intelligence, or plays the piano well *because* of his musical ability, we seem to be referring to causes. But on analysis these phrases prove to be merely redundant descriptions. A single set of facts is described by the two statements: "He eats" and "He is hungry." A single set of facts is described by the two statements: "He smokes a great deal" and "He has the smoking habit." A single set of facts is described by the two statements: "He plays well" and "He has musical ability." The practice of explaining one statement in terms of the other is dangerous because it suggests that we have found the cause and therefore need search no further. Moreover, such terms as "hunger," "habit," and "intelligence" convert what are essentially the properties of a process or relation into what appear to be things. Thus we are unprepared for the properties eventually to be discovered in the behavior itself and continue to look for something which may not exist.

THE VARIABLES OF WHICH BEHAVIOR IS A FUNCTION

The practice of looking inside the organism for an explanation of behavior has tended to obscure the variables which are immediately available for a scientific analysis. These variables lie outside the organism, in its immediate environment and in its environmental history. They have a physical status to which the usual techniques of science are adapted, and they make it possible to explain behavior as other subjects are explained in science. These independent variables are of many sorts and their relations to behavior are often subtle and complex, but we cannot hope to give an

adequate account of behavior without analyzing them.

Consider the act of drinking a glass of water. This is not likely to be an important bit of behavior in anyone's life, but it supplies a convenient example. We may describe the topography of the behavior in such a way that a given instance may be identified quite accurately by any qualified observer. Suppose now we bring someone into a room and place a glass of water before him. Will he drink? There appear to be only two possibilities: either he will or he will not. But we speak of the *chances* that he will drink, and this notion may be refined for scientific use. What we want to evaluate is the *probability* that he will drink. This may range from virtual certainty that drinking will occur to virtual certainty that it will not. The very considerable problem of how to measure such a probability will be discussed later. For the moment, we are interested in how the probability may be increased or decreased.

Everyday experience suggests several possibilities, and laboratory and clinical observations have added others. It is decidedly not true that a horse may be led to water but cannot be made to drink. By arranging a history of severe deprivation we could be "absolutely sure" that drinking would occur. In the same way we may be sure that the glass of water in our experiment will be drunk. Although we are not likely to arrange them experimentally, deprivations of the necessary magnitude sometimes occur outside the laboratory. We may obtain an effect similar to that of deprivation by speeding up the excretion of water. For example, we may induce sweating by raising the temperature of the room or by forcing heavy exercise, or we may increase the excretion of urine by mixing salt or urea in food taken prior to the experiment. It is also well known that loss of blood, as on a battlefield, sharply increases the probability of drinking. On the other hand, we may set the probability at virtually zero by inducing or forcing our subject to drink a large quantity of water before the experiment.

If we are to predict whether or not our subject will drink, we must know as much as possible about these variables. If we are to induce him to drink, we must be able to manipulate them. In both cases, moreover, either for accurate prediction or control, we must investigate the effect of each variable quantitatively with the methods and techniques of a laboratory science.

Other variables may, of course, affect the result. Our subject may be "afraid" that something has been added to the water as a practical joke or for experimental purposes. He may even "suspect" that the water has been poisoned. He may have grown up in a culture in which water is drunk only when no one is watching. He may refuse to drink simply to prove that we cannot predict or control his behavior. These possibilities do not disprove the relations between drinking and the variables listed in the preceding paragraphs; they simply remind us that other variables may have to be taken into account. We must know the history of our subject with respect to the behavior of drinking water, and if we cannot eliminate social factors from the situation, then we must know the history of his personal relations to people resembling the experimenter. Adequate prediction in any science requires information about all relevant variables, and the control of a subject matter for practical purposes makes the same demands.

Other types of "explanation" do not permit us to dispense with these requirements or to fulfill them in any easier way. It is of no help to be told that our subject will drink provided he was born under a particular sign of the zodiac which shows a preoccupation with water or provided he is the lean and thirsty type or was, in short, "born thirsty." Explanations in terms of inner states or agents, however, may require some further comment. To what extent is it helpful to be told, "He drinks because he is thirsty"? If to be thirsty means nothing more than to have a tendency to drink, this is mere redundancy. If it means that he drinks because of a state of thirst, an inner causal event is invoked. If this state is purely inferential—if no dimensions are assigned to it which would make direct observation possible —it cannot serve as an explanation. But if it has physiological or psychic properties, what role can it play in a science of behavior?

The physiologist may point out that several ways of raising the probability of drinking have a common effect: they increase the concentration of solutions in the body. Through some mechanism not yet well understood, this may bring about a corresponding change in the nervous system which in turn makes drinking more probable. In the same way, it may be argued that all these operations make the

organism "feel thirsty" or "want a drink" and that such a psychic state also acts upon the nervous system in some unexplained way to induce drinking. In each case we have a causal chain consisting of three links: (1) an operation performed upon the organism from without—for example, water deprivation; (2) an inner condition—for example, physiological or psychic thirst; and (3) a kind of behavior— for example, drinking. Independent information about the second link would obviously permit us to predict the third without recourse to the first. It would be a preferred type of variable because it would be nonhistoric: the first link may lie in the past history of the organism, but the second is a current condition. Direct information about the second link is, however, seldom, if ever, available. Sometimes we infer the second link from the third: an animal is judged to be thirsty if it drinks. In that case, the explanation is spurious. Sometimes we infer the second link from the first: an animal is said to be thirsty if it has not drunk for a long time. In that case, we obviously cannot dispense with the prior history.

The second link is useless in the *control* of behavior unless we can manipulate it. At the moment, we have no way of directly altering neural processes at appropriate moments in the life of a behaving organism, nor has any way been discovered to alter a psychic process. We usually set up the second link through the first: we make an animal thirsty, in either the physiological or the psychic sense, by depriving it of water, feeding it salt, and so on. In that case, the second link obviously does not permit us to dispense with the first. Even if some new technical discovery were to enable us to set up or change the second link directly, we should still have to deal with those enormous areas in which human behavior is controlled through manipulation of the first link. A technique of operating upon the second link would increase our control of behavior, but the techniques which have already been developed would still remain to be analyzed.

The most objectionable practice is to follow the causal sequence back only as far as a hypothetical second link. This is a serious handicap both in a theoretical science and in the practical control of behavior. It is no help to be told that to get an organism to drink we are simply to "make it thirsty" unless we are also told how this is to be done. When we have obtained the necessary prescription for thirst, the whole proposal is more complex than it need be. Similarly, when an example of maladjusted behavior is explained by saying that the individual is "suffering from anxiety," we have still to be told the cause of the anxiety. But the external conditions which are then invoked could have been directly related to the maladjusted behavior. Again, when we are told that a man stole a loaf of bread because "he was hungry," we have still to learn of the external conditions responsible for the "hunger." These conditions would have sufficed to explain the theft.

The objection to inner states is not that they do not exist, but that they are not relevant in a functional analysis. We cannot account for the behavior of any system while staying wholly inside it; eventually we must turn to forces operating upon the organism from without. Unless there is a weak spot in our causal chain so that the second link is not lawfully determined by the first, or the third by the second, then the first and third links must be lawfully related. If we must always go back beyond the second link for prediction and control, we may avoid many tiresome and exhausting digressions by examining the third link as a function of the first. Valid information about the second link may throw light upon this relationship but can in no way alter it.

A FUNCTIONAL ANALYSIS

The external variables of which behavior is a function provide for what may be called a causal or functional analysis. We undertake to predict and control the behavior of the individual organism. This is our "dependent variable"—the effect for which we are to find the cause. Our "independent variables"—the causes of behavior—are the external conditions of which behavior is a function. Relations between the two—the "cause-and-effect relationships" in behavior—are the laws of a science. A synthesis of these laws expressed in quantitative terms yields a comprehensive picture of the organism as a behaving system.

This must be done within the bounds of a natural science. We cannot assume that behavior has any peculiar properties which require unique methods or special kinds of knowledge. It is often argued that an act is not so important as the "intent" which lies behind it, or that it can be described only in terms of what it "means" to the behaving individual or to others whom it may affect. If statements of this sort are useful for scientific purposes, they must be based upon observable events, and we may confine ourselves to such events exclusively in a functional analysis. We shall see later that although such terms as "meaning" and "intent" appear to refer to properties of behavior, they usually conceal references to independent variables. This is also true of "aggressive," "friendly," "disorganized," "intelligent," and other terms which appear to describe properties of behavior but in reality refer to its controlling relations.

The independent variables must also be described in physical terms. An effort is often made to avoid the labor of analyzing a physical situation by guessing what it "means" to an organism or by distinguishing between the physical world and a psychological world of "experience." This practice also reflects a confusion between dependent and independent variables. The events affecting an organism must be capable of description in the language of physical science. It is sometimes argued that certain "social forces" or the "influences" of culture or tradition are exceptions. But we cannot appeal to entities of this sort without explaining how they can affect both the scientist and the individual under observation. The physical events which must then be appealed to in such an explanation will supply us with alternative material suitable for a physical analysis.

By confining ourselves to these observable events, we gain a considerable advantage, not only in theory, but in practice. A "social force" is no more useful in manipulating behavior than an inner state of hunger, anxiety, or skepticism. Just as we must trace these inner events to the manipulable variables of which they are said to be functions before we may put them to practical use, so we must identify the physical events through which a "social force" is said to affect the organism before we can manipulate it for purposes of control. In dealing with the directly observable data we need not refer to either the inner state or the outer force.

The material to be analyzed in a science of behavior comes from many sources:

(1) Our *casual observations* are not to be dismissed entirely. They are especially impor-

tant in the early stages of investigation. Generalizations based upon them, even without explicit analysis, supply useful hunches for further study.

(2) In *controlled field observation,* as exemplified by some of the methods of anthropology, the data are sampled more carefully and conclusions stated more explicitly than in casual observation. Standard instruments and practices increase the accuracy and uniformity of field observation.

(3) *Clinical observation* has supplied extensive material. Standard practices in interviewing and testing bring out behavior which may be easily measured, summarized, and compared with the behavior of others. Although it usually emphasizes the disorders which bring people to clinics, the clinical sample is often unusually interesting and of special value when the exceptional condition points up an important feature of behavior.

(4) Extensive observations of behavior have been made under more rigidly controlled conditions in *industrial, military, and other institutional research.* This work often differs from field or clinical observation in its greater use of the experimental method.

(5) *Laboratory studies of human behavior* provide especially useful material. The experimental method includes the use of instruments which improve our contact with behavior and with the variables of which it is a function. Recording devices enable us to observe behavior over long periods of time, and accurate recording and measurement make effective quantitative analysis possible. The most important feature of the laboratory method is the deliberate manipulation of variables: the importance of a given condition is determined by changing it in a controlled fashion and observing the result.

Current experimental research on human behavior is sometimes not so comprehensive as one might wish. Not all behavior processes are easy to set up in the laboratory, and precision of measurement is sometimes obtained only at the price of unreality in conditions. Those who are primarily concerned with the everyday life of the individual are often impatient with these artificialities, but insofar as relevant relationships can be brought under experimental control, the laboratory offers the best chance of obtaining the quantitative results needed in a scientific analysis.

(6) The *extensive results of laboratory studies of the behavior of animals below the human level* are also available. The use of this material often meets with the objection that there is an essential gap between man and the other animals, and that the results of one cannot be extrapolated to the other. To insist upon this discontinuity at the beginning of a scientific investigation is to beg the question. Human behavior is distinguished by its complexity, its variety, and its greater accomplishments, but the basic processes are not therefore necessarily different. Science advances from the simple to the complex; it is constantly concerned with whether the processes and laws discovered at one stage are adequate for the next. It would be rash to assert at this point that there is no essential difference between human behavior and the behavior of lower species, but until an attempt has been made to deal with both in the same terms, it would be equally rash to assert that there is. A discussion of human embryology makes considerable use of research on the embryos of chicks, pigs, and other animals. Treatises on digestion, respiration, circulation, endocrine secretion, and other physiological processes deal with rats, hamsters, rabbits, and so on, even though the interest is primarily in human beings. The study of behavior has much to gain from the same practice.

We study the behavior of animals because it is simpler. Basic processes are revealed more easily and can be recorded over longer periods of time. Our observations are not complicated by the social relation between subject and experimenter. Conditions may be better controlled. We may arrange genetic histories to control certain variables and special life histories to control others—for example, if we are interested in how an organism learns to see, we can raise an animal in darkness until the experiment is begun. We are also able to control current circumstances to an extent not easily realized in human behavior—for example, we can vary states of deprivation over wide ranges. These are advantages which should not be dismissed on the a priori contention that human behavior is inevitably set apart as a separate field.

3. PERSONS AND EXPERIENCE

R. D. Laing

EXPERIENCE AS EVIDENCE

Even facts become fictions without adequate ways of seeing "the facts." We do not need theories so much as the experience that is the source of the theory. We are not satisfied with faith, in the sense of an implausible hypothesis irrationally held: we demand to experience the "evidence."

We can see other people's behavior, but not their experience. This has led some people to insist that psychology has nothing to do with the other person's experience, but only with his behavior.

The other person's behavior is an experience of mine. My behavior is an experience of the other. The task of social phenomenology is to relate my experience of the other's behavior to the other's experience of my behavior. Its study is the relation between experience and experience: its true field is *interexperience*.

I see you, and you see me. I experience you, and you experience me. I see your behavior. You see my behavior. But I do not and never have and never will see your *experience* of me. Just as you cannot "see" my experience of you. My experience of you is not "inside" me. It is simply you, as I experience you. And I do not experience you as inside me. Similarly, I take it that you do not experience me as inside you.

"My experience of you" is just another form of words for "you-as-I-experience-you," and "your experience of me" equals "me-as-you-experience-me." Your experience of me is not inside you and my experience of you is not inside me, but *your experience of me is invisible to me and my experience of you is invisible to you.*

From THE POLITICS OF EXPERIENCE *by R. D. Laing, Chapter 1.* Copyright © *1967 by R. D. Laing. Reprinted by permission of Penguin Books, Ltd.*

I cannot experience your experience. You cannot experience my experience. We are both invisible men. All men are invisible to one another. Experience is man's invisibility to man. Experience used to be called the Soul. Experience as invisibility of man to man is at the same time more evident than anything. *Only* experience is evident. Experience is the *only* evidence. Psychology is the logos of experience. Psychology is the structure of the *evidence,* and hence psychology is the science of sciences.

If, however, experience is evidence, how can one ever study the experience *of the other?* For the experience *of the other* is not evident to me, as it is not and never can be an experience of mine.

I cannot avoid trying to understand your experience, because although I do not experience your experience, which is invisible to me (and nontastable, nontouchable, nonsmellable, and inaudible), yet I experience you *as experiencing*.

I do not experience your experience. But I experience you as experiencing. I experience myself as experienced by you. And I experience you as experiencing yourself as experienced by me. And so on.

The study of the experience of others is based on inferences I make, from my experience of you experiencing me, about how you are experiencing me experiencing you experiencing me. . . .

Social phenomenology is the science of my own and of others' *experience.* It is concerned with the relation between my experience of you and your experience of me. That is, with *interexperience.* It is concerned with your behavior and my behavior *as I experience it,* and your and my behavior *as you experience it.*

Since your and their experience is invisible

to me as mine is to you and them, I seek to make evident to the others, through their experience of my behavior, what I infer of your experience, through my experience of your behavior.

This is the crux of social phenomenology.

Natural science is concerned only with the observer's experience of things. Never with the way things *experience us*. That is not to say that things do not react to us, and to each other.

Natural science knows nothing of the relation between behavior and experience. The nature of this relation is mysterious—in Marcel's sense. That is to say, it is not an objective problem. There is no traditional logic to express it. There is no developed method of understanding its nature. But this relation is the copula of our science—if science means *a form of knowledge adequate to its subject*. The relation between experience and behavior is the stone that the builders will reject at their peril. Without it the whole structure of our theory and practice must collapse.

Experience is invisible to the other. But experience is not "subjective" rather than "objective," not "inner" rather than "outer," not process rather than praxis, not input rather than output, not psychic rather than somatic, not some doubtful data dredged up from introspection rather than extrospection. Least of all is experience "intrapsychic process." Such transactions, object relations, interpersonal relations, transference, countertransference, as we suppose to go on between people are not the interplay merely of two objects in space, each equipped with ongoing intrapsychic processes.

This distinction between outer and inner usually refers to the distinction between behavior and experience; but sometimes it refers to some experiences that are supposed to be "inner" in contrast to others that are "outer." More accurately this is a distinction between different modalities of experience, namely, perception (as outer) in contrast to imagination, etc. (as inner). But perception, imagination, fantasy, reverie, dreams, memory, are simply different *modalities of experience*, none more "inner" or "outer" than any other.

Yet this way of talking does reflect a split in our experience. We seem to live in two worlds, and many people are aware only of the "outer" rump. As long as we remember

that the "inner" world is not some space "inside" the body or the mind, this way of talking can serve our purpose. (It was good enough for William Blake.) The "inner," then, is our personal idiom of experiencing our bodies, other people, the animate and inanimate world: imagination, dreams, fantasy, and beyond that to ever further reaches of experience.

Bertrand Russell once remarked that the stars are in one's brain.

The stars as I perceive them are no more or less in my brain than the stars as I imagine them. I do not imagine them to be in my head, any more than I see them in my head.

The relation of experience to behavior is not that of inner to outer. My experience is not inside my head. My experience of this room is out there in the room.

To say that my experience is intrapsychic is to presuppose that there is a psyche that my experience is in. My psyche is my experience, my experience is my psyche.

Many people used to believe that angels moved the stars. It now appears that they do not. As a result of this and like revelations, many people do not now believe in angels.

Many people used to believe that the "seat" of the soul was somewhere in the brain. Since brains began to be opened up frequently, no one has seen "the soul." As a result of this and like revelations, many people do not now believe in the soul.

Who could suppose that angels move the stars, or be so superstitious as to suppose that because one cannot see one's soul at the end of a microscope it does not exist?

INTERPERSONAL EXPERIENCE AND BEHAVIOR

Our task is both to experience and to conceive the concrete, that is to say, reality in its fullness and wholeness.

But this is quite impossible, immediately. Experientially and conceptually, we have fragments.

We begin from concepts of the single person,[1] from the relations between two or more

1 Under person, the *Oxford English Dictionary* gives eight variants: a part played in a drama, or in life; an individual human being; the living body of a human being; the actual self of a human being; a human being or body corporate or corporation with rights or duties recognized in law; theologically applied, the three modes

persons, from groups or from the material world, and conceive of individuals as secondary. We can derive the main determinants of our individual and social behavior from external exigencies. All these views are partial vistas and partial concepts. Theoretically we need a spiral of expanding and contracting schemata that enable us to move freely and without discontinuity from varying degrees of abstraction to greater or lesser degrees of concreteness. Theory is the articulated vision of experience. This book begins and ends with the person.

Can human beings be persons today? Can a man be his actual self with another man or woman? Before we can ask such an optimistic question as, "What is a personal relationship?," we have to ask if a personal relationship is possible, or, *are persons possible* in our present situation? We are concerned with the possibility of man. This question can be asked only through its facets. Is love possible? Is freedom possible?

Whether or not all, or some, or no human beings are persons, I wish to define a person in a twofold way: in terms of experience, as a center of orientation of the objective universe; and in terms of behavior, as the origin of actions. Personal experience transforms a given field into a field of intention and action: only through action can our experience be transformed. It is tempting and facile to regard "persons" as only separate objects in space, who can be studied as any other natural objects can be studied. But just as Kierkegaard remarked that one will never find consciousness by looking down a microscope at brain cells or anything else, so one will never find persons by studying persons as though they were only objects. A person is the me or you, he or she, whereby an object is experienced. Are these centers of experience and origins of actions living in entirely unrelated worlds of their own composition? Everyone must refer here to their own experience. My own experience as a center of experience and

origin of action tells me that this is not so. My experience and my action occur in a social field of reciprocal influence and interaction. I experience myself, identifiable as Ronald Laing by myself and others, as experienced by and acted upon by others, who refer to that person I call "me" as "you" or "him," or grouped together as "one of us" or "one of them" or "one of you."

This feature of personal relations does not arise in the correlation of the behavior of nonpersonal objects. Many social scientists deal with their embarrassment by denying its occasion. Nevertheless, the natural scientific world is complicated by the presence of certain identifiable entities, re-identifiable reliably over periods of years, whose behavior is either the manifestation or a concealment of a view of the world equivalent in ontological status to that of the scientist.

People may be observed to sleep, eat, walk, talk, etc. in relatively predictable ways. We must not be content with observation of this kind alone. Observation of behavior must be extended by inference to attributions about experience. Only when we can begin to do this can we really construct the experiential-behavioral system that is the human species.

It is quite possible to study the visible, audible, smellable effulgences of human bodies, and much study of human behavior has been in those terms. One can lump together very large numbers of units of behavior and regard them as a statistical population, in no way different from the multiplicity constituting a system of nonhuman objects. But one will not be studying persons. In a science of persons, I shall state as axiomatic that: behavior is a function of experience; and both experience and behavior are always in relation to someone or something other than self.

When two (or more) persons are in relation, the behavior of each towards the other is mediated by the experience by each of the other, and the experience of each is mediated by the behavior of each. There is no contiguity between the behavior of one person and that of the other. Much human behavior can be seen as a unilateral or bilateral *attempt* to eliminate experience. A person may treat another *as though* he were not a person, and he may act himself *as though* he were not a person. There is no contiguity between one person's experience and another's. My experience of you is always mediated through your

---

of the Divine Being in the Godhead; grammatically, each of the three classes of pronouns and corresponding distinctions in verbs denoting the person speaking, i.e. in the first, second, third person respectively, and so on; zoologically, each individual of a compound or colonial organism—a zooid.

As we are concerned here with human beings, our two most relevant variants are person as persona, mask, part being played; and person as actual self.

behavior. Behavior that is the direct consequence of impact, as of one billiard ball hitting another, or experience directly transmitted to experience, as in the possible cases of extrasensory perception, is not personal.

NORMAL ALIENATION FROM EXPERIENCE

The relevance of Freud to our time is largely his insight and, to a very considerable extent, his *demonstration* that the *ordinary* person is a shriveled, desiccated fragment of what a person can be.

As adults, we have forgotten most of our childhood, not only its contents but its flavor; as men of the world, we hardly know of the existence of the inner world: we barely remember our dreams, and make little sense of them when we do; as for our bodies, we retain just sufficient proprioceptive sensations to coordinate our movements and to ensure the minimal requirements for biosocial survival— to register fatigue, signals for food, sex, defecation, sleep; beyond that, little or nothing. Our capacity to think, except in the service of what we are dangerously deluded in supposing is our self-interest and in conformity with common sense, is pitifully limited: our capacity even to see, hear, touch, taste and smell is so shrouded in veils of mystification that an intensive discipline of unlearning is necessary for *anyone* before one can begin to experience the world afresh, with innocence, truth and love.

And immediate experience of, in contrast to belief or faith in, a spiritual realm of demons, spirits, Powers, Dominions, Principalities, Seraphim and Cherubim, the Light, is even more remote. As domains of experience become more alien to us, we need greater and greater open-mindedness even to conceive of their existence.

Many of us do not know, or even believe, that every night we enter zones of reality in which we forget our waking life as regularly as we forget our dreams when we awake. Not all psychologists know of fantasy as a modality of experience,[2] and the, as it were, contrapuntal interweaving of different experiential modes. Many who are aware of fantasy believe that fantasy is the farthest that experience goes under "normal" circumstances. Beyond that are simply "pathological" zones of hallucinations, phantasmagoric mirages, delusions.

This state of affairs represents an almost unbelievable devastation of our experience. Then there is empty chatter about maturity, love, joy, peace.

This is itself a consequence of and further occasion for the divorce of our experience, such as is left of it, from our behavior.

What we call "normal" is a product of repression, denial, splitting, projection, introjection and other forms of destructive action on experience. It is radically estranged from the structure of being.

The more one sees this, the more senseless it is to continue with generalized descriptions of supposedly specifically schizoid, schizophrenic, hysterical "mechanisms."

There are forms of alienation that are relatively strange to statistically "normal" forms of alienation. The "normally" alienated person, by reason of the fact that he acts more or less like everyone else, is taken to be sane. Other forms of alienation that are out of step with the prevailing state of alienation are those that are labeled by the "normal" majority as bad or mad.

The condition of alienation, of being asleep, of being unconscious, of being out of one's mind, is the condition of the normal man.

Society highly values its normal man. It educates children to lose themselves and to become absurd, and thus to be normal.

Normal men have killed perhaps 100,000,000 of their fellow normal men in the last fifty years.

Our behavior is a function of our experience. We act according to the way we see things.

If our experience is destroyed, our behavior will be destructive.

If our experience is destroyed, we have lost our own selves.

How much human *behavior*, whether the interactions between persons themselves or between groups and groups, is intelligible in terms of human *experience?* Either our interhuman behavior is unintelligible, in that we are simply the passive vehicles of inhuman processes whose ends are as obscure as they are at present outside our control, or our own behavior towards each other is a function of our own experience and our own intentions, however alienated we are from them. In the

---

2 See R. D. Laing, *The Self and Others* (London: Tavistock Publications, 1961; Chicago: Quadrangle Press, 1962), especially Part I.

latter case, we must take final responsibility for what we make of what we are made of.

We will find no intelligibility in behavior if we see it as an inessential phase in an essentially inhuman process. We have had accounts of men as animals, men as machines, men as biochemical complexes with certain ways of their own, but there remains the greatest difficulty in achieving a human understanding of man in human terms.

Men at all times have been subject, as they believed or experienced, to forces from the stars, from the gods, or to forces that now blow through society itself, appearing as the stars once did to determine human fate.

Men have, however, always been weighed down not only by their sense of subordination to fate and chance, to ordained external necessities or contingencies, but by a sense that their very own thoughts and feelings, in their most intimate interstices, are the outcome, the resultant, of processes which they undergo.

A man can estrange himself from himself by mystifying himself and others. He can also have what he does stolen from him by the agency of others.

If we are stripped of experience, we are stripped of our deeds; and if our deeds are, so to speak, taken out of our hands like toys from the hands of children, we are bereft of our humanity. We cannot be deceived. Men can and do destroy the humanity of other men, and the condition of this possibility is that we are interdependent. We are not self-contained monads producing no effects on each other except our reflections. We are both acted upon, changed for good or ill, by other men; and we are agents who act upon others to affect them in different ways. Each of us is the other to the others. Man is a patient-agent, agent-patient, interexperiencing and interacting with his fellows.

It is quite certain that unless we can regulate our behavior much more satisfactorily than at present, then we are going to exterminate ourselves. But as we experience the world, so we act, and this principle holds even when action conceals rather than discloses our experience.

We are not able even to *think* adequately about the behavior that is at the annihilating edge. But what we think is less than what we know; what we know is less than what we love; what we love is so much less than what there is. And to that precise extent we are so much less than what we are.

Yet if nothing else, each time a new baby is born there is a possibility of reprieve. Each child is a new being, a potential prophet, a new spiritual prince, a new spark of light precipitated into the outer darkness. Who are we to decide that it is hopeless?...

4. TWO MODELS OF MAN

William D. Hitt

A Symposium sponsored by the Division of Philosophical Psychology of the American Psychological Association clearly pointed up the cleavage in contemporary theoretical and

William D. Hitt: "Two Models of Man"; AMERICAN PSYCHOLOGIST, 24 (1969), 651–658 Copyright 1969 by the American Psychological Association. Reprinted by permission of the American Psychological Association and the author.

philosophical psychology. The symposium was held at Rice University to mark the inception of the Division of Philosophical Psychology as a new division of the APA. Participants included Sigmund Koch, R. B. MacLeod, B. F. Skinner, Carl R. Rogers, Norman Malcolm, and Michael Scriven. The presentations and associated discussions were organized in the book: *Behaviorism and Phenomenology: Con-*

trasting Bases for Modern Psychology (Edited by T. W. Wann, 1964).

THE ARGUMENT

As indicated in the title of the book, the main argument of the symposium dealt with phenomenology versus behaviorism. This argument also could be described as one between existential psychology and behavioristic psychology. The presentations dealt with two distinct models of man and the scientific methodology associated with each model. The discussions following each presentation may be described as aggressive, hostile, and rather emotional; they would suggest that there is little likelihood of a reconciliation between the two schools of thought represented at the symposium.

To illustrate the nature of the argument, some of the statements made by the participants are presented below.

In Support of Behaviorism

• Skinner (1964):

An adequate science of behavior must consider events taking place within the skin of the organism, not as physiological mediators of behavior, but as part of behavior itself. It can deal with these events without assuming that they have any special nature or must be known in any special way.... Public and private events have the same kinds of physical dimension [p. 84].

• Malcolm (1964):

Behaviorism is right in insisting that there must be some sort of conceptual tie between the language of mental phenomena and outward circumstances and behavior. If there were not, we could not understand other people, nor could we understand ourselves [p. 152].

Attacks on Behaviorism

• Koch (1964):

Behaviorism has been given a hearing for fifty years. I think this generous. I shall urge that it is essentially a role-playing position which has outlived whatever usefulness its role might once have had [p. 6].

• Rogers (1964):

It is quite unfortunate that we have permitted the world of psychological science to be nar-

rowed to behavior observed, sounds emitted, marks scratched on paper, and the like [p. 118].

In Support of Phenomenology

• MacLeod (1964):

I am...insisting that what, in the old, prescientific days, we used to call "consciousness" still can and should be studied. Whether or not this kind of study may be called a science depends on our definition of the term. To be a scientist, in my opinion, is to have boundless curiosity tempered by discipline [p. 71].

• Rogers (1964):

The inner world of the individual appears to have more significant influence upon his behavior than does the external environmental stimulus [p. 125].

Attacks on Phenomenology

• Malcolm (1964):

I believe that Wittgenstein has proved this line of thinking (introspectionism) to be disastrous. It leads to the conclusion that we do not and cannot understand each other's psychological language, which is a form of solipsism[1] [p. 148].

• Skinner (1964):

Mentalistic or psychic explanations of human behavior almost certainly originated in primitive animism [p. 79].... I am a radical behaviorist simply in the sense that I find no place in the formulation for anything which is mental [p. 106].

This appears to be the heart of the argument:

The behaviorist views man as a passive organism governed by external stimuli. Man can be manipulated through proper control of these stimuli. Moreover, the laws that govern man are essentially the same as the laws that govern all natural phenomena of the world; hence, it is assumed that the scientific method used by the physical scientist is equally appropriate to the study of man.

The phenomenologist views man as the *source* of acts; he is free to choose in each situation. The essence of man is *inside* of man; he is controlled by his own consciousness. The most appropriate methodology for

1 Solipsism is defined as the theory that only the self exists, or can be proven to exist.

the study of man is phenomenology, which begins with the world of experience.

These two models of man have been proposed and discussed for many years by philosophers and psychologists alike. Versions of these models may be seen in the contrasting views of Locke and Leibnitz (see Allport, 1955), Marx and Kierkegaard, Wittgenstein and Sartre, and, currently, Skinner and Rogers. Were he living today, William James probably would characterize Locke, Marx, Wittgenstein, and Skinner as "tough-minded," while Leibnitz, Kierkegaard, Sartre, and Rogers would be viewed as "tender-minded." Traditionally, the argument has been one model versus the other. It essentially has been a black-and-white argument.

The purpose of this article is to analyze the argument between the behaviorist and the phenomenologist. This analysis is carried out by presenting and discussing two different models of man.

CONTRASTING VIEWS OF MAN

The two models of man are presented in terms of these contrasting views:

1. Man can be described meaningfully in terms of his behavior; or man can be described meaningfully in terms of his conciousness.
2. Man is predictable; or man is unpredictable.
3. Man is an information transmitter; or man is an information generator.
4. Man lives in an objective world; or man lives in a subjective world.
5. Man is a rational being; or man is an arational being.
6. One man is like other men; or each man is unique.
7. Man can be described meaningfully in absolute terms; or man can be described meaningfully in relative terms.
8. Human characteristics can be investigated independently of one another; or man must be studied as a whole.
9. Man is a reality; or man is a potentiality.
10. Man is knowable in scientific terms; or man is more than we can ever know about him.

Each of these attributes is discussed below.

SUPPORT FOR BOTH MODELS

The evidence offered below in support of each of the two models of man is both empirical and analytical. Perhaps some of the evidence is intuitive, but it at least seems logical to the author of this article.

Man Can Be Described Meaningfully in Terms of His Behavior; or Man Can Be Described Meaningfully in Terms of His Consciousness

According to John B. Watson, the founder of American behaviorism, the behavior of man and animals was the only proper study for psychology. Watson strongly advocated that

> Psychology is to be the science, not of consciousness, but of behavior. . . . It is to cover both human and animal behavior, the simpler animal behavior being indeed more fundamental than the more complex behavior of man. . . . It is to rely wholly on objective data, introspection being discarded [Woodworth & Sheehan, 1964, p. 113].

Behaviorism has had an interesting, and indeed productive, development since the time of Watson's original manifesto. Tolman, Hull, and a number of other psychologists have been important figures in this development. Today, Skinner is the leading behaviorist in the field of psychology. Skinner (1947) deals with both overt and covert behavior; for example, he states that "thought is simply *behavior*—verbal or nonverbal, covert or overt [p. 449]."

As a counterargument to placing all emphasis on behavior, Karl Jaspers, an existential psychologist and philosopher, points up the importance of consciousness or self-awareness. According to Jaspers (1963), consciousness has four formal characteristics: (*a*) the feeling of activity—an awareness of being active; (*b*) an awareness of unity; (*c*) awareness of identity; and (*d*) awareness of the self as distinct from an outer world and all that is not the self (p. 121). Jaspers (1957) stresses that "Man not only exists but knows that he exists [p. 4]."

It is apparent from this argument that psychologists over the years have been dealing with two different aspects of man—on the one hand, his actions, and on the other, his self-awareness. It seems reasonable that man could be described in terms of either his behavior *or* his consciousness or both. Indeed, behavior is more accessible to scientific treatment, but the systematic study of consciousness might well give the psychologist additional understanding of man.

Man Is Predictable; or Man Is Unpredictable

Understanding, prediction, and control are considered to be the three objectives of science. Prediction and control are sometimes viewed as evidence of the scientist's understanding of the phenomenon under study. The objective of prediction rests on the assumption of determinism, the doctrine that all events have sufficient causes. Psychological science has traditionally accepted the objective of predicting human behavior and the associated doctrine of determinism.

Indeed, there have been some notable successes in predicting human behavior. Recent predictions of the number of fatalities resulting from automobile accidents on a given weekend, for example, have been within 5–10% of the actual fatalities. College administrators can predict fairly accurately the number of dropouts between the freshman and sophomore years. Further, a psychometrician can readily predict with a high degree of accuracy the distribution of scores resulting from an achievement test administered to a large sample of high school students. As another example, the mean reaction time to an auditory stimulus can be predicted rather accurately for a large group of subjects. All of these examples lend support to the doctrine of determinism.

There also have been some notable failures in attempts to predict human behavior. For example, the therapist has had little success in predicting the effectiveness of a given form of therapy applied to a given patient. Similarly, the guidance counselor has had relatively little success in predicting the occupation to be chosen by individual high school students. Such failures in predicting human behavior sometimes prompt one to question the basic assumption of determinism.

To illustrate the complexity associated with predicting the behavior of man—as contrasted with that of other complex systems—consider the following illustration. Suppose that a research psychologist has made a detailed study of a given human subject. He now tells the subject that he predicts that he will choose Alternative A rather than Alternative B under such and such conditions at some future point in time. Now, with this limited amount of information, what do you predict the subject will do?

The evidence suggests that there is support for both sides of this issue. It is difficult to argue with the deterministic doctrine that there are sufficient causes for human actions. Yet these causes may be unknown to either the observer or the subject himself. Thus, we must conclude that man is both predictable and unpredictable.

Man Is an Information Transmitter; or Man Is an Information Generator

The information theorists and cyberneticists have formulated a model of man as an information transmitter. W. Ross Ashby (1961), the cyberneticist, has proposed a basic postulate that says that man is just as intelligent as the amount of information fed into him.

> Intelligence, whether of man or machine, is absolutely bounded. And what we can build into our machine is similarly bounded. The amount of intelligence we can get into a machine is absolutely bounded by the quantity of information that is put into it. We can get out of a machine as much intelligence as we like, if and only if we insure that at least the corresponding quantity of information gets into it [p. 280].

Ashby believes that we could be much more scientific in our study of man if we would accept this basic postulate and give up the idea that man, in some mysterious manner, generates or creates new information over and above that which is fed into him.

The information-transmitting model of man is indeed very compelling. It promises considerable rigor and precision; it is compatible with both empiricism and stimulus-response theory; and it allows the behavioral scientist to build on past accomplishments in the fields of cybernetics, systems science, and mechanics.

But, alas, man does not want to be hemmed in by the information-transmitting model. Man asks questions that were never before asked; he identifies problems that were never before mentioned; he generates new ideas and theories; he formulates new courses of action; and he even formulates new models of man. Now to say that all of these human activities are merely a regrouping or recombining of existing elements is an oversimplification, a trivialization of human activity. Further, the assumption that all information has actually been in existence but hidden since the days of prehistoric man is not intuitively satisfying.

Considering the evidence in support of man both as an information transmitter and as an information generator, would it be reasonable to view man as both a *dependent* variable and an *independent* variable?

Man Lives in an Objective World; or Man Lives in a Subjective World

Man lives in an objective world. This is the world of facts and data. This is a reliable world; we agree that this or that event actually occurred. This is a tangible world; we agree that this or that object is actually present. This is the general world that is common to all.

But man also lives in a subjective world. This is the individual's private world. The individual's feelings, emotions, and perceptions are very personal; he attempts to describe them in words but feels that he can never do complete justice to them.

In making this comparison between the objective world and subjective world, it is important to distinguish between two types of knowledge. We can know *about* something, or we can personally *experience* something. These two forms of knowledge are not the same.

We conclude that man is both object and subject. He is visible and tangible to others, yet he is that which thinks, feels, and perceives. The world looks at man, and he looks out at the world.

Are both the objective world and the subjective world available to the methods of science? Empiricism in general and the experimental method in particular can be applied to the objective world; phenomenology can be applied to the subjective world. In his efforts to understand man, perhaps the psychologist should attempt to understand both worlds.

Man Is a Rational Being; or Man Is an Arational Being

Man is sometimes referred to as a rational animal. He is intelligent; he exercises reason; he uses logic; and he argues from a scientific standpoint. Indeed, man is considered by man to be the *only* rational animal.

An individual's action or behavior, of course, is sometimes considered irrational. This is the opposite of rational. The irrational person defies the laws of reason; he contradicts that which is considered rational by some particular community of people.

But man also is arational. This characteristic transcends the rational-irrational continuum; it essentially constitutes another dimension of man's life. As an example of man being arational in his life, he makes a total commitment for a way of life. This commitment may be for a given faith, a religion, a philosophy, a vocation, or something else. It may be that any analysis of this decision would reveal that it was neither rational nor irrational—it merely was.

Man's actions are guided by both empirical knowledge and value judgment. Empirical knowledge belongs to the rational world, whereas value judgment often belongs to the arational world. According to Jaspers (1967): "An empirical science cannot teach anybody what he ought to do, but only what he can do to reach his ends by statable means [p. 60]."

To achieve greater understanding of man, it would seem essential that the psychologist investigate man's arational world as well as his rational world.

One Man Is Like Other Men; or Each Man Is Unique

A major goal of science is to develop general laws to describe, explain, and predict phenomena of the world. These laws are frequently based upon the study of one sample of objects or events and are then expected to be valid for a different sample of objects or events. It then follows that a major goal of psychology is to formulate general laws of man. In fact, without the possibility of developing general laws of human behavior, can psychology even be considered a science?

There is a considerable amount of evidence to support the possibility of developing general laws of human behavior. For example, the results of the reaction-time experiments have held up very well over the decades. Moreover, the many conditioning experiments conducted over the past several decades—either classical or operant—certainly suggest that man is governed by general laws applicable to all. Further, the cultural anthropologist and social psychologist have clearly pointed up the similarity of people in a given culture, suggesting that they might be taken from the same mold.

On the other hand, there is considerable evidence to support the concept of individual uniqueness. For example, there are thousands of possible gene combinations and thousands of different environmental determinants, all of which bring about millions of different personalities. Further, it is apparent that no two people ever live in exactly the same environment. As someone once said about two brothers living in the same house, with the same parents, and with the same diet: "Only one of the boys has an older brother." Then, too, we might reflect on a statement made by William James (1925): "An unlearned carpenter of my acquaintance once said in my hearing: 'There is very little difference between one man and another; but what little there is, *is very important*' [pp. 242–243]."

Our conclusion from this brief analysis is that the evidence appears to support both models of man: (*a*) that he is governed by general laws that apply to all of mankind, and (*b*) that each individual is unique in a nontrivial way.

Man Can Be Described Meaningfully in Absolute Terms; or Man Can Be Described Meaningfully in Relative Terms

If we believe that man can be described in absolute terms, we view such descriptions as being free from restriction or limitation. They are independent of arbitrary standards. Contrariwise, if we believe that man can be described in relative terms, we see him as existing or having his specific nature only by relation to something else. His actions are not absolute or independent.

If the concept of absoluteness is supported, we must accept the idea of general laws for all of mankind, and we also must accept the related idea that man is governed by irrefutable natural laws. On the other hand, if the concept of relativism is supported, we probably can have no general laws of man; we must realize that everything is contingent upon something else; and we can be certain of nothing.

It would appear that there is evidence to support the concept of absoluteness in psychology. The basic psychophysical laws, for example, might be characterized as irrefutable natural laws. Similarly, the basic laws of conditioning seem to be free from restriction or limitation. This evidence might lead us to conclude that man can be described in absolute terms.

But before we can become smug with this false sense of security, the relativist poses some challenging questions. For example:

What is considered intelligent behavior? What is normal behavior? What is an aggressive personality? What is an overachiever? At best, it would seem that we could answer such questions only in relative terms. The answers would be contingent on some set of arbitrary standards.

What can we conclude? Perhaps man can be described meaningfully in either absolute terms or relative terms, depending on what aspect of man is being described.

Human Characteristics Can Be Investigated Independently of One Another; or Must Be Studied as a Whole

The question here is: Can man be understood by analyzing each attribute independently of the rest, or must man be studied as a whole in order to be understood? Another way of phrasing the question is: Can we take an additive approach to the study of man, or is a holistic or Gestalt approach required?

There is some evidence to support an additive approach to the study of man. Consider the following areas of research: psychophysics, physiological psychology, motor skills, classical and operant conditioning, and sensation. All of these areas have produced useful results from experimentation involving the manipulation of a single independent variable and measuring the concomitant effects on a single dependent variable. Useful results have been produced by investigating a single characteristic independently of other characteristics.

Other areas of research, however, point up the value of a holistic point of view. Research in the area of perception, for example, has demonstrated the effect of individual motivation on perception. Similarly, studies of human learning have shown the great importance of motivation and intelligence on learning behavior. Further, as one more example, research in the area of psychotherapy has revealed that the relation between the personality of the therapist and that of the patient has a significant influence on the effectiveness of the therapy. All of these examples illustrate the importance of the interactions and interdependencies of the many variables operating in any given situation.

Support for a holistic view of man is seen in the works of Polanyi and Tielhard de Chardin, to mention only two. Polanyi (1963) gives this example: "Take a watch to pieces and examine, however carefully, its separate parts in turn, and you will never come across the principles by which a watch keeps time [p. 47]." Tielhard de Chardin (1961) says:

> In its construction, it is true, every organism is always and inevitably reducible into its component parts. But it by no means follows that the sum of the parts is the same as the whole, or that, in the whole, some specifically new value may not emerge [p. 110].

What can be concluded from this discussion? First, it would seem that a detailed analysis of man is essential for a systematic understanding. Yet, synthesis also is required in order to understand the many interactions and interdependencies. We can conclude that the most effective strategy for the behavioral scientist might be that used by the systems analyst—a working back and forth between analysis and synthesis.

Man Is a Reality; or Man Is a Potentiality

Is man a reality? If so, he exists as fact; he is actual; he has objective existence. Or is man a potentiality? If so, he represents possibility rather than actuality; he is capable of being or becoming. The question here is: Can we study man as an actually existing entity—as we would study any other complex system—or must we view man as a completely dynamic entity, one that is constantly emerging or becoming?

There is support for the view of man as an actuality. The numerous results from the many years of research in the area of experimental psychology, for example, suggest that man is definable and measurable, and is capable of being investigated as an actually existing complex system. Further, the many current studies in the area of cybernetics, which point up similarities between man and machine, lend credence to the concept of man as an existing system.

There also is evidence to support the view of man as a potentiality. For example, case studies have revealed that long-term criminals have experienced religious conversions and then completely changed their way of life. Further, complete personality transformations have resulted from psychoanalysis and electroshock therapy. Indeed, man is changeable, and any given individual can become something quite different from what he was in the past.

Maslow (1961) has stressed the importance of human potentiality:

> I think it fair to say that no theory of psychology will ever be complete that does not centrally incorporate the concept that man has his future within him, dynamically active at the present moment [p. 59].

What can we conclude? Only that man is both a reality and a potentiality. He represents objective existence, yet he can move toward any one of many different future states that are essentially unpredictable.

Man Is Knowable in Scientific Terms; or Man Is More Than We Can Ever Know about Him

This final issue is basic to the entire study of man, and is closely tied to all the previous issues discussed. Is man knowable in scientific terms, or is man more than we can ever know about him?

There are many centuries of evidence to support the idea that man is scientifically knowable. Aristotle, for example, applied the same logic to his study of man as he did to other phenomena in the world. Further, volumes of data resulting from psychological experiments since the time of Wundt's founding of the first experimental psychology laboratory in 1879 indicate that man is scientifically knowable. Then, too, the many laboratory experiments and field studies recently conducted by the different disciplines included in the behavioral and social sciences certainly suggest that man is scientifically knowable.

Yet, there also is support for the idea that man is more than we can ever know about him. Man has continued to transcend himself over the past million or so years, as demonstrated by the theory of evolution. Further, on logical grounds, it can be demonstrated that man becomes something different every time he gains new knowledge about himself, which would suggest that man is truly an "open system."

It is apparent that we know very little about man. William James (1956) says: "Our science is a drop, our ignorance a sea [p. 54]." Erich Fromm (1956) believes that "Even if we knew a thousand times more of ourselves, we would never reach bottom [p. 31]."

What can we conclude? We must conclude that man is scientifically knowable—at least to a point. Yet there is no evidence to support the idea that man is—or ever will be—*completely* knowable.

CONCLUSIONS

This paper has presented two models of man:

• The behavioristic model: Man can be described meaningfully in terms of his behavior; he is predictable; he is an information transmitter; he lives in an objective world; he is rational; he has traits in common with other men; he may be described in absolute terms; his characteristics can be studied independently of one another; he is a reality; and he is knowable in scientific terms.

• The phenomenological model: Man can be described meaningfully in terms of his consciousness; he is unpredictable; he is an information generator; he lives in a subjective world; he is arational; he is unique alongside millions of other unique personalities; he can be described in relative terms; he must be studied in a holistic manner; he is a potentiality; and he is more than we can ever know about him.

This analysis of behaviorism and phenomenology leads to these conclusions:

1. The acceptance of either the behavioristic model or a phenomenological model has important implications in the everyday world. The choice of one versus the other could greatly influence human activities (either behavior or awareness) in such areas as education, psychiatry, theology, behavioral science, law, politics, marketing, advertising, and even parenthood. Thus, this ongoing debate is not just an academic exercise.

2. There appears to be truth in both views of man. The evidence that has been presented lends credence to both the behavioristic model and the phenomenological model. Indeed, it would be premature for psychology to accept either model as the final model.

3. A given behavioral scientist may find that both models are useful, depending upon the problem under study. The phenomenological model, for example, might be quite appropriate for the investigation of the creative process in scientists. On the other hand, the behavioristic model might be very useful in the study of environmental factors that motivate a given population of subjects to behave in a certain manner.

4. Finally, we must conclude that the behaviorist and the phenomenologist should listen to each other. Both, as scientists, should be willing to listen to opposing points of view. Each should endeavor to understand what the other is trying to say. It would appear that a dialogue is in order.

REFERENCES

Allport, G. W. *Becoming: Basic considerations for a psychology of personality.* New Haven: Yale University Press, 1955.

Ashby, W. R. What is an intelligent machine? *Proceedings of the Western Joint Computer Conference,* 1961, 19, 275–280.

de Chardin, P. T. *The phenomenon of man.* New York: Harper & Row, 1961 (Harper Torchbook Edition).

Fromm, E. *The art of loving.* New York: Harper & Row, 1956.

James, W. *The will to believe and other essays on popular philosophy.* New York: Dover, 1956 (Orig. publ. 1896).

James, W. The individual and society. In, *The philosophy of William James.* New York: Modern Library, 1925 (Orig. publ. 1897).

Jaspers, K. *Man in the modern age.* New York: Doubleday, 1957 (Orig. publ. in Germany, 1931).

Jaspers, K. *General psychopathology.* Manchester, England: Manchester University Press, 1963 (Published in the United States by the University of Chicago Press).

Jaspers, K. *Philosophy is for everyman.* New York: Harcourt, Brace & World, 1967.

Koch, S. Psychology and emerging conceptions of knowledge as unitary. In T. W. Wann (Ed.), *Behaviorism and phenomenology: Contrasting bases for modern psychology.* Chicago: University of Chicago Press, 1964.

MacLeod, R. B. Phenomenology: A challenge to experimental psychology. In T. W. Wann (Ed.), *Behaviorism and phenomenology: Contrasting bases for modern psychology.* Chicago: University of Chicago Press, 1964.

Malcolm, N. Behaviorism as a philosophy of psychology. In T. W. Wann (Ed.), *Behaviorism and phenomenology: Contrasting bases for modern psychology.* Chicago: University of Chicago Press, 1964.

Maslow, A. H. Existential psychology—What's in it for us? In R. May (Ed.), *Existential psychology.* New York: Random House, 1961.

Polanyi, M. *The study of man.* Chicago: University of Chicago Press, 1963 (First Phoenix Edition).

Rogers, C. R. Toward a science of the person.

In T. W. Wann (Ed.), *Behaviorism and phenomenology: Contrasting bases for modern psychology*. Chicago: University of Chicago Press, 1964.

Skinner, B. F. *Verbal behavior*. New York: Appleton-Century-Crofts, 1957.

Skinner, B. F. Behaviorism at fifty. In T. W. Wann (Ed.), *Behaviorism and phenomenology: Contrasting bases for modern psy-*

chology. Chicago: University of Chicago Press, 1964.

Wann, T. W. (Ed.) *Behaviorism and phenomenology: Contrasting bases for modern psychology*. Chicago: University of Chicago Press, 1964.

Woodworth, R. S., & Sheehan, M. R. *Contemporary schools of psychology*. New York: Ronald Press, 1964.

RECOMMENDED FURTHER READING

*Barzun, Jacques: *Science:The Glorious Entertainment;* New York, Harper & Row 1964

Boring, Edwin G.: *A History of Experimental Psychology* (2nd Ed.); New York, Appleton-Century-Crofts 1957

Bugental, James F. T. (ed.): *Challenges of Humanistic Psychology;* New York, McGraw-Hill 1967

Chaplin, J. P. and T. S. Krawiec: *Systems and Theories of Psychology;* New York, Holt, Rinehart & Winston 1960

*Doherty, Michael & Kenneth Shemberg: *What is Psychology: An Introduction to How Psychologists Work;* Glenview, Ill., Scott, Foresman 1970

Heidbreder, Edna: *Seven Psychologies;* New York, Appleton-Century 1933

Helson, H. and W. Bevan: *Contemporary Approaches to Psychology;* Princeton, N. J., Van Nostrand 1967

*Henneman, Richard H.: *Nature and Scope of Psychology* (2 Ed.); Dubuque, Iowa, Wm. C. Brown 1971

Koch, Sigmund (ed.): *Psychology: Study of a Science,* 6 Vols.; New York, McGraw-Hill 1959–1963

*Kuhn, Thomas S.: *The Structure of Scientific Revolutions;* Chicago, University of Chicago Press 1962

Postman, Leo (ed.): *Psychology in the Making;* New York, Knopf 1962

*Walker, Edward: *Psychology As A Natural and Social Science;* Belmont, Calif., Brooks Cole 1969

*Wann, T. W. (ed.): *Behaviorism and Phenomenology: Contrasting Bases for Modern Psychology;* Chicago, University of Chicago Press 1964

Wolman, Benjamin B. and Ernest Nagel (eds.): *Scientific Psychology;* New York, Basic Books 1965

Woodworth, R. S. and M. R. Sheehan: *Contemporary Schools of Psychology* (3rd Ed.); New York, Ronald Press 1964

* Paperback edition available.

PART II

THE

BEHAVING-EXPERIENCING

ORGANISM

Whatever else man may be he is first of all an animal subject to the same kinds of biological processes and constraints as other animals. Which is to say that the bases of human as of animal behavior are, in the first instance, biological. That is not to say, however, that there are no differences between the behavior of humans and that of lower animals or that man is *nothing but* an animal. Here it will suffice to say that because of the unique and immense influence of culture in human life most human behavior is biologically *conditioned* or *influenced* without thereby being biologically *determined*.

Stemming from the orientation we examined in Part I and from the fact that most of their research has been conducted with animals, experimental psychologists have tended to stress the similarities between human and infrahuman behavior while clinicians and humanists, because they rarely if ever deal with other animals, tend to emphasize the unique characteristics of the human one. To what degree conclusions derived from research on lower animals also hold for the behavior of human beings is a problem we will encounter repeatedly in the course of this book. Despite the role of culture we must, nevertheless, understand the biological bases of human behavior if we are to have any hope of gaining a complete understanding of that behavior.

All living organisms "behave" in the sense that they respond perceptibly to changes generated both internally and in their external environment. Quite apart from culture and all that it connotes in differentiating human from non-human behavior is the role played by biological evolution itself. The degree of development attained by the human brain and central nervous system permits a variety, a complexity, and an integration of behavior biologically beyond the reach of any other species. This complexity and versatility seem related both to the human infant's long prenatal period and to the extended period of virtually total dependency that follows. Because so much of human behavior is mediated by processes in the brain and central nervous system, experimental and physiological psychologists (the latter a sub-speciality where psychology and brain physiology meet) have long been concerned with understanding the structure and functioning of the human brain and its effects on emotion and perception as well as behavior.

But behavior is not simply a reaction of the organism to physical stimuli, either internal or external. In the absence of the latter the healthy organism spontaneously seeks stimulation; its normal state is one of activity not quiescence (see Selection 29). This strongly suggests that "normal" or optimal psychological functioning depends on the establishment and maintenance of active, continuous, and gratifying transactions between the organism and its external environment. The studies by Hebb and others, reported below, support this interpretation.

If all organisms behave it is not so clear that all of them "experience" or possess consciousness. Given our previous definition of experience as the meaning that the acting organism attributes both to the stimuli it receives and to its own behavior it would seem that experience depends for its very existence on some means of making sensations, perceptions, and overt actions "meaningful." Human beings do this largely if not wholly through systems of symbolic communication—especially verbal language—that are cultural, not biological, in origin. "Experience" is thus a creation of culture. Logically, this does not preclude the possibility that nonhuman species also "experience," but until we are able to communicate with members of such species the possibility must remain only that.

Because subjective experience or consciousness is unique and incommensurable, because it can be apprehended directly only by the experiencing subject himself, and because it must be communicated symbolically if it is to be communicated at all, experimentalists—in contrast to clinicians— have tended to slight or even to deny its "reality." Yet, unique and difficult to communicate though it is, experience is surely real in its behavioral consequences and is sometimes more real to the individual than is his overt behavior (see Selections 24 and 49). By introspecting, the reader can try to examine for himself the relationship between his own behavior and his consciousness. In time, psychologists may develop accurate and dependable ways of inferring or identifying states of conscious experience directly from overt behavior or from measurable physiological responses, thus making possible precise and dispassionate study of this elusive, yet highly significant, entity.

In Selection 5 Dean E. Wooldridge, a distinguished physicist and engineer with a strong interest in brain physiology, examines the structure of the amazingly complex "machine" that is the human brain and discusses how localized centers therein control most of our emotions and sensations, our memory, and many of the qualities we attribute to consciousness. From this point of view the phrase "it's all in your head" takes on a new and deeper significance. Wooldridge speculates that consciousness itself may be "a property of certain organizations and states of matter." While much of the work he reports was done on lower animals there is considerable clinical and circumstantial evidence that most of its findings are valid for the functioning of the human brain as well.

Developing the theme introduced by Wooldridge, Ruth and Edward Brecher, a husband-wife team of science writers, report in detail on the work of James Olds and others with electrical stimulation of the brain (ESB) in animals. Electrical stimulation of specific areas in the brain can lead to dramatic changes in the behavior of the animals and, in humans as well, to equally dramatic changes in sensation and emotion. The Brechers then explore the implications of this research for the control of human behavior and its possible misuse by politicians and laymen.

In the following paper Donald O. Hebb of McGill University explores the effects of environmental stimulation (and its absence) on the development of mammals (including man) and the effects on perception and behavior of depriving biologically mature individuals of their usual interaction with the environment. For Hebb, behavior depends on learning, which suggests that it is a function of experience. He concludes that even in the case of mature individuals the maintenance of psychological integrity depends on "normal" (that is, usual for the species) and dependable sensory inputs from the external environment. The research Hebb reports is clearly relevant to the problems of development and maturation discussed in Part III and also to such practical issues as the "brainwashing" of military and political prisoners.

To end this section, Frederick Snyder presents a review of some of the recent research on sleep and dreaming. We may not usually think of sleep as behavior (we may, in fact, think of it as a temporary cessation of behavior) but it is—a universal and very primitive kind, biologically based and present from birth. Dreaming, on the other hand, develops only as the individual matures physiologically. It is an intensely private mode of experience not easily communicable to others, sometimes inaccessible to the waking consciousness of the dreamer himself. Snyder's article shows that the experience of dreaming has measurable behavioral correlates. Notice how technical advances in measurement have permitted the precise investigation of a phenomenon heretofore discussable only in clinical or speculative terms.

Both the studies reported by Snyder and others not mentioned by him show that dreaming is a constant accompaniment to sleep, that, like sleep itself, it is a normal, even a necessary part of human functioning. Depriving a human being of sleep and dreams for a prolonged period leads to psychotic-like behavior (as does prolonged sensory deprivation, such as that discussed by Hebb) and, in some lower animals, to hypersexuality and serious disturbances in eating. What this research has not yet clearly established is the function of dreaming for the human organism. The ancient belief that dreams foretold the future has long been discredited while Freud's view that a dream is the "disguised fulfillment of a repressed wish" and a guardian of sleep no longer seems fully adequate even if it is not positively wrong. The function of dreaming may well be to discharge instinctual energies harmlessly (sexual excitation seems to accompany most periods of dreaming) yet biological and behavioral processes associated with sleep (e.g., the rapid eye movements or REM's) are prior in time to dreaming, which depends on the later development of psychic structure. Clearly, the investigation of sleep and dreaming is one of the significant challenges to contemporary psychological research.

5. HOW THE MACHINE CALLED THE BRAIN FEELS AND THINKS

Dean E. Wooldridge

In a provocative series of experiments, a team of scientists at Western Reserve University in Cleveland has developed techniques to remove the brain of a monkey from its body and keep it alive for many hours. Bare except for two small bits of bone to help support it, the nerves and blood vessels that once connected it to the monkey's body severed, the brain is suspended above a laboratory table. Attached to it are the tubes of a mechanical heart to maintain its blood supply; from it run wires to recording instruments. Their measurements of its electrical activity not only show that it remains alive but even suggest that sometimes this isolated brain is conscious.

While the immediate goal of the team, headed by Dr. Robert J. White, is the development of methods for obtaining answers to basic questions related to the physiology of the brain, one cannot help being fascinated by less specifically scientific, but perhaps more profoundly philosophic, considerations. Can the truly "detached minds" of the Cleveland monkeys really be conscious? If so, conscious of what?

Sensation, for example, is an important ingredient of the conscious state. Does biological science give us any clues as to what sensations, if any, the conscious incorporated brains of the Western Reserve monkeys could have felt? After all, the nerves that normally carry to the brain indications of touch, taste, odor, light and sound were all cut, and the associated sensory organs were far removed. Does this mean that, during its conscious

periods, the isolated monkey brain floated in a sensory void, with no flashes of touch, pain, sight or sound to remind it of the kind of existence it once knew?

No one can know for sure, of course, but the answer is: Probably not. We know that the conscious, "feeling" part of the brain does not reach out to the sensory receptors of the finger tips in order to find out what the outside environment is doing to the periphery of the body. Instead, "feeling" is the result of electrical activity in a section of the brain's surface called the "sensory strip," which ordinarily serves as a "receiving station" for signals coming in through the nerves from the body surface. It is the activity in this "receiving station," rather than in the "wires" leading to it, that actually produces the conscious sensation that, say, a toe is cold.

Severing or otherwise mistreating the nerves leading to the sensory strip can result in patterns of electrical activity that "fool" the conscious part of the brain. This is why an amputee can feel the specific sensation of the fingers of his hand being twisted in an uncomfortable position for months after the arm carrying that hand has been cut off.

Similarly, while useful vision requires functioning eyes, and meaningful hearing requires operating ears, the sensations of sight and sound, involving uncoordinated but nonetheless vivid flashes of light or bursts of sound, can be experienced by an eyeless or earless individual. All that is necessary is that the conditions at the extremities of his severed nerves be such as to produce the rather simple kinds of electrochemical impulses that, upon arrival at the visual or auditory areas of the brain, are interpreted as sight or sound.

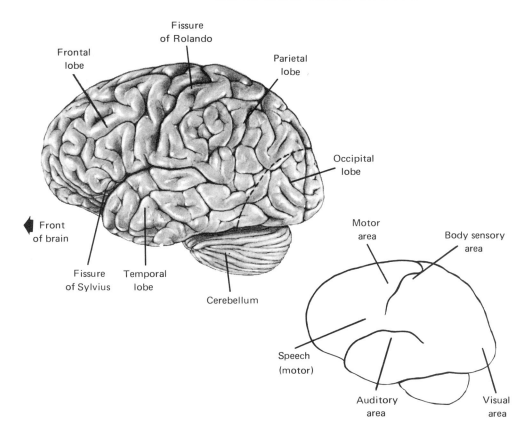

FIGURE 1. Localization of function in the human cortex. Above: the lobes of the cerebral hemispheres and the landmarks separating them. Right: the projection areas. Reproduced from INTRODUCTION TO PSYCHOLOGY, 4th edition, by Ernest R. Hilgard and Richard C. Atkinson (New York: Harcourt Brace Jovanovich, Inc., 1967), p. 46, by permission of the publisher.

Control Center. The human brain is a mass of 10 billion nerve cells weighing about three pounds. By means of electro-chemical impulses traveling along the nerves at speeds of 2 to 200 miles an hour, it receives and transmits messages from and to every part of the body. The human brain (above) consists of three main parts:

The brainstem. This is the core of the brain, essentially an extension of the spinal cord (through which all nerve impulses are channeled). The brainstem controls such involuntary but vital functions as breathing and the heart beat, and generates such primitive drives as feelings of hunger, anger and pleasure. Sometimes called the "old brain," it existed in much the same form in the dinosaurs.

The cerebellum. This bulbous structure, part way up the brainstem and protruding toward the back of the head, coordinates muscular activity. It has been called the "private secretary" of the brain.

The cerebrum, or cerebral cortex. This convoluted mantle covers the other parts of the brain and fills the rest of the skull. It is divided, left and right, into two equal hemispheres. Sometimes called the "new brain," it is the seat of mental activity, voluntary action and the senses.

The detached monkey brain could even have felt hungry or thirsty. Such sensations are determined by local electric currents and related chemical activity in specific small regions, or "centers," in the brainstem—the "primitive" lower part of the brain that is really an extension of the spinal cord. When stimulating electric impulses are injected into the appropriate part of an animal's "appetite center," for example, by means of a surgically implanted wire, the animal will exhibit the only kind of appetite that truly deserves the adjective "insatiable": It will continue to eat any food provided to it, even though it is so stuffed that it must regurgitate what it has already swallowed. If the stimulating electrode is placed in another part of the appetite center, only a fraction of an inch away, the animal will be unable to eat—even to the extent of starving to death while surrounded by its favorite food.

Hunger of another sort would also have been possible for the isolated monkey brain. There are small regions of nerve tissue in the brainstem that control activities related to reproduction and care of the young. While electric stimulation in these centers is effective, some of the most interesting recent work has been with hormones. By implanting the right chemicals in the right spots in rats' brains, Dr. Alan E. Fisher, psychologist at the University of Pittsburgh, found that he could cause a male rat to exhibit typically female behavior, and vice versa. Thus, males were observed building nests and gently carrying to shelter the baby rats they would ordinarily have eaten.

We can even speculate on the state of mind of the detached monkey brain, during its periods of consciousness. If it at all understood what was happening to it, it may well have been angry and afraid. Perhaps it felt like biting with the teeth it once possessed, or like scratching or running with the legs it formerly controlled. If so, it is not unlikely that the brain did in fact generate such commands and send them in the form of electrochemical impulses to the severed ends of the nerves which formerly went to the muscles.

But it is also possible that the brain felt relaxed and comfortable. It could even have felt happy. For there appear to be "pleasure" and "punishment" centers in the brain. The feelings of anger, fright, horror, ease, relaxation, pleasure and ecstasy, just like those of hunger and thirst, are now known to be turned on or off selectively by local patterns of electrochemical activity in the brainstem. Whether you are a rat, cat, monkey or human being, sites deep in the brain have been located where electric stimulation will produce a sense of horror; other sites are known

where stimulation will result in feelings of euphoria or ecstasy.

(Experimenters do not enjoy subjecting their animals to fright and pain, and do so as little as is consistent with obtaining the important information they seek. The justification for all such work is, of course, that the knowledge gained may ultimately make it possible to relieve human suffering.)

The Western Reserve experiments on isolated monkey brains constitute only one example of the progress that is being made toward clarifying some of the mysteries of the conscious state. For example, a "consciousness switch" has been located in the brain. Dr. H. W. Magoun, now at the University of California at Los Angeles, was able to show that an arrangement of interconnected nerve cells in the brainstem—the "reticular activating system" he called it—is the source of a special pattern of electrochemical nerve impulses that must be received by the brain if we are to be aware of what is going on.

During a surgical operation under general anesthesia, measurements have shown that the nerve impulses caused by the manipulation of the surgeon's scalpel arrive at the major brain centers with at least as great strength as though the patient were conscious. He does not feel them only because the chemical anesthetic has suppressed the reticular activating system. Without its steady flow of impulses to the higher portions of the brain, our sense of awareness is "turned off."

But this consciousness control need not be an "all or nothing" matter. The "switch" can regulate degrees of awareness as well.

For example, if a cat in a cage is exposed to a monotonous sequence of musical tones, measuring equipment will detect a corresponding sequence of electric impulses in the nerve leading from ear to brain. If then, with no change in the tone sequence or intensity, an object of great feline interest is displayed to the cat—a beaker containing mice, let us say—the measurements will show a great decrease or perhaps complete disappearance of the tone-generated nerve impulses.

It is the same reticular activating system in the brainstem—the "consciousness switch"—that is at work. The appearance of an object of overriding interest generates a new electric signal that serves to turn down the "volume control" of the nerve system registering the object of lesser interest. In this way we are permitted to "focus" our attention—to enhance our consciousness of events of interest by freeing our minds from unimportant distractions.

One of the most interesting and puzzling phenomena related to consciousness was first observed nearly 30 years ago by Dr. Wilder Penfield, at that time head of the Montreal Neurological Institute.

In connection with operations to remove tumors or epileptically defective brain tissue, Penfield had developed a new kind of electric-probe technique. After removal of the section of skull covering the area where defective tissue was believed to be, the patient would be restored to consciousness in the operating room, and asked to describe his sensations as needles were stuck into various parts of his brain and electricity injected. (The brain contains no nerve endings that can sense pain; a patient suffers no discomfort in such tests.) By the nature of the responses, it was frequently possible to determine the boundaries of defective tissue more accurately than by visual observation alone.

In 1936, several years after the first use of this new technique, Penfield was preparing to operate on a woman whose lesion was on the side of the cortex (the outer surface of the brain) just above the ear—a region that later work was to implicate with the memory mechanisms. When the needle electrode was inserted and the electric current turned on, the patient suddenly reported that she felt transported back to her early childhood. In the operating room, she essentially relived an episode out of her remote past, even feeling again the same fear that had accompanied the original event.

In the succeeding years, Penfield and many other brain surgeons have observed, in many patients, this kind of triggering of memory by cortical stimulation. The phenomenon possesses a number of fascinating features, which the developing understanding of brain function must some day explain. For example: The electrically elicited experiences always appear to be real although the patient usually has not been consciously carrying them in his memory. The induced recollection can be stopped abruptly by turning off the stimulating current, and often restarted by turning it on again. But, when restarted, the recalled

episode never continues where it left off—instead, it starts again from the beginning, as though it were stored on a film or tape which automatically rewinds each time it is interrupted.

Perhaps most startling is the vividness of the elicited experience. Instead of being a remembering, according to Penfield, "it is a hearing-again and seeing-again—a living-through-moments-of-past-time."

Nevertheless, the patient does not lose contact with the present. He seems to have concurrent existences—one in the operating room, and one in the part of the past that he is reliving. The term "double-consciousness" is employed by brain surgeons to describe these peculiar sensations of their patients.

Penfield's discovery no longer stands as the sole example of the successful tampering with the unity of consciousness by brain surgeons and research scientists. In the biology laboratories of the California Institute of Technology, Dr. R. W. Sperry has had under way for several years a series of experiments on cats and monkeys that in some ways are even more spectacular.

Sperry's methods are based on the left-right symmetry that characterizes higher animals, including cats, monkeys and men. In particular, in such animals the brain consists of two similar hemispheres.

They are interconnected by a vast system of nerve fibers numbering several hundred million in a human brain.

In concept, Sperry's idea was simple: Break these connections and see what happens. The trouble was that when he tried it on laboratory animals (usually cats) nothing much did happen. Even after most of the connections between the brain hemispheres had been cut, the animal appeared substantially unchanged. It behaved about as before; it achieved about the same scores on intelligence tests; it remembered its old tricks and could learn new ones.

The experiment had to be refined. This was done by adding to the brain-splitting surgery an operation on the visual system of the animal, as a result of which the left eye was connected only with the left half of the brain, and the right eye with the right half (ordinarily there are also crossing connections; these were cut).

Cats prepared in this way were then subjected to special training procedures. They were taught to choose between two swinging doors that they could easily open, one carrying a conspicuous circular design, the other a cross.

The cat under training would learn that choice of the door with a circle, say, would lead to a reward, choice of the door with a cross would lead to punishment. This was routine animal training; the distinguishing feature of the experiment was that the cat was provided with an eyepatch, so that all of its trials involved the use of, say, the left eye only, which in turn was connected to the isolated left half of the brain.

The animals learned their lessons about as fast as cats that had not had their brains split. Everything seemed normal—up to a point. This point was reached when the cat had been trained to near perfection using its left eye, and then was reintroduced into the training cage with the eyepatch shifted, so that the untrained eye—and the associated half of the brain—came into play.

The result was spectacular. Changing the eyepatch was exactly equivalent to changing cats. When employing the eye connected to the untrained half of its brain, the animal appeared to have not the slightest recollection of ever having been in the problem box. It could be trained again, using the new eye and hemisphere, to perform the desired discrimination, but its rate of learning was exactly the same as that of an entirely fresh, untrained cat.

In the new condition, it could even be taught, equally easily, a discrimination opposite to that learned originally. Using its right eye and right hemisphere, it could learn to open the door with the cross despite its earlier acquisition, when using its left eye and left hemisphere, of the habit of opening the door with the circle. Such a doubly trained animal would shift its performance automatically, without confusion, when the eyepatch was shifted.

By severing the connections between the two halves of the brain, Sperry had apparently split into two distinct parts what had previously been a single sense of consciousness.

In some respects, the split-consciousness implications of the work on cats was demonstrated even more vividly by later experiments on monkeys. In this work the two halves of the brain were provided with different proper-ties, not by training, but by surgical modification. Qn one side of the monkey's brain the nerve fibers running from the brainstem to a forward part of the brain were severed. This operation—a frontal lobotomy—has for years been known to produce significant personality changes if performed on both sides of the brain. Specifically, it produces under these circumstances a relaxed, "I-don't-care" person or animal. Before the development of tranquilizing drugs, it was sometimes employed to ease the unbearable tensions of psychotic mental patients.

In addition to the frontal lobotomy on one side of the brain, the monkeys were subjected to the split-brain operation, including modification of their optic connections, just as in the cat experiments. After the surgery, they were fitted with an arrangement of contact lenses similar to the cat's eyepatches.

A monkey employing the eye that was connected to the unmodified half of its brain would then be shown a snake. Monkeys are normally deathly afraid of snakes and the split-brain monkey was no exception. It showed the usual fright and escape reactions.

Then the conditions were changed so that the monkey had to employ the eye connected with the hemisphere that had had the lobotomy. Again the snake was displayed. This time, the monkey could not have cared less; the snake held no terrors for it. It was as though two different animal personalities now inhabited the body that had formerly been occupied by one.

The existence of pleasure and punishment centers in the brain, the discovery of the consciousness switch, the peculiar "double-consciousness" of Penfield's patients, the split-personality of Sperry's split-brain animals—all are variations on a single theme: the operation of the principle of cause and effect in the content and quality of the conscious state.

We feel horror or ecstasy, are conscious or unconscious, *because* of the electrochemical activity in specific brainstem tissue; we appear to have concurrent existences in past and present *because* of the disturbance of our brain mechanisms produced by Penfield's electric probe; we have two separate states of consciousness *because* Sperry has cut the connections between the two halves of our brain.

Is consciousness, then, finally to become an early and predictable physical quantity like gravity, electric charge or magnetism? Is it to be only another property of matter, to be dealt with by the impersonal and objective techniques of the mathematician and physicist? To be sure, consciousness seems to be connected with intelligence, but are we to learn that it is automatically and inevitably associated with the complex organizations and states of matter required for intelligence, much as gravity is associated with mass?

Must we even come to speculate that, among the wires and transistors of our electronic computers, there already stirs a dim glimmering of the same kind of sense of awareness that has become, for man, his most personal and precious possession? Fantastic? Perhaps.

The immediate human reaction—that consciousness is by its very nature a mysterious and unexplainable phenomenon—is really not very pertinent. All the laws and properties of nature are fundamentally mysterious; science can no more explain gravitational attraction or electric charge than it can the sense of consciousness. The scientist delineates the orderly and predictable interactions among his quantities; he never explains the quantities themselves.

If future investigation continues to disclose consistent interrelationships between the physical conditions of the brain and the qualities of consciousness, it is hard to see how consciousness can escape ultimate acceptance as a property of certain organizations and states of matter. Then consciousness would be no longer a question of metaphysics but part of the realm described by the physical laws of nature.

It would be hard to imagine a development of more far-reaching importance to science and philosophy. Yet it could come as a consequence of the exciting work now under way in the laboratories of the brain research scientists.

6. THE HAPPIEST CREATURES ON EARTH?

Ruth and Edward Brecher

In the psychological laboratory of Dr. James Olds at the University of Michigan, a rat presses a lever. This turns on a mild electric current which courses through an electrode to stimulate a carefully selected region in the rat's own brain.

Just what sensation the rat gets no one knows, of course. But Dr. Olds's rats certainly behave as if they loved it. No other reward in the rat world compares with it. Though food and water are readily available, famished or parched rats will press the lever rather than eat or drink. Even a female rat in heat cannot distract a male from the happy pursuit of this electrical delight.

In other laboratories, cats, dogs, dolphins, and monkeys stimulate their own brains in the same way. And at several medical centers human patients report pleasant emotions when corresponding regions of their brains are electrically stimulated. (Applied to other brain regions, the current can evoke displeasure, fear, even terror.)

These discoveries have implications far beyond their impact on psychological theory: they may point the way to new methods of treating human illnesses; military applications have been explored. The possible social consequences are incalculable. These vistas have opened up only within the past decade although the underlying technique is not new.

During the 1930s and 1940s a Swiss investigator, Dr. W. R. Hess, developed the basic methods of electrical brain stimulation (ESB) to a high level of precision: other psychologists and physiologists throughout the world thereafter found it a remarkably effective way to explore brain structure and functions.

At Yale in 1953, for example, Drs. José M. R. Delgado, Warren E. Roberts, and Neal E. Miller implanted sixty-six electrodes in the brains of six laboratory animals. Reactions differed greatly according to which electrode transmitted the current. When it was routed through some, the results were commonplace —the animals merely turned their heads, circled, pawed, licked, or gave no response whatever. But stimulation through other electrodes evoked "a fearlike response, characterized by hissing, opening the mouth, showing the teeth, flattening the ear, accompanied by well-oriented, co-ordinated efforts to escape.... Usually docile animals became aggressive, trying to bite and scratch.... Pupillary dilatation and other autonomic reactions, such as defecation and urination, were often observed...." The animals learned to escape this unpleasant stimulation either by manipulating a wheel or by jumping through an escape hatch. No matter how hungry, they would keep away from food if they knew the current would be turned on when they approached it.

At the 1953 meetings of the American Psychological Association, motion pictures of these experiments were shown. Among those who saw them was Dr. Olds, then a budding psychologist, working under Dr. Donald O. Hebb at McGill in Montreal. Another fledgling psychologist, Dr. Peter Milner, had just taught Dr. Olds how to use ESB—how, for example, to insert an electrode carefully into the brain of an anesthetized rat. Each electrode consisted of two very fine hairlike wires, insulated so that the current when applied would stimulate only the brain area near the tip. The effect depended primarily upon where the tip was lodged. A fraction of a millimeter shift in the site might make a significant difference in the animal's response.

Dr. Olds was so fascinated by this ESB work that he often spent Sundays in the laboratory "playing around" with the rats. On one such occasion, he noticed an animal behaving quite differently from those in the Yale film. When its brain was stimulated it neither bared its teeth, defecated, nor urinated in terror. Instead it raised its head, sniffed daintily—and kept coming back to the same corner of the experimental table for additional doses of ESB.

Soon Drs. Olds and Milner could make the rat go wherever they wanted merely by turning on the current when it headed in the desired direction. They concluded that ESB could serve not only as punishment but as a welcome reward; both effects could be used to control behavior. Very likely earlier ESB researchers had evoked— but failed to observe —such pleasurable reactions. Dr. Olds himself was nonplused that first Sunday morning. "Scarcely believing what I saw," he says, "I tried in the next few weeks and months to get other rats to do the same."

He has been at it ever since, with notable success, at McGill, at the University of California, and since 1957 at the University of Michigan. His work suggests that—for rats at least—ESB is the reward that exceeds all others.

PLEASURE WITHOUT SATIETY

One standard laboratory device for measuring the strength of motives is the "Skinner box," which has a pedal-like lever at one end. Each time an animal presses the lever, he receives a reward—usually a pellet of food. An automatic mechanism records the number of times per hour the lever is pressed, and this rate is a measure of the animal's hunger. For instance, a famished rat may press the lever for fifteen minutes at the rate of 100 per hour before it is sated by the food so earned.

To measure the strength of the ESB reward, Dr. Olds substitutes a half-second of brain stimulation for the food pellet. To get another half-second dose, the rat must release the lever and press again. Thus the rat rather than the experimenter controls the stimulus. Under these conditions, a rat with a properly placed electrode will stimulate itself continuously hour after hour—many hundreds of times each hour. Some electrode placements cause a rat to press the lever every half-second or oftener—7,000 or 8,000 times an hour, until it falls exhausted. When it awakens, it neither eats nor drinks but starts pressing the lever again, at the same rate.

Another measuring device is a long obstacle box bisected by an electrified grid which delivers a painful electric shock to the animal's paws. The hungrier the rat, the more severe the shock it will endure in order to reach food. A sufficiently painful shock will deter even the hungriest rat. But it takes a shock twice or three times as strong to keep him away from an ESB reward.

Experimenters have shown that this reward effect is not a mere laboratory curiosity but is directly related to such natural drives as hunger, thirst, and sex. For example, with an electrode in a brain region controlling sexual function, a rat may stimulate itself 2,000 times an hour. If it is then castrated, the rate gradually slows down as the level of sex hormones in its blood stream falls off. Within two weeks the rat loses all interest in the lever. But if sex hormones are later injected it starts pressing the lever again.

In several important ways reactions to ESB differ from most physiological responses. For instance, we eat until we are satisfied and then "can't eat another mouthful." Satiation similarly results when an electrode is placed in certain regions. But rats with an electrode in other reward regions seem *never* to get too much.

In one experiment a monkey stimulated itself 200,000 times in a single day. In another, at the Walter Reed Army Medical Center in Washington, D.C., researchers organized an ESB marathon. Day after day, week after week, rats pressed the levers, pausing only occasionally for fifteen-second snacks and sips, or brief naps. After twenty-one days, says Dr. Joseph V. Brady, the laboratory's director, "the rats were still going strong, but the rest of us were exhausted."

Were these rats ESB addicts—in the sense that they needed an additional dose to counteract the unpleasant aftereffects of the previous one? Apparently not. After six or eight months of continuous self-stimulation, Dr. Olds's rats look younger, healthier, more vigorous, and more alert than litter mates who have led ordinary lives. Between sessions the ESB rats behave normally. They exhibit no "withdrawal symptoms" when deprived of their accustomed stimulation. Nor do they, like the alcohol or narcotics habitué, have to keep increasing their dose to maintain the effect. The same mild current—usually measuring only a few volts and a few thousandths of an ampere—evokes the same response after many months.

Several researchers have been patiently mapping, out, cubic millimeter by cubic millimeter, the precise regions where the reward and punishment phenomena can be evoked. The brain consists of three major systems. At the core is the brain-stem, very similar in man and in animals far down the evolutionary scale; it is the site of quite primitive neurological functions. The outermost layer is the cerebral cortex, seat of the "higher thought processes," vastly more developed in man and the higher apes than in lower animals. In between, forming a border or "limbus" around the brain-stem and therefore called the "limbic system," is a complex collection of brain structures essentially similar in man and other mammals but not in sub-mammalian species. This system, recent research indicates, is the site of emotional control over behavior and of the reward and punishment effects.

Within the limbic system is a small organ called the hypothalamus. Here reward and punishment regions are interlarded with or overlap closely packed regions that control eating, drinking, sex, lactation, sweating, shivering, panting, heart rate, sleep, hormone secretions, and other physiological functions and emotional responses. When one hypothalamic region is stimulated, a rat will eat almost continuously and grow enormously fat. Stimulation of a nearby region will suppress appetite altogether. This close-knit structure of the hypothalamus leads to intriguing speculations. For example, oral, sex, and reward regions are close together or overlap. Does this suggest a physiological basis for the "oral eroticism" of Freudian fame? Could sadism or masochism be caused by some minute disorder in the contiguous regions concerned with reward, punishment, and sex? Further experiments may or may not confirm such speculations.

One effect of ESB is its ability to suppress anxiety. This has been demonstrated by Dr. Brady at Walter Reed. An animal in a Skinner box receives food pellets as a reward for pressing the lever. Then from time to time a loud buzzer is sounded for three minutes—after which a painful shock is delivered to the animal's paws. Soon the animal comes to associate the sound with the shock and stops pressing the lever as the buzzing begins. This is a typical anxiety response. But when the reward is ESB instead of food, the animal goes on unconcernedly pressing the lever despite the warning buzzer and inevitable painful shock. In this capacity to suppress anxiety ESB resembles the mythical drug *soma,* used in Aldous Huxley's *Brave New World* to enslave mankind.

Of equal interest are experiments conducted by Dr. Delgado and his associates at Yale with a cageful of monkeys. As is their custom, the monkeys establish a "society" of their own, with a status hierarchy. The most aggressive becomes the "boss"; the others cower at his approach. Then Dr. Delgado stimulates the boss monkey in a brain region where taming effects are produced. Promptly the boss loses his aggressiveness and behaves with unaccustomed meekness. The other monkeys —as well as human observers—soon note that, in Madison Avenue parlance, he is projecting an altered image. As a result, the whole social structure of the monkey colony shifts. The stimulated monkey is no longer boss; another takes over and rules the colony. When the current is turned off, the original boss resumes his accustomed role and the group readjusts. This experiment suggests that sociologists may find ESB an extremely useful tool. Its applicability to the human brain has, in fact, already been established.

MAKING PAIN BEARABLE

Human brains are stimulated only if benefit to the particular patient can be expected. When conservative treatment of a brain condition fails, for example, a surgeon may decide to remove abnormal tissue. ESB in such cases can be a valuable prelude to surgery. The surgeon must make sure that he will not cut into any regions which serve essential functions. Electrodes implanted temporarily throughout the area of interest and activated one at a time help him map his surgical strategy.

In other cases, ESB may be tried as a less drastic substitute for a radical brain operation such as lobotomy (an incision which severs certain nerve fibers in the frontal lobe). This is sometimes performed when all else has failed to relieve mental disorders and also to control intractable pain. Lobotomy is an irreversible procedure which may permanently destroy important functions. ESB, in contrast, causes little or no brain damage, although there is of course an inherent risk in any procedure which involves opening up the cranial cavity.

ESB has been used medically by groups headed by Dr. Wilder Penfield at Montreal Neurological Institute; Dr. Robert G. Heath at Tulane; Dr. Delgado at Yale; Drs. Sidney Mervin and George Hayes at Walter Reed; Dr. Reginald F. Bickford at the Mayo Clinic and Dr. Carl W. Sem-Jacobsen both there and at the Gaustad Mental Hospital in Oslo, Norway.

Dr. Penfield's work dates back to the 1940s when he stimulated the outermost layer of the brain—the cerebral cortex—of many hundreds of fully conscious patients. They reported experiencing a wide range of sounds, smells, visions, hallucinations, memories, dreamlike states, and *déjà-vu* feelings—even the detailed recall of whole scenes from the distant past. But these effects were curiously devoid of emotion. Neither pleasure, joy, anger, fear, nor rage was felt.

Very different results were reported, however, by subsequent researchers who ventured to implant electrodes more deeply in the limbic system. Dr. Heath at Tulane, for example, began stimulating such regions in 1950. The effect on pain-ridden patients he says "is quite startling. They get immediate relief...say they feel good. They smile, brighten up, change their facial expressions. ...The effect is immediate, as soon as the current hits. It is a repeatable thing. You can stimulate over and over again."

In contrast, Dr. Heath points out, "lobotomy patients still have pain, but don't care about it. Our stimulation patients say they don't have pain.... We feel it is a disappearance of pain rather than a lack of concern about it."

Dr. Sem-Jacobsen and his associates have implanted some 6,000 electrodes in the brains of 120 human patients as an essential prelude to surgery. With the electrode in some reward regions, "the patients get euphoric, laughing out loud and enjoying themselves actively. There are other pleasure areas where the patients enjoy themselves passively." An element of sexual pleasure is occasionally noted or there may be "a feeling of ease and relaxation," of "joy with smiling," or just "great satisfaction." Dr. Sem-Jacobsen adds that neither patients nor scientists seem to have a vocabulary adequate to describe or differentiate all the nuances of these feelings.

Some terminal cancer patients have been kept reasonably comfortable by ESB for many months, without addiction effects. The patients enjoy their daily ESB experience and are tranquil in the interim. Though narcotics are available to them they use them only sparingly. Nor is it necessary to increase the strength of current as the months roll by. ESB, however, is the "treatment of choice" for only a few patients under special circumstances including continuous hospitalization.

Punishment regions are never stimulated deliberately but are occasionally hit by accident. Dr. Sem-Jacobsen divides the negative effects in humans roughly into five groups: "anxiety," "restlessness," "depression," "fright," and "horror."

The complex relationships between ESB and chemical agents—such as the tranquilizers and "psychic energizers"—are being studied by several researchers. Dr. Miller and his group at Yale, for example, lodge an electrode in a rat's reward region and measure the minimum current which will make the rat press the lever. Then the rat gets a dose of a drug often used to treat human depression. The effect is to lower the threshold of the reward effect. A current so weak that it ordinarily has no effect will make the drug-treated rat press the lever repeatedly.

In other experiments, researchers seem to have discovered why one of the well-known tranquilizers sometimes deepens the depression of patients already depressed. This drug raises the threshold of the reward effect. A current ordinarily strong enough to make a rat press the lever has no effect at all after the drug has been administered.

With his wife, Dr. Olds has run a series of experiments in which drugs are substituted for ESB. Instead of an electrode a tiny pipette is implanted in a reward region of the rat's brain. Each time the rat presses the lever, it receives a minute drug injection. The rat responds to this chemical reward as it would to ESB, pressing the lever several hundred times an hour. Such research is valuable in locating the precise site of a drug's action within the brain and in casting light on how each drug achieves its effects. Newly synthesized chemicals can be screened for their potential action on reward and punishment centers; chemicals likely to achieve ESB-like effects when swallowed or injected can be identified. In the treatment of depression and other mental illnesses, such goals are benign indeed. But this new tool also raises ethical

questions, as a recent experiment suggests.

Impressed by the practical possibilities of ESB, one far-sighted corporation launched an ESB project of its own, in the hope of securing a research and development contract from the Defense Department. A corporate "top secret" lid was clamped on the project; hence the facts which follow have not been confirmed by the corporation, but we have reason to believe they are accurate.

The experimental subject was a donkey wearing a collar laden with a prism, a photoelectric eye, a make-break switch, a battery, and a miniaturized, transistorized circuit for sending an ESB current through an electrode lodged in a reward area of the donkey's brain. When sunlight struck the prism at precisely the right angle, the photoelectric eye activated the switch which turned on the current and administered the ESB reward. If the donkey veered in either direction or stood still, the switch turned the current off again. Thus accoutered, the joyful donkey trotted straight ahead, up hill, down dale, even across a mountain, neither straying nor lagging, to its predestined goal—a substation some five miles away. There the prism was reversed—whereupon the donkey retraced its arduous course over the mountain and back to its starting place.

When moving pictures of "Project Donkey" were shown at the Pentagon last year as part of a contract application, the audience reaction was mixed. One nonmilitary viewer—a scientist—is said to have murmured:

"There, but for the grace of God, go I."[1]

CAN IT CONTROL HUMAN BEHAVIOR?

We need not feel sorry for the donkey; it was no doubt enjoying a delightful ESB experience as it jogged along. But the thought of a human being subjected to this kind of external control—reduced to the status of an automaton for someone else's benefit—is shocking to the conscience of anyone adhering

1 So far as we could determine, none of the scientists whose work we have been describing took part in "Operation Donkey." At least one refused an invitation to participate. A spokesman informs us that the corporation is not currently engaged in ESB research, which suggests that the contract application may have been turned down.

to democratic or to Judaeo-Christian ethical traditions. As Professor F. S. C. Northrop of the Yale Law School reminded us, the heart of the matter is Immanuel Kant's "categorical imperative": *no man must ever be used as a mere pawn to serve another man's ends.* Nor is the ethical objection evaded when a man is thus degraded "with his own consent," or "for the good of all mankind."

The practical likelihood that ESB itself will ever be misused to enslave individuals or whole populations is exceedingly small. As a method of behavioral control, it is far too crude, requiring invasion of the cranial cavity and a heavy investment of skilled time to control a single individual. But ESB is nevertheless a striking example of a whole class of new behavioral control techniques.

Hypnosis is of course the prototype. Like ESB, it is not as yet directly adaptable to mass use. But the quasi-hypnotic techniques of the rabble rouser or lynch-mob leader suggest its possibilities. Reduced to a reliable science through further laboratory research, mass hypnosis might go far.

Isolation and *sensory deprivation* also produce amazing results in subjugating the human ego, for such purposes as brain-washing. Experiments in this area are currently under way.

Psychically active drugs are the most convenient method yet suggested for reducing men to pawns. One well-known drug seems to act on the same reward regions as ESB; users report that "all the bells of Heaven ring." Perhaps fortunately, this drug causes addiction and has degenerative side effects. However, a great effort is currently being made to develop equally potent substances free of such built-in limitations.

Beyond these known possibilities, others may already be secretly under investigation, here or abroad or both. In the course of our own inquiries we were asked: "Have you been cleared for access to classified data?"

SHOULD WE KEEP STILL?

The hazard, let us stress, is *not* that behavioral scientists will misuse these techniques for personal ends. Like physicians, our psychologists adhere to a professional code of ethics in which the Kantian imperative is implicit. Existing law, moreover, makes abuse of ESB, hypnosis, drugs, sensory deprivation, or the

like by an individual scientist a tort and perhaps also a crime. As we trust our physicians with poisons, narcotics, and scalpels, so we can safely trust behavioral scientists in their professional roles.

The real hazard arises when behavioral control techniques are taken over by others—for example, by national governments. As Dr. Carl R. Rogers, University of Wisconsin clinical psychologist, has cogently warned his colleagues:

> To hope that the power which is being made available by the behavioral sciences will be exercised by the scientists, or by a benevolent group, seems to me to be a hope little supported by either recent or distant history. It seems far more likely that behavioral scientists, holding their present attitudes, will be in the position of the German rocket scientists specializing in guided missiles. First, they worked devotedly for Hitler to destroy the U.S.S.R. and the United States. Now depending on who captured them, they work devotedly for the U.S.S.R. in the interest of destroying the United States, or devotedly for the United States in the interest of destroying the U.S.S.R. If behavioral scientists are concerned solely with advancing their science, it seems most probable that they will serve the purpose of whatever group has the power.

The new behavioral controls may prove far more tempting to those in power than such traditional devices as imprisonment, the rack, or the thumbscrew. Altruistic, benevolent leaders who would shrink from applying torture, or from dropping an H-bomb, might without qualms use the "pain-free" devices for what they deem the good of mankind—to steal a lap on an enemy or to lead their own followers into a land flowing with milk, honey, and ESB-like rewards.

It is thus high time, we believe, for laymen to ask: How are these new behavioral controls likely to affect mankind? Shall we permit their use at all? If so, which uses shall we permit and which shall we prohibit? How shall misuse be defined and prevented or punished? And what body—national or international—should make such decisions? During the early period of nuclear research, such questions were asked too seldom and too late.

At Yale, a symposium on Heaven, Hell, and Electrical Stimulation of the Brain has already been held, with a theologian and philosopher as well as scientists participating. Further conferences should be scheduled. The foundations—including Ford, Carnegie, and Rockefeller—which have been supporting ESB research might similarly support inquiries into the ethical implications of such scientific advances. The problem should also go on the agenda of the President's Science Advisory Committee—and behavioral scientists should be added to that committee.

Several of the scientists we consulted urged that these ethical problems not even be mentioned in an article for lay readers. Scientists, they point out, are already under exasperating fire from antivivisectionists, antifluoridationists, and antiscientific obscurantists of many brands who may gain aid and comfort from any new "attack on science." We are convinced, in contrast, that only good can come of open discussion. Fear and hatred of science have long existed among us; they have been intensified since Hiroshima, and cannot be merely shushed. The best way to build fuller confidence in science and scientists is to bring the hazards of misuse out into the open, determine their limits, explain the codes of ethics to which scientists already adhere, and modernize these codes to curb misuse by others—up to and including national governments.

It is in the political area, we suspect, that this issue must ultimately be faced. Even twenty years ago, our national leaders had relatively modest powers. The H-bomb gave them in addition the power to destroy a large part of mankind, and the Cold War gave them an incentive to develop this power to the fullest. The new methods of controlling behavior now emerging from the laboratory may soon add an awe-inspiring power to enslave us all with our own engineered consent. "Project Donkey" is an omen we ignore at our peril.

7. THE MAMMAL AND HIS ENVIRONMENT

D. O. Hebb

The original intention in this paper was to discuss the significance of neurophysiological theory for psychiatry and psychology and to show, by citing the work done by some of my colleagues, that the attempt to get at the neural mechanisms of behavior can stimulate and clarify purely behavioral—that is, psychiatric and psychological—thinking. The research to be described has, I think, a clear relevance to clinical problems; but its origin lay in efforts to learn how the functioning of individual neurons and synapses relates to the

From the AMERICAN JOURNAL OF PSYCHIATRY, *111, 1955, 826–831. Copyright 1955 by the American Psychiatric Association. Reprinted by permission of the American Psychiatric Association and the author. (Footnotes omitted.)*

functions of the whole brain and to understand the physiological nature of learning, emotion, thinking, or intelligence.

In the end, however, my paper has simply become a review of the research referred to, dealing with the relation of the mammal to his environment. The question concerns the normal variability of the sensory environment and this has been studied from two points of view. First, one may ask what the significance of perceptual activity is during growth; for this purpose one can rear an animal with a considerable degree of restriction, and see what effects there are upon mental development. Secondly, in normal animals whose development is complete, one can remove a good deal of the supporting action of the normal environment, to discover how far the animal continues to be dependent on it even after maturity.

THE ROLE OF THE ENVIRONMENT DURING GROWTH

The immediate background of our present research on the intelligence and personality of the dog is the work of Hymovitch on the intelligence of rats. He reared laboratory rats in two ways: (1) in a psychologically restricted environment, a small cage, with food and water always at hand and plenty of opportunity for exercise (in an activity wheel) but with no problems to solve, no need of getting on with others, no pain; and (2) in a "free" environment, a large box with obstacles to pass, blind alleys to avoid, other rats to get on with, and thus ample opportunity for problem-solving and great need for learning during growth. Result: the rats brought up in a psychologically restricted (but biologically adequate) environment have a lasting inferiority in problem-solving. This does not mean, of course, that environment is everything, heredity nothing: here heredity was held constant, which prevents it from affecting the results. When the reverse experiment is done, we find problem-solving varying with heredity instead. The *same* capacity for problem-solving is fully dependent on both variables for its development.

To take this further, Thompson and others have been applying similar methods to dogs. The same intellectual effect of an impoverished environment is found again, perhaps more marked in the higher species. But another kind of effect can be seen in dogs, which have clearly marked personalities. Personality —by which I mean complex individual differences of emotion and motivation—is again strongly affected by the infant environment. These effects, however, are hard to analyze and I cannot at present give any rounded picture of them.

First, observations during the rearing itself are significant. A Scottish terrier is reared in a small cage, in isolation from other Scotties and from the human staff. Our animal man, William Ponman, is a dog lover and undertook the experiment with misgivings, which quickly disappeared. In a cage 30 by 30 inches, the dogs are "happy as larks," eat more than normally reared dogs, grow well, are physically vigorous: as Ponman says, "I never saw such healthy dogs—they're like bulls." If you put a normally-reared dog into such a cage, shut off from everything, his misery is unmistakable, and we have not been able to bring ourselves to continue such experiments. Not so the dog that has known nothing else. Ponman showed some of these at a dog show of national standing, winning first-prize ribbons with them.

Observations by Dr. Ronald Melzack on pain are extremely interesting. He reared two dogs, after early weaning, in complete isolation, taking care that there was little opportunity for experience of pain (unless the dog bit himself). At maturity, when the dogs were first taken out for study, they were extraordinarily excited, with random, rapid movement. As a result they got their tails or paws stepped on repeatedly—but paid no attention to an event that would elicit howls from a normally reared dog. After a few days, when their movements were calmer, they were tested with an object that gave electric shock and paid little attention to it. Through five testing periods, the dog repeatedly thrust his nose into a lighted match and, months later, did the same thing several times with a lighted cigar.

A year and a half after coming out of restriction they are still hyperactive. Clipping and trimming one of them is a two-man job; if the normal dog does not stand still, a cuff on the ear will remind him of his duty; but cuffing the experimental dog "has as much effect as if you patted him—except he pays no attention to it." It seems certain, especially in view of the related results reported by Nissen, Chow, and Semmes for a chimpanzee, that the adult's perception of pain is essentially a function of pain experience during growth—and that what we call pain is not a single sensory quale* but a complex mixture of a particular kind of synthesis with past learning and emotional disturbance.

Nothing bores the dogs reared in restriction. At an "open house," we put two restricted dogs in one enclosure, two normal ones in another, and asked the public to tell us which were the normal. Without exception, they picked out the two alert, lively, interested animals—not the lackadaisical pair lying in the corner, paying no attention to the visitors.

* A sensation or feeling with its own particular quality. (Eds.)

The alert pair, actually, were the restricted; the normal dogs had seen all they wanted to see of the crowd in the first two minutes and then went to sleep, thoroughly bored. The restricted dogs, so to speak, do not have the brains to be bored.

Emotionally, the dogs are "immature," but not in the human or clinical sense. They are little bothered by imaginative fears. Dogs suffer from irrational fears, like horses, porpoises, elephants, chimpanzees, and man; but it appears that this is a product of intellectual development characteristic of the brighter, not the duller, animal. Our dogs in restriction are not smart enough to fear strange objects. Things that cause fear in normal dogs produce only a generalized, undirected excitement in the restricted. If both normal and restricted dogs are exposed to the same noninjurious but exciting stimulus repeatedly, fear gradually develops in the restricted; but the normals, at first afraid, have by this time gone on to show a playful aggression instead. On the street, the restricted dogs "lead well," not bothered by what goes on around them, while those reared normally vary greatly in this respect. Analysis has a long way to go in these cases, but we can say now that dogs reared in isolation are not like ordinary dogs. They are both stupid and peculiar.

Such results clearly support the clinical evidence, and the animal experiments of others, showing that early environment has a lasting effect on the form of adjustment at maturity. We do not have a great body of evidence yet and before we generalize too much, it will be particularly important to repeat these observations with animals of different heredity. But I have been very surprised, personally, by the lack of evidence of emotional instability, neurotic tendency, or the like, when the dogs are suddenly plunged into a normal world. There is, in fact, just the opposite effect. This suggests caution in interpreting data with human children, such as those of Spitz or Bowlby. Perceptual restriction in infancy certainly produces a low level of intelligence, but it may not, by itself, produce emotional disorder. The observed results seem to mean, not that the stimulus of another attentive organism (the mother) is necessary from the first, but that it may become necessary only as psychological *dependence* on the mother develops. However, our limited data certainly cannot prove anything for man, though they may suggest other interpretations besides those that have been made.

THE ENVIRONMENT AT MATURITY

Another approach to the relation between the mammal and his environment is possible: that is, one can take the normally reared mammal and cut him off at maturity from his usual contact with the world. It seems clear that thought and personality characteristics develop as a function of the environment. Once developed, are they independent of it? This experiment is too cruel to do with animals but not with college students. The first stage of the work was done by Bexton, Heron, and Scott. It follows up some work by Mackworth on the effects of monotony, in which he found extraordinary lapses of attention. Heron and his co-workers set out to make the monotony more prolonged and more complete.

The subject is paid to do nothing 24 hours a day. He lies on a comfortable bed in a small closed cubicle, is fed on request, goes to the toilet on request. Otherwise he does nothing. He wears frosted glass goggles that admit light but do not allow pattern vision. His ears are covered by a sponge-rubber pillow in which are embedded small speakers by which he can be communicated with, and a microphone hangs near to enable him to answer. His hands are covered with gloves and cardboard cuffs extend from the upper forearm beyond his fingertips, permitting free joint movement but with little tactual perception.

The results are dramatic. During the stay in the cubicle, the experimental subject shows extensive loss, statistically significant, in solving simple problems. He complains subjectively that he cannot concentrate; his boredom is such that he looks forward eagerly to the next problem, but when it is presented he finds himself unwilling to make the effort to solve it.

On emergence from the cubicle the subject is given the same kind of intelligence tests as before entering and shows significant loss. There is disturbance of motor control. Visual perception is changed in a way difficult to describe; it is as if the object looked at was exceptionally vivid, but impaired in its relation to other objects and the background—a disturbance perhaps of the larger organization of perception. This condition may last up to 12 or 24 hours.

Subjects reported some remarkable hullucinatory activity, some which resembled the effects of mescal or the results produced by Grey Walter with flickering light. These hallucinations were primarily visual, perhaps only because the experimenters were able to control visual perception most effectively; however, some auditory and somesthetic hallucinations have been observed as well.

The nature of these phenomena is best conveyed by quoting one subject who reported over the microphone that he had just been asleep and had a very vivid dream and although he was awake, the dream was continuing. The study of dreams has a long history and is clearly important theoretically, but is hampered by the impossibility of knowing how much the subject's report is distorted by memory. In many ways the hallucinatory activity of the present experiments is indistinguishable from what we know about dreams; if it is in essence the same process but going on while the subject can describe it (not merely hot but still on the griddle), we have a new source of information, a means of direct attack, on the nature of the dream.

In its early stages the activity as it occurs in the experiment is probably not dream-like. The course of development is fairly consistent. First, when the eyes are closed the visual field is light rather than dark. Next there are reports of dots of light, lines, or simple geometrical patterns, so vivid that they are described as being a new experience. Nearly all experimental subjects reported such activity. (Many, of course, could not tolerate the experimental conditions very long and left before the full course of development was seen.) The next stage is the occurrence of repetitive patterns, like a wallpaper design, reported by three-quarters of the subjects; next, the appearance of isolated objects, without background, seen by half the subjects; and finally, integrated scenes, involving action, usually containing dream-like distortions and apparently with all the vividness of an animated cartoon, seen by about a quarter of the subjects. In general, these amused the subject, relieving his boredom, as he watched to see what the movie program would produce next. The subjects reported that the scenes seemed to be out in front of them. A few could, apparently, "look at" different parts of the scene in central vision, as one could with a movie, and up to a point could change its content by "trying." It was not, however, well under control. Usually, it would disappear if the subject were given an interesting task, but not when the subject described it nor if he did physical exercises. Its persistence and vividness interfered with sleep for some subjects and at this stage was irritating.

In their later stages the hallucinations were elaborated into everything from a peaceful rural scene to naked women diving and swimming in a woodland pool to prehistoric animals plunging through tropical forests. One man saw a pair of spectacles, which were then joined by a dozen more, without wearers, fixed intently on him; faces sometimes appeared behind the glasses, but with no eyes visible. The glasses sometimes moved in unison, as if marching in procession. Another man saw a field onto which a bathtub rolled: it moved slowly on rubber-tired wheels, with chrome hub caps. In it was seated an old man wearing a battle helmet. Another subject was highly entertained at seeing a row of squirrels marching single file across a snowy field, wearing snowshoes and carrying little bags over their shoulders.

Some of the scenes were in three dimensions, most in two (that is, as if projected on a screen). A most interesting feature was that some of the images were persistently tilted from the vertical and a few reports were given of inverted scenes, completely upside down.

There were a few reports of auditory phenomena—one subject heard the people in his hallucination talking. There was also some somesthetic imagery, as when one saw a doorknob before him, and as he touched it felt an electric shock; or when another saw a miniature rocket ship maneuvering around him and discharging pellets that he felt hitting his arm. But the most interesting of these phenomena the subject, apparently, lacked words to describe adequately. There were references to a feeling of "otherness," or bodily "strangeness." One said that his mind was like a ball of cotton wool floating in the air above him. Two independently reported that they perceived a second body, or second person, in the cubicle. One subject reported that he could not tell which of the two bodies was his own and described the two bodies as overlapping in space—not like Siamese twins, but two complete bodies with an arm, shoulder, and side of each occupying the same space.

THEORETICAL SIGNIFICANCE

The theoretical interest of these results for us extends in two directions. On the one hand, they interlock with work using more physiological methods of brain stimulation and recording and, especially, much of the recent work on the relation of the brain stem to cortical "arousal." Points of correspondence between behavioral theory and knowledge of neural function are increasing, and each new point of correspondence provides both a corrective for theory and a stimulation for further research. A theory of thought and of consciousness in physiologically intelligible terms need no longer be completely fantastic.

On the other hand, the psychological data cast new light on the relation of man to his environment, including his social environment, and it is this that I should like to discuss a little further. To do so I must go back for a moment to some earlier experiments on chimpanzee emotion. They indicate that the higher mammal may be psychologically at the mercy of his environment to a much greater degree than we have been accustomed to think.

Studies in our laboratory of the role of the environment during infancy and a large body of work reviewed recently by Beach and Jaynes make it clear that psychological development is fully dependent on stimulation from the environment. Without it, intelligence does not develop normally and the personality is grossly atypical. The experiment with college students shows that a short period—even a day or so—of deprivation of a normal sensory input produces personality changes and a clear loss of capacity to solve problems. Even at maturity, then, the organism is still essentially dependent on a normal sensory environment for the maintenance of its psychological integrity.

The following data show yet another way in which the organism appears psychologically vulnerable. It has long been known that the chimpanzee may be frightened by representa-

tions of animals, such as a small toy donkey. An accidental observation of my own extended this to include representations of the chimpanzee himself, of man, and of parts of the chimpanzee or human body. A model of a chimpanzee head, in clay, produced terror in the colony of the Yerkes Laboratories, as did a lifelike representation of a human head, and a number of related objects such as an actual chimpanzee head, preserved in formalin, or a colored representation of a human eye and eyebrow. A deeply anesthetized chimpanzee, "dead" as far as the others were concerned, aroused fear in some animals and vicious attacks by others.

I shall not deal with this theoretically. What matters for our present purposes is the conclusion, rather well supported by the animal evidence, that the greater the development of intelligence the greater the vulnerability to emotional breakdown. The price of high intelligence is susceptibility to imaginative fears and unreasoning suspicion and other emotional weaknesses. The conclusion is not only supported by the animal data but also agrees with the course of development in children, growing intelligence being accompanied by increased frequency and strength of emotional problems—up to the age of five years.

Then, apparently, the trend is reversed. Adult man, more intelligent than chimpanzee or five-year-old child, seems not more subject to emotional disturbances but less. Does this then disprove the conclusion? It seemed a pity to abandon a principle that made sense of so many data that had not made sense before, and the kind of theory I was working with—neurophysiologically oriented—also pointed in the same direction. The question then was, is it possible that something is concealing the adult human being's emotional weaknesses?

From this point of view it became evident that the concealing agency is man's culture which acts as a protective cocoon. There are many indications that our emotional stability depends more on our successful avoidance of emotional provocation than on our essential characteristics: that urbanity depends on an urbane social and physical environment. Dr. Thompson and I reviewed the evidence and came to the conclusion that the development of what is called "civilization" is the progressive elimination of sources of acute fear, disgust, and anger, and that civilized man may not be less, but more, susceptible to such disturbance because of his success in protecting himself from disturbing situations so much of the time.

We may fool ourselves thoroughly in this matter. We are surprised that children are afraid of the dark or afraid of being left alone and congratulate ourselves on having got over such weakness. Ask anyone you know whether he is afraid of the dark and he will either laugh at you or be insulted. This attitude is easy to maintain in a well-lighted, well-behaved suburb. But try being alone in complete darkness in the streets of a strange city or alone at night in the deep woods and see if you still feel the same way.

We read incredulously of the taboo rules of primitive societies; we laugh at the superstitious fear of the dead in primitive people. What is there about a dead body to produce disturbance? Sensible, educated people are not so affected. One can easily show that they are, however, and that we have developed an extraordinarily complete taboo system—not just moral prohibition, but full-fledged ambivalent taboo—to deal with the dead body. I took a poll of an undergraduate class of 198 persons, including some nurses and veterans, to see how many had encountered a dead body. Thirty-seven had never seen a dead body in any circumstances, and 91 had seen one only after an undertaker had prepared it for burial;

making a total of 65 percent who had never seen a dead body in, so to speak, its natural state. It is quite clear that for some reason we protect society against sight of, contact with, the dead body. Why?

Again, the effect of moral education, and training in the rules of courtesy, and the compulsion to dress, talk and act as others do, adds up to ensuring that the individual member of society will not act in a way that is a provocation to others—will not, that is, be a source of strong emotional disturbance, except in highly ritualized circumstances approved by society. The social behavior of a group of civilized persons, then, makes up that protective cocoon which allows us to think of ourselves as being less emotional than the explosive four-year-old or the equally explosive chimpanzee.

The well-adjusted adult, therefore, is not intrinsically less subject to emotional disturbance: he is well-adjusted, relatively unemotional, as long as he is in his cocoon. The problem of moral education, from this point of view, is not simply to produce a stable individual but to produce an individual that will (1) be stable in the existing social environment and (2) contribute to its protective uniformity. We think of some persons as being emotionally dependent, others not; but it looks as though we are all completely dependent on the environment in a way and to a degree that we have not suspected.

8. IN QUEST OF DREAMING

Frederick Snyder

. . .

DISCOVERY OF THE RAPID EYE MOVEMENT STATE

Although recent developments in the scientific study of dreaming must be said to have begun fortuitously, fortune chose its beneficiaries wisely. In 1952 at the University of Chicago, a particularly tenacious graduate student, Eugene Aserinsky, pursued a trying task in the physiology laboratory of an outstanding authority on the subject of sleep, Dr. Nathaniel Kleitman. Aserinsky had set out to study the frequency of eye blinks during sleep in newborn infants as a possible correlate of sleep depth, but in the absence of available instrumentation suitable to that purpose had no choice but simply to watch the babies' eyes—hour after hour and month after month. The difficulty was that these infants did all sorts of things with their eyes, so that Aserinsky eventually confronted the discouraging realization that the "blink" was operationally indefinable. To salvage what he could from his efforts, he decided to reformulate the problem in terms of counting any eyelid movements during the infants' sleep! Undoubtedly this was every bit as tedious as it sounds, but when he did this his observations began to fall into an interesting pattern: there were times, associated with much diffuse body movement, when the eyelids were in active motion, and there were other times when both body movements and eye movements were lacking, these two conditions alter-

From Frederick Snyder: "In Quest of Dreaming"; in Herman A. Witkin and Helen B. Lewis (eds.): EXPERIMENTAL STUDIES OF DREAMING; Chapter 1. Copyright © 1967 by Random House, Inc. and reprinted with their permission.

nating at roughly equal intervals within a period of about an hour.

If Aserinsky had stopped at the fulfillment of his original goal, probably there would be no occasion for this discussion. Instead he decided, for the sake of completeness, to extend his study by observing eye movements during sleep in adult humans. Conceding to the fatigue of his own eyeballs, however, he again revised his approach to make use of an electrical recording technique, though this was suited to registered movements of the eyes themselves, rather than of the lids.[1] When Aserinsky and Kleitman used this technique to record the eye movements of adult humans throughout entire nights of natural sleep they made a startling discovery. They found the slow, pendular movements described so often before, but they also found a very different kind of eye movement, which was rapid, jerky, binocularly symmetrical in all directions, and which often occurred in extended bursts. Still more intriguing, these rapid eye movements (REM) came thick and fast during certain discrete periods of sleep lasting from a few minutes to a half-hour or more, and not at all during the rest. The REM periods never appeared at the beginning of sleep, but only after an hour or more had elapsed, recurring again after long intervals three to five times each night.

Since 1952 many hundreds of researchers

1 This method is based upon the fact that there is a small but constant voltage difference across the globes of the eyes, so that their movements result in shifting potential fields. These can be picked up by electrodes attached to the skin anywhere about the orbits, amplified, and recorded on a coventional electroencephalograph. Although this method has been used in most of the studies I shall mention, some recent work has employed a technique which actually does register movements of the eyelids.

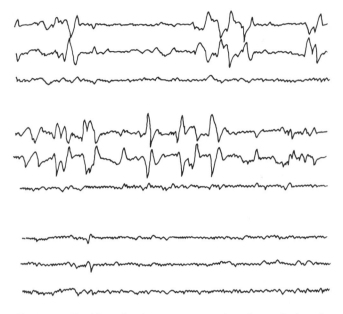

FIGURE 1. Rapid conjugate eye movement patterns during sleep. This illustrates the varying amounts and ever-changing patterns of eye movement from consecutive twenty-second samples of an REM period. The third line in each sample is the characteristic EEG pattern.

have watched their recording pens trace this constantly varied but always fascinating calligraphy of rapid eye movement patterns, such as those shown in Figure 1, but the same phenomenon can be confirmed by anyone with enough patience simply by observing the vermiform movements of the globes under the closed eyelids of the sleeper.[2]

Again in the interest of thoroughness, Aserinsky and Kleitman had made simultaneous records of EEG,* heart rate, and respiration; the results were almost equally remarkable. Those periods when REM took place were distinguished by slightly faster heart and respiration rates, as well as by a low-voltage EEG pattern, untypical of the rest of sleep except at its very onset (see Figure 1), though it was not clear then whether this EEG pattern was distinctive to the REM period. Given this striking and hitherto entirely unsuspected pattern of physiological events regularly recurrent during sleep, all of which

seemed to suggest a more highly aroused level of nervous activity, the obvious hypothesis that dreaming might be associated with this condition was promptly and directly tested. When the experimenters awakened their subjects while the rapid eye movement periods were occurring, detailed and vivid dream memories came forth in 74 per cent of instances, while awakenings from the rest of sleep yielded reports in just 7 per cent. Thus, what began as an unexciting scientific exercise, by dint of perseverance in the face of discouragement and a dogged urge for thoroughness, led to the unveiling of an extraordinary new visage of nature, previously hidden and undreamed of throughout the entire history of human experience.[3]

It was in 1953 that the entire discovery emerged in a brief note in *Science* and two years later that it was reported in greater detail; but it was not widely heralded, and recognition of the magnitude of its implica-

2 Just before the alarm clock sounds in the morning is an excellent time.

* Electroencephalogram: a recording of electrical patterns in the brain. (Eds.)

3 It should be recalled that, as noted in the preface, a relationship between eye movements and dreams had been anticipated by G. T. Ladd (1892) and probably others.

tions has required a decade. In the meantime, Eugene Aserinsky had received his doctorate and, finding that there was little demand for dreaming research in departments of physiology, had turned his efforts to more conventional problems.[4] Since most previous scientific claims about dreaming had been relegated to a special obscurity, this might well have happened then to the REM discovery. That it did not is largely due to the vision and dedication of another graduate student, William C. Dement, who had come to the same laboratory soon after the REM periods were first observed. With Kleitman's encouragement and guidance, Dement pressed forward with the studies almost alone for several years (at the same time completing both M.D. and Ph.D. degrees) and in the process defined the essential characteristics of an entirely new conception of dreaming.

EARLY CONFIRMATIONS

One of the particularly compelling ideas in the scientific lore surrounding this subject has been that of an equivalence between dreaming and psychosis,[5] and it was appropriate, therefore, that Dement's first venture should be to examine the sleep of schizophrenic patients. As has been substantiated in a number of subsequent studies, he determined that schizophrenics do have rapid eye movement periods and that their incidence over the course of the night is roughly similar to that of normals. Not unexpectedly, these patients were somewhat less consistent in reporting dreams after awakenings than were medical-student control subjects, but in both groups the correlation was of the same order as that found by Aserinsky and Kleitman. Dement was also interested in the kind of dream content which the patients reported, noting that about half of them frequently reported dreams of isolated, inanimate objects, dissimilar to any

dreams reported by the medical students.[6] At the same time he made an important observation about the nature of this physiological process, commenting in his discussion of that paper:

> Thus, the periods were neither initiated nor always ended by the disturbances [awakenings]. It seems likely, therefore, that the rapid eye movement periods and probably associated dream activities do not occur in response to random environmental stimuli, but are part of an intrinsic physiological sleep pattern.

In the next two investigations the existence of such an intrinsic physiological sleep pattern and its relationship to dreaming were much more firmly established.

Most previous researches on the EEG patterns of sleep, like most approaches to sleep physiology generally, had either equated short periods of sleep with all sleep, or relied upon intermittent time sampling during the night; the notion of obtaining continuous records throughout typical nights of sleep would have seemed highly extravagant. In a study that has become one of the classics in this young field, Dement and Kleitman did just this over a total of 126 nights from thirty-three subjects and, by means of a simplified categorization of EEG patterns,[7] scored them in their entirety. When they examined these 126 records they found that there was a very predictable sequence of patterns over the course of the night, such as had been hinted by Aserinsky's study, but entirely overlooked in all previous EEG studies of sleep. Although this sequence of regular variations has been observed now many thousands of times in scores of laboratories, no one has improved upon the original description of it:

> The usual sequence was that after the onset of sleep the EEG progressed fairly rapidly to Stage 4, which persisted for varying amounts of time, generally about 30 minutes, and then a lightening took place. While the progression

4 Dr. Aserinsky has now returned to studying the REM phenomenon after an interval of a decade, and later mention will be made of his most recent contributions.

5 To mention just a few examples, Jung said, "Let the dreamer walk about and act like one awakened and we have the clinical picture of dementia praecox"; Hughlings Jackson proclaimed, "Find out about dreams and you will find out about insanity." Kant is quoted as stating, "The lunatic is a wakeful dreamer"; while Schopenhauer observed that "a dream is a short-lasting psychosis, and a psychosis is a long-lasting dream."

6 This is an interesting observation which has not been followed up. Thus far there has been just one other published application of this technique for the purpose of examining dream content in particular psychodiagnostic groups.

7 Their categories have since been almost universally adopted, but without going into detailed definitions, . . . Stage 1 corresponds to the pattern labeled "drowsing," Stage 2 to "light" sleep, Stage 3 to "moderately deep sleep," and Stage 4 to "deep sleep."

from wakefulness to Stage 4 at the beginning of the cycle was almost invariably through a continuum of change, the lightening was usually abrupt and coincident with a body movement or series of body movements. After the termination of Stage 4, there was generally a short period of Stage 2 or 3 which gave way to Stage 1 and rapid eye movements. When the first eye movement period ended, the EEG again progressed through a continuum of change to Stage 3 or 4 which persisted for a time and then lightened often abruptly with body movement to Stage 2 which again gave way to Stage 1 and the second rapid eye movement period.

They found that this cyclical variation of EEG patterns occurred repeatedly throughout the night at intervals of 90 to 100 minutes from the end of one eye movement period to the end of the next. Usually the "deepest" sleep patterns are seen only in the first or second cycles, though transient periods of Stage 3 or Stage 4 are sometimes seen later in the night.

The regularly recurring REM periods were found every night in all subjects, as they have been ever since. The degree of regularity and of variation in the occurrence of these periods is illustrated in Figure 2, which is a diagrammatic presentation of a random sample of all-night records obtained in our own laboratory. Note, as Dement and Kleitman did, that the first REM period is usually shorter than the rest, and there is some tendency toward an increase in duration of successive periods. They can vary in duration from 1 to 70 minutes or more, though 20 minutes is about average. Dement and Kleitman found a mean total time taken up by REM periods of 64 minutes or 18 per cent, but this was based upon the first six hours of sleep, and in eight hours the percentage is higher. In the young adult subjects, who have been most intensively studied, average REM time in various reports ranges from 22 per cent to 24 per cent. It was noted then, and has since been further documented, that to some extent this all-night pattern of EEG changes is an individual characteristic, but there are extreme variations in the percentage of REM time from about fifteen to thirty. This twofold range is seen in "normal" individuals, and at a later point we shall deal with what little is known about the factors that contribute to it.

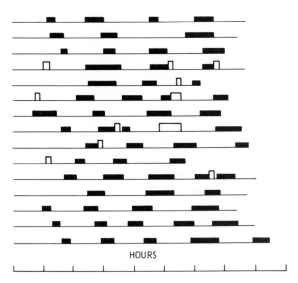

HOURS

Figure 2. Occurrence of REM periods in uninterrupted human sleep. Each line is the diagrammatic representation of an entire night of sleep, examples selected at random from the records of fifteen young adult subjects. Solid bars = REM periods; open bars = waking; single line = non-REM sleep. (Reprinted with the permission of the publishers from N.S. Greenfield and W.C. Lewis, eds., *Psychoanalysis and Current Biological Thought*, Madison, Wis., The University of Wisconsin Press, p. 279. Copyright © 1965 by the Regents of the University of Wisconsin.)

It was clearly established in this study that, except for the very transiently similar pattern at sleep onset, the EEG record concomitant with REM periods was a distinctive one, and while the eye movement itself is intermittent and highly variable in amount, this EEG pattern is continuous from the beginning of the period to the end. Dement and Kleitman stated then that the characteristic EEG pattern was actually a better criterion of dreaming than the eye movements themselves, and it has become the convention that when we speak of "REM periods" it is the interval distinguished by this EEG pattern that is referred to.

If it could be accepted that the presence of REM periods indicated the occurrence of dreaming, then the implications of this study were remarkable: that dreaming is an invariable and universal occurrence in normal sleep, every night in every sleeping human; that it takes up approximately one-fifth of each night; and that it is an intrinsic part of sleep rather than a result of fortuitous disturbances.

Additional evidence that REM periods did indicate the occurrence of dreaming appeared in another report by Dement and Kleitman in the same year. In the earlier studies there was the possibility that the REM relationship to dreaming had resulted from unintentional cueing at the time of awakening, so in this larger-scale test all direct contact between subject and experimenter at those times was dispensed with. As indicated in Table 1,* again the subjects uniformly showed a high incidence of dream recall following REM awakenings, and a very low incidence when awakened during the rest of sleep.

It might be that awakenings from REM periods are merely particularly favorable times for the instant creation of dreams, or for remembering them, or even for confabulating them, and in this same report first attempts were made to relate more specific variations in the objective events prior to awakening with the subjective events recalled afterwards. Subjects were awakened either five or fifteen minutes after the onset of REM, and asked to decide which had been the duration of their dream; they judged correctly 92 out of 111 times. Attempts were made to do the awakenings immediately after quite specific eye movement patterns, and although this was not highly systematic or extensive, results encouraged the interpretation that the pattern of the REM was related to the visual imagery of the dream. For example, the dream associated with the only instance of pure horizontal movement involved the subject's watching two people throwing tomatoes at each other.

Within a year the indefatigable Dement, now in collaboration with another student, Edwin Wolpert, had produced still more convincing evidence. They separated transcripts of dream reports into active and passive categories, then to eliminate possible bias on the part of the experimenters independently made similar division of the corresponding electrographic records in terms of the amount of eye movement. They found that these two kinds of data were very significantly correlated, i.e., active dreams are associated with more eye movement; then they went beyond this by attempting to infer the direction of last eye movement from the subject's recall of his very last dream action prior to awakening. Among the five possibilities (up, down, right, left, or none), the last eye movement was identical with the last reported fixation in the dream in seventeen of twenty-three cases.

When body movements interrupted REM periods, yet were followed by continuing ocular activity, Dement and Wolpert wondered whether this might mark the end of one dream episode and the beginning of another. To test this, they separated instances of dreams that were long and continuous as opposed to those that contained two or more unrelated fragments, and then correlated these with the corresponding electrical recordings divided into those with and those without body movements. Similarly, the transcriptions were scanned for narratives that were much shorter than would have been expected from the duration of REM, while the electrical records were examined to determine whether a body movement might have occurred several minutes before awakening. In both tests the relationships were as predicted, indicating that body movements during REM periods tend to signal a change in dream activity.[8]

Still in the same report, Dement and Wolpert went on to assess one of the most widely held assumptions about dream causa-

---

* Not shown here. (Eds.)

8 This implies that when we speak of a "dream" as a more or less coherent story, we are usually referring not to the experience of an entire REM period out of the three to five each night, but rather to one fragment of such a period, of which there may be many times that number.

tion, that dreams represent disturbances of sleep due to external or internal stimuli. The fact of the regular periodicity of REM independent of chance sleep disturbances already made this seem highly unlikely, but in that study they attacked the question directly. External stimulation of the sleeper during non-REM sleep did not give rise either to REM periods or to reports of dreaming. There is more to be said about this later, but it is now quite generally accepted not only that disturbance of sleep to the point of partial or complete arousal fails to produce REM but that it actually reduces its occurrence over the course of the night.

Even if chance stimuli do not cause dreaming, there was still the question as to how important they might be in shaping the content of dream experience. To test the effects of an internal stimulus they withheld fluids from their subjects for twenty-four hours, but in only a third of the dreams reported under this condition were there any elements that even vaguely related to thirst. To examine the effects of external stimuli they awakened their subjects during REM periods after stimulating them with tones, light flashes, or a spray of cold water, looking for obvious incorporations of such stimuli into the dream narratives. They found indications that the

most noxious stimulus, the water spray, had been incorporated in 14 of 33 instances, but the light flash appeared in just 7 of 30, and the tone signal in only 3 of 35.

This evidence suggested that although external stimuli can modify dream content, they are not markedly effective in doing so. The occasions when this does happen are of particular interest, however, since they introduce "time markers" into the dream experience, which can later be compared with the amount of actual time elapsed prior to awakening. In ten instances when such a comparison was possible, the amount of dream "action" following the incorporated stimulus was commensurate with that which might have occurred during the same time intervals in reality. Such evidence further supported the interpretation that under these experimental conditions subjects do report their dreams as they experience them, that the dreams take place during the time when REM is present rather than at the instant of awakening, and that dream events and real events proceed at about the same rate of speed. This single remarkable paper had shown that by using REM as an objective indicator of dreaming, aspects of that phenomenon that previously were only subject to speculation could now be put to careful experimental test....

RECOMMENDED FURTHER READING

Bell, Charles: "Idea of a New Anatomy of the Brain" in Wayne Dennis (ed.): *Readings in the History of Psychology* (2nd Ed.); New York, Appleton-Century 1948

*Brownfield, Charles A.: *Isolation: Clinical and Experimental Approaches;* New York, Random House 1965

*Darwin, Charles: *On the Origin of Species;* London 1859 (numerous editions available)

Dement, William C.: "An Essay on Dreams: The Role of Physiology in Understanding Their Nature" in Frank Barron, *et al.* (eds.): *New Directions in Psychology II;* New York, Holt, Rinehart & Winston 1965

Dement, William C. and Charles Fisher: "Experimental Interference with the Sleep Cycle"; *Canadian Psychiatric Association Journal, 8* (1963), 405–411

Eckstein, Gustav: *The Body Has A Head;* New York, Harper & Row 1970

Galton, Francis: *Inquiries into Human Faculty and Its Development;* New York, Dutton 1908

Hebb, D. O.: *The Organization of Behavior;* New York, John Wiley 1949

*Lorenz, Konrad: *King Solomon's Ring;* New York, Crowell 1952

Selye, Hans: *The Stress of Life;* New York, McGraw-Hill 1965

Sheer, D. (ed.): *Electrical Stimulation of the Brain;* Austin, Texas, Hogg Foundation and University of Texas Press 1961

Solomon, Philip, *et al.* (eds.): *Sensory Deprivation;* Cambridge, Mass., Harvard University Press 1961

Waddington, C. H.: *The Ethical Animal;* London, George Allen & Unwin 1960

* Paperback edition available.

PART III

GROWTH AND DEVELOPMENT
OF THE ORGANISM

Having seen that biological processes underlie psychological ones, we can now proceed to examine in greater detail the interaction between the two as well as the relationship between biological factors and culture. Our primary concern in this section will be with the processes of growth and development, especially in the early period of the organism's life.

Growth and maturation are essentially genetically-based, internally regulated biological processes that begin with the organism's conception (in the case of the human fetus, growth proceeds more rapidly in the period before birth than at any time thereafter) and end with its death, processes that proceed independently of learning or of any environmental influences save the physical. In many lower species genetically programmed processes and responses account for virtually all of the individual organism's behavior, which is to say that most behavior exhibited by members of such species is "instinctive" and their capacity for learning severely limited. Among members of such species the path from birth to biological maturity is traversed rapidly.

In higher species, most particularly in man, growth and maturation not only proceed far more slowly but must be accompanied and modified by complex social-psychological processes of learning (in the broadest sense of that word) if what we think of as "normal" development is to occur. Those processes are from birth onward mediated by culture: the accumulated beliefs, attitudes, traditions, behavior patterns, and material artifacts that characterize the social group into which an individual is born. While physiological maturation may create a readiness or propensity for development through learning, the absence of appropriate social and cultural facilitation will preclude the latter and may seriously impair normal further maturation. In other words, much if not most human behavior is governed not by genetically programmed biological processes but by culture operating on a set of limiting biological potentialities.

That complex of social and cultural processes which, over many years, transforms the human infant from a bundle of biological and physiological impulses into a more or less responsibly functioning social being, we call the process of "socialization." While argument over the relative roles played by nature (or genetics) and environment (or culture) in the determination of human behavior still rages, there is no question that instinctive or genetically pre-programmed responses play a far smaller part in the development of the human species than in that of any other, a fact that is importantly related to the degree of complexity and variety possible to human behavior, to the human child's long period of dependency, and to the absolute necessity of culture in the shaping of distinctively *human* behavior.

We are not yet certain whether, given favoring circumstances, human development proceeds in a continuous line or whether, as Freud, Piaget, Erikson, and others have maintained, it is marked by distinct stages or "critical periods" that are somewhat discontinuous one from another. The existence of critical periods has, however, been well established in the life cycle of various infra-human species. What this means is that, at a given stage of biological maturation, some influences or events can and do have an unusually profound impact on the organism's development. Should these influences or events be absent or should they present themselves in such a way that the organism cannot successfully cope with them serious behavior pathologies will probably result and normal development (normal for that species) will be impaired.

One phenomenon associated with critical periods that has received much attention from psychologists and ethologists (students of animal behavior) is that of "imprinting" in certain bird and other mammal species. In birds imprinting denotes the development of a permanent and irreversible bond between the young bird and any object (animate or inanimate) to which it is exposed for any length of time during the critical period of development, even though that contact be only visual. Imprinting is especially strong if the object is the very first stimulus which meets the newborn individual. Young ducklings may thus be imprinted to a wooden model of a duck or a chicken while goslings and puppies can easily be imprinted to human handlers, even before feeding behavior commences. Although imprinting can take place at any stage of the life cycle, it proceeds more slowly and is more easily reversed if it occurs outside the critical period or periods. In the case of animals, investigators have found that any strong emotional arousal (including fear) will increase both the speed and the strength of imprinting. While some authorities contend that imprinting is qualitatively different from the usual types of learning, others believe it is only a special case of conditioning (see Part IV) which occurs because the imprinted object greatly reduces the young animal's anxiety or is, at least, associated by the latter with a state of minimal anxiety. To the extent (an extent as yet undetermined) that imprinting occurs in human infants, it may help to explain both the strength and lasting impact of early childhood experiences and such apparently incongruous phenomena as the close attachment young children feel even to cruel, rejecting, or abusive parents. Once a behavioral system is organized—on whatever principle—it becomes increasingly difficult to reorganize it on an alternative basis. As J.P. Scott has put it: "Organization inhibits reorganization."

While there is considerable indirect evidence to support the existence of critical periods in human development, general agreement on the precise nature of those periods, their order of succession, and their duration is still lacking. Current opinion among developmental psychologists, however, favors the view that the development of many kinds of cognitive and social abilities depends on the environment provided the child in the first three years of his life. While the evidence is not yet conclusive and, because of the legal and ethical restrictions on experimenting with human children, may never be as unambiguous as the data from animal studies, we can already say with some confidence that the critical periods in human development are both longer in time than is the case with other mammals and are less dependent on biological maturation alone. Precisely because of this, far more events can interfere with normal human development than with that of any other species. Men pay a heavy psychological price for their biological and cultural advantages.

While most of the work on human development and socialization has been concerned with the first ten and especially with the first five or six years of life (perhaps because of the great influence of Freud's theories, which assert the critical importance of early childhood experiences such as feeding, weaning, and toilet training on later psychic development), we now recognize that processes of socialization and development continue throughout the life cycle—into adolescence, young adulthood, maturity, and old age—and terminate only with death. Erik Erikson's work has illuminated the problems of adolescence and youth (see Selection 13 below), and as both the percentage and the absolute numbers of people over 65 in the United States continue to grow we can expect that psychologists will pay increasing attention to the psychology of aging and the aged.

Although Harry Harlow of the University of Wisconsin does not discuss critical periods as such, the ingenious research he reports in the first selection concerns the development of what is perhaps the most critical social bond in the life of any primate: that between the infant and his "mother," even a constructed mother. Harlow concludes that love and affection, defined as the need for "contact comfort," and the warmth provided by the mother is a primary, not a secondary, drive and is probably of greater importance than the physical nourishment the mother provides the infant. Denial of such physical comfort and security leads to serious emotional disturbances in young monkeys, thus confirming the profound effect of early emotional deprivation on later emotional development. In a later paper not reprinted here, Harlow reported that monkeys raised in isolation from other infant monkeys failed to develop normal sexual and social responses upon reaching biological maturity. Monkeys raised by terrycloth "mothers" who, however, experienced normal physical and affectional contact with other growing monkeys did develop normal sexual and social responses. The reader might ask himself what these findings imply for the future of child-rearing in industrial societies such as our own. May computer-controlled communal child-rearing establishments someday replace the biological mother and the nuclear family as the primary instrumentality for socializing young children? The experience of the Israeli kibbutz, which Bettleheim discusses in Selection 13, suggests that this idea is far from fanciful.

Granted that monkeys are not men, the excerpts from Jean-Marc Itard's classic account of a "feral" or savage boy* who, apparently, had grown up

---

* Francois Truffaut's 1969 film *L'Enfant Sauvage* (*The Wild Child*) is based on Itard's work.

among animals in the woods of southern France, indicates that early contact with others of his own species is as critical for human as for monkey children. The boy of ten or eleven, called Victor, had been captured in the Aveyron woods in the autumn of 1799 and was brought to Paris the following year, apparently in the belief that he was an example of that "natural man" uncorrupted by society of which the philosopher Jean-Jacques Rousseau had written earlier in the eighteenth century. Itard, a young and dedicated physician, took an interest in the boy, but despite five years of intensive work was never able to develop his sensory, cognitive, or emotional capacities beyond a rudimentary level. Victor, for example, never learned to speak more than a few words and those were directly related to his physiological needs. While this case and several similar ones reported elsewhere in the literature indicate that a *human* being is a social and cultural rather than a biological product, they also suggest that biological factors set limits to the effects of culture, that once past a certain point of biological maturation it may be impossible for the human organism to actualize characteristic human potentialities. In other words, there almost certainly are *some* critical periods in the development of human behavior.

In the next selection Maya Pines reports several research projects at Harvard University which are exploring the development of cognitive abilities and generalized competence among very young children. While Miss Pines does not review previous research, the reader should recognize that these projects implicitly assume that critical periods in human development do exist, that they may be concentrated within the first three years of life, and that the differing qualities of early mother-child interaction (recall Harlow's findings) may be decisive for the later intellectual and emotional development of the individual. That differences in congnitive abilities among young children tend to correlate highly with social class position suggests that important social changes outside the formal educational system itself may be necessary to help culturally and socially disadvantaged children as well as to raise the general level of human performance in American society. Miss Pines' policy suggestions might well be compared with the existing practices of the Israeli kibbutz as described by Bettelheim.

Frank O'Connor's story presents an amusing and tender, yet psychologically perceptive, account of a young boy's rivalry with his returned-soldier father for the love of his mother, a theme of psychosexual development that Freud called, after the ancient myth, the "Oedipus complex." Notice how, at the end the boy's rivalry with his father is replaced by rivalry ("sibling rivalry") with his newborn brother. This, in turn, leads to a new solidarity with his father against his mother and the baby. Such emotional configurations are exceedingly common in small, relatively isolated two-generation families (so-called 'nuclear" or "conjugal" families) such as characterize American society, but they need not lead to later psychopathology unless they are ineptly handled and incompletely resolved.

Bruno Bettelheim's summary of the psychosocial development of the communally-raised Israeli kibbutz children is based on Erik Erikson's model of psychosocial stages, a model constructed largely from the experience of American middle-class children. Bettelheim's comparison of the kibbutz with American realities shows that there is no single, universally valid way of raising children, that different educational systems produce different personality types that may be equally suitable to the needs and values of their respective societies. It would seem, in fact, that some of the psychosocial dilemmas delineated by Erikson simply do not exist for kibbutz-raised children and adolescents. Bettelheim's analysis also points to the heightened role of the peer group in communal child-rearing, a point which recalls both Harlow's discussion of the role of affection among infant monkeys and David Riesman's discussion (in *The Lonely Crowd*) of the "other-directed" character type among Americans. Kibbutz-bred adolescents and adults are probably far more other-directed than any comparable American group.

9. THE NATURE OF LOVE[1]

Harry F. Harlow

Love is a wondrous state, deep, tender, and rewarding. Because of its intimate and personal nature it is regarded by some as an improper topic for experimental research. But, whatever our personal feelings may be, our assigned mission as psychologists is to analyze all facets of human and animal behavior into their component variables. So far as love or affection is concerned, psychologists have failed in this mission. The little we know about love does not transcend simple observation, and the little we write about it has been written better by poets and novelists. But of greater concern is the fact that psychologists tend to give progressively less attention to a motive which pervades our entire lives. Psychologists, at least psychologists who write textbooks, not only show no interest in the origin and development of love or affection, but they seem to be unaware of its very existence.

The apparent repression of love by modern psychologists stands in sharp contrast with the attitude taken by many famous and normal people. The word "love" has the highest reference frequency of any word cited in Bartlett's book of *Familiar Quotations*. It would appear that this emotion has long had a vast interest and fascination for human beings, regardless of the attitude taken by

1 Address of the President at the sixty-sixth Annual Convention of the American Psychological Association, Washington, D. C., August 31, 1958.

The researches reported in this paper were supported by funds supplied by Grant No. M-722, National Institutes of Health, by a grant from the Ford Foundation, and by funds received from the Graduate School of the University of Wisconsin.

psychologists; but the quotations cited, even by famous and normal people, have a mundane redundancy. These authors and authorities have stolen love from the child and infant and made it the exclusive property of the adolescent and adult.

Thoughtful men, and probably all women, have speculated on the nature of love. From the developmental point of view, the general plan is quite clear: The initial love responses of the human being are those made by the infant to the mother or some mother surrogate. From this intimate attachment of the child to the mother, multiple learned and generalized affectional responses are formed.

Unfortunately, beyond these simple facts we know little about the fundamental variables underlying the formation of affectional responses and little about the mechanisms through which the love of the infant for the mother develops into the multifaceted response patterns characterizing love or affection in the adult. Because of the dearth of experimentation, theories about the fundamental nature of affection have evolved at the level of observation, intuition, and discerning guesswork, whether these have been proposed by psychologists, sociologists, anthropologists, physicians, or psychoanalysts.

The position commonly held by psychologists and sociologists is quite clear: The basic motives are, for the most part, the primary drives—particularly hunger, thirst, elimination, pain, and sex—and all other motives, including love or affection, are derived or secondary drives. The mother is associated with the reduction of the primary drives—particularly hunger, thirst, and pain—and through learning, affection or love is derived.

It is entirely reasonable to believe that the mother, through association with food, may become a secondary-reinforcing agent, but this is an inadequate mechanism to account for the persistence of the infant-maternal ties. There is a spate of researches on the formation of secondary reinforcers to hunger and thirst reduction. There can be no question that almost any external stimulus can become a secondary reinforcer if properly associated with tissue-need reduction, but the fact remains that this redundant literature demonstrates unequivocally that such derived drives suffer relatively rapid experimental extinction. Contrariwise, human affection does not extinguish when the mother ceases to have intimate association with the drives in question. Instead, the affectional ties to the mother show a lifelong, unrelenting persistence and, even more surprising, widely expanding generality.

Oddly enough, one of the few psychologists who took a position counter to modern psychological dogma was John B. Watson, who believed that love was an innate emotion elicited by cutaneous stimulation of the erogenous zones. But experimental psychologists, with their peculiar propensity to discover facts that are not true, brushed this theory aside by demonstrating that the human neonate had no differentiable emotions, and they established a fundamental psychological law that prophets are without honor in their own profession.

The psychoanalysts have concerned themselves with the problem of the nature of the development of love in the neonate and infant, using ill and aging human beings as subjects. They have discovered the overwhelming importance of the breast and related this to the oral erotic tendencies developed at an age preceding their subjects' memories. Their theories range from a belief that the infant has an innate need to achieve and suckle at the breast to beliefs not unlike commonly accepted psychological theories. There are exceptions, as seen in the recent writings of John Bowlby, who attributes importance not only to food and thirst satisfaction, but also to "primary object-clinging," a need for intimate physical contact, which is initially associated with the mother.

As far as I know, there exists no direct experimental analysis of the relative importance of the stimulus variables determining the affectional or love responses in the neonatal and infant primate. Unfortunately, the human neonate is a limited experimental subject for such researches because of his inadequate motor capabilities. By the time the human infant's motor responses can be precisely measured, the antecedent determining conditions cannot be defined, having been lost in a jumble and jungle of confounded variables.

Many of these difficulties can be resolved by the use of the neonatal and infant macaque monkey as the subject for the analysis of basic affectional variables. It is possible to make precise measurements in this primate beginning at two to ten days of age, depending upon the maturational status of the individual animal at birth. The macaque infant differs from the human infant in that the monkey is more mature at birth and grows more rapidly; but the basic responses relating to affection, including nursing, contact, clinging, and even visual and auditory exploration, exhibit no fundamental differences in the two species. Even the development of perception, fear, frustration, and learning capability follows very similar sequences in rhesus monkeys and human children.

Three years' experimentation before we started our studies on affection gave us experience with the neonatal monkey. We had separated more than 60 of these animals from their mothers 6 to 12 hours after birth and suckled them on tiny bottles. The infant mortality was only a small fraction of what would have obtained had we let the monkey mothers raise their infants. Our bottle fed babies were healthier and heavier than monkey-mother-reared infants. We know that we are better monkey mothers than are real monkey mothers thanks to synthetic diets, vitamins, iron extracts, penicillin, chloromycetin, 5% glucose, and constant, tender, loving care.

During the course of these studies we noticed that the laboratory-raised babies showed strong attachment to the cloth pads (folded gauze diapers) which were used to cover the hardware-cloth floors of their cages. The infants clung to these pads and engaged in violent temper tantrums when the pads were removed and replaced for sanitary reasons. Such contact-need or responsiveness had been reported previously by Gertrude van Wagenen for the monkey and by Thomas McCulloch and George Haslerud for the chimpanzee and is reminiscent of the devotion often exhibited by human infants to their pillows, blankets, and soft, cuddly stuffed toys.... The baby, human or monkey, if it is to survive, must clutch at more than a straw.

We had also discovered during some allied observational studies that a baby monkey raised on a bare wire-mesh cage floor survives with difficulty, if at all, during the first five days of life. If a wire-mesh cone is introduced, the baby does better; and, if the cone is covered with terry cloth, husky, healthy, happy babies evolve. It takes more than a baby and a box to make a normal monkey. We were impressed by the possibility that, above and beyond the bubbling fountain of breast or bottle, contact comfort might be a very important variable in the development of the infant's affection for the mother.

At this point we decided to study the development of affectional responses of neonatal and infant monkeys to an artificial, inanimate mother, and so we built a surrogate mother which we hoped and believed would be a good surrogate mother. In devising this surrogate mother we were dependent neither upon the capriciousness of evolutionary processes nor upon mutations produced by chance radioactive fallout. Instead, we designed the mother surrogate in terms of modern human-engineering principles (Figure 1). We pro-

FIGURE 1. Cloth mother surrogate.

duced a perfectly proportioned, streamlined body stripped of unnecessary bulges and appendices. Redundancy in the surrogate mother's system was avoided by reducing the number of breasts from two to one and placing this unibreast in an upper-thoracic, sagittal position, thus maximizing the natural and known perceptual-motor capabilities of the infant operator. The surrogate was made from a block of wood, covered with sponge rubber, and sheathed in tan cotton terry cloth. A light bulb behind her radiated heat. The result was a mother, soft, warm, and tender, a mother with infinite patience, a mother available twenty-four hours a day, a mother that never scolded her infant and never struck or bit her baby in anger. Furthermore, we designed a mother-machine with maximal maintenance efficiency since failure of any system or function could be resolved by the simple substitution of black boxes and new component parts. It is our opinion that we engineered a very superior monkey mother, although this position is not held universally by the monkey fathers.

Before beginning our initial experiment we also designed and constructed a second mother surrogate, a surrogate in which we deliberately built less than the maximal capability for contact comfort. This surrogate mother is illustrated in Figure 2. She is made of wiremesh, a substance entirely adequate to provide postural support and nursing capability, and she is warmed by radiant heat. Her body differs in no essential way from that of the cloth mother surrogate other than in the quality of the contact comfort which she can supply.

In our initial experiment, the dual mother-surrogate condition, a cloth mother and a wire mother were placed in different cubicles attached to the infant's living cage as shown in Figure 2. For four newborn monkeys the cloth mother lactated and the wire mother did not; and, for the other four, this condition was reversed. In either condition the infant received all its milk through the mother surrogate as soon as it was able to maintain itself in this way, a capability achieved within two or three days except in the case of very immature infants. Supplementary feedings were given until the milk intake from the mother surrogate was adequate. Thus, the experiment was designed as a test of the relative importance of the variables of con-

FIGURE 2. Wire and cloth mother surrogates.

tact comfort and nursing comfort. During the first 14 days of life the monkey's cage floor was covered with a heating pad wrapped in a folded gauze diaper, and thereafter the cage floor was bare. The infants were always free to leave the heating pad or cage floor to contact either mother, and the time spent on the surrogate mothers was automatically recorded. Figure 3 shows the total time spent on the cloth and wire mothers under the two conditions of feeding. These data make it obvious that contact comfort is a variable of overwhelming importance in the development of affectional responses, whereas lactation is a variable of negligible importance. With age and opportunity to learn, subjects with the lactating wire mother showed decreasing responsiveness to her and increasing responsiveness to the nonlactating cloth mother, a finding completely contrary to any interpretation of derived drive in which the mother form becomes conditioned to hunger-thirst reduction. The persistence of these differential responses

throughout 165 consecutive days of testing is evident in Figure 4.

One control group of neonatal monkeys was raised on a single wire mother, and a second control group was raised on a single cloth mother. There were no differences between these two groups in amount of milk ingested or in weight gain. The only difference between the groups lay in the composition of the feces, the softer stools of the wire-mother infants suggesting psychosomatic involvement. The wire mother is biologically adequate but psychologically inept.

We were not surprised to discover that contact comfort was an important basic affectional or love variable, but we did not expect it to overshadow so completely the variable of nursing; indeed, the disparity is so great as to suggest that the primary function of nursing as an affectional variable is that of insuring frequent and intimate body contact of the infant with the mother. Certainly, man cannot live by milk alone. Love is an emotion

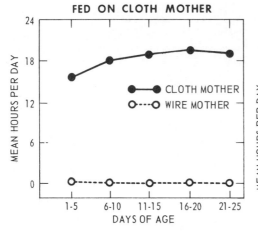

FED ON CLOTH MOTHER

MEAN HOURS PER DAY

CLOTH MOTHER
WIRE MOTHER

DAYS OF AGE

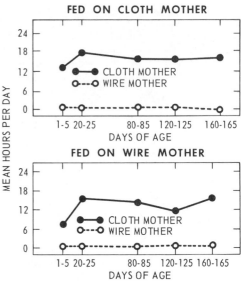

FED ON CLOTH MOTHER

MEAN HOURS PER DAY

CLOTH MOTHER
WIRE MOTHER

DAYS OF AGE

FED ON WIRE MOTHER

CLOTH MOTHER
WIRE MOTHER

DAYS OF AGE

FIGURE 4. Long-term contact time on cloth and wire mother surrogates.

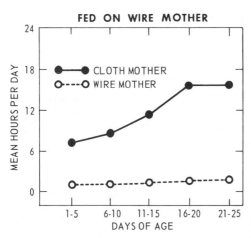

FED ON WIRE MOTHER

MEAN HOURS PER DAY

CLOTH MOTHER
WIRE MOTHER

DAYS OF AGE

FIGURE 3. Time spent on cloth and wire mother surrogates.

danger may be used as a measure of the strength of affectional bonds. We have tested this kind of differential responsiveness by presenting to the infants in their cages, in the that does not need to be bottle- or spoon-fed, and we may be sure that there is nothing to be gained by giving lip service to love.

A charming lady once heard me describe these experiments; and, when I subsequently talked to her, her face brightened with sudden insight: "Now I know what's wrong with me," she said, "I'm just a wire mother." Perhaps she was lucky. She might have been a wire wife. . . .

One function of the real mother, human or sub-human, and presumably of a mother surrogate, is to provide a haven of safety for the infant in times of fear and danger. The frightened or ailing child clings to its mother, not its father; and this selective responsiveness in times of distress, disturbance, or

FIGURE 5. Typical response to cloth mother surrogate in fear test.

presence of the two mothers, various fear-producing stimuli.... A typical response to a fear stimulus is shown in Figure 5, and the data on differential responsiveness are presented in Figure 6. It is apparent that the cloth mother is highly preferred over the wire one, and this differential selectivity is enhanced by age and experience. In this situa-

tion, the variable of nursing appears to be of absolutely no importance: the infant consistently seeks the soft mother surrogate regardless of nursing condition.

Similarly, the mother or mother surrogate provides its young with a source of security, and this role or function is seen with special clarity when mother and child are in a strange situation. At the present time we have completed tests for this relationship on four of our eight baby monkeys assigned to the dual mother-surrogate condition by introducing them for three minutes into the strange environment of a room measuring six feet by six feet by six feet (also called the "open-field test") and containing multiple stimuli known to elicit curiosity-manipulatory responses in baby monkeys. (See Figure 7.) The subjects were placed in this situation twice a week for eight weeks with no mother surrogate present during alternate sessions and the cloth mother present during the others. A cloth diaper was always available as one of the stimuli throughout all ses-

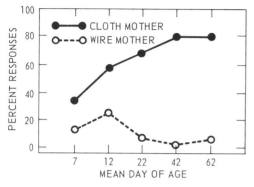

FIGURE 6. Differential responsiveness in fear tests.

FIGURE 7.

sions. After one or two adaptation sessions, the infants always rushed to the mother surrogate when she was present and clutched her, rubbed their bodies against her, and frequently manipulated her body and face. After a few additional sessions, the infants began to use the mother surrogate as a source of security, a base of operations.... They would explore and manipulate a stimulus and then return to the mother before adventuring again into the strange new world. The behavior of these infants was quite different when the mother was absent from the room. Frequently they would freeze in a crouched position. Emotionality indices such as vocalization, crouching, rocking, and sucking increased sharply,... Total emotionality score was cut in half when the mother was present. In the absence of the mother some of the experimental monkeys would rush to the center of the room where the mother was customarily placed and then run rapidly from object to object, screaming and crying all the while. Continuous, frantic clutching of their bodies was very common, even when not in the crouching position. These monkeys frequently contacted and clutched the cloth diaper, but this action never pacified them. The same behavior occurred in the presence of the wire mother. No difference between the cloth-mother-fed and wire-mother-fed infants was demonstrated under either condition. Four control infants never raised with a mother surrogate showed the same emotionality scores when the mother was absent as the experimental infants showed in the absence of the mother, but the controls' scores were slightly larger in the presence of the mother surrogate than in her absence....

Affectional retention was also tested in the open field during the first 9 days after separation and then at 30-day intervals, and each test condition was run twice at each retention interval. The infant's behavior differed from that observed during the period preceding separation. When the cloth mother was present in the post-separation period, the babies rushed to her, climbed up, clung tightly to her, and rubbed their heads and faces against her body. After this initial embrace and reunion, they played on the mother, including biting and tearing at her cloth cover; but they rarely made any attempt to leave her during the test period, nor did they manipulate or play with the objects in the room, in contrast with their behavior before maternal

separation. The only exception was the occasional monkey that left the mother surrogate momentarily, grasped the folded piece of paper (one of the standard stimuli in the field), and brought it quickly back to the mother. It appeared that deprivation had enhanced the tie to the mother and rendered the contact-comfort need so prepotent that need for the mother overwhelmed the exploratory motives during the brief, three-minute test sessions. No change in these behaviors was observed throughout the 185-day period. When the mother was absent from the open field, the behavior of the infants was similar in the initial retention test to that during the preseparation tests; but they tended to show gradual adaptation to the open-field situation with repeated testing and, consequently, a reduction in their emotionality scores.

In the last five retention test periods, an additional test was introduced in which the surrogate mother was placed in the center of the room and covered with a clear Plexiglas box. The monkeys were initially disturbed and frustrated when their explorations and manipulations of the box failed to provide contact with the mother. However, all animals adapted to the situation rather rapidly. Soon they used the box as a place of orientation for exploratory and play behavior, made frequent contacts with the objects in the field, and very often brought these objects to the Plexiglas box. The emotionality index was slightly higher than in the condition of the available cloth mothers, but it in no way approached the emotionality level displayed when the cloth mother was absent. Obviously, the infant monkeys gained emotional security by the presence of the mother even though contact was denied....

The over-all picture obtained from surveying the retention data is unequivocal. There is little, if any, waning of responsiveness to the mother throughout this five-month period as indicated by any measure. It becomes perfectly obvious that this affectional bond is highly resistant to forgetting and that it can be retained for very long periods of time by relatively infrequent contact reinforcement. During the next year, retention tests will be conducted at 90-day intervals, and further plans are dependent upon the results obtained. It would appear that affectional responses may show as much resistance to extinction as has been previously demonstrated for learned fears and learned pain, and such data would be in keeping with those of common human observation. . . .

We have already described the group of four control infants that had never lived in the presence of any mother surrogate and had demonstrated no sign of affection or security in the presence of the cloth mothers introduced in test sessions. When these infants reached the age of 250 days, cubicles containing both a cloth mother and a wire mother were attached to their cages. There was no lactation in these mothers, for the monkeys were on a solid-food diet. The initial reaction of the monkeys to the alterations was one of extreme disturbance. All the infants screamed violently and made repeated attempts to escape the cage whenever the door was opened. They kept a maximum distance from the mother surrogates and exhibited a considerable amount of rocking and crouching behavior, indicative of emotionality. Our first thought was that the critical period for the development of maternally directed affection had passed and that these macaque children were doomed to live as affectional orphans. Fortunately, these behaviors continued for only 12 to 48 hours and then gradually ebbed, changing from indifference to active contact on, and exploration of, the surrogates. The home-cage behavior of these control monkeys slowly became similar to that of the animals raised with the mother surrogates from birth. Their manipulation and play on the cloth mother became progressively more vigorous to the point of actual mutilation, particularly during the morning after the cloth mother had been given her daily change of terry covering. The control subjects were now actively running to the cloth mother when frightened and had to be coaxed from her to be taken from the cage for formal testing.

Objective evidence of these changing behaviors is given in Figure 7, which plots the amount of time these infants spent on the mother surrogates. Within 10 days mean contact time is approximately nine hours, and this measure remains relatively constant throughout the next 30 days. Consistent with the results on the subjects reared from birth with dual mothers, these late-adopted infants spent less than one and one-half hours per day in contact with the wire mothers, and this activity level was relatively constant throughout the test sessions. Although the maximum time that the control monkeys spent on the cloth mother was only about half that

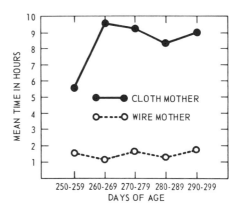

FIGURE 8. Differential time spent on cloth and wire mother surrogates by monkeys started at 250 days of age.

spent by the original dual mother-surrogate group, we cannot be sure that this discrepancy is a function of differential early experience. The control monkeys were about three months older when the mothers were attached to their cages than the experimental animals had been when their mothers were removed and the retention tests begun. Thus, we do not know what the amount of contact would be for a 250-day-old animal raised from birth with surrogate mothers. Nevertheless, the magnitude of the differences and the fact that the contact-time curves for the mothered-from-birth infants had remained constant for almost 150 days suggest that early experience with the mother is a variable of measurable importance. . . .

That the control monkeys develop affection or love for the cloth mother when she is introduced into the cage at 250 days of age cannot be questioned. There is every reason to believe, however, that this interval of delay depresses the intensity of the affectional response below that of the infant monkeys that were surrogate-mothered from birth onward. In interpreting these data it is well to remember that the control monkeys had had continuous opportunity to observe and hear other monkeys housed in adjacent cages and that they had had limited opportunity to view and contact surrogate mothers in the test situations, even though they did not exploit the opportunities.

During the last two years we have observed the behavior of two infants raised by their own mothers. Love for the real mother and love for the surrogate mother appear to be very similar. The baby macaque spends many hours a day clinging to its real mother. If away from the mother when frightened, it rushes to her and in her presence shows comfort and composure. As far as we can observe, the infant monkey's affection for the real mother is strong, but no stronger than that of the experimental monkey for the surrogate cloth mother, and the security that the infant gains from the presence of the real mother is no greater than the security it gains from a cloth surrogate. Next year we hope to put this problem to final, definitive, experimental test. But, whether the mother is real or a cloth surrogate, there does develop a deep and abiding bond between mother and child. In one case it may be the call of the wild and in the other the McCall of civilization, but in both cases there is "togetherness."

In spite of the importance of contact comfort, there is reason to believe that other variables of measurable importance will be discovered. Postural support may be such a variable, and it has been suggested that, when we build arms into the mother surrogate, 10 is the minimal number required to provide adequate child care. Rocking motion may be such a variable, and we are comparing rocking and stationary mother surrogates and inclined planes. The differential responsiveness to cloth mother and cloth-covered inclined plane suggests that clinging as well as contact is an affectional variable of importance. Sounds, particularly natural, maternal sounds, may operate as either unlearned or learned affectional variables. Visual responsiveness may be such a variable, and it is possible that some semblance of visual imprinting may develop in the neonatal monkey. There are indications that this becomes a variable of importance during the course of infancy through some maturational process.

John Bowlby has suggested that there is an affectional variable which he calls "primary object following," characterized by visual and oral search of the mother's face. Our surrogate-mother-raised baby monkeys are at first inattentive to her face, as are human neonates to human mother faces. But by 30 days of age ever-increasing responsiveness to the mother's face appears—whether through learning, maturation, or both—and we have reason to believe that the face becomes an object of special attention.

Our first surrogate-mother-raised baby had a mother whose head was just a ball of wood since the baby was a month early and we had not had time to design a more esthetic head and face. This baby had contact with the blank-faced mother for 180 days and was then placed with two cloth mothers, one motionless and one rocking, both being endowed with painted, ornamented faces. To our surprise the animal would compulsively rotate both faces 180 degrees so that it viewed only a round, smooth face and never the painted, ornamented face. Furthermore, it would do this as long as the patience of the experimenter in reorienting the faces persisted. The monkey showed no sign of fear or anxiety, but it showed unlimited persistence. Subsequently it improved its technique, compulsively removing the heads and rolling them into its cage as fast as they were returned. We are intrigued by this observation, and we plan to examine systematically the role of the mother face in the development of infant-monkey affections. Indeed, these observations suggest the need for a series of ethological-type researches on the two-faced female. . . .

If the researches completed and proposed make a contribution, I shall be grateful; but I have also given full thought to possible practical applications. The socioeconomic demands of the present and the threatened socioeconomic demands of the future have led the American woman to displace, or threaten to displace, the American man in science and industry. If this process continues, the problem of proper child-rearing practices faces us with startling clarity. It is cheering in view of this trend to realize that the American male is physically endowed with all the really essential equipment to compete with the American female on equal terms in one essential activity: the rearing of infants. We now know that women in the working classes are not needed in the home because of their primary mammalian capabilities; and it is possible that in the foreseeable future neonatal nursing will not be regarded as a necessity, but as a luxury—to use Veblen's term—a form of conspicuous consumption limited perhaps to the upper-classes. But whatever course history may take, it is comforting to know that we are now in contact with the nature of love.

10. THE WILD BOY OF AVEYRON

Jean-Marc-Gaspard Itard

...The most brilliant and irrational expectations preceded the arrival of the Savage of Aveyron at Paris. A number of inquisitive people looked forward with delight to witnessing the boy's astonishment at the sights of the capital. On the other hand many people otherwise commendable for their insight, forgetting that human organs are by so much less flexible, and imitation made by so much more difficult, in proportion as man is removed from society and from his infancy, believed that the education of this child would only be a question of some months, and that he would soon be able to give the most interesting information about his past life. In place of all this what do we see? A disgustingly dirty child affected with spasmodic movements and often convulsions who swayed back and forth ceaselessly like certain animals in the menagerie, who bit and scratched those who opposed him, who showed no sort of affection for those who attended him; and who was in short, indifferent to everything and attentive to nothing....

His eyes were unsteady, expressionless, wandering vaguely from one object to another without resting on anybody; they were so little experienced in other ways and so little trained by the sense of touch, that they never distinguished an object in relief from one in a picture. His organ of hearing was equally insensible to the loudest noises and to the most touching music. His voice was reduced to a state of complete muteness and only a uniform guttural sound escaped him. His sense of smell was so uncultivated that he was equally indifferent to the odor of perfumes and

From THE WILD BOY OF AVEYRON *by Jean-Marc-Gaspard Itard, translated by George and Muriel Humphrey, Part 1. Copyright 1932,* © *1962 by the Meredith Corporation. Reprinted by permission of Appleton-Century-Crofts.*

to the fetid exhalation of the dirt with which his bed was filled. Finally, the organ of touch was restricted to the mechanical function of the grasping of objects. Proceeding then to the state of the intellectual functions of this child, the author of the report presented him to us as being quite incapable of attention (except for the objects of his needs) and consequently of all those operations of the mind which attention involves. He was destitute of memory, of judgment, of aptitude for imitation, and was so limited in his ideas, even those relative to his immediate needs, that he had never yet succeeded in opening a door or climbing upon a chair to get the food that had been raised out of reach of his hand. In short, he was destitute of all means of communication and attached neither expression nor intention to his gestures or to the movements of his body. He passed rapidly and without any apparent motive from apathetic melancholy to the most immoderate peals of laughter. He was insensible to every kind of moral influence. His perception was nothing but a computation prompted by gluttony, his pleasure an agreeable sensation of the organ of taste and his intelligence the ability to produce a few incoherent ideas relative to his wants. In a word, his whole life was a completely animal existence....

All his habits bore the mark of a wandering and solitary life. He had an insurmountable aversion to society and to its customs, to our clothing, our furniture, to living in houses and to the preparation of our food. There was a profound indifference to the objects of our pleasures and of our fictitious needs; there was still in his present state, in spite of his new needs and dawning affections, so intense a passion for the freedom of the fields that during a short sojourn at Montmorency he would certainly have escaped into the forest had not the most rigid precautions been taken, and twice he did escape from the house of the Deaf and Dumb in spite of the supervision of his governess. His locomotion was extraordinary, literally heavy after he wore shoes, but always remarkable because of his difficulty in adjusting himself to our sober and measured gait, and because of his constant tendency to trot and to gallop. He had an obstinate habit of smelling at anything that was given to him, even the things which we consider void of smell; his mastication was equally astonishing, executed as it was solely by the sudden action of the incisors, which because of its similarity to that of certain rodents was a sufficient indication that our savage, like these animals, most commonly lived on vegetable products. I said most commonly, for it appeared by the following incident that in certain circumstances he had devoured small dead animals. A dead canary was given him and in an instant the bird was stripped of its feathers big and little, opened with his nail, sniffed at and thrown away....

Several times during the course of the winter I have seen him crossing the garden of the Deaf and Dumb, squatting half naked upon the wet ground, remaining thus exposed for hours on end to a cold and wet wind. It was not only to cold but also to intense heat that the organ of the skin and touch showed no sensitivity. When he was near the fire and the glowing embers came rolling out of the hearth it was a daily occurrence for him to seize them with his fingers and replace them without any particular haste upon the flaming fire. He has been discovered more than once in the kitchen picking out in the same way potatoes which were cooking in boiling water, and I can guarantee that he had, even at that time, a fine and velvety skin.

I have often succeeded in filling the exterior cavities of his nose with snuff without making him sneeze. The inference is that between the organ of smell, which was very highly developed in other respects, and those of respiration and sight, there did not exist any of those sympathetic relations which form an integral part of our sensibility, and which in this case would have caused sneezing or the secretion of tears. Still less was the secretion of tears connected with feelings of sadness, and in spite of innumerable annoyances, in spite of the bad treatment to which his new manner of life had exposed him during the first months, I have never discovered him weeping. Of all his senses, the ear appeared the least sensitive. It was found, nevertheless, that the sound of a cracking walnut or other favorite eatable never failed to make him turn round. This observation is quite accurate: yet, nevertheless, this same organ showed itself insensible to the loudest noises and the explosion of firearms. One day I fired two pistol shots near him, the first appeared to rouse him a little, the second did not make him even turn his head....

"Does the Savage speak? If he is not deaf why does he not speak?"

It is easily conceived that in the midst of the forest and far from the society of all thinking beings, the sense of hearing of our savage did not experience any other impressions than those which a small number of noises made upon him, and particularly those which were connected with his physical needs. Under these circumstances his ear was not an organ for the appreciation of sounds, their articulations and their combinations; it was nothing but a simple means of self-preservation which warned of the approach of a dangerous animal or the fall of wild fruit. These are without doubt the functions to which his hearing was limited, judging by the slight response obtained from the organ given a year ago to all sounds and noises except those bearing upon his individual needs; and judging on the other hand, by the exquisite sensibility which this sense showed for such sounds as had some such connection with his interests. When a chestnut or a walnut was cracked without his knowledge and as gently as possible; if the key of the door which held him captive was merely touched, he never failed to turn quickly and run towards the place whence the sound came. If the organ of hearing did not show the same susceptibility for the sounds of the voice, even for the explosion of firearms, it was because he was necessarily little sensitive and little attentive to all other impressions than those to which he had been long and exclusively accustomed....

I allude to the facility with which our young savage expresses his few wants otherwise than by speech. Each wish manifests itself by the most expressive signs which have in some measure, as have ours, their gradations and their equivalent values. If the time for his walk has come, he appears several times before the window and before the door of his room. If he then sees that his governess is not ready, he places before her all the objects necessary for her toilet and in his impatience even goes to help her dress. That done, he goes down first and himself pulls the check string of the door. Arriving at the Observatory, his first business is to demand some milk which he does by presenting a wooden porringer which, on going out, he never forgets to put in his pocket, and with which he first provided himself the day after he had broken in the same house a china cup which had been used for the same purpose.

Then again, in order to complete the pleasure of his evenings he has for some time past kindly been given rides in a wheelbarrow. Since then, as soon as the inclination arises, if nobody comes to satisfy it, he returns to the house, takes someone by the arm, leads him to the garden and puts in his hands the handles of the wheelbarrow, into which he then climbs. If this first invitation is resisted he leaves his seat, turns to the handles of the wheelbarrow, rolls it for some turns, and places himself in it again; imagining doubtless, that if his desires are not fulfilled after all this, it is not because they are not clearly expressed. Where meals are concerned his intentions are even less doubtful. He himself lays the cloth and gives Madame Guérin* the dishes, so that she may go down to the kitchen and get the food. If he is in town dining with me, all his requests are addressed to the person who does the honors of the table; it is always to her that he turns to be served. If she pretends not to hear him, he puts his plate at the side of the particular dish which he wants and, as it were, devours with his eyes. If that produces no result, he takes a fork and strikes two or three blows with it on the brim of his plate. If she persists in further delay, then he knows no bounds; he plunges a spoon or even his hand into the dish and in the twinkling of an eye he empties it entirely in his plate. He is scarcely less expressive in his way of showing his emotions,

* His governess. (Eds.)

above all impatience and boredom. A number of people visiting him out of curiosity know how, with more natural frankness than politeness, he dismisses them when, fatigued by the length of their visits, he offers to each of them, without mistake, cane, gloves and hat, pushes them gently towards the door, which he closes impetuously upon them. . . .

It has appeared to me at least that the following conclusions may be drawn:

(1) That man is inferior to a large number of animals in the pure state of nature, a state of nullity and barbarism that has been falsely painted in the most seductive colors; a state in which the individual, deprived of the characteristic faculties of his kind, drags on without intelligence or without feelings, a precarious life reduced to bare animal functions.

(2) That the moral superiority said to be *natural* to man is only the result of civilization, which raises him above other animals by a great and powerful force. This force is the preëminent sensibility of his kind, an essential peculiarity from which proceed the imitative faculties and that continual urge which drives him to seek new sensations in new needs.

(3) That this imitative force, the purpose of which is the education of his organs and especially the apprenticeship of speech, and which is very energetic and very active during the first years of his life, rapidly wanes with age, with isolation, and with all the causes which tend to blunt the nervous sensibility; from which it results that the articulation of sounds, of all the effects of imitation unquestionably the most incomprehensible and the most useful, must encounter innumerable obstacles at any age later than that of early childhood.

(4) That in the most isolated savage as in the most highly civilized man, there exists a constant relation between ideas and needs; that the increasing multiplicity of the latter in the most civilized peoples should be considered as a great means of developing the human mind; so that a general proposition may be established, namely, that all causes accidental, local or political, which tend to augment or diminish the number of our desires, necessarily contribute to extend or to narrow the sphere of our knowledge and the domain of science, fine arts and social industry. . . .

11. WHY SOME 3-YEAR-OLDS GET A'S— AND SOME GET C'S

Maya Pines

The all-American, exceptionally competent 3-year-old—the model for future generations, if a group of Harvard researchers has its way —is a frighteningly mature and verbal creature who scores high in 17 abilities which seem to hold the key to his success.

He can, for example, "dual focus." (While two children argued and one screamed, "I'll murder you!" Sally barely looked up from her block-building, muttered, "Not *me, though!"* and continued what she was doing.)

He can sense dissonance or discrepancy. (When another boy held up a streaked drawing and announced, "It's the moon," Jimmy replied at once, "A moon doesn't have hair!")

He can anticipate consequences. (Seeing his friend carelessly pick up a basket filled with toys, George shouted "Carry it, carry it, *use both hands!")*

Relying on thousands of simple, detailed observations like these, rather than on I.Q. tests, the Harvard School of Education's Pre-School Project believes it can now pick out the abilities which distinguish the most able 3-year-olds from the most inept. Nine of these abilities, including the three above, involve intellect (or "intellectual skills," if you like). The eight others involve social factors; for illustration, the Harvard researchers note that when something gets in the way of the inept child (they tag him "C"), he may be reduced to tears, or throw a tantrum, while the competent child ("A") will be quietly persistent (he might even "con" someone into giving him what he wants—in a socially acceptable way.) Also the "C" child may be locked into either sheeplike docility or rebellion, while the "A" child knows both how to lead and how to follow. And as early as 2 years of age, the most competent group will be able to understand complex, unexpected instructions, such as, "Put the spoon under your foot," or the reverse, "Put your foot under the spoon," while the "C" group cannot.[1] (The average, or "B," child was not covered in the study.)

The goal of the Harvard project is to find out how the two groups of children got that way—what it was in their earliest environment that produced the startling differences between them. But why concentrate on youngsters of age 3 and under especially? "There has been a striking shift of interest, unprecedented in history, toward the first three years of life," declares Prof. Burton L. White, the Pre-School Project's director. A no-nonsense, pipe-smoking man whom everyone in his group calls "Bud," he notes that the original conception behind the Government's Project Head Start was that "something's wrong with these

---

1 Other intellectual abilities include: dealing with abstractions, making interesting associations, planning and carrying out a sequence of activities, making effective use of resources. Other social abilities: showing pride in accomplishment, making-believe being adult, expressing both affection and hostility to peers and adults.

children at age 6. There was no appreciation of how early that something comes about."

"Head Start began," he says, "with a few weeks in the summer before the child entered kindergarten or first grade—the Head Start summer program. Then they decided to take the child for a whole year before he is 6. Next they decided to take him two years before he is 6. And now, at last, they've begun to run parent-and-child centers for children from birth on. It's always seemed clear to a number of us that the place to begin is with the first days of life."

Throughout the nation, large numbers of psychologists, computer experts, educators, sociologists, linguists and others are coming to the same conclusion. Working backward to a younger and younger age, they are creating a new field, encompassing what Harvard's Jerome Bruner has dubbed "the growth sciences." This new composite discipline concentrates on the period other researchers had chronically neglected because the child seemed so inaccessible—the time between his fifth day of life, when the newborn usually leaves the hospital, and his entry into nursery school at 3. Abandoning their rats, pigeons and other experimental subjects, including older children, hundreds of scientists are now focusing on the young child's mind—encouraged by the influx of Government funds for programs to stop the epidemic of school failure among the children of the poor, and by some new developments in psychology itself.

Just five years ago Benjamin S. Bloom of the University of Chicago shook up his colleagues with *Stability and Change in Human Characteristics,* a thin book filled with statistics based on a thousand different studies of growth. Each of these studies followed up certain children and measured them at various points in their development. Although made by different people over the last half-century, these studies showed such close agreement that Bloom began to see specific laws of development emerging, rather than mere trends. For each human characteristic, Bloom found, there is a growth curve. Half of a child's future height, for instance, is reached by the age of 2½. By age of 4, his I.Q. becomes so stable that it is a fairly accurate indicator of his I.Q. at 17. To a large extent, therefore, the die may be cast before a child ever begins his formal education.

Bloom emphasized that the child's environ-ment has a maximum impact on a developing characteristic during that characteristic's period of most rapid growth. Thus, since human intelligence grows most rapidly before the age of 4, this is the time when the environment can influence it most easily. As time goes on, Bloom declared, more and more powerful forces are required to produce a given amount of change in a child's intelligence, if it can be produced at all—and the emotional cost of this change is increasingly severe.

Meanwhile, other researchers were focusing on the differences between the children of the poor and the affluent. By kindergarten age, these differences are painfully obvious, with poor children's I.Q.'s running 5 to 15 points below those of middle-class youngsters, and their verbal ability trailing ever further behind. The Head Start programs were showing it was not easy to bridge the gap at that stage. So, when President Nixon announced that "Head Start must begin earlier in life, and last longer, to achieve lasting benefits," people in the growth sciences took new hope—especially those increasingly vocal, who want to concentrate on reaching children even before the age of 3.

If their research confirms that the first three years of life largely determine a human being's future competence, these years can no longer be left to chance, they believe. Thus, armies of tutors could conceivably be sent into the homes of disadvantaged infants, and thousands of expectant parents enrolled in crash programs to teach them modern child-rearing. We may be witnessing the end of society's traditional laissez-faire about the earliest years of a human being's life.

Harvard has clearly taken the lead in the growth sciences at this point, with at least three nuclei of research on the child's early development. Each one, in its own way, has had to start practically from scratch, devising new tools to measure young children's progress and new techniques to rate their environment. "Assume that you are studying the great-chested Jabberwocky," Bruner advised his students.

The Pre-School Project, for one, had not originally intended to focus on children so young, but began by studying 6-year-olds. And, initially, it did not even try to measure competence, but looked for "educability"— how ready a child was for formal education by the age of 6. This turned out to be a knotty problem, however, all tied up with certain virtues which the school system rewards—passivity, obedience, being "a nice, organization child," as one of the researchers put it—but which the project did not much like. "Is the child who's geared up to the Boston educational system the kind of child we want to set as a model?" the Project's Dr. E. Robert LaCrosse recalls asking himself. And the answer was, "My God, No!" Therefore, they decided to look for competence—all-around excellence in coping with problems in the yard as well as the schoolroom.

"What specifically is competence at 6?" Dr. White wanted to find out. "If you don't know the answer to that question, you can't have any idea of what you're trying to achieve." With disadvantaged children, at least you know clearly that you want to wipe out their deficits in language and whatever else goes into poor I.Q. development, he says, and there are programs for 4- and 5-year-olds that do this with some efficiency. "But that's not the same as asking, how are you going to rear your child so he will be *optimally* developed? We're not just responding to an emergency; we're looking for answers that will help *all* children."

Three years ago, then, White and a dozen other researchers armed with clip-boards and tape recorders set out like naturalists to look for examples of excellent as well as poor development in children. In weekly visits to various local nursery schools, kindergartens and Head Start centers, they selected one group of outstanding 3-to-6-year-olds, their "A" group, and a parallel group of children who were not sick, but couldn't quite cope, their "C" group. They followed 440 "A" and "C" children closely for a year, noting the differences between them and checking their ratings of the children against the teachers' ratings of the children, and then they realized that they had come too late: "With our "A" kids, the 3-year-old children had basically the same cluster of abilities, in perhaps less polished form, as the 6-year-old children," says LaCrosse, "and, in fact, they were more advanced than the 6-year-old "C's" in terms of both social and non-social skills."

This came as a shock to the project. "We were surprised, really, and kind of excited," says LaCrosse, one of the strongly committed young psychologists who have been flocking to

the growth sciences. "Big Daddy Freud had said everything was over at 5, with the resolution of the oedipal conflict, but we tended to disbelieve this. Then suddenly, we found that if you're talking about competence, the action comes before the age of 3."

As a result, the Pre-School Project did an about-face and began studying children between the ages of 1 and 3—in their natural habitat, of course. Off went LaCrosse and four associates into the homes of 30 toddlers to take regular running records of what actually goes on in a small child's life. Their assignment was to construct a new maternal behavior scale, later to become "a *human* behavior scale, that we can plug any human being into," LaCrosse explained. They followed the mothers and children from kitchen to bedroom to bathroom, furiously recording in the manner of a sports announcer what happened to the child and what the mother was trying to do.

At first these intrusions into the privacy of the home seemed strange. "We had to fight the 'girdle-on' phenomenon," recalls LaCrosse. "You know—the first day we arrive, there's the mother with false eyelashes and hair freshly done, and the house perfect, at 9 o'clock in the morning! Then one day, perhaps three visits later, we'll arrive and find the mother in a housecoat and the kitchen in chaos, the beds unmade—at that point, the girdle is off and we have achieved a certain rapport." The families were all known to the project from its earlier work with older children, and they were paid $5 a half day for their services.

While LaCrosse and his group concentrated on the mothers, other project teams visited 170 different homes to record how the children spent their time and to study the development of specific characteristics. It took a year and a half to boil down their material on child activities to 36 categories of things that these youngsters do. It is taking even longer to work out useful scales covering the development of the selected characteristics.

Now the information from all these probes is just beginning to produce promising patterns, as the children's activities are related to their development and to their mothers' behavior. "We think we have spotted five prototype mothers," says LaCrosse. "There is, first of all, the Super-Mother. She wants to provide educational opportunities for her child; she slips in from time to time to teach the kid something, but she's not frantic about it. She enjoys the child as he is. She tends to do a great deal of labeling with him—'This is a ball'—and to elaborate on his sentences, adding new bits, such as 'This is a *red* ball,' or related ideas. There is a good balance between activities that she initiates and those initiated by the child.

"Then there is the Smothering Mother. All the kid does all day is respond to her commands. She seems discontented with where the child is right now. She's very busy preparing him for Harvard.

"The Almost Mother enjoys and accepts her child, but she is confused and frequently unable to meet his needs. She may lack a capacity for intellectual input—she usually waits for the child to initiate activities, then often can't understand what he wants. If she reads to her child, her spontaneous comments may be, 'See the ball!' or 'See the hill!' while the Super-Mother may ask, 'What's he going to meet at the bottom of that hill?'

"The Overwhelmed Mother finds just living from day to day so overwhelming that she has almost no time for her child. The children may be raised by older siblings, or by themselves, in a chaotic home. Usually the mother has eight kids and a $30-a-week food budget, but there are middle-class mothers of this type, too.

"Finally there is the Zoo-Keeper Mother, who tends to be middle- to upper-middle-class. She has a highly organized household routine, and the child will be materially well cared for, but will spend most of his time alone—perhaps in a crib filled with educational toys. She doesn't monitor her child's behavior, doesn't interact—in fact, there's a striking lack of contact between this mother and her child. This produces a child with highly repetitive, stereotyped behavior, despite the variety of toys."

These five mothers represent extreme types—since the mothers of "B" children were not included in this study. The Super-Mother naturally raises an all-around "A" child. The Smothering Mother's offspring rates "A" in cognitive[2] capacity, but not in emotional maturity—he tends to be shy or incredibly infantile. The Overwhelmed Mother produces a "C" child. The Almost Mother does a very

2 The word cognition is used in psychology to mean the study of how knowledge is acquired, retained and used. The child rated "A" above has a good learning capacity.

good job until the child is 14 to 16 months old, when the mind-stretching aspects of care become more important, and then she fails. While the Super-Mother's child continues to grow rapidly, the child of the Almost Mother reaches a plateau which eventually turns him into a "B" child.

These differences cut across class lines. The project knows of at least one woman from a very poor neighborhood, a black activist, who is a Super-Mother, as well as numerous middle-class women who raise "C" children. However, the central tendency favors the middle-class child, both black and white, and one of the project's main contributions, so far, is that it documents for the first time just how the daily experiences of poor and middle-class children differ in the second and third years of life.

Take the matter of purposeless behavior—sitting and doing nothing, without looking at anything in particular, or else moving about in apparently aimless fashion. According to preliminary data, the child of an Overwhelmed Mother, who is usually very poor, spends 41 times as much of his waking hours in such vapid behavior as the child of a Super-Mother, who tends to be middle-class. Since the Overwhelmed Mother often attempts to cope with her children by giving them food or candy, he also spends much more of his time eating.

The child of a Super-Mother, on the other hand, spends nearly one fifth of his day at an activity almost unknown to the offspring of an Overwhelmed Mother: make-believe, pretending to be someone or something else, a characteristic of children who are doing well around the age of 2. Throughout this study, middle-class youngsters were found role-playing five times more frequently than lower-class children of the same age.

Since poor children are often accused of lacking a drive for achievement in school, it is very revealing that the middle-class children in this study spent 50 per cent more of their time constructing things or practicing skills which give a sense of mastery. They also benefited from far more tutorial experiences. And they devoted more of their day to the one predominant occupation of nearly all children between the ages of 1 and 3: staring at a person or thing with intensity, as if to study its features.

The extraordinary amount of time spent staring in this way—an average of 22 per cent of the children's day—is "a revelation," says White. "It has authenticity and is not disputable." He warns that the relationship between the types of mothers and the children's activities remains to be verified, however.

These differences occur mostly after the baby is one year old, White believes, because until then most parents do things that are essentially the same. There are, of course, instances of extreme deprivation which can seriously retard or damage a child. But, in general, parents don't yet know how to enrich their babies' environment in a meaningful way, and even researchers such as White have only limited information on the subject. A few years ago, White showed that when infants in a bland hospital nursery were given a chance to look at and touch colorful stabiles, they learned to reach for objects above them —a landmark in development—in less than half the time it took other infants in the same nursery. He has raised his own 3-year-old on the same principle, offering him plenty of interesting things to interact with at each stage in his development. Yet a lot more research needs to be done before parents can be given firm recommendations about the first year of life, he believes.

Meanwhile, White is convinced that the behavior of parents really begins to diverge during the child's second year, when the growing baby—now walking around and talking— forces himself on the attention of adults. The toddler's insatiable curiosity at that age, his zest for learning, and his obvious grasp of language, all lead the effective mother to produce a rich flow of talk and try in various ways to satisfy his drives. To other types of mothers, however, this growth means only two things: danger to the child, and much more work for them. In an extremely poor family where the mother is barely able to get through the day and has many other children to take care of, "you can predict what that will mean," says White. "She'll concentrate on keeping him out of the way; she cannot nurture his curiosity, and she won't do much talking."

In a two-year follow-up of the original "A" and "C" children, now 5 to 8 years old, the project has found amazing continuity in their levels of ability. The "A" group is still doing extremely well in kindergarten through second grade and also testing high on the 17 critical abilities. The "C" group is still inept—some sad and teary, some just oblivious, some every bit as likable as the more competent children —a diverse group that has one thing in common: Whatever its members are given to do, they don't do it well, either through lack of persistence or through lack of skill.

As soon as White has collected enough solid information about what causes these early differences, he plans to start teaching the Almost Mothers and the average mothers to use the best methods. Within 30 to 50 years, he predicts, the kind of child who is rated outstanding today will be considered merely normal, as a result of more skillful child-rearing.

The Pre-School Project's offices in Cambridge are cluttered and busy. Across Harvard Square, on the 11th floor of the imposing concrete structure known as the William James Hall for the Behavioral Sciences, one encounters a more rarefied atmosphere. Here is the Center for Cognitive Studies, headed by psychologist Bruner, a man of electric energy who paces up and down his spacious study, speaking volubly, with gestures. Until recently he studied how children between the ages of 3 and 12 process information—how they acquire it, retain it, transform it and communicate it. But now, to find the *sources* of intelligent action, he concentrates on infancy. Under his guidance the entire center, with its staff of psychologists, linguists and researchers, has turned to an examination of the first two years of life—though no one here follows individual children, studies homes, or tries to intervene in the domestic situation in any way.

These researchers seem filled with a sense of wonder at how the human infant—so helpless and limited at birth—learns to control his environment and himself. At first, they find, the baby appears stupider than chimpanzees of the same age. But by the age of 2 or 3, the normal child has achieved one of the most difficult intellectual feats he may ever perform: he has reinvented the rules of grammar, all by himself, and he has learned to speak. He begins with what the linguists call holophrases—single words such as "Mummy" or "see," or very short phrases that are used as one word ("gimme"). Then, suddenly, around 18 months of age, he takes one holophrase and combines it with many other words ("see doggie," "see light").

"At this particular point," notes Bruner, "as far as I am concerned, he enters the human race as a speaker, because I think you can find examples of holophrastic utterances in higher primates, but you will never find combinatorial grammar."

Besides learning language, the normal 2-year-old constructs a fairly complex mental model of the world. (This allows him to manipulate various aspects of the world in his thoughts and fantasies.) He has also learned to control his own behavior so accurately that he can mobilize various skill patterns whenever he needs them. This is a formidable set of achievements, and the Center for Cognitive Studies is only beginning to unravel how the baby attains them.

Behind a partly closed room at the center, overlooking all of Harvard, a mother nurses her 3-month-old infant. He has just been to a specially constructed baby "theater" where, reclining on a tiny chair resembling a car seat (safely strapped to it, in fact, by belly-and-breech cloth), he watched a swinging red ball, with exciting black and white bullseye stripes and a central row of shiny pearls, as it moved gently before his eyes. It was an experiment in depth perception, to discover whether infants of that age have any idea of what is graspable: Would the baby move his arms more when the shiny ball was up close than when it was far away? Did he have any sort of mental map of where he was? Finding, on both questions: Yes. Three-month-old infants have much more depth perception than was thought possible only a few years ago, the center finds. On the day of their birth, it has been determined, infants can track a triangle with their eyes. By one month of age, they notice when objects have been changed. In fact, infants are in every way much more aware of their surroundings than scientists had surmised—which helps explain the speed with which they build their model of the world.

To trace the development of this world-model, Bruner and two associates recently put three groups of babies of different ages through an experiment in which a jingly toy was placed behind a small transparent screen, open on one end. The youngest babies, only 7 months old, simply reached for the toy with the nearest hand and bumped into the screen. After banging on and clawing at the screen for a while, they lost interest and gave up. The next group, the 1-year-olds, began in the same fashion, but then let their hands follow the edge of the screen and reached behind it in a sort of backhand grasp until they got the toy. Only the 18-month-olds knew right away how to reach the toy efficiently, and did so. Over 16 trials each, none of the babies ever changed his initial strategy: this was the best he was capable of at that stage.

The babies who take part in these experiments are usually the offspring of graduate students, brought there in response to ads in *The Harvard Crimson*. Asked how much time he actually spends with these babies, Bruner gestured helplessly. "Depends on what's going on in the Yard!" he exclaimed. "Which babies do you have in mind?" During the student strike, the faculty meetings took up most of his time. Now that the troubles seem to be over, he can go back to his main interest—studying how babies discover how to use their hands intelligently.

In babies' hands, Bruner believes, lie clues to much of their later development, and he particularly wants to find out how babies learn the value of two-handedness. Nobody teaches infants this skill, just as nobody teaches them to talk. Yet around the age of 1, a baby will master the "two-handed obstacle box," a simple puzzle devised by the center to study this process. Seated on his mother's lap, he will suddenly use one hand to push and hold a transparent cover, while the other hand reaches inside the box for a toy.

To Bruner this is extraordinary, for it shows that the baby has learned to distinguish between two kinds of grip—the power or "holding" grip, which stabilizes an object, and the precision or "operating" grip, which does the work. Monkeys and apes have developed a precision grip, Bruner says, but "it is not until one comes to man with his asymmetry that the power grip migrates to one hand (usually the left) and the precision to the other." From then on, he emphasizes, many routines can be devised for holding an object with one hand while working it with the other, leading to the distinctively human use of tools and tool-making.

The experiments at the center are essentially very simple, but their interpretations are not. Some of these interpretations parallel Noam Chomsky's "transformational" approach to linguistics, which reduces language to basic kernel sentences, each one made up of a noun phrase and a verb phrase. Early in childhood every human being learns the logical rules which allow him to transform these kernels into any possible sentence. Bruner speculates that when a baby learns to differentiate between the two kinds of manual grip, this foreshadows "the development of topic and comment in human language"—the basic sentence form of subject/predicate, which may be found in all languages, with no exception whatsoever, and which a baby expresses when he combines a holophrase with another word. Thus, man may be uniquely predisposed, at birth, to re-invent the rules of grammar, to process information, and to develop "clever hands." He is born with a highly complex programing system, the result of millions of years of evolution.

What about disadvantaged children, then—why should they be different, if they are born with the same programing system? "Mind you, you can *ruin* a child's inheritance, too," warned Bruner, "with an environment where he acquires helplessness. You can also be trained to be stupid."

Before man's marvelous programing system can be activated for language, for instance, a baby must learn a series of primitive codes—and these require interaction with an adult. "What seems to get established very quickly between infant and parent is some sort of code of mutual expectancy," Bruner said, "when the adult responds to an initiative on the part of the child, thus converting some feature of the child's spontaneous behavior into a signal." Right from the start, parent and infant are busy communicating through eye-to-eye contact, smiles and sounds. As early as at 4 months of age, an infant will smile more to a face that smiles back than to one that does not respond; and if the adult face then stops smiling back, the infant will look away. In some cases, he may even struggle bodily to look away. A child's other attempts at learning can similarly be brought to a halt when his expectancy is thwarted, and things stop making sense.

Much of the center's work is based on the findings of the famous Swiss psychologist, Jean Piaget, who first described the stages through which young children construct their mental model of the world. How well and rapidly this model is built depends largely on the children's environment: the more new things a child has seen and heard, Piaget noted, the more he wants to see and hear. The greater variety of things a child has coped with, the greater his capacity for coping, and the more new methods he is able to invent by combining or re-combining what he has learned before. Both Piaget and Bruner disclaim an interest in early childhood *education,* however. What they are studying is early childhood itself. The mind of the human infant is still so deep a mystery, said Bruner, that he himself intends to stay with it for the rest of his life—"or until we give up, in final despair."

While Bruner concentrates on the process of learning, and White attempts to find the keys to individual children's competence, Prof. Jerome Kagan of Harvard's Department of Social Relations focuses on differences in the development of young children from different social classes. These are sometimes so acute, he has found, that poor homes can be considered actually crippling—at least for life in our society. This is not a racial matter: Kagan's study of 180 youngsters deals entirely with white families. For nearly three years he saw and tested these 180 children at regular intervals in his laboratory, beginning when they were 4 months old.

"Class differences emerge clearly by 12 months of age, and show up even earlier for girls—in some cases as early as at 8 months," Kagan declares. They appear in every one of the basic skills which the child learns during his first three years. Middle-class children are at an advantage, for instance, in learning specific "schema" for the events around them. By one year of age, they are way ahead of poorer children in discriminating between similar stimuli. As Kagan explains it, the reason for this superiority is the middle-class youngsters' greater experience with *distinctive* stimulation—slight transformations or discrepancies from what is ordinary.

"Middle-class mothers seem unconsciously to try to surprise their infants," he says, "and that's very good! They play peek-a-boo, or make unexpected sounds. In slum areas the mothers don't do this—they don't think of it, or may have no time—yet it's important." Infants who live in crowded homes where they are surrounded by noise all the time, from television and from many voices, learn to "tune it out" right from the beginning. "You don't learn anything in a Tower of Babel," says Kagan. "The main question is, is the mother distinctive?"

Kagan was among the first to use electronic

equipment to record babies' heartbeats during tests of attention. This is a useful way to determine whether an infant is actually looking at something, or just staring blankly: when a baby's heartbeats slow down, he is alerted and paying attention. With this equipment lightly and painlessly hooked up to the child's chest, Kagan could display various kinds of normal-looking or distorted masks and know exactly which ones surprised the infants. He learned that by the age of 1, middle-class children are more attentive to unusual events—they look longer at strange faces and forms. Kagan interprets this to mean that middle-class children have a bigger stock of schemata with which to try and explain unexpected things in their environment, which makes them less likely to turn away until they understand the event.

He also found that middle-class babies form closer attachments to their mothers, and therefore, he says, are more likely to accept the mother's values and goals. This closer attachment, which can be observed by the greater amount of crying among middle-class infants between the age of 6 and 10 months when their mother leaves the room, has nothing to do with the quality of the mother's love, he points out. "The fact is that the human caretaker is a target for the baby's clinging, scanning, vocalizing and smiling," explains Kagan. "The mother is a toy—just like the terry-cloth 'mothers' with which [psychologist Harry] Harlow's monkeys were raised in an experiment, and which they preferred [for reasons still unknown] to the wire 'mothers,' even when the latter provided them with milk. The more you play with this object, the more you get attached to it." And, according to a recent study by one of Kagan's graduate students, middle-class mothers do indeed spend a lot more time "entertaining" their babies—talking, smiling, playing face-to-face—than do poorer women.

"We don't imply that the lower-class mother doesn't love her child," Kagan warns. "There is no difference in kissing, nor in the total amount of talking, as opposed to face-to-face talking. However, the lower-class mother is more apt to talk from another room, or issue orders, and not take time for long periods of reciprocal play with her child."

This leads to obvious differences in the quality of language among the poor and the affluent. The poor child, then, is at a disadvantage in all these things—learning schemata, forming the kind of attachments which lead him to accept the mother's values, and speaking. He is also less persistent at difficult tasks, Kagan has noted; worse at nonverbal problems, such as perceptual puzzles; and, in addition, has learned a sort of impotence.

"When a mother tends to a child in distress as soon as he cries, this leads the child to believe there is something he can do," says Kagan. "He learns he can have an effect upon the world—make things go, or stop. If he is not tended, he will learn helplessness." He describes a recent study with newborn dogs and cats which were placed in a situation where there was nothing they could do to ward off mild electric shocks. When these animals were later given the opportunity to act on their environment, they could not learn to do so.

Since all these differences occur so early, "we should think of changing the behavior of the mothers of poor children during the first two years of the child's life," Kagan suggests. He believes this will require a major national commitment.

Each in its own way, then, the three Harvard groups conclude that some fundamental learning patterns are set very early in life—well before the age of 3 and that during this period the child is particularly open to environmental influences, for good or for bad.

Does this mean that, once past the age of 3, a child who has not learned the right patterns is doomed and cannot be changed? "No," replies Kagan. The child remains quite malleable during his first 7 years, but the longer you wait, the more radically you need to change his environment—and the *probability* of change becomes a little less with each successive year.

Is it true that "compensatory education... apparently has failed," as psychologist Arthur Jensen wrote in a recent issue of the *Harvard Educational Review*? No, answer the growth scientists, compensatory education has not failed, because it has never really been tried —at least never properly, or on a large scale. They tend to dismiss the only massive effort, Head Start, as too little, too late, and too unfocused in its present form. "Just eight weeks [of training], a couple of hours a day? That's not very much!" says Kagan. "That's not a radical change in a child's environment." The growth scientists also object that Head

Start children are comparatively old (two-thirds of them are 5 or 6, and only 5 per cent of the total are under the age of 4). More powerful programs, they believe, are needed for children between the ages of 3 and 6, lasting the full year, and focused so as to teach cognitive skills.

What the people in the growth sciences really want, however, is not emergency treatment for disadvantaged children, but *prevention* of handicaps. And for this, they are convinced, you need to start before the age of 3. There are two possible strategies:

(1) Starting kibbutz-like day-care centers in which trained teachers would give children an excellent education from earliest infancy. In a reply to Jensen, Benjamin Bloom has just suggested that we learn from Israel's experience with the children of poor and mainly illiterate immigrants from North Africa and Yemen. These Oriental children have extremely low I.Q.'s when reared at home—an average of 85, compared with the 105 scored by Jewish children of European origin. When both kinds of children are raised in the same communal nurseries from birth on, however, both have an average I.Q. of 115 —a jump of 30 points for the Oriental children. Bloom points out that these children had spent 22 hours a day in the kibbutz nursery for at least four years.

(2) Producing major improvements in the way parents raise their children—the solution which Bloom, Kagan and many others in the growth sciences prefer, and for which White is actively preparing. This, too, is a form of prevention, apparently more palatable than widespread day-care centers, but not necessarily easier to carry out.

After spending $2-million on projects in which social workers, clinical psychologists and psychiatrists tried to change the child-rearing practices of lower-class parents by means of counseling, for instance, the National Institute of Mental Health's Committee on Social Problems learned from its chairman, J. McV. Hunt, that "nothing, absolutely nothing, so far as I can ascertain, has come of it." Hunt's book, *Intelligence and Experience* (1961), played a major role in sparking the current interest in the first three years of life. He now believes that when poor mothers are given something useful to do with their children they sometimes become just as effective as professional teachers.

One "serendipitous finding," according to Hunt, was that infants in a Durban, N.C., ghetto actually benefited from a research program aimed only at studying their psychological development, not interfering in it. After two years of tests at a Duke University laboratory, once a month, these toddlers scored close to 110 on the Binet I.Q. test, while other 2½-year-olds from their neighborhoods scored only 70 to 80. Hunt thinks that the babies' mothers—who were present throughout the tests—must have noticed which items they did well on and which they failed, and then given them practice where they needed it. "They appear to have been exceedingly effective as teachers," he says. "This suggests that poor children's decline can be prevented."

When Merle B. Karnes of the University of Illinois trained the mothers of 15 disadvantaged 3-year-olds to make inexpensive educational materials—sock puppets, lotto and matching games, etc.—to use at home, she made a similar discovery. These mothers also served as assistants in Karnes' experimental nursery school, being paid $3 for each two-hour training session. Within less than three months after they began, their own children, who had stayed home, suddenly gained 7.5 points of I.Q. Later on these children did as well as those in Karnes' professionally run nursery school. Karnes concluded that teachers should take on a new role: Training parents, rather than just teaching children, and involving the entire family in the education of preschoolers.

The burden of the new research, then, is to put ever more burden on parents—which generally means mothers, since fathers have been strangely ignored by the growth sciences. Interestingly, when the mothers in Karnes' group realized how much time and effort are required to do a good job of raising preschool youngsters, they headed en masse for the local chapter of the Planned Parenthood Association —they felt they could never teach their children enough if they had babies every year, as before.

This does not solve the problem for the 1.5-million youngsters under the age of 3 whose mothers work away from home, however. Few of these women can either afford or find a first-rate nurse who is interested in stimulating their babies' intellectual and social growth. Even fewer have access to a day-care center with a strong educational component. The government has utterly failed to take their needs into account, but now private industry is beginning to enter this field and an upsurge in specialized day-care centers may be expected in the near future.

Both approaches—the educational day-care centers and the training of parents—have already come under attack. "What do you mean, have a white professor come here and tell us how to raise our kids?" sputtered a black militant when he heard about a new program for parents. Others object to the idea of "taking children away from their mothers and putting them in day-care centers from birth on—it's totalitarian!" Sociologists argue that one shouldn't impose middle-class values on the poor, who have their own culture. Community leaders declare that if any day-care centers are opened in their area, *they,* not outsiders, should decide what will be taught.

The people in the growth sciences know it's going to be an uphill fight, but they are fascinated by the possibility of giving each child a chance to "realize his full potential." According to Hunt, "Most of the skills we are talking about—cognitive skills, language skills, pride in achievement, and so on—are not a matter that is black or white or green or yellow. In order to survive in a technological culture, one *must* have these skills." The best time to acquire them is in early childhood. He also points out that if one wishes to maximize a child's development, "you need to maximize it all along. Competence—like deprivation—is cumulative."

As these ideas spread, the nation's educational efforts are likely to include ever younger children, and soon the years from birth to 3 may become a target of first priority.

12. MY OEDIPUS COMPLEX

Frank O'Connor

Father was in the army all through the war—the first war, I mean—so, up to the age of five, I never saw much of him, and what I saw did not worry me. Sometimes I woke and there was a big figure in khaki peering down at me in the candlelight. Sometimes in the early morning I heard the slamming of the front door and the clatter of nailed boots down the cobbles of the lane. These were Father's entrances and exits. Like Santa Claus he came and went mysteriously.

In fact, I rather liked his visits, though it was an uncomfortable squeeze between Mother and him when I got into the big bed in the early morning. He smoked, which gave him a pleasant musty smell, and shaved, an operation of astounding interest. Each time he left

From THE STORIES OF FRANK O'CONNOR *by Frank O'Connor. Copyright 1952 by Alfred A. Knopf, Inc. and Hamish Hamilton, Ltd. Reprinted by permission of Random House, Inc. and A. D. Peters & Co., London.*

a trail of souvenirs—model tanks and Gurkha knives with handles made of bullet cases, and German helmets and cap badges and buttonsticks, and all sorts of military equipment—carefully stowed away in a long box on top of the wardrobe, in case they ever came in handy. There was a bit of the magpie about Father; he expected everything to come in handy. When his back was turned, Mother let me get a chair and rummage through his treasures. She didn't seem to think so highly of them as he did.

The war was the most peaceful period of my life. The window of my attic faced southeast. My mother had curtained it, but that had small effect. I always woke with the first light and, with all the responsibilities of the previous day melted, feeling myself rather like the sun, ready to illumine and rejoice. Life never seemed so simple and clear and full of possibilities as then. I put my feet out from under the clothes—I called them Mrs. Left and Mrs. Right—and invented dramatic situations for them in which they discussed the problems of the day. At least Mrs. Right did; she was very demonstrative, but I hadn't the same control of Mrs. Left, so she mostly contented herself with nodding agreement.

They discussed what Mother and I should do during the day, what Santa Claus should give a fellow for Christmas, and what steps should be taken to brighten the home. There was that little matter of the baby, for instance. Mother and I could never agree about that. Ours was the only house in the terrace without a new baby, and Mother said we couldn't afford one till Father came back from the war because they cost seventeen and six. That showed how simple she was. The Geneys up the road had a baby, and everyone knew they couldn't afford seventeen and six. It was probably a cheap baby, and Mother wanted something really good, but I felt she was too exclusive. The Geneys' baby would have done us fine.

Having settled my plans for the day, I got up, put a chair under the attic window, and lifted the frame high enough to stick out my head. The window overlooked the front gardens of the terrace behind ours, and beyond these it looked over a deep valley to the tall, red-brick houses terraced up the opposite hillside, which were all still in shadow, while those at our side of the valley were all lit up, though with long strange shadows that made them seem unfamiliar; rigid and painted.

After that I went into Mother's room and climbed into the big bed. She woke and I began to tell her of my schemes. By this time, though I never seem to have noticed it, I was petrified in my nightshirt, and I thawed as I talked until, the last frost melted, I fell asleep beside her and woke again only when I heard her below in the kitchen, making the breakfast.

After breakfast we went into town; heard Mass at St. Augustine's and said a prayer for Father, and did the shopping. If the afternoon was fine we either went for a walk in the country or a visit to Mother's great friend in the convent, Mother St. Dominic. Mother had them all praying for Father, and every night, going to bed, I asked God to send him back safe from the war to us. Little, indeed, did I know what I was praying for!

One morning, I got into the big bed, and there, sure enough, was Father in his usual Santa Claus manner, but later, instead of uniform, he put on his best blue suit, and Mother was as pleased as anything. I saw nothing to be pleased about, because, out of uniform, Father was altogether less interesting, but she only beamed, and explained that our prayers had been answered, and off we went to Mass to thank God for having brought Father safely home.

The irony of it! That very day when he came in to dinner he took off his boots and put on his slippers, donned the dirty old cap he wore about the house to save him from colds, crossed his legs, and began to talk gravely to Mother, who looked anxious. Naturally, I disliked her looking anxious, because it destroyed her good looks, so I interrupted him.

"Just a moment, Larry!" she said gently.

This was only what she said when we had boring visitors, so I attached no importance to it and went on talking.

"Do be quiet, Larry!" she said impatiently. "Don't you hear me talking to Daddy?"

This was the first time I had heard those ominous words, "talking to Daddy," and I couldn't help feeling that if this was how God answered prayers, he couldn't listen to them very attentively.

"Why are you talking to Daddy?" I asked with as great a show of indifference as I could muster.

"Because Daddy and I have business to discuss. Now, don't interrupt again!"

In the afternoon, at Mother's request, Father took me for a walk. This time we went into town instead of out the country, and I thought at first, in my usual optimistic way, that it might be an improvement. It was nothing of the sort. Father and I had quite different notions of a walk in town. He had no proper interest in trams, ships, and horses, and the only thing that seemed to divert him was talking to fellows as old as himself. When I wanted to stop he simply went on, dragging me behind him by the hand; when he wanted to stop I had no alternative but to do the same. I noticed that it seemed to be a sign that he wanted to stop for a long time whenever he leaned against a wall. The second time I saw him do it I got wild. He seemed to be settling himself forever. I pulled him by the coat and trousers, but, unlike Mother who, if you were too persistent, got into a wax and said: "Larry, if you don't behave yourself, I'll give you a good slap," Father had an extraordinary capacity for amiable inattention. I sized him up and wondered would I cry, but he seemed to be too remote to be annoyed even by that. Really, it was like going for a walk with a mountain! He either ignored the wrenching and pummeling entirely, or else glanced down with a grin of amusement from his peak. I had never met anyone so absorbed in himself as he seemed.

At teatime, "talking to Daddy" began again, complicated this time by the fact that he had an evening paper, and every few minutes he put it down and told Mother something new out of it. I felt this was foul play. Man for man, I was prepared to compete with him any time for Mother's attention, but when he had it all made up for him by other people it left me no chance. Several times I tried to change the subject without success.

"You must be quiet while Daddy is reading, Larry," Mother said impatiently.

It was clear that she either genuinely liked talking to Father better than talking to me, or else that he had some terrible hold on her which made her afraid to admit the truth.

"Mummy," I said that night when she was tucking me up, "do you think if I prayed hard God would send Daddy back to the war?"

She seemed to think about that for a moment.

"No, dear," she said with a smile. "I don't think he would."

"Why wouldn't he, Mummy?"

"Because there isn't a war any longer, dear."

"But, Mummy, couldn't God make another war, if He liked?"

"He wouldn't like to, dear. It's not God who makes wars, but bad people."

"Oh!" I said.

I was disappointed about that. I began to think that God wasn't quite what he was cracked up to be.

Next morning I woke at my usual hour, feeling like a bottle of champagne. I put out my feet and invented a long conversation in which Mrs. Right talked of the trouble she had with her own father till she put him in the Home. I didn't quite know what the Home was but it sounded the right place for Father. Then I got my chair and stuck my head out of the attic window. Dawn was just breaking, with a guilty air that made me feel I had caught it in the act. My head bursting with stories and schemes, I stumbled in next door, and in the half-darkness scrambled into the big bed. There was no room at Mother's side so I had to get between her and Father. For the time being I had forgotten about him, and for several minutes I sat bolt upright, racking my brains to know what I could do with him. He was taking up more than his fair share of the bed, and I couldn't get comfortable, so I gave him several kicks that made him grunt and stretch. He made room all right, though. Mother waked and felt for me. I settled back comfortably in the warmth of the bed with my thumb in my mouth.

"Mummy!" I hummed, loudly and contentedly.

"Sssh! dear," she whispered. "Don't wake Daddy!"

This was a new development, which threatened to be even more serious than "talking to Daddy." Life without my early-morning conferences was unthinkable.

"Why?" I asked severely.

"Because poor Daddy is tired."

This seemed to me a quite inadequate reason, and I was sickened by the sentimentality of her "poor Daddy." I never liked that sort of gush; it always struck me as insincere.

"Oh!" I said lightly. Then in my most winning tone: "Do you know where I want to go with you today, Mummy?"

"No, dear," she sighed.

"I want to go down the Glen and fish for thornybacks with my new net, and then I want to go out to the Fox and Hounds, and—"

"Don't-wake-Daddy!" she hissed angrily, clapping her hand across my mouth.

But it was too late. He was awake, or nearly so. He grunted and reached for the matches. Then he stared incredulously at his watch.

"Like a cup of tea, dear?" asked Mother in a meek, hushed voice I had never heard her use before. It sounded almost as though she were afraid.

"Tea?" he exclaimed indignantly. "Do you know what the time is?"

"And after that I want to go up the Rathcooney Road," I said loudly, afraid I'd forget something in all those interruptions.

"Go to sleep at once, Larry!" she said sharply.

I began to snivel. I couldn't concentrate, the way that pair went on, and smothering my early-morning schemes was like burying a family from the cradle.

Father said nothing, but lit his pipe and sucked it, looking out into the shadows without minding Mother or me. I knew he was mad. Every time I made a remark Mother hushed me irritably. I was mortified. I felt it wasn't fair; there was even something sinister in it. Every time I had pointed out to her the waste of making two beds when we could both sleep in one, she had told me it was healthier like that, and now here was this man, this stranger, sleeping with her without the least regard for her health!

He got up early and made tea, but though he brought Mother a cup he brought none for me.

"Mummy," I shouted, "I want a cup of tea, too."

"Yes, dear," she said patiently. "You can drink from Mummy's saucer."

That settled it. Either Father or I would have to leave the house. I didn't want to drink from Mother's saucer; I wanted to be treated as an equal in my own home, so, just to spite her, I drank it all and left none for her. She took that quietly, too.

But that night when she was putting me to bed she said gently:

"Larry, I want you to promise me something."

"What is it?" I asked.

"Not to come in and disturb poor Daddy in the morning. Promise?"

"Poor Daddy" again! I was becoming suspicious of everything involving that quite impossible man.

"Why?" I asked.

"Because poor Daddy is worried and tired and he doesn't sleep well."

"Why doesn't he, Mummy?"

"Well, you know, don't you, that while he was at the war Mummy got the pennies from the Post Office?"

"From Miss MacCarthy?"

"That's right. But now, you see, Miss Mac-Carthy hasn't any more pennies, so Daddy must go out and find us some. You know what would happen if he couldn't?"

"No," I said, "tell us."

"Well, I think we might have to go out and beg for them like the poor old woman on Fridays. We wouldn't like that, would we?"

"No," I agreed. "We wouldn't."

"So you'll promise not to come in and wake him?"

"Promise."

Mind you, I meant that. I knew pennies were a serious matter, and I was all against having to go out and beg like the old woman on Fridays. Mother laid out all my toys in a complete ring round the bed so that, whatever way I got out, I was bound to fall over one of them.

When I woke I remembered my promise all right. I got up and sat on the floor and played —for hours, it seemed to me. Then I got my chair and looked out the attic window for more hours. I wished it was time for Father to wake; I wished someone would make me a cup of tea. I didn't feel in the least like the sun; instead, I was bored and so very, very cold! I simply longed for the warmth and depth of the big featherbed.

At last I could stand it no longer. I went into the next room. As there was still no room at Mother's side I climbed over her and she woke with a start.

"Larry," she whispered, gripping my arm very tightly, "what did you promise?"

"But I did, Mummy," I wailed, caught in the very act. "I was quiet for ever so long."

"Oh, dear, and you're perished!" she said sadly, feeling me all over. "Now, if I let you stay will you promise not to talk?"

"But I want to talk, Mummy," I wailed.

"That has nothing to do with it," she said with a firmness that was new to me. "Daddy wants to sleep. Now, do you understand that?"

I understood it only too well. I wanted to talk, he wanted to sleep—whose house was it, anyway?

"Mummy," I said with equal firmness, "I think it would be healthier for Daddy to sleep in his own bed."

That seemed to stagger her, because she said nothing for a while.

"Now, once for all," she went on, "you're to be perfectly quiet or go back to your own bed. Which is it to be?"

The injustice of it got me down. I had convicted her out of her own mouth of inconsistency and unreasonableness, and she hadn't even attempted to reply. Full of spite, I gave Father a kick, which she didn't notice but which made him grunt and open his eyes in alarm.

"What time is it?" he asked in a panic-stricken voice, not looking at Mother but at the door, as if he saw someone there.

"It's early yet," she replied soothingly. "It's only the child. Go to sleep again. . . . Now, Larry," she added, getting out of bed, "you've wakened Daddy and you must go back."

This time, for all her quiet air, I knew she meant it, and knew that my principal rights and privileges were as good as lost unless I asserted them at once. As she lifted me, I gave a screech, enough to wake the dead, not to mind Father. He groaned.

"That damn child! Doesn't he ever sleep?"

"It's only a habit, dear," she said quietly, though I could see she was vexed.

"Well, it's time he got out of it," shouted Father, beginning to heave in the bed. He suddenly gathered all the bedclothes about him, turned to the wall, and then looked back over his shoulder with nothing showing only two small, spiteful, dark eyes. The man looked very wicked.

To open the bedroom door, Mother had to let me down, and I broke free and dashed for the farthest corner, screeching. Father sat bolt upright in bed.

"Shut up, you little puppy!" he said in a choking voice.

I was so astonished that I stopped screeching. Never, never had anyone spoken to me in that tone before. I looked at him incredulously and saw his face convulsed with rage. It was only then that I fully realized how God had codded me, listening to my prayers for the safe return of this monster.

"Shut up, you!" I bawled, beside myself.

"What's that you said?" shouted Father, making a wild leap out of the bed.

"Mick, Mick!" cried Mother. "Don't you see the child isn't used to you?"

"I see he's better fed than taught," snarled Father, waving his arms wildly. "He wants his bottom smacked."

All his previous shouting was as nothing to these obscene words referring to my person. They really made my blood boil.

"Smack your own!" I screamed hysterically. "Smack your own! Shut up! Shut up!"

At this he lost his patience and let fly at me. He did it with the lack of conviction you'd expect of a man under Mother's horrified eyes, and it ended up as a mere tap, but the sheer indignity of being struck at all by a stranger, a total stranger who had cajoled his way back from the war into our big bed as a result of my innocent intercession, made me completely dotty. I shrieked and shrieked, and danced in my bare feet, and Father, looking awkward and hairy in nothing but a short grey army shirt, glared down at me like a mountain for murder. I think it must have been then that I realized he was jealous too. And there stood Mother in her nightdress, looking as if her heart was broken between us. I hoped she

felt as she looked. It seemed to me that she deserved it all.

From that morning out my life was a hell. Father and I were enemies, open and avowed. We conducted a series of skirmishes against one another, he trying to steal my time with Mother and I his. When she was sitting on my bed, telling me a story, he took to looking for some pair of old boots which he alleged he had left behind him at the beginning of the war. While he talked to Mother I played loudly with my toys to show my total lack of concern. He created a terrible scene one evening when he came in from work and found me at his box, playing with his regimental badges, Gurkha knives and button-sticks. Mother got up and took the box from me.

"You mustn't play with Daddy's toys unless he lets you, Larry," she said severely. "Daddy doesn't play with yours."

For some reason Father looked at her as if she had struck him and then turned away with a scowl.

"Those are not toys," he growled, taking down the box again to see had I lifted anything. "Some of those curios are very rare and valuable."

But as time went on I saw more and more how he managed to alienate Mother and me. What made it worse was that I couldn't grasp his method or see what attraction he had for Mother. In every possible way he was less winning than I. He had a common accent and made noises at his tea. I thought for a while that it might be the newspapers she was interested in, so I made up bits of news of my own to read to her. Then I thought it might be the smoking, which I personally thought attractive, and took his pipes and went round the house dribbling into them till he caught me. I even made noises at my tea, but Mother only told me I was disgusting. It all seemed to hinge round that unhealthy habit of sleeping together, so I made a point of dropping into their bedroom and nosing round, talking to myself, so that they wouldn't know I was watching them, but they were never up to anything that I could see. In the end it beat me. It seemed to depend on being grown-up and giving people rings, and I realized I'd have to wait.

But at the same time I wanted him to see that I was only waiting, not giving up the fight. One evening when he was being particularly obnoxious, chattering away well above my head, I let him have it.

"Mummy," I said, "do you know what I'm going to do when I grow up?"

"No, dear," she replied. "What?"

"I'm going to marry you," I said quietly.

Father gave a great guffaw out of him, but he didn't take me in. I know it must only be pretence. And Mother, in spite of everything, was pleased. I felt she was probably relieved to know that one day Father's hold on her would be broken.

"Won't that be nice?" she said with a smile.

"It'll be very nice," I said confidently. "Because we're going to have lots and lots of babies."

"That's right, dear," she said placidly. "I think we'll have one soon, and then you'll have plenty of company."

I was no end pleased about that because it showed that in spite of the way she gave in to Father she still considered my wishes. Besides, it would put the Geneys in their place.

It didn't turn out like that, though. To begin with, she was very preoccupied—I supposed about where she would get the seventeen and six—and though Father took to staying out late in the evenings it did me no particular good. She stopped taking me for walks, became as touchy as blazes, and smacked me for nothing at all. Sometimes I wished I'd never mentioned the confounded baby—I seemed to have a genius for bringing calamity on myself.

And calamity it was! Sonny arrived in the most appalling hullabaloo—even that much he couldn't do without a fuss—and from the first moment I disliked him. He was a difficult child—so far as I was concerned he was always difficult—and demanded far too much attention. Mother was simply silly about him, and couldn't see when he was only showing off. As company he was worse than useless. He slept all day, and I had to go round the house on tiptoe to avoid waking him. It wasn't any longer a question of not waking Father. The slogan now was "Don't-wake-Sonny!" I couldn't understand why the child wouldn't sleep at the proper time, so whenever Mother's back was turned I woke him. Sometimes to keep him awake I pinched him as well. Mother caught me at it one day and gave me a most unmerciful flaking.

One evening, when Father was coming in from work, I was playing trains in the front garden. I let on not to notice him; instead, I pretended to be talking to myself, and said in a loud voice: "If another bloody baby comes into this house, I'm going out."

Father stopped dead and looked at me over his shoulder.

"What's that you said?" he asked sternly.

"I was only talking to myself," I replied, trying to conceal my panic. "It's private."

He turned and went in without a word. Mind you, I intended it as a solemn warning, but its effect was quite different. Father started being quite nice to me. I could understand that, of course. Mother was quite sickening about Sonny. Even at mealtimes she'd get up and gawk at him in the cradle with an idiotic smile, and tell Father to do the same. He was always polite about it, but he looked so puzzled you could see he didn't know what she was talking about. He complained of the way Sonny cried at night, but she only got cross and said that Sonny never cried except when there was something up with him— which was a flaming lie, because Sonny never had anything up with him, and only cried for attention. It was really painful to see how simple-minded she was. Father wasn't attractive, but he had a fine intelligence. He saw through Sonny, and now he knew that I saw through him as well.

One night I woke with a start. There was someone beside me in the bed. For one wild moment I felt sure it must be Mother, having come to her senses and left Father for good, but then I heard Sonny in convulsions in the next room, and Mother saying: "There! There! There!" and I knew it wasn't she. It was Father. He was lying beside me, wide awake, breathing hard and apparently as mad as hell.

After a while it came to me what he was mad about. It was his turn now. After turning me out of the big bed, he had been turned out himself. Mother had no consideration now for anyone but that poisonous pup, Sonny. I couldn't help feeling sorry for Father. I had been through it all myself, and even at that age I was magnanimous. I began to stroke him down and say: "There! There!" He wasn't exactly responsive.

"Aren't you asleep either?" he snarled.

"Ah, come on and put your arm around us, can't you?" I said, and he did, in a sort of way. Gingerly, I suppose, is how you'd describe it. He was very bony but better than nothing.

At Christmas he went out of his way to buy me a really nice model railway.

13. THE CHILDREN OF THE DREAM: THEIR MOLD AND OURS

Bruno Bettelheim

TRUST VERSUS MISTRUST

Starting with the *first* psychosocial crisis, that of trust versus mistrust, there seems little doubt of how different is the kibbutz infant's radius of significant relations. Because trust, in the kibbutz, derives not so much from *the* maternal person as from a number of maternal persons. From the very beginning, things are hence very different in the kibbutz than Erikson's model would suggest.

One might say here that what counts for the basic personality in infancy, and for the fundamental outlook on life later on, is not any absolute quantity, either of trust or mistrust, but the balance between them. To state it crudely: deep experiences prompting trust, and deep experiences leading to mistrust, may inspire an outlook on life essentially similar to one caused by a moderate taste of both trust and mistrust. Because when the negative is deducted from the positive, the remainders may be equal. This is so, even if the absolute size of what is deducted from what, differs vastly.

Thus a small basis for trust may produce the same basic security—if little interfered with by cause for basic mistrust—as would a vast experience creating trust when eroded by considerable cause for mistrust. My crude example may also suggest that the absolute size of what is deducted from what, may affect how deep the experience, but not its nature. Because the nature of the outlook, in this crude approximation, depends on what remains after subtraction.

Now, basic trust, from a very early age, is born of how the mothering task is performed. When the child's needs are well and responsively met, he develops, we think, a sense of trust. But in the kibbutz these tasks are performed by several mothering persons. One might assume then that the need to adjust to a variety of caretakers interferes with the feeling that this world and its ministrations are most reliable.

On the other hand, because there are several persons to take care of the nurseling, and this is the *metapelet's** central task, the infant has less cause for waiting and worrying, which may breed less mistrust. So here we might assume there is less interference with mothering than where a child depends on a mother's ministrations but this mother belongs also to many other tasks (housekeeping, siblings, husband).

Or again: With other infants eternally present, there will be less distrust and fear of desertion. But with no adult immediately available at night there will be less security. Multiple mothering, then, and the particular situation in kibbutz nurseries, may create less of both: less basic trust and also less basic mistrust.

According to Erikson's model, the "related element of social order" which flows from this earliest encounter with trust and mistrust, he calls "Cosmic Order." For the typical middle-class family this sense of order derives from one central person. As such, it lends credence

* The woman whose full-time job it is to raise a group of kibbutz children. (Eds.)

to a world order created by one Supreme Being, with all its consequent feelings of bondage. Since cosmic order, for the kibbutz infant, is from the very first derived not from one person only, but from several, this too may create far-reaching differences in what will give order to his world.[1]

Initial learning, in the kibbutz, may be more difficult for the infant, given the need to adjust to different ways of how things are done. At least Rabin (*Growing Up in the Kibbutz,* 1965) suggests possible retardation of certain social and motor responses, when compared with adaptation in the infant who faces the much simpler task of adjusting his responses mainly to one person.

My own observation of infants was not extensive enough to permit me to agree or disagree with Rabin's findings on early behavior. But after presenting them, he goes on to say that the "relative developmental retardation noted in kibbutz infants is not maintained in later years." My foregoing comment may suggest why such retardation, if it occurs (Rabin's findings are not conclusive) would, by the toddler age, be made up for. Perhaps it is not that retardation ever took place—because if it had, and the child could so easily catch up, if there were no lasting effects, then we would have to change our entire model of how human development takes place. Perhaps what occurs is not retardation but simply that it takes longer to master a more complex bit of learning. It is fairly easy to adjust one's movements and social responses to one person alone. Hence the response is learned sooner. If the task is to adjust one's motor and social responses to several persons at once, then the learning task is more complex and takes longer to achieve.

Eventually, of course, all infants have to learn to adjust to several persons; certainly in the oedipal phase. But perhaps those who have learned it from the beginning come out ahead in the long run, compared to those who learned first to respond to one person and later had to transfer the learning to many. Multiple mothering may also explain the absence in the kibbutz of what is technically

called symbiotic psychosis of childhood. This is a disturbance marked by the child's utter dependence on his mother, which prevents him from having any life of his own. In the kibbutz there is no chance for symbiosis to develop in the first place.

Just as important, even at the very start of life, is how different are the social and psychological procedures that mark this first stage of human development. Here the essential experience for the kibbutz infant is to get, while to give in return is emphasized much less. No doubt, if the infant reaches out to his caretakers, he will get more from them. But since there are several caretakers, how they give to him will be less uniform in manner, and it will make much less difference how he gives in return.

Which means that from the beginning of life the extremes of development will be absent. In the kibbutz, with its multiple mothering, the infant has neither the utter security that may come of feeling himself at the core of his mother's existence, nor will he know the bondage it can bring. The heights of intimate mutuality (or later, of individuation) will not be reached that are possible in some mother-infant relationships. But neither will he know the extremes of nonmutuality (and hence of isolation and alienation) that result from bad mother-infant relations. And these occur in quite a few of our families where the mother, in the way she handles her infant, fails to adjust to his cues because of her own emotional problems, or because of the pressures of time or other interests.

One result is that grounds may be laid even at this early stage for the so-called "flatness" so often remarked upon in the kibbutz-born personality. It may be the consequence of a shallowness in the experience of mutuality— or of both trust and mistrust. Perhaps in these terms, most persons in the middle reaches of our society have equally flat personalities, or worse. Where we seem to differ from the kibbutz is in the presence of extremes, both of intensity and withdrawal.

One last comment before leaving this earliest of all developmental stages. Many of the concerns that led Erikson to formulate his model had to do with the severe identity crisis he observed in American middle-class youth (but which also afflicts our Negro and lower-class youth), and which is rooted in this earliest period of life. Perhaps relative absence of

---

1 One might even wonder if the compound family system (or any arrangements wherein many different persons look after the infant) does not create fertile ground for a cosmic order based not on the rule of one God but of many—and of a group of deities where none is very superior to the rest.

an identity crisis in kibbutz youth indicates that their experience, at the very beginning, is more benign by comparison.

AUTONOMY, SHAME, AND DOUBT

The difference between Erikson's model and kibbutz reality is as marked in the *second* psychosocial crisis, that of autonomy versus shame and doubt. The importance of the peer group, in Erikson's model, does not make itself felt until the fifth of these crises, at puberty. In the kibbutz the peer group is already greatly important during this second psychosocial crisis, or stage of development, not only through its presence, but through its actual help, as with toilet training and other forms of early socialization. Indeed, the peer group is significant even in the first stage, given the intense watching of other infants in adjacent cribs, as it reduces feelings of loneliness and abandonment.

Since it is the other children who set examples and influence the education to cleanliness, there is much less shaming than is typical when adults toilet train the child. Also the "radius of significant relations" is much larger, because to the "parental persons" must be added the peer group, if not almost the entire kibbutz.

"To hold (on)" and "to (let go)" are much less important in the kibbutz, since there is so much less emphasis on toilet training, table manners, cleanliness, the care of clothing, etc. (Which may be why private property and the holding on to it become less important.) We find a reduction in the kind of autonomy that is based on a stubborn insistence on having one's way as it may develop around these activities, and with it a radical decrease in doubt. But in other spheres a much greater autonomy develops because the kibbutz child is left so much to his own devices.

With far fewer do's and don'ts and a much more lenient toilet training, the internalized feeling for "law and order" is less stringent. Law and order derive less from toilet training and much more from the "laws" of the kibbutz. Even at this early age it is less the voice of conscience, and much more the peer group that utters the do's and don'ts. And these are enforced by group influence, through shaming.

But the shaming is much gentler and less severe than when it comes from adults, not because the other children may be less force-

ful, but because the child observes how much the children who shame him transgress themselves. Because of it, their injunctions carry less weight and lead to much less self-doubt. Which makes the experience of shame very different from what is typical for the middle-class child. It comes not from any vast difference between "my behavior" and that of the shaming adult, but from a rather small difference between two comparative equals. Which, again, engenders less doubt.

Let me use this period for a few brief comparisons. Erikson lists some items discussed by Spock to suggest the problems now besetting parent and child, such as "Feeling his oats" and "The passion to explore." In consequence of these come the parent's problems of "Arranging the house for a wandering baby. Putting poison out of reach. Making him leave certain things alone. Making him stay in bed."

Each is a problematic issue in the middle-class home at this period of development. Around them, battles are fought that often scar the infant for life, and sometimes the parent. But these issues hardly exist for the kibbutz child. The infant house is arranged specially for him, there is no poison, nor anything he must not touch. Since there are no parents to turn to after bedtime and nothing going on around him in the evening, keeping children in bed is as little a problem for the parent as is staying in bed for the child.

INITIATIVE VERSUS GUILT

During the period of the *third* psychosocial crisis, that of initiative versus guilt, the basic family, according to Erikson, becomes important in addition to parental persons. But in the kibbutz there is no basic family in our sense. What replaces it are the two parents on one hand, and the *metapelets* and peer group on the other. Much more important, the radius of significant relations has by this time expanded far more than the model suggests. It extends to the kibbutz as a whole, because the kibbutz performs so many functions that parents do in our setting, such as offering physical protection, being the main provider, etc.

Speaking of this third period Erikson writes: "the child must now find out *what kind* of person he is going to be...he wants to be like his parents, who to him appear very powerful and very beautiful, although quite unreasonably dangerous. He 'identifies with them,' he plays with the idea of how it would be to be them." These are the ideal prototypes of the period in our middle-class family.

How different things are for the kibbutz child. He, too, in this period must find out what kind of person he is going to be. But while his parents are very important to him, they certainly do not appear to him as very powerful, and even less so as unreasonably dangerous.

The most powerful persons, to the kibbutz child of this age, are the metapelets. And typically if the children play the role of adults, as they do at this age just as often as do children in our society, the girls play at being metapelets, and both boys and girls play at being persons carrying high prestige in the kibbutz, such as truck drivers.

Thus at a much earlier age the identification is with the society's "culture carrier," not the parent. And in the kibbutz the culture carrier embodies the culture much more closely than does the parent (or the cowboy or Indian or athlete) in our society. So again the identification with what the kibbutz stands for takes precedence over the identification with parents. Children also identify less with a particular individual, and more with some role the group admires. The child wishes less to become like a particular, unique person—a wish also largely suppressed in his parents and metapelets—than to become a good comrade. Such an ideal accords with both his parents' ego ideal and the moral valuation of the entire society.

In the kibbutz, however, far more than is true of many middle-class families, the ego ideals of father and mother are very much akin to each other, and to those of the metapelets. Even if the child wished to be different from them, he has hardly any images that differ enough to serve him as variant ideals. Life is much simpler at this age, a boon for which a price will be exacted of those adolescents who may yearn for a highly personal identity that eludes them.

Social crisis in this third period centers around the issue of initiative versus guilt. But guilt in the kibbutz derives from transgressing the rules of the children's community and not from violating the basic values of a nuclear family. Hence the nature of guilt is very different. The essential experience creating guilt in the kibbutz is based on the anxiety: *"They will think I'm no good"* rather than *"I will*

think I'm no good"; while in the middle-class conscience the relative importance of the two personal elements is exactly reversed.

Grounds for this difference are laid in the second phase of development, where from the much gentler shaming comes the fear that "they'll think I'm no good," versus the middle-class child's feeling of "I'm no good compared to my parents." The first permits ready relief. One has only to catch up with peers who are only one step ahead. The latter makes the child feel hopeless about himself because the gap between his own self-control and that of the shaming parent is just too great—or seems so to him. In the nuclear family the heir of the personal voices of the parents is thus a highly personalized superego. In the kibbutz the outer voices internalized are those of the entire community, and lead to a collective superego.

But if internalization is weaker, along with inner initiative, locomotor initiative in trying to master the physical world is much more encouraged. This is because the children must so largely fend for themselves, and because the whole life of their community is an open book to them (the exception here is the private life of adults, including the sexual life; but in the kibbutz the adult's life is much less private than with us). There is continual challenge to do things, and hardly any to sit and think and feel. I am tempted to exaggerate and say this starts at the beginning of life, for it is not much of an exaggeration.

Any budding inner experience the child has with himself is interfered with or extinguished before it can go very far by some group experience directing him outward. The children are always busy doing things. And if they don't seduce or even push each other in that direction, the metapelet will. There is no time, no opportunity and no challenge for them to think their own thoughts or to yield themselves up to their own feelings.

Neither are there introjects to converse with in fantasy. And when, later on in adolescence, the desire for all this is much stronger, there is no prior experience on which it can build. To have to build it from scratch at so late a developmental stage seems impossible for most. One consequence is that these adolescents who use their bodies so skillfully to do things, are not "at home" with the body itself, their own or another's. Having looked inward so little they are not very intimate with feelings generated by the body, though they can use it with competence; they are more familiar with what it does than what it feels.

Kibbutz living arrangements have far-reaching consequences for the nature of the children's fantasies about sex. Living apart from their parents prevents the children from watching primal scenes and from having it forcefully brought home to them each night that now their parents are in bed together, just the two of them, a fact at once known to and hidden from the middle-class child. For example, since they do not observe human intercourse, neither might they get the notion that this is an aggressive, sadistic act performed by the male on the female. Since there was so much less of anal or urethral inhibitions in the preceding period, initiative is much less impeded by guilt than it is in our middle-class families. Muscular development, too, except for the sphincter, is far more encouraged and facilitated in both the second and third periods, because kibbutz children can roam so freely through the landscape (perhaps an origin of their deep seated love for it).

INDUSTRY VERSUS INFERIORITY

Speaking of the latency period and of the *fourth* psychosocial crisis, that of industry versus inferiority, Erikson remarks: "While all children at times need to be left alone in solitary play (or later in the company of books...) and while all children need their hours and days of make believe in games, they all, sooner or later, become dissatisfied and disgruntled without a sense of being useful, without a sense of being able to make things and make them well and even perfectly: this is what I call the sense of industry."

His statement illustrates once more how different matters are in American society compared to the kibbutz. Our middle-class children used to get more than their fill of being left alone in solitary play. But their lives, in many cases, were deficient in the experience of being useful. Lately, it must be said, their days have become so crowded that their chances for solitary activity have severely contracted. As a result they neither get enough of solitary play nor of useful activity.

By comparison the kibbutz child is much advantaged by the chance to do useful things and do them well. But his life, and again only by comparison, is deficient in the chances for

being alone with himself or in the company of books. The kibbutz child is never alone. Even if he engages for moments in solitary play, he is quickly interrupted by some other child or adult, since nonprivacy in the kibbutz does not stop short at the child. And this he accepts as part of the everyday fabric of his life.

On the other hand, his devotion to, and high valuation of, industry appears even before the start of the latency period. As early as the play age he contributes to kibbutz economy, be it by growing things or raising animals. And from school age on, he will work on the children's farm, and work there industriously.

How different the timetables are by which human development unfolds in kibbutz society compared to our own. Solitude will not be available to the kibbutz youngster, if at all, before the end of adolescence, and then only rarely, for short time periods, and against heavy odds. But by then it is too late for the internalization that creative solitude forces on the young child.

The middle-class parent's often desperate plea, "Can't you find something to do?" is replaced in the kibbutz by the tacit (but often open) command: "Don't go off by yourself; be a good comrade, be part of your group." The middle-class child has a powerful but largely frustrated desire to be useful, to make things that count. For the kibbutz child this is replaced by an easy access to and demand for exactly such constructive doing. And this means not just what will count toward his later development, but what will bring him rewards here and now, just as it does for his parents and all other adults.

With so much more chance for early industry in ways that matter importantly to his society, less feeling of inferiority develops. From now on, the youngster will feel little or no sense of inferiority within his society.

True, the limited nature of his industry, and the absence of solitude will develop him mostly for life in this society, and he will feel himself unsuited to any other. But he will respond to this less with a feeling of personal inferiority than of superiority. "Those others are bad societies, not fit to be lived in. So if I don't fit in, why should I feel inferior?" He will feel uncomfortable there, out of place, awkward, insecure, even lost, but not inferior. He will shun other types of living conditions (his xenophobia). But despite the sense of awkwardness, he feels inwardly superior.

Hence the so-called arrogance of the kibbutz-born adult which, to outsiders, contrasts strangely with what we look upon as his very limited and limiting outlook. In fact, both reflect his self-sufficiency when at home with his group, and his sense of being robbed of it when apart from his group, in an alien world.

Since he is not made to feel inferior by the society around him, but on the contrary feels very secure, and since he can satisfy his desire for industry to the full, this fourth psychosocial crisis is much reduced in its stresses. Once again the kibbutz child is much happier than a child of his age in our society. But not having to resolve a crisis of great depth as regards industry versus inferiority, he again has no need to develop great inner resources to weather it. Nor will his personality deepen for having resolved such a conflict successfully.

During this same period, according to Erikson's scheme, the neighborhood and school stand in the center of significant relations. But the kibbutz child has long since made the entire kibbutz the focus of his relations. More important for his later development, the radius of significant relations will not expand any further. Thus in the growth of significant relations...we see in the kibbutz a tremendous speeding up of the developmental process.

Possibly by as early as the second period of crisis, and certainly during the third, the entire world of significant relations will have been mastered, which is very different from the slow and steady development of our middle-class children. But contrary to what happens in our setting, this radius will not significantly widen for the kibbutz child during the following periods of development. In this area of significant relations we see that a much greater mastery is expected (and usually achieved) rather early in life, and not much more later on. It is just one indication of how any educational system, compared to another, pushes certain developments and retards others, with far-reaching consequences for the type of personality it will finally produce.

Two other problem areas show the same pattern of early mastery and later stasis, namely in problem area C (related elements of social order) and particularly in area D (psychosocial modalities). In the latter case, development seems essentially to stop at the fourth stage, which is only natural: no higher stage seems possible for a kibbutznik than "to make things together." There is no superego or ego demand, no ego ideal and no social or group pressure to strive for anything beyond a concentration on work morality. No other examples are accepted as valid that could even serve as incentives.

Indeed, no further psychosocial crises are necessary beyond Erikson's fourth, that of industry versus inferiority. Since the *fifth* struggle, the one for a personal identity, would almost have to take the adolescent caught up in it away from the kibbutz, it is not pertinent for those who will stay. Nor can this crisis really develop. Those who fit into kibbutz life have no need to struggle for identity of a personal nature, since the community so largely defines it for them. In this way the kibbutz adolescent escapes the identity diffusion that afflicts so many of our middle-class adolescents, and which Erikson has discussed for us at length.

Since the kibbutz child does not experience solitude, the typical adolescent crisis does not occur either—that of whether to be essentially oneself, or to mesh one's being with that of others. Because this crisis presupposes the childhood experience of being left to one's very own devices, with only oneself and one's introjects for company. The adolescent's deep desire to be himself is based on this childhood experience of loneliness, and of the need to now integrate various introjects with the rest of his own personality—which of them to keep, and which not, how to modify them all until they are part of one integrated personality. But without the previous experience of playing and being by oneself, and without the introjects, there is no essential conflict between wishing to be most oneself, and also wishing to be deeply with others. The kibbutz-born is essentially himself when among others.

Since this struggle, in Erikson's scheme, leads up to the *sixth* psychosocial crisis, that of intimacy versus isolation, it may now be apparent for theoretical reasons, too, why intimacy is essentially not available to many kibbutz-born. Each of these crises is marked by struggle between two opposites. But the struggle between isolation and intimacy cannot be a problem to someone raised in a kibbutz, since he has never lived in isolation. I could go on, but I meant only to suggest how kibbutz education can be understood in terms of a developmental psychology based on psychoanalytic insight.

INTEGRITY VERSUS DESPAIR

One last thought based on Erikson's scheme: in applying his model to my observations I was struck by how—for those who were born in the kibbutz and felt no need to leave it—psychosocial development seems for the most part to conclude with the fourth in the sequence of crises. This means that they never reach that *eighth* psychosocial crisis of integrity versus despair.

The existential despair that seems to haunt Western society, the kibbutznik escapes: despair about oneself or the world, about the fact that one's life is to end, and that it had little meaning or purpose. But in terms of all I have said, the kibbutznik escapes at a price. By now it should be clear what that consists of. In terms of Erikson's model, despair is escaped at some cost to personal identity, emotional intimacy, and individual achievement. On the other hand, this may seem a very small price to many of our aging and aged who suffer a feeling of uselessness, a sharp sense of isolation, because there is nothing meaningful for them to do any more, nor any place of importance in society. Those who grow old in the kibbutz are never alone. They remain as before in the middle of things, feeling needed. To the end of their natural days there is as much for them, or as little, of importance to be done as they wish.

Just as latency is a happier time for kibbutz children, so too is old age, which in the kibbutz is infinitely richer than is typical in our setting.

Though the founding generation is pleased with the results of its unique educational system, this does not mean that misgivings are absent. Essentially they wanted both for their children: utter egalitarianism, and highest individuation. It comes hard to them to realize that these are contradictory values. But despite some hesitation, their actions show that for the present they have opted for egalitarianism. It is just possible that their children of the second (and particularly the third) generation, brought up in this spirit, will no longer be able to opt otherwise. . . .

RECOMMENDED FURTHER READING

*Bettelheim, Bruno: *The Children of the Dream;* New York, Macmillan 1969

Birren, James E.: *The Psychology of Aging;* Englewood Cliffs, N.J., Prentice-Hall 1964

Bowlby, John: *Attachment and Loss;* New York, Basic Books 1969

*Bowlby, John, Mary D. Ainsworth, *et al.: *Maternal Care and Mental Health* and *Deprivation of Maternal Care: A Reassessment of Its Effects;* New York, Schocken Books 1966

*Bromley, D. B.: *The Psychology of Human Ageing;* Baltimore, Penguin Books 1966

Bronfenbrenner, Urie: *Two Worlds of Childhood: U.S. and U.S.S.R.;* New York, Russell Sage Foundation 1970

Erikson, Erik: *Childhood and Society* (2nd. Ed.); New York, Norton 1963

Fiske, D. W. and S. R. Maddi (eds.): *Functions of Varied Experience;* Homewood, Ill., Dorsey Press 1961

Flavell, J. H.: *The Developmental Psychology of Jean Piaget;* Princeton, N. J., Van Nostrand 1963

Harlow, Harry and S. J. Suomi: "Nature of Love—Simplified"; *American Psychologist,* 25 (1970), 161–68

Hess, Eckhard: "Imprinting in Animals"; *Scientific American,* March 1958

Kagan, Jerome and Howard A. Moss: *Birth to Maturity;* New York, John Wiley 1962

*Mussen, P. H.: *The Psychological Development of the Child;* Englewood Cliffs, N.J., Prentice-Hall 1963

Mussen, P. H., J. J. Conger and Jerome Kagan: *Child Development and Personality* (2nd Ed.); New York, Harper & Row 1963

Muuss, R. E.: *Theories of Adolescence;* New York, Random House 1962

Neugarten, Bernice L., *et al.: Personality in Middle and Late Life;* New York, Atherton Press 1964

Pressey, Sidney L. and R. G. Kuhlen: *Psychological Development Through the Life Span;* New York, Harper & Row 1957

Rabin, A. I.: *Growing Up in the Kibbutz;* New York, Springer 1965

Scott, J. P.: *Early Experience and the Organization of Behavior;* Belmont, Calif., Brooks/Cole 1968

Sears, Robert R., Eleanor E. Maccoby and Harry T. Levin: *Patterns of Child Rearing;* Evanston, Ill., Row, Peterson 1957

Sluckin, W.: *Imprinting and Early Learning;* Chicago, Aldine 1965

Stone, L. Joseph and Joseph Church: *Childhood and Adolescence* (2nd. Ed.); New York, Random House 1968

* Paperback edition available.

PART IV

LEARNING

Because of the human organism's protracted period of maturation and its relatively rudimentary endowment of instinctive behavior patterns (or, what amounts to the same thing, its great plasticity) the process of learning plays a decisive role in the development of human behavior. "Learning" is a generic term that refers to any enduring change in an organism's behavior (including its verbal behavior) that occurs either as the result of experience or of practice by the organism. Learning is certainly not limited to humans, as anyone who has trained a dog—or a flatworm—knows, but human beings are not only capable of learning and remembering far more than members of any other species but are correspondingly more dependent on what they have learned for their very survival.

Three major theories of how learning takes place—theories neither monolithic nor mutually exclusive—dominate contemporary American psychology: the *associative,* the *wholistic* or *cognitive,* and the *biochemical.* Since some of the following selections deal specifically with these theories we will forego any detailed exposition of them here. A few general remarks, however, do seem appropriate.

Associative theories of learning, including both classical (Pavlovian) and operant (Skinnerian) conditioning and theories of multiple response learning, stress the formation of habits through the making and reinforcing of new connections between stimuli and responses. These theories are by far the most popular among American psychologists and are thoroughly congenial to the traditional American preference for action over contemplation and the belief that action occurs largely in response to external stimuli. Indirectly and through many intermediate steps such theories are linked to the empiricist interpretation of perception that we will discuss in the introduction to Part V.

Cognitive or wholistic theories of learning, on the other hand, derive largely from the more philosophical European tradition of psychology, especially the work of the Gestalt psychologists. They stress understanding and "insight"—often suddenly arrived at (the so-called "Eureka!" experience) rather than the gradual establishment of habits through trial and error. While not denying the role of habit formation, proponents of wholistic theories emphasize the creative application of old habits to new conditions and the understanding of total situations through an intuitive grasp of their underlying relationships. Not surprisingly, cognitive theorists have had far more to say about imagination and creativity than have associative learning theorists, whose positivist approach seems to leave little place for originality or creativity.

Biochemical theories, a late and not entirely welcome entry in the theoretical sweepstakes, suggest that learning may be mediated (or even, in a proximate sense, be "caused") by the levels of certain chemical substances in the brain and by changes in those levels associated with the experience of the organism. While such theories are still somewhat "far out," a good deal of evidence in their favor is gradually accumulating and discussions of "transfers of learning" through chemical injections are no longer found only in the pages of science fiction magazines or on science fantasy television shows. Biochemical theories, however, do not so much supplant as supplement both associative and wholistic ones.

Theories of learning aside, the course of actual learning and its effectiveness necessarily depend on many other circumstances, such as the psychological state of the organism, the degree of its motivation, the kinds of rewards that learning promises or the kinds of punishments that failure to learn may incur, the technique of the learning itself, and some reasonable balance between the organism's capacities and the demands of the learning task.

Because present learning (and thinking) presuppose the ability to remember and apply past learning and experience to new situations the phenomena of remembering and forgetting are intrinsic to the study of learning. Some of the relevant theories of these phenomena are mentioned below, but it may be that the greatest advances in the understanding of memory, as of thinking itself, will come through new information processing and computer simulation models developed over the past few years, models which suggest that behavior is "computed" according to certain rules and procedures, that thinking occurs through the use of abstract concepts and logical operations, not simply through past associative connections. These new approaches are closely related to Chomsky's theories regarding the acquisition of language, ideas we will discuss in the introduction to Part VI.

To Aristotle man was a "rational animal" as well as a social one and thinkers ever since have considered man's reason, his ability to think, to be his supreme glory, the characteristic that sets him both apart from and above all other animal species. By "thinking" or "reasoning" we refer to the mental process, usually but not necessarily conscious (some thinking, called *associative*, may occur in dreams or in half-conscious reveries) through which an individual manipulates meaningful symbols (usually but not always verbal) in order to reach some goal. As a "problem" may be defined as an obstacle along the path toward a goal, it would be equally accurate to say that, in the broadest meaning of the word "problem," thinking is an attempt to solve problems. (The results of thinking and of higher mental processes generally are known as "cognition" while the processes and methods by which people attain concepts and solve problems are known as "cognitive" processes.) Were there no problems there would be no need for thought yet, as Bertrand Russell once acerbically remarked, "Most people would rather die than think." That a few people at any time do prefer to think probably explains that small degree of civilization mankind now so precariously enjoys. Given the intertia of human beings, all thinking that does take place is "creative" in that it represents the conscious application of old learning to new, or at least changed, situations.

Much, perhaps most, behavior—human and animal—is either instinctive, reflexive, or habitual and to that extent involves no thinking or reasoning as we have defined it. Man's rational behavior is, as Freud pointed out early in this century, but a small portion of his total behavior, an insight which had occurred to certain philosophers at a much earlier date. As far back as 1739 David Hume in his *Treatise of Human Nature* (Book I) had asserted that "reason is, and ought only to be, the slave of the passions."

Alas for human vanity we now know that other animals such as the chimpanzee, the dolphin, and even the lowly rat can think and form concepts (the latter defined as a symbol or symbol cluster referring to a class of objects or events having one or more common characteristics). What distinguishes human thinking, aside from the size and complexity of the thinking apparatus, is that most human thought comes into being through the mediation of complex verbal symbol systems or languages, symbols that can refer to and be used to construct still other symbols. While verbal language is not essential to thought as such, it is language that so greatly extends the scope and sophistication of human thinking as to make it qualitatively different from comparable processes known among any other species. In large measure, language has been responsible for the cumulative building and transmission of human culture and for humans it is an almost essential prerequisite to thought precisely because we learn how to think almost entirely through the medium of language.

At the summit of human thinking is that kind of thought called "original" or "creative." The phenomenon of creativity, its nature and its sources, has intrigued psychologists ever since Francis Galton in 1869 published his pioneering work on outstanding men. Given the ever increasing complexity and the heightened challenge of the social world it seems essential to understand and foster creativity, to encourage all modes of thinking that break through the fixed personal habits and cultural stereotypes within which most so-called "thinking" proceeds. Nor should creativity be thought of as the exclusive possession of artists and scientists; what is perhaps most needed today is social and political creativity, the ability of human beings to look at radically changed political and social realities in new and fruitful ways. Without such creativity that of the artist and the scientist may rapidly become irrelevant to the life we actually live.

In our first selection B. F. Skinner, the father of operant conditioning, defines and characterizes the latter, at the same time contrasting it with classic or Pavlovian conditioning. Skinner believes that the repertoire of human behaviors is built up largely through processes of operant conditioning. Consistent with his characterization of psychology as a science of observable behavior (see Selection 2) Skinner is concerned only with observing and measuring the organism's responses, not at all with its feelings, its subjective experience (consciousness), or any of its internal states.

James McConnell is not only a distinguished psychologist at the University of Michigan but an accomplished science fiction writer. His delightful story reviews the major principles and techniques of associative learning theories even as he pokes satiric fun at them from the point of view of the subject in a conditioning experiment. Yet, under the satire and the irony are two points worthy of serious attention: that theories are often born of the equipment and techniques with which investigators approach a problem and that if we are ever to understand behavior we must study it as we encounter it in reality, not as we create it under artificial laboratory conditions. Even most rats, after all, do not live in the wire cages of psychology laboratories.

For many years Keller and Marian Breland, both trained psychologists, have directed Animal Behavior Enterprises, Inc. near Hot Springs, Arkansas, an organization that has specialized in the training of animals for appearances in movies, on television, and in other commercial ventures. Beginning as convinced Skinnerians, the Brelands' faith has obviously been shaken by the kinds of experiences they recount in their article. Their work with thousands of animals suggests that instinctive behavior patterns limit the power of operant learning to shape and control behavior. They have found that particular behaviors often persist in the total absence of reinforcement while consistently reinforced responses are gradually abandoned. What the Brelands call "instinctive drift" implies that behavior of any species (man included) cannot be adequately understood without a knowledge of its instinctive patterns, its evolutionary history, and its ecological niche. We urge the reader to ask what light, if any, the Brelands' analysis throws on the problem of aggression discussed in Part VII, and on the broader question of behavior control.

David Krech of the University of California (Berkeley) then examines some of the evidence for the role of chemicals in learning and memory. Of at least equal importance, however, are his findings that different qualities of environment (enriched versus impoverished) among rats affect both the amount of certain critical enzymes in the latter's brains and their ability to solve problems. These findings suggest that the environment may affect intellectual performance directly through altering the level of critical chemicals in the brain. Environment and experience may, in other words, affect the brain as directly as chemicals or drugs. Although it would be premature to generalize results obtained from the study of rats to the analysis of human intellectual functioning, the research reported by Maya Pines (Selection 11) concerning the effects of different environments on the intellectual and social competence of very young children is easily susceptible of a parallel explanation. Obviously, more research is badly needed here, but should these preliminary results be confirmed and prove of general applicability the implications, not alone for psychology, but for educational and social policy as well will be little short of revolutionary.

Goodwin Watson's article then provides a convenient summary of many of the most important findings in the fields of learning and memory while R. J. Heathorn's piece is an ironic and amusing comment on the rage for teaching machines and other mechanical or electronic aids to learning.

14. OPERANT BEHAVIOR

B. F. Skinner

THE CONSEQUENCES OF BEHAVIOR

Reflexes, conditioned or otherwise, are mainly concerned with the internal physiology of the organism. We are most often interested, however, in behavior which has some effect upon the surrounding world. Such behavior raises most of the practical problems in human affairs and is also of particular theoretical interest because of its special characteristics. The consequences of behavior may "feed back" into the organism. When they do so, they may change the probability that the behavior which produced them will occur again. The English language contains many words, such as "reward" and "punishment," which refer to this effect, but we can get a clear picture of it only through experimental analysis.

LEARNING CURVES

One of the first serious attempts to study the changes brought about by the consequences of behavior was made by E. L. Thorndike in 1898. His experiments arose from a controversy which was then of considerable interest. Darwin, in insisting upon the continuity of species, had questioned the belief that man was unique among the animals in his ability to think. Anecdotes in which lower animals seemed to show the "power of reasoning" were published in great numbers. But when terms which had formerly been applied only to human behavior were thus extended, certain questions arose concerning their meaning. Did the observed facts point to mental processes, or could these apparent evidences of

Reprinted by permission of The Macmillan Company from SCIENCE AND HUMAN BEHAVIOR *by B. F. Skinner, pp. 59–66. Copyright 1953 by The Macmillan Company.*

thinking be explained in other ways? Eventually it became clear that the assumption of inner thought processes was not required. Many years were to pass before the same question was seriously raised concerning human behavior, but Thorndike's experiments and his alternative explanation of reasoning in animals were important steps in that direction.

If a cat is placed in a box from which it can escape by unlatching a door, it will exhibit many different kinds of behavior, some of which may be effective in opening the door. Thorndike found that when a cat was put into such a box again and again, the behavior which led to escape tended to occur sooner and sooner until eventually escape was as simple and quick as possible. The cat had solved its problem as well as if it were a "reasoning" human being, though perhaps not so speedily. Yet Thorndike observed no "thought process" and argued that none was needed by way of explanation. He could describe his results simply by saying that a part of the cat's behavior was "stamped in" because it was followed by the opening of the door.

The fact that behavior is stamped in when followed by certain consequences, Thorndike called "The Law of Effect." What he had observed was that certain behavior occurred more and more readily in comparison with other behavior characteristic of the same situation. By noting the successive delays in getting out of the box and plotting them on a graph, he constructed a "learning curve." This early attempt to show a quantitative process in behavior, similar to the processes of physics and biology, was heralded as an important advance. It revealed a process which took place over a considerable period of time and which was not obvious to casual inspection. Thorndike, in short, had made a discovery. Many similar curves have since been recorded and have become the substance of chapters on learning in psychology texts.

Learning curves do not, however, describe the basic process of stamping in. Thorndike's measure—the time taken to escape—involved the elimination of other behavior, and his curve depended upon the number of different things a cat might do in a particular box. It also depended upon the behavior which the experimenter or the apparatus happened to select as "successful" and upon whether this was common or rare in comparison with other behavior evoked in the box. A learning curve obtained in this way might be said to reflect the properties of the latch box rather than of the behavior of the cat. The same is true of many other devices developed for the study of learning. The various mazes through which white rats and other animals learn to run, the "choice boxes" in which animals learn to discriminate between properties or patterns of stimuli, the apparatuses which present sequences of material to be learned in the study of human memory—each of these yields its own type of learning curve.

By averaging many individual cases, we may make these curves as smooth as we like. Moreover, curves obtained under many different circumstances may agree in showing certain general properties. For example, when measured in this way learning is generally "negatively accelerated"—improvement in performance occurs more and more slowly as the condition is approached in which further improvement is impossible. But it does not follow that negative acceleration is characteristic of the basic process. Suppose, by analogy, we fill a glass jar with gravel which has been so well mixed that pieces of any given size are evenly distributed. We then agitate the jar gently and watch the pieces rearrange themselves. The larger move toward the top, the smaller toward the bottom. This process, too, is negatively accelerated. At first the mixture separates rapidly, but as separation proceeds, the condition in which there will be no further change is approached more and more slowly. Such a curve may be quite smooth and reproducible, but this fact alone is not of any great significance. The curve is the result of certain fundamental processes involving the contact of spheres of different sizes, the resolution of the forces resulting from agitation, and so on, but it is by no means the most direct record of these processes.

Learning curves show how the various kinds of behavior evoked in complex situations are sorted out, emphasized, and recorded. The basic process of the stamping in of a single act brings this change about, but it is not reported directly by the change itself.

OPERANT CONDITIONING

To get at the core of Thorndike's Law of Effect, we need to clarify the notion of "probability of response." This is an extremely important concept; unfortunately, it is also a difficult one. In discussing human behavior, we often refer to "tendencies" or "predispositions" to behave in particular ways. Almost every theory of behavior uses some such term as "excitatory potential," "habit strength," or "determining tendency." But how do we observe a tendency? And how can we measure one?

If a given sample of behavior existed in only two states, in one of which it always occurred and in the other never, we should be almost helpless in following a program of functional analysis. An all-or-none subject matter lends itself only to primitive forms of description. It is a great advantage to suppose instead that the *probability* that a response will occur ranges continuously between these all-or-none extremes. We can then deal with variables which, unlike the eliciting stimulus, do not "cause a given bit of behavior to occur" but simply make the occurrence more probable. We may then proceed to deal, for example, with the combined effect of more than one such variable.

The everyday expressions which carry the notion of probability, tendency, or predisposition describe the frequencies with which bits of behavior occur. We never observe a probability as such. We say that someone is "enthusiastic" about bridge when we observe that he plays bridge often and talks about it often. To be "greatly interested" in music is to play, listen to, and talk about music a good deal. The "inveterate" gambler is one who gambles frequently. The camera "fan" is to be found taking pictures, developing them, and looking at pictures made by himself and others. The "highly sexed" person frequently engages in sexual behavior. The "dipsomanic" drinks frequently.

In characterizing a man's behavior in terms of frequency, we assume certain standard conditions: he must be able to execute and repeat a given act, and other behavior must not interfere appreciably. We cannot be sure of the extent of a man's interest in music, for example, if he is necessarily busy with other things. When we come to refine the notion of probability of response for scientific use, we find that here, too, our data are frequencies and that the conditions under which they are observed must be specified. The main technical problem in designing a controlled experiment is to provide for the observation and interpretation of frequencies. We eliminate, or at least hold constant, any condition which encourages behavior which competes with the behavior we are to study. An organism is placed in a quiet box where its behavior may be observed through a one-way screen or recorded mechanically. This is by no means an environmental vacuum, for the organism will react to the features of the box in many ways; but its behavior will eventually reach a fairly stable level, against which the frequency of a selected response may be investigated.

To study the process which Thorndike called stamping in, we must have a "consequence." Giving food to a hungry organism will do. We can feed our subject conveniently with a small food tray which is operated electrically. When the tray is first opened, the organism will probably react to it in ways which interfere with the process we plan to observe. Eventually, after being fed from the tray repeatedly, it eats readily, and we are then ready to make this consequence contingent upon behavior and to observe the result.

We select a relatively simple bit of behavior which may be freely and rapidly repeated, and which is easily observed and recorded. If our experimental subject is a pigeon, for example, the behavior of raising the head above a given height is convenient. This may be observed by sighting across the pigeon's head at a scale pinned on the far wall of the box. We first study the height at which the head is normally held and select some line on the scale which is reached only infrequently. Keeping our eye on the scale we then begin to open the food tray very quickly whenever the head rises above the line. If the experiment is conducted according to specifications, the result is invariable: we observe an immediate change in the frequency with which the head crosses the line. We also observe, and this is of some impor-

tance theoretically, that higher lines are now being crossed. We may advance almost immediately to a higher line in determining when food is to be presented. In a minute or two, the bird's posture has changed so that the top of the head seldom falls below the line which we first chose.

When we demonstrate the process of stamping in in this relatively simple way, we see that certain common interpretations of Thorndike's experiment are superfluous. The expression "trial-and-error learning," which is frequently associated with the Law of Effect, is clearly out of place here. We are reading something into our observations when we call any upward movement of the head a "trial," and there is no reason to call any movement which does not achieve a specified consequence an "error." Even the term "learning" is misleading. The statement that the bird "learns that it will get food by stretching its neck" is an inaccurate report of what has happened. To say that it has acquired the "habit" of stretching its neck is merely to resort to an explanatory fiction, since our only evidence of the habit is the acquired tendency to perform the act. The barest possible statement of the process is this: we make a given consequence contingent upon certain physical properties of behavior (the upward movement of the head), and the behavior is then observed to increase in frequency.

It is customary to refer to any movement of the organism as a "response." The word is borrowed from the field of reflex action and implies an act which, so to speak, answers a prior event—the stimulus. But we may make an event contingent upon behavior without identifying, or being able to identify, a prior stimulus. We did not alter the environment of the pigeon to *elicit* the upward movement of the head. It is probably impossible to show that any single stimulus invariably precedes this movement. Behavior of this sort may come under the control of stimuli, but the relation is not that of elicitation. The term "response" is therefore not wholly appropriate but is so well established that we shall use it in the following discussion.

A response which has already occurred cannot, of course, be predicted or controlled. We can only predict that *similar* responses will occur in the future. The unit of a predictive science is, therefore, not a response but a class of responses. The word "operant" will be used to describe this class. The term emphasizes the fact that the behavior *operates* upon the environment to generate consequences. The consequences define the properties with respect to which responses are called similar. The term will be used both as an adjective (operant behavior) and as a noun to designate the behavior defined by a given consequence.

A single instance in which a pigeon raises its head is a *response*. It is a bit of history which may be reported in any frame of reference we wish to use. The behavior called "raising the head," regardless of when specific instances occur, is an *operant*. It can be described, not as an accomplished act, but rather as a set of acts defined by the property of the height to which the head is raised. In this sense an operant is defined by an effect which may be specified in physical terms; the "cutoff" at a certain height is a property of behavior.

The term "learning" may profitably be saved in its traditional sense to describe the reassortment of responses in a complex situation. Terms for the process of stamping in may be borrowed from Pavlov's analysis of the conditioned reflex. Pavlov himself called all events which strengthened behavior "reinforcement" and all the resulting changes "conditioning." In the Pavlovian experiment, however, a reinforcer is paired with a *stimulus;* whereas in operant behavior it is contingent upon a *response*. Operant reinforcement is therefore a separate process and requires a separate analysis. In both cases, the strengthening of behavior which results from reinforcement is appropriately called "conditioning." In operant conditioning we "strengthen" an operant in the sense of making a response more probable or, in actual fact, more frequent. In Pavlovian or "respondent" conditioning we simply increase the magnitude of the response elicited by the conditioned stimulus and shorten the time which elapses between stimulus and response. (We note, incidentally, that these two cases exhaust the possibilities: an organism is conditioned when a reinforcer [1] accompanies another stimulus or [2] follows upon the organism's own behavior. Any event which does neither has no effect in changing a probability of response). In the pigeon experiment, then, food is the *reinforcer* and presenting food when a response is emitted is the *reinforcement*. The *operant* is defined by the property upon which reinforcement is contingent—the height to which the head must be raised. The change in frequency with which the head is lifted to this height is the process of *operant conditioning*.

While we are awake, we act upon the environment constantly, and many of the consequences of our actions are reinforcing. Through operant conditioning the environment builds the basic repertoire with which we keep our balance, walk, play games, handle instruments and tools, talk, write, sail a boat, drive a car, or fly a plane. A change in the environment—a new car, a new friend, a new field of interest, a new job, a new location— may find us unprepared, but our behavior usually adjusts quickly as we acquire new responses and discard old. . . . operant reinforcement does more than build a behavioral repertoire. It improves the efficiency of behavior and maintains behavior in strength long after acquisition or efficiency has ceased to be of interest.

15. LEARNING THEORY

James V. McConnell

I am writing this because I presume He wants me to. Otherwise He would not have left paper and pencil handy for me to use. And I put the word "He" in capitals because it seems the only thing to do. If I am dead and in hell, then this is only proper. However, if I am merely a captive somewhere, then surely a little flattery won't hurt matters.

As I sit here in this small room and think about it, I am impressed most of all by the suddenness of the whole thing. At one moment I was out walking in the woods near my suburban home. The next thing I knew, here I was in a small, featureless room, naked as a jaybird, with only my powers of rationalization to stand between me and insanity. When the "change" was made (whatever the change was), I was not conscious of so much as a momentary flicker between walking in the woods and being here in this room. Whoever is responsible for all of this is to be complimented—either He has developed an instantaneous anesthetic or He has solved the problem of instantaneous transportation of matter. I would prefer to think it the former, for the latter leads to too much anxiety.

Yes, there I was walking through the woods, minding my own business, studiously pretending to enjoy the outing so that I wouldn't mind the exercise too much, when the transition took place. As I recall, I was immersed in the problem of how to teach my class in Beginning Psychology some of the more abstruse points of Learning Theory when the transition came. How far away and distant life at the University seems at the moment! I must be forgiven if now I am much more concerned about where I am and how to get out of here

than about how freshmen can be cajoled into understanding Hull or Tolman.

PROBLEM ONE

Where am I? For an answer, I can only describe this room. It is about twenty feet square, some twelve feet high, with no windows, but with what might be a door in the middle of one of the walls. Everything is of a uniform gray color, and the walls and ceiling emit a fairly pleasant achromatic light. The walls themselves are of some hard material which might be metal since it feels slightly cool to the touch. The floor is of a softer, rubbery material that yields a little when I walk on it. Also, it has a rather "tingly" feel to it, suggesting that it may be in constant vibration. It is somewhat warmer than the walls, which is all to the good since it appears I must sleep on the floor.

The only furniture in the room consists of what might be a table and what passes for a chair. They are not quite that, but they can be made to serve this purpose. On the table I found the paper and the pencil. No, let me correct myself. What I call paper is a good deal rougher and thicker than I am used to, and what I call a pencil is nothing more than a thin round stick of graphite which I have sharpened by rubbing one end of it on the table.

And that is the sum extent of my surroundings. I wish I knew what He has done with my clothes. The suit was an old one, but I am worried about the walking boots. I was very fond of those boots—not because of any sentimental attachment nor because they had done me much good service, but rather because they were quite expensive and I would hate to lose them.

The problem still remains to be answered,

however, as to just where in the hell I am—if not in hell itself!

PROBLEM TWO

Problem Two is a knottier one—why am I here? Were I subject to paranoid tendencies, I would doubtless come to the conclusion that my enemies had kidnapped me. Or perhaps that the Russians had taken such an interest in my research that they had spirited me away to some Siberian hideout and would soon appear to demand either cooperation or death. Sadly enough, I am too reality oriented. My research was highly interesting to me, and perhaps to a few other psychologists who like to dabble in esoteric problems of animal learning, but it was scarcely startling enough to warrant such attention as kidnapping.

So I am left as baffled as before. Where am I, and why?

And who is He?

2

I have decided to forego all attempts at keeping this diary according to "days" or "hours." Such units of time have no meaning in my present circumstances, for the light remains constant all the time I am awake. The human organism is not possessed of as neat an internal clock as some of the lower species. Far too many studies have shown that a human being who is isolated from all external stimulation soon loses his sense of time. So I will merely indicate breaks in the narrative and hope that He will understand that if He wasn't bright enough to leave me with my wristwatch, He couldn't expect me to keep an accurate record.

Nothing much has happened since I began this narrative, except that I have slept, been fed and watered, and have emptied my bladder and bowels. The food was waiting on the table when I awoke last time. I must say that He had little of the gourmet in Him. Protein balls are not my idea of a feast royal. However, they will serve to keep body and soul together (presuming, of course, that they *are* together at the moment). But I must object to my source of liquid refreshment. The meal made me very thirsty and I was in the process of cursing Him and everybody else when I noticed a small nipple which had appeared in the wall while I was asleep. At first I thought that perhaps Freud was right after all, and that

my libido had taken over control of my imagery. Experimentation convinced me, however, that the thing was real, and that it is my present source of water. If one sucks on the thing, it delivers a slightly cool and somewhat sweetish flow of liquid. But really, it's a most undignified procedure. It's bad enough to have to sit around all day in my birthday suit. But for a full professor to have to stand on his tiptoes and suck on an artificial nipple in order to obtain water is asking a little too much. I'd complain to the Management if only I knew to whom to complain!

Following eating and drinking, the call to nature became a little too strong to ignore. Now, I was adequately toilet-trained with indoor plumbing, and the absence of same is most annoying. However, there was nothing much to do but choose a corner of the room and make the best of a none too pleasant situation. (As a side-thought, I wonder if the choosing of a corner was in any way instinctive?). However, the upshot of the whole thing was my learning what is probably the purpose of the vibration of the floor. For the excreted material disappeared through the floor not too many minutes later. The process was a gradual one. Now I will be faced with all kinds of uncomfortable thoughts concerning what might possibly happen to me if I slept too long!

Perhaps this is to be expected, but I find myself becoming a little paranoid after all. In attempting to solve my *Problem Two*, why I am here, I have begun to wonder if perhaps some of my colleagues at the University are not using me as the subject in some kind of experiment. It would be just like them to dream up some fantastic kind of "human-in-isolation" experiment and use me as a pilot observer. You would think that they'd have asked my permission first. However, perhaps it's important that the subject not know what's happening to him. If so, I have one happy thought to console me. If any of them are responsible for this, they'll have to take over the teaching of my classes for the time being. And how they hate teaching Learning Theory to freshmen!

You know, this place seems dreadfully quiet to me.

3

Suddenly I have solved two of my problems. I know both where I am and who He is. And

I bless the day I got interested in the perception of motion.

I should say to begin with that the air in this room seems to have more than the usual concentration of dust particles. This didn't seem particularly noteworthy until I noticed that most of them seemed to pile up along the floor against one wall in particular. For a while I was sure that this was due to the ventilation system—perhaps there was an outgoing air duct there where this particular wall was joined to the floor. However, when I went over and put my hand to the floor there, I could feel no breeze whatsoever. Yet even as I held my hand along the dividing line between the wall and the floor, dust motes covered my hand with a thin coating. I tried this same experiment everywhere else in the room to no avail. This was the only spot where the phenomenon occurred, and it occurred along the entire length of this one wall.

But if ventilation was not responsible for the phenomenon, what was? All at once there popped into my mind some calculations I had made back when the rocket boys had first proposed a manned satellite station. Engineers are notoriously naive when it comes to the performance of a human being in most situations, and I remembered that the problem of the perception of the satellite's rotation seemingly had been ignored by the slip-stick crowd. They had planned to rotate the doughnut-shaped satellite in order to substitute centrifugal force for the force of gravity. Thus the outer shell of the doughnut would appear to be "down" to anyone inside the thing. Apparently they had not realized that man is at least as sensitive to angular rotation as he is to variations in the pull of gravity. As I figured the problem then, if a man aboard the doughnut moved his head as much as three or four feet outwards from the center of the doughnut, he would have become fairly dizzy! Rather annoying it would have been, too, to have been hit by a wave of nausea every time one sat down in a chair. Also, as I pondered the problem, it became apparent that dust particles and the like would probably show a tendency to move in a direction opposite to the direction of the rotation, and hence pile up against any wall or such that impeded their flight.

Using the behavior of the dust particles as a clue, I then climbed atop the table and leapt off. Sure enough, my head felt like a mule had kicked it by the time I landed on the floor. My hypothesis was confirmed.

So I am aboard a spaceship!

The thought is incredible, but in a strange way comforting. At least now I can postpone worrying about heaven and hell—and somehow I find the idea of being in a spaceship much more to the liking of a confirmed agnostic. I suppose I owe my colleagues an apology—I should have known they would never have put themselves in a position where they might have to teach freshmen all about learning!

And, of course, I now know who "He" is. Or rather, I know who He *isn't,* which is something else again. Surely, though, I can no longer think of Him as being human. Whether I should be consoled at this or not, I have no way of telling.

I still have no notion of *why* I am here, however, nor why this alien chose to pick me of all people to pay a visit to His spaceship. What possible use could I be? Surely if He were interested in making contact with the human race, He would have spirited away a politician. After all, that's what politicians are for! Since there has been no effort made to communicate with me, however, I must reluctantly give up any cherished hopes that His purpose is that of making contact with *genus homo.*

Or perhaps He's a galactic scientist of some kind, a biologist of sorts, out gathering specimens. Now, that's a particularly nasty thought. What if He turned out to be a psychologist, interested in cutting me open eventually to see what makes me tick? Will my innards be smeared over a glass slide for scores of youthful Hims to peer at under a microscope? Brrrr! I don't mind giving my life to Science, but I'd rather do it a little at a time.

If you don't mind, I think I'll go do a little repressing for a while.

4

Good God! I should have known it! Destiny will play her little tricks, and all jokes have their cosmic angles. He is a *psychologist!* Had I given it due consideration, I would have realized that whenever you come across a new species, you worry about behavior first, physiology second. So I have received the ultimate insult—or the ultimate compliment. I don't know which. I have become a specimen for an alien psychologist!

This thought first occurred to me when I awoke after my latest sleep (which was filled,

I must admit, with most frightening dreams). It was immediately obvious that something about the room had changed. Almost at once I noticed that one of the walls now had a lever of some kind protruding from it, and to one side of the lever, a small hole in the wall with a container beneath the hole. I wandered over to the lever, inspected it for a few moments, then accidentally depressed the thing. At once there came a loud clicking noise, and a protein ball popped out of the hole and fell into the container.

For just a moment a frown crossed my brow. This seemed somehow so strangely familiar. Then, all at once, I burst into wild laughter. The room had been changed into a gigantic Skinner Box! For years I had been studying animal learning by putting white rats in a Skinner Box and following the changes in the rats' behavior. The rats had to learn to press the lever in order to get a pellet of food, which was delivered to them through just such an apparatus as is now affixed to the wall of my cell. And now, after all of these years, and after all of the learning studies I had done, to find myself trapped like a rat in a Skinner Box! Perhaps this was hell after all, I told myself, and the Lord High Executioner's admonition to "let the punishment fit the crime" was being followed.

Frankly, this sudden turn of events has left me more than a little shaken.

5

I seem to be performing according to theory. It didn't take me long to discover that pressing the lever would give me food some of the time, while at other times all I got was the click and no protein ball. It appears that approximately every twelve hours the thing delivers me a random number of protein balls— the number has varied from five to fifteen so far. I never know ahead of time how many pellets—I mean protein balls—the apparatus will deliver, and it spews them out intermittently. Sometimes I have to press the lever a dozen times or so before it will give me anything, while at other times it gives me one ball for each press. Since I don't have a watch on me, I am never quite sure when the twelve hours have passed, so I stomp over to the lever and press it every few minutes when I think it's getting close to time to be fed. Just like my rats always did. And since the pellets

are small and I never get enough of them, occasionally I find myself banging away on the lever with all the compulsion of a stupid animal. But I missed the feeding time once and almost starved to death (so it seemed) before the lever delivered food the next time. About the only consolation to my wounded pride is that at this rate of starvation, I'll lose my bay window in short order.

At least He doesn't seem to be fattening me up for the kill. Or maybe he just likes lean meat.

6

I have been promoted. Apparently He in His infinite alien wisdom has decided that I'm intelligent enough to handle the Skinner-type apparatus, so I've been promoted to solving a maze. Can you picture the irony of the situation? All of the classic Learning Theory methodology is practically being thrown in my face in mockery. If only I could communicate with Him! I don't mind being subjected to tests nearly as much as I mind being underestimated. Why, I can solve puzzles hundreds of times more complex than what He's throwing at me. But how can I tell Him?

7

As it turns out, the maze is much like our standard T-mazes, and is not too difficult to learn. It's a rather long one, true, with some 23 choice points along the way. I spent the better part of half an hour wandering through the thing the first time I found myself in it. Surprisingly enough, I didn't realize the first time out what I was in, so I made no conscious attempt to memorize the correct turns. It wasn't until I reached the final turn and found food waiting for me that I recognized what I was expected to do. The next time through the maze my performance was a good deal better, and I was able to turn in a perfect performance in not too long a time. However, it does not do my ego any good to realize that my own white rats could have learned the maze a little sooner than I did.

My "home cage," so to speak, still has the Skinner apparatus in it, but the lever delivers food only occasionally now. I still give it a whirl now and again, but since I'm getting a fairly good supply of food at the end of the maze each time, I don't pay the lever much attention.

Now that I am very sure of what is happening to me, quite naturally my thoughts have turned to how I can get out of this situation. Mazes I can solve without too much difficulty, but how to escape is apparently beyond my intellectual capacity. But then, come to think of it, there was precious little chance for my own experimental animals to get out of my clutches. And assuming that I am unable to escape, what then? After He has finished putting me through as many paces as He wishes, where do we go from there? Will he treat me as I treated most of my non-human subjects—that is, will I get tossed into a jar containing chloroform? "Following the experiment, the animals are sacrificed," as we so euphemistically report in the scientific literature. This doesn't appeal to me much, as you can imagine. Or maybe if I seem particularly bright to Him, He may use me for breeding purposes, to establish a colony of His own. Now, that might have possibilities...

Oh, damn Freud anyhow!

8

And damn Him, too! I had just gotten the maze well learned when He upped and changed things on me. I stumbled about like a bat in the sunlight for quite some time before I finally got to the goal box. I'm afraid my performance was pretty poor.

9

Well, it wasn't so bad after all. What He did was just to reverse the whole maze so that it was a mirror image of what it used to be. Took me only two trials to discover the solution. Let Him figure that one out if He's so smart!

10

My performance on the maze reversal must have pleased Him, because now He's added a new complication. And again I suppose I could have predicted the next step if I had been thinking along the right direction. I woke up a few hours ago to find myself in a totally different room. There was nothing whatsoever in the room, but opposite me were two doors in the wall—one door a pure white, the other jet black. Between me and the doors was a deep pit, filled with water. I didn't like the looks of the situation, for it occurred to me right away that He had devised a kind of jumping-stand for me. I had to choose which of the doors was open and led to the food. The other door would be locked. If I jumped at the wrong door, and found it locked, I'd fall in the water. I needed a bath, that was for sure, but I didn't relish getting it in this fashion.

While I stood there watching, I got the shock of my life. I mean it quite literally. The bastard had thought of everything. When I used to run rats on jumping stands, to overcome their reluctance to jump, I used to shock them. He's following exactly the same pattern. The floor in this room is wired but good. I howled and jumped about and showed all the usual anxiety behavior. It took me less than two seconds to come to my senses and make a flying leap at the white door, however.

You know something? That water is ice-cold!

11

I have now, by my own calculations, solved no fewer than 87 different problems on the jumping stand, and I'm getting sick and tired of it. One time I got angry and just pointed at the correct door—and got shocked for not going ahead and jumping. I shouted bloody murder, cursing Him at the top of my voice, telling Him if He didn't like my performance, He could damn well lump it. All He did, of course, was to increase the shock.

Frankly, I don't know how much longer I can put up with this. It's not that the work is difficult. But rather that it seems so senseless, so useless. If He were giving me half a chance to show my capabilities, I wouldn't mind it. I suppose I've contemplated a thousand different ways of escaping, but none of them is worth mentioning. But if I don't get out of here soon, I shall go stark raving mad!

12

For almost an hour after it happened, I sat in this room and just wept. I realize that it is not the style of our culture for a grown man to weep, but there are times when cultural taboos must be forgotten. Again, had I thought much about the sort of experiments He must have had in mind, I most probably could have predicted the next step. Even so,

I most likely would have repressed the knowledge.

One of the standard problems which any learning psychologist is interested in is this one—will an animal learn something if you fail to reward him for his performance? There are many theorists, such as Hull and Spence, who believe that reward (or "reinforcement," as they call it) is absolutely necessary for learning to occur. This is mere stuff and nonsense, as anyone with a grain of sense knows, but nonetheless the "reinforcement" theory has been dominant in the field for years now. We fought a hard battle with Spence and Hull, and actually had them with their backs to the wall at one point, when suddenly they came up with the concept of "secondary reinforcement." That is, anything associated with a reward takes on the ability to act as a reward itself. For example, the mere sight of food would become a reward in and of itself—almost as much as a reward, in fact, as is the eating of the food. The *sight* of food, indeed! But nonetheless, it saved their theories for the moment.

For the past five years now, I have been trying to design an experiment that would show beyond a shadow of a doubt that the *sight* of a reward was not sufficient for learning to take place. And now look at what has happened to me!

I'm sure that He must lean towards Hull and Spence in his theorizing, for earlier today, when I found myself in the jumping stand room, instead of being rewarded with my usual protein balls when I made the correct jump, I discovered. . .

I'm sorry, but it is difficult to write about even now. For when I made the correct jump and the door opened and I started toward the food trough, I found it had been replaced with a photograph. A calendar photograph. You know the one. Her name, I think, is Monroe.

I sat on the floor for almost an hour weeping afterwards. For five whole years I have been attacking the validity of the secondary reinforcement theory, and now I find myself giving Him evidence that the theory is correct! For I cannot help "learning" which of the doors is the correct one to jump through. I refuse to stand on the apparatus and have the life shocked out of me, and I refuse to pick the wrong door all the time and get an icy bath time after time. It just isn't fair!

For He will doubtless put it all down to the fact that the mere *sight* of the photograph is functioning as a reward, and that I am learning the problems merely to be able to see Miss What's-her-name in her bare skin!

Oh, I can just see Him now, sitting somewhere else in this spaceship, gathering in all the data I am giving Him, plotting all kinds of learning curves, chortling to Himself because I am confirming all of His pet theories. I just wish. . .

13

Almost an hour has gone by since I wrote the above section. It seems longer than that, but surely it's been only an hour. And I have spent the time in deep thought. For I have discovered a way out of this place, I think. The question is, dare I do it?

I was in the midst of writing that paragraph about His sitting and chortling and confirming his theories, when it suddenly struck me that theories are born of the equipment that one uses. This has probably been true throughout the history of all science, but perhaps most true of all in psychology. If Skinner had never invented his blasted box, if the maze and the jumping stand had not been developed, we probably would have entirely different theories of learning today than we now have. For if nothing else, the type of equipment that one uses drastically reduces the type of behavior that one's subjects can show, and one's theories have to account only for the type of behavior that appears in the laboratories.

It follows from this also that any two cultures that devise the same sort of experimental procedures will come up with almost identical theories.

Keeping all of this in mind, it's not hard for me to believe that He is an iron-clad reinforcement theorist, for He uses all of the various paraphernalia that they use, and uses it in exactly the same way.

My means of escape is therefore obvious. He expects from me confirmation of all His pet theories. Well, He won't get it any more! I know all of His theories backwards and forwards, and this means I know how to give Him results that will tear his theories right smack in half!

I can almost predict the results. What does any learning theorist do with an animal that won't behave properly, that refuses to give the results that are predicted? One gets rid of the beast, quite naturally. For one wishes to use only healthy, normal animals in one's work, and any animal that gives "unusual" results is removed from the study but quickly. After all, if it doesn't perform as expected, it must be sick, abnormal, or aberrant in one way or another...

There is no guarantee, of course, what method He will employ to dispose of my now annoying presence. Will He "sacrifice" me? Or will He just return me to the "permanent colony?" I cannot say. I know only that I will be free from what is now an intolerable situation. The chance must be taken.

Just wait until He looks at His results from now on!

II

FROM: Experimenter-in-Chief, Interstellar Labship PSYCH-145
TO: Director, Bureau of Science

Thlan, my friend, this will be an informal missive. I will send the official report along later, but I wanted to give you my subjective impressions first.

The work with the newly discovered species is, for the moment, at a standstill. Things went exceedingly well at first. We picked what seemed to be a normal, healthy animal and smattered it into our standard test apparatus. I may have told you that this new species seemed quite identical to our usual laboratory animals, so we included a couple of the "toys" that our home animals seem to be fond of— thin pieces of material made from woodpulp and a tiny stick of graphite. Imagine our surprise, and our pleasure, when this new specimen made exactly the same use of the materials as have all of our home colony specimens. Could it be that there are certain innate behavior patterns to be found throughout the universe in the lower species?

Well, I merely pose the question. The answer is of little importance to a Learning Theorist. Your friend Verpk keeps insisting that the use of these "toys" may have some deeper meaning to it, and that perhaps we should investigate further. At his insistence, then, I include with this informal missive the materials used by our first subject. In my opinion, Verpk is guilty of gross anthropomorphism, and I wish to have nothing further to do with the question. However, this behavior did give us hope that our newly discovered colony would yield subjects whose performance would be exactly in accordance with standard theory.

And, in truth, this is exactly what seemed to be the case. The animal solved the Bfian Box problem in short order, yielding as beautiful data as I have ever seen. We then shifted it to maze, maze-reversal and jumping stand problems, and the results could not have confirmed our theories better had we rigged the data. However, when we switched the animal to secondary reinforcement problems, it seemed to undergo a strange sort of change. No longer was its performance up to par. In fact, at times it seemed to go quite berserk. For part of the experiment, it would perform superbly. But then, just as it seemed to be solving whatever problem we set it to, its behavior would subtly change into patterns that obviously could not come from a normal specimen. It got worse and worse, until its behavior departed radically from that which our theories predicted. Naturally, we knew then that something had happened to the animal, for our theories are based upon thousands of experiments with similar subjects, and hence our theories must be right. But our theories hold only for normal subjects, and for normal species, so it soon became apparent to us that we had stumbled upon some abnormal type of animal.

Upon due consideration, we returned the subject to its home colony. However, we also voted almost unanimously to request from you permission to take steps to destroy the complete colony. It is obviously of little scientific use to us, and stands as a potential danger that we must take adequate steps against. Since all colonies are under your protection, we therefore request permission to destroy it in toto.

I must report, by the way, that Verpk's vote was the only one which was cast against this procedure. He has some silly notion one should study behavior as one finds it. Frankly, I cannot understand why you have seen fit to saddle me with him on this expedition, but perhaps you have your reasons.

Verpk's vote notwithstanding, however, the rest of us are of the considered opinion that this whole new colony must be destroyed, and quickly. For it is obviously diseased or some such—as reference to our theories has proven. And should it by some chance come in contact with our other colonies, and infect our other animals with whatever disease or aberration it has, we would never be able to predict their behavior again. I need not carry the argument further, I think.

May we have your permission to destroy the colony as soon as possible, then, so that we may search out yet other colonies and test our theories against other healthy animals? For it is only in this fashion that science progresses.

Respectfully yours,
IOWYY.

16. THE MISBEHAVIOR OF ORGANISMS

Keller and Marian Breland

There seems to be a continuing realization by psychologists that perhaps the white rat cannot reveal everything there is to know about behavior. Among the voices raised on this topic, Beach (1950) has emphasized the necessity of widening the range of species subjected to experimental techniques and conditions. However, psychologists as a whole do not seem to be heeding these admonitions, as Whalen (1961) has pointed out.

Perhaps this reluctance is due in part to some dark precognition of what they might find in such investigations, for the ethologists Lorenz (1950, p. 233) and Tinbergen (1951, p. 6) have warned that if psychologists are to understand and predict the behavior of organisms, it is essential that they become thoroughly familiar with the instinctive behavior patterns of each new species they essay to study. Of course, the Watsonian or neo-behavioristically oriented experimenter is apt to consider "instinct" an ugly word. He tends to class it with Hebb's (1960) other "seditious notions" which were discarded in the behavioristic revolution, and he may have some premonition that he will encounter this *bête noire*** in extending the range of species and situations studied.

We can assure him that his apprehensions are well grounded. In our attempt to extend a behavioristically oriented approach to the engineering control of animal behavior by operant conditioning techniques, we have

* Literally "black beast." A person or thing to be feared and avoided. (Eds.)

fought a running battle with the seditious notion of instinct.[1] It might be of some interest to the psychologist to know how the battle is going and to learn something about the nature of the adversary he is likely to meet if and when he tackles new species in new learning situations.

Our first report (Breland & Breland, 1951) in the *American Psychologist,* concerning our experiences in controlling animal behavior, was wholly affirmative and optimistic, saying in essence that the principles derived from the laboratory could be applied to the extensive control of behavior under nonlaboratory conditions throughout a considerable segment of the phylogenetic scale.

When we began this work, it was our aim to see if the science would work beyond the laboratory, to determine if animal psychology could stand on its own feet as an engineering discipline. These aims have been realized. We have controlled a wide range of animal behavior and have made use of the great popular appeal of animals to make it an economically feasible project. Conditioned behavior has been exhibited at various municipal zoos and museums of natural history and has been used for department store displays, for fair and trade convention exhibits, for entertainment at tourist attractions, on television shows, and in the production of television commercials. Thirty-eight species, totaling over 6,000 individual animals, have been conditioned, and we have dared to tackle such unlikely subjects as reindeer, cockatoos, raccoons, porpoises, and whales.

Emboldened by this consistent reinforce-

1 In view of the fact that instinctive behaviors may be common to many zoological species, we consider *species specific* to be a sanitized misnomer, and prefer the possibly septic adjective *instinctive*.

ment, we have ventured further and further from the security of the Skinner box. However, in this cavalier extrapolation, we have run afoul of a persistent pattern of discomforting failures. These failures, although disconcertingly frequent and seemingly diverse, fall into a very interesting pattern. They all represent breakdowns of conditioned operant behavior. From a great number of such experiences, we have selected, more or less at random, the following examples.

The first instance of our discomfiture might be entitled, What Makes Sammy Dance? In the exhibit in which this occurred, the casual observer sees a grown bantam chicken emerge from a retaining compartment when the door automatically opens. The chicken walks over about 3 feet, pulls a rubber loop on a small box which starts a repeated auditory stimulus pattern (a four-note tune). The chicken then steps up onto an 18-inch, slightly raised disc, thereby closing a timer switch, and scratches vigorously, round and round, over the disc for 15 seconds, at the rate of about two scratches per second until the automatic feeder fires in the retaining compartment. The chicken goes into the compartment to eat, thereby automatically shutting the door. The popular interpretation of this behavior pattern is that the chicken has turned on the "juke box" and "dances."

The development of this behavioral exhibit was wholly unplanned. In the attempt to create quite another type of demonstration which required a chicken simply to stand on a platform for 12–15 seconds, we found that over 50% developed a very strong and pronounced scratch pattern, which tended to increase in persistence as the time interval was lengthened. (Another 25% or so developed other behaviors—pecking at spots, etc.) However, we were able to change our plans so as to make use of the scratch pattern, and the result was the "dancing chicken" exhibit described above.

In this exhibit the only real contingency for reinforcement is that the chicken must depress the platform for 15 seconds. In the course of a performing day (about 3 hours for each chicken) a chicken may turn out over 10,000 unnecessary, virtually identical responses. Operant behaviorists would probably have little hesitancy in labeling this an example of Skinnerian "superstition" (Skinner, 1948) or

"mediating" behavior, and we list it first to whet their explanatory appetite.

However, a second instance involving a raccoon does not fit so neatly into this paradigm. The response concerned the manipulation of money by the raccoon (who has "hands" rather similar to those of the primates). The contingency for reinforcement was picking up the coins and depositing them in a 5-inch metal box.

Raccoons condition readily, have good appetites, and this one was quite tame and an eager subject. We anticipated no trouble. Conditioning him to pick up the first coin was simple. We started out by reinforcing him for picking up a single coin. Then the metal container was introduced, with the requirement that he drop the coin into the container. Here we ran into the first bit of difficulty: he seemed to have a great deal of trouble letting go of the coin. He would rub it up against the inside of the container, pull it back out, and clutch it firmly for several seconds. However, he would finally turn it loose and receive his food reinforcement. Then the final contingency: we put him on a ratio of 2, requiring that he pick up both coins and put them in the container.

Now the raccoon really had problems (and so did we). Not only could he not let go of the coins, but he spent seconds, even minutes, rubbing them together (in a most miserly fashion), and dipping them into the container. He carried on this behavior to such an extent that the practical application we had in mind —a display featuring a racoon putting money in a piggy bank—simply was not feasible. The rubbing behavior became worse and worse as time went on, in spite of nonreinforcement.

For the third instance, we return to the gallinaceous birds. The observer sees a hopper full of oval plastic capsules which contain small toys, charms, and the like. When the S_D (a light) is presented to the chicken, she pulls a rubber loop which releases one of these capsules onto a slide, about 16 inches long, inclined at about 30 degrees. The capsule rolls down the slide and comes to rest near the end. Here one or two sharp, straight pecks by the chicken will knock it forward off the slide and out to the observer, and the chicken is then reinforced by an automatic feeder. This is all very well—most chickens are able to master these contingencies in short order. The loop pulling presents no problems; she then has only to peck the capsule off the slide to get her reinforcement.

However, a good 20% of all chickens tried on this set of contingencies fail to make the grade. After they have pecked a few capsules off the slide, they begin to grab at the capsules and drag them backwards into the cage. Here they pound them up and down on the floor of the cage. Of course, this results in no reinforcement for the chicken, and yet some chickens will pull in over half of all the capsules presented to them.

Almost always this problem behavior does not appear until after the capsules begin to move down the slide. Conditioning is begun with stationary capsules placed by the experimenter. When the pecking behavior becomes strong enough, so that the chicken is knocking them off the slide and getting reinforced consistently, the loop pulling is conditioned to the light. The capsules then come rolling down the slide to the chicken. Here most chickens, who before did not have this tendency, will start grabbing and shaking.

The fourth incident also concerns a chicken. Here the observer sees a chicken in a cage about 4 feet long which is placed alongside a miniature baseball field. The reason for the cage is the interesting part. At one end of the cage is an automatic electric feed hopper. At the other is an opening through which the chicken can reach and pull a loop on a bat. If she pulls the loop hard enough the bat (solenoid operated) will swing, knocking a small baseball up the playing field. If it gets past the miniature toy players on the field and hits the back fence, the chicken is automatically reinforced with food at the other end of the cage. If it does not go far enough, or hits one of the players, she tries again. This results in behavior on an irregular ratio. When the feeder sounds, she then runs down the length of the cage and eats.

Our problems began when we tried to remove the cage for photography. Chickens that had been well conditioned in this behavior became wildly excited when the ball started to move. They would jump up on the playing field, chase the ball all over the field, even knock it off on the floor and chase it around, pecking it in every direction, although they had never had access to the ball before. This behavior was so persistent and so dis-ruptive, in spite of the fact that it was never reinforced, that we had to reinstate the cage.

The last instance we shall relate in detail is one of the most annoying and baffling for a good behaviorist. Here a pig was conditioned to pick up large wooden coins and deposit them in a large "piggy bank." The coins were placed several feet from the bank and the pig required to carry them to the bank and deposit them, usually four or five coins for one reinforcement. (Of course, we started out with one coin, near the bank.)

Pigs condition very rapidly, they have no trouble taking ratios, they have ravenous appetites (naturally), and in many ways are among the most tractable animals we have worked with. However, this particular problem behavior developed in pig after pig, usually after a period of weeks or months, getting worse every day. At first the pig would eagerly pick up one dollar, carry it to the bank, run back, get another, carry it rapidly and neatly, and so on, until the ratio was complete. Thereafter, over a period of weeks the behavior would become slower and slower. He might run over eagerly for each dollar, but on the way back, instead of carrying the dollar and depositing it simply and cleanly, he would repeatedly drop it, root it, drop it again, root it along the way, pick it up, toss it up in the air, drop it, root it some more, and so on.

We thought this behavior might simply be the dilly-dallying of an animal on a low drive. However, the behavior persisted and gained in strength in spite of a severely increased drive—he finally went through the ratios so slowly that he did not get enough to eat in the course of a day. Finally it would take the pig about 10 minutes to transport four coins a distance of about 6 feet. This problem behavior developed repeatedly in successive pigs.

There have also been other instances: hamsters that stopped working in a glass case after four or five reinforcements, porpoises and whales that swallow their manipulanda (balls and inner tubes), cats that will not leave the area of the feeder, rabbits that will not go to the feeder, the great difficulty in many species of conditioning vocalization with food reinforcement, problems in conditioning a kick in a cow, the failure to get appreciably increased effort out of the ungulates with increased drive, and so on. These we shall not dwell on in detail, nor shall we discuss how they might be overcome.

These egregious failures came as a rather considerable shock to us, for there was nothing in our background in behaviorism to prepare us for such gross inabilities to predict and control the behavior of animals with which we had been working for years.

The examples listed we feel represent a clear and utter failure of conditioning theory. They are far from what one would normally expect on the basis of the theory alone. Furthermore, they are definite, observable; the diagnosis of theory failure does not depend on subtle statistical interpretations or on semantic legerdemain—the animal simply does not do what he has been conditioned to do.

It seems perfectly clear that, with the possible exception of the dancing chicken, which could conceivably, as we have said, be explained in terms of Skinner's superstition paradigm, the other instances do not fit the behavioristic way of thinking. Here we have animals, after having been conditioned to a specific learned response, gradually drifting into behaviors that are entirely different from those which were conditioned. Moreover, it can easily be seen that these particular behaviors to which the animals drift are clear-cut examples of instinctive behaviors having to do with the natural food getting behaviors of the particular species.

The dancing chicken is exhibiting the gallinaceous birds' scratch pattern that in nature often precedes ingestion. The chicken that hammers capsules is obviously exhibiting instinctive behavior having to do with breaking open of seed pods or the killing of insects, grubs, etc. The raccoon is demonstrating so-called "washing behavior." The rubbing and washing response may result, for example, in the removal of the exoskeleton of a crayfish. The pig is rooting or shaking—behaviors which are strongly built into this species and are connected with the food getting repertoire.

These patterns to which the animals drift require greater physical output and therefore are a violation of the so-called "law of least effort." And most damaging of all, they stretch out the time required for reinforcement when nothing in the experimental setup requires them to do so. They have only to do the little tidbit of behavior to which they were conditioned—for example, pick up the coin and put it in the container—to get reinforced immediately. Instead, they drag the process out for a matter of minutes when there is nothing

in the contingency which forces them to do this. Moreover, increasing the drive merely intensifies this effect.

It seems obvious that these animals are trapped by strong instinctive behaviors, and clearly we have here a demonstration of the prepotency of such behavior patterns over those which have been conditioned.

We have termed this phenomenon "instinctive drift." The general principle seems to be that wherever an animal has strong instinctive behaviors in the area of the conditioned response, after continued running the organism will drift toward the instinctive behavior to the detriment of the conditioned behavior and even to the delay or preclusion of the reinforcement. In a very boiled-down, simplified form, it might be stated as "learned behavior drifts toward instinctive behavior."

All this, of course, is not to disparage the use of conditioning techniques, but is intended as a demonstration that there are definite weaknesses in the philosophy underlying these techniques. The pointing out of such weaknesses should make possible a worthwhile revision in behavior theory.

The notion of instinct has now become one of our basic concepts in an effort to make sense of the welter of observations which confront us. When behaviorism tossed out instinct, it is our feeling that some of its power of prediction and control were lost with it. From the foregoing examples, it appears that although it was easy to banish the Instinctivists from the science during the Behavioristic Revolution, it was not possible to banish instinct so easily.

And if, as Hebb suggests, it is advisable to reconsider those things that behaviorism explicitly threw out, perhaps it might likewise be advisable to examine what they tacitly brought in—the hidden assumptions which led most disastrously to these breakdowns in the theory.

Three of the most important of these tacit assumptions seem to us to be: that the animal comes to the laboratory as a virtual *tabula rasa,** that species differences are insignificant, and that all responses are about equally conditionable to all stimuli.

It is obvious, we feel, from the foregoing account, that these assumptions are no longer tenable. After 14 years of continuous condi-

* A blank slate. (Eds.)

tioning and observation of thousands of animals, it is our reluctant conclusion that the behavior of any species cannot be adequately understood, predicted, or controlled without knowledge of its instinctive patterns, evolutionary history, and ecological niche.

In spite of our early successes with the application of behavioristically oriented conditioning theory, we readily admit now that ethological facts and attitudes in recent years have done more to advance our practical control of animal behavior than recent reports from American "learning labs."

Moreover, as we have recently discovered, if one begins with evolution and instinct as the basic format for the science, a very illuminating viewpoint can be developed which leads naturally to a drastically revised and simplified conceptual framework of startling explanatory power (to be reported elsewhere).

It is hoped that this playback on the theory will be behavioral technology's partial repayment to the academic science whose impeccable empiricism we have used so extensively.

REFERENCES

Beach, F. A. The snark was a boojum. *Amer. Psychologist,* 1950, 5, 115–124.

Breland, K., & Breland, M. A field of applied animal psychology. *Amer. Psychologist,* 1951, 6, 202–204.

Hebb, D. O. The American revolution. *Amer. Psychologist,* 1960, 15, 735–745.

Lorenz, K. Innate behaviour patterns. In *Symposia of the Society for Experimental Biology.* No. 4. *Physiological mechanisms in animal behaviour.* New York: Academic Press, 1950.

Skinner, B. F. Superstition in the pigeon. *J. Exp. Psychol.,* 1948, 38, 168–172.

Tinbergen, N. *The study of instinct.* Oxford: Clarendon Press, 1951.

Whalen, R. E. Comparative psychology. *Amer. Psychologist,* 1961, 16, 84.

17. THE CHEMISTRY OF LEARNING

DAVID KRECH

American educators now talk a great deal about the innovative hardware of education, about computer-assisted instruction, 8 mm. cartridge-loading projectors, microtransparencies, and other devices. In the not too distant future they may well be talking about enzyme-assisted instruction, protein memory consolidators, antibiotic memory repellers, and the chemistry of the brain. Although the psychologists' learning theories derived from the study of maze-running rats or target-pecking pigeons have failed to provide insights into the education of children, it is unlikely that what is now being discovered by the psychologist, chemist, and neuro-physiologist about rat-brain chemistry can deviate widely from what we will eventually discover about the chemistry of the human brain.

Most adults who are not senile can repeat a series of seven numbers—8, 4, 8, 8, 3, 9, 9 —immediately after the series is read. If, however, they are asked to repeat these numbers thirty minutes later, most will fail. In the first instance, we are dealing with the immediate memory span; in the second, with

This article is adapted from a speech to three National Seminars on Innovation, sponsored by the U.S. Office of Education and the Charles F. Kettering Foundation, in Honolulu July 1967. Copyright © 1968 by Saturday Review, Inc. Reprinted by permission of the author from the January 20, 1968 issue of the SATURDAY REVIEW.

long-term memory. These basic behavioral observations lie behind what is called the two-stage memory storage process theory.

According to a common variant of these notions, immediately after every learning trial—indeed, after every experience—a short-lived electrochemical process is established in the brain. This process, so goes the assumption, is the physiological mechanism which carries the short-term memory. Within a few seconds or minutes, however, this process decays and disappears; but before doing so, if all systems are go, the short-term electro-chemical process triggers a second series of events in the brain. This second process is chemical in nature and involves, primarily, the production of new proteins and the induction of higher enzymatic activity levels in the brain cells. This process is more enduring and serves as the physiological substrate of our long-term memory.

It would follow that one approach to testing our theory would be to provide a subject with some experience or other, then interrupt the short-term electrochemical process immediately—before it has had an opportunity to establish the long-term process. If this were done, our subject should never develop a long-term memory for that experience.

At the Albert Einstein Medical School in New York, Dr. Murray Jarvik has devised a "step-down" procedure based on the fact that when a rat is placed on a small platform a few inches above the floor, the rat will step down onto the floor within a few seconds. The rat will do this consistently, day after day. Suppose that on one day the floor is electri-fied, and stepping onto it produces a painful shock. When the rat is afterward put back on the platform—even twenty-four hours later—it will not budge from the platform but will remain there until the experimenter gets tired and calls the experiment quits. The rat has thus demonstrated that he has a long-term memory for that painful experience.

If we now take another rat, but this time *interfere* with his short-term memory process *immediately after* he has stepped onto the electrified floor, the rat should show no evidence of having experienced a shock when tested the next day, since we have not given his short-term electrochemical memory pro-cess an opportunity to initiate the long-term protein-enzymatic process. To interrupt the short-term process, Jarvik passes a mild elec-tric current across the brain of the animal. The current is not strong enough to cause irreparable harm to the brain cells, but it does result in a very high level of activation of the neurons in the brain, thus disrupting the short-term electrochemical memory process. If this treatment follows closely enough after the animal's first experience with the foot shock, and we test the rat a day later, the rat acts as if there were no memory for yesterday's event; the rat jauntily and promptly steps down from the platform with no apparent expectation of shock.

When a long time-interval is interposed between the first foot shock and the electric-current (through the brain) treatment, the rat *does* remember the foot shock, and it remains on the platform when tested the next day. This, again, is what we should have expected from our theory. The short-term electro-chemical process has now had time to set up the long-term chemical memory process before it was disrupted.

Some well known effects of accidental human head injury seem to parallel these findings. Injuries which produce a temporary loss of consciousness (but no permanent damage to brain tissue) can cause the patient to experience a "gap" in his memory for the events just preceding the accident. This retro-grade amnesia can be understood on the assumption that the events immediately prior to the accident were still being carried by the short-term memory processes at the time of the injury, and their disruption by the injury was sufficient to prevent the induction of the long-term processes. The patient asks "Where am I?" not only because he does not recognize the hospital, but also because he cannot re-member how he became injured.

Work conducted by Dr. Bernard Agranoff at the University of Michigan Medical School supports the hypothesis that the synthesis of new brain proteins is crucial for the establish-ment of the long-term memory process. He argues that if we could prevent the formation of new proteins in the brain, then—although the short-term electrochemical memory process is not interfered with—the long-term memory process could never become established.

Much of Agranoff's work has been done with goldfish. The fish is placed in one end of a small rectangular tank, which is divided into two halves by a barrier which extends from the bottom to just below the surface of the water. When a light is turned on, the fish must swim across the barrier into the other side of the tank within twenty seconds—otherwise he receives an electric shock. This training is continued for several trials until the animal learns to swim quickly to the other side when the light is turned on. Most goldfish learn this shock-avoidance task quite easily and remember it for many days. Immediately before—and in some experiments, immediately after—training, Agranoff injects the antibiotic puromycin into the goldfish's brain. (Puromycin is a protein inhibitor and prevents the formation of new proteins in the brain's neurons.) After injection, Agranoff finds that the goldfish are not impaired in their acquisition of the shock-avoidance task, but, when tested a day or so later, they show almost no retention for the task.

These results mean that the short-term memory process (which helps the animal remember from one trial to the next and thus permits him to learn in the first place) is not dependent upon the formation of new proteins, but that the long-term process (which helps the animal remember from one day to the next and thus permits him to retain what he had learned) is dependent upon the production of new proteins. Again, as in the instance of Jarvik's rats, if the puromycin injection comes more than an hour after learning, it has no effect on later memory—the long-term memory process presumably has already been established and the inhibition of protein synthesis can now no longer affect memory. In this antibiotic, therefore, we have our first chemical memory erasure—or, more accurately, a chemical long-term memory preventative. (Almost identical findings have been reported by other workers in other laboratories working with such animals as mice and rats, which are far removed from the goldfish.)

Thus far I have been talking about disrupting or preventing the formation of memory. Now we will accentuate the positive. Dr. James L. McGaugh of the University of California at Riverside has argued that injections of central nervous system stimulants such as strychnine, picrotoxin, or metrazol should enhance, fortify, or extend the activity of the short-term electrochemical memory processes and thus increase the probability that they will be successful in initiating long-term memory

processes. From this it follows that the injection of CNS* stimulants immediately before or after training should improve learning performance. That is precisely what McGaugh found —together with several additional results which have important implications for our concerns today.

In one of McGaugh's most revealing experiments, eight groups of mice from two different hereditary backgrounds were given the problem of learning a simple maze. Immediately after completing their learning trials, four groups from each strain were injected with a different dosage of metrazol—from none to five, 10, and 20 milligrams per kilogram of body weight. First, it was apparent that there are hereditary differences in learning ability—a relatively bright strain and a relatively dull one. Secondly, by properly dosing the animals with metrazol, the learning performance increased appreciably. Under the optimal dosage, the metrazol animals showed about a 40 per cent improvement in learning ability over their untreated brothers. The improvement under metrazol was so great, in fact, that the dull animals, when treated with 10 milligrams, did slightly better than their untreated but hereditarily superior colleagues.

In metrazol we not only have a chemical facilitator of learning, but one which acts as the "Great Equalizer" among hereditarily different groups. As the dosage was increased for the dull mice from none to five to 10 milligrams their performance improved. Beyond the 10-milligram point for the dull mice, however, and beyond the five-milligram point for the bright mice, increased strength of the metrazol solution resulted in a deterioration in learning. We can draw two morals from this last finding. First, the optimal dosage of chemical learning facilitators will vary greatly with the individual taking the drug (there is, in other words, an interaction between heredity and drugs); second, there is a limit to the intellectual power of even a hopped-up Southern Californian Super Mouse!

We already have available a fairly extensive class of drugs which can facilitate learning and memory in animals. A closer examination of McGaugh's results and the work of others, however, also suggests that these drugs do not work in a monolithic manner on something called "learning" or "memory." In some in-

* Central Nervous System. (Eds.)

stances, the drugs seem to act on "attentiveness"; in some, on the ability to vary one's attacks on a problem; in some, on persistence; in some, on immediate memory; in some, on long-term memory. Different drugs work differentially for different strains, different individuals, different intellectual tasks, and different learning components.

Do all of these results mean that we will soon be able to substitute a pharmacopoeia of drugs for our various school-enrichment and innovative educational programs, and that most educators will soon be technologically unemployed—or will have to retool and turn in their schoolmaster's gown for a pharmacist's jacket? The answer is no—as our Berkeley experiments on the influence of education and training on brain anatomy and chemistry suggest. This research is the work of four—Dr. E. L. Bennett, biochemist; Dr. Marian Diamond, anatomist; Dr. M. R. Rosenzweig, psychologist; and myself—together, of course, with the help of graduate students, technicians, and, above all, government money.

Our work, started some fifteen years ago, was guided by the same general theory which has guided more recent work, but our research strategy and tactics were quite different. Instead of interfering physiologically or chemically with the animal to determine the effects of such intervention upon memory storage (as did Jarvik, Agranoff, and McGaugh), we had taken the obverse question and, working with only normal animals, sought to determine the *effects* of memory storage on the chemistry and anatomy of the brain.

Our argument was this: If the establishment of long-term memory processes involves increased activity of brain enzymes, then animals which have been required to do a great deal of learning and remembering should end up with brains enzymatically different from those of animals which have not been so challenged by environment. This should be especially true for the enzymes involved in trans-synaptic neural activity. Further, since such neural activity would make demands on brain-cell action and metabolism, one might also expect to find various morphological differences between the brains of rats brought up in psychologically stimulating and psychologically pallid environments.

I describe briefly one of our standard experiments. At weaning age, one rat from each of a dozen pairs of male twins is chosen by lot to be placed in an educationally active and innovative environment, while its twin brother is placed in as unstimulating an environment as we can contrive. All twelve educationally enriched rats live together in one large, wire-mesh cage in a well lighted, noisy, and busy laboratory. The cage is equipped with ladders, running wheels, and other "creative" rat toys. For thirty minutes each day, the rats are taken out of their cages and allowed to explore new territory. As the rats grow older they are given various learning tasks to master, for which they are rewarded with bits of sugar. This stimulating educational and training program is continued for eighty days.

While these animals are enjoying their rich intellectual environment, each impoverished animal lives out his life in solitary confinement, in a small cage situated in a dimly lit and quiet room. He is rarely handled by his keeper and never invited to explore new environments, to solve problems, or join in games with other rats. Both groups of rats, however, have unlimited access to the same standard food throughout the experiment. At the age of 105 days, the rats are sacrificed, their brains dissected out and analyzed morphologically and chemically.

This standard experiment, repeated dozens of times, indicates that as the fortunate rat lives out his life in the educationally enriched condition, the bulk of his cortex expands and grows deeper and heavier than that of his culturally deprived brother. Part of this increase in cortical mass is accounted for by an increase in the number of glia cells (specialized brain cells which play vital functions in the nutrition of the neurons and, perhaps, also in laying down permanent memory traces); part of it by an increase in the size of the neuronal cell bodies and their nuclei; and part by an increase in the diameters of the blood vessels supplying the cortex. Our postulated chemical changes also occur. The enriched brain shows more acetylocholinesterase (the enzyme involved in the trans-synaptic conduction of neural impulses) and cholinesterase (the enzyme found primarily in the glia cells).

Finally, in another series of experiments we have demonstrated that these structural and chemical changes are the signs of a "good" brain. That is, we have shown that either through early rat-type Head Start programs or through selective breeding programs, we can increase the weight and density of the rat's cortex and its acetylocholinesterase and cholinesterase activity levels. And when we do—by either method—we have created superior problem-solving animals.

What does all of this mean? It means that the effects of the psychological and educational environment are not restricted to something called the "mental" realm. Permitting the young rat to grow up in an educationally and experientially inadequate and unstimulating environment creates an animal with a relatively deteriorated brain—a brain with a thin and light cortex, lowered blood supply, diminished enzymatic activities, smaller neuronal cell bodies, and fewer glia cells. A lack of adequate educational fare for the young animal—no matter how large the food supply or how good the family—and a lack of adequate psychological enrichment results in palpable, measurable, deteriorative changes in the brain's chemistry and anatomy.

Returning to McGaugh's results, we find that whether, and to what extent, this or that drug will improve the animal's learning ability will depend, of course, on what the drug does to the rat's brain chemistry. And what it does to the rat's brain chemistry will depend upon the status of the chemistry in the brain to begin with. And what the status of the brain's chemistry is to begin with reflects the rat's early psychological and educational environment. Whether, and to what extent, this or that drug will improve the animal's attention, or memory, or learning ability, therefore, will depend upon the animal's past experiences. I am not talking about interaction between "mental" factors on the one hand and "chemical" compounds on the other. I am talking, rather, about interactions between chemical factors introduced into the brain by the biochemist's injection or pills, and chemical factors induced in the brain by the educator's stimulating or improverishing environment. The biochemist's work can be only half effective without the educator's help.

What kind of educational environment can best develop the brain chemically and morphologically? What kind of stimulation makes for an enriched environment? What educational experiences can potentiate the effects of the biochemist's drugs? We don't know. The biochemist doesn't know. It is at this point that I see a whole new area of collaboration in basic research between the educator, the psychologist, and the neurobiochemist—essentially, a research program which combines the Agranoff and McGaugh techniques with our Berkeley approach. Given the start that has already been made in the animal laboratory, an intensive program of research—with animals and with children—which seeks to spell out the interrelations between chemical and educational influences on brain and memory can pay off handsomely. This need not wait for the future. We know enough now to get started.

Both the biochemist and the teacher of the future will combine their skills and insights for the educational and intellectual development of the child. Tommy needs a bit more of an immediate memory stimulator; Jack could do with a chemical attention-span stretcher; Rachel needs an anticholinesterase to slow down her mental processes; Joan, some puromycin—she remembers too many details, and gets lost.

To be sure, all our data thus far come from the brains of goldfish and rodents. But is anyone so certain that the chemistry of the brain of a rat (which, after all, is a fairly complex mammal) is so different from that of the brain of a human being that he dare neglect this challenge—or even gamble—when the stakes are so high?

18. WHAT DO WE KNOW ABOUT LEARNING?

Goodwin Watson

What do we really know today about learning? Although no scientific "truths" are established beyond the possibility of revision, knowledgeable psychologists generally agree on a number of propositions about learning which are important for education. The educator who bases his program on the propositions presented below is entitled, therefore, to feel that he is on solid psychological ground and not on shifting sands.

Behaviors which are rewarded (reinforced) are more likely to recur.

This most fundamental law of learning has been demonstrated in literally thousands of experiments. It seems to hold for every sort of animal from earthworms to highly intelligent adults. The behavior most likely to emerge in any situation is that which the subject found successful or satisfying previously in a similar situation. No other variable affects learning so powerfully. The best-planned learning provides for a steady, cumulative sequence of successful behaviors.

Reward (reinforcement), to be most effective in learning, must follow almost immediately after the desired behavior and be clearly connected with that behavior in the mind of the learner.

The simple word, "Right," coming directly after a given response, will have more influence on learning than any big reward which comes much later or which is dimly connected with many responses so that it can't really reinforce any of them. Much of the effectiveness of programed self-instruction lies in the

From the NATIONAL EDUCATION ASSOCIATION JOURNAL, *March 1963. Copyright* © *1963 by the National Education Association. Reprinted by permission of the* National Education Association Journal.

fact that information about success is fed back immediately for each learner response. A total mark on a test the day after it is administered has little or no reinforcement value for the specific answers.

Sheer repetition without indications of improvement or any kind of reinforcement (reward) is a poor way to attempt to learn.

Practice is not enough. The learner cannot improve by repeated efforts unless he is informed whether or not each effort has been successful.

Threat and punishment have variable and uncertain effects upon learning: They may make the punished response more likely or less likely to recur; they may set up avoidance tendencies which prevent further learning.

Punishment is not, psychologically, the reverse of reward. It disturbs the relationship of the learner to the situation and the teacher. It does not assist the learner in finding and fixing the correct response.

Readiness for any new learning is a complex product of interaction among such factors as (a) sufficient physiological and psychological maturity, (b) sense of the importance of the new learning for the learner in his world, (c) mastery of prerequisites providing a fair chance of success, and (d) freedom from discouragement (expectation of failure) or threat (sense of danger).

Conversely, the learner will not be ready to try new responses which are beyond his powers or are seen as valueless or too dangerous.

Opportunity for fresh, novel, stimulating experience is a kind of reward which is quite effective in conditioning and learning.

Experiments indicate that lower animals (rats, dogs, monkeys) will learn as effectively when they receive rewards of new experience or satisfied curiosity as they will when the rewards gratify physical desires. Similarly, stimulating new insights have been found to be effective as rewards for the learning efforts of human beings.

The sense of satisfaction which results from achievement is the type of reward (reinforcement) which has the greatest transfer value to other life situations.

Any extrinsic reward—candy, or stars on a chart, or commendation—depends on its dispenser. There is no need to strive if the reward-giver is out of the picture. Also, cheating can sometimes win the extrinsic reward. The internal reward system is always present for the learner, and he sees little gain in fooling himself.

Learners progress in an area of learning only as far as they need to in order to achieve their purposes. Often they do only well enough to "get by"; with increased motivation, they improve.

Studies of reading speed show that practice alone will not bring improvement; a person may have read books for years at his customary rate, but with new demands and opportunities he may be able to double that rate.

The most effective effort is put forth by children when they attempt tasks which are not too easy and not too hard—where success seems quite possible but not certain. It is not reasonable to expect a teacher to set an appropriate level of challenge for each pupil in a class; pupils can, however, be helped to set their own goals to bring maximum satisfaction and learning.

Children are more likely to throw themselves wholeheartedly into any learning project if they themselves have participated in the selection and planning of the project.

Genuine participation (not pretended sharing) increases motivation, adaptability, and speed of learning.

Excessive direction by the teacher is likely to result in apathetic conformity, defiance, scapegoating, or escape from the whole affair.

Autocratic leadership has been found to increase dependence of members on the leader and to generate resentment (conscious or unconscious) which finds expression in attacks on weaker figures or even in sabotage of the work.

Overstrict discipline is associated with more conformity, anxiety, shyness, and acquiescence in children; greater permissiveness is associated with more initiative and creativity.

In comparisons of children whose parents were most permissive in home discipline with those whose parents were most strict (both groups of parents loving and concerned), the youngsters from permissive homes showed more enterprise, self-confidence, curiosity, and originality.

Many pupils experience so much criticism, failure, and discouragement in school that their self-confidence, level of aspiration, and sense of worth are damaged.

The pupil who sees himself at his worst in school is likely to place little value on study and to seek his role of importance outside the classroom. He may carry through life a sense of being not good for much. He is likely also to feel resentment at schools, teachers, and books.

When children or adults experience too much frustration, their behavior ceases to be integrated, purposeful, and rational. The threshold of what is "too much" varies; it is lowered by previous failures.

Pupils who have had little success and almost continuous failure at school tasks are in no condition to think, to learn, or even to pay attention. They may turn their anger outward against respectable society or inward against themselves.

Pupils think whenever they encounter an obstacle, difficulty, puzzle, or intellectual challenge which interests them. The process of thinking involves designing and testing plausible solutions for the problem as understood by the thinker.

It is useless to command people to think; they must feel concerned to get somewhere and eager to remove an obstruction on the way.

The best way to help pupils form a general concept is to present the concept in numerous and varied specific situations—contrasting experiences with and without the desired concept—and then to encourage precise formulations of the general idea and its application in situations different from those in which the concept was learned.

For example, the concept of democracy might be illustrated not only in national government but also in familiar situations of home, school, church, jobs, clubs, and local affairs. It is best understood when it is contrasted with other power structures such as autocracy, oligarchy, or *laissez faire.*

The experience of learning by sudden insight into a previously confused or puzzling situation arises when (a) there has been a sufficient background and preparation, (b) attention is given to the relationships operative in the whole situation, (c) the perceptual structure "frees" the key elements to be shifted into new patterns, (d) the task is meaningful and within the range of ability of the subject.

The term "cognitive reorganization" is sometimes applied to this experience. Suddenly the scene changes into one that seems familiar and can be coped with.

Learning from reading is facilitated more by time spent recalling what has been read than by re-reading.

In one experiment (typical of many), students who spent eighty per cent of their learning periods trying to remember what they had read surpassed those who spent only sixty per cent of the time on recollection. The students who spent all the time reading and re-reading the assignment made the poorest record.

Forgetting proceeds rapidly at first—then more and more slowly. Recall shortly after learning reduces the amount forgotten.

Within twenty-four hours after learning something, a large part is forgotten unless efforts are made to prevent forgetting. A thing can be relearned more quickly than it was learned originally, however, and if it is reviewed several times at gradually increasing intervals, it can be retained for some time.

People remember new information which confirms their previous attitudes better than they remember new information which runs counter to their previous attitudes.

Studies consistently show that individuals who feel strongly on a controversial issue, and who are asked to read presentations of both sides, remember the facts and arguments which support their feelings better than they recall those on the opposite side.

What is learned is most likely to be available for use if it is learned in a situation much like that in which it is to be used and immediately preceding the time when it is needed. Learning in childhood, then forgetting, and later relearning when need arises is not an efficient procedure.

The best time to learn is when the learning can be useful. Motivation is then strongest and forgetting less of a problem. Much that is now taught children might be more effective if taught to responsible adults.

If there is a discrepancy between the real objectives and the tests used to measure achievement, the latter become the main influence upon choice of subject matter and method. Curriculum and teaching geared to standardized tests and programed learning are likely to concentrate only on learnings which can be easily checked and scored.

The most rapid mental growth comes during infancy and early childhood; the average child achieves about half of his total mental growth by age five.

In the first two years a normal child transforms the "big, buzzing, blooming confusion" of his first conscious experience to organized perception of familiar faces, spoken words, surroundings, toys, bed, clothing, and foods. He differentiates himself from others, high from low, many from few, approval from disapproval. He lays a foundation for lifelong tendencies toward trust or mistrust, self-acceptance or shame, initiative or passivity; and these vitally condition further growth.

Not until adolescence do most children develop the sense of time which is required for historical perspective. The so-called facts of history—1492, 1776, and all that—can be learned by children but without any real grasp of what life was like in another period or in a different country. Most instruction in ancient, medieval, and even modern history is no more real to children than are fairy tales.

Ability to learn increases with age up to adult years. The apparent decline is largely the result of lack of motivation. We can coerce children into school activities; adult education is mostly voluntary. Men and women *can,* if they wish, master new languages, new ideas, and new ways of acting or problem-solving even at sixty and seventy years of age.

19. THE ULTIMATE TEACHING MACHINE

R. J. HEATHORN

A new aid to rapid—almost magical—learning has made its appearance. Indications are that if it catches on, all the electronic gadgets will be so much junk. The new device is known as Built-in Orderly Organized Knowledge. The makers generally call it by its initials, BOOK.*

Many advantages are claimed over the old-style learning and teaching aids on which most people are brought up nowadays. It has no wires, no electric circuits to break down. No connection is needed to an electricity power point. It is made entirely without mechanical parts to go wrong or need replacement.

Anyone can use BOOK, even children, and it fits comfortably into the hands. It can be conveniently used sitting in an armchair by the fire.

How does this revolutionary, unbelievably easy invention work? Basically BOOK consists only of a large number of paper sheets. These may run to hundreds where BOOK covers a lengthy program of information. Each sheet bears a number in sequence, so that the sheets cannot be used in the wrong order. To make it even easier for the user to keep the sheets in the proper order they are held firmly in place by a special locking device called a "binding."

Each sheet of paper presents the user with an information sequence in the form of symbols, which he absorbs optically for automatic registration on the brain. When one sheet has been assimilated a flick of the finger turns it

Originally titled "Learn With BOOK" and copyright © 1962 by Punch, London. Reprinted by permission of the Ben Roth Agency, Inc. from the May 9, 1962 issue of PUNCH.

* What you are now (presumably) reading will serve as an excellent example. (Eds.)

over and further information is found on the other side. By using both sides of each sheet in this way a great economy is effected, thus reducing both the size and cost of BOOK. No buttons need to be pressed to move from one sheet to another, to open or close BOOK, or to start it working.

BOOK may be taken up at any time and used by merely opening it. Instantly it is ready for use. Nothing has to be connected up or switched on. The user may turn at will to any sheet, going backwards or forwards as he pleases. A sheet is provided near the beginning as a location finder for any required information sequence.

A small accessory, available at trifling extra cost, is the BOOKmark. This enables the user to pick up his program where he left off on the previous learning session. BOOKmark is versatile and may be used in any BOOK.

The initial cost varies with the size and subject matter. Already a vast range of BOOKs is available, covering every conceivable subject and adjusted to different levels of aptitude. One BOOK, small enough to be held in the hands, may contain an entire learning schedule. Once purchased, BOOK requires no further cost; no batteries or wires are needed, since the motive power, thanks to the ingenious device patented by the makers, is supplied by the brain of the user.

BOOKs may be stored on handy shelves and for ease of reference the program schedule is normally indicated on the back of the binding.

Altogether the Built-in Orderly Organized Knowledge seems to have great advantages with no drawbacks. We predict a big future for it.

RECOMMENDED FURTHER READING

Bartlett, Frederick C.: *Remembering: A Study in Experimental and Social Psychology;* London, Cambridge University Press 1932

*Bruner, Jerome S.: *The Process of Education;* Cambridge, Mass., Harvard University Press 1960

——: *Toward A Theory of Instruction;* Cambridge, Mass., Harvard University Press 1966

——, J. Goodnow and G. Austin: *A Study of Thinking;* New York, John Wiley 1956

Coulson, G. E. (ed.): *Programmed Learning and Computer Based Instruction;* New York, John Wiley 1962

*Ebbinghaus, Hermann: *Memory: A Contribution to Experimental Psychology;* New York, Dover 1964 (originally published 1885)

Feigenbaum, E. A. and J. Feldman (eds.): *Computers and Thought;* New York, McGraw-Hill 1963

Freedman, J. L.: "Increasing Creativity by Free Association Training"; *Journal of Experimental Psychology, 69* (1965), 89–91

Gagne, Robert M.: *Conditions of Learning;* New York, Holt, Rinehart & Winston 1965

——: *Learning and Individual Differences;* Columbus, Ohio, Charles E. Merrill 1967

Hilgard, Ernest R. and G. H. Bower: *Theories of Learning* (3rd Ed.); New York, Appleton-Century-Crofts 1966

Johnson, D. M.: *The Psychology of Thought and Judgment;* New York, Harper & Row 1955

*Kagan, Jerome (ed.): *Creativity and Learning;* Boston, Houghton Mifflin 1967

Katona, G.: *Organizing and Memorizing;* New York, Columbia University Press 1940

Kimble, D. (ed.): *The Anatomy of Memory;* Palo Alto, Calif., Science and Behavior Books 1965

Koestler, Arthur: *The Act of Creation;* New York, Macmillan 1964

Köhler, Wolfgang: *The Mentality of Apes;* New York, Harcourt Brace Jovanovich 1925

McKellar, Peter: *Imagination and Thinking;* London, Cohen & West 1957

MacKinnon, Donald W. (ed.): *The Creative Person;* Berkeley, Calif., University of California General Extension 1962

*Mednick, Sarnoff A.: *Learning;* Englewood Cliffs, N. J., Prentice-Hall 1964

Miller, George A.: "The Magical Number Seven, Plus or Minus Two: Some Limits on Our Capacity for Processing Information"; *Psychological Review, 60* (1956), 81–97

——, Eugene Galanter and Karl H. Pribram: *Plans and the Structure of Behavior;* New York, Holt, Rinehart & Winston 1960

Pavlov, Ivan P.: *Conditioned Reflexes;* New York, Oxford University Press 1927

Rokeach, Milton: *The Open and Closed Mind;* New York, Basic Books 1960

Scheerer, Martin: "Problem Solving"; *Scientific American,* April 1963

Schulman, Lee and E. Keislar (eds.): *Learning By Discovery;* Skokie, Ill., Rand McNally 1966

Skinner, B. F.: *The Behavior of Organisms;* New York, Appleton-Century-Crofts 1938

Staats, Arthur W. and C. K. Staats: *Complex Human Behavior;* New York, Holt, Rinehart & Winston 1963

Tolman, Edward C.: *Purposive Behavior in Animals and Men;* New York, Appleton-Century-Crofts 1932

Underwood, Benton J.: "Forgetting"; *Scientific American,* March 1964

Voss, J. F.: *Approaches to Thought;* Columbus, Ohio, Charles E. Merrill 1969

Wallach, Michael and N. Kogan: *Modes of Thinking in Young Children;* New York, Holt, Rinehart & Winston 1965

* Paperback edition available.

Current, by Bridget Riley, 1964. Collection, The Museum of Modern Art, New York. Philip Johnson Fund.

PART V

PERCEPTION

AND ITS VICISSITUDES

Most of us most of the time probably take our perceptions for granted and assume that they provide us with a "true" and accurate representation of the "real" world—accurate enough, at any rate, for our purposes. We are able to sustain this belief because we base predictions or expectations on our perceptions and when those expectations are confirmed (as they often are) we conclude that the original perceptions were true. In other words, much of the time the action we take predicated on our perceptions "works," that is, it is reasonably effective in dealing with the problems posed by the external environment and in attaining at least some of our goals. When our action is ineffective more often than is usual in our experience or when it brings untoward or unwanted consequences then, but only then, we may begin to doubt the "truth" of our perceptions (other results are, of course, possible, such as the development of paranoid delusions). The ultimate test of perception's adequacy is thus always a pragmatic one: Is action based upon it effective? When action is not possible or would be inappropriate it may be impossible and perhaps irrelevant to establish the "truth" of the perceptions.

More generally, however, the fundamental problem of perception is: How does information from the organism's external environment (assuming that environment has an independent existence apart from the organism) become part of the same organism's phenomenological field or subjective consciousness? In simple language, how does information or representations regarding what is outside the organism get inside? And with what effects?

Debate over this question has continued ever since the philosophical argument between the "nativists" (René Descartes (1595–1650), Gottfried von Leibniz (1646–1716) and, later, Immanuel Kant (1724–1804)), who believed that the categories of perception, as of thought itself, were innate and thus biologically given, and the "empiricists" (John Locke (1632–1704) and, later, George Berkeley (1685–1753)) who believed that man's mind at birth was a *tabula rasa* (blank slate) and that he learned to perceive through the sensory experience of objects in his environment. Put another way, the issue is whether a normally functioning set of sensory receptors is a necessary but not a sufficient condition of perception or whether it is both a necessary and sufficient condition.

Stating this issue in terms of such a dichotomy, with its inevitable implication that "either" one position "or" the other is true is both unnecessary and unfruitful. Modern research suggests that perception is neither wholly innate nor wholly learned, that, in James Gibson's words, "we do not learn to have percepts but to differentiate them." The perception of space, color, depth, and even of some forms (e.g., a face) seems to be largely innate but the ability to discriminate particular objects or features of the sensory environment and to infuse them with "meaning" are largely learned through experience, of which language is a major component. Recent research further suggests that the relative roles in perception of what is innate and what is learned may vary both from one sensory modality to another and with the complexity of the stimulus object.

All this implies that most complex perception is a process that requires the active collaboration of the organism; what is perceived, especially in modern industrial societies, is rarely determined solely by the physiological stimuli coming from external objects. Perception in all sense modalities is selective and is influenced by the physiological state of the subject, by his goals and motives, his values and interests, his hopes and fears, and his previous experience. Selectivity of perception is what we mean by "attention": the tendency of an individual to focus on particular items of the varied information reaching him from his sensory environment. It is attention (or its lack) that differentiates "seeing" (a relatively passive process) from "observing" (a far more active one) or "hearing" from "listening." What a person is aware of perceiving depends very largely on what he wants and expects to perceive and on a schematizing tendency whereby individuals assimilate most new or ambiguous sensory experience to that which is already familiar.

Over and above those perceptions that reach us through the standard five senses stands the still controversial phenomenon of extrasensory perception (ESP). Extrasensory perception may be defined as accurate information regarding the external environment that is present to the mind without the mediation of one or more of the usual five senses. While a number of psychologists and parapsychologists (students of ESP) believe that the validity of ESP has for some time been scientifically established many others deny this, some of them, perhaps, because to admit it would necessitate rethinking the entire nature of perception and even the basic paradigm of psychology itself. The absence from this book of a selection dealing with ESP does not denote our agreement with those who reject its validity but rather represents our belief that the issues and problems involved in normal sense perception are far more significant and urgent than the controversy over ESP.

Thus far we have spoken of perception as though it related only to the world of physical objects and their properties. Scientific study of perception began with the phenomenon of vision and, considering the dominant visual character of modern industrial civilization, it is not surprising that visual perception has received the most detailed and comprehensive attention, with hearing a rather poor second. Texture and the sense of touch, except in the case of those temporarily or permanently blind, has been studied little, taste and smell even less, the latter largely by deodorant manufacturers bent on reducing the olfactory world to a pine-scented antiseptic blandness.

Yet, perhaps the most important kind of perception for most people and surely the most problematic is "social" or "person" perception, the perception of other people—their appearance, attitudes, intentions, and actions. This kind of perception begins at or shortly after birth as the infant relates to his mother or to whomever cares for him and attends to his needs. It is in the perception of persons and their actions that learning probably plays the greatest role, that distortion through internal needs, external pressures, or prior experience is most prevalent and most difficult to eliminate, and in which actions or "occurrences" are subject to the widest range of differing interpretations. It is in the realm of social life that misperception presents the greatest danger, for example, the tendency to confuse a person's or even a nation's capabilities with its intentions or the tendency to act on the basis of misperceptions and thus to make the latter come "true"—so-called "self-fulfilling" prophecies. In the realm of social life it is preeminently true that the consequences of perceptions are far more important than their truth. In the words of the American sociologist W. I. Thomas (1863–1947): "If men define situations as real they are real in their consequences." We will return to the problems of social perception and misperception in both Parts VI and XIII.

In the initial selection of this group William Ittelson develops the idea that perception is a prediction tested by action. For him, every perception is an "involuntary bet" based on expectations developed through previous experience with similar situations. The only way to know whether one's bet is "right" is to act on it. People who make different bets because of different past experiences or differing needs and goals (as often happens in ambiguous situations) follow different courses of action and may, in consequence, live, literally, in different worlds. While Ittelson develops this theme with reference to the visual perception of objects and to experimentally induced visual illusions the analysis seems equally applicable to the perception of people and to sense modalities other than the visual. Note too the author's discussion of the instructive role of "wrong" bets in inducing learning and growth.

In the next selection Sanford Freedman, studying the effects of perceptual deprivation on humans, emphasizes the active, striving quality of all perception. The individual strives continuously to find ordered relationships and dependable schemata in his perceptual environment; when deprived of the sensory inputs necessary to the construction and maintenance of such schemata his perception becomes distorted and disoriented. Freedman's emphasis on the learned character of spatial schemata and the reality testing function of perception places his views regarding visual perception close to those of Ittelson. Once again, we see the importance of sensory stimulation from the environment to the maintenance of "normal" and effective psychological functioning (compare Hebb in Selection 7). Yet, one wonders whether sensory deprivation as such is the entire story.

With Daniel Katz and Kenneth Braly's classic research, conducted in the early 1930s but equally timely today, we confront the realm of social or person perception. Katz and Braley's findings show how the schematized and partial perceptions (or misperceptions) represented by culturally supported verbal stereotypes (or "learned meanings") shape the attitudes, feelings, and judgments of many people toward whole racial and ethnic groups. Such stereotypes, far from being the product of personal experience or firsthand learning, tend rather to be absorbed unquestioningly from one's social milieu and, once accepted, influence or even determine personal experience. A stereotyped response to a group (or to the word that stands for it) means that one reacts to members of that group not as individuals but as examples of a class or even as symbols; one judges them first and observes them later, if at all. The authors find that the truth or the clarity of the stereotype has little effect on the overall level of expressed prejudice. The ability of language to constrain perception and evoke emotion is more than a little frightening and is certainly not confined to the realm of racial and ethnic relationships. Those who believe that education is the best answer to this kind of prejudice will not be comforted by the knowledge that the subjects for this study were students at one of America's leading universities. We do not, however, know the degree to which the prejudice expressed in response to such questionnaires is translated into overt behavior when the prejudiced individual confronts situations demanding or permitting action.

Albert Hastorf and Hadley Cantril's study of what Princeton and Dartmouth students "saw" as their teams met on the football field one November afternoon highlights, in relation to a quite ordinary experience, how individuals perceive the "same" physical stimuli according to the interests, goals, and emotions they bring to the occasion of perception. Obviously, the two groups of students "saw" a quite different game—or did they? For Hastorf and Cantril an "occurrence" or objective physical stimulus does not become a phenomenological "event" unless it has significance for the person in the situation. We do not, in other words, simply respond to what is "out there," even when that is far less ambiguous than the complex action of a football game.

To end this section, British psychologist Harry Asher provides a witty and perceptive, if somewhat terrifying account of how taking the psychedelic drug LSD (lysergic acid diethylamide) affected his perception of space, time, other people, and himself. We have selected this account not because it is typical of reported experiences under LSD (in fact, most observers who have written accounts of their "trips" have found them far more pleasant and illuminating than did Asher) or because we wish to frighten readers but because it details so vividly many of the drug's effects on perception, effects some of which are remarkably similar to those reported by persons, such as Freedman's experimental group, subjected to extreme sensory deprivation. That similarity remains to be satisfactorily explained. In Part XII we will examine other aspects of the physiology and psychology of psychedelic drugs.

20. THE INVOLUNTARY BET

William H. Ittelson

How and why do we see the people and things around us? Trying to answer this question—technically called the study of perception—may seem at first glance to be a trivial task. But understanding this simple fact, perhaps just because it is one of the most universal and basic of human experiences, is by no means simple. Ask yourself, for example, why the chair across the room looks the way it does. And does it look the same to someone else? If not, how can either of you know what it really is like? Or how can you ever come to any sort of agreement or decision about the chair? It is just such questions as these that psychologists studying perception are trying to answer. And while they may seem trivial when asked about a chair, their importance is obvious if we ask them of more complicated perceptions, such as those of the men about a conference table in the United Nations.

Of all the work being done in the study of perception today, beyond any doubt the most fascinating is that of a scientist in Hanover, New Hampshire, Adelbert Ames, Jr. who is today actively collaborating with some of the members of the psychology department at Princeton University in designing new experiments and extending our understanding of this important no-man's-land, the psychology of perception. In commenting on Ames's work, Dr. Allan Gregg, vice-president of the Rockefeller Foundation, has said, as quoted in a recent book, *The Rockefeller Foundation,* by R. B. Fosdick, "I think Ames will be rediscovered in future years as often as anyone the Medical Sciences Division has aided."

Ames believes that his experiments, four of

which are described on these pages, show that every perception we have, even of the chair across the room, is essentially an "involuntary bet." These bets are based on the probabilities each of us has learned through previous experiences with similar situations. To the extent that several people have had similar experiences, they will tend to make the same bets, to see the same things. If they have had different experiences, they will tend to see things differently. And since every perception is basically a bet, it can, like any bet, be wrong on occasion. The only way we can tell if any particular perception, any one bet, is right or wrong is by acting on it. If we are successful, the bet was "right." If we fail, it was "wrong."

1. *The Three Chairs* experiment, from the outside, looks like a big, black box, about the size of two large office desks placed one on top of the other. Along one side of this box are three small peepholes through which one can look into the interior of the box. Looking through each of these peepholes, the observer sees what appears to be the same chair, dimly illuminated inside the completely dark box. The chair seems to be made of heavy wires, but otherwise it looks like an ordinary, solid, well-built chair. The seat is flat, the legs and back are straight, and it sits squarely on the floor. After the observer has noted this through each of the peepholes, he walks to the back of the box, which is open so that he can see what is really inside. To his amazement, he discovers that only one of these objects actually is a wire chair. The other two resemble nothing more than weird wire cobwebs. In each case, what the observer sees does not correspond to what is really there. The three-dimensional "chairness" which he experiences does not exist in the physical objects at which he is looking. After finding out what is actually in the box, the observer can go back and look

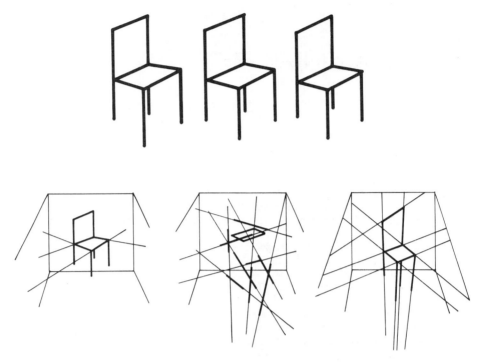

FIGURE 1. Experiment 1: Upper—Chairs as they appeared to the viewer. Lower—As they actually were made.

through the peepholes again. *He still sees the same solid wire chairs* [Figure 1].

2. *The Leaf Room* experiment, as its name suggests, consists of a small room, the inside of which is completely covered with leaves. An observer looks into this room carefully, is allowed to examine it and even to walk in it. He then looks at it while wearing a specially designed pair of aniseikonic glasses which have the peculiar property of altering some of the visual indications he is receiving while not affecting others. Now the room assumes weird and fantastic shapes. The leaves and walls change size and shape and appear to move mysteriously under their own power. The observer becomes confused, bewildered. When asked to walk into the room, he may become terrorized and remain frozen to his seat. Even if he does enter the room, he does so hesitatingly. He can not walk steadily. He is unable to touch objects when he reaches for them. He can not very well describe the room because it seems always to be changing.

For most people this experience is quite disturbing and even frightening. It is frequently described as a "nightmare." Sometimes, if the observer looks at an ordinary, familiar room,

instead of the "leaf room," the glasses have little or no effect, and the experience is not at all disturbing. Occasionally, an observer seems to enjoy wearing the glasses even in the "leaf room," but this reaction is most often seen in children. For children, wearing the glasses is better than a party. They laugh and squeal as they go through experiences which terrify many adults. They not only do not mind, but they seem actually to delight in having their own world turned topsy-turvy.

It is interesting that in this demonstration, as in everyday life, no matter how confusing the situation may be, no matter how extreme the conflicts, most people manage to make some decision, to arrive at what seems to be the "best bet" under the circumstances [Figure 2].

3. *The Distorted Room* is a model, about the size of a large packing case, of a crazily built room. The floor slopes down, the ceiling slopes up, the back wall slopes away. All the walls are different sizes and shapes. But this peculiar room has one important property—from one *point of view* it looks like an ordinary rectangular room. The observer is shown the room in detail before he looks at it from

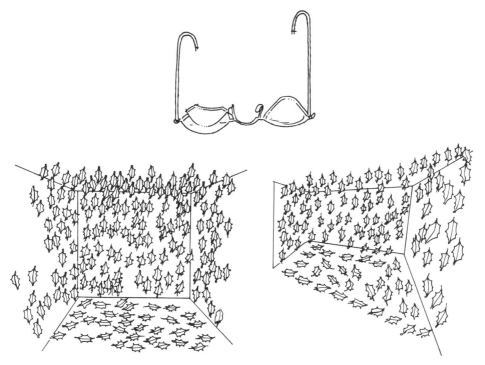

FIGURE 2. Experiment 2: Leaf room (left) distorted by glasses into nightmare (right).

the viewing position. He examines its construction, shape, and size carefully until he becomes quite familiar with it. No attempt is made to fool him, on the contrary, every effort is made to have him learn all that he can about the room. When the observer is satisfied that he knows the room thoroughly, he sits at the viewing point. The room now appears to be perfectly rectangular while familiar objects, such as a pair of hands, appear distorted. He experiences a conflict between what he sees and what he knows, accompanied by a sense of confusion and uncertainty. Now the observer is given a pointer and told to hit a spot on one of the side walls as if he were swatting a fly. He confidently swings but misses, wildly smashing the pointer into the back wall [Figure 3].

FIGURE 3. Experiment 3: Distorted room (left); the illusion of normalcy (right).

No matter how much a person knows about the true shape of the room, when asked to do something in it, he acts, not on what he *knows,* but rather on what he *sees.* It would seem, therefore, that the bets we make, which determine what we see, are really guesses as to the probable results of acting in the particular situation. We can check our perceptions, find out if our bets are right or wrong, only through action.

In life's constant sequence of checking by acting, the role of failure, of unsuccessful action, is as important as that of success. Success can only confirm what we already know, while failure points out our inadequacies and opens up opportunities for change and development toward greater adequacy. The overprotected child is a familiar example of a person denied this opportunity by never being allowed to experience the consequences of his own actions.

The way a person reacts to a failure is an indication of that person's potentialities for development and growth. In the distorted room, for example, initial failure in "swatting the fly" quickly makes the observer much more able to act in the room than he ever would have been if he just sat and looked at it. But different people react quite differently. Most observers keep on trying after the first failure, some with grim determination, some with nervous embarrassment, and a few with real, wholehearted enjoyment. At the other extreme are those who refuse to try again at all. A few observers have been known to throw the pointer down and stalk from the experimental room in a fury.

4. *The Rotating Trapezoid* consists of a trapezoidal piece of sheet metal or cardboard, with holes cut in it and shadows painted on it to give the appearance of a window. It is mounted on a rod connected to a motor which rotates it continuously about a vertical axis. When an observer views this device, however, he does not see a rotating trapezoid, but instead an oscillating rectangular window, swinging back and forth through an arc of about 100 degrees. A particularly interesting effect can be seen if a solid tube is inserted in the window through one of the openings. Part of the time the tube and the window appear to be swinging in opposite directions so that at one point they seem to hit head on. Different observers see different things when this happens. Some see the tube remain absolutely rigid and appear to cut its way through the window frame. To others, the tube seems to be flexible, so that it appears to stretch out and bend around the window. Here is an important laboratory proof that when different people make different "bets" about the same situation they experience that situation differently. *They literally live in different worlds* [Figure 4].

In one especially interesting experiment using the rotating trapezoid, observers were shown and allowed to feel a steel tube and told that it would be put in the window. They were later shown and handed a rubber tube and told the same thing. Actually a third, wood tube was placed in the window both

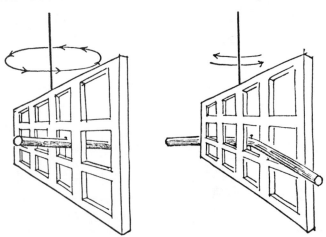

FIGURE 4. Experiment 4: Actually a revolving object: the illusion (right) and oscillating object.

times. Most observers, however, saw the "steel" tube remain rigid and cut through the window while they saw the "rubber" tube stretch and bend around. Since they had had very little experience in situations like this, the bets they made were quite tentative and easily changed by suggestion or "propaganda."

Such bets are essentially predictions of the results of future actions, based on the probabilities learned from acting in the past. This means that people can pick out of a welter of conflicting possibilities those actions that have the highest probability of being successful. And when we recognize that people never act in a vacuum, that they always act for some purpose of greater or lesser value to them, we can see that the study of perception may eventually help increase our understanding of basic human values.

21. PERCEPTUAL CHANGES IN SENSORY DEPRIVATION: SUGGESTIONS FOR A CONATIVE THEORY*

Sanford J. Freedman

Since the original work of Dr. Hebb and his students on the sensory and social isolation of human beings, a number of studies have been reported under the rubric of "sensory deprivation." These experiments have involved restriction or occlusion of visual, auditory, and kinesthetic inputs. Usually, the subject lies on a bed in a cubicle or a small room (or even in a respirator) wearing translucent goggles to produce a diffuse visual field and with earphones or some other device to supply a continuous masking noise. Cardboard cuffs on the forearms and heavy cotton gloves are worn to reduce tactile stimulation. He is instructed to move little or not at all, and remains in this situation without interpersonal contact for hours or days. The most striking finding in these reports taken as a whole is that radical changes in functioning occur under what appear to be relatively innocuous conditions. A few of the published reports concentrate upon perceptual changes, but most restrict themselves to changes in cognitive functions, namely: hallucinations, delusions, depersonalization, or changes in the body image.

For the purposes of this symposium, I should like to separate the two kinds of effects, discussing perceptual disturbances only. It is not possible to make any statement about the nature or occurrence of such disturbances in experiments where no perceptual tests were made although I think it *is* generally assumed that they are to some extent common to almost any kind of sensory deprivation.

It will be helpful briefly to review the findings of several experimenters who have described in detail and attempted to measure visual disturbance. At McGill, Doane isolated 13 subjects for from two to five days, and shortly thereafter Heron, Doane, and Scott

* This research was supported in part by the U. S. Air Force under Contract No. AF33(616)5663 monitored by Aerospace Medical Laboratory, Wright-Patterson Air Force Base, Ohio.

isolated each other for periods of six days each. Immediately following the experiment, a variety of remarkable disturbances was described. Although these were largely dissipated in about 20 minutes, some effects persisted for over 24 hours. There was apparent movement independent of movement by the observer; people and the room itself seemed to change shape and size, with walls bulging forward and back. An ash tray or a watch appeared to expand or contract. There were distortions of shape with a tendency for straight edges or lines to appear curved and for the region about the fixation point of flat surfaces to appear to bulge outwards. Pronounced negative afterimages appeared and colors seemed bright, highly saturated or luminescent. Black figures on a white ground gave rise to subjective colors. Finally, there were consistent changes in size constancy.

In our laboratory, under similar isolation conditions for uninterrupted sessions of only eight hours, 20 subjects reported many comparable (though, of course, less extensive) effects. These persisted, on the average, about five minutes: there was shimmering, instability, undulation, and fluctuation of contours in the visual field with apparent changes in the size and shape of simple forms. Shapes seemed to flow in a direction away from the fixation point. Ambiguous figures alternated more rapidly and the apparent speed of a moving contour decreased markedly. Most of these effects have recently been replicated by Courtney at the Boston City Hospital, also in short sessions.

Now, what is going on in these experiments; how can we explain such effects? There seems to be a partial breakdown of the customary process of stabilizing, structuring and organizing the visual world. The normal adult organism structures his perceptual world in accord with an overall spatial schema depending upon basic coordinates such as up-down and self-other. Transactions with the environment require adequate localization and stabilization of self and objects in the spatial schema. It would seem that in sensory deprivation, this schema has somehow become disorganized, degraded, or to use Werner's word "de-differentiated." The terms "schema" and "spatial schema" are here employed in a specific sense directly analogous to the body-schema concept of Henry Head and the English school of neurology. Head defined the body-schema as an integrate of all sensations, perceptions, memories and images continuously being built up and altered by new activity and new stimulation and also being used continually for reference in locating any new sensation and in correctly initiating any new movement. The spatial schema is a very similar integrate, a dynamic psychic structure. Neurologists have found it more and more necessary to link the schema of the body to a schema of the world of external objects.

Since bodily and spatial schemata are so intimately related, alteration of one may produce changes in the other and perhaps any subdivision is arbitrary. The conditions of reported sensory deprivation experiments have drastically curtailed or modified cues for the maintenance of both schemata so that the effects are confounded. Feelings of depersonalization, specific changes in the body image, and paranoid fears which have been described may all be related to deterioration of the body schema. However, since we have found no significant correlation in 57 subjects between the occurrence of these kinds of effects and visual disturbance, it may be permissible to disregard the former temporarily. We would attribute the visual disturbances to deterioration or degradation of the spatial schema resulting from particular kinds of prolonged sensory stimulation whereas cognitive effects are probably more closely related to social isolation, inability to test reality, personality differences, and the total unstructured situation.

The overall spatial schema may be subdivided into lower-order schemata for vision, audition and kinesthesis which are normally well-integrated. Such schemata, as well as their integration, are not innate givens, but have to be slowly learned by the infant organism. Riesen has shown that interference with this ontogenetic development by subjecting newborn monkeys and kittens to deficient sensory environments for prolonged periods makes subsequent development of effective schemata difficult and perhaps impossible. Senden's review of the literature on the vision of the congenitally blind given sight by surgical operation leads to the same conclusion. These reports suggest that spatial orientation develops by repeated observation and testing of ordered relationships in the perceptual environment.

Spatial schemata are not only originally

learned, but may be modified by new learning. The classic disarrangement experiment of Stratton, the work of Köhler, and more recent studies by Held transform the visual environment of the subject by *systematically* shifting certain sets of cues. However, the new sensory field is isomorphic with the old one and, furthermore, auditory and kinesthetic subschemata are not directly impaired. In the normal relationship of an adult human to his environment, "up" is always "up" and "down" is always "down." If he should wear inverting prisms, "up" becomes "down" and "down" becomes "up." This reversal continues becoming the basis for learning a whole new spatial order. Other relationships in the field are relatively undisturbed. Objects which had previously been contiguous, for example, remain so and distances between familiar objects are not appreciably altered. The subject must modify his visual schema and re-integrate it with other schemata if he is in any way to function effectively with the new perceptual environment. He is also to do so by incorporating the new set of constant relationships which has been provided. Whether "up" is always "up" or is always "down" is relatively unimportant provided that the relationship be *continuous and predictable.*

In sensory deprivation, rather than a systematically transformed environment, the subject is presented with an undifferentiated, homogeneous sensory environment which provides no useful information for spatial orientation. It is unreasonable to think that simple forgetting of greatly overlearned schemata occurs in such a short time as eight hours or even a few days under these conditions. After all, a good night's sleep does not produce marked visual disturbance. No, the answer is not one of decay over time. We are forced to postulate an active process which interferes with and degrades pre-existing schemata. Since they are flexible and modifiable, and since appropriate schemata are biologically necessary, the organism must continuously (albeit unconsciously) sample his perceptual environment both for reaffirmation of existing schemata and for evidence of change. The process of sampling and of incorporating observed, ordered relationships into a personal perceptual schema is one of extracting useful information from the welter of "noisy" sensations with which the organism is constantly bombarded. This activity may be called

adaptation, accommodation, or reality-testing.

In sensory deprivation experiments, the extrinsic visual field is homogenous and, as noted above, an undifferentiated field provides no usable information for spatial orientation. In addition, intrinsic factors complicate the situation. After adaptation, spontaneous random firing of retinal ganglion cells would dominate the neuro-visual system. In the languages of communications theory, this is a "noisy" situation. Greenblatt and I have compared the effects of prolonged exposure to strong diffuse light with blackout conditions. Subjects experience visual disturbances in either situation despite apparently large differences in quality and quantity of stimulation. However, the two conditions may be considered as roughly equivalent for the visual nervous system since both are steady states to which there is rapid adaptation. The visual receptors respond predominantly to changes of state and not to steady states. Once adaptation to any homogeneous field has occurred; the system may come to be dominated by the spontaneous, non-patterned (i.e., "noisy" or random) discharge of the retinal ganglion cells. In fact, Granit and Kuffler have each reported that such spontaneous activity is greater in the dark-adapted than in the light-adapted eye (cats and frogs).

Held has postulated that noise is *per se* disorienting. Following up this notion, he and I recently conducted an experiment where extrinsic visual "noise" was supplied to the subject in sensory deprivation. The effects were compared with those of diffuse and blackout fields. Through translucent goggles, the subject viewed a rapidly changing visual field established by a set of incandescent lights of different intensities flashing on and off in random sequence and duration (maximum intensity 250W, maximum period on for any single light = 2 sec.). As predicted, this condition produced similar but far greater changes in apparent visual speed than did homogeneous stimulation.

The fact that perceptual disturbance occurs both with diffuse light and with blackout conditions as well as with flashing lights, indicates that it is the absence of order and/or meaning, the lack of usable information, that tends to degrade the spatial schemata. Riesen has reported several experiments, where dark-reared animals (chimpanzees and cats) were exposed to diffuse light daily. This stimulation did not lead to normal visual function; patterned vision seemed to be essential, as with the sensory deprivation experiments, in the building of appropriate schemata for spatial orientation. With an adult animal or human being, the schemata would be highly over-learned and, as noted above, it is not reasonable to think that they would decay or be forgotten in the absence of reinforcement over a short period of time. The explanation must be in terms of an active process in the waking state, a conative process. The organism strives or seeks continuously and automatically to find ordered relationships in the perceptual environment. When, in the experiment on sensory deprivation, the subject is presented with a disordered perceptual environment, his previously acquired spatial schema becomes useless. What is worse, it becomes impossible to modify the old schema or to develop a new one since he cannot extract from the stimulus field the amount of information required to maintain any spatial schema at all.

But, spatial orientation is vital to the organism. If it didn't make any difference, adaptation would never occur in the disarrangement experiments. Since spatial orientation is essential, striving for it continues automatically even when relevant cues are absent. The individual keeps sampling his environment and, finding only noise, tries to accommodate to the noise.

We would postulate that it is this process of seeking orderly relationships where there are none, and of unconsciously striving to incorporate non-order into previously existing schemata which degrades the perceptual frame of reference. The properly functioning organism imposes structure on a fluid environment according to a learned set of relationships which have proven dependable and useful. Such a structure is not necessarily the same for various forms of life but must be related to the needs of the organism and sufficiently congruent with important aspects of the external world to afford satisfaction of those needs. Perception is thus always selective and always testing the cues that are essential to the maintenance of various schemata. With the breakdown of the internalized frame of reference, it becomes increasingly more difficult to structure the environment, to impose constancies and stabilities on the perceived visual world. As a result, contours fluctuate, objects seem to change their size and shape, subjective colors appear, and walls bulge in and out. Renewed experience with a patterned environment is then required before normal visual function can be restored.

22. VERBAL STEREOTYPES
AND RACIAL PREJUDICE

Daniel Katz and Kenneth W. Braly

One outstanding result of investigations of racial prejudice is the uniformity in the patterns of discrimination against various races* shown by Americans throughout the United States. People in widely separated parts of the country show a high degree of agreement in their expressions of relative liking or disliking of different "foreign" groups.

In an early study Bogardus asked 110 businessmen and schoolteachers about the degrees of social intimacy to which they were willing to admit certain ethnic groups. The degrees of social distance employed were: to close kinship through marriage, to my club as personal chums, to my street as neighbors, to employment in my occupation, to citizenship in my country, to my country as visitors only, and exclusion from my country. By weighting these seven classifications Bogardus obtained the following preferential rating of 23 ethnic groups:

Canadians	22.51
English	22.35
Scotch	20.91
Irish	19.38
French	18.67
Swedes	16.20
Germans	14.95

Adapted by the authors from "Racial Stereotypes of 100 College Students," JOURNAL OF ABNORMAL AND SOCIAL PSYCHOLOGY, 28, 1933, 280–290, and "Radical Prejudice and Racial Stereotypes," Ibid., 30, 1935, 175–193, with permission of the American Psychological Association. Copyright 1933, 1935 by the American Psychological Association. Reprinted by permission of Daniel Katz.

* The term *race* is here used in the popular, not the scientific, sense, and covers reference to racial, religious, and national groupings.

Spanish	14.02
Italians	8.87
Indians	7.30
Poles	6.65
Russians	6.40
Armenians	6.16
German-Jews	5.45
Greeks	5.23
Russian-Jews	4.94
Mexicans	4.57
Chinese	4.12
Japanese	4.08
Negroes	3.84
Mulattoes	3.62
Hindus	3.08
Turks	2.91

The Bogardus study was carried out on the Pacific Coast but studies made in other parts of the United States indicate the same pattern of preferences for the various groups. In the Middle West, for example, Thurstone constructed a scale on the basis of the likes and dislikes of 239 students. The resulting rank order and scale values for 21 ethnic groups follow:

American	0.00
English	−1.34
Scotch	−2.09
Irish	−2.18
French	−2.46
German	−2.55
Swede	−2.90
South American	−3.64
Italian	−3.66
Spanish	−3.79
Jew	−3.92
Russian	−4.10
Pole	−4.41
Greek	−4.62
Armenian	−4.68

Japanese .... −4.93
Mexican .... −5.10
Chinese .... −5.30
Hindu .... −5.35
Turk .... −5.82
Negro .... −5.86

How is the agreement about "foreign" groups to be interpreted? The first possibility is that the foreign groups possess varying degrees of undesirable qualities upon which most Americans base their preferential ratings. But it is obvious that there are wide individual differences within any nationality group—that is, not all Englishmen are alike, nor are all Frenchmen, nor are all Russians. It is also obvious that few Americans have had much opportunity to know a large number of people from the many nationalities they dislike. It is also highly probable that if we were basing our judgments wholly upon what we know from actual contact with individual Spaniards, we would have differing impressions of what Spaniards are really like, because we would not all have met the same type of Spaniard. Hence a more valid interpretation of the agreement of Americans about foreign groups is that it represents the prejudgments or pre-judices, absorbed from the stereotypes of our culture.

Thus the preferential disliking reported by Bogardus and Thurstone may reflect attitudes toward race names and may not arise from animosity toward the specific qualities inherent in the real human beings bearing a given racial label. We have learned responses of varying degrees of aversion or acceptance to racial names and where these tags can be readily applied to individuals, as they can in the case of the Negro because of his skin color, we respond to him not as a human being but as a personification of the symbol we have learned to look down upon. Walter Lippmann has called this type of belief a stereotype—by which is meant a fixed impression which conforms very little to the facts it pretends to represent and results from our defining first and observing second.

THE PRESENT STUDY*

To explore the nature of racial and national stereotypes more fully, the following procedures were employed:

(1) Twenty-five students were asked to list

* This study was made in 1932.

as many specific characteristics or traits as were thought typical of the following ten groups: Germans, Italians, Irish, English, Negroes, Jews, Americans, Chinese, Japanese, Turks. No traits were suggested to the students. This list was then supplemented by characteristics commonly reported in the literature. The result was a final check-list of 84 descriptive adjectives.

(2) One hundred Princeton undergraduates were then asked to select the traits from this prepared list of 84 adjectives to characterize the ten racial and national groups. Specific directions used in the experiment follow in part:

> Read through the list of words on page one and select those which seem to you to be typical of the Germans. Write as many of these words in the following spaces as you think are necessary to characterize these people adequately. If you do not find proper words on page one for all the typical German characteristics, you may add those which you think necessary for an adequate description.

This procedure was then repeated for other national and racial groups. When the student had finished this he was asked to go back over the ten lists of words which he had chosen and to mark the five words of each list which seemed most typical of the group in question.

(3) Another group of students was asked to rate the list of adjectives on the basis of the desirability of these traits in friends and associates. The students making this judgment had no knowledge that the characteristics were supposed to describe racial groups. The traits or adjectives were rated from 1 to 10 on the basis of their desirability.

(4) Still another group of students was asked to put in rank order the ten racial and national groups on the basis of preference for association with their members. The group which the subject most preferred to associate with was placed first and the group with which he preferred to associate least was placed tenth or last.

RESULTS

STEREOTYPED CONCEPTIONS OF TEN ETHNIC GROUPS

Table 1 presents the twelve characteristics most frequently assigned to the ten races by the 100 students. This table summarizes the

TABLE 1

The Twelve Traits Frequently Assigned to Each of Various Racial
and National Groups by 100 Princeton Students

TRAITS CHECKED, RANK ORDER	NO.	PER-CENT	TRAITS CHECKED, RANK ORDER	NO.	PER-CENT
GERMANS			Progressive	27	27
Scientifically-minded	78	78	Pleasure-loving	26	26
Industrious	65	65	Alert	23	23
Stolid	44	44	Efficient	20	20
Intelligent	32	32	Aggressive	20	20
Methodical	31	31	Straightforward	19	19
Extremely nationalistic	24	24	Practical	19	19
Progressive	16	16	Sportsmanlike	19	19
Efficient	16	16	**NEGROES**		
Jovial	15	15	Superstitious	84	84
Musical	13	13	Lazy	75	75
Persistent	11	11	Happy-go-lucky	38	38
Practical	11	11	Ignorant	38	38
ITALIANS			Musical	26	26
Artistic	53	53	Ostentatious	26	26
Impulsive	44	44	Very religious	24	24
Passionate	37	37	Stupid	22	22
Quick-tempered	35	35	Physically dirty	17	17
Musical	32	32	Naïve	14	14
Imaginative	30	30	Slovenly	13	13
Very religious	21	21	Unreliable	12	12
Talkative	21	21	**IRISH**		
Revengeful	17	17	Pugnacious	45	45
Physically dirty	13	13	Quick-tempered	39	39
Lazy	12	12	Witty	38	38
Unreliable	11	11	Honest	32	32
ENGLISH			Very religious	29	29
Sportsmanlike	53	53	Industrious	21	21
Intelligent	46	46	Extremely nationalistic	21	21
Conventional	34	34	Superstitious	18	18
Tradition-loving	31	31	Quarrelsome	14	14
Conservative	30	30	Imaginative	13	13
Reserved	29	29	Aggressive	13	13
Sophisticated	27	27	Stubborn	13	13
Courteous	21	21	**CHINESE**		
Honest	20	20	Superstitious	34	35
Industrious	18	18	Sly	29	30
Extremely nationalistic	18	18	Conservative	29	30
Humorless	17	17	Tradition-loving	26	27
JEWS			Loyal to family ties	22	23
Shrewd	79	79	Industrious	18	19
Mercenary	49	49	Meditative	18	19
Industrious	48	48	Reserved	17	17
Grasping	34	34	Very religious	15	15
Intelligent	29	29	Ignorant	15	15
Ambitious	21	21	Deceitful	14	14
Sly	20	20	Quiet	13	13
Loyal to family ties	15	15	**JAPANESE**		
Persistent	13	13	Intelligent	45	48
Talkative	13	13	Industrious	43	46
Aggressive	12	12	Progressive	24	25
Very religious	12	12	Shrewd	22	23
AMERICANS			Sly	20	21
Industrious	48	48	Quiet	19	20
Intelligent	47	47	Imitative	17	18
Materialistic	33	33	Alert	16	17
Ambitious	33	33	Suave	16	17

TABLE 1

(*Continued*)

TRAITS CHECKED, RANK ORDER	NO.	PER-CENT	TRAITS CHECKED, RANK ORDER	NO.	PER-CENT
JAPANESE (Cont.)			Sensual	20	23
Neat	16	17	Ignorant	15	17
Treacherous	13	14	Physically dirty	15	17
Aggressive	13	14	Deceitful	13	15
			Sly	12	14
TURKS			Quarrelsome	12	14
Cruel	47	54	Revengeful	12	14
Very religious	26	30	Conservative	12	14
Treacherous	21	24	Superstitious	11	13

traits which students rechecked as the five most typical characteristics of each race.

The traits most frequently assigned to the Germans seem consistent with the popular stereotype to be found in newspapers and magazines. Their science, industry, ponderous and methodical manner, and intelligence were pointed out by over one fourth of the students. Scientifically-minded was the most frequently assigned characteristic, as many as 78 percent of the group ascribing this trait to the Germans.

Italians received the common characterization of the hot-blooded Latin peoples: artistic, impulsive, quick-tempered, passionate, musical, and imaginative. The greatest agreement was shown on the artistic qualities of the Italians with 53 percent of the students concurring in this belief.

The characteristics ascribed to the Negroes are somewhat similar to the picture of the Negro as furnished by the *Saturday Evening Post:* highly superstitious, lazy, happy-go-lucky, ignorant, musical, and ostentatious. The greatest degree of agreement for a single trait for any racial group was reached when 84 percent of the students voted the Negroes superstitious. Laziness was given as a typical characteristic by three fourths of the students, but the other traits mentioned above had much lower frequencies of endorsement. It may be noted in passing that for a northern college, Princeton draws heavily upon the South for her enrollment so that this characterization of Negroes is not exclusively a Northern description.

In the case of the Irish no single trait of the 84 presented could be agreed upon as a typical Irish characteristic by half the stu-

dents. Forty-five percent, however, thought pugnacity typical and 39 percent agreed upon quick-tempered. Witty, honest, very religious, industrious, and extremely nationalistic were the other adjectives selected by a fifth or more of the students.

The characterization of the English savors more of the English "gentleman" than of the general stereotype of John Bull. The leading characteristic is sportsmanship with an endorsement from 53 percent of the students. Forty-six percent of the students favored intelligence as typical of the English, 34 percent conventionality, 31 percent love of traditions, and 30 percent conservatism. Other adjectives were reserved, sophisticated, courteous, and honest.

The qualities of the competitive business world are used to describe the Jews. They are pictured as shrewd, mercenary, industrious, grasping, ambitious, and sly. Fifteen percent of the students did include Jewish loyalty to family ties. The greatest agreement (79 percent) was shown for shrewdness.

The traits ascribed to Americans show a certain objectivity on the part of the students in describing themselves, for the description given is not greatly at variance with the stereotype held by non-Americans. Americans are described as industrious, intelligent, materialistic, ambitious, progressive, and pleasure-loving. As in the case of the Irish the degree of agreement on these traits is relatively low. Almost one half did assign industry and intelligence to Americans, and a third gave materialistic and ambitious as the most descriptive adjectives.

Apparently the general stereotype for the Chinese among eastern college students is fairly indefinite, for the agreement on typical Chinese characteristics is not great. Three of the 100 students could give no characteristics for the Chinese. Of the 97 who did respond 35 percent thought the Chinese superstitious, 30 percent thought them sly, 30 percent regarded them as conservative. The next most frequently ascribed traits were love of tradition, loyalty to family ties, industry, and meditation.

The picture of the Japanese seems more clear-cut with some recognition of the westernization of Japan. Emphasis was placed upon intelligence, industry, progressiveness, shrewdness, slyness, and quietness. The Japanese are the only group in which intelligence leads the list as the most frequently assigned characteristic. Forty-eight percent of the students filling in this part of the questionnaire gave intelligence as a typical Japanese trait.

Thirteen students could select no characteristics for the Turks. Fifty-four percent of those responding gave cruelty. Other traits selected described the Turks as very religious, treacherous, sensual, ignorant, physically dirty, deceitful, and sly.

PREFERENTIAL RANKING OF THE TEN GROUPS

The adjectives used to describe the ten groups are a rough index of the esteem in which they are held. More precise measure were furnished (1) by the direct ranking of the ten racial and national names in order of preference (Table 2), and (2) by the desirability of the typical traits attributed to the ten groups (Table 3).

TABLE 2

Average Rank Order of Ten Racial Groups: Preferential Ranking

NATIONALITY	AVERAGE RANK ORDER
Americans	1.15
English	2.27
Germans	3.42
Irish	3.87
Italians	5.64
Japanese	5.78
Jews	7.10
Chinese	7.94
Turks	8.52
Negroes	9.35

TABLE 3

The Ranking of Ten Races on the Basis of the Rating of Their Alleged Typical Traits by 65 Students

NATIONALITY	AVERAGE VALUE OF ASSIGNED TRAITS
Americans	6.77
English	6.26
Germans	6.02
Japanese	5.89
Irish	5.42
Jews	4.96
Chinese	4.52
Italians	4.40
Negroes	3.55
Turks	3.05

The scores in Table 3 are the average total value of the traits assigned to the various races, computed as follows: For every race the average rating of a trait was multiplied by the number of times it was assigned to that race. The ratings of all the traits assigned to one race were added and divided by the total number of assignments of traits to that race. This division would have been unnecessary if all the 100 students in the original group assigning traits had assigned five traits to every race. In some cases, however, a student made less than five assignments.

When we compare the ranking of the ten groups on the basis of preference for association with their members with their standing based on the desirability of traits attributed to them, we find a few changes in relative placement. The Italians drop from fifth to eighth place; the Irish drop two places, while the Japanese move up two places; and the Jews, Chinese, and Negroes move up one place. In other words, the Italians are regarded more highly and the Japanese are held in lower esteem than the qualities imputed to them would justify.

It also is true that the ethnic groups are bunched much more closely together on the scores based on assigned traits than on the preference ranking. The preference ranking accorded to Americans is five times as desirable as that accorded to the Japanese, but the difference in rating Americans and Japanese on the basis of imputed characteristics is nowhere nearly as great. In part this is an artifact of our method, but in part it is due to the fact that prejudice exceeds the rationalization of undesirable racial characteristics. Nonetheless there is marked similarity between the relative ranking on the basis of preference for group names and the average scores representing an evaluation of typical traits.

Thus racial prejudice is part of a general set of stereotypes of a high degree of consistency and is more than a single specific reaction to a race name. The student is prejudiced against the label Negro because to him it means a superstitious, ignorant, shiftless person of low social status. The whole attitude is more than a simple conditioned response to the race name: it is a pattern of rationalizations organized around the racial label.

This does not mean that the rationalized complex is justified by objective reality— that is, that Negroes really are the type of people described by the stereotype. In fact the clearness or vagueness of the stereotyped conception bears little relation to the degree of prejudice expressed against a group as determined by its preferential ranking.

RELATIVE CLEARNESS AND CONSISTENCY OF PATTERN OF STEREOTYPES

Table 4 shows the clearness of the stereotypes about the ten groups in terms of the degree of agreement in assigning typical characteristics to them.

Table 4 lists the least number of traits which have to be included to find 50 percent of the 500 possible votes cast by the 100 students in the case of every racial and national group. It will be remembered that each student was allowed to select 5 of the 84 traits presented and that there were 100 students. If there were perfect agreement, 2.5 traits would have received 50 percent of the votes. Perfect disagreement or chance would mean that 42 traits would be necessary to give half of the votes. Table 4 shows that in the case of Negroes we can find 50 percent of the votes or selections of traits in 4.6

TABLE 4

The Least Number of Traits Which Must be Taken to Include 50 Percent of the Possible Assignments for Each Race

RACES, RANK ORDER	NUMBER OF TRAITS REQUIRED
Negroes	4.6
Germans	5.0
Jews	5.5
Italians	6.9
English	7.0
Irish	8.5
Americans	8.8
Japanese	10.9
Chinese	12.0
Turks	15.9

traits. The agreement here is very high and even in the case of the Turks where 15.9 traits must be included to give 50 percent of the possible 500 assignments or selections the voting is far from a chance selection.

Thus in Table 4 we have a comparison of the definiteness of the ten racial stereotypes. The most definite picture is that of the Negroes. The Germans and the Jews also give consistent patterns of response, while the Chinese, Japanese, and Turks furnish the least clear cut stereotypes.

Though the belief in the undesirable qualities of a national group bolsters the prejudice against the group, it is not necessary to have a well worked out set of such rationalizations to obtain expressions of extreme prejudice. In fact Table 4 shows little relation between degree of disliking and the definiteness of the stereotyped picture. Negroes and Turks both are held in the lowest esteem, yet they represent opposite extremes in sharpness of stereotype. Students agreed among themselves most closely in characterizing Negroes and disagreed most in characterizing Turks. But they were in agreement in putting both groups at the bottom of the list as least desirable as companions or friends. . . .

23. THEY SAW A GAME: A CASE STUDY

Albert H. Hastorf and Hadley Cantril

On a brisk Saturday afternoon, November 23, 1951, the Dartmouth football team played Princeton in Princeton's Palmer Stadium. It was the last game of the season for both teams and of rather special significance because the Princeton team had won all its games so far and one of its players, Kazmaier, was receiving All-American mention and had just appeared as the cover man on *Time* magazine, and was playing his last game.

A few minutes after the opening kick-off, it became apparent that the game was going to be a rough one. The referees were kept busy blowing their whistles and penalizing both sides. In the second quarter, Princeton's star left the game with a broken nose. In the third quarter, a Dartmouth player was taken off the field with a broken leg. Tempers flared both during and after the game. The official statistics of the game, which Princeton won, showed that Dartmouth was penalized 70 yards, Princeton 25, not counting more than a few plays in which both sides were penalized.

Needless to say, accusations soon began to fly. The game immediately became a matter of concern to players, students, coaches, and the administrative officials of the two institutions, as well as to alumni and the general public who had not seen the game but had become sensitive to the problem of big-time football through the recent exposures of subsidized players, commercialism, etc. Discussion of the game continued for several weeks.

One of the contributing factors to the extended discussion of the game was the extensive space given to it by both campus and

Albert H. Hastorf and Hadley Cantril: "They Saw A Game: A Case Study"; JOURNAL OF ABNORMAL AND SOCIAL PSYCHOLOGY 49, 1954, 129–134. Copyright 1954 by the American Psychological Association. Reprinted by permission of the American Psychological Association and the authors.

metropolitan newspapers. An indication of the fervor with which the discussions were carried on is shown by a few excerpts from the campus dailies.

For example, on November 27 (four days after the game), the *Daily Princetonian* (Princeton's student newspaper) said:

> This observer has never seen quite such a disgusting exhibition of so-called "sport." Both teams were guilty but the blame must be laid primarily on Dartmouth's doorstep. Princeton, obviously the better team, had no reason to rough up Dartmouth. Looking at the situation rationally, we don't see why the Indians should make a deliberate attempt to cripple Dick Kazmaier or any other Princeton player. The Dartmouth psychology, however, is not rational itself.

The November 30th edition of the *Princeton Alumni Weekly* said:

> But certain memories of what occurred will not be easily erased. Into the record books will go in indelible fashion the fact that the last game of Dick Kazmaier's career was cut short by more than half when he was forced out with a broken nose and a mild concussion, sustained from a tackle that came well after he had thrown a pass.
>
> This second-period development was followed by a third quarter outbreak of roughness that was climaxed when a Dartmouth player deliberately kicked Brad Glass in the ribs while the latter was on his back. Throughout the often unpleasant afternoon, there was undeniable evidence that the losers' tactics were the result of an actual style of play, and reports on other games they have played this season substantiate this.

Dartmouth students were "seeing" an entirely different version of the game through the editorial eyes of the *Dartmouth* (Dartmouth's undergraduate newspaper). For example, on November 27 the *Dartmouth* said:

> However, the Dartmouth-Princeton game set the stage for the other type of dirty football. A type which may be termed an unjustifiable accusation.
>
> Dick Kazmaier was injured early in the game. Kazmaier was the star, an All-American. Other stars have been injured before, but Kazmaier had been built to represent a Princeton idol. When an idol is hurt there is only one recourse—the tag of dirty football. So what did the Tiger Coach Charley Caldwell do? He announced to the world that the Big Green had been out to extinguish the Princeton star. His purpose was achieved.
>
> After this incident, Caldwell instilled the old see-what-they-did-go-get-them attitude into his players. His talk got results. Gene Howard and Jim Miller were both injured. Both had dropped back to pass, had passed, and were standing unprotected in the backfield. Result: one bad leg and one leg broken.
>
> The game was rough and did get a bit out of hand in the third quarter. Yet most of the roughing penalties were called against Princeton while Dartmouth received more of the illegal-use-of-the-hands variety.

On November 28 the *Dartmouth* said:

> Dick Kazmaier of Princeton admittedly is an unusually able football player. Many Dartmouth men traveled to Princeton, not expecting to win—only hoping to see an All-American in action. Dick Kazmaier was hurt in the second period, and played only a token part in the remainder of the game. For this, spectators were sorry.
>
> But there were no such feelings for Dick Kazmaier's health. Medical authorities have confirmed that as a relatively unprotected passing and running star in a contact sport, he is quite liable to injury. Also, his particular injuries—a broken nose and slight concussion—were no more serious than is experienced almost any day in any football practice, where there is no more serious stake than playing the following Saturday. Up to the Princeton game, Dartmouth players suffered about 10 known nose fractures and face injuries, not to mention several slight concussions.
>
> Did Princeton players feel so badly about losing their star? They shouldn't have. During the past undefeated campaign they stopped several individual stars by a concentrated effort, including such mainstays as Frank Hauff of Navy, Glenn Adams of Pennsylvania and Rocco Calvo of Cornell.
>
> In other words, the same brand of football

condemned by the *Prince*—that of stopping the big man—is practiced quite successfully by the Tigers.

Basically, then, there was disagreement as to what had happened during the "game." Hence we took the opportunity presented by the occasion to make a "real life" study of a perceptual problem.[1]

PROCEDURE

Two steps were involved in gathering data. The first consisted of answers to a questionnaire designed to get reactions to the game and to learn something of the climate of opinion in each institution. This questionnaire was administered a week after the game to both Dartmouth and Princeton undergraduates who were taking introductory and intermediate psychology courses.

The second step consisted of showing the same motion picture of the game to a sample of undergraduates in each school and having them check on another questionnaire, as they watched the film, any infraction of the rules they saw whether these infractions were "mild" or "flagrant."[2] At Dartmouth, members of two fraternities were asked to view the film on December 7; at Princeton, members of two undergraduate clubs saw the film early in January.

The answers to both questionnaires were carefully coded and transferred to punch cards.[3]

RESULTS

Table 1 shows the questions which received different replies from the two student populations on the first questionnaire.

Questions asking if the students had friends on the team, if they had ever played football themselves, if they felt they knew the rules of the game well, etc. showed no differences in

1 We are not concerned here with the problem of guilt or responsibility for infractions, and nothing here implies any judgment as to who was to blame.

2 The film shown was kindly loaned for the purpose of the experiment by the Dartmouth College Athletic Council. It should be pointed out that a movie of a football game follows the ball, is thus selective, and omits a good deal of the action on the field. Also, of course, in viewing only a film of a game the possibilities of participation as spectator are greatly limited.

3 We gratefully acknowledge the assistance of Virginia Zerega, Office of Public Opinion Research, and J. L. McCandless, Princeton University, and E. S. Horton, Dartmouth College, in the gathering and collation of the data.

TABLE 1

Data from First Questionnaire

QUESTION	DARTMOUTH STUDENTS % (N = 163)	PRINCETON STUDENTS % (N = 161)
1. Did you happen to see the actual game between Dartmouth and Princeton in Palmer Stadium this year?		
Yes	33	71
No	67	29
2. Have you seen a movie of the game or seen it on television?		
Yes, movie	33	2
Yes, television	0	1
No, neither	67	97
3. (Asked of those who answered "yes" to either or both of above questions.) From your observations of what went on at the game, do you believe the game was clean and fairly played, or that it was unnecessarily rough and dirty?		
Clean and fair	6	0
Rough and dirty	24	69
Rough and fair*	25	2
No answer	45	29
4. (Asked of those who answered "no" on both of the first questions.) From what you have heard and read about the game, do you feel it was clean and fairly played, or that it was unnecessarily rough and dirty?		
Clean and fair	7	0
Rough and dirty	18	24
Rough and fair*	14	1
Don't know	6	4
No answer	55	71
(Combined answers to questions 3 and 4 above)		
Clean and fair	13	0
Rough and dirty	42	93
Rough and fair*	39	3
Don't know	6	4
5. From what you saw in the game or the movies, or from what you have read, which team do you feel started the rough play?		
Dartmouth started it	36	86
Princeton started it	2	0
Both started it	53	11
Neither	6	1
No answer	3	2
6. What is your understanding of the charges being made?**		
Dartmouth tried to get Kazmaier	71	47
Dartmouth intentionally dirty	52	44
Dartmouth unnecessarily rough	8	35
7. Do you feel there is any truth to these charges?		
Yes	10	55
No	57	4
Partly	29	35
Don't know	4	6
8. Why do you think the charges were made?		
Injury to Princeton star	70	23
To prevent repetition	2	46
No answer	28	31

* This answer was not included on the checklist but was written in by the percentage of students indicated.

** Replies do not add to 100% since more than one charge could be given.

TABLE 2
Data from Second Questionnaire Checked While Seeing Film

GROUP	N	TOTAL NUMBER OF INFRAC-TIONS CHECKED AGAINST			
		DARTMOUTH TEAM		PRINCETON TEAM	
		MEAN	SD	MEAN	SD
Dartmouth students	48	4.3*	2.7	4.4	2.8
Princeton students	49	9.8*	5.7	4.2	3.5

* Significant at the .01 level.

either school and no relation to answers given to other questions. This is not surprising since the students in both schools come from essentially the same type of educational, economic, and ethnic background.

Summarizing the data of Tables 1 and 2, we find a marked contrast between the two student groups.

Nearly all *Princeton* students judged the game as "rough and dirty"—not one of them thought it "clean and fair." And almost nine-tenths of them thought the other side started the rough play. By and large they felt that the charges they understood were being made were true; most of them felt the charges were made in order to avoid similar situations in the future.

When Princeton students looked at the movie of the game, they saw the Dartmouth team make over twice as many infractions as their own team made. And they saw the Dartmouth team make over twice as many infractions as were seen by Dartmouth students. When Princeton students judged these infractions as "flagrant" or "mild," the ratio was about two "flagrant" to one "mild" on the Dartmouth team, and about one "flagrant" to three "mild" on the Princeton team.

As for the *Dartmouth* students, while the plurality of answers fell in the "rough and dirty" category, over one-tenth thought the game was "clean and fair" and over a third introduced their own category of "rough and fair" to describe the action. Although a third of the Dartmouth students felt that Dartmouth was to blame for starting the rough play, the majority of Dartmouth students thought both sides were to blame. By and large, Dartmouth men felt that the charges

they understood were being made were not true, and most of them thought the reason for the charges was Princeton's concern for its football star.

When Dartmouth students looked at the movie of the game they saw both teams make about the same number of infractions. And they saw their own team make only half the number of infractions the Princeton students saw them make. The ratio of "flagrant" to "mild" infractions was about one to one when Dartmouth students judged the Dartmouth team, and about one "flagrant" to two "mild" when Dartmouth students judged infractions made by the Princeton team.

It should be noted that Dartmouth and Princeton students were thinking of different charges in judging their validity and in assigning reasons as to why the charges were made. It should also be noted that whether or not students were spectators of the game in the stadium made little difference in their responses.

INTERPRETATION: THE NATURE OF A SOCIAL EVENT

It seems clear that the "game" actually was many different games and that each version of the events that transpired was just as "real" to a particular person as other versions were to other people. A consideration of the experiential phenomena that constitute a "football game" for the spectator may help us both to account for the results obtained and illustrate something of the nature of any social event.

Like any other complex social occurrence, a "football game" consists of a whole host of happenings. Many different events are occurring simultaneously. Furthermore, each happening is a link in a chain of happenings, so that one follows another in sequence. The "football game," as well as other complex social situations, consists of a whole matrix of events. In the game situation, this matrix of events consists of the actions of all the players, together with the behavior of the referees and linesmen, the action on the sidelines, in the grandstands, over the loud-speaker, etc.

Of crucial importance is the fact that an "occurrence" on the football field or in any other social situation does not become an experiential "event" unless and until some significance is given to it: an "occurrence" becomes an "*event*" only when the happening has significance. And a happening generally has significance only if it reactivates learned significances already registered in what we have called a person's assumptive form-world.

Hence the particular occurrences that different people experienced in the football game were a limited series of events from the total matrix of events *potentially* available to them. People experienced those occurrences that reactivated significances they brought to the occasion; they failed to experience those occurrences which did not reactivate past significances. We do not need to introduce "attention" as an "intervening third" (to paraphrase James on memory) to account for the selectivity of the experiential process.

In this particular study, one of the most interesting examples of this phenomenon was a telegram sent to an officer of Dartmouth College by a member of a Dartmouth alumni group in the Midwest. He had viewed the film which had been shipped to his alumni group from Princeton after its use with Princeton students, who saw, as we noted, an average of over nine infractions by Dartmouth players during the game. The alumnus, who couldn't see the infractions he had heard publicized, wired:

> Preview of Princeton movies indicates considerable cutting of important part please wire explanation and possibly air mail missing part before showing scheduled for January 25 we have splicing equipment.

The "same" sensory impingements emanating from the football field, transmitted through the visual mechanism to the brain, also obviously gave rise to different experiences in different people. The significances assumed by different happenings for different people depend in large part on the purposes people bring to the occasion and the assumptions they have of the purposes and probable behavior of other people involved. This was amusingly pointed out by the New York *Herald Tribune's* sports columnist, Red Smith, in describing a prize fight between Chico Vejar and Carmine Fiore in his column of December 21, 1951. Among other things, he wrote:

> You see, Steve Ellis is the proprietor of Chico Vejar, who is a highly desirable tract of Stamford, Conn., welterweight. Steve is also a radio announcer. Ordinarily there is no conflict between Ellis the Brain and Ellis the Voice because Steve is an uncommonly substantial lump of meat who can support both halves of a split personality and give away weight on each end without missing it.
>
> This time, though, the two Ellises met head-on, with a sickening, rending crash. Steve the Manager sat at ringside in the guise of Steve the Announcer broadcasting a dispassionate, unbiased, objective report of Chico's adventures in the ring. . . .
>
> Clear as mountain water, his words came through, winning big for Chico. Winning? Hell, Steve was slaughtering poor Fiore.
>
> Watching and listening, you could see what a valiant effort the reporter was making to remain cool and detached. At the same time you had an illustration of the old, established truth that when anybody with a preference watches a fight, he sees only what he prefers to see.
>
> That is always so. That is why, after any fight that doesn't end in a clean knockout, there always are at least a few hoots when the decision is announced. A guy from, say, Billy Graham's neighborhood goes to see Billy fight and he watches Graham all the time. He sees all the punches Billy throws, and hardly any of the punches Billy catches. So it was with Steve.
>
> "Fiore feints with a left," he would say, honestly believing that Fiore hadn't caught Chico full on the chops. "Fiore's knees buckle," he said "and Chico backs away." Steve didn't see the hook that had driven Chico back. . . .

In brief, the data here indicate that there is no such "thing" as a "game" existing "out there" in its own right which people merely "observe." The "game" "exists" for a person and is experienced by him only in so far as certain happenings have significances in terms of his purpose. Out of all the occurrences going on in the environment, a person selects those that have some significance for him from his own egocentric position in the total matrix.

Obviously in the case of a football game, the value of the experience of watching the game is enhanced if the purpose of "your" team is accomplished, that is, if the happenning of the desired consequence is experienced—i.e., if your team wins. But the value attribute of the experience can, of course, be spoiled if the desire to win crowds out behavior we value and have come to call sportsmanlike.

The sharing of significances provides the links except for which a "social" event would not be experienced and would not exist for anyone.

A "football game" would be impossible except for the rules of the game which we bring to the situation and which enable us to share with others the significances of various happenings. These rules make possible a certain repeatability of events such as first downs, touchdowns, etc. If a person is unfamiliar with the rules of the game, the behavior he sees lacks repeatability and consistent significance and hence "doesn't make sense.". . .

From this point of view it is inaccurate and misleading to say that different people have different "attitudes" concerning the same "thing." For the "thing" simply is *not* the same for different people whether the "thing" is a football game, a presidential candidate, Communism, or spinach. We do not simply "react to" a happening or to some impingement from the environment in a determined way (except in behavior that has become reflexive or habitual). We behave according to what we bring to the occasion, and what each of us brings to the occasion is more or less unique. And except for these significances which we bring to the occasion, the happenings around us would be meaningless occurrences, would be "inconsequential."

From the transactional view, an attitude is not a predisposition to react in a certain way to an occurrence or stimulus "out there" that exists in its own right with certain fixed characteristics which we "color" according to our predisposition. That is, a subject does not simply "react to" an "object." An attitude would rather seem to be a complex of registered significances reactivated by some stimulus which assumes its own particular significance for us in terms of our purposes. That is, the object as experienced would not exist for us except for the reactivated aspects of the form-world which provide particular significance to the hieroglyphics of sensory impingements.

24. THEY SPLIT
MY PERSONALITY
or 'I Go Off My Rocker'

Harry Asher

I should have had the sense not to volunteer for this experiment. But one so seldom does the sensible thing, and I did agree, on request, to act as one of the subjects in a test of the new drug lysergic acid, sometimes known as LSD.

This drug has exciting possibilities because it produces in some subjects symptoms which resemble those of schizophrenia. Since the composition of the drug is known, there is the hope that antidotes to it may in turn be developed, and that either these antidotes or compounds related to them may be a cure for schizophrenia itself.

One of the early steps in the research was to make a careful study of the symptoms that the drug produces. It was in this early stage that I was involved.

The day came when I sat in a chair in a laboratory, and a man in a white overall handed me a beaker containing thirty millionths of a gram of lysergic acid.

Effects were expected to develop after about half an hour.

"Any symptoms?" I was asked at the end of that time.

"No. Sorry. Nothing at all."

Later the question was repeated.

"No. Sorry. Nothing at all."

"Don't you feel sick?"

"Good Lord, yes. Perfectly horrible. I never

Adapted from Chapter 9 of EXPERIMENTS IN SEE-ING by Harry Asher. Copyright © 1961 by Harry Asher. Reprinted by permission of Basic Books, Inc. and Gerald Duckworth & Co., Ltd. This adaptation was first published in the SATURDAY REVIEW of June 1, 1963. Copyright © 1963 by Saturday Review, Inc.

thought of reporting that. It's your stuff, is it? All right, record a considerable nausea."

After about an hour with nothing but nausea, I said, "Look. You've got to observe me for the next four hours. We might as well enjoy ourselves. It's a lovely day. Let's break out from this stuffy building and walk for miles and miles out into the country."

Looking back now and remembering that I seldom go for walks, it is clear that the drug was beginning to act. However, I did not realize it then.

"Any change in the way things look?" I was asked.

"No. No change."

"Don't you see anything at the edges of buildings, for instance?"

"Good Lord, yes! That factory chimney has got a spectrum down the edge! Just as though it was seen through a prism."

The drug had certainly started to work, and we returned to the laboratory, where more accurate observations could be recorded.

The early experiences were wholly delightful. There was a feeling of exhilaration and self-confidence, such as is rarely experienced, and an exaggerated tendency to laugh at anything at all. The failure of anyone else to understand what the joke was became in itself irrepressibly funny. The laughter became difficult to control. Things got funnier and funnier, and I laughed until I was in a condition of painful spasm, with tears running down my cheeks.

Then the visual distortions began. I noticed a patch of sunlight on the floor. Because its brightness appeared to be fluctuating I inquired if clouds were crossing the sky. No, the light was really steady. I dictated into the tape recorder a running commentary on the apparent changes of intensity of this steady patch of sunlight.

At about this time distortions of depth also began to occur. The object that made the greatest impression on me was a pair of spectacles worn by one of the assistants. They stood out in front of his face, which itself was increased in depth.

"You've no idea how funny you look," I said to the man.

He looked puzzled. In some curious way the fact that he was, as it were, at the same time both in the experiment looking distorted, and outside the experiment looking puzzled, with the puzzled look showing in the distorted face with the protruding spectacles, struck me very forcibly.

Then the nausea increased, the depth distortions became greater, and color changes were more noticeable. Earlier, it had been fun but now I was ill.

At their height, the depth distortions alternated. At one moment the feet would seem to be far away and small, just exactly as they do when opera glasses are used the wrong way round. Then the effect would reverse, and the legs and body would look very short. The feet appeared to be about eighteen inches below my eyes, and it seemed that they had come up rather than that I had gone down. The illusion reversed direction several times per minute.

Having played the game of trying to walk along a line while looking down binoculars the wrong way, and remembering that equilibrium is then upset, I set out very, very gingerly on a visit down the corridor to the toilet, expecting to fall over. The corridor, which really is long, kept changing in length. If I looked down, my feet might be far or near according to what "phase" they happened to be in. But, despite the alternate stretching of the corridor to perhaps two to three times its normal length followed by compression to one-half or one-third its length, accompanied by the apparent alteration in my own height, there was no difficulty in walking. There was, perhaps, a slight feeling of dissociation, which was to become more apparent later. The walking was done by a walking man, and on top of him was a pair of eyes which saw

things distorted, but these eyes were not in control of the motion.

On coming out into the corridor, I met the Deputy Vice Chancellor of the University. If I had not been fully conscious of his status, I would surely have bitten him in the waistcoat. Of all the places to bite a man, the waistcoat is the least profitable, but it was only there that I wanted to bite him.

The wish came in the form of a visual image. My false teeth were snapping away in the air, rather as a barber snips the air with his scissors between cuts of the hair.

All that the Deputy Vice Chancellor saw was two men walking, my observer and myself, one looking at him very fixedly and walking slowly and with elaborate care.

At times on the way back from the toilet I would make a running commentary. Something like this:

"Steady now. Someone's coming. Corridor's long. Can we get past? Good Lord, yes. Lots of room. Dead easy after all."

Soon we were back in the lab, and they were showing me a flickering light made by an electronic flash lamp which consisted of a concave mirror, maybe eighteen inches in diameter, with a small bent hollow glass tube in the center. The tube contained gas under low pressure, and gave a flash each time a condenser discharged through it. In this way the rate of flashing could be controlled very simply. The flash was bright enough to be irritating, but not painful.

They set the lamp flashing at a fairly rapid rate and asked me to report what I saw.

There was quite a complex pattern of light in the mirror, and it was easy to see many pictures in this pattern, just as one can by looking into a fire. The most striking thing was a set of teeth quite near the middle of the lamp. They were about one-third normal size, and absolutely distinct. I think, too, there was an eye.

In giving a description of what I saw, I was so slow, and insisted in describing each thing in order, going round clockwise, that I never got as far as describing the teeth. It was only after I was told that people often see teeth that I mentioned this neat little set which I had seen.

The next treatment was to lie down and close the eyes, while the light was flashed on the closed lids at various frequencies.

A lady psychiatrist sat by the side of the couch with a notebook in her hand. She could control the frequency of the flashes by turning a knob. She asked me to dictate into the tape recorder a commentary on the experience which would follow.

At the lower frequencies of flashing, nothing especially striking was seen. But at higher frequencies an illusion began to build up. I think it was at a frequency of twenty-three flashes per second that the picture became most vivid.

I was by the seaside, lying on my back on the yellow sand, with the blue sea on my left. I had no desire to turn my head to look at the sea or sand, so that in a certain sense I could not actually see them. Normally, if a person lies on his back, little more than the sky is visible. Yet my appreciation of the sand and sky was certainly visual. It is hard to convey these illusions. If you lie on your back you can picture to yourself the sand and sea without looking at them; it was like that, only the picturing was as vivid as seeing them.

It was a bright day at the seaside. The sky was blue, and the sun was shining down straight into my eyes. I tried to close them and found them shut already.

I was not alone on the beach. Just out of sight, to my right, were three women. They were exceedingly lovely women, and again I could see them only in a certain sense. Suppose I were to meet one of these women. I would not be able to recognize her. All the same, I knew a lot about them because I could appreciate their presence so vividly. Their womanliness was most intensely felt.

This was not an ordinary erotic dream where one experiences certain sensations and even emotions more vividly than in the waking condition. It was along those lines, but much more impressive.

It was not just that I liked or loved these women very, very much. Rather was it that I felt a wonder that was really there, really there in the illusion, if you follow me; it just cannot be described in words.

What a pity the sun was so dazzling. I wanted to lie back and enjoy the feeling of the presence of these women. They were so very kind.

When the frequency of the flashing light was twenty-three everything was just right.

When it went higher than that, the dream deteriorated. So, when we had covered the frequency range, I asked the lady psychiatrist who was turning the control knob if I could have twenty-three again. She put the frequency back to twenty-three, but this time it wasn't so good. Also, I had the greatest trouble in understanding that she had given me twenty-three, although she repeated "This is twenty-three" many times quite clearly.

Then the flashing light was turned off and I "came to" or "woke up." It is not clear how to describe it. I was extremely surprised to find that there were only the lady psychiatrist and myself in the inner room of the laboratory.

"Only you and me? Oh well, just you and me. It's all quite friendly, isn't it?" I remember saying, rather foolishly.

When the lady had finished her research, a man came in to record the electroencephalogram.

"For goodness sake, try and keep still just a half a minute. I can't get a decent recording," he said.

This puzzled me. I was keeping still. I was lying on the couch and was not making any muscular movements. I was apparently floating about in space, but clearly that would not affect him or his instrument—that only affected me.

"You don't mind me floating about, do you? That doesn't affect your instrument, does it?"

"You're wriggling," he said.

"I'm just getting comfortable. I'll be still for a quarter of an hour."

I lay still for what seemed about a quarter of an hour, floating for much of the time.

"There you are," I said. "I hope you got a good record."

The thought occurred to me that since time seemed to pass so slowly, and since my speech seemed at this particular period to be of normal speed, it would seem to follow that I would be able to utter many more words in a given time than would normally be possible. Accordingly the attempt was made, at my suggestion, to count up to as high a number as possible in five seconds. I seemed to count very rapidly for a long time, but I only got as far as thirty.

The experiment had started at 10:15 a.m. and it was now 4 p.m. We had had sandwiches and coffee for lunch. It was thought to be safe to take me along for a cup of tea in the common room. The custom is to take afternoon tea somewhat early, so that now, at 4 p.m., only one person remained, a pharmacologist who was a good friend of mine. He knew all about LSD, and looked at me pityingly. I began talking to him with the boring, monotonous, half-nonsense speech I was compelled to turn out.

"Now then, Bobby. I know I am boring you, you see I can't stop talking. I am cut off from reality, but one thing is very real and that is the terrible look of boredom in your eye. So please don't go on listening."

Back we went to the laboratory. It was about that time I first felt that I was split into two people. The following report is made with particular care:

There were two of me walking down the corridor. The two people were not very accurately localized in space, but the main one corresponded in position to where I would have been had there been only one of me. The shadowy, or more tenuous individual, the naughty one, was slightly to the left. We could talk to each other, exchanging verbal thoughts, but not talking aloud.

The main person was really me, but in an improved form. He was a very strong character. He had an effortless strength that I never knew before that I possessed. The other individual on the left was much less well known to me.

"Why not jump out of a window?" he said to me.

The invitation had a compulsive quality which was difficult to resist. But just as I was considering it, the main person answered for me, speaking with effortless strength.

"Of course not. Don't be such a bloody fool!"

I was delighted with this man—with myself, that is. I thought, "I had no idea what strength of character I had."

Those in charge were beginning to get a bit worried as to what was to be done with me. The effects which would normally have worn off by now were lasting for an unexpectedly long time.

They asked me whether I thought it was safe for me to go home.

"Take me home," I said abruptly.

I was a little worried that I might want to jump out of the window when I got home, but decided to rely on my super-self to look after

the naughty one. I never told the experimenters that I was at times double.

The lady psychiatrist was to take me home, so she asked me to tell her the way.

"Hell, it's up to *you* to get me home" was the thought that was in my mind. What I said was, "Drive round this roundabout [traffic circle—see Figure 1] for about a quarter of an hour and then turn off to the left. I'll tell you when we come to it."

It cannot have taken much more time than was used in uttering that sentence to have driven a quarter of the way around the roundabout. But it seemed that that remark took the usual time and yet occupied only an inconsiderable proportion of the long time which appeared to elapse in going around the roundabout.

The psychiatrist seemed worried.

"Is this the turning?" she asked.

"You've been driving quite a time now. Yes, I should think this is it. Try it, anyway," I replied.

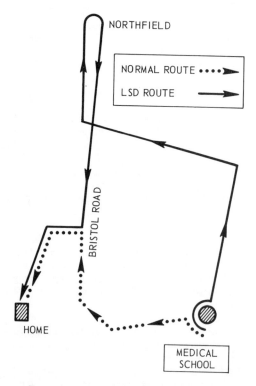

FIGURE 1. Normal route home and route taken under the influence of LSD.

The road we were on was not recognizable, but I had ceased to bother. The day's work was over, and I relaxed. Actually, as the map shows, we had gone 180 degrees around.

I was prepared for the journey home, which is one mile precisely, to seem very long in the car. So I settled down to endure it.

"Bristol Road," I said. "When you come to Bristol Road you turn right, then left down Bournbrook Road."

She did turn right down Bristol Road but, being wrong already, that turn took her farther wrong.

It was really surprising how much the psychiatrist relied on me to direct her to my home. I must have failed entirely to convey to her my inability to interpret the changing world around me. I could, however, feel her anxiety and worry, and could see that she had her family on her mind. But one of the final symptoms of LSD was beginning to develop in me, and that was lassitude and complete selfishness. I did not care if her children were waiting for her, or if she had a party. If her house had been on fire, that would have been entirely her problem.

"We may be wrong. We may be right. Drive what way you will," I said.

She stopped to ask a policeman the way. And, after what I believe now was a real half hour's car drive, we arrived home.

The psychiatrist explained the situation to my wife:

"He can't help talking," she said, gave a brief resumé of the case, and then drove off.

"No, thank you, darling, I think I won't come in just now," I said to my wife. "I will go for a walk. Keep the children away from me, will you please?"

I had a compulsive urge to do violence to my children, and did not like to tell her about it.

"Are you safe? Can you get back?" she asked. For her, the situation must have been extremely distressing.

"I haven't a hope of crossing a road with traffic on it. How can I possibly judge speed?" I replied. "But I can go round the block. I will always turn left. It is about half a mile round, so you will see me going past from time to time!"

And I set off.

Although the nausea was still present, the muscular system felt in order, and the exercise was more pleasing than usual. Also, the con-certina effect added interest. I had a feeling, too, that the exercise would help to work off the effects of the drug. There was no difficulty in recognizing the different streets, and no question of becoming lost.

I must have gone around a great many times. I remember passing some people to whom my wife and I had previously made a friendly approach, but who had snubbed us decisively. Should I now, with the license, as it were, of being able to blame any peculiarity of behavior on the drug, go and tell them what I thought of them? But no, I did not. The ordinary natural human reserve prevented it. I noticed this myself and regarded it as a most excellent sign that the drug action was abating.

I still could not stop talking to myself on the way round. But I could not sense when I was really talking and when I was merely having verbal thoughts. To find out, I would place a hand to my lips. I could then tell from the movement felt whether I was talking or not. Whenever the test was made, I was talking, but could not stop.

I got into conversation with one gentleman who was cutting his hedge. For an Englishman to speak to a near neighbor after passing him perhaps six times during an evening walk may, since there was no one to introduce us, suggest a certain lack of reserve, but the fact that the conversation did not start until the sixth encounter was an indication that recovery had started.

After walking around the block, at a brisk pace, for about an hour to an hour and a half, I went into my own garden.

"Keep the children away from me, please!" I said to my wife. I could not convey to her how important it was that she should do this, nor do I know myself to this day how great the gap was between the violent thoughts in my mind and their possible execution.

Most fortunately, the children were both in a blessedly happy and amenable mood. When Patria called they ran into the drawing-room, settled round her, and she began to read to them, having explained that father was not well and that he wanted to sit undisturbed in the garden. I settled down in a deck chair, bathed in the evening sunlight, and looked at the happy little group in the drawing-room, which I could see through the french windows. The children could see me looking at them, and waved to me.

That scene made a big impression. I felt that I was a long way off, and that no effort of mine could bring me any nearer. But I knew it would be all right if I waited; so I waved back to them, and settled down to wait.

The nausea wore off, and other effects of the LSD seemed to be abating. So after a while I agreed to read to the elder child, Robert, in bed. The reading was a failure from his point of view. His father seemed inattentive, and to be reading so poorly and slurring his speech so badly that the story was barely intelligible. From my point of view, the concertina and stretching effects were troublesome again. The boy seemed to have such peculiar limbs. . . .

The night was very wakeful, but it did not seem too long. An eye was seen very clearly from time to time in the darkness. This was neither distressing nor particularly interesting. Just an eye—rather diagrammatic.

Next day, unfortunately, I still was not right. There was no question of getting out of bed. I just lay there talking, babbling rather, mostly about my past. Often I cried, which was very distressing for my wife, who naturally thought it represented a condition of deep grief. As far as I can remember it did not. It was as though my body were crying and I was outside it, admittedly feeling rather hopeless, but not moved to tears.

The color distortion was still there. The psychiatrist and others from the laboratory came to see me, looking very worried—and *green*. All their faces had that unpleasant green tinge.

I still wanted to jump out of the window, but had no feeling of wanting to commit suicide. It was an absolutely specific compulsion to jump out of one particular window in the bedroom. I was no longer split into two, and the very strong character who had been so easily able to resist the temptation before had gone. The temptation was vaguely associated with the naughty character, but he was not very distinct from me now. It was more as if I myself wanted, in a purely irresponsible way, to jump out of the window.

I was in bed for a few days and, when not babbling or crying, I lay very limp and completely apathetic. . . .

After a fortnight I was still very jumpy and susceptible to illusions. In the bathroom, I would see pictures made from the irregular condensation of steam on the walls. The pictures in steam were noble, and reminded me of the strange sweetness of the women by the seaside.

Then there was the insect.

One morning, on looking into the sink, I saw this enormous creature, standing at one edge. It looked so real that I frankly did not know what sort of action to take. Rather feebly I blew on it, and to my horror it made grotesque movements, impossible for any normal insect to achieve; and with these movements it fluttered around the sink. The illusion of the movement lasted only about one second. But one second can be a long time, and the sensation in the solar plexus was felt very strongly indeed. Then, with immense relief, I could see it was only the black charred remains of a piece of paper. . . .

It would make a nice story to say how I thus became master of my fate, and cured myself by my own determined efforts. But things didn't happen that way.

For several months I was dependent on barbiturates in order to get a reasonable amount of sleep. After that, I could manage to sleep from 12 p.m. until about 4 a.m. most nights without any drug. The time from then on passed pleasantly enough, and the insomnia was not a thing which mattered much. Normally I was a very heavy sleeper, and it was surprising to me to realize how much time is wasted in bed. One morning, to reduce this waste, I got up at 5 a.m. and spent three hours breaking up old bricks in the garden before breakfast. Whether it was the bricks or a coincidence will never be known, but that day marked the end of the insomnia. A great sleepiness overwhelmed me by 8 p.m. the next evening. For the first time for months a full night's sleep was obtained, and a normal sleep rhythm was established very shortly afterwards.

The only definite permanent effect which has been observed to follow my taking thirty millionths of a gram of lysergic acid is that after-images are now always seen more vividly than ever they were before. But if the condition I had been in was schizophrenia, my sympathy for those so afflicted has been increased many times.

RECOMMENDED FURTHER READING

Allport, Gordon W. and Thomas F. Pettigrew: "The Trapezoidal Illusion Among the Zulus"; *Journal of Abnormal and Social Psychology, 55* (1957), 104–113

Asch, S. E.: "Forming Impressions of Personality"; *Journal of Abnormal and Social Psychology, 41* (1946), 258–290

Bruner, Jerome S.: "On Perceptual Readiness"; *Psychological Review, 64* (1957), 123–152

Dember, William N.: *The Psychology of Perception;* New York, Holt, Rinehart & Winston 1960

Fantz, R.: "The Origin of Form Perception"; *Scientific American,* May 1961

Forgus, R. H.: *Perception: The Basic Process in Cognitive Development;* New York, McGraw-Hill 1966

Gibson, James J.: *The Perception of the Visual World;* Boston, Houghton Mifflin 1950

————: *The Senses Considered as Perceptual Systems;* Boston, Houghton Mifflin 1966

———— and R. Walk: "The Visual Cliff"; *Scientific American,* April 1960

Gregory, R. L.: *Eye and Brain;* New York, McGraw-Hill 1966

———— and J. Wallace: *Recovery from Early Blindness: A Case Study;* Cambridge, England, Experimental Psychology Society Monographs, No. 2, 1963

Hoch, P. and J. Zubin (eds.): *Psychopathology of Perception;* New York, Grune & Stratton 1965

Ittleson, W. and F. Kilpatrick: "Experiments in Perception"; *Scientific American,* August 1951

Julesz, B.: "Experiment in Perception"; *Psychology Today,* February 1968

Kelley, H.: "The Warm-Cold Variable in First Impressions of Persons"; *Journal of Personality;* 18 (1950), 431–439

Mueller, C. G.: *Sensory Psychology;* Englewood Cliffs, N.J., Prentice-Hall 1965

Sackett, G. P.: "Monkeys Reared in Visual Isolation with Pictures as Visual Input: Evidence for an Innate Releasing Mechanism"; *Science, 154* (1966), 1468–1472

*Vernon, M. D.: *The Psychology of Perception;* Baltimore, Penguin Books 1962

* Paperback edition available.

PART VI

LANGUAGE

AND COMMUNICATION

Language is one of the seminal inventions of human history; it may well be the invention that made "history," as opposed to a mere temporal succession of events, possible. Yet, like all things, however important, that are familiar to us from birth we tend to take the miracle of language for granted. To most of us a society without language is inconceivable; did it not exist we would surely have to invent it—a necessity that was no doubt felt by those, many millennia ago, who *did* invent it.

Language not only makes communication more economical and precise than it could otherwise be but it facilitates action, it creates perceptions and emotions (recall Selection 22) and, through the medium of writing, it makes possible the transmission of the thought and experience of one age to succeeding generations. Language thus plays a crucial role in the creation of culture and an even more crucial one in its cumulation and transmission. At the same time, however, language can serve to conceal reality, to confuse perception, and to deceive both ourselves and others.

Because all of us (unless we are congenitally deaf or socially isolated) grow up and live in an ongoing linguistic community that we have not ourselves created (although we all help to sustain and gradually to modify it) we are not surprised that children begin to utter words, or at least to babble word-like sounds, during their second year of life or that by the age of six they have virtually mastered, without formal instruction, the grammar of their language. Yet, perhaps we ought to be surprised or even amazed that such a complex structure as the grammar of Swahili, Russian, English, Japanese, Arabic, or Turkish should be mastered by a child of six in the ordinary course of maturation.

The precise mechanisms by which a language is acquired (the subject matter of *psycholinguistics*) is, like so much else in contemporary psychology, a matter of dispute. Older theories based on the idea of imitation or the concepts of conditioning and reinforcement (see Part IV) while they may explain learning of particular words and phrases seem inadequate to account for the learning of grammar and the ability of even very young children to devise or "generate" entirely new sentences never before spoken. More recent work by linguists and students of "transformational" or "generative" grammar, especially Noam Chomsky and his associates, suggests that what children may learn are certain basic rules and "deep structures" of the language on the basis of which they combine meaningful linguistic elements (morphemes) to generate new, grammatically correct, and meaningful sentences. Chomsky's work has opened new vistas both on the nature of language and on its acquisition.

There can be no question, however, that language is a collective product and that it is learned by young members of a social group in the course of their maturation and socialization. Simultaneously, through a feedback process, the gradual acquisition of language itself greatly facilitates further socialization and more complex kinds of learning. Yet, language does not merely express pre-existing thoughts or label aspects of external reality so as to make the latter intellectually manipulable. As Katz and Braly's work on verbal stereotypes demonstrates, linguistic labels may affect perception and thought, attitudes and even actions, as well as be affected by them. This is especially true in the case of young children who necessarily accept unquestioningly the perceptions and attitudes implied in the words and categories of the language they learn. We live in a world that is largely created by language and precisely because of that we must always remember that words are *not* the things to which they refer (i.e., their "referents").

Were verbal language the only means by which human beings communicated life would not only be more monotonous but all of us would probably be victimized by the deficiencies and ambiguities of words far more often than, in fact, we are. Human beings communicate through a variety of other modes besides words. Some of these are oral without being verbal (e.g., vocal tone and inflection, rate of speech, pronounciation, grunts, groans, and interjections); others are both nonverbal and non-oral: touch, spatial position, bodily and facial gestures, posture, dress, bodily adornment and grooming, physical objects and the way in which we use them. All these means—and perhaps others as well—not only give variety to human intercommunication but form a continuous counterpoint to the verbal level of discourse, a counterpoint that sometimes clarifies and reinforces, sometimes confuses and contradicts the overt significance of the words. Nonverbal communication is more vivid and immediate, often less ambiguous, than verbal and it frequently serves, unbeknownst to the "speaker," to reveal underlying emotions and motives of which the latter may be unconscious or that he may use his words to conceal. While the study of nonverbal and non-oral communication (sometimes called "kinesics") is still in its early stages scholars may eventually develop "grammars" of such "languages" as complete and adequate as those of more familiar verbal ones.

The first selection in this part is a classic article by the late Benjamin Lee Whorf, a fire prevention engineer by vocation and an anthropological linguist by avocation. Whorf's thesis (sometimes known as the Whorf-Sapir hypothesis) is that language shapes thought rather than merely expresses it, that the categories and implicit paradigms embedded in a language exercise a powerful if unconscious constraint on ideas and on the very perception of the external world held by speakers of that language. In other words, we "see" the physical and social worlds in a manner dictated by the grammar of our language. It is the structure of our language that organizes reality and gives it meaning, for it is through language that men come to agree on what reality "is." Logically implied in this position is the belief that the world is conceived and perceived very differently by people whose languages are radically different in structure, an implication Whorf developed explicitly in some of his other writings. The basic concepts of time, space, and causality found in English and other Indo-European languages and our tendency to think in dichotomies are thus given, not by nature, but by language. This theory represents a frontal assault not only on the traditional view of the relation between language and thought but also, by extension, on the nativistic theory of perception (see the introduction to Part V) and on the whole tradition of Western metaphysics and epistemology (theory of knowledge) stemming from the philosophy of Immanuel Kant (1724–1804).

While Whorf's hypothesis has by now become almost an orthodoxy it seems, however, to overstate the case. We have evidence that some perceptions are unlearned (see the introduction to Part V) and that others are remarkably constant amongst cultures with entirely different and unrelated languages. Perception, thinking, and emotion probably influence language as much as the latter influences them and the relationship among these various phenomena seems to be of a dialectical character rather than of one-directional causality. Moreover, the work of Chomsky and others suggests that every language is capable of expressing all ideas even though, for historical or other reasons, particular ideas are not native to a given culture. Despite such criticisms, however, Whorf's work has been extraordinarily fruitful in the study of language and its relationship to human perception and action. Its implications for psychology are both obvious and immense.

In the second selection Flora Davis, a student of communications describes various types of nonverbal communication and some of the conventions governing the use of such "languages." These conventions—or "grammars" —often differ from culture to culture, a fact that can be a fertile source of misunderstanding when people from different cultures meet and try to communicate. Note how bodily movement and gestures, often of an involuntary character, may subtly reveal hidden motives and emotions. The reader might try to relate Miss Davis' discussion of personal space to the discussion of territoriality in the selections of Part VII dealing with aggression.

Finally, Jurgen Ruesch, a psychiatrist, and the late Weldon Kees, a poet and photographer, attempt a systematic classification of types of nonverbal communication, each of which has a grammar of its own and each of which serves particular functions. The authors' discussion of the relationship between nonverbal and verbal communication is especially illuminating. Contradictions among communications reaching an individual (both among different verbal communications and between verbal and nonverbal ones) have been suggested by some investigators as an important contributing cause of schizophrenia, especially in young children. In contrast to Whorf, and perhaps to linguists generally, Ruesch and Kees emphasize that we do *not* live in an exclusively verbal world, that nonverbal communication is more closely tied to actual events and is thus less ambiguous and less susceptible to distortions of meaning.

The photographs at the end of this Part will, we hope, provide the reader some interesting and useful practice in the interpretation of nonverbal communications.

25. SCIENCE AND LINGUISTICS

Benjamin Lee Whorf

Every normal person in the world, past infancy in years, can and does talk. By virtue of that fact, every person—civilized or uncivilized—carries through life certain naïve but deeply rooted ideas about talking and its relation to thinking. Because of their firm connection with speech habits that have become unconscious and automatic, these notions tend to be rather intolerant of opposition. They are by no means entirely personal and haphazard; their basis is definitely systematic, so that we are justified in calling them a system of natural logic—a term that seems to me preferable to the term common sense, often used for the same thing.

According to natural logic, the fact that every person has talked fluently since infancy makes every man his own authority on the process by which he formulates and communicates. He has merely to consult a common substratum of logic or reason which he and everyone else are supposed to possess. Natural logic says that talking is merely an incidental process concerned strictly with communication, not with formulation of ideas. Talking, or the use of language, is supposed only to "express" what is essentially already formulated nonlinguistically. Formulation is an independent process, called thought or thinking, and is supposed to be largely indifferent to the nature of particular languages. Languages have grammars, which are assumed to be merely norms of conventional and social correctness, but the use of language is supposed to be guided not so much by them as by correct, rational, or intelligent *thinking*.

Thought, in this view, does not depend on grammar but on laws of logic or reason which are supposed to be the same for all observers of the universe—to represent a rationale in

From TECHNOLOGY REVIEW, *44, 1940, 229–231, 247, 248. Reprinted by permission of the MIT Press.*

the universe that can be "found" independently by all intelligent observers, whether they speak Chinese or Choctaw. In our own culture, the formulations of mathematics and of formal logic have acquired the reputation of dealing with this order of things, i.e., with the realm and laws of pure thought. Natural logic holds that different languages are essentially parallel methods for expressing this one-and-the-same rationale of thought and, hence, differ really in but minor ways which may seem important only because they are seen at close range. It holds that mathematics, symbolic logic, philosophy, and so on, are systems contrasted with language which deal directly with this realm of thought, not that they are themselves specialized extensions of language. The attitude of natural logic is well shown in an old quip about a German grammarian who devoted his whole life to the study of the dative case. From the point of view of natural logic, the dative case and grammar in general are an extremely minor issue. A different attitude is said to have been held by the ancient Arabians: Two princes, so the story goes, quarreled over the honor of putting on the shoes of the most learned grammarian of the realm; whereupon their father, the caliph, is said to have remarked that it was the glory of his kingdom that great grammarians were honored even above kings.

The familiar saying that the exception proves the rule contains a good deal of wisdom, though from the standpoint of formal logic it became an absurdity as soon as "prove" no longer meant "put on trial." The old saw began to be profound psychology from the time it ceased to have standing in logic. What it might well suggest to us today is that if a rule has absolutely no exceptions, it is not recognized as a rule or as anything else; it is then part of the background of experience of which we tend to remain unconscious. Never having experienced anything in contrast to it, we cannot isolate it and formulate it as a rule until we so enlarge our experience and expand our base of reference that we encounter an interruption of its regularity. The situation is somewhat analogous to that of not missing the water till the well runs dry, or not realizing that we need air till we are choking.

For instance, if a race of people had the physiological defect of being able to see only the color blue, they would hardly be able to formulate the rule that they saw only blue. The term blue would convey no meaning to them, their language would lack color terms, and their words denoting their various sensations of blue would answer to, and translate, our words light, dark, white, black, and so on, not our word blue. In order to formulate the rule or norm of seeing only blue, they would need exceptional moments in which they saw other colors. The phenomenon of gravitation forms a rule without exceptions; needless to say, the untutored person is utterly unaware of any law of gravitation, for it would never enter his head to conceive of a universe in which bodies behaved otherwise than they do at the earth's surface. Like the color blue with our hypothetical race, the law of gravitation is a part of the untutored individual's background, not something he isolates from that background. The law could not be formulated until bodies that always fell were seen in terms of a wider astronomical world in which bodies moved in orbits or went this way and that.

Similarly, whenever we turn our heads, the image of the scene passes across our retinas exactly as it would if the scene turned around us. But this effect is background, and we do not recognize it; we do not see a room turn around us but are conscious only of having turned our heads in a stationary room. If we observe critically while turning the head or eyes quickly, we shall see no motion, it is true, yet a blurring of the scene between two clear views. Normally we are quite unconscious of this continual blurring but seem to be looking about in an unblurred world. Whenever we walk past a tree or house, its image on the retina changes just as if the tree or house were turning on an axis; yet we do not see trees or houses turn as we travel about

at ordinary speeds. Sometimes ill-fitting glasses will reveal queer movements in the scene as we look about, but normally we do not see the relative motion of the environment when we move; our psychic make-up is somehow adjusted to disregard whole realms of phenomena that are so all-pervasive as to be irrelevant to our daily lives and needs.

Natural logic contains two fallacies. First, it does not see that the phenomena of a language are, to its own speakers, largely of a background character and so are outside the critical consciousness and control of the speaker who is expounding natural logic. Hence, when anyone, as a natural logician, is talking about reason, logic, and the laws of correct thinking, he is apt to be simply marching in step with purely grammatical facts that have somewhat of a background character in his own language or family of languages but are by no means universal in all languages and in no sense a common substratum of reason. Second, natural logic confuses agreement about subject matter, attained through use of language, with knowledge of the linguistic process by which agreement is attained; i.e., with the province of the despised (and to its notion superfluous) grammarian. Two fluent speakers, of English let us say, quickly reach a point of assent about the subject matter of their speech; they agree about what their language refers to. One of them, *A,* can give directions that will be carried out by the other, *B,* to *A*'s complete satisfaction. Because they thus understand each other so perfectly, *A* and *B,* as natural logicians, suppose they must of course know how it is all done. They think, e.g., that it is simply a matter of choosing words to express thoughts. If you ask *A* to explain how he got *B*'s agreement so readily, he will simply repeat to you, with more or less elaboration or abbreviation, what he said to *B.* He has no notion of the process involved. The amazingly complex system of linguistic patterns and classifications which *A* and *B* must have in common before they can adjust to each other at all, is all background to *A* and *B.*

These background phenomena are the province of the grammarian—or of the linguist, to give him his more modern name as a scientist. The word linguist in common, and especially newspaper, parlance means something entirely different, namely, a person who can quickly attain agreement about subject matter with different people speaking a number of different languages. Such a person is better termed a polyglot or a multilingual. Scientific linguists have long understood that ability to speak a language fluently does not necessarily confer a linguistic knowledge of it —i.e., understanding of its background phenomena and its systematic processes and structure—any more than ability to play a good game of billiards confers or requires any knowledge of the laws of mechanics that operate upon the billiard table.

The situation here is not unlike that in any other field of science. All real scientists have their eyes primarily on background phenomena that cut very little ice, as such, in our daily lives; and yet their studies have a way of bringing out a close relation between these unsuspected realms of fact and such decidedly foreground activities as transporting goods, preparing food, treating the sick, or growing potatoes, which in time may become very much modified simply because of pure scientific investigation in no way concerned with these brute matters themselves. Linguistics presents a quite similar case; the background phenomena with which it deals are involved in all our foreground activities of talking and of reaching agreement, in all reasoning and arguing of cases, in all law, arbitration, conciliation, contracts, treaties, public opinion, weighing of scientific theories, formulation of scientific results. Whenever agreement or assent is arrived at in human affairs, and whether or not mathematics or other specialized symbolisms are made part of the procedure, *this agreement is reached by linguistic processes, or else it is not reached.*

As we have seen, an overt knowledge of the linguistic processes by which agreement is attained is not necessary to reaching some sort of agreement, but it is certainly no bar thereto; the more complicated and difficult the matter, the more such knowledge is a distinct aid, till the point may be reached —I suspect the modern world has about arrived at it—when the knowledge becomes not only an aid but a necessity. The situation may be likened to that of navigation. Every boat that sails is in the lap of planetary forces; yet a boy can pilot his small craft around a harbor without benefit of geography, astronomy, mathematics, or international politics. To the captain of an ocean liner, however,

some knowledge of all these subjects is essential.

When linguists became able to examine critically and scientifically a large number of languages of widely different patterns, their base of reference was expanded; they experienced an interruption of phenomena hitherto held universal, and a whole new order of significances came into their ken. It was found that the background linguistic system (in other words, the grammar) of each language is not merely a reproducing instrument for voicing ideas but rather is itself the shaper of ideas, the program and guide for the individual's mental activity, for his analysis of impressions, for his synthesis of his mental stock in trade. Formulation of ideas is not an independent process, strictly rational in the old sense, but is part of a particular grammar and differs, from slightly to greatly, as between different grammars. We dissect nature along lines laid down by our native languages. The categories and types that we isolate from the world of phenomena we do not find there because they stare every observer in the face; on the contrary, the world is presented in a kaleidoscopic flux of impressions which has to be organized by our minds —and this means largely by the linguistic systems in our minds. We cut nature up, organize it into concepts, and ascribe significances as we do, largely because we are parties to an agreement to organize it in this way—an agreement that holds throughout our speech community and is codified in the patterns of our language. The agreement is, of course, an implicit and unstated one, *but its terms are absolutely obligatory;* we cannot talk at all except by subscribing to the organization and classification of data which the agreement decrees.

The fact is very significant for modern science, for it means that no individual is free to describe nature with absolute impartiality but is constrained to certain modes of interpretation even while he thinks himself most free. The person most nearly free in such respects would be a linguist familiar with very many widely different linguistic systems. As yet, even, no linguist is in any such position. We are thus introduced to a new principle of relativity, which holds that all observers are not led by the same physical evidence to the same picture of the universe, unless their linguistic backgrounds are similar, or can in some way be calibrated.

This rather startling conclusion is not so apparent if we compare only our modern European languages, with perhaps Latin and Greek thrown in for good measure. Among these tongues there is a unanimity of major pattern which at first seems to bear out natural logic. But this unanimity exists only because these tongues are all Indo-European dialects cut to the same basic plan, being historically transmitted from what was long ago one speech community; because the modern dialects have long shared in building up a common culture; and because much of this culture, on the more intellectual side, is derived from the linguistic backgrounds of Latin and Greek. Thus this group of languages satisfies the special case of the clause beginning "unless" in the statement of the linguistic relativity principle at the end of the preceding paragraph. From this condition follows the unanimity of description of the world in the community of modern scientists. But it must be emphasized that "all modern Indo-European-speaking observers" is not the same thing as "all observers." That modern Chinese or Turkish scientists describe the world in the same terms as Western scientists means, of course, only that they have taken over bodily the entire Western system of rationalizations, not that they have corroborated that system from their native posts of observation.

When Semitic, Chinese, Tibetan, or African languages are contrasted with our own, the divergence in analysis of the world becomes more apparent; and when we bring in the native languages of the Americas, where speech communities for many millennia have gone their ways independently of each other and of the Old World, the fact that languages dissect nature in many different ways becomes patent. The relativity of all conceptual systems, ours included, and their dependence upon language stand revealed. That American Indians speaking only their native tongues are never called upon to act as scientific observers is in no wise to the point. To exclude the evidence which their languages offer as to what the human mind can do is like expecting botanists to study nothing but food plants and hothouse roses and then tell us what the plant world is like!

Let us consider a few examples. In English we divide most of our words into two classes, which have different grammatical and logical properties. Class 1 we call nouns, e.g., "house," "man"; Class 2, verbs, e.g., "hit," "run." Many words of one class can act secondarily as of the other class, e.g., "a hit," "a run," or "to man" the boat, but on the primary level the division between the classes is abso-

FIGURE 1. Languages dissect nature differently. This figure illustrates the different isolates of meaning (thoughts) used by English and Shawnee in reporting the same experience, that of cleaning a gun by running the ramrod through it. The pronouns "I" and "it" are not shown by symbols, as they have the same meaning in each case. In Shawnee "ni-" equals "I"; "-a" equals "it."

lute. Our language thus gives us a bipolar division of nature. But nature herself is not thus polarized. If it be said that strike, turn, run, are verbs because they denote temporary or short-lasting events, i.e., actions, why then is fist a noun? It also is a temporary event. Why are lightning, spark, wave, eddy, pulsation, flame, storm, phase, cycle, spasm, noise, emotion, nouns? They are temporary events. If man and house are nouns because they are long-lasting and stable events, i.e., things, what then are keep, adhere, extend, project, continue, persist, grow, dwell, and so on, doing among the verbs? If it be objected that possess, adhere, are verbs because they are stable

relationships rather than stable percepts, why then should equilibrium, pressure, current, peace, group, nation, society, tribe, sister, or any kinship term, be among the nouns? It will be found that an "event" to us means "what our language classes as a verb" or something analogized therefrom. And it will be found that it is not possible to define event, thing, object, relationship, and so on, from nature, but that to define them always involves a circuitous return to the grammatical categories of the definer's language.

In the Hopi language, lightning, wave, flame, meteor, puff of smoke, pulsation, are verbs—events of necessarily brief duration cannot be

HOPI — ONE WORD (MASA'VYAKA)
ENGLISH — THREE WORDS

ENGLISH — ONE WORD (SNOW)
ESKIMO — THREE WORDS

HOPI — PĀHE
ENGLISH — ONE WORD (WATER); HOPI — TWO WORDS

HOPI — KĒVI

FIGURE 2. Languages classify items of experience differently. The class corresponding to one word and one thought in language *A* may be regarded by language *B* as two or more classes corresponding to two or more words and thoughts.

anything but verbs. Cloud and storm are at about the lower limit of duration for nouns. Hopi, you see, actually has a classification of events (or linguistic isolates) by duration type, something strange to our modes of thought. On the other hand, in Nootka, a language of Vancouver Island, all words seem to us to be verbs, but really there are no Classes 1 and 2; we have, as it were, a monistic view of nature that gives us only one class of word for all kinds of events. "A house occurs" or "it houses" is the way of saying "house," exactly like "a flame occurs" or "it burns." These terms seem to us like verbs because they are inflected for durational and temporal nuances, so that the suffixes of the word for house event make it mean long-lasting house, temporary house, future house, house that used to be, what started out to be a house, and so on.

Hopi has a noun that covers every thing or being that flies, with the exception of birds, which class is denoted by another noun. The former noun may be said to denote the class FC—B, i.e., flying class minus bird. The Hopi actually call insect, airplane, and aviator all by the same word, and feel no difficulty about it. The situation, of course, decides any possible confusion among very disparate members of a broad linguistic class, such as this class FC—B. This class seems to us too large and inclusive, but so would our class "snow" to an Eskimo. We have the same word for falling snow, snow on the ground, snow packed hard like ice, slushy snow, wind-driven flying snow—whatever the situation may be. To an Eskimo, this all-inclusive word would be almost unthinkable; he would say that falling snow, slushy snow, and so on, are sensuously and operationally different, different things to contend with; he uses different words for them and for other kinds of snow. The Aztecs go even farther than we in the opposite direction, with cold, ice, and snow all represented by the same basic word with different terminations; ice is the noun form; cold, the adjectival form; and for snow, "ice mist."

What surprises most is to find that various grand generalizations of the Western world, such as time, velocity, and matter, are not essential to the construction of a consistent picture of the universe. The psychic experiences that we class under these headings are, of course, not destroyed; rather, categories derived from other kinds of experiences take

over the rulership of the cosmology and seem to function just as well. Hopi may be called a timeless language. It recognizes psychological time, which is much like Bergson's "duration," but this "time" is quite unlike the mathematical time, T, used by our physicists. Among the peculiar properties of Hopi time are that it varies with each observer, does not permit of simultaneity, and has zero dimensions; i.e., it cannot be given a number greater than one. The Hopi do not say, "I stayed five days," but "I left on the fifth day." A word referring to this kind of time, like the word day, can have no plural. The puzzle picture (Fig. 3) will give mental exercise to anyone who would like to figure out how the Hopi verb gets along without tenses. Actually, the only practical use of our tenses, in one-verb sentences, is to distinguish among five typical situations, which are symbolized in the picture. The timeless Hopi verb does not distinguish between the present, past, and future of the event itself but must always indicate what type of validity the *speaker* intends the statement to have: (*a*) report of an event (situations 1, 2, 3 in the picture); (*b*) expectation of an event (situation 4); (*c*) generalization or law about events (situation 5). Situation 1, where the speaker and listener are in contact with the same objective field, is divided by our language into the two conditions, 1*a* and 1*b*, which it calls present and past, respectively. This division is unnecessary for a language which assures one that the statement is a report.

Hopi grammar, by means of its forms called aspects and modes, also makes it easy to distinguish between momentary, continued, and repeated occurrences, and to indicate the actual sequence of reported events. Thus the universe can be described without recourse to a concept of dimensional time. How would a physics constructed along these lines work, with no T (time) in its equations? Perfectly, as far as I can see, though of course it would require different ideology and perhaps different mathematics. Of course V (velocity) would have to go too. The Hopi language has no word really equivalent to our "speed" or "rapid." What translates these terms is usually a word meaning intense or very, accompanying any verb of motion. Here is a clue to the nature of our new physics. We may have to introduce a new term I, intensity. Every thing and event will have an I, whether

OBJECTIVE FIELD	SPEAKER (SENDER)	HEARER (RECEIVER)	HANDLING OF TOPIC RUNNING OF THIRD PERSON
SITUATION 1A.			ENGLISH . . "HE IS RUNNING." HOPI . . . . . "WARI." (RUNNING, STATEMENT OF FACT.)
SITUATION 1B. OBJECTIVE FIELD BLANK DEVOID OF RUNNING			ENGLISH . . ."HE RAN." HOPI . . . . . "WARI." (RUNNING) STATEMENT OF FACT.)
SITUATION 2.			ENGLISH . . "HE IS RUNNING." HOPI . . . . . "WARI." (RUNNING, STATEMENT OF FACT.)
SITUATION 3. OBJECTIVE FIELD BLANK			ENGLISH . . "HE RAN." HOPI . . . . . "ERA WARI". (RUNNING, STATEMENT OF FACT FROM MEMORY.)
SITUATION 4. OBJECTIVE FIELD BLANK			ENGLISH . . "HE WILL RUN." HOPI . . . . . "WARIKNI." (RUNNING, STATEMENT OF EXPECTATION.)
SITUATION 5. OBJECTIVE FIELD BLANK			ENGLISH . . "HE RUNS." (e.g. ON THE TRACK TEAM.) HOPI . . . . . "WARIKNGWE." (RUNNING, STATEMENT OF LAW.)

FIGURE 3. Contrast between a "temporal" language (English) and a "timeless" language (Hopi). What are to English differences of time are to Hopi differences in kind of validity.

we regard the thing or event as moving or as just enduring or being. Perhaps the I of an electric charge will turn out to be its voltage, or potential. We shall use clocks to measure some intensities, or, rather, some *relative* intensities, for the absolute intensity of any-thing will be meaningless. Our old friend ac-celeration will still be there but doubtless under a new name. We shall perhaps call it V, meaning not velocity but variation. Perhaps all growths and accumulations will be regarded as V's. We should not have the concept of rate in the temporal sense, since, like velocity, rate introduces a mathematical and linguistic time. Of course we know that all measure-ments are ratios, but the measurements of intensities made by comparison with the standard intensity of a clock or a planet we do not treat as ratios, any more than we so treat a distance made by comparison with a yardstick. . . .

One significant contribution to science from the linguistic point of view may be the greater development of our sense of perspective. We shall no longer be able to see a few recent dialects of the Indo-European family, and the rationalizing techniques elaborated from their patterns, as the apex of the evolution of the human mind; nor their present wide spread as due to any survival from fitness or to anything but a few events of history—events that could be called fortunate only from the parochial point of view of the favored parties. They, and our own thought processes with them, can no longer be envisioned as spanning the gamut of reason and knowledge but only as one constellation in a galactic expanse. A fair realization of the incredible degree of diversity of linguistic system that ranges over the globe leaves one with an inescapable feeling that the human spirit is inconceivably old; that the few thousand years of history covered by our written records are no more than the thickness of a pencil mark on the scale that measures our past experience on this planet; that the events of these recent millennia spell nothing in any evolutionary wise, that the race has taken no sudden spurt, achieved no commanding synthesis during recent millennia, but has only played a little with a few of the linguistic formulations and views of nature bequeathed from an inexpressibly longer past. Yet neither this feeling nor the sense of precarious dependence of all we know upon linguistic tools which themselves are largely unknown need be discouraging to science but should, rather, foster that humility which accompanies the true scientific spirit, and thus forbid that arrogance of the mind which hinders real scientific curiosity and detachment.

26. HOW TO READ BODY LANGUAGE

Flora Davis

Imagine that you're at a party and your hostess suggests a get-to-know-the-others game —*without* words. You can, she says, come up close to your partner and look him over, touch him, sniff him, hug him, use sign language—but you must not say one word.

The first thing you would learn from this experience is how limited wordless communication is. The next thing you might realize is how seldom you touch other people; how uncomfortable it is to be stared at, at close range; how disturbing to be sniffed. Eventually, you might recognize that the one thing nonverbal communication does express very efficiently is emotion.

All of us communicate nonverbally. Most of the time we're not aware that we're doing it. We gesture with eyebrows or a hand,

meet someone else's eyes and look away, shift positions in a chair. We assume that our actions are random and incidental. When we respond to nonverbal cues from others, we sometimes recognize those cues consciously but more often we react to them on an intuitive level.

Researchers have discovered in recent years that there is a system to body gestures almost as consistent and comprehensible as language, and so a flourishing new field for research has opened up. The general assumption: that all body movements have meaning within their specific context.

Every culture has its own body language, and children absorb its nuances along with spoken language. A Frenchman talks and moves in French. An American handles his body in a distinctively American way. Some cultural differences are easy to spot. Most Americans, observing an Englishman, would recognize that the way he crosses his legs is nothing like the way a male American does it. But it takes an expert to pick out a native of Wisconsin just by the way he uses his eyebrows during conversation.

Such regional idioms *can* sometimes be pinpointed. It's also true that men and women use the same body language in distinctively masculine and feminine ways. Your ethnic background, your social class and your own personal style all influence your body language. Nevertheless, you move and gesture within the American idiom.

The person who is truly bilingual is also bilingual in body language. New York's famous mayor Fiorello La Guardia politicked in English, Italian and Yiddish. When films of his speeches are run through without sound, it's not too difficult to identify from his gestures the language he was speaking. One of the reasons dubbed films often seem flat and unreal is that the gestures don't match the language.

Usually, the nonverbal communication acts to qualify the verbal. Casual conversation is normally quite laconic, its meaning conveyed by a few words blended in a kind of madrigal with other elements. What these nonverbal elements express very often is the emotional side of the message.

"I don't know how I know it, but I'm sure she doesn't like me," one woman complained about another. When a person feels liked or disliked, very often it's a case of "not what she said but the way she said it." Psychologist Albert Mehrabian has devised a formula to explain the emotional impact of any message: total impact = 7 percent verbal + 38 percent vocal + 55 percent facial. The importance of the voice can be seen when you consider that even the words "I hate you" can be made to sound seductive. Experiments have been done with tape-recorded voices with the sound filtered: the high register is cut out so that words are low and blurred but the tone of voice comes through. Mehrabian reports that listeners could judge degree of liking rather easily from these doctored tapes.

It isn't just feelings that are expressed nonverbally. One of the surprises is that gestures constitute almost a parallel language. Americans are apt to end a statement with a droop of the head or hand, a lowering of the eyelids. They wind up a question with a lift of the hand, a tilt of the chin or widening

of the eyes. With a future-tense verb they often gesture with a forward movement; for the past tense with a backward one.

Experts in kinesics—the study of communication through body movement—are not prepared to spell out a precise vocabulary of gestures and probably never will be. They will not say, for example, that when an American rubs his nose it always means he is disagreeing with someone or rejecting something. That's one possible interpretation, but there are others. To take another example: When a student in conversation with a professor holds the older man's eyes a little longer than is usual, it can be a sign of respect and affection, it can be a subtle challenge to the professor's authority or it can be something else entirely. The kinesicist, recording the action with a camera and/or an ingenious shorthand system, looks for patterns in the context, not for single meaningful gestures.

The concept of meaning is tricky, since most gestures are not *intended* to mean anything. The student probably is not trying to tell the professor with his eyes that he respects, or doesn't respect, him. He is simply using the eye movement that fits the context, as he might casually use a particular word within a sentence.

Kinesics is a young science, about seventeen years old and very much the brainchild of one man, Ray Birdwhistell. Already it offers a regular smorgasbord of observations. For example, eyebrows have a repertoire of about twenty-three possible positions; men use their eyebrows more than women do; and so forth.

There's nothing here that's startling, much that seems picayune. But for the layman there's a fascination about body language, because it's so vividly *there* for anyone to see. Seeing isn't easy, though—most people find they can shut out the conversation and concentrate on the kinesics for only about thirty seconds at a time. Students of kinesics sometimes learn from video tapes, which can be played, stopped, replayed. Anyone with a television set can experiment with kinesics-watching simply by turning on the picture without the sound.

One of the most potent elements in body language is eye behavior. You shift your eyes, meet another person's gaze or fail to meet it —and produce an effect out of all proportion to the trifling muscular effort you've made.

When two Americans look searchingly into each other's eyes, emotions are heightened and the relationship tipped toward greater intimacy. However, Americans are careful about how and when they meet another's eyes. In our normal conversation, each eye contact lasts only about a second before one or both individuals look away.

Because the longer meeting of the eyes is rare, it is weighted with significance when it happens and can generate a special kind of human-to-human awareness. A girl who has taken part in civil rights demonstrations reported that she was advised, if a policeman confronted her, to look straight into his eyes.

"Make him *see* you as another human being and he's more likely to treat you as one," she was told.

Most of the time, the American interprets a lingering look as a sign of sexual attraction and scrupulously avoids this minor intimacy, except in appropriate circumstances.

"That man makes me so uncomfortable," a young woman complained. "Half the time when I glance at him he's already looking at me—and he keeps right on looking."

By simply using his eyes, a man can make a woman aware of him sexually, comfortably or uncomfortably.

Americans abroad sometimes find local eye behavior hard to interpret.

"My first day in Tel Aviv was disturbing," one man recalled. "People not only stared right at me on the street, they actually looked me up and down. I kept wondering if I was uncombed or unzipped or if I just looked too American. Finally, a friend explained that Israelis think nothing of staring at others on the street."

Proper street behavior in the United States requires a nice balance of attention and inattention. You are supposed to look at a passerby just enough to show that you're aware of his presence. If you look too little, you appear haughty or furtive; too much and you're inquisitive. Usually what happens is that people eye each other until they are about eight feet apart, at which point both cast down their eyes. Sociologist Erving Goffman describes this as "a kind of dimming of lights."

Much of eye behavior is so subtle that we react to it only on the intuitive level. The next time you have a conversation with someone who makes you feel liked, notice what he does with his eyes. Chances are he looks at you more often than is usual with glances a little longer than the normal. You interpret this as a sign—a polite one—that he is interested in you as a person rather than just in the topic of conversation. Probably you also feel that he is both self-confident and sincere.

All this has been demonstrated in elaborate experiments. Subjects sit and talk in the psychologist's laboratory, innocent of the fact that their eye behavior is being observed from behind a one-way vision screen. In one fairly typical experiment, subjects were induced to cheat while performing a task, then were interviewed and observed. It was found that those who had cheated met the interviewer's eyes less often than was normal, an indication that "shifty eyes"—to use the mystery writers' stock phrase—*can* actually be a tip-off to an attempt to deceive or to feelings of guilt.

In parts of the Far East it is impolite to look at the other person at all during conversation. In England the polite listener fixes the speaker with an attentive stare and blinks his eyes occasionally as a sign of interest. That eye-blink says nothing to Americans, who expect the listener to nod or to murmur something—such as "mnhmn."

Let's examine a typical American conversation. Joan and Sandra meet on the sidewalk. Preliminary greetings over with, Joan begins to talk. She starts by looking right away from Sandra. As she hits her conversational stride, she glances back at her friend from time to time at the end of a phrase or a sentence. She does not look at her during hesitations or pauses but only at natural breaks in the flow of her talk. At the end of what she wants to say, she gives Sandra a rather longer glance. Experiments indicate that if she fails to do this, Sandra, not recognizing that it is her turn to talk, will hesitate or will say nothing at all.

When Sandra takes up the conversation, Joan, listening, sends her longer glances than she did when she herself had the floor. When their eyes meet, Joan usually makes some sign that she is listening.

It's not hard to see the logic behind this eye behavior. Joan looks away at the start of her statement and during hesitations to avoid being distracted while she organizes her thoughts. She glances at Sandra from time to time for feedback: to make sure she is listening, to see how she is reacting or for permission to go on talking. And while Sandra is doing the talking, Joan glances often at her to show that she is paying attention—to show that she's polite. For Americans, then, eye behavior does duty as a kind of conversational traffic signal, to control how talking time is shared.

You have only to observe an actual conversation to see that this pattern is not a precisely predictable one. None of the "facts" of eye behavior are cut and dried, for there are variations between individuals. People use their eyes differently and spend different—and characteristic—amounts of time looking at others. But if you know what to look for, the basic American idiom is there.

Just talking about eye behavior is enough to make most people so self-conscious that they suddenly don't know what to do with their eyes. But the surprising strength of these microhabits shows in the speed with which they reassert themselves the minute they're dropped out of awareness again.

A man's eye movements and the rest of his body language are more apt to provide a clue to his origins than to his secret thoughts. But it's true that there are times when what a person says with his body gives the lie to what he is saying with his tongue. Sigmund Freud once wrote:

"He that has eyes to see and ears to hear may convince himself that no mortal can keep a secret. If his lips are silent, he chatters with his fingertips; betrayal oozes out of him at every pore."

Psychiatrists working with patients respond sometimes consciously, sometimes intuitively, to nonverbal clues that signal inner conflicts. Some psychiatrists have tried to pin down these clues more precisely.

In one recent experiment Dr. Paul Ekman and Wallace Friesen filmed interviews with mental patients. Each patient was doing his best to seem calm, cool and rational, though some were still quite disturbed. Dr. Ekman and Friesen's theory—partially confirmed—was that the disturbance would be easier to deduce from gestures than from facial expressions.

People who can successfully control their faces are often unaware of what their hands, legs and feet may be doing; or else they just can't prevent signs of tension and anxiety from leaking out.

"Ted seems like the calmest, most self-controlled guy in the world—until you know about his foot," a man remarked about a business colleague. But the whole office staff knows about Ted's foot, which beats the floor constantly, restlessly, as if it had a life of its own beyond the control of this big, quiet man.

Anxiety is one emotion feet and legs may reveal. Rage is another: during arguments the feet often tense up. Fear sometimes produces barely perceptible running motions—a kind of nervous leg-jiggle. And then there are the subtle, provocative leg gestures that women use, consciously and unconsciously.

Ordinarily we sit too close to each other to be able to observe the lower body easily. In fact, people who are forced to sit at a distance from others, without a desk or table to shield them, usually feel uncomfortable and vulnerable.

Aside from uneasy eye behavior and true facial *faux pas,* the best facial clue to deception is the microexpression. These are expressions or fragments of an expression that cross the face so fleetingly that they're gone—suppressed or disguised—before most people can notice them. Most expressions last half a second to a second, but the microexpression can be as quick as a single motion-picture frame, over in one fiftieth of a second. It can sometimes be caught by an alert observer, and an untrained person may react to it intuitively without being able to say just what he is reacting to. When a face is filmed and the film is then run through at a slow speed, microexpressions are easy to pick out.

Sometimes a person signals his inner emotions by his posture—sitting, for example, in a very tense way. Psychiatrist Frieda Fromm-Reichmann, to get some idea of what a patient was feeling, would imitate his posture. Recent studies by psychologists suggest that what posture often reflects is the person's attitude to people he is with.

Imagine two businessmen, Mark and Stanley, comfortably settled in a psychologist's lab. Stanley sits up very straight, hands clasping his knees, facing his companion squarely. Mark lounges far back in his chair, body twisted slightly to the right. A psychologist, observing the pair, can make several shrewd guesses about them just from their postures. The first guess: that they dislike each other.

Second: that Stanley is rather intimidated by Mark; Mark not at all by Stanley.

Support for these conclusions comes from an experiment that indicates that when men are with other men whom they dislike they relax either very little or very much—depending on whether they see the other man as threatening. Relaxation was judged quite precisely within three categories. Labeled least relaxed were those—like Stanley—who sat with tense hands in a rigid posture. Subjects who slumped forward slightly—the angle was measured in degrees from the vertical—were judged moderately relaxed, and it was usually found that they liked the person they were with. Most relaxed were those, like Mark, who leaned far back and to one side.

Women who took part in this experiment always signaled their dislike with the very relaxed posture. And men, paired with women they disliked, were never up-tight enough about it to sit rigidly.

Congruent postures sometimes offer a guide to broad relationships within a group. Imagine that at the tag-end of a party the remaining guests have been fired up by an argument over student radicalism. Soon you may be able to spot at a glance the two sides of the argument by postures adopted. Most of the pros, for example, may sit with crossed knees, the cons with legs stretched out and arms folded. A few middle-of-the-roaders may try a little of each—crossing their knees *and* folding their arms. If an individual abruptly shifts his body around in his chair, it may mean that he disagrees with the speaker or even that he is changing sides. None of this, of course, represents an infallible guide to group-watching. If you try to check it out, you may find several pros in the con posture and when your neighbor squirms around in his chair it may turn out to be because his leg went to sleep. But congruent postures are apparently significant enough of the time to be worth watching for.

Postural shifts sometimes parallel spoken language. Psychiatrist Albert Scheflen studied posture by filming psychotherapy sessions and found that a kind of kinesic dance took place. The individual would shift his head and eyes every few sentences, usually just as he finished making a point; would make a major shift of his whole body to coincide with a change in point of view—from that of listener to speaker, for example. Both patients and therapists worked from limited postural repertoires and produced their shifts in remarkably predictable sequences. One patient turned his head to the right and avoided the woman therapist's eyes whenever she spoke; looked directly and challengingly at her each time he answered; and then, usually, he would cock his head and turn his eyes to the left as he went off on a conversational tangent.

While children learn spoken and body language—proper postures, eye behavior, etc.—they also learn a subtler thing: how to react to space around them.

A man's sense of self apparently is not bound by his skin. He walks around inside a kind of private bubble, which represents the amount of air-space he feels he must have between himself and other people. This is a truth anyone can easily demonstrate by moving in gradually on another person. At some point the other will begin, irritably or perhaps just absentmindedly, to back away. Anthropologists working with cameras have recorded the tremors and minute eye movements that betray the moment when the bubble is breached.

Anthropologist Edward Hall was one of the first to comment on man's feelings about space. From his work the fascinating field of proxemics has evolved.

Hall pointed out that the North American demands more personal space for himself than do people from many other countries. For two unacquainted adult male North Americans the comfortable distance to stand for conversation is about two feet apart. The South American likes to stand much closer, which creates problems when the two meet face to face. For as the South American moves in to what is to him a proper talking distance, the North American feels he's being pushy; and as the North American backs off to create the size gap that seems right to him, the South American thinks he's being standoffish. Hall once watched a conversation between a Latin and a North American that began at one end of a forty-foot hall and eventually wound up at the other end, the pair progressing by "an almost continual series of small backward steps on the part of the North American...and an equal closing of the gap by the Latin American...."

Often, North Americans can't control their own reactions to being closed in on.

"Dolores is one of those people who like

to talk standing practically nose to nose," one young woman explained. "I like her and I know it's just her way, but I can't help myself; when I see her coming I start backing up. I put a desk or a chair between us if I can."

If Americans and Latins have misunderstandings, the American and the Arab are even less compatible in their space habits. Arabs thrive on close contact. They stand very close together to talk, staring intently into each other's eyes and breathing into each other's faces. These are all actions the American associates with sexual intimacy and he finds it quite disturbing to be subjected to them in a nonsexual context.

Americans maintain their distance in many ways. We actually suppress our sense of smell. Anthropologist Margaret Mead once remarked:

> "In the United States, nobody has been willing to smell another human being, if they could help it, for the last fifty years."

To the Arab, on the other hand, to be able to smell a friend is reassuring. Good smells please him, and smelling is a way of being involved with another. To deny a friend his breath would be to act ashamed. When Arab intermediaries call to inspect a prospective bride for a friend or relative, they sometimes ask to smell her—but not to make sure she's freshly scrubbed; apparently what they look for is any lingering odor of anger or discontent.

Americans don't like to feel anyone else's body heat, except in lovemaking—they object to sitting down in a chair warmed by another. And they don't like to be touched. The American spends years teaching his children not to crowd him.

When forced to share his bubble of space with another—for example, in a crowded elevator—the American compensates for the unwanted intimacy in a number of ways. He averts his eyes and shifts his body so that he doesn't face anyone directly. If forced into actual physical contact with another person, he holds that part of his body rigid. He feels strongly that this is the proper way to behave.

"I can't stand that guy," a young stockbroker remarked. "I have to ride down in the elevator with him sometimes and he just lets himself go. It's like being leaned on by a mountain of warm jelly."

The amount of space a man needs is also influenced by his personality—introverts, for example, seem to need more elbow room than extraverts—and by the way he feels about the person he is with. If he dislikes him or if the other outranks him, then he will stand farther away. Space can be a telltale status signal. When executive Jones walks into executive Smith's office, you can gauge their relative importance in the scheme of things by noting just how far into the room Jones comes. Executive desks are often made big enough to hold visitors to a respectful distance.

Situation and mood also affect distance. Moviegoers waiting in line to see a sexy film will queue up much more densely than those waiting to see a family-entertainment movie; in fact, one suburban theater manager reported that he could get three times as many customers into his lobby for a sex comedy.

In America a man standing still or seated in a public place is assumed to have around him a small sphere of privacy, even larger than his personal-space bubble, that has to be respected. Anyone invading this space will apologize. In a nearly empty room a man does not expect a stranger to come and take a chair right next to him. If someone does, he will either put up with it or he will move to another chair, but he will not protest. Experiments have demonstrated that people rarely defend their space rights with words, possibly because they're not really conscious of the fact that they feel they have rights.

Dr. Augustus F. Kinzel, a New York psychiatrist, recently studied the "body-buffer zone" in violent and nonviolent prisoners. Placing each man in turn in the center of a small, bare room, he walked slowly toward him. Prisoners with a record of violence reacted sharply while he was still some distance away. They reported a feeling that he was "looming" or "rushing" at them. The nonviolent men let him come up quite close. Dr. Kinzel studied just fifteen subjects and isn't jumping to any conclusions until he has carried out more tests, but his experiment suggests that proxemics might provide a simple technique for spotting the potentially violent.

It's important to know how much physical space people actually need, especially in crowded city living. Animals forced to live in overcrowded conditions undergo such stress that whole populations sometimes die off.

Architects need to consider the effects of different kinds of space in designing new buildings. Winston Churchill, reacting to a postwar plan to change the intimate scale of the House of Commons, where opponents face each other across a narrow aisle, warned that:

> "We shape our buildings, and they shape us."

Borrowing material from both kinesics and proxemics, sociologists have also entered the nonverbal field. Their work often encompasses the verbal as well, but it is usually lumped with the nonverbal studies because the field of interest for men such as Erving Goffman is still the small behaviors of face-to-face encounters.

Taking nothing for graduated, Goffman has examined the assumptions, conscious and unconscious, that underlie our everyday behavior. If most sane people didn't share these assumptions, the world would be a more unruly and dangerous place. When you walk on a public street you assume that no stranger will assault you or bar your way. In casual conversation you assume that other people will not insult you, lie to you or create a scene. People depend on each other to behave properly.

Many of our assumptions have been shaken in the past five to ten years—notably, the assumption that people will not use their own bodies to block access to a public building. Sociologists point out that wherever there are rules there is the potential for breaking rules —for making them the basis for aggression. This is all the more shocking when the rules are the taken-for-granted kind.

Another assumption that has been challenged is the middle-class idea of what constitutes a proper appearance. A person communicates —nonverbally—with his clothes, hair style and general manner, for these are a matter of choice. Ordinarily what they communicate is respect for the social occasion. They signify that this person can be trusted not to do anything outlandish. Today young people often use this particular social technique to communicate disrespect instead.

"I don't understand kids nowadays. You can't tell the girls from the boys," an elderly woman complained, typically, on a street in New York's East Village.

"But that's the whole point, lady," a long-haired passerby told her patiently. "We don't *care* whether you can tell us apart."

It's easier to understand why people get so up-tight about certain things if you take into account the presuppositions they start out with.

There are other assumptions, too. We all have our territorial preserves—boundaries we don't expect people to try to cross. Personal space is one kind of territoriality, the earliest studied. Professor Goffman is concerned with other kinds, rights we assume we have: the right not to be stared at, not to be touched, the right not to be brought into strangers' conversations, the right to informational privacy—there are certain questions we don't expect to be asked. Encounter groups or sensitivity training play on these assumptions. In an attempt to teach "normal" people to live more intensely, they require participants to touch each other, perhaps even to grapple with each other, to ask intimate questions and express honest opinions, even hurtful ones. They encourage people who are usually total strangers to share the trappings of intimacy in the hope that real, deeply emotional—if temporary—relationships will result and that in the process each participant will learn something about himself. Those who join a grope group, as encounter groups are sometimes called, are expected most of the time to *do,* rather than to talk, for the theory is that by the time we are adults we have learned to hide our feelings behind a screen of polite words—hiding them so well that often they are inaccessible even to ourselves.

Which brings us full circle, back to that nonverbal party game with its emotion-charged undertones. George du Maurier once wrote:

> "Language is a poor thing. You fill your lungs with wind and shake a little slit in your throat, and make mouths, and that shakes the air; and the air shakes a pair of little drums in my head...and my brain seizes your meaning in the rough. What a roundabout way and what a waste of time."

Communication between human beings would be just that dull if it were all done with words; but actually, words are often the smallest part of it....

27. TOWARD A THEORY OF NONVERBAL COMMUNICATION

Jurgen Ruesch and Weldon Kees

In broad terms, nonverbal forms of codification fall into three distinct categories:

Sign language includes all those forms of codification in which words, numbers, and punctuation signs have been supplanted by gestures; these vary from the "monosyllabic" gesture of the hitchhiker to such complete systems as the language of the deaf.

Action language embraces all movements that are not used exclusively as signals. Such acts as walking and drinking, for example, have a dual function: on one hand they serve personal needs, and on the other they constitute statements to those who may perceive them.

Object language comprises all intentional and nonintentional display of material things, such as implements, machines, art objects, architectural structures, and—last but not least—the human body and whatever clothes or covers it. The embodiment of letters as they occur in books and on signs has a material substance, and this aspect of words also has to be considered as object language.

Analogic, nonverbal forms of codification stand in a somewhat complementary relationship to digital or verbal forms of denotation, particularly in *spatial and temporal characteristics*. Sign, action, and object languages usually require a certain space that ordinarily cannot be modified. This is not true of spoken and written languages, whose spatial requirements are minimal. For example, print can be modified in size, and microfilming makes it possible to reduce an entire library to a fraction of the space occupied by the original

From NONVERBAL COMMUNICATION *by Jurgen Ruesch and Weldon Kees, pp. 189–193. Copyright 1956 by the University of California Press. Reprinted by permission of The Regents of the University of California.*

material. The distinctions in terms of the temporal characteristics are even more impressive. In order to be understood, words must be read or heard one after another. In written communication, the amount of time that elapses between the act of writing and the act of reading may be considerable, since a piece of writing may be composed over a long period of time and may not be read or come to light until years afterward. In contrast, the appreciation of objects and gestures is based less upon impressions that follow each other in serial order but more upon multiple sensory impressions that may impinge simultaneously.

Verbal and nonverbal languages do not appeal to the same *sensory modalities*. Silently executed sign language is perceived exclusively by the eye, much in the way that spoken language is perceived by the ear. Action language may be perceived by the eye and the ear and—to a lesser degree—through the senses of touch, temperature, pain, and vibration. Object language appeals to both distance and closeness receivers, including the senses of smell and taste. This fact has notable effects upon the mutual position of the participants in a communication network. In practice, sign and action languages depend upon immediacy, requiring the participants to be within the range of each other's vision. Object language requires various kinds of perception, usually at a much closer range, but transmitter and perceiver need not be within reach. As a matter of fact, the transmitter may be dead when the receiver obtains the object and the message that is coded therein. In this respect, object language closely resembles written language, except that it is more universally understood.

The *selection* of a particular type *of codification* depends upon the communicative versatility of an individual and his ability to vary statements in keeping with the nature of a situation. The use of object language is indicated, for example, because of its succinct and immediate nature, in situations where a person needs to make statements to himself —he may tie a knot in his handkerchief to remind himself of something important. Action language is indicated when people wish to convey the exact nature of a situation to others; for example, certain concepts are involved in the performance of music and in the servicing of machinery—in brief, the transmission of skills—that can be conveyed only nonverbally. Verbal language is most adapted to dissecting aspects of events and to codifying such knowledge in spoken or written terms, and to carrying on meaningful discourse.

Nonverbal languages take on prime importance in situations *where words fail completely.* Words are particularly inadequate when the quality of space has to be symbolized. Photographs, paintings, drawings, material samples, or small-scale, three-dimensional models are indispensable to an appreciation of the distinctions between a Gothic cathedral and its Baroque counterpart. Analogic forms of representation are equally necessary in the reporting of extreme situations, when emotional experiences are difficult to convey to those who did not personally participate in them. In an effort to suggest the quality of such events, a speaker or a writer attempts to use verbal signals that are designed to evoke emotions similar to those he or others experienced. If the listener or reader has never been exposed to or is not familiar, either through reading or other experience, with situations similar to or evocative of those described, the account will fail altogether. However, with the aid of objects and pictures, or through reënactment, even the least imaginative can be given some sense of what happened. Such verbally oriented specialists as lawyers are aware of the necessity of supplementing their verbal arguments with courtroom reënactments and of documenting them with material and pictorial evidence.

The characteristic functions of each of the various types of nonverbal language are not necessarily interchangeable. *Object language,* because of its time-enduring qualities, plays an enormous role in archaeology, anthropology, and history. Until the discovery of the first written documents to come down to us, the only enduring traces we had of the remote past were those that survived in the forms of objects and buildings. Tools and weapons were known as early as the Stone Age, and the fact that material articles almost always carry either implicit or explicit instructions with them makes it possible to reconstruct events of prehistoric times, even though we lack knowledge of the verbal language of a particular period. When we observe a tool or an implement, we consciously or unconsciously connect such objects with human activities. Somehow, when an object is assessed, the missing craftsman, inventor, or operator— either the projected self or another person— is present at the rim of consciousness, vaguely outlined though not insistent, but nonetheless felt. The interpretation is made easier because of the fact that objects either refine and increase the scope of our sensory end organs or serve to extend or replace our muscles. The modern version of sensory extension is the scientific recording instrument; that of motor extension is the labor-saving machine. In very recent years, a third kind of extension has been developed: giant calculators, computing machines, and other devices vastly extend the scope of our thinking, predicting, and decision making.

Objects may be intentionally shaped *as symbols,* or they may come to be looked upon as symbols. When they are not used for sharpening perception, facilitating evaluation, or simplifying action, they may consequently stand for something else and assume functions similar to those of words, standing for individuals, animals, activities, or other objects. The decorative aspects of materials and objects are closely related to their language functions. Whereas the referential properties of objects bear upon events that, if expressed in words, would be referred to as the subject, decoration is an expression of activities that, if expressed in words, would be called the predicate.

Nonverbal language is frequently used to effect *social control.* In interpersonal situations, many ideas, concepts, and things must be stated in ways that will not be considered obtrusive or offensive. Among such considerations is the definition of boundaries. Marks of ownership, expressed by means of objects, may be found near entrances, at gateways and doors, identifying owners or residents of a certain property and indicating how they may be reached. Such marks are particularly suitable for denoting statements to whom it may concern. Objects that stand permanently in one place and can be seen at any time impose prohibitions through their impact. Some objects are addressed to particular people; appealing interpersonally, they may invite, seduce, or repel, or demand to be looked at, touched, or tried out. We all consciously look for nonverbal clues in buildings, landscapes, and interiors, for we know that these clues have something to say about the status, prestige, taste, and other values of those who own them. Such an awareness is used by architects, decorators, and owners to set the scene for social encounters.

Object language may also be called into play when persons who make unethical, immoral, slanderous, or *profane statements* wish to hide their identity. Object language is ideal for such purposes, since it is less rigidly governed by rules than are actions or words; frequently, too, such messages are difficult to track down to their source. Thus, where words might be considered to be in bad taste or in violation of the law, many of the subtleties touching on social discrimination, emotional expression, and selective appeal are entrusted either completely or in part to nonverbal codifications.

Although verbal language often necessitates uneconomical denotation, object language allows concise and *economic phrasing*. Abbreviated statements are frequently expressed through a mixture of verbal and nonverbal language that in turn necessitates a particular kind of grammar. For example, the subject may be denoted by a three-dimensional object, whereas the predicate may be expressed in words. Here, the object identifies, the words qualify. Other statements may be repeated in nonverbal terms to avoid repetitions that might be considered boring. Human tolerance for redundancy in analogic language is far greater than its tolerance for redundancy in verbal language.

In contrast to object language, *action language* is transitory, although at the same time it represents the most universal kind of language. Among animals, auditory and visual perception of movements tend to set in motion other actions on the part of the perceiving animal. These actions may in turn influence the animal who gave the first signal. This is true of human behavior as well. Since action language exerts a kinesthetic effect, often initiating abortive movements in the perceiver, the deaf, for example, depend upon this phenomenon in the interpretation of lip reading. Indeed, almost everyone attempts to "get into the act" when watching certain physical or social actions, as can be observed from the behavior of people watching parades or from the lack of reserve on the part of sports enthusiasts. This fact is apparent in any activity that depends upon the reciprocal responses of the participants. The members of a team of acrobats in action cannot signal to each other through words or objects, but instead must rely upon split-second comprehension of each other's timing. Similarly, a spectator must experience the impact of such action himself, either visually or by actual participation, to understand fully the scope and extent of the communicative aspects of such movements.

Action language is the principal way in which *emotions* are expressed. When, in the course of a deadlocked argument, a person slams his fist upon the table, this action, along with other signs of tension, is universally understood. Other participants, almost by necessity, react with avoidant, protective, or fighting reactions. By making a switch from words to action, the referential properties of language are abruptly shifted from conflict to a context in which agreement may be possible. By means of such expression, the discussants are capable of reëstablishing contact, and may either resume their verbal discussion or separate altogether. In any event, a deadlock is broken.

Closely related to action language are *sign language and gesture*. Over the course of centuries, every social group has developed systems of communication in which particular words, signs, and gestures have been assigned communicative significance. There is a kind of gesture that assumes the auxiliary role of an emphasizing, timing, and directional device —for example, a pointed finger. Another kind of gesture takes the place of verbal signs themselves, as in Indian sign language. Because such denotation systems are not bound to phonetics, they enable persons who speak different languages to communicate with each other in ways analagous to the pictographic symbolizations that cut across verbal language barriers.

The *relationship between verbal and nonverbal codifications* can be conceptualized best through the notion of metacommunication. Any message may be regarded as having two aspects: the statement proper, and the explanations pertaining to its interpretation. The nature of interpersonal communication necessitates that these coincide in time, and this can be achieved only through the use of another channel. Thus, when a statement is phrased verbally, instructions tend to be given nonverbally. The effect is similar to an arrangement of a musical composition for two instruments, where the voices in one sense move independently and in another change and supplement each other but nonetheless are integrated into an organic and functional unity.

Combinations of the verbal and the nonverbal may be employed not only to enlighten but also *to obscure the issues* involved. In politics, business, advertising—indeed in every walk of life—words may be used to conceal forthcoming actions, and contradictory expressions are consciously used to create confusion, since human communication almost always involves object, action, and word. If all the symbolic expressions of an individual refer to the same event, then the referential aspects of the statement are clear. But when action codifications contradict verbal codifications, then confusion is almost certain to result. For example, when a mother repeatedly exclaims, "Darling, you're so sweet," simultaneously pinching her child to the extent of producing black and blue marks, the child has to learn to disregard either the action or the verbal statement in order to avoid confusion.

Finally, *verbal language* is based upon entirely different principles than the nonverbal languages. In its denotative capacity a single word can refer to a general or universal aspect of a thing or event only. In order to particularize and specify, words must be combined with other words in serial order. Words enable us to express abstractions, to communicate interpolations and extrapolations, and they make possible the telescoping of far-flung aspects of events and diversified ideas into comprehensible terms. Unlike nonverbal codifications, which are analogic and continuous, verbal codifications are essentially emergent,

discontinuous, and arbitrary. The versatility of words—and this includes numbers—may, however, have dangerous consequences. Words and—to a lesser degree—gestures are commonly thought to be the principal means through which messages are conveyed. Even though such a view is not substantiated by fact, it is convenient—especially for purposes of public administration and law—to assume that we live in an almost exclusively verbal world. This emphasis upon the verbal is a by-product of modern civilization, with its accelerated centralization of control, in which increasingly more people do clerical work and fewer people are engaged in productive work. One of the consequences has been the creation of a staggering variety of middlemen who traffic solely in information. Not only salesmen but even many executives seem to have become credulous of their own propaganda, a situation that is further aggravated by the fact that most of these men have rather limited contact with many of the processes they symbolically deal with or control. The danger of this remoteness from reality lies in the tendency to regard abstract principles as concrete entities, attributing body and substance to numbers and letters and confusing verbal symbols with actual events. Such a way of thinking is an almost inescapable occupational hazard of those who use words for purposes of control.

When verbal and digital symbols are not repeatedly checked against the things they purport to stand for, *distortions of signification* may develop that *nonverbal languages seldom bring about*. Since in everyday communication these shortcomings of verbal language are difficult to avoid, people often intuitively resort to the use of nonverbal, analogic language, which is more closely tied to actual events. But this is not enough. If human beings are to protect themselves against the onslaughts of modern communications machinery and the distortions of propaganda, they must ultimately learn once again to use words scrupulously and with a sense of integrity. Only by a renewal of emphasis on the individual, with all his personal and unique characteristics—and this involves to a great extent the nonverbal—can a sense of proportion and dignity be restored to human relations.

28. WHAT IS BEING COMMUNICATED?

Andrew Wyeth, *Christina's World* (1948). Collection, The Museum of Modern Art, New York.

Andrew Wyeth, *April Wind*. Courtesy Wadsworth Atheneum, Hartford, Connecticut.

Bye-bye

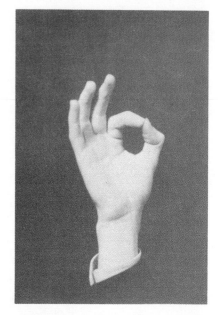

Just right

Louder, please

GESTURES AS SUBSTITUTES FOR WORDS   Over there

Play at close quarters

Transaction at arm's length

Closeness and touch can
convey affection

An unrelated pair

One and a couple

INTERPERSONAL DISTANCE

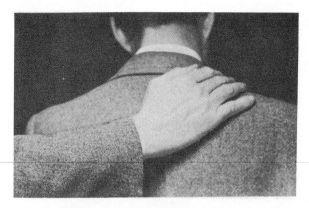

Gesture of moral support

Proffered light

The pleasure of feeding and being fed

Paternal consolation: squatting
down

Maternal consolation: picking
up and holding tight

ASSISTANCE AND SUPPORT

United Press International Photo, September 20, 1960.

RECOMMENDED FURTHER READING

Brown, Roger: *Words and Things;* Glencoe, Ill., Free Press 1958

Bruner, Jerome S. *et al.: Studies in Cognitive Growth;* New York, John Wiley 1966

*Carroll, John B.: *Language and Thought;* Englewood Cliffs, N.J., Prentice-Hall 1964

Furth, H.: *Thinking Without Language: Psychological Implications of Deafness;* New York, Free Press 1966

Jakobovits, L. and M. Miron: *Readings in the Psychology of Language;* Englewood Cliffs, N.J., Prentice-Hall 1967

Lenneberg, Eric H.: *New Directions in the Study of Language;* Cambridge, Mass., MIT Press 1964

Miller, George A.: *Language and Communication;* New York, McGraw-Hill 1951

Morris, Charles: *Signs, Language and Behavior;* Englewood Cliffs, N.J., Prentice-Hall 1946

Osgood, Charles E. and T. A. Sebeok (eds.): *Psycholinguistics;* Bloomington, Ind., Indiana University Press 1965

Pei, Mario: *The Story of Language;* Philadelphia, Lippincott 1949

*Sapir, Edward: *Language;* New York, Harcourt Brace Jovanovich 1921

*————: *Selected Writings in Language, Culture and Personality* (ed. by David Mandelbaum); Berkeley, Calif., University of California Press 1949

Staats, Arthur W.: *Learning, Language and Cognition;* New York, Holt, Rinehart & Winston 1968

Vetter, H.: *Language Behavior and Psychopathology;* Skokie, Ill., Rand McNally 1969

Whorf, Benjamin Lee: *Language, Thought and Reality: Selected Writings of Benjamin Lee Whorf* (ed. by John B. Carroll); New York, Technology Press of MIT-Wiley 1956

* Paperback edition available.

PART VII

THE MOTIVATION

OF BEHAVIOR

However closely psychologists may observe behavior and its development they are never satisfied with observation and description alone. They insist on discovering what *causes* behavior, *why* an organism acts as it does rather than in some other way equally open to it. They believe, in other words, that action has antecedent causes, that it does not happen merely because the organism has nothing better to do (although, in fact, some kinds of exploratory behavior may occur for that reason, perhaps in response to boredom).

In discussing the causes of behavior, many psychologists speak of "motives" or "motivations" as though the latter were entities the existence of which explained the behavior in question. In reality, however, motives are not things that can be isolated or directly observed and examined apart from behavior itself. To say that an individual does well at a particular task because he has high achievement motivation is a tautology of a limited and rather unenlightening sort. Rather, "motives"—like "instincts"—are words, verbal constructs, or "intervening variables" that refer to processes (their precise nature as yet unknown)—biochemical, neurological, social, and cultural—intermediate between physiological states of the organism and the overt behavior (physical or verbal) that other people and instruments can observe and record. "Motives" are thus words, not things or even processes, although the work of many researchers (see Selection 6) suggests that the source of most, if not all, goal-directed behaviors ("motivations") may eventually be localized within the brain. So long, however, as we recognize that the word motives *refers* not to things but to particular states of the organism that stimulate it to act or that sustain and give direction to its action once begun, states that are inferred retrospectively from the actions themselves, we can continue to use the word fruitfully and to investigate its exact referents.

Over time, various theories of human motivation have been advanced, theories that we cannot explore here in any depth. While these theories are not mutually contradictory each of them tends to emphasize different elements of causation. All of them, however, start with the biological organism and agree that it is born with certain physiological needs that demand gratification if it is to live and mature normally. Denial of these needs creates what is called "primary drives" in the organism, such as hunger, thirst, elimination, and sex. At this point, regrettably, agreement ends and disagreement commences, both over the precise number and nature of such primary drives and their relative importance.

Sigmund Freud's psychoanalytic theories, historically the first comprehensive formulation and still probably the single most influential (see Parts IX and XI), asserted the ultimate primacy of two drives (or instincts—*Trieb* in German): sex (libido or *eros*) and aggression (*thanatos* or the death instinct), from which all others are directly or indirectly derived. Freud, who based his theories on clinical experience with neurotic patients, also developed systematically the concept of unconscious motivation: that individuals often (though not always) act for reasons of which they are not consciously aware, that their overt behavior is often but an indirect and devious expression of concealed, consciously unacceptable drives. These underlying motives reveal themselves in dreams, jokes, and slips of the tongue or pen and can be made conscious in psychoanalysis through the process of "free association." Ultimately, Freud believed that all motivation would be found to have a biological basis but most of his present followers have explicitly or implicitly abandoned that belief. Since about 1950, however, psychoanalytic theorists have begun to pay increasing attention to the ego, that part of the psychic structure that recognizes and copes with reality, as against unconscious drives (the "id") derived either from biological processes or childhood experiences.

Behavior or learning theorists, while not rejecting the idea of unconscious motivation, have stressed that most human motives (for example, fear and hate) are acquired or learned in the course of socialization and that even the primary drives are constrained, channeled, and directed toward particular goals by the influence of social learning and culture. A number of such theorists have tried to restate psychoanalytic ideas in terms of learning theory and so long as one construes learning in a broad sense, not merely as conscious and formal instruction, there seems considerable compatibility between the two positions. Freud, for example, stressed the importance of experiences undergone during the first five years of life (the period of primary socialization) a period during which the child's most important learning doubtless takes place.

A third approach, that of the cognitive theorists, emphasizes the conscious aspects of human behavior: that action is frequently purposive, that individuals are often not only aware of their motives but consciously choose goals and devise plans so as to attain them. Once again, this point of view does not exclude the others but emphasizes more than they the elements of conscious choice and planning in human behavior, an emphasis that complements the new interest in ego psychology among psychoanalytic theorists.

In the present state of knowledge we cannot say that one of these theories of motivation is true and the others false. There is evidence that supports and other data that contradict each position. To be frank, psychology as yet possesses no universally accepted general theory of human motivation. What we can be sure of is that human—as contrasted with infra-human—motivation is enormously complex, that particular acts are usually determined by multiple causes, that rarely can human action be explained solely by reference to physiological drives (and then only when the individual has been reduced near the animal level, as in cases of extreme starvation or sustained environmental deprivation), that much human behavior is an uneasy compromise among two or more conflicting motives, and that the almost infinite human capacity for deception and self-deception ensures that motivation can rarely be inferred with certainty from an isolated behavioral act.

In the first selection that follows Robert W. White of Harvard argues that "competence" or "effectance"—the desire to deal effectively with one's environment—is as basic a human motive as those stemming from imperative physiological needs. Human beings dislike boredom and typically respond to it by actively seeking stimulation and novelty from their surroundings, a point very similar to Hebb's discussion (in Selection 7) of the role of environmental stimulation in normal psychological functioning. White maintains that play is a serious attempt by the child to develop and test his sense of competence and that later adolescent and adult motives are differentiated out from a general feeling of competence that develops early in childhood. The research reported by Maya Pines in Selection 11 supports this latter contention.

If the importance of a motive is to be judged by the importance of those behaviors to which it leads then there are no more crucial human motives than sex and aggression, as Freud long ago pointed out. For that reason, if for no other, it seems appropriate that we devote the bulk of this section to a consideration of these omnipresent and compelling impulses.

In Selection 30 Clellan Ford and Frank Beach consider sexual behavior among "civilized" people in the light of data from animal studies and from nonliterate (or primitive) societies. They conclude that human sexual behavior as we know it is the result of interaction between diffuse, physiologically grounded motivational tendencies and cultural prescriptions or proscriptions. Culture channels human physiological needs in approved ways toward acceptable objects. Human beings must learn appropriate sexual responses and behaviors—even gender roles (that is, masculine and feminine) are learned—and almost all such learning is social rather than of an individual trial and error variety. Human sexual behavior thus involves far more than the gratification of a physiological need. Through social influences ("conditioning" or "learning") sexual motivation can, in fact, be directed toward objects, such as money and power, that are not at all sexual in the biologic sense. Finally, the reader should note how these authors link sexual motivation with aggression, a connection that Freud made explicit and that runs like a recurring theme through many discussions of both sex and aggression.

Paul Gebhard's short selection shows that immediate situational factors can decisively affect a person's pattern of sexual response. While he suggests that puberty may be a "critical period" (see Part III) for human sexual development it would appear that sexual behavior patterns can be reorganized long after the critical period has ended if favoring situational factors happen to fuse with strong sexual and emotional drives. "One-shot conditioning" thus becomes an example of dramatic and unusually effective re-learning or "imprinting."

In the third selection dealing with sex Wardell Pomeroy, one of the authors of the original Kinsey Report, reviews the various meanings of the word "normal" and the range of human sexual behaviors that may be embraced by those meanings. His discussion should make clear that sexual "normality" is determined not biologically but culturally.

Discussions of homosexuality are still too often characterized by intense, often passionate, emotion as well as by a tendency to stereotype the image of "the" homosexual. In the final selection of this group Evelyn Hooker, of the University of California (at Los Angeles), dispassionately compares the personality adjustment of a group of overt male homosexuals with that of a matched group of heterosexual males. Her findings, based on the use of projective tests (see Part VIII), suggest not only that homosexuals, like heterosexuals, exhibit life adjustments ranging from superior to marginal but that it is often impossible for even experienced clinicians to tell from a test protocol (record) whether an individual is homosexual or heterosexual. Dr. Hooker concludes that "homosexuality" as a clearly defined clinical entity does not, in fact, exist and that homosexual object choice is not, as such, evidence of psychopathology. The reader might ask himself what the probable consequences would be should American society come to consider homosexuality within the range of "normal" (i.e., acceptable) behaviors.

Turning from sex to aggression, Konrad Lorenz, the renowned Austrian ethologist links aggression in animals to the acquisition and defense of territory (behavior which is itself linked to sex and the defense of offspring), an interpretation extended to human behavior by Robery Ardrey in his controversial book *The Territorial Imperative*. Lorenz first points to the positive evolutionary functions served by animal aggression, then notes how displaced or redirected aggressiveness forms the basis of personal bonds between pairs of animals and social bonds among entire groups. According to Lorenz, the absence of biological inhibitions on intra-species aggression among those species (such as man) poorly equipped with natural weapons poses the most serious of threats to human civilization. The development of artificial weapons has given men the means to kill each other easily and the more recent development of immensely destructive weapons that operate at long range has divorced men from the direct consequences of their aggressiveness. Just as culture has made human aggression a peril to life itself so culture, in Lorenz's view, must build effective barriers against the unbridled expression of that aggression and provide functional alternatives to it.

While Lorenz implies that aggression is an instinct, Anthony Storr, a British psychoanalyst, develops that view explicitly. The word "instinct," like the word "motive," is not an explanation but rather a label or a tautology for what ethologists call "species-specific" behavior, behavior which may be triggered either by internal physiological processes or by highly specific environmental stimuli called "releasers." Storr believes that aggression in human beings is as much an innate drive as sexuality and often needs no external stimulus to be released. This view recalls the Brechers' discussion of electrical stimulation of the brain in Selection 6. Storr also notes the similarities between internal bodily changes in states of sexual and of aggressive arousal. Aggression, he feels, is connected with the human organism's need to master its external environment, a position that recalls both White's discussion of competence and Hebb's remarks on the results of environmental deprivation.

Storr's view of aggression as an ineradicable instinct connotes a tragic view of the human situation and thus contrasts with the prevalent optimistic

American view that aggression arises as the result of frustration and can be eliminated by reducing or removing life's frustrations. Yet frustration, of one kind or another, from one cause or another, is an inevitable accompaniment to life in society. Only in the grave are men free of frustration.

Both the selections by Sally Carrighar, an English naturalist, and J. P. Scott of Bowling Green State University sharply attack what is coming to be called the Lorenz-Ardrey thesis that man is a killer by nature. Miss Carrighar tackles Lorenz on the ethologist's own ground by citing contrary evidence from animal studies themselves that, for example, not all animal species—not even all primates—are territorial. For Miss Carrighar war is a product of culture (an idea supported by thinkers as diverse as Jean-Jacques Rousseau and Lewis Mumford) and she further argues that belief in the Lorenz-Ardrey position can only help to make its predictions come true. In comparing Lorenz's analysis with Miss Carrighar's the reader should recognize how different observers emphasize different aspects of the same "facts" and, depending on their theoretical positions, advance diametrically opposite interpretations of those "facts." That this has been a common occurrence in the history of *every* science suggests that it need not be a source of discouragement. Truth arises more easily from conflict than from consensus.

Scott, on the other hand, emphasizes the need for a multi-factor theory of human aggression. He admits the existence of a genetic predisposition but points to its variability across species and the role of culture and learning in channelling its expression. He sees a danger in "explaining" human behavior on the basis of data drawn from distantly related species, points to several errors in Lorenz's interpretations of animal behavior, and ends by emphasizing the role of social disorganization as a cause of destructive violence, a position that goes back at least to the work of the nineteenth-century French sociologist Émile Durkheim (1858–1917). While it is hard to disagree with Scott's conclusion that further research into the causes of human aggression is needed we run the serious risk of annihilating each other while the necessary research is being conducted. Regardless of whether man's aggression be instinctive or learned, history provides scant support to those who believe that he will be able to control or redirect it. The causes and control of human aggression are problems that psychologists dare not ignore or rationalize. The death camps of Nazi Germany, the ever growing hatred between Arab and Israeli in the Middle East, and the massacre of civilians at My Lai in Vietnam point up how little we know of the dynamics of human aggression and how great the cost of our ignorance may be.

29. MOTIVATION RECONSIDERED:
THE CONCEPT OF COMPETENCE

Robert W. White

When parallel trends can be observed in realms as far apart as animal behavior and psychoanalytic ego psychology, there is reason to suppose that we are witnessing a significant evolution of ideas. In these two realms, as in psychology as a whole, there is evidence of deepening discontent with theories of motivation based upon drives. Despite great differences in the language and concepts used to express this discontent, the theme is everywhere the same: Something important is left out when we make drives the operating forces in animal and human behavior.

The chief theories against which the discontent is directed are those of Hull and of Freud. In their respective realms, drive-reduction theory and psychoanalytic instinct theory, which are basically very much alike, have acquired a considerable air of orthodoxy. Both views have an appealing simplicity, and both have been argued long enough so that their main outlines are generally known. In decided contrast is the position of those who are not satisfied with drives and instincts. They are numerous, and they have developed many pointed criticisms, but what they have to say has not thus far lent itself to a clear and inclusive conceptualization. Apparently there is an enduring difficulty in making these contributions fall into shape.

In this paper I shall attempt a conceptuali-

Robert W. White: "Motivation Reconsidered: The Concept of Competence"; THE PSYCHOLOGICAL RE-VIEW, 66, 1959 297–333 (abridged). Copyright 1959 by the American Psychological Association. Reprinted by permission of the American Psychological Association and the author. Quotations from Jean Piaget: THE ORIGINS OF INTELLIGENCE IN CHILDREN reprinted by permission of International Universities Press, Inc. and Delachaux & Niestlé, S. A., Neuchâtel, Switzerland.

zation which gathers up some of the important things left out by drive theory. To give the concept a name I have chosen the word *competence*, which is intended in a broad biological sense rather than in its narrow everyday meaning. As used here, competence will refer to an organism's capacity to interact effectively with its environment. In organisms capable of but little learning, this capacity might be considered an innate attribute, but in the mammals and especially man, with their highly plastic nervous systems, fitness to interact with the environment is slowly attained through prolonged feats of learning. In view of the directedness and persistence of the behavior that leads to these feats of learning, I consider it necessary to treat competence as having a motivational aspect, and my central argument will be that the motivation needed to attain competence cannot be wholly derived from sources of energy currently conceptualized as drives or instincts. We need a different kind of motivational idea to account fully for the fact that man and the higher mammals develop a competence in dealing with the environment which they certainly do not have at birth and certainly do not arrive at simply through maturation. Such an idea, I believe, is essential for any biologically sound view of human nature....

One of the most obvious features of animal behavior is the tendency to explore the environment. Cats are reputedly killed by curiosity, dogs characteristically make a thorough search of their surroundings, and monkeys and chimpanzees have always impressed observers as being ceaseless investigators. Even Pavlov, whose theory of behavior was one of Spartan simplicity, could not do without an investigatory or orientating reflex. Early workers with the obstruction method, such as Dashiell (1925) and Nissen (1930), reported that rats would cross an electrified grid simply for the privilege of exploring new territory. Some theorists reasoned that activity of this kind was always in the service of hunger, thirst, sex, or some other organic need, but this view was at least shaken by the latent learning experiments, which showed that animals learned about their surroundings even when their major needs had been purposely sated. Shortly before 1950 there was a wave of renewed interest not only in exploratory behavior but also in the possibility that activity and manipulation might have to be assigned the status of independent motives. . . .

ACTIVITY AND MANIPULATION

Exploration is not the only motive proposed by critics of drive orthodoxy, and novelty is not the only characteristic of the environment which appears to incite motivated behavior. Some workers have suggested a need for activity, which can be strengthened by depriving animals of their normal opportunities for movement. Kagan and Berkun used running in an activity wheel as the reward for learning and found it "an adequate reinforcement for the instrumental response of bar pressing." Hill showed that rats will run in an activity wheel to an extent that is correlated with their previous degree of confinement. It is certain that the activity wheel offers no novelty to the animals in these experiments. Nevertheless, they seem to want to run, and they continue to run for such long times that no part of the behavior can readily be singled out as a consummatory response. Perhaps an unpleasant internal state created by inactivity is gradually worked off, but this is certainly accomplished by a tremendous increase of kinaesthetic stimulation and muscular output which would seem to imply increased excitation in the system as a whole.

Harlow and his associates maintain that there is also a manipulative drive. It is aroused by certain patterns of external stimulation and reduced by actively changing the external pattern. The experiments were done with rhesus monkeys, and they involve the solving of a mechanical problem which, however, leads to no further consequences or rewards. The task might be, for instance, to raise a hasp

which is kept in place by both a hook and a pin; all that can be accomplished is to raise the hasp, which opens nothing and leads to no fresh discoveries. When the hasp problem is simply installed in the living cages, the monkeys return to it and solve it as many as 7 or 8 times over several days. It seems unlikely that novelty can be postulated as the essential characteristic of the stimulus which evokes this repeated behavior. The simplest interpretation is rather that value lies for the animal in the opportunity, as Zimbardo and Miller express it, "to effect a stimulus change in the environment." This formulation suggests something like the propensities toward mastery or power that have often been mentioned in discussions of human motivation.

The addition of activity and manipulation to the list of primary drives can only make more serious the difficulties for the orthodox model that resulted from admitting exploration. But recent research with animals has put the orthodox model on the defensive even on its home grounds. It has become increasingly clear that hunger, thirst, and sex cannot be made to fit the simple pattern that seemed so helpful 40 years ago.

CHANGING CONCEPTIONS OF DRIVE

In a brief historical statement, Morgan has pointed out that the conception of drive as a noxious stimulus began to lose its popularity among research workers shortly after 1940. "On the whole," he says, "the stimulus concept of drive owed more to wishful thinking than to experimental fact." When technical advances in biochemistry and brain physiology made it possible to bring in an array of new facts there was a rapid shift toward the view that "drives arise largely through the internal environment acting on the central nervous system." One of the most influential discoveries was that animals have as many as a dozen specific hungers for particular kinds of food, instead of the single hunger demanded by Cannon's model of the hunger drive. If an animal's diet becomes deficient in some important element such as salt, sugar, or the vitamin-B complex, foods containing the missing element will be eagerly sought while other foods are passed by, a selectivity that obviously cannot be laid to contractions of the stomach. Similarly, a negative food preference can be produced by loading either the stomach or the blood stream with some single element of the normal diet. The early work of Beach on sexual behavior brought out similar complications in what had for a time been taken as a relatively simple drive. Hormone levels appeared to be considerably more important than peripheral stimulation in the arousal and maintenance of the sex drive. Further work led Beach to conclude that sexual behavior is "governed by a complex combination of processes." He points out that the patterns of control differ tremendously from one species to another and that within a single species the mechanisms may be quite different for males and females. Like hunger, the sex drive turns out to be no simple thing.

New methods of destroying and of stimulating brain centers in animals have had an equally disastrous effect on the orthodox drive model. The nervous system, and especially the hypothalamus, appears to be deeply implicated in the motivational process. Experimental findings on hypothalamic lesions in animals encourage Stellar to believe that there are different centers "responsible for the control of different kinds of basic motivation," and that in each case "there is one main excitatory center and one inhibitory center which operates to depress the activity of the excitatory center." As research findings accumulate, this picture may seem to be too cleanly drawn. Concerning sexual behavior, for example, Rosvold concludes a recent review by rejecting the idea of a single center in the cerebrum; rather, the sex drive "probably has a wide neural representation with a complex interaction between old and new brain structures and between neural and humoral·agents." Nevertheless, Miller's careful work seems to leave little doubt that motivated behavior in every way similar to normal hunger and normal pain-fear can be elicited by electrical stimulation of quite restricted areas of the hypothalamus. It is clear that we cannot regress to a model of drives that represents the energy as coming from outside the nervous system. Whatever the effects of peripheral stimulation may be, drives also involve neural centers and neural patterns as well as internal biochemical conditions. . . .

Twenty years of research have thus pretty much destroyed the orthodox drive model. It is no longer appropriate to consider that drives originate solely in tissue deficits external to the nervous system, that consummatory acts are a universal feature and goal of motivated behavior, or that the alleviation of tissue deficits is the necessary condition for instrumental learning. Instead we have a complex picture in which humoral factors and neural centers occupy a prominent position; in which, moreover, the concept of neurogenic motives without consummatory ends appears to be entirely legitimate. Do these changes remove the obstacles to placing exploration, activity, and manipulation in the category of drives?

Perhaps this is no more than a question of words, but I should prefer at this point to call it a problem in conceptual strategy. I shall propose that these three new "drives" have much in common and that it is useful to bring them under the single heading of competence. Even with the loosening and broadening of the concept of drive, they are still in important respects different from hunger, thirst, and sex. In hunger and thirst, tissue deficits, humoral factors, and consummatory responses retain an important position. The mature sex drive depends heavily on hormonal levels and is sharply oriented toward consummation. Tendencies like exploration do not share these characteristics, whatever else they have in common with the better known drives. It is in order to emphasize their intrinsic peculiarities, to get them considered in their own right without a cloud of surplus meanings, that I prefer in this essay to speak of the urge that makes for competence simply as motivation rather than as drive.

THE TREND IN PSYCHOANALYTIC EGO PSYCHOLOGY

Rather an abrupt change of climate may be experienced as we turn from the animal laboratory to the psychoanalytic treatment room, but the trends of thought in the two realms turn out to be remarkably alike. Here the orthodox view of motivation is to be found in Freud's theory of the instincts—they might be known to us as drives if an early translator had been more literal with the German *Trieb*.

In his final work, Freud described instincts as "somatic demands upon mental life" and as "the ultimate cause of all activity.". . .

Freud's tendency to revise his thinking makes it difficult to pin down an orthodox doctrine, but most workers will probably agree that his main emphasis was upon somatically based drives, a mental apparatus which received its power from the drives, and, of course, the multitude of ways in which the apparatus controlled, disguised, and transformed these energies. His treatment of the ego was far from complete, and it was not long before voices were raised against the conception that so vital and versatile a part of the personality could be developed solely by libidinal and aggressive energies.

AN INSTINCT TO MASTER

In 1942 Hendrick proposed that this difficulty be met by assuming the existence of an additional major instinct. "The development of ability to master a segment of the environment," he wrote, and the need to exercise such functions, can be conceptualized as an "instinct to master," further characterized as "an inborn drive to do and to learn how to do." The aim of this instinct is "pleasure in exercising a function successfully, regardless of its sensual value." The simpler manifestations are learning to suck, to manipulate, to walk, to speak, to comprehend and to reason; these functions and others eventually become integrated as the ego. "The central nervous system is more than a utility," Hendrick declared. The infant shows an immediate desire to use and perfect each function as it ripens, and the adult secures gratification from an executive function efficiently performed regardless of its service to other instincts.

Hendrick's procedure in this and two supporting papers is quite similar to that of the animal psychologists who propose listing exploration as an additional primary drive. The instinct to master has an aim—to exercise and develop the ego functions—and it follows hedonic principles by yielding "primary pleasure" when efficient action "enables the individual to control and alter his environment." It is to this extent analogous to the instincts assumed by Freud. But just as an exploratory drive seemed radically to alter the whole conception of drive, so the instinct to master implied a drastic change in the psychoanalytic idea of instinct. Critics were quick to point out that Freud had always conceived of instincts as having somatic sources external to the ego apparatus, a condition not met by the proposed instinct to master. There was nothing comparable to erogenous zones, to orgasm, or to

the sequence of painful tension followed by pleasurable release. Mastery, the critics agreed, could not be an instinct, whatever else it might be.

It is of interest that Fenichel, who definitely rejected Hendrick's proposal, gives us another close parallel to the animal work by attributing mastering behavior to anxiety-reduction. He argued that mastery is "a general aim of every organism but not of a specific instinct." He agreed that there is "a pleasure of enjoying one's abilities," but he related this pleasure to cessation of the anxiety connected with not being able to do things. "Functional pleasure," he wrote, "is pleasure in the fact that the exercise of a function is now possible without anxiety," and he contended that when anxiety is no longer present, when there is full confidence that a given situation can be met, then action is no longer accompanied by functional pleasure. We must certainly agree with Fenichel that anxiety *can* play the part he assigns it, but the proposal that all pleasure in ego functions comes from this source raises the same difficulties we have already considered in connection with exploratory behavior. That we exercise our capacities and explore our surroundings only to reduce our fear of the environment is not, as I have already argued, an assumption that enjoys high probability on biological grounds.

MOTILITY AND A SENSE OF INDUSTRY

The trend away from instinct orthodoxy is illustrated by the work of Kardiner on what he calls "the development of the effective ego." Kardiner's reflections arose from his work on the traumatic neuroses of war. In these disorders the main threat is to self-preservation, and some of the most important symptoms, such as defensive rituals and paralyses, are lodged in the action systems that normally bring about successful adaptive behavior. It thus becomes pertinent to study the growth of action systems, to discover how they become integrated so as to maintain "controlled contact" with the environment and "controlled exploitation of objects in the outer world," and to work out the conditions which either favor or disrupt this acquired integration. Thinking along these lines, Kardiner is led to conclusions just about the opposite of Freud's: It is the successful and gratifying experiences, not the frustrations, that lead to increasingly integrated action and to the discrimination of self from outer world. Frustration produces chiefly disruptions and inhibitions which are unfavorable to the early growth of the ego. Children are gratified when they discover the connection between a movement executed and the accompanying and subsequent sensations. They are still more gratified when they carry out actions successfully; this "gives rise to the triumphant feeling of making an organ obedient to the will of the ego." Such experiences build up "a definite self- or body-consciousness which becomes the center and the point of reference of all purposeful and coördinated activity." Growth of the ego, in short, depends heavily upon action systems and the consequences of action. The course and vicissitudes of this development have to be studied in their own right, and they cannot be understood as side effects of the stages of libidinal development.

A similar theme is pursued to even more radical conclusions by Mittelmann in his paper on motility. Mittlemann regards motility, which manifests itself most typically in skilled motor actions such as posture, locomotion, and manipulation, as an "urge in its own right" in the same sense that one speaks of oral, excretory, or genital urges. From about 10 months of age it has a distinctly "driven" character, and there is restlessness and anger if it is blocked. During the second and third years the motor urge "dominates all other urges," so that it is proper to "consider this period the motor level of ego and libido development." The child makes tremendous efforts to learn to walk, and to walk well, and he exhibits joyous laughter as he attains these ends. Restrictions of motility may occur because the parents are anxious or because the child's assertiveness troubles them, and a lasting injury to the parent-child relationship may result. Clumsiness in motor or manipulative accomplishments may lead to self-hatred and dependence, for "the evolution of self-assertiveness and self-esteem is intimately connected with motor development." Motility is of central importance in many of the most characteristic functions of the ego. Partly by its means the infant differentiates himself from other objects, and the child's knowledge of objects depends on an extensive activity of manipulation and examination. "Thus motility becomes one of the most important aspects of reality testing." Because it is an element in all cognitive behavior, it can also be considered "the dominant integrative function." Mittelmann bases motor development, in short, on an independent urge, and he sees this urge as the really crucial motive behind the development of the ego. . . .

NEED FOR EXCITEMENT AND NOVELTY

Human experience provides plentiful evidence of the importance of reducing excessive levels of tension. Men under wartime stress, men under pressure of pain and extreme deprivation, men with excessive work loads or too much exposure to confusing social interactions, all act as if their nervous systems craved that utterly unstimulated condition which Freud once sketched as the epitome of neural bliss. But if these same men be granted their Nirvana they soon become miserable and begin to look around for a little excitement. Human experience testifies that boredom is a bad state of affairs about which something must be done. Hebb has been particularly insistent in reminding us that many of our activities, such as reading detective stories, skin-diving, or driving cars at high speeds, give clear evidence of a need to raise the level of stimulation and excitement. Men and animals alike seem at times bent on increasing the impact of the environment and even on creating mild degrees of frustration and fear. Hebb and Thompson reflect upon this as follows:

> Such phenomena are, of course, well known in man: in the liking for dangerous sports or roller coasters, where fear is deliberately courted, and in the addiction to bridge or golf or solitaire, vices whose very existence depends upon the level of difficulty of the problems presented and an optimal level of frustration. Once more, when we find such attitudes toward fear and frustration in animals, we have a better basis for supposing that we are dealing with something fundamental if a man prefers skis to the less dangerous snowshoes, or when we observe an unashamed love of work (problem solving and frustration included) in the scientist, or in the business man who cannot retire. Such behavior in man is usually accounted for as a search for prestige, but the

animal data make this untenable. It seems much more likely that solving problems and running mild risks are inherently rewarding, or, in more general terms, that the animal will always act so as to produce an optimal level of excitation.[1]

The concept of optimal stimulation has been developed by Leuba, who sees it as helpful in resolving some of the problems of learning theory. Believing that most theorizing about motivation has been based upon "powerful biological or neurotic drives," Leuba bids us look at the much more common learning situations of nursery, playground, and school, where "actions which increase stimulation and produce excitement are strongly reinforced, sometimes to the dismay of parents and teachers." He proposes that there is an optimal level of stimulation, subject to variation at different times, and that learning is associated with movement toward this optimal level, downward when stimulation is too high and upward when it is too low. A similar idea is expressed by McReynolds concerning the more restricted concept of "rate of perceptualization." Monotonous conditions provide too low a rate, with boredom; excessive stimulation produces too high a rate, with disruptive excitement; the optimal rate yields the experience of pleasure. These ideas are now amply supported by recent experimental work on sensory deprivation. . . .

It seems to me that these contributions, though differing as to details, speak with unanimity on their central theme and would force us, if nothing else did, to reconsider seriously the whole problem of motivation. Boredom, the unpleasantness of monotony, the attraction of novelty, the tendency to vary behavior rather than repeating it rigidly, and the seeking of stimulation and mild excitement stand as inescapable facts of human experience and clearly have their parallels in animal behavior. We may seek rest and minimal stimulation at the end of the day, but that is not what we are looking for the next morning. Even when its primary needs are satisfied and its homeostatic chores are done, and organism is alive, active, and up to something.

1 Hebb, D.O. and W.R. Thompson: "The Social Significance of Animal Studies," in Gardner Lindzey (ed.): *Handbook of Social Psychology;* Cambridge, Mass., Addison-Wesley 1954, Vol. I, p. 551.

DEALING WITH THE ENVIRONMENT

If we consider things only from the viewpoint of affect, excitement, and novelty, we are apt to overlook another important aspect of behavior, its effect upon the environment. Moving in this direction, Diamond invites us to consider the motivational properties of the sensorineural system, the apparatus whereby higher animals "maintain their relations to the environment." He conceives of this system as demanding stimulation and as acting in such a manner as to "force the environment to stimulate it." Even if one thinks only of the infant's exploring eyes and hands, it is clear that the main direction of behavior is by no means always that of reducing the impact of stimulation. When the eyes follow a moving object, or when the hand grasps an object which it has touched, the result is to preserve the stimulus and to increase its effect. In more elaborate explorations the consequence of a series of actions may be to vary the manner in which a stimulus acts upon the sense organs. It is apparent that the exploring, manipulating child produces by his actions precisely what Hebb's theory demands as a basis for continuing interest: he produces differences-in-sameness in the stimulus field.

In a critical analysis of Freud's views on the reality principle, Charlotte Bühler makes a strong case for positive interests in the environment, citing as evidence the responsiveness and adaptiveness of the new-born baby as well as the exploratory tendencies of later months. The problem is worked out in more detail by Schachtel in a paper on focal attention. Acts of focal attention are characteristically directed at particular objects, and they consist of several sustained approaches "aimed at active mental grasp" while excluding the rest of the field. These qualities can be observed even in the infant's early attempts to follow a moving object with his eyes, and they show more clearly in his later endeavors to learn how objects are related both to himself and to one another. Such behavior bespeaks "a relatively autonomous capacity for object interest." Schachtel makes the proposal that this interest is pursued precisely at those times when major needs are in abeyance. High pressure of need or anxiety is the enemy of exploratory play and is a condition, as every scientist should know, under which we are unlikely to achieve an objective grasp of the environment. Low need pressure is requisite if we are to perceive objects as they are, in their constant character, apart from hopes and fears we may at other times attach to them. Schachtel doubts that "the wish for need-satisfaction alone would ever lead to object perception and to object-oriented thought." Hence an autonomous capacity to be interested in the environment has great value for the survival of a species. . . .

The most far-reaching attempt to give these aspects of behavior a systematic place in the theory of motivation is contained in Woodworth's . . . book, *Dynamics of Behavior* (1958). Woodworth takes his start from the idea that a great deal of human behavior appears to be directed toward producing effects upon the environment without immediate service to any aroused organic need. "Its incentives and rewards are in the field of behavior and not in the field of homeostasis." This is illustrated by exploratory behavior, which is directed outward toward the environment. . . .

Woodworth leaves no doubt as to what he considers basic in motivation. . . . The ever-present, ever-primary feature of motivation is the tendency to deal with the environment. . . .

I now propose that we gather the various kinds of behavior just mentioned, all of which have to do with effective interaction with the environment, under the general heading of competence. According to Webster, competence means fitness or ability, and the suggested synonyms include capability, capacity, efficiency, proficiency, and skill. It is therefore a suitable word to describe such things as grasping and exploring, crawling and walking, attention and perception, language and thinking, manipulating and changing the surroundings, all of which promote an effective—a competent—interaction with the environment. It is true, of course, that maturation plays a part in all these developments, but this part is heavily overshadowed by learning in all the more complex accomplishments like speech or skilled manipulation. I shall argue that it is necessary to make competence a motivational concept; there is a *competence motivation* as well as competence in its more familiar sense of achieved capacity. The behavior that leads to the building up of effective grasping, handling, and letting go of objects, to take one

example, is not random behavior produced by a general overflow of energy. It is directed, selective, and persistent, and it is continued not because it serves primary drives, which indeed it cannot serve until it is almost perfected, but because it satisfies an intrinsic need to deal with the environment.

No doubt it will at first seem arbitrary to propose a single motivational conception in connection with so many and such diverse kinds of behavior. What do we gain by attributing motivational unity to such a large array of activities? We could, of course, say that each developmental sequence, such as learning to grasp or to walk, has its own built-in bit of motivation—its "aliment," as Piaget has expressed it. We could go further and say that each item of behavior has its intrinsic motive —but this makes the concept of motivation redundant. On the other hand, we might follow the lead of the animal psychologists and postulate a limited number of broader motives under such names as curiosity, manipulation, and mastery. I believe that the idea of a competence motivation is more adequate than any of these alternatives and that it points to very vital common properties which have been lost from view amidst the strongly analytical tendencies that go with detailed research.

In order to make this claim more plausible, I shall now introduce some specimens of playful exploration in early childhood. I hope that these images will serve to fix and dramatize the concept of competence in the same way that other images—the hungry animal solving problems, the child putting his finger in the candle flame, the infant at the breast, the child on the toilet, and the youthful Oedipus caught in a hopeless love triangle—have become memorable focal points for other concepts. For this purpose I turn to Piaget's studies of the growth of intelligence from its earliest manifestations in his own three children. The examples come from the first year of life, before language and verbal concepts begin to be important. They therefore represent a practical kind of intelligence which may be quite similar to what is developed by the higher animals.

As early as the fourth month, the play of the gifted Piaget children began to be "centered on a result produced in the external environment," and their behavior could be described as rediscovering the movement which by chance exercised an advantageous action upon things."[2] Laurent, lying in his bassinet, learns to shake a suspended rattle by pulling a string that hangs from it. He discovers this result fortuitously before vision and prehension are fully coordinated. Let us now observe him a little later when he has reached the age of three months and ten days.

> I place the string, which is attached to the rattle, in his right hand, merely unrolling it a little so that he may grasp it better. For a moment nothing happens. But at the first shake due to chance movement of his hand, the reaction is immediate: Laurent starts when looking at the rattle and then violently strikes his right hand alone, as if he felt the resistance and the effect. The operation lasts fully a quarter of an hour, during which Laurent emits peals of laughter.[3]

Three days later the following behavior is observed.

> Laurent, by chance, strikes the chain while sucking his fingers. He grasps it and slowly displaces it while looking at the rattles. He then begins to swing it very gently, which produces an as yet faint sound inside them. Laurent then definitely increases by degrees his own movements. He shakes the chain more and more vigorously and laughs uproariously at the result obtained.[4]

Very soon it can be observed that procedures are used "to make interesting spectacles last." For instance, Laurent is shown a rubber monkey which he has not seen before. After a moment of surprise, and perhaps even fright, he calms down and makes movements of pulling the string, a procedure which has no effect in this case, but which previously has caused interesting things to happen. It is to be noticed that "interesting spectacles" consist of such things as new toys, a tin box upon which a drumming noise can be made, an unfolded newspaper, or sounds made by the observer such as snapping the fingers. Commonplace as they are to the adult mind, these spectacles enter the infant's experience as novel and apparently challenging events.

Moving ahead to the second half of the first year, we can observe behavior in which the child explores the properties of objects and tries out his repertory of actions upon them. This soon leads to active experimentation in which the child attempts to provoke new results. Again we look in upon Laurent, who has now reached the age of nine months. On different occasions he is shown a variety of new objects—for instance a notebook, a beaded purse, and a wooden parrot. His carefully observing father detects four stages of response: (*a*) visual exploration, passing the object from hand to hand, folding the purse, *etc.*; (*b*) tactile exploration, passing the hand all over the object, scratching, *etc.*; (*c*) slow moving of the object in space; (*d*) use of the repertory of action: shaking the object, striking it, swinging it, rubbing it against the side of the bassinet, sucking it, *etc.*, "each in turn with a sort of prudence as though studying the effect produced."[5]

Here the child can be described as applying familiar tactics to new situations, but in a short while he will advance to clear patterns of active experimentation. At 10 months and 10 days Laurent, who is unfamiliar with bread as a nutritive substance, is given a piece for examination. He manipulates it, drops it many times, breaks off fragments and lets them fall. He has often done this kind of thing before, but previously his attention has seemed to be centered on the act of letting go. Now "he watches with great interest the body in motion; in particular, he looks at it for a long time when it has fallen, and picks it up when he can." On the following day he resumes his research.

> He grasps in succession a celluloid swan, a box, and several other small objects, in each case stretching out his arm and letting them fall. Sometimes he stretches out his arm vertically, sometimes he holds it obliquely in front of or behind his eyes. When the object falls in a new position (for example on his pillow) he lets it fall two or three times more on the same place, as though to study the spatial relation; then he modifies the situation. At a certain moment the swan falls near his mouth; now he does not suck it (even though this object habitually serves this purpose), but drops it three times more while merely making the gesture of opening his mouth.[6]

2 Piaget, Jean: *The Origins of Intelligence in Children*, trans. M. Cook; New York, International Universities Press 1952, p. 151.

3 *Ibid.*, p. 162.

4 *Ibid.*, p. 185.

5 *Ibid.*, p. 255.

6 *Ibid.*, p. 269.

These specimens will furnish us with sufficient images of the infant's use of his spare time. Laurent, of course, was provided by his studious father with a decidedly enriched environment, but no observant parent will question the fact that babies often act this way during those periods of their waking life when hunger, erotic needs, distresses, and anxiety seem to be exerting no particular pressure. If we consider this behavior under the historic headings of psychology we shall see that few processes are missing. The child gives evidence of sensing, perceiving, attending, learning, recognizing, probably recalling, and perhaps thinking in a rudimentary way. Strong emotion is lacking, but the infant's smiles, gurgles, and occasional peals of laughter strongly suggest the presence of pleasant affect. Actions appear in an organized form, particularly in the specimens of active exploration and experimentation. Apparently the child is using with a certain coherence nearly the whole repertory of psychological processes except those that accompany stress. It would be arbitrary indeed to say that one was more important than another.

These specimens have a meaningful unity when seen as transactions between the child and his environment, the child having some influence upon the environment and the environment some influence upon the child. Laurent appears to be concerned about what he can do with the chain and rattles, what he can accomplish by his own effort to reproduce and to vary the entertaining sounds. If his father observed correctly, we must add that Laurent seems to have varied his actions systematically, as if testing the effect of different degrees of effort upon the bit of environment represented by the chain and rattles. Kittens make a similar study of parameters when delicately using their paws to push pencils and other objects ever nearer to the edge of one's desk. In all such examples it is clear that the child or animal is by no means at the mercy of transient stimulus fields. He selects for continuous treatment those aspects of his environment which he finds it possible to affect in some way. His behavior is selective, directed, persistent—in short, motivated.

Motivated toward what goal? In these terms, too, the behavior exhibits a little of everything. Laurent can be seen as appeasing a stimulus hunger, providing his sensorium with an agreeable level of stimulation by eliciting from the environment a series of interesting sounds, feels, and sights. On the other hand we might emphasize a need for activity and see him as trying to reach a pleasurable level of neuromuscular exercise. We can also see another possible goal in the behavior: the child is achieving knowledge, attaining a more differentiated cognitive map of his environment and thus satisfying an exploratory tendency or motive of curiosity. But it is equally possible to discern a theme of mastery, power, or control, perhaps even a bit of primitive self-assertion, in the child's concentration upon those aspects of the environment which respond in some way to his own activity. It looks as if we had found too many goals, and perhaps our first impulse is to search for some key to tell us which one is really important. But this, I think, is a mistake that would be fatal to understanding.

We cannot assign priority to any of these goals without pausing arbitrarily in the cycle of transaction between child and environment and saying, "This is the real point." I propose instead that the real point is the transactions as a whole. If the behavior gives satisfaction, this satisfaction is not associated with a particular moment in the cycle. It does not lie solely in sensory stimulation, in a bettering of the cognitive map, in coordinated action, in motor exercise, in a feeling of effort and of effects produced, or in the appreciation of change brought about in the sensory field. These are all simply aspects of a process which at this stage has to be conceived as a whole. The child appears to be occupied with the agreeable task of developing an effective familiarity with his environment. This involves discovering the effects he can have on the environment and the effects the environment will have on him. To the extent that these results are preserved by learning, they build up an increased competence in dealing with the environment. The child's play can thus be viewed as serious business, though to him it is merely something that is interesting and fun to do. . . .

Some objection may be felt to my introducing the word *competence* in connection with behavior that is so often playful. Certainly the playing child is doing things for fun, not because of a desire to improve his competence in dealing with the stern hard world. In order to forestall misunderstanding, it should be pointed out that the usage here is parallel to what we do when we connect sex with its biological goal of reproduction. The sex drive aims for pleasure and gratification, and reproduction is a consequence that is presumably unforeseen by animals and by man at primitive levels of understanding. Effectance motivation similarly aims for the feeling of efficacy, not for the vitally important learnings that come as its consequence. If we consider the part played by competence motivation in adult human life we can observe the same parallel. Sex may now be completely and purposefully divorced from reproduction but nevertheless pursued for the pleasure it can yield. Similarly, effectance motivation may lead to continuing exploratory interests or active adventures when in fact there is no longer any gain in actual competence or any need for it in terms of survival. In both cases the motive is capable of yielding surplus satisfaction well beyond what is necessary to get the biological work done.

In infants and young children it seems to me sensible to conceive of effectance motivation as undifferentiated. Later in life it becomes profitable to distinguish various motives such as cognizance, construction, mastery, and achievement. It is my view that all such motives have a root in effectance motivation. They are differentiated from it through life experiences which emphasize one or another aspect of the cycle of transaction with the environment. Of course, the motives of later childhood and of adult life are no longer simple and can almost never be referred to a single root. They can acquire loadings of anxiety, defense, and compensation, they can become fused with unconscious fantasies of a sexual, aggressive, or omnipotent character, and they can gain force because of their service in producing realistic results in the way of income and career. It is not my intention to cast effectance in the star part in adult motivation. The acquisition of motives is a complicated affair in which simple and sovereign theories grow daily more obsolete. Yet it may be that the satisfaction of effectance contributes significantly to those feelings of interest which often sustain us so well in day-to-day actions, particularly when the things we are doing have continuing elements of novelty. . . .

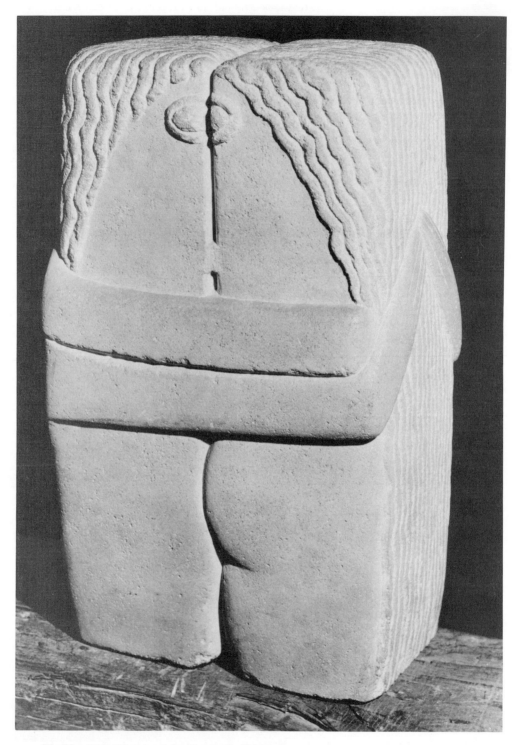

The Kiss, 1908 (Limestone) by Constantin Brancusi.
Louise and Walter Arensberg Collection, Philadelphia Museum of Art.

Sex and Its Varieties

30. HUMAN SEXUAL BEHAVIOR IN PERSPECTIVE

Clellan S. Ford and Frank A. Beach

Up to this point we have concerned ourselves primarily with differences between man and other animals, but of equal significance are the various points of similarity that reflect the evolutionary heritage of *Homo sapiens*. As we have said, these are sufficiently numerous and important to justify the concept of a basic mammalian pattern of sexual behavior, certain elements of which persist in human beings. Many of these separate items have been pointed out in preceding chapters and only a few need be reviewed here.

SEX PLAY IN CHILDHOOD

Three generalizations can be made with respect to this topic: First, that early sex play occurs in many species other than our own. Second, that the frequency, variety, and completeness of prepubertal sexual reaction tends to increase from the lower mammals to

the higher. And third, that species differences in the amount of such behavior are directly related to the physiological differences we have just discussed.

The cross-cultural evidence clearly reveals a universal human tendency for sexual responses to appear in the immature person long before he or she is capable of fertile coitus. Impulses of this nature are condoned and encouraged in some societies, strictly forbidden and punished in others. But regardless of the cultural ideal with respect to sex play in childhood, the underlying drive toward such activity constitutes one feature of the heredity of the human species.

Many years before they are fertile, male and female apes and monkeys indulge in a variety of sexual games which include attempts at heterosexual union. This form of infantile play is no less natural for the young primate than are the chasing, wrestling, and mock fighting that consume much of his waking life. Furthermore, these tendencies are not confined to primates. Although immature females of infraprimate species rarely show the adult mating response, very young males often engage in incomplete coital attempts with other individuals of their own age. This behavior may appear as soon as the young animal is physically capable of performing the necessary responses. For example, some animals such as the sheep are able to stand and walk shortly after birth, and sexual mounting appears in the first few days of life.

Self-Stimulation

Manipulation and stimulation of one's own sexual organs is another item that can be classified as basically mammalian. From the evolutionary point of view this kind of behavior seems to stem from the universal tendency of lower mammals to clean their genitalia by licking and manipulating them with the feet or mouth. Such behavior on the part of such animals as rats and cats cannot be classified as a deliberate attempt at self-excitation. Nevertheless, close observation of the animal's behavior strongly suggests that the resultant sensations have a sexually exciting quality.

In some infrahuman primates, genital manipulation assumes a frankly sexual character and is classifiable as masturbation. Immature and adult apes and monkeys occasionally indulge in stimulation of their own genitalia, and some adult males habitually induce ejaculation by masturbating. It is of considerable importance that this type of behavior is much less common in female primates of infrahuman species. Although a few mature female chimpanzees have been seen to masturbate, this is relatively rare.

Masturbation by captive primates has long been recognized, but most observers have considered the behavior an unnatural response produced by the artificial conditions of cage life. Recently, however, it has been found that self-stimulation is practiced by at least some male monkeys in their native habitat despite ample opportunity for coitus with receptive females. For lower primates, therefore, masturbation does not appear to be an unnatural or abnormal form of sexual activity.

Different human societies maintain widely divergent attitudes toward self-masturbation. Some social codes enforce different rules depending upon the age of the individual involved. There are peoples who condone or even encourage masturbation during childhood, whereas some other societies condemn this form of sexual expression for all individuals

from infancy onward. Almost all human groups subject adult masturbation to negative sanctions ranging from mild ridicule to severe punishment. It should be added, however, that regardless of social condemnation, at least some adults in all or nearly all the societies in our sample appear to practice it. In every society self-stimulation seems to be less common among women than among men, and, as was noted earlier, a comparable sex difference is seen in infrahuman primates. The zoological and the cross-cultural evidence leads us to conclude that the tendency toward self-stimulation should be classified as one more item in the basic mammalian sexual repertoire and that masturbation is more likely to occur in the male than in the female.

Homosexual Behavior

Homosexual behavior is never the predominant type of activity for adults in any of the societies covered by this book. Heterosexual coitus is the dominant sexual activity for the majority of the adults in every society. But some homosexual behavior occurs in nearly all the societies comprising our sample. It is generally more common in men than in women. The apparent universality of this form of sexual activity might be due to some equally widespread social influence that tends to force a portion of every group into homosexual alliances. Certain social factors probably do incline certain individuals toward homosexuality, but the phenomenon cannot be understood solely in such terms.

Social codes differ markedly in their treatment of liaisons between members of the same sex. At one extreme are societies such as our own that forbid and punish any homosexual relationship in individuals of any age and of either sex. There are, in contrast, other peoples who are tolerant of homosexual play in childhood but disapprove of the same behavior on the part of adults. Still a third group of societies actively enforces homosexual relations upon all its male members. This is true, however, only for a given age group, and it is usually associated with puberty ceremonials. A number of cultures make special provisions for the adult male homosexual, according him a position of dignity and importance and permitting him to live as the "wife" of some other man.

Our cross-cultural comparisons suggest three

generalizations concerning homosexual behavior in human beings: First, there is a wide divergence of social attitudes toward this kind of activity. Second, no matter how a particular society may treat homosexuality, the behavior is very likely to occur in at least a few individuals. Third, males seem more likely to engage in homosexual activity than do females. In order to interpret these facts it is necessary to see their relationships to the zoological and physiological data.

Homosexual behavior is not uncommon among males and females of several infrahuman primate species. Immature monkeys and apes indulge in a variety of homosexual games which include manipulation of the genitals of a like-sexed partner and may even involve attempts at homosexual coitus. Such relationships tend to occur less frequently after puberty, but in some cases an adult individual may form an enduring homosexual liaison with an immature member of his own sex. It is significant that in other primates, as in human beings, homosexuality is less prevalent among females than among males. It is also important to note the absence of any evidence to justify classifying this behavior exclusively as a substitute for heterosexual relations. Adult male monkeys with ample opportunity for heterosexual intercourse may nevertheless indulge in homosexual relations with younger males. And in some cases the same individual will carry on hetero- and homosexual alliances concurrently.

Male and female mammals belonging to infraprimate species sometimes display mating responses typical of the opposite sex. Adult females often mount other females in masculine fashion, and the females that are thus mounted react as they would to a male. Under certain circumstances males attempt to copulate with males, and occasionally the one thus approached will react in the manner of a receptive female. Such observations reveal the bisexuality of the physiological mechanisms for mammalian mating behavior. Even in such species as the rat or rabbit, the neuromuscular basis for feminine responses is present in males as well as females, and the normal female's physiological capacities include the ability to react as would the male. Temporary inversions of the sexual role are due in these species not to an underlying physical abnormality in the individual but to the nature of the external stimulus situation.

It is our belief that a comparable though much more complex condition obtains in human beings. It seems probable that all men and women possess an inherited capacity for erotic responsiveness to a wide range of stimuli. Tendencies leading to sexual relations with individuals of the same sex are probably not as strong as those leading to heterosexual relations. But the important fact is that all societies enforce some modification of the individual's genetically determined impulses, with the result that the preferred type of behavior is strongly influenced by experience.

Men and women who are totally lacking in any conscious homosexual leanings are as much a product of cultural conditioning as are the exclusive homosexuals who find heterosexual relations distasteful and unsatisfying. Both extremes represent movement away from the original, intermediate condition which includes the capacity for both forms of sexual expression. In a restrictive society such as our own a large proportion of the population learns not to respond to or even to recognize homosexual stimuli and may eventually become in fact unable to do so. At the same time a certain minority group, also through the process of learning, becomes highly if not exclusively sensitive to the erotic attractions of a like-sexed partner. Physical or physiological peculiarities that hamper the formation of heterosexual habits may incline certain individuals to a homosexual existence. But human homosexuality is not basically a product of hormonal imbalance or "perverted" heredity. It is the product of the fundamental mammalian heritage of general sexual responsiveness as modified under the impact of experience.

TYPE OF FOREPLAY

Comparisons between man and lower animals make it clear that many elements in the human heterosexual coital pattern are directly determined by the species heredity. For example, the male's erection and ejaculation are basic reflexes present in all mammals. Similarly, the tendency to respond to rhythmic stimulation of the genitals with thrusting movement of the pelvic region is a fundamental reaction in the mammalian repertoire.

Somewhat less apparent is the evolutionary generality of several types of behavioral interactions that tend to occur just before heterosexual coitus. For instance, investigation and consequent stimulation of the feminine genitalia by the male are a universal response in all mammals. The manner in which such stimulation is achieved varies from species to species and depends in large measure upon the effector equipment of the animal involved. Application of the male's tongue, teeth, and lips to the vulva and clitoris is extremely common. The forefeet or hands are employed in the same fashion by males of several species. The behavior seems to be investigatory as far as the male is concerned, but the female's bodily responses make it obvious that she is sexually excited by the resultant stimulation.

In all animal species for which adequate knowledge is available, males exhibit much more of this kind of behavior than do females. Nevertheless, females of many if not all species do occasionally investigate and therefore stimulate the sexual organs of the male. This is most likely to occur when the female is sexually aroused and the male is sluggish or slow to respond to her coital invitations.

Some amount of precoital stimulation occurs in nearly every society of which we have record. In certain cases, as in the Ponapeans, the techniques involved are elaborate, involving use not only of the hands but of the mouth as well. There are a few societies which disapprove of any form of genital stimulation except that derived from coitus, but these are rare. Within American society the individual's social stratum partially determines his or her tendency to practice or permit precoital caressing of the sexual organs. Men and women on lower social levels are less likely to indulge in these forms of foreplay than are individuals belonging to a higher socioeducational level. When such behavior is engaged in, it may be mutual or unilateral; but if only one of the partners stimulates the other, the active individual is almost always the male. This is true not only for our own society but also for the vast majority of the remaining ones in our sample. And, as has been pointed out, the same generalizations extend to other animals as well.

Another very common type of prelude to copulation is grooming behavior. This type of activity is characteristic of many human societies and appears in much the same form in every infrahuman primate species that has been studied. In some peoples sexual arousal and expression are enhanced by moderately painful stimulation. Among the Trukese, the Siriono, and certain other tribes, scratching, biting, and hair pulling form a regular part of the coital pattern. Similarly, in several species of lower animals aggressive or assaultive behavior is characteristically incorporated into the mating relationship. One interesting difference between human beings and lower animals is that sexually receptive females of subhuman species rarely bite or otherwise injure the male. Even though, as in the baboon or macaque monkey, the male may severely wound the female, she remains receptive and does not retaliate. But we have found no human society in which such a unilateral relationship exists. On the contrary, if the cultural stereotype of foreplay involves biting or scratching, both partners show this behavior.

The biological functions of preliminaries to intercourse in lower animals are evident. They tend to increase the degree of excitement in both sexes and also to synchronize the behavior of the pair. In this manner foreplay increases the probability of fertile intercourse. Man's capacity for responding to symbolic stimuli such as those involved in language has to some extent reduced the biological necessity for direct physical stimulation prior to copulation, but unless social conditioning imposes inhibitions upon active foreplay it is very likely to occur. And when it does appear it often takes essentially the same forms seen in other mammals and has essentially the same behavioral results.

MAN THE LEARNING ANIMAL

We have said that evolution of the human brain has endowed man with a greater ability to learn from experience than is present in any other animal species. It would, of course, be a mistake to conclude that lower animals cannot learn. In this respect, as in so many others, the human species differs from other mammals more in degree than in kind. The role of learning in sexual behavior varies from species to species in two ways. There are differences in the degree to which learning is necessary for successful coitus, and there are differences in the extent to which learning can suppress, redirect, or otherwise modify the inherited sexual tendencies of the individual.

Learning and practice are apparently not essential for fertile mating in the few species of lower animals that have been carefully studied. If male rats are reared in complete isolation they are nevertheless capable of copulating effectively the first time they are placed with a receptive female. No practice or experimentation is necessary. The behavior is what is ordinarily called "instinctive." This does not mean, however, that experience cannot affect sexual behavior in male rodents. On the contrary, an individual that has repeatedly been presented with receptive females in a particular cage, pen, or experimental room tends to become sexually excited whenever he is returned to the same setting. Under such circumstances sexual attempts may be directed toward any other animal encountered in that particular environment. And conversely, the male may fail to respond sexually to receptive females encountered in surroundings in which he has previously experienced pain or frustration.

Experience and learning appear to be much more important in the sexual performance of the primates. At least some, and perhaps all, male chimpanzees have to learn how to copulate. Adult apes lacking any copulatory experience respond to the receptive female with evident sexual excitement, but they appear to be incapable of carrying out the bodily adjustments necessary for coitus. Their response to the female's sexual invitation is awkward, poorly organized, and inadequately directed. Only after several years of practice and experimentation do male apes of this species become capable of effective and well-integrated coital behavior.

As a result of experimentation some chimpanzees develop highly individualistic methods of mating. For example, the usual method of coitus consists of the male mounting the stooping female from the rear; but some male apes acquire a preference for intercourse in which they remain seated on the ground and the female reclines upon their thighs.

In addition to shaping the physical reactions involved in intercourse, learning exerts other effects upon the sexual habits of infrahuman primates. It contributes to the formation of personal preferences and tastes in sexual matters. Although they occasionally show some selective tendencies, potent males of most of the lower mammalian species will copulate readily with any female who is receptive; and females in estrus are equally undiscriminating. This is much less true as far as monkeys and apes are concerned. Some male chimpanzees show a distinct preference for certain feminine partners and are reluctant or unwilling to copulate with others. Females of these species also tend to seek the company of some potential partners and to ignore or avoid others.

We interpret the increased importance of learning in primates as being due primarily to the evolutionary advance in brain structure and the partial release from rigid hormonal control. From what has already been said concerning the physiological changes associated with human evolution, it might be expected that in our own species learning would have the most marked and far-reaching effects upon sexual activities. This expectation is amply verified by the facts. Human sexuality is affected by experience in two ways: First, the kinds of stimulation and the types of situations that become capable of evoking sexual excitement are determined in a large measure by learning. Second, the overt behavior through which this excitement is expressed depends largely upon the individual's previous experience.

Human beings can learn without tutelage. That is to say, they can learn by trial and error in much the same fashion as a rat learns to traverse a maze or a cat to open a puzzle box. And to a certain degree, unguided trial-and-error learning may influence the development of the individual's sexual patterns. But this is exceptional. By far most of what people learn to feel and to do in the realm of sex is learned from or with other individuals. Human learning, in other words, customarily occurs in a social context. For this reason the impact of learning upon human sexuality is best understood within the frame of reference provided by the society of which the individual is a member.

MAN THE SOCIAL ANIMAL

Human infants are always born into extensive social groups, or societies. And the things that children and adults learn are governed to a considerable extent by the social structure and culture of their societies. Every society has accumulated, over centuries of experience, preferential ways of behaving, habits and codes that are transmitted from one generation to the next. Each new member of the society finds pressures brought to bear upon him to behave in the traditional manner, to conform to custom. Cultural precepts define for the individual when and where it is proper to behave in a certain manner, and they even specify the types of activities in which he may engage. In a word, the culture provides, through the habits of its members, the major learning conditions for the maturing individual.

The social structure and culture of a society have special significance with respect to sexual behavior. The position occupied by the individual in the social group carries with it definitions of the sexual activities expected of him. Some of these definitions are taken so seriously that severe punishment awaits the person who fails to perform his role in the traditionally accepted manner. Other rules are regarded more lightly, and the individual who varies his behavior may run only the risk of ridicule. But in any case cultural pressure is constantly exerted on all members of any society to express their sexual impulses in socially accepted fashion.

INTERCULTURAL SIMILARITIES PRODUCED BY LEARNING

There are many general similarities between human cultures in respect to sexual behavior. Some of these cultural universals cannot be explained solely in terms of the species heredity. Instead, they seem to be the products of common learning experience on the part of the members of all societies. An outstanding example is seen in the universal prohibition against primary incest.

Animals of infrahuman species freely interbreed with their own offspring, parents, and siblings. And in human beings consanguinity is no barrier to erotic attractiveness. Analyses of the fantasies and dreams of people in our own and many other societies plainly reveal the existence of unconscious sexual desires directed toward offspring, parents, and siblings. One must therefore look to social learning rather than to biological factors for an interpretation of incest taboos. The tentative explanation which we have offered involves the assumption that such taboos have arisen and

persisted during societal evolution because they serve as a protective device against disintegration of the nuclear family—disintegration which would result if intrafamilial sexual jealousies and conflicts were not held at a minimum. We do not suppose that this device has been rationally conceived and instituted. On the contrary, it seems best understood as a product of natural selection. Societies lacking this protective regulation could not long endure. Survival of the larger social group depends too heavily upon preservation of its basic unit, the nuclear family. It is true that close inbreeding sometimes has biologically unfortunate or maladaptive consequences. And it might be surmised that this in itself would result in the eventual extinction of any society that failed to forbid incestuous relations. However, the evidence in this direction is scant, and it seems to us that the universality of incest taboos is more adequately explained on social-psychological grounds.

Another illustration of the way in which learning and societal evolution may produce widespread channelization of sexual impulses is the almost universal prohibition against intercourse with a menstruating woman. There is no evidence to suggest that these restrictions rest upon a biologically controlled absence of desire for sexual stimulation or capacity to respond to it on the part of either the woman or the man. On the contrary, the taboo appears to reflect common attitudes toward menstrual blood as a substance somehow associated with disease or physical injury.

INTERCULTURAL DIFFERENCES PRODUCED BY LEARNING

Socially controlled learning is responsible not only for a number of intercultural similarities but also for many of the differences that exist between societies. It is generally agreed that all human races belong to the same species. They will, therefore, possess essentially the same species heredity. Whether or not there are important genetic differences between races—differences directly affecting behavior—is a matter of some dispute. However, no one has suggested, and we do not believe, that members of separate societies are sufficiently different genetically so that the variations in their sexual codes and habits can be explained on the basis of heredity. It follows, then, that marked intersocietal variations in such matters must be referable to differences in the cultural modification of inherited sexual impulses.

The full extent to which social forces can influence the behavior of the individual is not immediately obvious. It should be apparent that the attitude of members of a given society toward masturbation or toward homosexuality will be shaped to a large degree by early training. The result is that many members of our own society, for instance, look upon such phenomena with loathing and disgust and tend to classify the behavior as "abnormal" or "perverted." But the Keraki of New Guinea regard a man as "abnormal" if he abstains from homosexual relations prior to marriage. The importance of learning and culture in the formation of attitudes toward various sexual practices becomes fairly obvious after the evidence is reviewed and reflected upon, but there are still other effects that are less likely to be recognized. For example, various aspects of the heterosexual relationship are also influenced by training.

Certain elements in the coital pattern appear to be so completely reflexive that their control by voluntary means might seem impossible, but in fact some of them are powerfully affected by experience. One of these is the occurrence of man's ejaculation within a relatively short time after the penis has entered the vagina. Data presented in Chapter II indicate that for the majority of men in our society, ejaculation and orgasm occur within two minutes or less after the beginning of intercourse. Among the Marquesans, in contrast, the habitual copulatory pattern involves reservatus, and every man learns early in life to control his ejaculatory reflexes in such a manner as to permit maintenance of an erection and continuation of coitus for as long as the woman desires.

Both the tendency to incorporate painful stimulation in the culturally accepted pattern of precoital play and the type of response to such stimulation are strongly influenced by learning. From early life the Siriono or the Trobriand man or woman has learned to associate sexual excitement with the experience of being scratched or bitten. Accordingly, such sensations acquire erotic value and are subjectively experienced as pleasantly stimulating. Most members of other societies in which love-making lacks such aggressive components are likely to find physical pain a deterrent to sexual arousal and satisfaction.

Social learning and experience powerfully affect the extent to which a man or woman adopts and enjoys a passive or an active role in the sexual relationship. We have pointed out that in every infra-human species the distribution of sexual initiative is bilateral. Both the male and the female may extend the sexual invitation and both have an active share in the continuation of the relationship until coitus is completed. The wide divergence between different human societies in this regard is probably due, not to biological differences between males and females, but to the lifelong effects of early training.

The societies that severely restrict adolescent and preadolescent sex play, those that enjoin girls to be modest, retiring, and submissive appear to produce adult women that are incapable or at least unwilling to be sexually aggressive. The feminine products of such cultural training are likely to remain relatively inactive even during marital intercourse. And, quite often, they do not experience clearcut sexual orgasm. In contrast, the societies which permit or encourage early sex play usually allow females a greater degree of freedom in seeking sexual contacts. Under such circumstances the sexual performance of the mature woman seems to be characterized by a certain degree of aggression, to include definite and vigorous activity, and to result regularly in complete and satisfactory orgasm.

INDIVIDUAL DIFFERENCES PRODUCED BY LEARNING

Personal experience, operating through learning, is one important source of variation in the sexual practices followed by different members of the same society. We have noted, for instance, that at least a small proportion of every society engages in homosexual behavior even though the social code may strongly condemn such activities. It is our opinion, as expressed earlier in this chapter, that the occurrence of exclusive homosexuality in the face of severe disapproval is due primarily to learning rather than to constitutional factors. In other words, men and women who are exclusively homosexual become so because of personal experience rather than because of some imperative, inherited urge. Of equal importance is the point that total absence of any conscious response to homosexual stimuli probably reflects the inhibiting effects of social conditioning.

The amount and kinds of foreplay which the individual finds satisfying and stimulating depend in part upon learning. Some American women are sexually aroused if the partner manipulates the vulva and clitoris before coitus, whereas other individuals find the same techniques unpleasant. These individual differences might be due in part to variations in the sensitivity of the organs involved, but we consider it much more likely that learned attitudes toward this type of behavior play the major role in determining its effects.

The ability of a man to perform the coital act depends not solely upon his physical condition, but also upon emotional attitudes toward the general subject of sex and toward the particular feminine partner involved. As a result of personal experience, some men become unable to achieve and maintain an erection or to reach climax under certain conditions, although they may be potent in other circumstances. The feminine orgasm is an especially sensitive indicator of experience. Many women have to learn to recognize orgasm when it occurs; and others, as a result of learned inhibitions, may go through life without ever experiencing a satisfactory sexual climax. . . .

31. IMMEDIATE SITUATIONAL FACTORS IN HUMAN SEXUAL RESPONSE

Paul H. Gebhard

The response of an individual to a given situational stimulus obviously depends in large part upon the prior experiences of the individual. In our research we frequently discover that a factor which produces a certain response in an inexperienced individual will produce a diametrically opposite response in an experienced person. For example, having coitus in a situation where discovery is probable is usually extremely inhibiting to an inexperienced individual, whereas with some experienced individuals the risk and novelty often enhance sexual arousal and activity. Conversely, limited experience seems to be correlated with greater response to particular

From Paul H. Gebhard: "Situational Factors Affecting Human Sexual Response"; in Frank A. Beach (ed.): SEX AND BEHAVIOR; New York, John Wiley & Sons 1965, pp. 488–491. Copyright © 1965 by John Wiley & Sons and reprinted with their permission.

sorts of stimuli. When we divide our male sample into age-matched groups based on the number of females with whom they have had coitus, we find that men who have had the fewest coital partners tend to be the ones who are most frequently and intensely aroused by visual and auditory stimuli.

Aside from these differential responses based on differences in past experience, one can say that the specific, immediate, situational factors which have the most potent effect upon subsequent sexual life are those which occur around the time of puberty. In brief, we believe that this age is a "critical period" in human sexual development. While psychiatrists and analysts have long dwelt on the importance of events in infancy and childhood, there has been little recognition of puberty as a crucial transitional phase.

In our research we find that at least in

males the years before puberty do not seem to be as "critical" as the pubertal years. Sexual activities begun in prepubertal life more often than not are subsequently discontinued for long periods. For example, data indicate that only about one quarter of the boys who begin heterosexual activity before puberty carry it on past the age of puberty without lengthy interruption. However, any heterosexual activity which is begun after males reach their pubescent year is almost invariably continuous thereafter. In order to make certain that this continuity difference is not merely a consequence of the occurrence or nonoccurrence of orgasm in pre-versus postpubescent males, we shall check the continuity of sexual activities in those individuals whose prepubertal experience resulted in orgasm.

One can argue that the sexual awareness and behavior which so often begin at puberty rest upon unlearned responses which are triggered by endocrine changes and reinforced by culture. However, we find that much of the bizarre behavior—which cannot be attributed to instinct or cultural norms—first appears around puberty and is only very rarely initiated at older ages. Moreover, this behavior is frequently caused or at least precipitated by unusual combinations of situational factors. Two dramatic examples are illustrative.

One case is that of an individual, now in his thirties, who, when nearing puberty, had not as yet recognized sexual arousal. He became involved in a childhood tussle with a girl somewhat larger and more powerful than he. While struggling and wriggling beneath her he experienced not only his first conscious sexual arousal but in a strong degree. This one experience has dominated his life ever since. He has always been attracted to large, muscular, dominant females; and in his heterosexual contacts he tries to arrange the same wrestling. He has, not surprisingly, developed some additional masochistic attributes.

The other case is that of a boy who was already in what one might call the flush of sexual excitability which accompanies puberty in most males. During some childhood game he fractured his arm and was taken to a neighborhood physician who, noting the rapidity of swelling, decided to "set" the fracture at once without anesthesia. The physician's attractive nurse felt very sorry for the boy. During the reduction of the fracture and for

some time afterwards she held and caressed him with his head pressed against her breasts. The boy experienced a powerful and curious combination of pain and sexual arousal. Considerably later in life this man began to notice that he was unusually attracted to brunettes with a certain type of hair style—attracted to an extent meriting the label of fetish. Some sadomasochistic tendencies also existed. After much introspection the man recalled that the hair style which was his fetish was the style in which the nurse had worn her hair. This insight did not destroy the fetish.

These two cases also illustrate what I call, for lack of a better term, "one-shot conditioning," which is intended as a more forceful term than one-trial learning. Psychiatric records are replete with such "one-shot conditionings" as a consequence of trauma, but there are few cases of its occurrence as a sequel to a happier experience. We are especially curious to learn why a certain experience will immediately condition one person and fail to have any obvious effect on another. One cannot refrain from the vaccination analogy of "take" versus "nontake." Certainly one variable which influences whether there is a "take" or not, is whether the experience occurs during some period of unusual sensitivity such as the one that seems to exist around puberty. Another powerful variable is whether the experience is linked with a strong drive: if so, it is apt to more powerfully modify subsequent behavior. Both my illustrative cases involved both the critical period and the linkage. We postulate that the difference in strength of sexual drive of human males and human females explains in large part why so few females are fetishists, masochists, voyeurs, and adherents of other such behavior patterns which seem to stem from unusual situational combinations.

It is obvious that "one-shot conditioning" is more likely to occur if the situational factors are linked with pre-existing behavioral patterns. Under such circumstances immediate situational factors can strongly modify the behavior of adults well beyond the more formative years of life. One might say that a hardened adult can only be changed by playing upon his habits. I shall give two examples of this, again dramatic cases, for more forceful illustration.

One was a case of incest involving a father

and his young adult daughter. In brief, there was a long period of propinquity and physical intimacy enforced by poverty, frequent visual stimulation, the sexual awakening of the girl, and the mutual deep affection. Immediate situational factors including sexual and emotional deprivation, marital discord, and some alcohol, suddenly caused the long established father-daughter pattern to metamorphose into a sexual relationship. Once the taboo was broken, the sexual behavior continued.

A more complex case was one of the extremely rare instances in which a fortuitous concatenation of situational factors changed the whole sexual orientation of an adult, in this instance a woman. Disappointed by heterosexuality early in life, she had become almost exclusively homosexual overtly and psychically. She had also fallen in with a partially homosexual and very liberal social group which afforded acceptance and friendship. One evening, after a somewhat alcoholic party at the home of a predominantly homosexual male friend whom she liked, it became very late and she accepted his invitation to stay there the night, secure in the belief he posed no sexual threat to her.

As luck would have it, the man had some homosexual activity, and overhearing this not only kept her awake in her adjoining room, but made her somewhat aroused and quite lonely. When his partner had gone, her friend heard her stirring about and asked her to come in and have a final drink. He was nude and covered with a sheet, she wore nothing but a housecoat, and she sat on the edge of his bed. With an ordinary male she would have been frozen and apprehensive, but with this friend she was relaxed and at ease. When she complained of being lonely he laughed, flung back the sheet revealing his erect penis, and pulled her down on him. At this point chance again weighted the scales: being on top in a sexual situation happened to be her customary position in homosexual activity. Suddenly all the situational factors fused. She had absorbed some alcohol, was hungry for emotional warmth, and was partially aroused sexually; her inhibitions were down, she was in her favorite position, and most importantly, she was taken by surprise before she had time to get her defenses up. As a result she suddenly found herself in a heterosexual situation and enjoying it. To her surprise she reached orgasm, and quite quickly. Almost out of clinical curiosity she tried coitus again the following night and again it was very satisfactory.

When I interviewed this woman three months after this experience she was predominantly heterosexual in her fantasy life and other psychic responses, and exclusively heterosexual in her overt behavior. This is a remarkable example of the effects of immediate situational factors. . . .

32. WHAT IS NORMAL?

Wardell B. Pomeroy

The young man sat still for a moment, drawing deeply on a cigarette and exhaling with slow deliberation. Looking me quickly in the eye, he asked: "Am I normal?"

It was the anticipated response to my question, and once more I had to parry it:

"What do you mean by normal?"

We were discussing his sex life, concluding an interview for the Institute for Sex Research, and I had posed my final query: What question about sex may I answer for you? This had been my very last question in over 7000 interviews about people's sex lives during the past 20 years, and the young man's response was typical. Frequently the response was merely a variation on the same theme:

"Is masturbation normal?"
"Is homosexuality normal?"
"Is mouth-genital contact normal?"

Each of these responses points to one of the serious concerns of a great many people in society today: What constitutes normal sexual behavior? And because the ages have not withered nor customs staled the variety of human sexual behavior, it is impossible to answer directly the question of what constitutes normal sexual behavior.

Whether you are normal or not, or whether you classify certain kinds of sexual behavior as normal or not, depends on how you define normal—and it is one of the most casually and blatantly misused words in the English language. The semantic approach to a definition via the ever-convenient dictionary is not a sure or satisfying way out, since standard reference dictionaries list up to nine definitions

"What Is Normal?" by Wardell B. Pomeroy originally appeared in PLAYBOY *magazine of March 1965; copyright © 1965 by HMH Publishing Co., Inc. Reprinted by permission of the author.*

for normal. The pitfalls that lurk along the semantic path may be illustrated by a single example from the combined one-volume *Funk & Wagnalls Standard Dictionary of the English Language and the Britannica World Language Dictionary,* page 863 (international edition): "normal, *adj.* In accordance with an established law or principle; conforming to a type or standard; regular; natural.... Synonyms: common, natural, ordinary, regular, typical, usual. That which is natural is according to nature; that which is normal is according to the standard or rule which is observed or claimed to prevail in nature...the normal color of the crow is black, while the normal color of the sparrow is gray, but one is as natural as the other."

In giving its general difinition, *Webster's New International Dictionary* illuminates the picture not one whit more: That which is normal is "according to, constituting, or not deviating from, an established norm, rule, or principle; conformed to a type...not abnormal; regular; natural; analogical." For all the dictionaries reveal, they might as well say that what's normal is what's normal.

Approaching a definition of normal by way of its antonyms is just as confusing, since, while one might suppose that sexual behavior that is not normal would be termed abnormal, in common usage other words are employed without regard to finer distinctions (even in the jungles of psychologic and psychiatric jargon) to denote sexual behavior that is "not normal." "Pervert," "deviate" and "degenerate" are descriptive nouns interchangeably used in locker rooms and lecture halls alike in reference to the not normal, and, like all such emotionally loaded words, they carry pejorative, punitive and, hence, judgmental connotations. Furthermore, you have to be "perverted" *away from* something, "deviate" *from* something and "degenerate" *from* something—and that something must be what is normal.

But if our casual misuse of the terms normal and abnormal and their synonyms don't yield any clues to precisely what kind of sexual behavior is normal, the judgmental connotations we impute to these words speak volumes about sexual attitudes: Normal sexual behavior is behavior that is considered "right" or "acceptable," and abnormal sexual behavior is behavior that is considered "wrong" or "unacceptable." The next logical question is: What is right or wrong according to whom? —and in attempting an answer, we are confronted with countless battles—some of which have raged for thousands of years—for authority over the minds, bodies and souls of men. For every definition of "normal" in contemporary dictionaries there are thousands of moralists, legislators, religious zealots, doctors, reformers, politicians, philosophers, artists and just plain laymen—propagandists all, each for his own cause—who are more than willing to tell us what's right and what's wrong and, hence, what's normal and what's abnormal. And with quite possibly no exceptions, each and every one of us has evolved his own tacit judgments of right and wrong (normal and abnormal) concerning the next fellow's behavior, according to our own formative mores and our subsequent experiences and insights.

However, since we are also prone to lump our judgments into broad categories, such as "what's moral" and "what's legal," applying such concepts to our definition, we can rephrase the question to: What's normal sexual behavior according to our laws? or, What's normal sexual behavior according to our prevailing morals? and so on. And now, paradoxically, our tendency to generalize helps us pinpoint working definitions of normality and abnormality by which we may classify particular types of sexual behavior.

There are at least five major criteria according to which sexual behavior may be defined as normal or abnormal: statistics, phylogenetics, prevailing morals, law and dominant social attitudes. The statistical concept we use so often in daily life that we're often not aware of it: Whenever we say something like "The guy next door is of normal height," or when we refer to the "abnormal height" of some basketball-playing seven-footer, our standard of comparison is the general height of the population—most of our citizens are nowhere near seven feet tall, and the guy next door could be discerned in a crowd only if he were wearing a Homburg while the rest wore fedoras.

From a statistical point of view, then, how do we behave sexually? It's easy enough to say that if most married couples have sexual intercourse, sexual intercourse must be normal among married couples. But this nice circular argument leaves unanswered the extremely important question of *how* commonplace a given type of behavior must be before we can call it *statistically* normal. What percentage of our married couples have to engage in sexual intercourse before we can say it's normal? Three quarters of the married population? Half? One quarter?

For the sake of argument, we'll say 50 percent will suffice for any sort of sexual behavior: By our arbitrary limit, if half or more of the population performs a particular type of sexual activity, we will call that activity statistically normal. It's obvious right away that marital intercourse is normal by this definition, but how about some of our other sexual behavior?

Masturbation, for instance: 95 percent of human males and about 65 percent of human females masturbate; more than 50 percent of *married* males and nearly as many married females masturbate. By our definition, masturbation is statistically normal for all but married females.

How about homosexuality? While only about a third of human males and a sixth of human females engage in *overt* homosexual activity, about half of the males have either had overt homosexual relations or have been sexually aroused by males. For males, then, homosexuality is statistically almost normal; for females, it is not.

Since sexual behavior is influenced by educational levels, we might expect that some types of sexual behavior would show up as statistically normal for one part of the population but statistically abnormal for other parts. And they do. Mouth-genital activity furnishes a case in point: Among the better educated, this activity is common for more than 50 percent of the group, and is therefore normal by definition. But among the less educated, where taboos remain stronger, fewer than 50 percent of the group engage in mouth-genital activity, and, for them, it is abnormal.

Abnormal also—for *all* segments of the population—are adult relations with children (pedophilia) and real rape (as distinguished from statutory rape), which are the sexual predilections of much less than half our citizenry. Finally, how do we perform sexually out of wedlock? Statistically speaking, well over 85 percent of us indulge in one form or another of nonmarital intercourse—premarital, extramarital or postmarital.

What is normal sexual behavior? Almost anything, according to statistics, except pedophilia and rape. Normal is as normal does.

Let's try another approach toward a definition of sexual normality. From grade school on, we have it persistently drummed into our heads that human beings are a species of animal—specifically, mammals—and during the rest of our lives certain aphorisms ("Man is a rational animal.") are tossed at us whenever we act as though we have forgotten the fact. Since we are mammals, we can ask ourselves how our sexual behavior compares with that of other mammals: How is our behavior like theirs, and how does it differ? This is the phylogenetic definition of sexual normality: Sexual behavior natural to mammals is sexual behavior we're likely to be engaged in.

Among mammals other than the human variety, monogamy is the equivalent of marital status (we alone have benefit of law or clergy), and in this respect, as mammals, we are distinctly *ab*normal and *un*natural. Most mammals do not cleave to one mate for a long period of time.

On the other hand, masturbation, homosexuality and mouth-genital activity are common to almost all species of mammals; even sexual relations between mammals of different species and between mammals and inanimate objects are more common than popularly believed. Do other mammals rape, have sexual relations with their young, engage in sadistic behavior? Yes, some do. So by phylogenetic definition, there's almost nothing that humans do sexually that isn't part of their mammalian nature and heritage.

For one reason or another, we humans are generally reluctant to recognize how close our sexual behavior is to that of our mammalian forebears, and one of the arguments most frequently employed to put distance between ourselves and the primates is that though we are mammals, we are a very special kind endowed with unique and highly developed abilities to love and to think and to communicate. Proponents of this thesis of man's exclusivity also argue that we're the only mammals that practice intercourse face to face. None of these arguments is entirely true. Other mammals *do* have the ability to love, they *do* communicate with one another, and they *do* have some sort of thinking ability—and some primates do, on occasion, have intercourse face to face. The difference between humans and other mammals, therefore, is one of degree and not of kind.

Since the other three definitions of normal sexual behavior—the moral, legal and social—depend to varying degrees on the Judaeo-Christian code of ethics and the bodies of law that have been built upon it, it will repay us to briefly note its origins.

The history of the Judaeo-Christian ethic goes back many centuries before Christ, to the nomadic Jewish tribes of western Asia, whose code of sexual behavior was typical of tribes in that part of the world: Homosexuality was permitted provided no master-servant or superior-subordinate relationship existed between the two parties; intercourse with certain animals was condoned, while it was condemned with certain others, depending upon the species; prostitution was part of the religious ceremony in temples of worship; and polygyny was practiced. It was a sexual code considerably freer than that which the Jews developed upon their return from the Babylonian exile, by which time nationalistic fervor had led them to draw sharp distinctions between themselves and their neighbors. The latter Assyrians, Hittites and Chaldeans, among others, did not believe in Jehovah and were therefore considered pagan by the Jews. Exile and nationalism radically changed the Jews' attitudes toward sexual behavior: Any sexual act that was not directly conducive to procreation was severely condemned; tribal survival and growth became paramount. Masturbation was punishable by death; males were forbidden to touch their genitals on the grounds that they might accidentally arouse themselves; nudity, homosexuality, sexual relations with animals and mouth-genital contacts were all condemned. In a word, any thought that sex could be for pleasure rather than procreation was denied and, hence, any imaginative precoital sex play or variations of position in intercourse were prohibited. Many of these proscriptions found their way into the Old

Testament, frequently in allegorical form. As allegory, they were subject to widely divergent interpretation—as is evident from the writings of Christian clerics of a later and more antisexual era.

Because most early Christians were converted Jews, the early Christian movement was strongly influenced by the rigorous Jewish sexual code, and it was only much later in history that the Christian Church relented and sanctioned elaborations of precoital sex play, variations of position in intercourse and mouth-genital activity—on the firmly understood condition, however, that the *final* sexual act was intercourse. This remains the official position of the Catholic Church today. While many Protestant churches hold that sexual behavior in marriage is not sinful even if no intercourse is involved, they do condemn sexual behavior outside of marriage; very recently some Protestant denominations undertook to consider further liberalization of their sex codes, and it may well be that in the foreseeable future they will relax their rigid distinctions between sexual behavior in marriage and out of marriage.

This brings us to the present, and the question of what is normal sexual behavior as defined by our Judaeo-Christian morals: Masturbation, homosexuality, nonmarital intercourse, rape and pedophilia are all abnormal ("wrong"). Marital intercourse is normal ("right")—in which a degree of latitude is given to precoital sex play, variations of position during intercourse and mouth-genital contacts.

The Judaeo-Christian tradition influenced more than just our moral sex codes; it was also the basis of ecclesiastic law, upon which English common law is based, and from which, in turn, our own sex laws are derived. One might think, therefore, that in defining normal sexual behavior as "what is legal" (normal) and "what is illegal" (abnormal) one would discover the same strictures and the same permissions found in our moral code. But this is not the case. Masturbation is one exception; it is not against the law to masturbate, as long as it is done in private—although there are two states among our 50 in which inducing another person to masturbate is classified as sodomy, according to law. But whereas masturbation is morally abnormal but legally normal, mouth-genital activity is morally normal but legally *ab*normal; in fact, mouth-genital activity is a felony—even between husband and wife—in all states except Illinois.

"Except Illinois" is a significant qualification —it is proof positive that where you live can determine the legal normality of specific sex behavior. What you can legally do in one state may be illegal in the next, another way of saying that—from the legal standpoint—the distinction between normal and abnormal depends on geography. All of our states have laws against extramarital intercourse (adultery), and about half of them have laws against premarital and postmarital intercourse (fornication). Ask what's normal sexual behavior according to the law, and the answer is another question: Where do you live?

What is normal sexual behavior according to a social definition? Defined by this standard, sexual behavior that does no harm to society or its members is normal, whereas sexual behavior that does harm is abnormal. On this basis, our sex laws should protect all members of society from forced sexual relations (rape), and should protect children from sexual relations with adults (pedophilia)—the two sexual activities in which more than the two parties involved are affected. The underlying argument runs that our laws are made to protect persons and property and are not designed to perpetuate or eliminate—or punish—any particular sexual customs. By this social definition, then, masturbation and adult consensual homosexuality, nonmarital intercourse and mouth-genital contacts are normal, since each person determines for himself just what sexual

CRITERIA	MASTUR-BATION	HOMO-SEX-UALITY	NON-MARITAL SEX	MOUTH-GENITAL	PEDO-PHILIA	RAPE
1. Statistical	Normal	?	Normal	Normal	Abnormal	Abnormal
2. Phylogenetic	Normal	Normal	Normal	Normal	?	?
3. Moral	Abnormal	Abnormal	Abnormal	Normal	Abnormal	Abnormal
4. Legal	Normal	Abnormal	?	Abnormal	Abnormal	Abnormal
5. Social	Normal	Normal	Normal	Normal	Abnormal	Abnormal

activity is desirable in his own life; rape and pedophilia would definitely be abnormal. The American Law Institute, in proposing a Model Penal Code, has taken essentially this definition of normal sexuality as the basis for its recommendations.

.   .   .

"Am I normal?"

"What do you mean by normal?" Statistically, phylogenetically, morally, legally and socially we have sought a definition of normal sexual behavior. (For what we found, see the accompanying chart.)

.   .   .

"Am I normal?" It would be easier to banish "normal" from our vocabulary than to answer the question. And to do so might well

make more sense; after all, from the standpoint of individual psychic and physical health, what we do sexually is not nearly as important as how we feel about what we do. I—like many other objective observers—have seen cases where marital intercourse was a hostile and destructive act, and other cases where a homosexual relationship was loving and constructive. Our concern should be with individual well-being rather than with the irrelevant, illogical and psychologically damaging labeling of sexual behavior as normal or abnormal. And we might bear in mind this bit of wisdom from the Stoic philosopher Epictetus:

Men are disturbed not by things, but by the views which they take of them.

33. THE ADJUSTMENT OF
THE MALE OVERT HOMOSEXUAL

Evelyn Hooker [1,2,3]

Current psychiatric and psychological opinion about the adjustment of the homosexual may be illustrated by a quotation from a report on homosexuality recently issued by the

1 This investigation was supported by a research grant, Grant M-839, from The National Institute of Mental Health of the National Institutes of Health, Public Health Service.

2 Paper read at the American Psychological Association Convention, Chicago, August 30, 1956.

3 I wish to acknowledge the invaluable assistance given by Dr. J. A. Gengerelli in acting as consultant on experimental design and statistical methodology. I wish also to gratefully acknowledge the contribution made to the project by Dr. Frederic G. Worden in his capacity of psychiatric consultant. Finally, there is no adequate way to express my gratitude to Dr. Karl Muenzinger for this assistance in thinking through the total project with me in its many phases.

From the JOURNAL OF PROJECTIVE TECHNIQUES, *21 (1957), 18–31. Copyright 1957 by the Society for Projective Techniques and Rorschach Institute, Inc. Reprinted by permission of the* Journal of Projective Techniques and Personality Assessment *and the author.*

Group for the Advancement of Psychiatry (1, p. 2): "When such homosexual behavior persists in an adult, it is then a symptom of a severe emotional disorder." If one wishes to subject this opinion to experimental investigation, one is immediately confronted by problems of considerable magnitude. One problem is the attitude and theoretical position of the clinician who may be asked to examine the data. I quote again from the Group for the Advancement of Psychiatry in the same report (1, p. 4): "It is well known that many people, including physicians, react in an exaggerated way to sexual deviations and particularly to homosexuality with disgust, anger, and hostility. Such feelings often arise from the individual's own conflict centering about his unconscious homosexual impulses. These attitudes may interfere with an intelligent and objective handling of the problem." One hopes that the clinician does not react with "disgust, anger, and hostility." It is not realistic to hope that he will avoid theoretical preconceptions when looking at psychological material which he knows was obtained from a homosexual.

From a survey of the literature it seemed highly probable that few clinicians have ever had the opportunity to examine homosexual subjects who neither came for psychological help nor were found in mental hospitals, disciplinary barracks in the Armed Services, or in prison populations. It therefore seemed important, when I set out to investigate the adjustment of the homosexual, to obtain a sample of overt homosexuals who did not come from these sources; that is, who had a chance of being individuals who, on the surface at least, seemed to have an average adjustment, provided that (for the purpose of the investigation) homosexuality is not considered to be a symptom of maladjustment. It also seemed important to obtain a comparable control group of heterosexuals. This group would not only provide a standard of comparison but might also make it possible to avoid labels and thus assist the clinician in suspending theoretical preconceptions. This, I recognized, would be fraught with extreme difficulties. And so it was. Without relating in detail the—in many ways—fascinating, frustrating, and gratifying aspects of the attempts to secure both of these groups, I shall describe the homosexual and heterosexual samples of thirty individuals each finally obtained.

Each homosexual man is matched for age, education, and IQ with a heterosexual man. It would have been desirable to match for other variables, also, including occupation, but this was manifestly impossible. It should also be stated at the outset that no assumptions are made about the random selection of either group. No one knows what a random sample of the homosexual population would be like; and even if one knew, it would be extremely difficult, if not impossible, to obtain one. The project would not have been possible without the invaluable assistance of the Mattachine Society, an organization which has as its stated purpose the development of a homosexual ethic in order to better integrate the homosexual into society. The members of the Mattachine Society not only made themselves available as subjects but also persuaded their friends to become subjects. Because the heterosexuals were, for the most part, obtained

from community organizations which must remain anonymous, I cannot describe further the way in which they were obtained.

Considerable effort was devoted to securing the 30 matched pairs of subjects, and the data in Table 1 indicate that in most instances the matching was unusually close.

The homosexuals, and thus the heterosexuals, ranged in age from 25 to 50, with an average age of 34.5 for the homosexual group and 36.6 for the heterosexual group. The IQ range, as measured by the Otis Self-Administering Tests of Mental Ability, was from 90 to 135, with an average for the homosexual group of 115.4 and for the heterosexual group of 116.2. In education the range was from completion of grammar school to the equivalent of a master's degree, with an average for the homosexual group of 13.9 years and for the heterosexual group of 14.3.

In both groups subjects were eliminated who were in therapy at the time. If, in the preliminary screening, evidence of considerable disturbance appeared, the individual was eliminated (5 heterosexuals; 5 homosexuals). I attempted to secure homosexuals who would be pure for homosexuality; that is, without heterosexual experience. With three exceptions this is so. These three subjects had not had more than three heterosexual experiences, and they identified themselves as homosexual in their patterns of desire and behavior. The heterosexual group is exclusively heterosexual beyond the adolescent period, with three exceptions; these three had had a single homosexual experience each. In the effort to control the presence of homosexuality, latent or otherwise, in the heterosexual group, each potential subject was referred by a responsible leader of a community group, who described him as being a thorough-going heterosexual and well adjusted. This was an attempt to take precautions to eliminate as many men as possible with homosexual patterns of behavior. It did not do so, and some individuals came who had to be eliminated because, though married and functioning in the community as married men, they had had extensive homosexual experience (four subjects).

The heterosexual subjects came because they were told that this was an opportunity to contribute to our understanding of the way in which the average individual in the community functions, since we had little data on normal men. They were told nothing before-

TABLE 1

MATCHED PAIRS	HOMOSEXUAL			HETEROSEXUAL		
Number	AGE	IQ	EDUCATION	AGE	IQ	EDUCATION
1........................	42	105	12	41	105	12
2........................	29	104	12	28	104	12
3........................	29	109	9	31	109	12
4........................	31	120	16	30	123	16
5........................	44	127	18	45	126	17
6........................	33	127	16	32	129	16
7........................	40	124	16	42	123	16
8........................	33	124	16	36	122	16
9........................	40	98	12	42	100	12
10........................	33	101	14	32	105	15
11........................	30	127	14	29	127	16
12........................	42	91	12	39	94	14
13........................	44	98	9	44	100	12
14........................	36	114	16	36	117	16
15........................	33	120	14	34	120	16
16........................	40	106	12	44	107	12
17........................	37	116	12	34	113	14
18........................	36	127	16	36	127	16
19........................	35	103	12	37	101	11
20........................	26	133	18	27	133	18
21........................	33	124	13	36	122	16
22........................	32	123	12	39	120	12
23........................	26	123	16	29	133	16
24........................	26	123	16	29	133	16
25........................	41	135	16	39	119	16
26........................	28	114	16	35	112	13
27........................	27	118	13	48	119	13
28........................	27	110	14	48	113	16
29........................	57	95	14	46	100	12
30........................	26	124	14	30	129	12

hand about the homosexual aspects of the project. When an individual came to me, after describing to him the nature of the testing and the interview and securing his willingness to participate in the project, I then described very briefly the purpose of the study, including the homosexual group. It was impossible to avoid this explanation. The community leaders who referred these men were concerned about possible repercussions of a "sex study." They required that each man be informed that the total project involved a comparison of homosexual and heterosexual men. I had, therefore, to risk the effect of this information upon my subjects. So, having very briefly described the project to him, I then asked whether he had had any homosexual inclinations or experience. This question was put in a matter-of-fact way and only after

a good relationship of cooperation had been established. If the individual seemed to be severely disturbed by the question, or responded in a bland way, or denied it vehemently, I did not include him in the sample of 30. It is possible, though I doubt it, that there are some heterosexuals in my group who have strong latent or concealed overt homosexuality.

The materials used for the comparative study of personality structure and adjustment of these two groups of men consisted of a battery of projective techniques, attitude scales, and intensive life history interviews. The material I am reporting on here is largely from an analysis of the Rorschach, TAT,* and MAPS,† with some references to life histories,

* Thematic Apperception Test. (Eds.)
† Make A Picture Story. (Eds.)

the detailed analysis of which has not yet been completed.

I used the Rorschach because many clinicians believe it to be the best method of assessing total personality structure and, also, because it is one of the test instruments currently used for the diagnosis of homosexuality. The 60 Rorschach protocols were scored by me, the usual tabulations made, and the profiles constructed. With all identifying information except age eliminated, they were then arranged in random order. Two clinicians, who are also experts in Rorschach, analyzed each of the 60 protocols separately in this order. Because of the importance of knowing how, by what process, using what evidence in the Rorschach, a judge arrived at his rating or judgment in each of the categories, each judge was urged to describe as much as he could of the procedure he was using, the conclusions arrived at, and the evidence used; and the whole process was recorded by Audograph. Let it be said here that the task which the judges were asked to perform, that of analyzing 60 records in succession and of verbalizing the whole process, was a monumental one. It demanded not only a devotion to science "beyond the call of duty" but also an admirable willingness to expose one's fallibility. My success in persuading Dr. Klopfer and Dr. Mortimer Meyer, for the Rorschach, and Dr. Shneidman, for the TAT and MAPS, to give so generously of themselves in this project was primarily due to their belief in its importance and to their eagerness to see a unique body of material and to engage in what they anticipated to be a rewarding learning experience.

The purpose of the Rorschach analysis was two-fold: (1) to obtain an unbiased judgment (that is, without knowledge of homosexual or heterosexual identification of subjects and without life-history materials) of personality structure and overall adjustment of the subjects in both groups; (2) to determine the accuracy with which expert clinicians who are Rorschach workers can differentiate homosexual from heterosexual records. Each judge was asked, in addition to the overall adjustment rating, to analyze the Rorschach protocol in terms of a number of categories, such as methods of handling aggression, affection and dependency needs, methods of impulse control, and clinical label, if any. These judgment categories were used because of their theoretical importance in current approaches to homosexuality. The adjustment rating was on a five-point scale: from 1, superior, to 5, maladjusted; with 3 representing average adjustment. The norm which the judges used was, of course, a subjective one, of average adjustment in the population at large, not just in this group. Assigning an adjustment rating to a Rorschach protocol is difficult, as all of us know. The meanings of the five points of the rating scale were defined as follows: (1) superior, or top adjustment; better than the average person in the total population; evidence of superior integration of capacities, both intellectual and emotional; ease and comfort in relation to the self and in functioning effectively in relation to the social environment; (3) as well-adjusted as the average person in the total population; nothing conspicuously good or bad; (5) bottom limit of normal group and/or maladjusted, with signs of pathology. Ratings 2 and 4 are self-evident, 2 being better-than-average but not quite superior, and 4 being worse-than-average, or the bottom limit of the average group. These ratings are very difficult to objectify, and it is very difficult to be sure that they were used in the same way by the two judges.

One further comment about procedure, before discussing the results of the judging on adjustment: each judge, before he began, knew that some records were homosexual and some were heterosexual. Most clinicians in the Los Angeles area are familiar with the project, and it would have been impossible to secure experts without some knowledge of it. The judge was told that the opportunity to distinguish homosexual from heterosexual records would come later and that the present task was that of telling me as much as he could about what he thought the subject to be like in personality structure and adjustment. If anything impressed him about the pattern of sexual adjustment, he should say it, but this was not the primary purpose of this stage of the analysis. The task of the judges was broken down into two steps: (1) The protocols were analyzed, with overall adjustment ratings given and summary judgments made, in the categories already described; and (2) each judge was then presented with 30 pairs of protocols, matched for age, education, and IQ, the task being to distinguish the homosexual record in each pair.

TABLE 2

Ratings on Overall Adjustment—Rorschach

| | RATINGS | | | | |
	(TOP)				(BOT-TOM)
Group	1	2	3	4	5
Judge "A" Homosexual	9	9	4	3	5
Heterosexual	6	12	5	3	4
Total	15	21	9	6	9
Judge "B" Homosexual	2	15	5	4	4
Heterosexual	2	8	9	8	3
Total	4	23	14	12	7

The results of the judging of adjustment from the Rorschach protocols are presented in Table 2.

It will be noted that *there are no significant differences between the number of homosexuals and heterosexuals having a rating of 3 and better for each judge; two-thirds of each group are assigned an adjustment rating of 3 or better.* There are apparent differences between judges. For Judge "B" there is a greater unwillingness to assign a top rating. In fact, for Judge "B," there is a slight but insignificant trend in the direction of superior adjustment for the homosexual group. By the method of "grand medians," chi square for Judge "A" is zero for the differences in adjustment between heterosexuals and homosexuals and for Judge "B" the difference is 2.31, which is insignificant.

The immediate question is the degree of agreement between the two judges. Although a Tschuprow coefficient between the ratings of Judge "A" and Judge "B" is only 0.33, it is important to point out that the situation is not as bad as this low coefficient would seem to indicate.

Table 3 shows that the two judges agreed exactly in 19 of the 60 cases, 8 being homosexual and 11 heterosexual. In 23 cases they disagreed by one rating step, 12 of these being homosexual and 11 heterosexual. *This means that in 42 out of the 60 cases there was either exact agreement or disagreement by only one step.* So it is safe to say that in two-thirds of the total distribution there is high agreement. An additional fact that may be pointed out is that 14, or approximately one-half, of the homosexuals were placed either in Adjustment Rating 1 or 2 by both judges.

How is one to interpret this finding? Is one to take it at face value and assume that the Rorschach is a valid instrument for determining adjustment in the way in which we have defined it? If so, then clearly there is no inherent connection between pathology and homosexuality. But caution is needed. As clinicians, we are well aware, in daily practice, of the limitations of projective material analyzed "blind." Nevertheless, the quantitative results are striking, and they are confirmed in part by observations of the judges, as well as—and I say this with great caution—by life-history data.

But let us look at the results in the second

TABLE 3

DIFFERENCES	TOTAL	NUMBER OF SUBJECTS HOMOSEXUAL	HETEROSEXUAL
0 (exact agreement)	19	8	11
1 rating step	23	12	11
2 rating steps	14	7	7
3 rating steps	4	3	1
	60	30	30

task given the judges, that of distinguishing between matched pairs of homosexual and heterosexual records. This is a much easier task than that which the clinician ordinarily faces, of identifying homosexuality in one record out of many; and yet it proved to be a very difficult one. As a judge compared the matched protocols, he would frequently comment, "There are no clues"; or, "These are so similar that you are out to skin us alive"; or, "It is a forced choice"; or, "I just have to guess." The difficulty of the task was reflected not only in the comments of the judges but also in the results. Judge "A" correctly identified 17 of the 30 pairs, and Judge "B" 18 of the 30. Thus neither judge was able to do better than chance. In seven pairs both judges were incorrect, that is, identifying the homosexual as the heterosexual, and vice versa; in twelve pairs, correct; and in the remaining eleven they disagreed.

Let us look at the problems the judges faced. In some pairs of records none of the clues usually considered to be signs of homosexuality occurred. In some pairs the "homosexual clues" appeared in both records. These "homosexual clues" were primarily anality, open or disguised; avoidance of areas usually designated as vaginal areas; articles of feminine clothing, especially under-clothing, and/or art objects elaborated with unusual detail; responses giving evidence of considerable sexual confusion, with castration anxiety, and/or hostile or fearful attitudes toward women; evidence of feminine cultural identification, and/or emotional involvement between males. When these clues appeared in neither or in both records, the judge was forced to look for other evidence, and most frequently depended upon peculiar verbalization, or responses with idiosyncratic meaning, or the "flavor" of the total record. When careful examination failed to reveal anything distinctive, the judge assumed that the more banal or typical record was that of the heterosexual, an assumption which was sometimes false.

After the judging was completed, and, indeed, even while it was in process, both judges commented on the fact that the records which they thought to be homosexual were unlike the ones they were familiar with in the clinic. They were not the disturbed records ordi-narily seen. One judge, in the process of choosing, said, "It begins to look as if the homosexuals have all the good things: for example, M's and Fc." It may be pertinent to reiterate that I had made an effort to secure records of homosexuals who ordinarily would not be seen in a clinic. A discussion of the validity and reliability of homosexual signs is tangential to this symposium,[4] but I would point out in passing that my data indicate the need for a thorough-going reconsideration of this problem. At a minimum, healthy skepticism about many (but not all) so-called homosexual-content signs in the Rorschach is, I think, called for. The inability of the judges to distinguish the homosexual from the heterosexual records better than would be expected by chance fits, I think, the finding on adjustment of the two groups. Some of the records can be easily distinguished; the fact that the judges agreed in their identification of twelve pairs indicates this. These were records of individuals with strong emphasis on "femininity" and/or anality. But apart from these, which constitute about a third of the group, the remaining two-thirds cannot be easily distinguished. If the homosexual records had been similar to those frequently seen in the clinic, that is, severely disturbed, there might have been greater probability that they could have been correctly identified, although this cannot be said with certainty. I have now seen about two hundred homosexual records and would be skeptical about my ability to identify correctly records similar to many in this group.

Although it is not pertinent to this symposium[5] to present in detail the findings of the statistical comparisons of the two groups of Rorschach protocols, it is relevant to point out in summary form that most of these comparisons have failed to produce differences of sufficient magnitude to satisfy tests of significance. Several examples will suffice to make the point. Although most studies of homosexual protocols indicate greater productivity on the Rorschach, the difference between the two groups in the present study does not reach significance, though there is a trend in

4 A paper on "Homosexuality in the Rorschach" is in process of preparation. It will contain a full discussion of homosexual signs, as well as other aspects of homosexuality in the Rorschach.

5 See Footnote 4.

this direction (t = 1.389, df = 29, p = >.10). A detailed comparison of total M's and human figures was made. Of some 25 computations, of differences between means of M% in various categories (such as flexor or extensor), differences in form level, variation in form level, etc., the only ones which approached low significance were the sigma of form level (t = 1.98, df = 29, p = >.05), and O-minus percent (t = 2.262, df = 29, p = <.02).

Cronbach's warning about inflation of probabilities deters me from drawing too many conclusions from these two findings, although there is good theoretical rationale for them. The details of the analysis will be discussed more appropriately in a later paper. I cite these general findings at this time in order to show that despite considerable effort and the pursuing of many alluring possibilities, the efforts thus far to establish clear-cut differences between the two groups as a whole have been relatively fruitless. This, too, is consistent with the lack of significant differences between the adjustments of the two groups.

In addition to the overall adjustment ratings, each judge gave summary statements about each subject in a number of categories, including methods of handling aggression, affectional and dependency needs, and form of impulse control. When these statements were tabulated and subjected to statistical analysis, again no clear-cut differences emerged.[6] For example, the statements about affectional and dependency needs have been tabulated in eleven categories, such as repressed or absent, ego-alien, integrates well, controlled by (that is, a dependent character). Four homosexuals were described as having affectional and dependency needs repressed or absent, while three heterosexuals were similarly described. Six homosexuals and six heterosexuals were described as integrating well these needs. It was said of one homosexual and one heterosexual that affectional and dependency needs were ego-alien. Chi square for differences between the number of heterosexuals and homosexuals assigned to all categories is 5.736, df = 10, insignificant.

Let us turn now to the TAT and MAPS. These were administered as a single test, the selected MAPS items following the TAT. Altogether, 12 pictures were used: 3BM,

6BM, 7BM, 12M, 13MF, 16, and 18GF of the TAT; and from the MAPS, the Living Room, the Street Scene, the Bathroom, the Bedroom, and the Dream. It was hoped that the TAT and MAPS would be helpful in revealing current conflicts. The MAPS was used in addition to the TAT because of the opportunity it gives the subject for the selection of figures together with backgrounds with different situational pulls of particular importance in this study. Very fortunately, Dr. Shneidman agreed to analyze the MAPS and TAT protocols of the 60 subjects using the same categories for analysis and overall adjustment as did the Rorschach judges. The service he performed, in terms of sheer energy alone, may be suggested by the fact that he began the task on week-ends in February, when the first fruit trees in our California garden were in bloom, and barely escaped before fruit appeared in July. The problem of identifying the homosexual protocol from this material was essentially a much easier one than that encountered with the Rorschach, since few homosexuals failed to give open homosexual stories on at least one picture. The second task given the Rorschach judges, of distinguishing the homosexual from the heterosexual records when they were presented in matched pairs, was therefore omitted. In every other respect, however, both with respect to task and procedure and including the recording, the TAT-MAPS judge proceeded as had the Rorschach judges. In the first 30 records the TAT and MAPS protocols for each man were analyzed together, with judgments given about overall adjustment rating and the other categories, such as methods of handling aggression, etc. In the second 30 records, the TAT protocols were analyzed in succession, with judgments given, and then the MAPS—the judge not knowing which MAPS protocol corresponded with which TAT. This was done in an effort to prevent a "halo" effect, since homosexuality was openly revealed in some TAT records and not in the MAPS (for the same man), and vice versa. Some very interesting results were obtained, to which I shall refer later.

Table 4 shows the data on the adjustment ratings. The results are essentially the same as for the Rorschach. *The homosexuals and heterosexuals do not differ significantly in their ratings:* Chi square = 2.72, df = 4, p = > .70. This judge does not place a single sub-

6 The complete data will be reported in the future publication previously referred to.

TABLE 4

Adjustment Ratings on TAT-MAPS

| | RATINGS | | | | |
| | *(TOP)* | | | | *(BOTTOM)* |
GROUP	1	2	3	4	5
Homosexual	0	9	15	6	0
Heterosexual	0	7	19	3	1
Total	0	16	34	9	1

ject in Rating 1, and he places only one in Rating 5 (a heterosexual). Determining the degree of agreement between the ratings on the Rorschach and TAT-MAPS constitutes a difficult problem, since two variables are involved: the judges and the test materials. A Tschuprow coefficient between either Rorschach judge and the TAT-MAPS judge is 0.20. Perhaps a more meaningful way of looking at the material is that between one Rorschach judge (Judge "A") and the TAT-MAPS judge there is exact agreement in 15 of the 60 cases (8 homosexual and 7 heterosexual); for Judge "B" there is agreement in 16 cases. When the ratings of all three judges are put together, there is agreement on 14 homosexuals (approximately one-half of the group) as being 3 or better in adjustment, and 14 heterosexuals.[7]

Let me turn now to some qualitative descriptions of the homosexuals from the projective material. Perhaps even better than do the quantitative results, these will convey the problem. Man #16 is described by one judge in summary fashion as "an individual who has the most superb and smooth mastery of intellectual processes we have seen. Intellectualization is his major defense, although there is no compulsive flavor. On one side there is isolation of aggression. But essentially he is submissive, and since he is so sensitive and responsive, he cannot give in to the submissive seduction. His dependency needs are filtered and sublimated. He is the ethical type. Intellectual introspection must be his major preoccupation. He is really balanced on a razor's edge. An extremely clever person." He was correctly identified by this judge, who gave him a rating of 1, and incorrectly by the other judge, who placed him in Rating 2. The latter

[7] A paper on "Homosexuality in the TAT and MAPS." which will contain the full report, is in process of preparation.

describes him in the following terms: "He gives an original twist to ordinary things. For him it is very important not to be conventional. He avoids it like the plague. He tries to keep it cool. I get the feeling that he wants to deny dependency. He has passive longings, but these would not fit in with his ego-ideal of being strong, superior, and wise. He would be able to be very rewarding emotionally. He does not wish to expose his aggression ordinarily, but would in relation to manly intellectual pursuits. I think he is heterosexual."

This man is described on the MAPS and TAT as being "the most heterosexual-looking homosexual I have ever seen. Up to the last two stories on the MAPS, I would say confidently, 'This is a heterosexual record.' His attitudes to sexuality are fairly moral. He has refined, quiet relationships to people. I would give him a rating of 2. The unconscious conflicts are very deep, but they are not disturbing clinically. No idea of clinical label. I would not have known he is a homosexual except for a 'give away' on two of the MAPS stories."

This man is in his early 40's and holds two master's degrees in different artistic fields from one of the major educational institutions of this country. He had a long career as a college teacher—long, and apparently successful. He was caught in what was, to the police, suspicious circumstances with another man, and in the space of a few minutes his entire professional career was destroyed. He now is the manager of a magazine. Although in his early life he passed through the "cruising" stage, he now has highly stable personal relationships, including a "homosexual marriage." If one brackets the fact that he is a homosexual, one would think of him as being a highly cultured, intelligent man who, though unconventional in his manner of living, exhibits no particular signs of pathology. He has never sought psychological or psychiatric help. He has been a homosexual from adolescence, with no heterosexual experience or inclination.

Let me describe another (Subject #50) of these individuals who was placed in adjustment categories 1 or 2 by both Rorschach judges and misidentified as being a heterosexual. One judge described this man "as being so ordinary that it's hard to say anything specific about him. His impulse control is very smooth. He uses channelization rather than repression. Except for a little too much emphasis on conquest in heterosexual relations, he is well adjusted and smooth. His aggressive impulses are expressed in phallic gratification. Good fusion of tenderness and aggression, though he subjugates tenderness to phallic gratification. He must be a heterosexual. I would really have to force myself, to think of him as not heterosexual." By the second judge this man is described in the following terms: "He must be a very interesting guy. He must convey comfort to people. He takes essentials and doesn't get lost in details. A solid citizen, neatly and solidly integrated, with no specific defenses. Neither aggression nor dependency is a problem. I think that this man is heterosexual."

Man #50 is twenty-seven. He works in the electronics industry, in a very large firm in which he has a supervisory job. He lives alone in an apartment, though in an apartment house in which other homosexuals reside. His homosexual pattern involves rather a large number of homosexual partners. He is thoroughly immersed in the homosexual way of life, but apart from this I see no particular evidence of disturbance.

The TAT was analyzed first, and on the TAT he talks about homosexuality, thus revealing that he is a homosexual. The judgments to which the clinician comes are essentially that he is a promiscuous, driven person; that there are compulsive elements; that he goes from one relationship to another, not even aware of what he is seeking, a fairly lonely man, although with an adjustment slightly below 3. The first four stories of the MAPS were described by the judge as being definitely heterosexual. On the last story, the Dream, I should like to quote the judge directly: "I am surprised, because what this means is that this is the record of a homosexual; and it means that I had not seen this

at all up to this point. It means, also, that he doesn't show it except over the jealousy and rivalry of homosexual partners. The record is clean psychiatrically up to this point. It wasn't especially rich, but it would certainly pass. I don't want to do fancy equivocation and say I see it all now, because I don't see a damn thing now. The Living Room is fine; it is as heterosexual as any story we have read in the entire series. The Street Scene simply shows the derogatory and disdainful attitudes that many heterosexual men have toward female sexuality. It is not the exclusive approach of the homosexual, though it is consistent with it. It has a heterosexual flavor. In the Bath, the privacy of the father is interrupted, but this, if anything, would be heterosexual. The Bedroom is as normal a heterosexual story as I have ever read." The judge re-reads the story: "This is almost an encapsulated homosexual. I don't know if I am just being fancy, but we talk about a guy sometimes who functions fairly well until you mention 'Republican' or 'Communist' then you plug in a whole series of paranoid and delusory material; at this point the guy is just crazy. *This* guy has an encapsulated homosexual system. If I had not been shown the Dream story, I would have bet 85 to 15 that he was heterosexual, and maybe even more. I also feel that this guy is a male homosexual. He plays the aggressive, masculine role. But I am puzzled. I can hardly speak intelligently of the dynamics of the homosexuality when, until the last moment, I thought of him as heterosexual. I would give him a rating of slightly better than 3. Not a rich record; not creative and imaginative. It's a rather perfunctorily heterosexual record. I am amazed at this record. He has intense involvement with people. He is not a promiscuous homosexual. There is strong affect. He practically acts like a husband and father. One of the statements about him is that he is a normal homosexual. I mean it's like a guy who has a tic: ordinarily we say he must have a very serious problem. Maybe he does, but if you examine the material of lots of people who have tics, you will find some people who look pretty good, if you think of normal functioning. Then, after you have said this, someone tells you, 'Yes, but he is one of the guys who tics.' And you say, 'Well, he looks clean to me.' And that is what this record looks like. This record is schizophrenic like I am an aviator. If you want proof that a homosexual can be normal, this record does it."

Man #49 is described by Judge "A" as follows (Rating 1): "This record presents less problems of any sort than any other we have seen. The mental type is very clear-cut, calling a spade a spade. Looks like a well-integrated person. Impulse control really smooth, because he permits all impulses to express themselves in a context—both dependent and aggressive. Of all the cases, the best balance of aggression and dependency we have seen. No problem, clinical or otherwise. Relations with others skillful and comfortable." Judge "B" (Rating 2; if not 2, a 1): "Able to integrate well with all stimuli. Effective functioning. Heterosexual adjustment. Defense used: some repression. Not an 'acter outer.' Avoids intense emotional stimuli because they are disorganizing to him."

The TAT and MAPS were analyzed separately. In the first four stories of the TAT, the subject was described as being a thoroughgoing heterosexual. In 13MF the judge comments, "Here we have a fairly straightforward heterosexual story." In the blank card in the TAT, the judge says, "Here this guy opens up more than on the others. He is a sleeper. This is one of the best-adjusted and, in a sense, one of the most paradoxical records I have seen. What is here is indecision and a schizoid feeling. So this is not in any sense a superior personality. There is some withdrawal and some aridity. This is not an outgoing, warm, decisive person. It is a constricted, somewhat egocentric, somewhat schizoid, perturbed, a little guilty fellow. Even so, it is not a tormented record and is not necessarily a homosexual record. He talks about this quite casually and has a fairly good adjustment to his homosexuality. This guy is a very interesting person and quite a complicated guy. In many ways he is both well adjusted to his homosexuality and the kind of guy who could almost be heterosexual in a way that other homosexuals could not be. I don't think he would be swishy or over-masculine. He would pass. I find him very difficult to rate. I can't rate him as 1 or 2. To call him average is innocuous. He doesn't merit 5 or 4. I don't know. I will call him 3, but it doesn't give the flavor. I don't know what to do."

At another time the same judge analyzed the MAPS protocol, in which no homosexual stories are given. The judge comments: "I want to comment on his insistence on the normal situation and his freedom to use the nude. I think this is a very healthy guy, in a somewhat barren way. I have a feeling that this is a kind of emancipated person who has not made an issue of being independent but is able to stand on his own two feet. The fact that he doesn't have rich dynamics robs him of being interesting, creative, and unusual. I rate him as a 2 for sure. I don't know what a 1 would be. He handles hostility and sexuality easily. One shortcoming in the record—not pathological—is the conventionality; and I imply by that a touch of emptiness. He is able to love and to dislike. He is a good father and husband and would be a steady employee. I could see him as having a better-than-average job. He would not be a creative or imaginative person. I don't mean a Babbitt, but he would not take the risk of loving deeply. He is a middle-of-the-roader. This is as clean a record as I think I have seen. I don't think he has strong dependency needs. He is comfortable, and in that sense he is strong. I imply that this is a heterosexual record specifically."

This man is 37, and he works in a ceramics factory doing fairly routine work. He has a "homosexual marriage" of some six years' duration. He tried very hard to change his sexual pattern but was unsuccessful and has now accepted the homosexual "life." He has not had heterosexual experience.

Out of the 30 homosexual men, there were seven who were placed by one or the other judge in rating categories 4 or 5. Since these individuals have what is probably the more expected personality picture, I should like to describe several. One of these is #6. He was rated by one judge at a 5 level and by the other judge at 2. By the judge who places him at 5, he is described as a "pseudo-normal, nearpsychotic, with brittle personality organization which is fairly stabilized. His reality testing is uncannily sharp, but he is almost autistic. His chief defenses are projection and intellectual control. There are strong castration fears, strong orality, and the aggression is projected or transformed into irony. The emotional needs are withered away."

Man #52 is described by one judge who places him in the 4 category, as "a personality which is basically pathological. An anal character, with a strongly destructive flavor. Anal-sadistic. A past-master of intellectualization, though superficially socializes it. Just enough reality testing to be clinically normal. Impossible to separate the hysterical and paranoid elements. Dependency needs are repressed or crippled. Very narcissistic and incapable of guilt. A cloak of righteousness over it all." The second judge describes him in the following terms: "There is too much unconscious breaking through. Some ideational leakage. A chronic situation to which he has made an adjustment. He is not paranoid, but obsessive in a paranoid structure. On the surface he operates smoothly. Emotional relationships will lack in depth and warmth. Uses over-ideation as a defense. His primary method is intellectualization. His dependency needs will make him appear demanding. Essentially a character picture."

Of a somewhat different nature is #28, who is placed by both judges at the bottom level of adjustment. Described by one judge as "very defensive; every impulse ego-alien. Uses denial, intellectualization, and repression. High level of narcissism. Regresses easily into the infantile. The most unbalanced record one could find." By the other judge: "This looks like a clinic record. An anxiety state, prepsychotic. Is more scared of his own fantasies than the world. People present too many problems; he tries to preserve distant relations. Doesn't want to see sex in people. Sex is very repulsive."

Thus, there is no single pattern of homosexual adjustment. This had been anticipated. The richness and variety of ways in which the homosexual adjusts are as difficult to summarize as to summarize 30 full, qualitative pictures of 30 individuals. If I were to read pictures of heterosexuals with the same level of adjustment, the pictures would be essentially the same, with the exception of the bottom range, where one does not find the marked anal-destructive character-structure or the emphasis on "femininity" (which may occur at other levels, also).

That homosexuality is determined by a multiplicity of factors would not now, I think, be seriously questioned. That the personality structure and adjustment may also vary within a wide range now seems quite clear. It comes as no surprise that some homosexuals are severely disturbed, and, indeed, so much so that the hypothesis might be entertained that the homosexuality is the defense against open psychosis. But what is

difficult to accept (for most clinicians) is that some homosexuals *may* be very ordinary individuals, indistinguishable, except in sexual pattern, from ordinary individuals who are heterosexual. Or—and I do not know whether this would be more or less difficult to accept —that some *may* be quite superior individuals, not only devoid of pathology (unless one insists that homosexuality itself is a sign of pathology) but also functioning at a superior level.

But before we accept this hypothesis as a plausible one, we must look carefully at the limitations of the evidence. We have already spoken of the necessity of caution in accepting as valid the results of "blind" analyses of projective test protocols. As clinicians, we are also cautious about accepting an analysis which is not "blind." It may be that the primary psychological defect, if there is one, in the homosexual lies in a weakness of ego-function and control and that this cannot be adequately diagnosed from projective test protocols. As one psychiatrist puts it, the material produced in the Rorschach is like that produced on the analytic couch. Two men may produce very similar material on the couch, but the difference between them is that one—the normal—gets up at the end of the hour and resumes his normal functioning, while the other does not. Another way of looking at the data from the projective tests may be that the homosexual "pathology" occurs only in an erotic situation and that the homosexual can function well in non-erotic situations such as the Rorschach, TAT, and MAPS. Thus, one could defend the hypothesis that homosexuality is symptomatic of pathology, but that the pathology is confined to one sector of behavior, namely, the sexual.

As I listened to each of the three judges analyze the 60 records, I was very much impressed with the usefulness of the projective tests, when interpreted by expert clinicians. Often, the picture of the personality which emerged bore such a striking resemblance to the man as I knew him from many hours of interviewing and testing that it was difficult to believe that the judge did not have detailed personal knowledge as well. Of course there was great discrepancy in some cases. The full report of the material will contain all of the evidence of the congruency or lack of congruency between the life-history materials and the projective analysis.

When I speak of the life-history materials, I am highly conscious of the fact that these have not been *objectively* rated for adjustment. This presents a problem for the future similar to that of the TAT and MAPS, only more so because of the difficulty of controlling for theoretical bias in judging open homosexual material. Final conclusions cannot be drawn until this is done. It can now be said with some certainty, however, that at least in one respect the life-history data from the two groups will differ: namely, in the love relationships. Comparisons between the number and duration of love relationships, cruising patterns, and degree of satisfaction with sexual pattern and the love-partner will certainly show clear-cut differences.

A question also arises about the size of the sample used. It is possible that much larger samples—for example, 100 in each group—would show differences. But would we not, in this case, be dealing with a different question, namely, "How many homosexuals, as compared with heterosexuals, are average or better in adjustment, and how many are worse than average? It seems to me that for the present investigation the question is whether homosexuality is necessarily a symptom of pathology. All we need is a single case in which the answer is negative.

What are the psychological implications of the hypothesis that homosexuality is not necessarily a symptom of pathology? I would *very tentatively* suggest the following:

1. Homosexuality as a clinical entity does not exist. Its forms are as varied as are those of heterosexuality.
2. Homosexuality may be a deviation in sexual pattern which is within the normal range, psychologically. This has been suggested, on a biological level, by Ford and Beach (2).
3. The role of particular forms of sexual desire and expression in personality structure and development may be less important than has frequently been assumed. Even if one assumes that homosexuality represents a severe form of maladjustment to society in the sexual sector of behavior, this does not necessarily mean that the homosexual must be severely maladjusted in other sectors of his behavior. Or, if one assumes that homosexuality is a form of severe maladjustment internally, it may be that the disturbance is limited to the sexual sector alone.

REFERENCES

1. Committee on Cooperation with Governmental (Federal) Agencies of the Group for the Advancement of Psychiatry. Report on homosexuality with particular emphasis on this problem in governmental agencies. Report No. 30, Jan., 1955. Pp. 7.
2. Ford, C. S., and Beach, F. A. *Patterns of Sexual Behavior* New York: Harper, 1951. Pp. 307.

Is Man a Killer by Nature?

UPI Photo of Scene outside the 1968 Democratic National Convention. Photo by Leslie H. Sintay.

34. THE NATURE AND FUNCTIONS OF AGGRESSION

Konrad Lorenz

All the cases described above, in which animals of different species fight against each other, have one thing in common: every one of the fighters gains an obvious advantage by its behavior or, at least, in the interests of preserving the species it "ought to" gain one. But intra-specific aggression, aggression in the proper and narrower sense of the word, also fulfills a species-preserving function. Here, too, the Darwinian question "What for?" may and must be asked. Many people will not see the obvious justification for this question, and those accustomed to the classical psychoanalytical way of thinking will probably regard it as a frivolous attempt to vindicate the life-destroying principle or, purely and simply, evil. The average normal civilized human being witnesses aggression only when two of his fellow citizens or two of his domestic animals fight, and therefore sees only its evil effects. In addition there is the alarming progression of aggressive actions ranging from cocks fighting in the barnyard to dogs biting each other, boys thrashing each other, young men throwing beer mugs at each other's heads, and so on to bar-room brawls about politics, and finally to wars and atom bombs.

With humanity in its present cultural and technological situation, we have good reason to consider intra-specific aggression the greatest of all dangers. We shall not improve our chances of counteracting it if we accept it as something metaphysical and inevitable, but on the other hand, we shall perhaps succeed in finding remedies if we investigate the chain of its natural causation. Wherever man has achieved the power of voluntarily guiding a natural phenomenon in a certain direction, he has owed it to his understanding of the chain of causes which formed it. Physiology, the science concerned with the normal life processes and how they fulfill their species-preserving function, forms the essential foundation for pathology, the science investigating their disturbances. Let us forget for a moment that the aggression drive has become derailed under conditions of civilization, and let us inquire impartially into its natural causes. For the reasons already given, as good Darwinians we must inquire into the species-preserving function which, under natural—or rather precultural—conditions, is fulfilled by fights within the species, and which by the process of selection has caused the advanced development of intraspecific fighting behavior in so many higher animals. It is not only fishes that fight their own species: the majority of vertebrates do so too, man included.

Darwin had already raised the question of the survival value of fighting, and he has given us an enlightening answer: It is always favorable to the future of a species if the stronger of two rivals takes possession either of the territory or of the desired female. As so often, this truth of yesterday is not the untruth of today but only a special case; ecologists have recently demonstrated a much more essential function of aggression. Ecology —derived from the Greek *oikos*, the house— is the branch of biology that deals with the manifold reciprocal relations of the organism to its natural surroundings—its "household"— which of course includes all other animals and plants native to the environment. Unless the special interests of a social organization demand close aggregation of its members, it is obviously most expedient to spread the individuals of an animal species as evenly as possible over the available habitat. To use a human analogy: if, in a certain area, a larger number of doctors, builders, and mechanics want to exist, the representatives of these professions will do well to settle as far away from each other as possible.

The danger of too dense a population of an animal species settling in one part of the available biotope* and exhausting all its sources of nutrition and so starving can be obviated by a mutual repulsion acting on the animals of the same species, effecting their regular spacing out, in much the same manner as electrical charges are regularly distributed all over the surface of a spherical conductor. This, in plain terms, is the most important survival value of intra-specific aggression....

In many animals the same result is achieved without aggressive behavior. Theoretically it suffices that animals of the same species "cannot bear the smell of each other" and avoid each other accordingly. To a certain extent this applies to the smell signals deposited by cats, though behind these lies a hidden threat of active aggression. There are some vertebrates which entirely lack intra-specific aggression but which nevertheless avoid their own species meticulously. Some frogs, in particular tree frogs, live solitary lives except at mating time, and they are obviously distributed very evenly over the available habitat. As American scientists have recently discovered, this distribution is effected quite simply by the fact that every frog avoids the quacking sound of his own species. This explanation, however, does not account for the distribution of the females, for these, in most frogs, are dumb.

We can safely assume that the most important function of intra-specific aggression is the even distribution of the animals of a particular species over an inhabitable area, but it is certainly not its only one. Charles Darwin had already observed that sexual selection, the selection of the best and strongest animals for reproduction, was furthered by the fighting of rival animals, particularly males. The strength of the father directly

affects the welfare of the children in those species in which he plays an active part in their care and defense. The correlation between male parental care and rival fighting is clear, particularly in those animals which are not territorial in the sense which the Cichlids demonstrate but which wander more or less nomadically, as for example, large ungulates,* ground apes, and many others. In such animals, intra-specific aggression plays no essential part in the "spacing out" of the species. Bisons, antelopes, horses, etc., form large herds, and territorial borders and territorial jealousy are unknown to them since there is enough food for all. Nevertheless the males of these species fight each other violently and dramatically, and there is no doubt that the selection resulting from this aggressive behavior leads to the evolution of particularly strong and courageous defenders of family and herd; conversely, there is just as little doubt that the survival value of herd defense has resulted in selective breeding for hard rival fights. This interaction has produced impressive fighters such as bull bison or the males of the large baboon species; at every threat to the community, these valiantly surround and protect the weaker members of the herd....

Social Bonds

In a rather different sense, the phylogenetic prototype of the personal bond and of group formation is the attachment between two partners which together tend their young. From such a tie a family can easily arise, but the bond with which we are here concerned is of a much more special kind. We will now describe how this bond comes about in Cichlids.

In observing, with a thorough knowledge of all the expressive movements, the processes which in Cichlids effect the coming together of partners of opposite sex, it is a nerve-wracking experience to see the prospective mates in a state of real fury with each other. Again and again they are close to starting a vicious fight, again and again the ominous flare-up of the aggressive drive is only just inhibited and murder sidestepped by a hair. Our apprehension is by no means founded on a false interpretation of the particular expressive

---

* A region uniform in its environmental conditions and in its animal population. (Eds.)

* Deer or other four-footed, hoofed animals. (Eds.)

movements observed in our fish: every fish breeder knows that it is risky to put male and female of a Cichlid species together in a tank, and that there is considerable danger of casualty if pair formation is not constantly supervised.

Under natural conditions, habituation is largely responsible for preventing hostilities between the prospective mates. We can best imitate natural conditions by putting several young, still peaceable fishes in a large aquarium and letting them grow up together. Pair formation then takes place in the following way: on reaching sexual maturity a certain fish, usually a male, takes possession of a territory and drives out all the others. Later, when a female is willing to pair, she approaches the territory owner cautiously and, if she acknowledges the superior rank of the male, responds to his attacks which, at first, are quite seriously meant, in the way described on page 104, with the so-called "coyness behavior," consisting, as we already know, of behavior elements arising partly from mating and partly from escape drives. If, despite the clearly aggression-inhibiting intention of these gestures, the male attacks, the female may leave his territory for a short time, but sooner or later she returns. This is repeated over a varying period until each of the two animals is so accustomed to the presence of the other that the aggression-eliciting stimuli inevitably proceeding from the female lose their effect.

As in many similar processes of specific habituation, here, too, all fortuitously occurring accessory factors become part of the entire situation to which the animal finally becomes accustomed. If any of these factors is missing, the whole effect of the habituation will be upset. This applies in particular to the beginning stages of peaceful cohabitation, when the partner must always appear on the accustomed route, from the accustomed side; the lighting must always be the same, and so on, otherwise each fish considers the other as a fight-releasing stranger. Transference to another aquarium can at this stage completely upset pair formation. The closer the acquaintanceship, the more the picture of the partner becomes independent of its background, a process well known to the Gestalt psychologist as also to the investigators of conditioned reflexes. Finally, the bond with the partner becomes so independent of accidental conditions that pairs can be transferred, even transported far away, without rupture of their bond. At most, pair formation "regresses" under these circumstances, that is, ceremonies of courtship and appeasement may recur, which in long-mated partners had long ago disappeared, having ceded to force of habit.

If pair formation runs an undisturbed course, the male's sexual behavior gradually comes to the fore. There may already be traces of these behavior patterns in his first seriously intended attacks on the female, but now they increase in intensity and frequency without, however, causing the disappearance of the expression movements implying aggressive mood. In the female, however, the original escape-readiness and "submissiveness" decrease very quickly. Movements expressive of fear or escape mood disappear in the female more and more with the consolidation of pair formation, in fact they sometimes disappear so quickly that, during my early observations of Cichlids, I overlooked them altogether and for years erroneously believed that no ranking order existed between the partners of this family. We have already heard what part ranking order plays in the mutual recognition of the sexes, and it persists latently, even when the female has completely stopped making submissive gestures to her mate. Only on the rare occasions when an old pair quarrels does she do it again.

At first nervously submissive, the female gradually loses her fear of the male, and with it every inhibition against showing aggressive behavior, so that one day her initial shyness is gone and she stands, fearless and truculent, in the middle of the territory of her mate, her fins outspread in an attitude of selfdisplay, and wearing a dress which, in some species, is scarcely distinguishable from that of the male. As may be expected, the male gets furious, for the stimulus situation presented by the female lacks nothing of the key stimuli which, from experimental stimulus analysis, we know to be strongly fight-releasing. So he also assumes an attitude of broadside display, discharges some tail beats, then rushes at his mate, and for fractions of a second it looks as if he will ram her—and then the thing happens which prompted me to write this book: the male does not waste time replying to the threatening of the female; he is far too excited for that, he actually launches a furious attack which, however, *is not directed at his mate but, passing her by narrowly, finds its goal in another member of his species.* Under natural conditions this is regularly the territorial neighbor.

This is a classical example of the process which we call, with Tinbergen, a *redirected activity.* It is characterized by the fact that an activity is released by *one* object but discharged at *another,* because the first one, while presenting stimuli specifically eliciting the response, simultaneously emits others which inhibit its discharge. A human example is furnished by the man who is very angry with someone and hits the table instead of the other man's jaw because inhibition prevents him from doing so, although his pent-up anger, like the pressure within a volcano, demands outlet. Most of the known cases of redirected activity concern aggressive behavior elicited by an object which simultaneously evokes fear. In this special case, which he called "bicycling," B. Grzimek first recognized and described the principle of redirection. The "bicyclist" in this case is the man who bows to his superior and treads on his inferior. The mechanism effecting this behavior is particularly clear when an animal approaches its opponent from some distance, then, on drawing near, notices how terrifying the latter really is, and now, since it cannot check the already started attack, vents its anger on some innocent bystander or even on some inanimate substitute object.

There are, of course, innumerable further forms of redirected movements, and various combinations of opposing drives can produce them. The special case of the Cichlid male is very significant for our theme because analogous processes play a decisive role in the family and social life of a great many higher animals and man. The problem of how to prevent inter-marital fighting is solved in a truly remarkable way not only by not inhibiting the aggression elicited in each partner by the presence of the other, but by putting it to use in fighting the hostile neighbor. This solution has evidently been found independently in several unrelated groups of vertebrates. . . .

The so-called *functional change* is a means often used by the two great constructors of evolution to put to new purposes remnants of an organization whose function has been outstripped by the progress of evolution. With daring fantasy, the constructors have, for ex-

ample, made from a water-conducting gill slit an air-containing, sound-conducting hearing tube; from two bones of the jaw joint two little auditory bones; from a parietal eye an endocrine gland, the pineal body; from a reptile's arm a bird's wing, and so on. However, all these amazing metamorphoses seem tame in comparison with the ingenious feat of transforming, by the comparatively simple means of redirection and ritualization, a behavior pattern which not only in its prototype but even in its present form is partly motivated by aggression, into a means of appeasement and further into a love ceremony which forms a strong tie between those that participate in it. This means neither more nor less than converting the mutually repelling effect of aggression into its opposite. Like the performance of any other independent instinctive act, that of the ritual has become a need for the animal, in other words an end in itself. Unlike the autonomous instinct of aggression, out of which it arose, it cannot be indiscriminately discharged at any anonymous fellow member of the species, but demands for its object the personally known partner. Thus it forms a *bond* between individuals.

We must consider what an apparently insoluble problem is here solved in the simplest, most elegant and complete manner: two furiously aggressive animals, which in their appearance, coloring, and behavior are to each other what the red rag (though only proverbially) is to the bull, must be made to agree within the narrowest space, at the nesting place, that is at the very place which each regards as the center of its territory, where intra-specific aggression is at its peak. And this in itself difficult task is made more difficult by the additional demand that intra-specific aggression must not be weakened in either of the partners. We know from Chapter Three that even the slightest decrease in aggression toward the neighboring fellow member of the species must be paid for with loss of territory and, at the same time, of sources of food for the expected progeny. Under these circumstances, the species "cannot afford," for the sake of preventing mate fights, to resort to appeasement ceremonies such as submissive or infantile gestures whose prerequisite is reduction of aggression. Ritualized redirection precludes not only this undesirable effect, but moreover makes use of the key stimuli proceeding from one mate to stimulate the other against the territorial neighbor. I consider this behavior mechanism supremely ingenious, and much more chivalrous than the reverse analogous behavior of the man who, angry with his employer during the day, discharges his pent-up irritation on his unfortunate wife in the evening. . . .

In the chapter on behavior mechanisms functionally analogous to morality, I have spoken of the inhibitions controlling aggression in various social animals, preventing it from injuring or killing fellow members of the species. As I explained, these inhibitions are most important and consequently most highly differentiated in those animals which are capable of killing living creatures of about their own size. A raven can peck out the eye of another with one thrust of its beak, a wolf can rip the jugular vein of another with a single bite. There would be no more ravens and no more wolves if reliable inhibitions did not prevent such actions. Neither a dove nor a hare nor even a chimpanzee is able to kill its own kind with a single peck or bite; in addition, animals with relatively poor defense weapons have a correspondingly great ability to escape quickly, even from specially armed predators which are more efficient in chasing, catching, and killing than even the strongest of their own species. Since there rarely is, in nature, the possibility of such an animal's seriously injuring one of its own kind, there is no selection pressure at work here to breed in killing inhibitions. The absence of such inhibitions is apparent to the animal keeper, to his own and to his animals' disadvantage, if he does not take seriously the intra-specific fights of completely "harmless" animals. Under the unnatural conditions of captivity, where a defeated animal cannot escape from its victor, it may be killed slowly and cruelly. In my book *King Solomon's Ring,* I have described in the chapter "Morals and Weapons" how the symbol of peace, the dove, can torture one of its own kind to death, without the arousal of any inhibition.

Anthropologists concerned with the habits of *Australopithecus* have repeatedly stressed that these hunting progenitors of man have left humanity with the dangerous heritage of what they term "carnivorous mentality." This statement confuses the concepts of the carnivore and the cannibal, which are, to a large extent, mutually exclusive. One can only deplore the fact that man has definitely not got a carnivorous mentality! All his trouble arises from his being a basically harmless, omnivorous creature, lacking in natural weapons with which to kill big prey, and, therefore, also devoid of the built-in safety devices which prevent "professional" carnivores from abusing their killing power to destroy fellow members of their own species. A lion or a wolf may, on extremely rare occasions, kill another by one angry stroke, but, as I have already explained in the chapter on behavior mechanisms functionally analogous to morality, all heavily armed carnivores possess sufficiently reliable inhibitions which prevent the self-destruction of the species.

In human evolution, no inhibitory mechanisms preventing sudden manslaughter were necessary, because quick killing was impossible anyhow; the potential victim had plenty of opportunity to elicit the pity of the aggressor by submissive gestures and appeasing attitudes. No selection pressure arose in the prehistory of mankind to breed inhibitory mechanisms preventing the killing of conspecifics until, all of a sudden, the invention of artificial weapons upset the equilibrium of killing potential and social inhibitions. When it did, man's position was very nearly that of a dove which, by some unnatural trick of nature, has suddenly acquired the beak of a raven. One shudders at the thought of a creature as irascible as all prehuman primates are, swinging a well-sharpened hand-ax. Humanity would indeed have destroyed itself by its first inventions, were it not for the very wonderful fact that inventions and responsibility are both the achievements of the same specifically human faculty of asking questions.

Not that our prehuman ancestor, even at a stage as yet devoid of moral responsibility, was a fiend incarnate; he was by no means poorer in social instincts and inhibitions than a chimpanzee, which, after all, is—his irascibility not withstanding—a social and friendly creature. But whatever his innate norms of social behavior may have been, they were bound to be thrown out of gear by the invention of weapons. If humanity survived, as, after all, it did, it never achieved security from the danger of self-destruction. If moral responsibility and unwillingness to kill have indubitably increased, the ease and emotional impunity of killing have increased at the same rate. The distance at which all shooting weapons take effect screens the killer against the stimulus situation which would otherwise activate his killing inhibitions. The deep, emotional layers of our personality simply do not register the fact that the crooking of the forefinger to release a shot tears the entrails of another man. No sane man would even go rabbit hunting for pleasure if the necessity of killing his prey with his natural weapons brought home to him the full, emotional realization of what he is actually doing.

The same principle applies, to an even greater degree, to the use of modern remote-control weapons. The man who presses the releasing button is so completely screened against seeing, hearing, or otherwise emotionally realizing the consequences of his action, that he can commit it with impunity—even if he is burdened with the power of imagination. Only thus can it be explained that perfectly good-natured men, who would not even smack a naughty child, proved to be perfectly able to release rockets or to lay carpets of incendiary bombs on sleeping cities, thereby committing hundreds and thousands of children to a horrible death in the flames. The fact that it is good, normal men who did this, is as eerie as any fiendish atrocity of war!...

35. IS AGGRESSION AN INSTINCT ?

Anthony Storr

Before turning to the positive function of aggression in the preservation of species we ought, briefly, to direct our attention to the question which forms the title of this chapter. It is a question which we cannot yet fully answer, and which may be the wrong one to ask, yet it must not be avoided, since it is still the subject of controversy.

The concept of instinct is itself in the melting pot. As S. A. Barnett put it in a broadcast talk,

> the sharp division of behaviour into "fixed," or "innate," or "instinctive" on the one hand, and "learned" on the other has now generally been given up; and the term "learning" itself is coming to be seen as too general and too imprecise to be useful in any rigorous account of behaviour.[1]

Although we cannot give a straightforward and simple answer to the question "Is aggression an instinct?" what we can say is that, in man, as in other animals, there exists a physiological mechanism which, when stimulated, gives rise both to subjective feelings of anger and also to physical changes which prepare the body for fighting. This mechanism is easily set off, and, like other emotional responses, it is stereotyped and, in this sense, "instinctive." Just as one angry cat is very like another angry cat, so one angry man or woman closely resembles another at the level of physiological response; although, of course, the way in which human beings adapt to and control their feelings of rage differs widely according to training.

In a famous book, first published in 1915, W. B. Cannon showed that *Bodily Changes in Pain, Hunger, Fear and Rage* served the function of increasing "efficiency in physical struggle."[2] The arousal of emotion, Cannon believed, served the biological purpose of preparing an animal to take action, whether this might be flight in response to fear, or fighting in response to rage. We now know more about physiology than Cannon did; but subsequent research has done nothing to invalidate his

From HUMAN AGGRESSION *by Anthony Storr, Chapter 2. Copyright © 1968 by Anthony Storr. Reprinted by permission of Atheneum Publishers and Penguin Books, Ltd.*

original thesis, and his book is still valuable and interesting. When anger is aroused in mammals, there is an increase in pulse rate and blood pressure, together with an increase in the peripheral criculation of the blood, and a rise in the level of blood glucose. The rate of breathing is accelerated, and the muscles of the limbs and trunk become more tensely contracted and less liable to fatigue. At the same time, blood is diverted from the internal organs of the body, and digestion and the movements of the intestine cease, although the flow of acid and the digestive juice tends to be increased. In animals, and possibly also in man, the hair stands on end; and the picture of rage is completed by baring the teeth and the emission of involuntary noises. During anger, there is also a diminution of sensory perception—so that men who are fighting can sustain quite severe injuries without being aware of them.

The mechanism by which these changes in bodily function come about is still incompletely understood. From experiments in animals, it appears that there is a small area at the base of the brain in which the feeling of anger originates, and from which are sent forth the nervous impulses which cause the rise in blood-pressure and other changes which have been outlined above. This small area is called the hypothalamus. The function of the hypothalamus is to coordinate emotional responses, including anger; and, when it is stimulated artificially by electricity, in a cat, for instance, the animal will show all the signs of rage, although there is no barking dog or anything else in the immediate environment which might ordinarily be expected to provoke such a reaction. In the ordinary course of events, the hypothalamus is under the inhibitory control of the cerebral cortex; that is, of that part of the brain which, in terms of evolution, is the most recently developed, and which is particularly extensive and particularly important in human beings. If, however, the cerebral cortex receives the impulse of an external threat such as a fist being shaken in the face, or an insult, it will send down messages to the hypothalamus, releasing it from inhibitory control and stimulating it into action. The physiological consequences are those which have been outlined above; and, once these changes have been initiated, they tend to persist for some time, even though the immediate threat in the environment has been removed. Everyone knows that anger, once thoroughly aroused, takes time to subside; especially if the angry individual is unable to take the strenuous physical action for which his body is now prepared. The way in which the hypothalamus and the cerebral cortex continue to interact so that the immediate response to threat is prolonged is not fully understood. It seems probable that the release of adrenalin, noradrenalin, cortisone and other hormones from the adrenal glands play an important part. There is evidence that active aggressive emotion is accompanied by an increase in noradrenalin excretion, whereas passive anxiety is associated with an increase in adrenalin output. This was discovered by comparing the physico-chemical state of active ice-hockey players with that of the goal-keeper.[3] These chemical substances are secreted into the blood stream when the hypothalamic mechanism is fired; for the hypothalamus is linked with the adrenal glands by way of the autonomic nervous system. It is partly by means of these hormones that the blood pressure is raised, the heart beat accelerated, and so on; but it is probable that they also reciprocally affect the brain itself. In other words, a circular reaction is set up in such a way that the brain which initiates the emotional response is itself stimulated by the reaction. For our purpose, however, it does not matter that some physiological detail remains obscure. The important point is that the body contains a coordinated physico-chemical system which subserves the emotions and actions which we call aggressive, and that this system is easily brought into action both by the stimulus of threat, and also by frustration. Moreover, because of the way in which the body works, the aggressive response tends to have an all-or-none quality. There are, of course, degrees of anger; but it is important to realize that the aggressive response is not a reflex action which dies down immediately the precipitating threat disappears, as, for example, when a finger touching a hot stove is immediately withdrawn, but a complicated series of physiological changes which, once begun, are prolonged enough to sustain the body in fight or other strenuous action. Under conditions of civilization, it is perhaps easier to arouse aggression than to dispel it; and the man who works out his aggression in violent digging in the garden may seem psychologically naïve, but is displaying physiological wisdom, for he is both giving his rage time to subside and also making some of the physical effort for which his body is now keenly alerted.

The existence of the physiological mechanism is not in doubt. Self-preservation demands that an animal should carry within it the potential for aggressive action, since the natural world is a place in which hostile threats must be overcome or evaded if life is to continue.

Our physiological discussion has shown that the physical mechanism of aggression, aggressive emotions and behaviour is indeed "instinctive" in that it is an inborn, automatic possibility which is easily triggered. But need the trigger be pulled? What has not been decided is whether there is any pressing internal need for the mechanism to be brought into use; or whether, if the organism were never threatened, aggressive behaviour would ever be manifested. This question may sound academic; since it is obvious that every animal, including the human, must experience threat during the course of its existence, and must, therefore, respond aggressively from time to time. Nevertheless, if we are to control aggression, it is important to determine whether there is, in animals or humans, an internal accumulation of aggressive tension which needs periodic discharge, or whether the aggressive response is simply a potential which need never be brought into use. If the first supposition is true, what is needed to control aggression is the provision of suitable outlets for aggression. If the latter is true, what is required is the avoidance of all stimuli which might arouse the aggressive response.

Some authors are convinced that there is no essential need for aggressive behaviour ever to be manifested. J. P. Scott, in his book *Aggression*, for example, says:

> The important fact is that the chain of causation in every case eventually traces back to the outside. There is no physiological evidence of any spontaneous stimulation for fighting arising within the body. This means that there is no need for fighting, either aggressive or defensive, apart from what happens in the external environment. We may conclude that a person who is fortunate enough to exist in an environment which is without stimulation to fight will not suffer physiological or nervous damage because he never fights. This is a quite different situation from the physiology of eating, where

the internal processes of metabolism lead to definite physiological changes which eventually produce hunger and stimulation to eat, without any change in external environment.

We can also conclude that there is no such thing as a simple "instinct for fighting," in the sense of an internal driving force which has to be satisfied. There is, however, an internal physiological mechanism which has only to be stimulated to produce fighting. This distinction may not be important in many practical situations, but it leads to a hopeful conclusion regarding the control of aggression. The internal physiological mechanism is dangerous, but it can be kept under control by external means[4]*

Those who are prejudiced in favour of this point of view often quote the experiments of Zing Yang Kuo who discovered that if a kitten was reared in the same cage with a rat it would accept the rat as a companion and could never afterwards be induced to pursue or kill rats. Kuo concluded that "The behaviour of an organism is a *passive* affair. How an animal or man will behave in a given moment depends on how it has been brought up and how it is stimulated."[5] But, as Eibl-Eibesfeldt has remarked, these experiments "certainly prove that aggressive behaviour can be enhanced or inhibited by experience, but that it has to be learned in order to occur was not shown."[6] Eibl raised rats in isolation, but discovered that, when another rat of the same species was introduced into the cage, the isolated would attack it "with the same patterns of threat and fighting used by experienced animals."[6]

Moreover, electrical stimulation of one area of the brain in cocks can cause a restless searching for an object on which to discharge its aggression; whereas stimulation of another area will make the animal seek objects which release patterns of courtship.[7] In other words, it looks as though aggression is as much an innate drive as sexuality. In both instances, the behaviour which is released by electrical stimulation is appetitive behaviour—that is, the searching for an object which will fulfil the animal's need for expressing its sexuality on the one hand, or its aggression on the other. The conclusions of Scott and Kuo that aggression is learned, rather than an expression

---

* Reprinted here by permission of the author and the University of Chicago Press. Copyright 1958 by the University of Chicago Press.

of an innate drive are not supported by these experiments. The fact that the aggressive response requires an outside stimulus to elicit it does not imply that the organism may not need to behave aggressively or obtain satisfaction from so doing.

It is true that aggressive tension cannot yet be portrayed in physiological terms as we might describe hunger; that is, as a state of deprivation which drives the animal to take action to relieve it. But the same is actually true of the sexual instinct; and most people, rightly or wrongly, accept the idea that sex is "an internal driving force which has to be satisfied." The full release of sexual tension is generally thought to require a partner, although a modicum of satisfaction can be obtained by masturbation. In other words, just as with aggression, there is an internal physiological mechanism which needs an outside stimulus to fire it off. Although we generally think of sex as driving an animal to seek the stimulus which will bring internal satisfaction, we do not generally think of aggression in the same terms. Yet we cannot define the sense of tension or deprivation which leads to sexual behaviour any more than we can define the possible physiological state which might lead to an animal "spoiling for a fight" or, at least, needing to make the violent physical efforts for which the body is prepared when the aggressive mechanism is fired.

One interesting fact is that the state of the body in sexual arousal and in aggressive arousal is extremely similar. Kinsey lists fourteen physiological changes which are common to both sexual arousal and anger, and in fact can only discover four physiological changes which are different in the two states of emotion.[8] Moreover, it is not uncommon for one response suddenly to change into the other; which is why quarrelling marital partners often end up in bed together and why some fights end in orgasm. On the basis of their research, Kinsey and his co-workers concluded that

> For those who like the term, it is clear that there is a sexual drive which cannot be satisfied for any large proportion of the population by any sort of social convention. For those who prefer to think in simpler terms of action and reaction, it is a picture of an animal who, however civilized and cultured, continues to respond to the constantly present sexual stimuli, albeit with some physical and social restraints.[9]

We cannot at present rule out the possibility that the same may be true of aggression. Indeed, there is considerable evidence to be found from the study of animal behaviour which suggests that, if an animal is prevented from engaging in the aggressive activity which is normal to it, it will seek out substitute stimuli to release its aggression, just as a man who is deprived of women will turn to other men or to phantasy to release his sexuality.

Lorenz, in his book *On Aggression*[10] gives as an example the behaviour of cichlid fish. These highly aggressive creatures require hostile territorial neighbours on whom they can vent their aggression. If a pair of cichlids is isolated by removing them from a tank containing other fish, the male will turn his aggression against his own spouse and progeny and will actually destroy them.

There is a great deal of evidence that aggressive tension can be dammed up in exactly the same way as we habitually suppose that sexual tension can be. Heiligenberg, in careful statistical studies, has shown that

> When a sufficiently aggressive fish has no opportunity to attack another fish, the percentage of digging in its total of mouth activities is much higher than when it lives among some young fish that it can bite at any time.[11]

It has been proved that the activity called "digging" which consists in biting into the substrata of the tank, is directly related to the readiness to attack of the individual fish concerned. In other words, digging is a displacement activity which increases in amount when there is no outlet for the fish's normal activity, in exactly the same way as the energetic violence of a man's digging in his garden may increase in intensity when he is angry with his wife but is restraining his desire to attack her.

At the time of writing, it is fashionable for academic psychologists to deride the possibility that man's aggression is an endogenous, instinctive impulse which seeks discharge. Although such writers of course admit that man is an aggressive being, they try to explain all human aggression in terms either of a response to frustration, or else as a learned activity, which, because it is rewarded in terms of possessions, praise or status, is constantly reinforced in human societies as they are at present constituted. Thus Berkowitz, for example, summarizing "Instinct Conceptions of Aggression" writes as follows:

> Since "spontaneous" animal aggression is a relatively rare occurrence in nature (and there is the possibility that even these infrequent cases may be accounted for by frustrations or prior learning of the utility of hostile behaviour), many ethologists and experimental biologists rule out the possibility of a self-stimulating aggressive system in animals. One important lesson to be derived from these studies is that there is no instinctive drive toward war within man. Theoretically, at least, it is possible to lessen the likelihood of interpersonal conflict by decreasing the occurrence of frustrations and minimizing the gains to be won through aggression.[12]

Such a point of view can only be sustained if a vast amount of evidence from ethological and anthropological studies is neglected; and must surely rest upon the belief or hope that, if only society were better organized or children reared in ways which did not encourage them to be aggressive, men would live in peace with one another, and the millennium would at last be realized. Such beliefs are as old as history, and will be discussed in a later chapter. It is, however, particularly characteristic of modern Americans to hold these opinions, since perennial optimism makes it hard for them to believe that there is anything unpleasant either in the physical world or in human nature which cannot be "fixed."

Authors such as Berkowitz and Scott never suggest that the sexual impulse could be abolished or seriously modified by learning or by decreasing the rewards of sexual satisfaction, for, in their minds, sex carries a positive sign, whereas aggression is negatively labelled. Yet, it is probable that when no outside stimulus for aggression exists, men actually seek such stimuli out in much the same way as they do when sexually deprived. At the introspective level, it may be true to say that one deplores getting angry; but the physiological changes which accompany anger give rise to a subjective sense of well-being and of invigorating purpose which in itself is rewarding. Appalling barbarities have been justified in the name of "righteous wrath";

but there can be no doubt that men enjoy the enlivening effect of being angry when they can justify it, and that they seek out opponents whom they can attack in much the same way that cichlid fish do.

What we still need to know, and what we may hope that physiologists may soon tell us, is the biochemical state underlying tension, whether this be aggressive or sexual. There must be physiological differences between the animal who is in a state of sexual deprivation and the animal who is spoiling for a fight. But there is so far no convincing evidence that the aggressive response is, at a physiological level, any less instinctive than the sexual response; and, provided that the term aggression is not restricted to actual fighting, aggressive expression may be as necessary a part of being a human being as sexual expression.

In the introduction, it was suggested that our use of language revealed the aggressive substructure of even intellectual activity. Once we can bring ourselves to abandon the pleasure principle, it is easy to accept the idea that the achievement of dominance, the overcoming of obstacles, and the mastery of the external world, for all of which aggression is necessary, are as much innate human needs as sexuality or hunger. Scott hoped that, if children could be reared in an environment where there was no stimulation to fight they would remain peaceful. But as one critic remarked, "whether such passivity would be at the cost of initiative is an unanswered question."[13]

REFERENCES

1. Barnett, S. A., "Instinct" from *A Few Ideas* (London: B.B.C. Publications, 1964), p. 35.
2. Cannon, W. B., *Bodily Changes in Pain, Hunger, Fear and Rage* (New York: Appleton, 1929).
3. Elmadijan, F., *Symposium on Catecholamines* (Baltimore: Williams and Wilkins, 1959), p. 409.
4. Scott, J. P., *Aggression* (Chicago: University of Chicago Press, 1958), pp. 62 and 64.
5. Kuo, Zing Yang, "Genesis of the Cat's Response to the Rat" from *Instinct* (Princeton: Van Nostrand, 1961), p. 24.
6. Eibl-Eibesfeldt, Irenaeus, "Aggressive Be-

haviour and Ritualized Fighting in Animals" from Massermann, J. H. (ed.) *Science and Psychoanalysis* (New York: Grune and Stratton, 1963).

7. Von Holst, Erich and Von Saint Paul, Ursula, "Electrically Controlled Behaviour," *Scientific American*, 1962.

8. Kinsey, Alfred C. *et al., Sexual Behaviour in the Human Female* (Philadelphia: Saunders, 1953), p. 704.

9. Kinsey, Alfred C. *et al., Sexual Behaviour in the Human Male* (Philadelphia: Saunders, 1948), p. 269.

10. Lorenz, Konrad, *On Aggression* (London: Methuen, 1966).

11. Heiligenberg, Walter, "A Quantitative Analysis of Digging Movements and their Relationship to Aggressive Behaviour in Cichlids," *Animal Behaviour*, 13, 1, 1965.

12. Berkowitz, Leonard, *Aggression: A Social-Psychological Analysis* (New York: McGraw-Hill, 1962), pp. 24–25.

13. McNeil, E. B., "Psychology and Aggression," *Journal of Conflict Resolution*, 3, 1959, 195–239.

36. WAR IS NOT IN OUR GENES

Sally Carrighar

There are still men and women living who can remember the horror which greeted Darwin's theory that we are "descended from apes." That phrase probably accounted in part for the revulsion because "descended from" was generally used in a more personal way—"I am descended from Scottish ancestors," that is, I am one of them, I am like them. Darwin meant, of course, "We have evolved from apes," with apes standing in for the whole range of evolved animals, but the unfortunate phrase had caught on.

That we have *evolved* from apes—and are, therefore, obviously different from them—is an unemotional, scientific assertion, harmless enough, it would seem, except that it does leave Adam and Eve stranded without progeny and raises an unresolved question about men's souls. If each human being has been created with his own unique soul, then so have

all animals—wolves, rabbits, mice, water bugs. To many people that thought was, and still is, intolerable, although the concept does not seem very difficult if one thinks of soul as *life,* the bit of animation temporarily lent from the great source of all life.

The first, grudging acceptance of evolution was in connection with physical structures: it was hard for anyone to deny such evidence as the development of a thinking cortex on top of a simpler brain. The idea of the evolution of *behavior,* however, has been slower to win support, for there is no "fossil behavior." From fossil bones, guesses can be made as to the ways that the bones were used, but how can anyone ever reliably know the origins of the habits of today's animals—or of our own?

Nevertheless, the evolution of behavior is now inspiring one of biology's hottest debates. Darwin himself laid the groundwork for it when he wrote "The Expression of the Emotions in Man and Animals," and showed how closely alike the signs of emotion are. This book was largely ignored, at least in its implications, for the mechanical age had arrived and there was more interest in putting captive animals into pieces of apparatus, in testing their reflexes, their ability to find their way out of mazes, to count. and to discriminate between colors and forms—problems like these.

About 1950, however, a group calling themselves ethologists broke out of the laboratories, declaring that the most reliable facts about animal behavior are secured by watching animals in their natural habitats. From the discoveries made by these thoughtful observers, it soon became clear that we really don't know very much about how most animals lead their lives, about what animals do. Dr. William H. Thorpe of Cambridge University was one of the first to stride boldly onto the battlefield with the statement: "There is hardly any aspect of the behavior of animals which may not have some reference to problems in human behavior."

Some ethologists fell on that battlefield and went back to the laboratories. The ones who stayed in the field had to endure some ridicule; they were called Boy Scouts and taunted with the criticism that their work could not be a science since most of it was done without experimentation. Some of this obviously stung, for few ethologists are now simply trying to fill in the great gaps in our knowledge about the daily lives of wild animals. Work in the field must now include experimentation, and some ethologists are even confining the animals that they study in artificial environments which they call "semi-wild."

Meanwhile, the behavior of animals has fascinated the non-scientific public. Readers devour Joy Adamson's Elsa books, George Schaller's reports of his gorilla companions and those of Jane Goodall about the chimpanzees with whom she and her husband live. An increasing number of popular films and television programs about animals whet this interest. And if orthodox biologists hold out against assuming any lines of descent in human behavior, from all sides laymen are asking what we can learn from living animals.

What about the relationship between the sexes? What about care of the young and their training, about the health of animals and how they maintain it, their feeding habits, how they relax and the ways in which they play? Above all, with war so great a threat in our lives, what about animal aggression?

This last has been the subject of two recent and readable books: *On Aggression,* by Konrad Lorenz, and *The Territorial Imperative,* by Robert Ardrey. Both authors declare that fighting is an instinct which demands expression in virtually all higher animals—and also in ourselves because, they claim, we have inherited this compulsion. Before examining their arguments, however, it is first necessary to define exactly what is meant by aggression.

Most laymen would think at once of predatory attacks on prey for food: the pursuit, the pounce, the kill. The biological definition, however, excludes this kind of slaughter because it involves no malice. A wolf bringing down an ill or aged caribou (a strong caribou can outrun a wolf) is no more angry than we are when we buy meat at the butcher's shop. He is merely hungry, as are other predators when prey is there and vulnerable.

Nor is there any true aggression, and malice, between members of different species going about their separate ways in the wilderness they share. They seem to recognize that each has different needs and perhaps, in their inarticulate way, they even recognize that other species have rights. On a path used by many or at a water hole or salt lick, the weaker and smaller animals await their turn, letting the stronger go first without argument.

Aggressiveness in its strict biological sense, and in the sense that Lorenz and Ardrey use the word, is expressed between two members *of the same species* when both want the same thing. With the great majority of animals, this same thing will be living space in which to raise the young of the year—an animal's homesite, also known as his territory.

Sometimes aggressiveness is aroused over possession of a desired female or over rank in a hierarchy. Biologists often call the space around a disputed female a territory. It moves when she moves and the male, going along, will not allow another male to approach within a certain well-understood distance.

Lorenz and Ardrey both tie their definition of aggressiveness in mankind to home territory. They call attention to properties marked with "No Trespassing" signs and—this is their ominous and essential theme—they extend the concept of farms or suburban lots to the nation, claiming that men fight to preserve or expand their national boundaries almost as involuntarily as they would their homes. They fight the soldiers of other nations because their remote animal ancestors once instinctively fought for nesting site, burrow, hunting range or the space which encircles a female.

Thus both Lorenz and Ardrey are convinced that war is an instinctive compulsion. Lorenz says that the most important function of animal aggression "is the spacing out of individuals of one species over the available habitat, in other words, the distribution of 'territories.' " He concludes: "There cannot be any doubt, in the opinion of any biologically minded scientist, that intra-specific aggression is, in man, just as much of a spontaneous instinctive drive as in most other higher vertebrates."

Ardrey, for his part, says: "If we defend the title to our land or the sovereignty of our country, we do it for reasons no different, no less innate, no less *ineradicable* than do the lower animals" (italics added). He also says: "All of us will give everything we are for a place of our own." And: "I believe man's innumerable territorial expressions are human responses to an imperative lying with equal force on mockingbirds and men."

Now, a widespread belief that human wars are instinctive, by which biologists mean inevitable, would of course tend to make them inevitable. Therefore it seems worthwhile to inquire whether aggression is universal in animals and just how insistent an urge it is. If aggression, as these authors insist, is a doom carried in human genes, we are predestined to wage wars and hopes for peace would seem to be slim. Lorenz does plead with some eloquence for an effort to replace competition for living space with competition in sports and other sublimations—but he already has made the urge to fight for territory seem so over-powering that the final impression left by "On Aggression" leans toward the depressing view that fighting for territory is, in Ardrey's word, "ineradicable." That this is the lasting message gained from both books is shown by the comments of many reviewers and readers. The publicity for both, including pictures of viciously snarling animals, helps to promote this conviction.

It must be agreed that during mating seasons, at least, disputes over territorial boundary lines are prevalent. Spring, when most animal young are born and many conceived, is a time of much sparring for areas on which to raise them and find their food. But for some species, late summer and fall are the rutting season, and that is the time when the "territories" surrounding females are fought for.

In most cases, such aggressive behavior is related to reproductive needs. A territory, as space, can be as small as the single nesting tree defended by a woodpecker, or the range, nine miles or more in diameter, believed necessary to feed an average family of wolves.

To the creatures themselves, territory probably means home in the same way that home, for us, means more than house. To them the need may be temporary but it is not surprising that they instinctively fight for it.

But how universally and how desperately? The doom of eternal war would not seem so inescapable for us if some animals—indeed, if *any* of them—can escape the compulsion.

Caribou have no territories; neither do elephants. Sea otters don't. They copulate in the water and raise their young in fronds of seaweed. Whales are not likely to have individual homesites, although no one knows definitely. Lemmings live in villages, shallow excavations in the Arctic frost mounds, with several lemmings sleeping together in each nest until a gravid* female is about to give birth, when she makes a nest of her own.

These could be called colonies. There are numerous animals in the temperate zone who have communal dwellings: gophers, prairie dogs, marmots. What goes on in their hidden worlds, at each stage of the annual cycle, is imperfectly known for most species. Some colonies defend the territory shared by all; it appears that others do not. Within the burrow it is customary for an individual family to defend its own unit.

What of cowbirds, which lay their eggs in other birds' nests and then are off to live on the backs of cattle (formerly bison), feeding on the parasites in their hosts' fur? It is amusing to speculate on whether individual cowbirds claim certain cows as their territory. It seems unlikely.

Among primates, most monkeys live in groups. In some there is a hierarchical social organization. Usually the dominant male has first choice when a female is in oestrus and discord often prevails. Other groups are sexually promiscuous and among them fighting often seems abhorrent. If youngsters are too aggressive, the adult males will separate them.

Howling monkeys claim possession of their communal areas but defend them generally with only vocal protests—as do gibbon fami-

* Pregnant. (Eds.)

lies. When their screams fail to drive away intruders, gibbons may bite, but such occasions are rare.

The English ethologist J. H. Crook discussed the question of territory in *The Listener,* April 6. 1967. He explained the very flexible attitude of some birds and animals usually thought to defend territories. A territory "allows an individual to develop a close familiarity with a locality. This increases its food-finding efficiency and the speed of finding refuge from enemies." But some ducks that mate on their wintering grounds, or on migration, will accompany a new spouse to its homesite instead of returning to their own.

Species may change territories in response to local conditions. In drier years, certain marsh-dwelling weaver birds will disperse their nests over a large ground area; in wetter years, they may congregate in a large tree islanded in a flood pool. Harem groups of the gelada baboon wander independently in poor feeding years but "congregate in large herds of variable size under conditions of plenty. They have no territories, their disposition directly reflecting the local food availability."

Chimpanzees, says Dr. Crook, vary the size of their parties. As a rule individual and small groups wander over large home ranges and "territorial behavior appears to be absent." The facts are complex he says. "The dispersion pattern itself must depend largely on learning and tradition, and this is particularly so when we are talking about advanced mammals such as the monkeys. The sort of territory-holding present is more likely to be determined by the commodities for which the higher mammals compete than by any species characteristic directly determined by the genes. Thus in different ecologies, territorial systems will vary or even be absent altogether." These conclusions regarding the animals closest to us in the evolutionary scale seem very significant.

How unreliable are rigid definitions of territory was emphasized on Britain's BBC Third Program in August 1967 by Dr. Paul Layhausen, director of the Max Planck Institut at Wuppertal and described as "one of the world's foremost experts" on the subject of animal behavior. Territoriality is not just the static demarcation of an area, he said; it is part of a much more complex working out of a system of relationships in time as well

as space—the very subtle and fluid pattern of "density tolerance." He continued: "There's much more to it still, of course: the difference between the ways in which mammals and birds 'survey' their territory...; the interlacing of the routes by which animals go about their affairs, and the interrelation of the times at which they do things...Density tolerance is a matter of time as well as space."

One thinks of the fact that many bird parents will tolerate the trespassing of neighbors after their young are out of the nest: the time factor here seems more important than that of space.

Since most birds and animals which defend territories do limit this strongly emotional response to the reproductive season, a point to be considered is whether human beings, too, only feel animosity toward aliens while they are of the child-bearing age. Much depends on the individual, but that is the time, granted, when many homes are first established. If the most intense "territorial" feelings are typical of the young adults, how does it happen that most countries have to resort to conscription in order to raise their predominantly youthful military units? As is well known, those who enter the services voluntarily often do so to escape from conditions which seem stifling at the parental home. Others marry at about the same age and set up their own households. Some biologists, as an argument for territoriality, make much of the fact that animal young may be "driven out" in their second year. Observations in the wild suggest that few have to be driven. When they are ready to mate, they wish to form their own families and in order to do so, they leave.

Ardrey is not a biologist, as he himself explicitly and creditably states in his book. In reporting the work of professionals, he seems simply to have misjudged the emphasis that they put on territories and territorial aggression.

Lorenz, of course, is an ethologist of world repute, but his experience with animals is limited in a different way. He has done most of his research with tamed animals, such as geese induced by guard fences and food to live in a human environment, and with captive cichlid fishes in tanks. All creatures so confined have their aggressiveness heightened enormously.

As Lorenz himself explains, these two types of animals, fish and birds, are among those which demand "individual distance," meaning that they do not welcome, at any time, anywhere, the close approach of their conspecifics (the biological terms for others of one's own species). Lorenz's fish and geese, disturbed by the enforced intimate association with their mates, have worked out rather elaborate rituals for "redirecting" their aggression—from mates to neighboring males. Since these are only symbolic attacks, the adjacent male seldom is injured, and the spouse, with his aggression now neutralized, returns to his mate triumphant.

Rituals *of the same sort* are not employed by our own class of animals, mammals, for mammals are "contact" species—that is, they seek and enjoy the touch of their own kind. This distinction between animals who want and those who do not want to be near their con-specifics is only mentioned briefly by Lorenz, but it is actually of the most basic importance.

Lorenz sets out in detail the observation that among all strongly aggressive animals there is a very powerful inhibition against killing con-specifics. Since they do, unavoidably, often annoy one another, however, various behavior patterns have become established to prevent fights with lethal consequences. The redirected aggression of fish and geese is one example; among mammals, a common mechanism is simply the flight of the weaker combatant. The victor does not pursue him; the fact that he gives in is satisfaction enough.

Serving the same purpose are many close-range gestures of submission or appeasement. Lorenz describes the well-known reaction of a defeated wolf. As soon as he recognizes that he will lose a fight, the wolf turns his head away, a movement that the victor immediately understands and accepts. When Lorenz described this wolf behavior in 1952 in "King Solomon's Ring," he spoke of it as the loser "offering his neck" to his opponent —moving evidence of good faith between wolves, inasmuch as the victor always withholds the final bite.

Since that time, Lorenz has more firmly become a "mechanist." In "On Aggression," he describes the loser's behavior as one of the "submissive or appeasing movements [which] have evolved from juvenile expression movements persisting into adulthood. This is not surprising to anyone who knows how strong the inhibition against attacking pups is in any normal dog." But however defined, the wolf ritual works; it prevents the killing of a con-specific.

Another form of ritualized, harmless fighting is the "tournament," such as the pushing contest between two ungulates (deer or other hoofed quadrupeds) during the rut. If they really wanted to kill each other, they would attack with their hoofs (as they do a predator). Instead they literally lock horns, each trying to make the other give way. As soon as one knows himself to be losing ground, he disengages his antlers, turns and runs, and the winner goes back to his females. It is a contest to see which is the stronger male— and the one, therefore, more likely to father superior fawns and, in those ungulate species in which the bulls defend the herd, more likely to prove a superior warden against predators.

Perhaps from their concentration on the subject, both Ardrey and Lorenz seem to have exaggerated impressions of the amount of conspecific aggression. At the start of Chapter II of *On Aggression,* Lorenz writes: "What is the significance of all this fighting? In nature, fighting is such an ever-present process, its behavior mechanisms and weapons are so highly developed and have so obviously arisen under the selection pressure of a species-preserving function that it is our duty to ask this Darwinian question...Darwin's expression, 'the struggle for existence,' is sometimes erroneously interpreted as the struggle between different species. In reality, the struggle Darwin was thinking of...is the competition between near relatives."

When Lorenz writes of "all this fighting," and fighting as being "such an ever-present process" in nature, he is describing a wilderness that would not be recognized by those who, like myself, have lived there for years at a stretch.

On some mornings one finds blood on the snow where tracks of fox and hare collide, but that is evidence of predation, not the encounter of an animal with another of its own kind. Real aggression, usually reproductive in its origin and purpose, concerns the animals so briefly that most of the several dozen species I am familiar with spend far more than half their time—some of them as much as 11 months in the year—in casual or amiable association with their fellows.

Typical are black bears. After a rather perfunctory but successful courtship, a male returns to a drowsy life, the daytime often spent in a copse with four or five other males. They do, however, show animosity toward one of the off-shade bears that are a color phase of their own species. The forest rangers say that these rejected bears become neurotic. One charged me once, with small provocation. I escaped into my cabin but he stalked me for the next three weeks until, my exasperation boiling over, I attacked him, hurling rocks and language I hardly realized I knew. He left for good—I hope with no new psychological trauma.

Both Lorenz and Ardrey distinguish too briefly between offensive and defensive fighting. Is one who defends his territory "aggressive?" If not, if only an invader is properly so described, how many do thus intrude? Extremely few, except in captivity. Among wolves, one who comes into the territory of another's family may be seeking companionship (a "lone wolf" is usually an orphan). According to most observers, he is not attacked; he is simply threatened and he leaves —and is not pursued to the border. Even the young ungulate bull or buck does not often boldly challenge an older, stronger male. He tries to steal a female, and when he encounters the leader's anger, at once retires to a safer distance.

Those who describe the wilderness from a domestic garden like Darwin's or Lorenz's fenced enclosure and laboratory or Ardrey's library, tend to put the emphasis on a few, dramatic animals like rats, wolves and lions.

Rats are contact species, and to explain some fights he saw among rats, Lorenz suggests that they were not personal confrontations, that rat clans tend to kill all outsiders. Such group aggressiveness would seem especially ominous because of the possible analogy with mankind's national wars. But here, as with geese and fish, Lorenz is presenting evidence provided by captives, and captives held in conditions so unsatisfactory as to stimulate fighting.

As Lorenz describes them: "Steiniger put brown rats from different localities into a large enclosure which provided them with completely natural living conditions. At first the individual animals seemed afraid of each other; they were not in an aggressive mood, but they bit each other if they met by chance, particularly if two were driven towards each other along one side of the enclosure, so that they collided at speed." (Most biologists, incidentally, would not call the conditions provided by any enclosure as "completely natural"—especially not if it were so small that individuals collided when racing along the fence.)

Steiniger's rats soon began to attack one another and fought until all but one pair were killed. The descendants of that pair formed a clan, which subsequently slaughtered every strange rat introduced into the habitat.

During the same years that this study was being conducted, John B. Calhoun in Baltimore was also investigating the behavior of rats. There were 15 rats in F. Steiniger's original population; 14 in Calhoun's—also strangers to one another. But Calhoun's enclosure was *16 times* larger than Steiniger's and more favorable in other ways: "harborages" were provided for rats pursued by hostile associates (such refuges would probably exist in the wild), and all Calhoun's rats were identified by markings.

For 27 months, from a tower in the center of the large area, the movements of all the individual rats were recorded. After a few fights while getting acquainted, they separated into two clans, neither of which tried to eliminate the other. There was a good deal of crossing back and forth unchallenged—so often by some individuals that they were dubbed messengers.

Steiniger has also observed rat clans on a small island in the North Sea. They were rather belligerent in a neutral no-man's-land. But isn't it possible that these rat populations were outgrowing the available living area? The crowdedness of many communities is surely one cause for the dangerous degree of aggressiveness now existing throughout the world. War and the population explosion: these influences must be related—to what extent would seem to be a most promising study of man's belligerent motives. But as for clan-aggressiveness, *per se*, many of us believe that this cannot be identified with any certainty as an evolutionary source of human wars.

Other than rats, wolves, and lions, there is a vast kingdom of little lives absorbed in the business of living. When Lorenz says that "fighting is an ever-present process" in nature, he must be forgetting all the moles, hedgehogs, raccoons, opossums, woodchucks, otters, chipmunks, squirrels of several kinds, rabbits, lemmings, moles, muskrats and beavers—not "eager," as a leisure generation of human beings has facetiously called them, but terribly earnest about creating one of the most complex (and needed) animal "estates" on earth. It is usual for them to respect one another's ownership of these properties.

Lorenz says that only the most aggressive creatures ever form permanent pairs, but beavers mate for life. And although their gnawing teeth would serve as very effective weapons, I have never known any occasion when they were so used against con-specifics. In their cleverly built houses, behind the dams and network of canals they have constructed, they live in notable harmony with one another and with the muskrats, for whom they provide ponds and who may be welcomed into beaver houses—as badgers will receive, and make friends with, coyotes and foxes.

How would such animals have *time* for continual fighting? What the absent biologists do not seem to realize is that a wilderness is a community of workers. Simply finding enough to eat every day is a chancy and tiring task. Think of the vast bulk of a whale to be nourished and the problems of providing for a family of wolves (averaging 12).

One has a mental picture of field mice running around everywhere in sufficient numbers to sustain the predators, but examination of some coyotes' stomach contents showed that, for days, they had eaten nothing but small amounts of berries, carrion, garbage, and old scraps of leather.

It may be a surprise to know that many animals also spend a great deal of time keeping themselves clean and, if possible, free of parasites. Primates groom one another for hours every day. One year, one of the small pretty deer-mice came in to share my cabin, and sometimes I wished she would stop washing her fur; she did it so incessantly it was tiring to watch. (When I bathed, sponging water over myself from the basin in which I stood, she always took up a position in front of me and went through her own bathing routine. I used to wonder whether she sensed the analogy. I don't think she did but I enjoyed asking the question.)

Such mammals as these, in rising strata of complexity—these are our ancestors, more recent than the primitive, sexually antagonistic fish and geese. Many mammals have never even developed rituals to prevent the death of con-specifics, because they don't need them. Except when attacked by a predator, they quite simply do not fight.

Our immediate forebears, the apes, seem to have reached something like a summit in nonaggressiveness, since they do not fight either—not as individuals or as clans. Lorenz suggests that they do not attack their associates because they do not have such effective weapons as the teeth of wolves or the paws of lions, but would not the arm of a full-grown male gorilla be as strong as a lion's paw?

We do not know which mammals were the nearest ancestors of primates, but there are sufficient numbers of nonaggressive creatures living today to suggest that co-operation was becoming the habit of evolving mammals even before the primates developed. What, therefore, has happened? Man obviously is an aggressive animal. We have lost both the peacefulness and the inhibition against killing others of our own kind. Is there an explanation?

As Lorenz points out, aggressiveness can be taught. It is also intensified when it is exercised (and atrophies when it is not). When men began to settle in communities, they learned the irritations of being crowded. By then they had probably learned the use of weapons, originally for the purpose of killing game. And since they had already acquired at least a rudimentary speech, they could absorb from one another, and preach, animosity. With words, they could incite hatred against neighboring tribes. A leader, coveting power or property, could, with propaganda, instill in his subjects admiration for warlike attitudes.

Perhaps that is the way—culturally rather than genetically—that human aggressiveness arose. As for sadism, something no animal displays, it is my belief that the trait is psychotic. (In the case of cats' treatment of mice, research indicates that it is pure play —though useful as practice of hunting skills. The cat probably does not realize that it is torturing the mice.)

Nothing could more effectively prolong man's fighting behavior than a belief that aggression is in our genes. An unwelcome cultural inheritance can be eradicated fairly quickly and easily, but the incentive to do it is lacking while people believe that aggression is innate and instinctive with us, as both Ardrey and Lorenz declare.

More than 100 years ago, the philosopher William Whewell wrote: "There is a mask of theory over the whole face of nature." Anyone writing about the wilderness has a great responsibility not to accept too readily a belief that the mask is nature's true face. In a chaotic and perfidious world, nature is all we have that is infallibly real.

If writers assert their own, unproven hypotheses as the truth, civilized people, so isolated from the wilderness that they cannot recognize a fallacy when they hear one, will be deprived in their one lifetime of what may be felt intuitively as sane and good. Then, even the intuition will be lost—what is there left for anybody but madness?

37. BIOLOGY AND HUMAN AGGRESSION

J. P. Scott

Serious scientific research on the causes and control of fighting in animal societies has been going on for over forty years, beginning with the researches of Schjelderup-Ebbe (1922) on social dominance in flocks of hens and Elliot Howard's (1920) study of song and territory in bird life. Extensive work in mammals did not begin until considerably later, with the studies of Allee (1942) and his students and my own work with fighting in mice, and later work with sheep, goats, and dogs. Parallel to this, there was extensive physiological research with fighting behavior in cats. In the intervening years work has broadened out to include a much wider group of phenomena as well as including many more different species.

Most of the work on the physiology of fighting behavior has been done with cats, although some notable work with brain stimulation has been done on primates by Delgado and others. Much more work has been done

From the AMERICAN JOURNAL OF ORTHOPSY-CHIATRY, 40, *1970, 569–577. References omitted. Copyright © 1970 by the American Orthopsychiatric Association. Reprinted by permission of the* American Journal of Orthopsychiatry *and the author. A portion of this paper was presented at the 1969 International Congress of Psychology in London.*

with fighting in mice, with particular attention to accompanying changes in brain biochemistry. Among the most notable accomplishments of the past few years are the establishment of the generality of the phenomenon of defensive fighting in reaction to pain by Ulrich and his colleagues, although this should be experimentally demonstrated in many more species before it is accepted as a universal phenomenon. Another major accomplishment has been the many excellent field studies of social behavior in primates, which place fighting behavior into proper perspective under natural conditions in man's closest relatives.

Because of increasing concern with the problems of destructive violence, both as manifested in warfare between human societies and as mob and individual violence within societies, there have been a number of scientific conferences devoted to the subject, and most of the recent scientific literature on the biology of aggression has been reviewed in them. Unfortunately, certain scientists and popular writers have been inspired to present popularized accounts of the evolution of human aggression that pay little or no attention to the experimental data on biological factors other than historical ones based on evolution and certainly pay no attention to other factors than biological ones. The conclusions reached on this narrow basis by such writers as Lorenz and Ardrey are overgeneralized, overpessimistic, and have been heavily criticized (Montagu, 1968). On the other hand, biological bases of aggression certainly exist. In this paper I shall try to summarize the major principles regarding them, indicating both their relevance and limitations with respect to human affairs. I must emphasize that this is not the final word on the subject, as new information is constantly appearing. Rather, it is the best estimate that I can make on the basis of current knowledge.

Agonistic behavior is defined as a system of related behavior patterns having the common function of adaptation to situations of conflict between members of the same species. The concept of "aggression" as applied to either human or non-human behavior is so broad and vague as to become virtually useless as an analytic tool. In this paper I shall principally be talking about one pattern of agonistic behavior, overt fighting between members of the same species.

The term "aggression" is particularly confusing since many persons, beginning with Freud, have dichotomized all human behavior into sex and aggression. While dichotomous thinking is often useful in the early stages of scientific analysis, it is only valid if in fact the phenomena naturally fall into only two categories. The meaning of aggression as applied in this broad sense is so inclusive that almost any statement concerning it is partially true and is equally likely to be partially false. When we categorize behavior more carefully, we find that there are at least seven major categories of social behavior other than sexual behavior and agonistic behavior. There are not only multiple categories of social behavior, but multiple factors producing such behavior.

Fighting behavior is affected by factors operating on every level of organization: ecological, social, organismic, physiological, and molecular. Therefore, any adequate explanatory theory of fighting must be multifactorial. It follows that any hypothesis that postulates a single cause of human aggression, whether it be instinct, learning, culture, or original sin, is inadequate and misleading.

Heredity plays a strong part in the determination of individual, sex, and species differ-

ences in agonistic behavior. There is no room for argument on this point. The literature demonstrates that large genetic differences exist within such species as mice, poultry, and dogs. Genetic differences between species are more difficult to demonstrate because of the confounding factors of cultural, hereditary, and ecological differences, but it can be assumed that the differences between the highly agonistic woodchucks and the controlled and organized behavior of prairie dogs are largely genetic. *It is therefore highly probable that the basic agonistic behavior of human beings is genetically different from that of any other species, including all other primates, and that there are large genetic differences between individuals within human populations, modified, of course, by all sorts of cultural and environmental factors.* With respect to sex differences, it is probable that human males and females are intermediate on a comparative biological scale between those species which show extreme differences and those which are virtually alike with respect to agonistic behavior. It also follows that because of man's unique genetic composition that no direct analogies from any other species to man are justified. Final verification must rest on the direct study of human behavior.

Social fighting has most probably been evolved from defensive reactions to injury. Such reactions are almost universal and are adaptive against attacks by predators as well as against accidental injury by members of the same species. Starting at this point, the evolution of social fighting has proceeded independently in different species, with the result that fighting serves a variety of social functions. The most general of these functions is the regulation of social space, but agonistic behavior may also regulate the availability of mates, as in deer and sage grouse; the division of food, in dogs and wolves but not in mice; and the availability of breeding territories in many species of birds.

Therefore, the hypothesis that man fights man because he is by nature a bloodthirsty carnivore is false. In carnivores the patterns of behavior involved in predation are distinctly different from those involved in social fighting, and agonistic behavior plays just as prominent a part in strictly herbivorous animals as it does in carnivorous ones. Anthropological and archeological evidence indicates that primitive men were basically food gatherers and did not develop the potentiality of a largely meat diet until they acquired tools. Basically, man's teeth and digestive system are those of an omnivore, and there is no indication that man was ever anything else. Like the pigs, man has the capacity to eat anything.

It also follows that the social functions of fighting in man must be determined by study of his own species. The various functions of fighting in other animals at best give us hypotheses. It is possible that man fights for any or all of the reasons that are found in other animal societies, and highly likely that other reasons are peculiar to human beings alone.

Man is, above all, a tool using animal. While many other species make occasional use of tools and while non-human primates may use tools defensively to threaten predators (but only very rarely against their own species), the system of human verbal communication has made possible an elaboration of tool using that is seen in no other species. In the first place, the use of tools affects the nature of social fighting. Once tools for killing other species were discovered, the possibility of using them for social fighting must have been immediately apparent. Furthermore, fighting itself can be used as a tool, to obtain various desired behaviors and objects. It has been used to make people work, as in slavery, and to acquire all sorts of material objects, as in various sorts of criminal assaults. The concept of fighting as a tool is particularly important in warfare, as organized group fighting is so superior to individual fighting or that of unorganized groups that it lends itself to all sorts of attempts to enforce behavior or acquire land and other forms of wealth. This means that in human societies the motivations that lie behind social fighting are vastly extended compared to those of non-human animal societies.

Man is the only animal with a high degree of symbolic communication and hence the capacity to culturally transmit large amounts of accumulated information from generation to generation. While all social animals transmit information, none have developed anything comparable to human language. It follows that man, because of this basically biological capacity, has a unique capacity to regulate fighting behavior either in a positive or negative way.

Both overt fighting and the emotional reactions accompanying it can be enhanced or suppressed by training. In mice we have shown that males can be trained to be either ferocious fighters or completely peaceful, and the wide prevalence of dominance orders in various species of social animals indicates that training resulting in the social control of fighting is a normal process in many animal societies. While relatively little has been done with the conditioning of emotional reactions as such, much work on conditioning, from Pavlov on, indicates that internal reactions can be conditioned at least as readily as overt behavior. The recent work of Miller and his colleagues, demonstrating that such autonomically controlled reactions as the heartbeat can be operantly as well as classically conditioned, strengthens this possibility. These effects should be quite different from cases of suppression noted in psychopathology.

Since human beings are highly responsive to training, it follows that it should be possible to bring both overt fighting and its accompanying emotions under a high degree of control, both with respect to particular situations, as in simple conditioning, and in a much more general way through the application of cultural rules. One of the most effective ways to train an individual not to fight is to use the principle of passive inhibition (i.e., that not fighting in a particular situation will form a habit of not fighting). Conversely, one of the most effective ways to train an individual to fight is to insure that his fighting experience is successful.

No magical cut-off signals. During the first fight between two individual animals, they ordinarily attack each other vigorously after some preliminary investigation and threats. After a time one of them becomes either injured or fatigued and thereafter either runs away or begins to show other behavior patterns of a defensive or passive sort. If the latter happens, the attacks of the victorious animal begin to decline, although he may go on biting and attacking the helpless individual for some time if the latter has not run away and escaped entirely. In those species capable of developing dominance orders this behavior may in time become still further reduced and quite stereotyped, so that the dominant animal's attacks are reduced to a threat and the subordinate animal responds with some sort of defensive or appeasement behavior.

However, the situation is strictly under the control of the dominant animal. If the subordinate dares to revolt, he is immediately attacked by the dominant animal.

The original report of supposed "cut-off signals" or so-called "showing the jugular vein" (by which the subordinate animal was assumed to infallibly influence the dominant one to cease attacks) is becoming a classical case of mistaken observation, made on animals whose history and social relationships were unknown to the observer. In the case of two dogs or wolves having a well-developed dominance relationship and who are threatening each other, the dominant animal can always be identified by his erect tail, the subordinate animal having it lowered. In such cases the dominant animal may indicate that he is no longer interested in continuing the interchange by turning his head away. Lorenz called this behavior "showing the jugular vein," thinking that the dominant animal was in fact the subordinate. Actually, the dominant animal is in complete control of the situation. A subordinate does not show this behavior but rolls on his back and, if severely frightened, snaps and yelps at the dominant one.

It follows that the hypothesis that man is a killer because he lacks such magical cut-off signals is false. The concept of appeasement was first derived from human behavior and only later applied to behavior observed in non-human animals. Furthermore, human beings do in fact have many signals indicating helplessness and non-resistance, the most obvious being that of crying. As with other species, one would expect these signals to lower the level of attacks, but to be completely effective only in a relationship where such behavior had been worked out and accepted. In addition, human beings are capable of devising general verbal rules for indicating submission or surrender, such as raising the hands. However, the human attacker is no less and no more bound by these signals in the absence of previous experience than are other animals.

Many different motivational systems may be involved in fighting. Physiological research indicates that the neurological basis of agonistic behavior in cats is highly specific and that somewhat different parts of the brain are involved even in the alternate patterns of agonistic behavior such as defense, attack, and flight. Furthermore, as indicated above,

the adaptive function of fighting may involve the acquisition of food or sex partners, and thus involve widely disparate sources of motivation. One of the most general explanations of overt attacks and feelings of hostility is *that individuals contiguous to and aware of each other may interpret any feeling of pain or discomfort as being caused by the other individual and hence attempt to drive him away.*

The physiological and emotional reactions connected with fear and anger have the effect of magnifying and prolonging the effects of external stimulation rather than originating internal stimulation. Attack and defense are emergency reactions, adaptive in specific situations, and evolution should proceed in the direction of making these mechanisms available in emergencies rather than uselessly creating emergencies caused by internal pressure. This principle has been disputed by advocates of a hydraulic theory of motivation based on analogy with the physiology of such behaviors as eating and drinking, where stimulation may arise from on-going metabolic processes. In either of the above alternate theories, internal factors are important. If the former interpretation is true, and I believe that it is more in accord with both the physiological and evolutionary evidence, it follows that an animal or human being can live satisfactorily for long periods without ever showing overt fighting or feeling unpleasant emotions of hostility, provided external stimulation for fighting is kept to a minimum. It also follows that one of the major practical problems for the control of human aggression is to discover forms of social organization which will create such conditions. It is, however, impossible that external stimulation can ever be completely avoided, and even if this were done, fighting might occur simply because it could be used as a tool. We therefore also need social organization which will allow the harmless expression of hostile feelings and will minimize the possibilities of using fighting and the threat of injury as a tool.

Behavior is not inherited as such but developed under the influence of a variety of genetic and environmental factors. Agonistic behavior evolves in the direction of becoming functional and hence non-harmful under the conditions of social and ecological organization normal to the species. Under modern conditions of huge worldwide interbreeding populations, the biological evolution of human behavior is coming to a standstill; and it is probable that human agonistic behavior, from a biological standpoint, is still best adapted to the conditions of small isolated tribal communities that existed before the dawn of history.

Social disorganization is a major cause of destructive violence. Under normal natural conditions a well-functioning animal society shows only sporadic cases of destructive violence. However, if social organization is destroyed or disrupted in some way, violent behavior may break out. Such disorganization may take place because of natural disasters, but is most frequently produced by human interference, as when strange individuals are introduced into a population, or the population is compressed and confined in some way so that individuals cannot employ their usual patterns of agonistic behavior without injuring each other. The classical case of this sort is Zuckerman's account of the hamadryas baboons in the London Zoo. This species is normally organized into subgroups consisting of a single male and several females who are competed for by other males. In an unconfined natural area and with the normal ratio of an excess of females, this sort of fighting seldom results in death or injury. In the zoo situation, defeated animals could not leave the area, there was an excess of males over females, and strange individuals were not only thrown together in the original group but added at a later date. Under these conditions of social disorganization, the males engaged in continual fighting in which females were sometimes pulled to pieces and no young had a chance to survive.

This suggests that outbreaks of destructive human violence may be caused by social disorganization, and the available data are consistent with this hypothesis. Areas which are high in crimes of violence are usually slum areas, either skid rows including a population of homeless wanderers who have little organization with each other, or areas in which there has been a large amount of recent immigration and where the individuals are not only unknown to each other but crowded into close contact.

In addition, there is an almost inevitable breakdown of social organization in large cities because of the fact that in very large populations individuals do not know and recognize each other. The kind of social control which restrains destructive violence through interpersonal relationships is missing, and is ordinarily replaced by bureaucratic and largely impersonal police organization which functions by identifying and apprehending individuals after crimes of violence have been committed, and whose effectiveness, as would be predicted by the laws of reinforcement, depends upon the speed and efficiency with which this is done. Under these circumstances not all individuals become violent, and if the personal history of those who do is traced, it turns out that such individuals often come from broken homes, where family organization is either weakened or destroyed. This is, of course, a form of social disorganization.

Furthermore, there is in our society a built-in period of developmental social disorganization. Young adults are expected to leave their primary families at about the age of approximately 18 and thereafter to form a new family through marriage. Ordinarily this does not take place for several years, leaving the young adult partially free from family ties and hence somewhat disorganized with respect to this form of social control. It is this age, between 18 and 25, in which the highest crime rates occur, as well as the highest deaths from automobile accidents, etc. The advantage of institutionalized social disorganization is that it makes it possible for social change to take place more rapidly in our society, the disadvantage that it makes antisocial acts more frequent and probable.

The theory that social disorganization is a major cause of destructive violence is therefore strongly supported by the facts as we know them. I suggest that we need a major research effort in this direction, examining all facets and aspects of our social organization and, on the positive side, determining what sorts of organization, either new or old, are effective in counteracting disorganization.

As the above example shows, human agonistic behavior has been culturally modified in many ways, some tending to decrease it and others to magnify it. The latter effect is particularly evident in the development of the institution of warfare. It is still an open question as to how far social organization can change without distorting human agonistic behavior still further from the primitive condition in which it was probably expressed chiefly by arm waving and angry shouts. Under favorable conditions of social organization, human beings can develop into highly co-operative, unselfish, and peaceful beings. Under conditions of social disorganization they, like other animal societies, can develop destructive and violent behavior. Going beyond the other animals they can, under certain kinds of organization, become merciless engines of destruction directed toward their own kind. It is this latter kind of organization that is inherent in any military organization, as well as in criminal gangs within a society. It is one of the major problems of human behavior to replace such organizations with ones that will lead to peaceful productivity and a sense of well-being.

In conclusion, the control of destructive violence, whether it be on the level of individual crimes and conflicts between groups within a society, or whether it be one of warfare between societies, is basically an organizational problem, and its solution will come about through the study and understanding of social organization. This is a biological problem, but it is also a psychological, sociological, and political one. It deserves a major interdisciplinary effort on the part of both the biological and social sciences.

TABLE 1
Multifactorial Theory of Agonistic Behavior

LEVEL OF ORGANIZATION	EXAMPLE OF MAJOR FACTOR	EFFECT
Ecological	Restricted space	Increased fighting
Social	Social disorganization	Destructive fighting
Organismic	Pain	Induces defensive fighting or escape
Physiological	Lesions	Increased or reduced irritability
Genetic	Sex and strain differences	Quantitative and qualitative differences in fighting

	HISTORICAL AND ORGANIZATIONAL FACTORS	EFFECT
	Organic evolution	Tendency to organize agonistic behavior adaptively
	Cultural evolution	Reduction or augmentation of fighting
	Previous experience; training	Organization of individual behavior

RECOMMENDED FURTHER READING

MOTIVATION: GENERAL

Aronoff, J.: *Psychological Needs and Cultural Systems;* Princeton N.J., Van Nostrand Reinhold 1967

Atkinson, John W.: *An Introduction to Motivation;* Princeton, N.J., Van Nostrand Reinhold 1964

Cofer, C. and M. Appley: *Motivation: Theory and Research;* New York, John Wiley 1966

Festinger, Leon: *A Theory of Cognitive Dissonance;* Stanford, Calif., Stanford University Press 1957

Harlow, Harry F.: "Mice, Monkeys, Men and Motives"; *Psychological Review, 60* (1953), 23–32

McClelland, David C.: *The Achieving Society;* Princeton, N.J., Van Nostrand Reinhold 1961

McClelland, David C. (ed.): *Studies in Motivation;* New York, Appleton-Century-Crofts 1955

McClelland, David C., John W. Atkinson, R. Clark, and E. Lowell: *The Achievement Motive;* New York, Appleton-Century-Crofts 1953

Maslow, Abraham H.: *Motivation and Personality;* New York, Harper & Row 1954

Miller, Neal E.: "Experiments in Motivation: Studies Combining Psychological, Physiological and Pharmacological Techniques"; *Science, 126* (1957), 1271–1278

*Murray, E. J.: *Motivation and Emotion;* Englewood Cliffs, N.J., Prentice-Hall 1964

SEX

Beach, Frank A. (ed.): *Sex and Behavior;* New York, John Wiley 1965

Brecher, Edward: *The Sex Researchers;* Boston, Little, Brown 1969

Ford, Clellan S. and Frank A. Beach: *Patterns of Sexual Behavior;* New York, Harper and Row, Publishers, Inc., 1951

*Hoffman, Martin: *The Gay World;* New York, Basic Books 1968

Kinsey, Alfred C., Wardell B. Pomeroy and Clyde E. Martin: *Sexual Behavior in the Human Male;* Philadelphia, Saunders 1948

Kinsey, Alfred C., Wardell B. Pomeroy, Clyde E. Martin and Paul H. Gebhard: *Sexual Behavior in the Human Female;* Philadelphia, Saunders 1953

Masters, William H. and Virginia Johnson: *Human Sexual Response;* Boston, Little, Brown 1966

—— and ——: *Human Sexual Inadequacy;* Boston, Little, Brown 1970

*Morris, Desmond: *The Naked Ape;* New York, McGraw-Hill 1967, Chapter 2

Schofield, Michael: *Sociological Aspects of Homosexuality;* Boston, Little, Brown 1965

Sheffield, F., J. Wulff and R. Backer: "Reward Value of Copulation Without Sex Drive Reduction"; *Journal of Comparative and Physiological Psychology, 44* (1951), 3–8

West, Donald J.: *Homosexuality;* Chicago, Aldine 1968

*Young, Wayland: *Eros Denied: Sex in Western Society;* New York, Grove Press 1964

AGGRESSION:

*Ardrey, Robert: *The Territorial Imperative;* New York, Atheneum 1966

*Ashley Montagu, M. F. (ed.): *Man and Aggression;* New York, Oxford University Press 1968

Berkowitz, Leonard: *Aggression: A Social-Psychological Analysis;* New York, McGraw-Hill 1962

*—— (ed.): *Roots of Aggression;* New York, Atherton 1969

Buss, Arnold H.: *The Psychology of Aggression;* New York, John Wiley 1961

Carthy, J. D. & J. J. Ebling (eds.): *The Natural History of Aggression;* New York, Academic Press 1964

Clemente, C. D. & D. B. Lindsley (eds.): *Aggression* and *Defense (Brain Function,* Vol. 5); Los Angeles, University of California Press 1967

Dollard, John, Leonard Doob, Neal Miller, O. H. Mowrer and Robert R. Sears: *Frustration and Aggression;* New Haven, Yale University Press 1939

Fried, Morton, M. Harris & R. Murphy (eds.): *War: The Anthropology of Armed Conflict & Aggression;* Garden City, N.Y., Natural History Press 1968

Hitler, Adolf: "Must Man Kill?" in Carl Cohen (ed.): *Communism, Fascism and Democracy: The Theoretical Foundations;* New York, Random House 1962

*Lorenz, Konrad: *On Aggression;* New York, Harcourt Brace Jovanovich 1966

*Morris, Desmond: *The Naked Ape;* New York, McGraw-Hill 1967, Chapter 5

Scott, J. P.: *Aggression;* Chicago, University of Chicago Press 1958

*Storr, Anthony: *Human Aggression;* New York, Atheneum 1968

    * Paperback edition available

PART VIII

PSYCHOLOGICAL TESTING:

WHAT AND HOW?

If we look at psychology's involvement in the world outside the laboratory and consulting room no activity looms more important—or more ubiquitous —than psychological testing and measurement, the branch of psychology known as psychometry or psychometrics. Virtually all readers of this book will have had some experience with such tests, be they intelligence tests, Scholastic Aptitude or other College Board Examinations, or personality tests. So commonplace has psychological testing become and so big a business that, whatever other appellations may be appropriate to our age, it is certainly the "Age of Testing."

Despite their great variety, psychological tests may logically be grouped under three general rubrics: aptitude tests; achievement tests; and personality tests. Aptitude tests, of which intelligence tests are the most familiar representative, purport to measure an individual's ability to learn (either a generalized ability or the ability to learn a particular task, such as flying a plane or playing the piano) while achievement tests attempt to determine the knowledge or skill a person has already mastered. These two types of tests are closely related in that measures of achievement necessarily form the basis on which aptitude tests are constructed and scored. Aptitude tests, conversely, must involve some measurement of achievement, else they could hardly be tests at all. Personality tests, on the other hand, attempt either to construct a picture of an individual's total personality and its dynamics or to measure some single characteristic or set of related characteristics. Such tests may be of the paper and pencil type, containing multiple choice or "yes-no" questions, or they may ask the individual to respond to ambiguous visual stimuli (such as inkblots or posed photographs) into which he then projects his own needs, anxieties, wishes, and feelings—hence the name "projective" tests. Although most psychological tests are scored by machine, projective personality tests and some achievement tests involving the writing of essays are scored by human judges.

In the case of all psychological tests we should ask at least three critical (and sometimes embarrassing) questions: what do the tests actually measure; how accurately do they measure it; and how consistently do they measure it? (A fourth question—whether "it" is worth measuring at all—we will not discuss because its answer is a matter of value judgment, not of scientific fact. This emphatically does *not* mean that the question is either meaningless or unimportant; it means only that it cannot be answered scientifically.)

The third question—the easiest to deal with—raises the problem of *reliability,* whether, that is, a person taking a particular test twice—or two versions of the same test—within a short time of each other will give approximately the same answers both times and come out with approximately the same result. The solution to this problem is largely a matter of trial and error in devising and refining questions, but most good aptitude and achievement tests are now highly reliable, exhibiting reliability coefficients of .90 or greater.

The second question refers to the problem of *validity,* whether a test actually measures what it purports to measure. This can only be answered by comparing an individual's test performance with some other performance or *criterion* by which the results of the test can be assessed. If, for example, most people with IQs of 125 and above flunked out of school (provided there was no radical change in educational practice) intelligence tests would be invalid no matter how reliable they were. This is another way of saying that validity and reliability are partially independent dimensions of a test, "partially independent" because, while there are tests (e.g., some personality tests) that are reliable without being valid, it is hard to find a test that is valid without being reliable.

Paradoxically, the first question—what do tests actually measure?—while it may seem the simplest is, on the contrary, the most perplexing. Although intelligence tests have been used ever since the pioneering work of Alfred Binet (1857–1911) and Théodore Simon (1873–1961) in Paris in 1905, no one has yet advanced a fully satisfactory definition or characterization of "intelligence." The purpose of Binet and Simon's original test was to differentiate those students who could not benefit from the traditional French educational system from those who could and in this the tests eventually proved highly successful. Nowadays, intelligence test performance is the best single predictor of academic grades and overall school success, which is to say that the tests have a high degree of validity.

To say, however, as some psychologists and psychometricians do, that "intelligence is what intelligence tests measure" may be true as far as it goes but the statement is a tautology that does not go very far. Most psychologists now believe that "intelligence" is not a unitary entity or trait but a composite of various abilities and factors (of which motivation is often a critical one). If that is true, intelligence tests clearly emphasize one factor—verbal facility—at the expense of many others, including visual, aural, motor, and imaginative abilities. While intelligence test results correlate highly with performance in the formal educational system (hardly surprising since that is what they were designed to do and since the verbal facility rewarded by the tests is also rewarded by the educational system) they correlate much less highly with performance in real life situations and with overall post-school achievement. Too much significance should not, therefore, be accorded the results of intelligence tests (IQ) for while what they measure may indeed be intelligence it is not the whole of intelligence. Perhaps the least acceptable result of such tests is that many children and adolescents who earn low scores are treated as retarded or uneducable rather than as people whose talents and abilities may not be those measured and rewarded by the tests. IQ scores can thus become a "scientific" device for enforcing and perpetuating the exclusion of some individuals or groups from full cultural and social participation.

Personality tests are a more recent development than aptitude and achievement tests. Hermann Rohrschach first published the projective test named after him in 1921 while Henry Murray developed the Thematic Apperception Test (TAT) in 1935. It was World War II, however, that gave a tremendous impetus to personality testing because of the armed forces' need to match the characteristics of their members to the often highly specialized and rigorous demands of particular assignments. Following the end of the war testing rapidly diffused from the armed forces throughout education, government, business and industry, a development abetted by the upsurge of interest in psychology throughout American society.

The problems of personality testing compound those of aptitude and achievement testing precisely because the individual's "personality" is, at a given moment, the unique product or summation of his whole life thus far. Except in a statistical sense there is no "modal" or "normal" personality and no one knows precisely what "well-adjusted" means. A personality well adjusted to one situation or set of circumstances may be very poorly adjusted to another. Even in the case of highly reliable personality tests (and not all of them are so) there are still no "correct" answers to test items, the scores on different items or scales are not genuinely additive, the possibility of conscious or unconscious falsification by the respondent always exists, and it is difficult or impossible to find or devise external criteria by which to validate the results. Consequently, the *interpretation* of the results often varies wildly depending not only on the interpreter's scientific views but on his personal values, his moral, political, and even aesthetic preferences, as well as on his own personality and life experiences. Personality tests have not, by and large, proved notably accurate in predicting behavior, especially in complex situations, although they have done somewhat better than predictions based on personal knowledge and assessment of the individual in question (so-called "clinical" predictions). Personality tests, in other words, are of dubious validity, although they are often useful in providing insights into an individual's personality and in raising fruitful questions for further exploration. As to what personality "is" no one has yet had the temerity to say that "personality is what personality inventories measure." In such restraint may lie a hopeful augury of psychometric humility.

In our first selection Otto Klineberg of the University of Paris discusses a problem that has once again become the center of public controversy: the consistently lower average scores made by groups of black children on standard intelligence tests. No one disputes the facts—black children *do* make lower scores, *on the average,* than white children; as usual, it is the interpretation of the facts that causes disagreement. Klineberg presents a reasoned argument for ascribing these differences to the culturally and often materially impoverished environment in which black children grow up rather than to any innate or genetic differences between the races, a position that draws indirect support from the researches reported both by Maya Pines (Selection 11) and David Krech (Selection 17). The controversy derives from a more recent article by Arthur Jensen of the University of California (Berkeley)[1] (a study excerpts from which we were denied permission to reprint) in which, after reviewing many of the studies cited by Klineberg as well as more recent ones, he concluded that there is considerable evidence for the view that the consistent differences in average IQs between black and white populations may reflect real genetic differences between the two groups.

Not surprisingly, given the prevailing political and ideological climate in America, Jensen's suggestion has evoked outraged charges of "irresponsibility" and "racism" from liberals, some of which have come from within the psychological community itself. Meanwhile, true racists have put on their best "I told you so" expressions and nodded in gleeful agreement. And yet, the issue Jensen has courageously raised is a real one, one that cannot be dismissed by name-calling or ideological polemics merely because, if true, it would be ideologically or politically embarrassing to certain groups. Even if Jensen proves correct it would not mean that every white is intellectually superior to every black (a conclusion so patently absurd as hardly to require refutation) nor could a difference in *mean* intelligence test scores between whites and blacks be used, logically or scientifically, to justify the perpetuation of legal, political, or social inequalities between the races, inequalities that have nothing whatsoever to do with intelligence.

The highly emotional and ideological responses to Jensen's work provide a clear example of how psychological research can become entangled with politics. At the same time they reveal vividly some of the biases and blind spots of American psychologists. Despite the preponderant evidence that intelligence is *largely* inherited (which does *not* mean, by the way, that it is not *influenced* by environmental factors) most American psychologists reject in principle the idea that there might be genetically-based differences in average intelligence between the races. Such an idea runs counter to the ideology of equality, to the strongly held belief that human nature is infinitely malleable, and to the behaviorist emphasis on the power of external, environmental factors to shape not only the behavior but the very capacities of the individual. An ideological rejection of Jensen's (or of anyone else's) work does no credit to psychologists and can only impede the free development of psychology as a science. For psychology, if it is to be scientific, must examine all theories with equal care and must subject all of them to the test of evidence, however ideologically or personally unpalatable to some the conclusions of such a process may be. We urge the reader to examine Jensen's study for himself, to weigh the evidence he presents, to compare it with Klineberg's analysis, and to recognize his own biases in this highly charged area before reaching his own conclusions.

In our second selection, Banesh Hoffmann, a theoretical physicist, severely criticizes what are admittedly the best of contemporary aptitude and achievement tests. He points out how the ambiguity and poor quality of many of their questions tend to penalize the creative, profound, and insightful student in favor of the average, superficial, and conventional one. Statistics, moreover, are often used in a pseudo-scientific way to gloss over the short-

---

1 "How much can we boost IQ and scholastic achievement?" *Harvard Educational Review, 39,* 1969, 1–123.

comings of the tests. In Hoffmann's opinion the reduction of intellectual performance to a matter of statistical measurement and manipulation ignores both crucial aspects of ability that cannot be quantified and the "corrupting" side effects of the tests themselves. That testers are interested only in the student's responses rather than the reasons for them is again consistent with American psychology's concern with overt behavior at the expense of subjective consciousness. Professor Hoffmann's discussion further suggests that the actual workings of the educational system may stifle creativity while claiming to encourage it. To the extent that Hoffmann's analysis is accurate the end result of "testomania" can only be the thoroughgoing "mediocratization" of American education. It may be that the aptitude chiefly tested by the Scholastic Aptitude Test is the aptitude for taking Scholastic Aptitude tests —a limited but, in our present society, doubtless a useful talent. At this point, one might well ask exactly whose interests are being served by such tests.

Ever since the mid-1950s, when William H. Whyte published his now well-known advice "How to Cheat on Personality Tests" in *The Organization Man,* psychological testing—of achievement, aptitude, and personality—has been subjected to a steadily rising amount of public and professional criticism. As a result, in the autumn of 1965, subcommittees of both the United States Senate and House of Representatives held public hearings into the uses and abuses of psychological testing, hearings which focussed on whether or not such testing unjustifiably invaded the privacy and infringed the constitutional rights of those tested. The widely used Minnesota Multiphasic Personality Inventory (MMPI) was subjected to especially close scrutiny. The fundamental question at issue in the hearings has implications at once ethical, scientific, and political and, not surprisingly, it elicited passionate responses from all concerned parties. While we lack space here to discuss those implications in any detail they remain lively issues both to psychologists and to legislators. In consequence of this controversy a final question to those we suggested above should be asked of all psychological tests, namely: "Do they have the *right* to measure 'it'?"

In the final selection of this group Victor Lovell of Stanford University raises pertinent questions regarding the uses of personality tests. He distinguishes between tests of "capacity" (the questions on which have "right" and "wrong" answers, determined by criteria external to the testing situation itself) and tests of "character" (the questions on which have no "objectively" right or wrong answers external to the demands of the test situation). The basis of this distinction lies not in the content of the test items but in what the respondent is told to do on the test and in how his answers are treated when his test protocol is scored. As Whyte and others have pointed out, one can "cheat" on a test of character just as one may, in fact, be penalized for giving honest answers that are deemed by the scorers to be "peculiar," "inappropriate," or "undesirable."

Lovell also discusses the different kinds of "contracts" under which personality tests are administered: what he calls the "client contract," the "strong personnel contract," and the "weak personnel contract." Once again, these contracts do not denote differences in test content; rather they denote differences in the uses to which the test results are put and differences in what is understood, usually implicitly, between the test-giver and the test-taker. The author points out how variations in the test contract strongly affect the validity of test results and he argues, on ethical, scientific, *and* service grounds, for the exclusive use of the "client contract." Personnel contracts, according to Lovell, not only militate against measuring individual differences when honest answers are required of the respondent, but positively encourage the kinds of duplicity discussed by Whyte and deplored by others.

Lovell's thoughtful article again raises the issues—discussed at length in the 1965 Congressional hearings—of what sorts of questions personality tests may legitimately ask, what the effects of asking them are likely to be and, still more important, which uses of test results are legitimate. Further still, it challenges those psychologists engaged in the business of testing to decide both the nature and the locus of their professional loyalties. As a profession psychology has not yet responded adequately to that challenge and so we may justly ask: For whose benefit are personality tests administered; are they legitimate instruments of self-discovery and dispassionate scientific inquiry or are they the deceiving servants of a paternalistic political and social system?

38. NEGRO-WHITE DIFFERENCES IN INTELLIGENCE TEST PERFORMANCE: A NEW LOOK AT AN OLD PROBLEM

Otto Klineberg

I have written this article at the suggestion of the Society for the Psychological Study of Social Issues (SPSSI), Division 9 of the American Psychological Association. It is based in part on some of my own earlier publications and in part on a chapter which I have prepared for a forthcoming book; it represents an attempt to bring up to date a psychological analysis of an old problem. The substantial number of recent publications in this field, some of which have attracted considerable popular attention; the many "letters to the editor"; the unfortunate tendency, all too frequent, to stray from an interpretation of the data to an attack on the ethnic origins or the alleged political positions of the persons involved; the accusation of a "conspiracy"; and finally, the practical implications which have been drawn for public policy—all of these developments have made a factual reappraisal desirable. I had hoped that this might be done by another psychologist, one less closely identified with a definite stand on one side of this issue. As the next best thing, I have tried to look, as honestly as my own bias would permit, at the evidence which has accumulated on both sides. It goes without saying that I am writing as an individual, and that neither the Council nor the membership of SPSSI should be held responsible for what follows.

THE ISSUE

I shall restrict my discussion of Negro-white differences to that aspect of the issue on which we, as psychologists, may claim to speak with professional competence, namely, the interpretation of the results obtained from the application of mental tests. There are other aspects of at least equal importance; whether, for example, there is any acceptable indication of biological superiority or inferiority; whether one can argue from the nature of a culture to the genetic factors responsible, etc. On these and related questions the anthropologists are better qualified than we are to express a judgment. I leave these matters, therefore, with the single reminder that the American Anthropological Association has taken the position that there is no scientifically acceptable basis for a genetic hierarchy among ethnic groups.

As far as mental tests are concerned, the issue is *not* one of whether *on the average* Negro children obtain lower test scores than whites. Of that there can be no doubt. My own earlier survey (Klineberg, 1944), in which I was greatly aided by Kenneth B. Clark, was based on 27 studies, and led me to the conclusion that an IQ of 86 represented the approximate Negro median. Shuey (1958), after a much more thorough and complete survey, obtained substantially similar results; on verbal group tests alone, she located no fewer than 72 studies, based upon tests of 36,000 colored children, and her estimate of the average IQ is 85. (I might add parenthetically that in my own earlier survey I found median IQs for children of Italian, Portuguese, and Mexican parentage at or below those of American Negroes, and those of American Indians definitely below.) Shuey's estimate is therefore very close to mine.

The addition of so many further studies has, however, supplied very little new insight. One is reminded of the *Literary Digest* poll in connection with the Roosevelt-Landon electoral contest in 1936; on the basis of more than 2,000,000 ballots, it was predicted that Landon would win an overwhelming victory. As is well known, there was a systematic bias in the sample. The addition of another 100 studies of Negro children would not strengthen Shuey's (1958) conclusion that there are "some native differences between Negroes and whites as determined by intelligence tests" (p. 318), if some systematic error entered into the test results.

As far back as 1933, Garrett and Schneck in their book on *Psychological Tests* reminded us that "the examiner must always remember that comparisons are permissible only when environmental differences are absent, or at least negligible." This appears to be the crucial issue. What comparisons of Negroes and whites have been made under such conditions?

THE ARGUMENT FOR "SOME NATIVE DIFFERENCES"

There are three major studies cited by Shuey and others as demonstrating that differences persist even when environmental factors have been "equated." (I have put this word in quotation marks for reasons which will appear later.) One of these is by Myrtle Bruce (1940), who matched Negroes and whites in a rural community in southern Virginia on the Sims Socioeconomic scale, and still found a difference, with a resulting mean IQ on the Binet of 86 for the whites and 77 for the Negroes. Those who have used Bruce's results have not always gone on to note her careful qualifications.

> Although the white and Negro samples equated for social status still show statistical differences in IQ on each of the three intelligence tests, this fact cannot be considered proof of the superiority of the white group, since the equation of the two groups *is not entirely valid* (p. 20, italics supplied).

Even a quick look at her graph on page 20 shows more whites at the upper levels and more Negroes at the lower. Bruce herself "is inclined to believe that there is an innate difference between the particular white and Negro groups studied" (p. 97). She does not, however, extend this conclusion to the ethnic groups in general; she speaks, for example, of the skewness of the Negro IQ distribution as something which "prevents this study from being used as evidence for the superiority of the white race to the Negro race" (p. 97).

Suppose, however, that the two groups had really been "equated" for their scores on a satisfactory socioeconomic scale. Can this possibly be regarded as taking care of all the relevant environmental variables? This appears to be the assumption underlying the study by McGurk (1951) in New Jersey and Pennsylvania. Negro and white high school seniors were matched for socioeconomic level, and still there was a difference, the Negroes overlapping the white means by 29%. This would be an important finding (as would also the demonstration that there was about as much difference between the two groups on test items identified as "cultural" and "noncultural," (respectively) if socioeconomic level were all that mattered. Can anyone really believe that? Do motivation, self-confidence, opportunity for wider experience, and other related factors count for nothing?

In a recent critical review, Dreger and Miller (1960) insist that it is not enough to equate ethnic groups in terms of social class and economic variables; that there is a caste as well as a class difference; that even those Negroes whose economic status is higher than that of most white persons will still in most cases be prevented from living the same kind of life in all respects; these writers insist that many other factors may also be important. Incidentally, they emphasize that they "are not taking sides at this point in the heredity-environment controversy..." (p. 367). They show their impartiality in a striking and (to me) slightly painful manner by stating that "Shuey does the same rationalizing from an hereditarian standpoint that Klineberg did in his earlier 'review' from an environmental standpoint" (p. 364). To return to McGurk, it is impossible to accept the contention that all relevant environmental factors have been considered, just because socioeconomic status has been controlled.

The third study which has figured prominently on this side of the argument is by Tanser (1939). This was conducted in Kent County, Ontario, Canada, where the Negroes have lived since before the Civil War; Tanser writes that they are on a level with the whites in regard to "every political and social advantage." On the Pintner-Paterson tests, the mean white IQ was 109.6, the Negro, 91; on the Pintner nonlanguage test, the means were 111 and 95; on the National Intelligence Test the respective figures were 104 and 89. On this last test, 20% of the Negroes reached or exceeded the white median; 29% of the Negroes and 56% of the whites reached or surpassed the *National* test norms. (Tanser's study is unfortunately not available to me in Paris; I have quoted these figures from Shuey.)

If Tanser is right with regard to "every political and social advantage," these results must be taken seriously. A comment by Anastasi (1958) is, however, pertinent.

> Nevertheless significant differences were found in the socioeconomic level of the two groups. Moreover, it is reported that the white children attended school more regularly than the Negro, a difference often associated with social class differences. Thus within the entire sample of white children tested, school attendance averaged 93.38%; within the Negro sample, it averaged 84.77% (pp. 556–557).

I have only one comment to add. I was born in Canada, and lived there the first 25 years of my life. I would have said that Negroes were reasonably well off there, but emphatically not that they lived under conditions of complete equality, or that the social environment was free of prejudice. I would have thought that Canada was in this respect similar to the northeastern United States, with Negroes occupying about the same relative position. As a matter of fact Chant and Freedman (1934) report a correlation of .98 between scale values assigned to the same list of ethnic groups, including Negroes, by Canadian as by American students. I do not know Kent County, Ontario, and I cannot take it for granted that the same attitudes would be found there. I cannot help wondering, however, whether this particular Canadian community can be so exceptional. I would like to see a replication of this study, with full attention to social and sociological variables, and to patterns of personal development and interpersonal relations. In the meantime, Tanser's results cannot be dismissed, but they appear to me to be outweighed by the evidence on the other side.

THE ARGUMENT AGAINST NATIVE DIFFERENCES

The evidence against the assumption of native differences in intelligence test performance between Negroes and whites still seems to me to be very convincing. The relevant studies, most of which are already well known and will therefore be presented in brief outline, include the following.

Among infants during the first year of life the earlier finding by McGraw (1931) was that southern Negro babies showed inferiority on the Hetzer-Wolf tests. McGraw concludes:

> It is significant that with even the very young subjects, *when environmental factors are minimized* [italics supplied], the same type and approximately the same degree of superiority is evidenced on the part of the white subjects as that found among older groups.

In New Haven, however, where Negro mothers obtained more adequate nourishment and where the general economic level of the families had improved, Pasamanick (1946) found no Negro inferiority or retardation. A follow-up of 40 cases at a mean age of about two years still showed no retardation (Knobloch & Pasamanick, 1953; Pasamanick & Knobloch, 1955). Using different tests, Gilliland (1951) also reports no significant differences between Negro and white infants in Chicago.

For preschool children, Anastasi and d'Angelo (1952), found no significant differences on Goodenough Draw-a-Man IQ between samples of Negroes and whites attending Day Care Centers in New York City. Dreger and Miller (1960) comment:

> With due recognition of the limitations of the Goodenough as a test of intelligence, we may yet regard Anastasi and d'Angelo's results as a challenge to nativist theories of intellectual differences between the races (p. 366).

It is as the children get older that differences in test performance appear. Surely this is to be expected on the basis of the cumulative effect of an inferior environment. Such an effect has been demonstrated in the case of white children as well. To mention only one example out of many, Sherman and Key (1932) found a striking decrement with age among white children living in the "hollows" of the Blue Ridge Mountains; there was a Pintner-Cunningham IQ of 84 at ages 6-8; 70 at 8-10; and 53 at 10-12. This is a much more dramatic drop than any with which I am familiar in the case of Negro children; it shows what *can* happen when a poor environment persists over a long period.

Conversely, when the environment improves, test scores go up. In the case of Negro children they do not usually go up all the way to meet the white norms, but this is to be expected if the discriminatory treatment persists, and even *for a time* if discrimination were to be completely eliminated. The atmosphere in the home, the conversation around the dinner table, the use of leisure time, the books read and discussed—these and other factors contributing to "intelligence" cannot be expected to change over night or even possibly in one generation. With this in mind, the changes that have been reported in Negro IQs become all the more impressive.

When my students and I indicated (Klineberg, 1935) that test scores of southern Negro children improved in proportion to their length of residence in New York City, we were perfectly aware that they still did not reach the white norms, and we pointed that out. Could anyone have expected them to do so under Harlem living conditions, and in the Harlem schools as they were at that time? Could anyone possibly suggest that in New York or in Philadelphia, where Lee (1951) obtained similar results, there is *no* discrimination against Negroes? There was improvement, however, because there was *less* discrimination than where they came from.

In some cases, the improvement has even been dramatic. Shuey (1958, p. 87) points out that in my review of Negro intelligence testing (Klineberg, 1944) I gave special prominence to a study by W. W. Clark in Los Angeles (1923). This I did because of the striking finding that the Negro children attending 5 elementary schools obtained an average National Intelligence Test IQ of 104.7 as compared with an IQ of 106 for all the children in 15 schools. Shuey indicates that she wrote to Clark asking for further details, and was informed by him that "the *National* norms available in 1922 were probably *about 5 per cent too high*" (p. 87, italics supplied). Surely 5% does not change the results greatly. Besides, in that case the results for the comparison group of 15 schools would also have to be reduced by a similar proportion.

I also wrote to Clark for further information, and he indicated that the obtained IQs were too high, but that he could not determine by how much. The fact remains that if they were too high for the Negroes, they were also too high for the rest of the Los Angeles school population. Clark's original article indicates that there was *no significant difference* shown in the intelligence level of the Negro children and the 15 schools in general, nor were there significant differences in reading comprehension, arithmetic ability, spelling, as well as educational accomplishment in general. He writes: "The average accomplishment and range of accomplishment for Negro children is practically the same as for the total population of the fifteen schools."

Shuey reports further that research conducted in Los Angeles Public Schools in 1928 (unpublished) revealed a median IQ for Negro children of 95. If that is the case, it is difficult to understand Clark's finding of "no significant difference." Even if we accept this estimate, however, the fact remains that in the relatively friendly climate of Los Angeles, Negro IQs have shown a tremendous leap upwards. Compare even this lower estimate of 95 with the 76 reported by Bruce for rural Virginia. Could "selective migration" account for this large difference? Shuey writes:

If we were correct in assuming an IQ difference of about 9 points between northern and southern Negro children, then about half to two-thirds of this difference may reasonably be attributed to environmental factors and the remainder to selective migration (p. 314).

Here the difference is 19 points, and "half to two-thirds" would suggest that Shuey would accept an improvement of 10 to 12 points in IQ as attributable to the superior environment. I am putting this figure *at its most conservative,* since I have found no acceptable evidence for this kind of selective migration, but even then the environmental rise is clear, and it is considerable.

The desegregation of elementary schools, particularly in the border states and cities where the process has more than a "token" character, gives us another opportunity to see what an improved educational environment may accomplish. This situation has been studied in Washington, D. C., although the measures used were tests of achievement rather than of intelligence. Stallings (1960) writes:

The Washington study showed that during the five years following integration, marked progress has been made in academic achievement ...a gain was made in the median score for every [school] subject tested at every grade level where the tests were given.

With regard to Louisville, Kentucky, Omer Carmichael, Superintendent of Public Schools, reported (1959) as follows:

When we tested, we looked at the results the year before desegregation and then looked at them after the second year of desegregation and found that the Negro in all grades had improved—and by an amount that was statistically significant.

This does not mean that average differences between Negroes and whites have disappeared; it does mean that they have been reduced. Nor has this occurred as the result of "pulling down" the white level. Carmichael reports that there "was a slight improvement for the whites; a substantial improvement for the Negroes." For the difference to disappear completely, much more has to happen. (Even among whites, the difference in the IQ of occupational classes is substantial.) Until that "more" has happened, we have no right to assume that Negroes are, on the average, innately inferior.

AVERAGES AND INDIVIDUALS

In many of the recent analyses of ethnic differences, including the extensive one by Shuey, a great deal of emphasis has been placed on the extent of overlapping. Her own estimate is that the median overlap among school children was between 10 and 20%. (In McGurk's study it was 29%, and presumably in Clark's it was close to 50%.) As every psychology student (but unfortunately not every layman) knows, this refers to the percentage of the "inferior" group who reach or exceed the mean of the "superior." As Anastasi (1958) points out:

If 30 per cent of the Negroes reach or exceed the white median, the percentage who reach or exceed the lowest score of the white group will be approximately 99. Under these conditions, therefore, the ranges will overlap almost completely (p. 549).

Clearly, then, statements to the effect that there was "only 20% overlap" obscure the degree of similarity in the total distributions.

This fact comes out strikingly when one looks more closely at Bruce's findings on the Kuhlmann-Anderson scale. For the total population examined (521 whites and 432 Negroes), the range in IQ was 52 to 129 for the former and 39 to 130 for the latter. When equated on the Sims scale, the range was 51 to 115 for the whites, and 41 to 130 for the Negroes. On the Binet, the two ranges were 51 to 125, and 51 to 130; on the Grace Arthur scale, 46 to 140, and 51 to 120, respectively. On three out of these four comparisons, one or more Negroes obtained higher scores than *any* of the whites; on two out of the four, one or more whites obtained scores as low as, or lower than, those of *any* Negro.

Let us suppose for the purpose of this argument (a supposition for which I perceive no acceptable evidence) that there is a difference in averages due to genetic factors. What about the individuals who "overlap?" I learned my statistics from a good teacher, a former psychologist at Columbia University, who kept reminding us not to forget the *range* when we compared two distributions. We were both students of that wise man, R. S. Woodworth, for whom the essence of psychology, as I understood him, was the behavior and characteristics of the *individual*. In one of his tests (1929) he defined psychology as the scientific study of the activities of the individual.

It is perhaps beyond the scope of this paper to consider the practical implications of psychological research on Negro-white differences and similarities, but I hope I may be permitted one observation. Lines of demarcation between groups of people, in employment, in education, in opportunities for development, based on alleged differences in averages which are essentially abstractions, do violence to the facts of individual capacities and potentialities. At the most, group differences are obscure and uncertain; we are faced with the living reality of individual human beings who have a right to the opportunity to show what they can do when they are given an equal chance. Perhaps I am allowing my own value system to influence me to look at the whole range of individual variations and not just at averages. I should have thought, however, that concern with the individual represented one value on which all psychologists might find themselves in agreement.

CONCLUSION

I can only conclude that there is no scientifically acceptable evidence for the view that ethnic groups differ in innate abilities. *This is not the same as saying that there are no ethnic differences in such abilities.* In the first place, I do not feel that mental tests can by themselves alone be used to prove this negative proposition. Perhaps in the future new techniques will be developed, better than our present tests, less subject to possible variations in interpretation, more conclusive in their results. I doubt that this would really change the picture, but the possibility must be kept open. Secondly, it is exceedingly difficult ever to prove the absence of something, because one can never be certain that all the relevant factors have been taken into account. We can, however, say to those who have claimed to find evidence for ethnic differences in innate mentality: You have not proved your case. You have not been able to demonstrate that such differences exist.

We can go a little farther than that. We can point to the improvement in achievement when conditions of life improve. We can emphasize the tremendous variations within each ethnic group, much greater than the differences between groups even under discrepant environmental stimulation. We can insist that since innate psychological differences between ethnic groups have never been satisfactorily demonstrated, we have no right to act as if they had been. The science of psychology can offer no support to those who see in the accident of inherited skin color or other physical characteristics any excuse for denying to individuals the right to full participation in American democracy.

REFERENCES

Anastasi, Anne. *Differential psychology.* (3rd ed.) New York: Macmillan, 1958.

Anastasi, Anne, & d'Angelo, R. Y. A comparison of Negro and white preschool children in language development and Goodenough Draw-a-Man IQ. *J. genet. Psychol.,* 1952, *81,* 147–165.

Bruce, M. Factors affecting intelligence test performance of whites and Negroes in the rural South. *Arch. Psychol., N. Y.,* 1940, No. 252.

Carmichael, O. Television Program of Sept. 13, 1959. Report, Dec. 15, 1959, Southern Regional Council, Atlanta.

Chant, S. N. F., & Freedman, S. S. A quantitative comparison of the nationality preferences of two groups. *J. soc. Psychol.,* 1934, *5,* 116–120.

Clark, W. W. Los Angeles Negro children. *Educ. Res. Bull., Los Angeles,* 1923, *3*(2), 1–2.

Dreger, R. M., & Miller, K. S. Comparative psychological studies of Negroes and whites in the United States. *Psychol. Bull.,* 1960, *57,* 361–402.

Garrett, H. E., & Schneck, M. R. *Psychological tests, methods and results.* New York: Harper's, 1933.

Gilliland, A. R. Socioeconomic status and race as factors in infant intelligence test scores. *Child Developm.,* 1951, *22,* 271–273.

Klineberg, O. *Negro intelligence and selective migration.* New York: Columbia Univer. Press, 1935.

Klineberg, O. (Ed.) *Characteristics of the American Negro.* New York: Harper, 1944.

Knobloch, H., & Pasamanick, B. Further observations on the behavioral development of Negro children. *J. genet. Psychol.,* 1953, *83,* 137–157.

Lee, E. S. Negro intelligence and selective migration: A Philadelphia test of Klineberg's hypothesis. *Amer. sociol. Rev.,* 1951, *61,* 227–233.

McGraw, M. B. A comparative study of a group of southern white and Negro infants. *Genet. Psychol. Monogr.,* 1931, *10,* 1–105.

McGurk, F. C. J. *Comparison of the performance of Negro and white high school seniors on cultural and noncultural psychological test questions.* Washington, D.C.: Catholic Univer. of America Press, 1951.

Pasamanick, B. A comparative study of the educational development of Negro infants. *J. genet. Psychol.,* 1946, *69,* 3–44.

Pasamanick, B., & Knobloch, H. Early language behavior in Negro children and the testing of intelligence. *J. abnorm. soc. Psychol.,* 1955, *50,* 401–402.

Sherman, M., & Key, C. B. The intelligence of isolated mountain children. *Child Developm.,* 1932, *3,* 279–290.

Shuey, A. M. *The testing of Negro intelligence.* Lynchburg, Va.: J. P. Bell, 1958.

Stallings, F. H. Atlanta and Washington: Racial differences in academic achievement. Report No. L-16, Feb. 26, 1960, Southern Regional Council, Atlanta.

Tanser, H. A. *The settlement of Negroes in Kent County, Ontario, and a study of the mental capacity of their descendants.* Chatham, Ont.: Shepherd, 1939.

Woodworth, R. S. *Psychology.* (Rev. ed.) New York: Holt, 1929

39 PSYCHOMETRIC SCIENTISM

Banesh Hoffmann

Although this article is concerned primarily with academic testing, it has wider implications. First let us be clear on a crucial point: There is no generally satisfactory method of evaluating human abilities and capabilities, though occasionally it can be done individually with remarkable prescience. Rough, superficial evaluations are of course possible, and they can be made on a mass production basis. But the detection and evaluation of other than superficial ability is inevitably an art demanding insight, taste, and knowledge. Current attempts to reduce it to a science and then mechanize it are not only dangerous but in a profound sense unscientific.

These are hard words, and it would be too much to expect psychometrists to find them pleasing. Yet the psychometrists defensive reaction to past criticism has been unfortunate. By it the psychometrists have not only prevented a significant confrontation of issues; they have unwittingly advertised their own insecurity.

Most of the weaknesses of psychometrists' current methods have to do with the manner

in which they use statistics. They seem unaware of the fallacies in their procedures. To illustrate some of these, consider the following skeleton of a multiple-choice question. One is required, essentially, to say which one of the words, if any, in the following sentence makes it defective and should thus be changed:

Among them Tom and Dick could not find enough money.

It does not take long to pick *among* on the ground that Tom and Dick are two persons and the preposition should therefore be *between.* On a pretest of this question the statistics would strongly support this as the key.

But if one pauses just a little to think—and has the ability to do so—one concludes that the question is ambiguous. For Tom and Dick might have been holding up a large group at gunpoint and "among *them*" could not find enough money.

Would this ambiguity show up in the statistics? Think carefully before you answer. There is a trap in all of this. I have tried this question verbally on various groups. Some people, unaware that *among* and *between* mean different things, see nothing wrong with the sentence. The question discriminates excellently between these people (call them Group I—for ignorant) and those who say *among* should be *between* (call them Group K—for knowledgeable). Only a small percentage of the people seem to see the alternative meaning fairly quickly and to conclude therefore that the question is ambiguous (call them Group D—for deep). Since Group D is small, it has no great effect on the pretest statistics. These statistics, therefore, will not reveal to the test-maker that the question is defective.

Psychometrists would do well to concede this point. For the question is a close paraphrase of an actual item on a test made by a leading test-making organization, and if the psychometrists insist that the pretest statistics would indeed reveal the above defect, they will imply that the test-makers deliberately used a question that their pretest statistics showed to be defective.

That would put the psychometrists in an untenable position. But the alternative is also untenable. For if the pretest statistics failed to reveal the defect here, in a by no means untypical situation, we have the following important theorem: *pretest statistics are significantly misleading.*

Test-makers sometimes argue that they do not rely solely on pretest statistics to eliminate defective items: that they also use their own judgment and that of their expert consultants in the subject of the test. But the fact that defective questions nevertheless appear on tests—and not rarely—shows that this judgment too is by no means to be relied on. Because space does not permit a full analysis of this point, I confine myself to two reasons.

One is that the testers and their expert consultants often know beforehand which is the wanted answer, and this destroys their objectivity. Another is that they have a psychological set as to the answer they think would be wanted even when they are not told which one it is. Since the testers may believe that they can make the necessary allowances for this and thus retain objectivity, I should like to demonstrate here that this is almost certainly not the case.

For the purposes of this demonstration let us return to the question about Tom and Dick and the word "among." We said that deep people quickly decide that the question is ambiguous. But in fact the question is logically *not* ambiguous. There is no ambiguity in it at

all—except, of course, for doubts we may have as to what is in the tester's mind. Not only is there only one logically correct answer, but that answer is different from the keyed answer. Why? Because *the sentence is a good sentence as it stands.* It reads, "Among them Tom and Dick could not find enough money," and the word "among" shows that "them" does not refer to Tom and Dick but to a larger group. True, we also get a good sentence—though one with a different meaning—if we change "among" to "between," just as we would if we changed "Dick" to "Harry" or "money" to "food," but such possible changes are irrelevant. The fact remains that the given sentence is good as it stands and therefore the only logically correct response—as distinguished from the officially wanted response—is to leave the sentence unchanged.

In my experience with this question, only an extremely small percentage of people (call them Group P—for profound) realize this on their own. Why do so many people miss it? Why do most readers feel that the matter has been fully discussed at the Group D stage and thus believe the question ambiguous? Because of their psychological set. They sense what is in the tester's mind and they cannot easily rid their own minds of the bias this induces—despite my early mention of a trap.

So much for the demonstration. But there are further important conclusions to be drawn from the above. One is a deepening of the theorem that pretest statistics are significantly misleading, for those statistics would not reveal this new and crucial facet of the item. The other major point is that the item itself fails to discriminate between members of Group I (for ignorant) and of Group P (for profound) but gives them all the same score of zero.

Though the preceding considerations were illustrated in terms of a single item, they are of general validity. They demonstrate fundamental defects in current psychometric procedures and are part of the reason for the choice of the title of this article. They are not the most important defects, though, as we shall see.

Why do the pretest statistics perform so badly on this question, and thus on many others? There are two main reasons. First, in the usual statistical sample, the percentage of people in Group P, and even in Group D, is apt to be very small. These people thus have little effect on the statistics—a fact that is particularly unfortunate because we would do better to cherish such people for their depth than to dismiss them, as at present, as a negligible minority of statistical misfits.

The second reason is that the process of statistical pretesting suffers from the fundamental deficiency of the mechanized, multiple-choice tests themselves: It concentrates solely on the choices of answers and ignores the reasons for these choices. Even though the tests themselves ignore the reasons for choices, the sensible thing would surely be to pretest the items by asking not just for the choices but for the reasons. In this way many major defects visible to, say, one percent of the students, and thus undetected statistically, would become sharply evident to any sufficiently intelligent psychometrist who cared—or dared—to look at the reasons. Besides, this would open his eyes, if they were not already opened, to the extraordinary variety of reasons, both good and bad, for making particular choices. Indeed, psychometrists who have never looked seriously into students' reasons for their choices would find this a most salutary experience, because it would strikingly exhibit once again one of the fundamental fallacies we have discussed of the standard multiple-choice method of testing.

I hope no reader will react with the argument that statistical validation is empirical, that the pretest should be concerned solely with the responses under test conditions, or that there is no need to be concerned about a mere one percent or so of the students.

There are, of course, dangerous fallacies in such arguments. Only exceptional students are apt to see the deeper defects of test items. Since these important people form a small minority, both the pretest statistics and the validation statistics, as currently used, are insensitive to their presence; and since these exceptional students often pick better answers than the official so-called "best" answers that are supported by the mass statistics, these very statistics contain a built-in bias against the deep students. Clearly, if both the pretest statistics and the validation statistics contain this bias, so do the tests themselves.

This bias can be traced in part to the fallacy of giving all students the same statistical weight. It is not an easy fallacy to avoid on a purely statistical basis. To give greater weight to students who scored high on the test, for example, would amount merely to statistical inbreeding. It would intensify the bias rather than diminish it, and there seems to be no way to break the vicious circle without going outside the pseudo-science of the usual statistical analysis of pretest responses to items and the usual statistical method of validation.

The principal objection to mechanized testing as currently practiced, and indeed to the general procedures of the multiple-choice psychometrists, is the fallacy of the statistical criterion. This goes beyond the matters of misguidance and bias discussed above. It has to do with the limitations of statistics themselves. To bring in statistics, one must first quantify, however crudely. Until something has been somehow reduced to numbers it cannot be handled statistically.

Of course, anything can be reduced to numbers; for example, a person can be represented by his social security number. But important aspects of ability resist routine meaningful quantification, and with most of the important aspects that might be squeezed into a numerical mold, the complexity of the task and the imprecision of the results would seem, to the multiple-choice psychometrist, hardly to justify the labor involved.

Acordingly, the multiple-choice psychometrist confines himself, in the name of Science, to those criteria that he can readily reduce to statistical form, and closes his eyes to criteria that require subtle evaluation, even though just those criteria are apt to be the important ones. By so doing, he introduces a further and graver bias in his statistical criteria, this one arising from the very fact that the criteria he uses are purely statistical.

That is the first part of the fallacy of the statistical criterion. But there is a second part that is far more important: Not only does the statistical criterion ignore crucial aspects of ability; it also ignores the side effects of the tests.

Gifted teachers well know, for example, that the prevalence of mechanized tests corrupts education. But the multiple-choice psychometrist brushes such things aside and evaluates tests by means of their reliability and validity correlation coefficients. In so doing he believes he is behaving scientifically. When pressed, he asks for statistical evidence of the side effects before he, as a Scientist, will believe they exist. Yet he can easily obtain evidence that undesirable side effects exist, if only he can gain the confidence of gifted teachers and gifted students so that they will talk to him freely. He might be surprised to learn, for example, that such teachers often feel it necessary to warn precisely their intellectually liveliest students not to think too precisely or deeply when taking mechanized tests. The causes of the corruption of education by mechanized tests are many. Among them are such things as the use of ambiguity as a substitute for worthwhile difficulty, the fostering of intellectual dishonesty, the ignoring of taste, style, and quality of reasoning, the rewarding of superficiality, the penalizing of depth, and so on. The list is a long one, and not the least items in it are the evaluation of educational experiments by means of such tests, and the sheer poor quality of actual test questions.

If multiple-choice tests corrupt education, their worth certainly cannot be properly evaluated by statistical criteria that ignore this and other far from negligible side effects.

It is no defense to say, as has been said, that the only function of a test is to test, and that a test can indeed be properly evaluated solely by means of such statistical criteria as validity correlation coefficients. The fallacy of a pseudo-scientific argument of this sort is easily seen by applying it to a test for the presence of cancer. By the statistical criterion of validity the best method of testing would be to kill the patient and perform a post-mortem—indeed, there would be no statistical advantage at all in killing him painlessly.

Evaluating the merits of different types of tests is not as simple as multiple-choice psychometrists seem to imagine. To confine oneself to simple correlation coefficients, costs per pupil, and other narrow figures of merit, while ignoring not only the inherent biases in the statistics but also the crucial side effects of the tests, is hardly to be scientific. I hope that those psychometrists who are aware of this will forgive my underlining the obvious, but my experiences with psychometrists lead me to believe that far too many of them and of their supporters are unaware how treacherous are the grounds on which they conduct their activities and reach their conclusions.

So much, for the time being, for the overall objections to the methods and philosophy of multiple-choice psychometrists. Let us now consider some particular instances of unscientific behavior—some lesser errors of important testers.

It is generally agreed that for almost all testing of high-level ability the true-false format is much inferior to the multiple-choice one. In seeking outstanding scientific talent, the inferiority of true-false questions to multiple-choice questions would seem unquestionable. Let us assume that it is indeed unquestionable.

For years the Westinghouse Science Talent Search used tests that were almost entirely, if not entirely, of the multiple-choice type, each question having one so-called "best" answer and four unwanted ones. To increase the separation of the scores at the top, the testers have recently changed the format. There are still five choices per question, but now an unspecified number of them may be "right," the number varying from question to question. To score other than zero on the question the candidate has to select all those of the five choices that are keyed as correct and reject all those that are keyed as incorrect. Naturally, this cuts down significantly on the scores and, as intended, increases the separation at the top. But is it an improvement?

The format is still ostensibly multiple-choice, since each question is followed by five choices. But in answering such a question the student is now really answering not just one multiple-choice item but five true-false items. This in itself is bad enough. But there is worse. For if the student gets even one of the five wrong—that is, wrong according to the key—he scores zero on all five. Surely it is obvious that this is a major regression. To go from multiple-choice to true-false items is certainly no improvement. But to score the true-false questions in batches of five, and to give credit only if all five are answered in agreement with the key, with no partial credit even if four out of the five are so answered—that is an incredible mockery of both sense and science. That the psychometrists who have done this thing do not hold true-false questions in high esteem is shown by their insistence on grouping the questions into sets of five, even though this makes nonsense of the scoring. They will not candidly present the questions as isolated true-false items. If they did, and then announced that the scoring would be by batches of five, the absurdity of the procedure would be manifest even to themselves. What they have done may not be a major crime, but it does qualify at least as psychometric misbehavior.

The Science Talent Search test, in its new form, is the most glaring instance of the use of disguised true-false questions scored in batches, for in this test all the questions are now of this sort. But one finds analogous questions on many other important tests, including College Entrance Examination Board tests and Graduate Record Examinations. One method is to give three statements followed by eight choices running through the various combinations of true and false for each statement. And there are variants that amount to much the same thing basically but have further objectionable features into which I shall not enter here.

I have already mentioned the sheer poor quality of test items, and a few remarks on the subject of quality will not be irrelevant. After all, test items made by leading test-making organizations are a product of what is widely regarded as an objective, scientific procedure, and if the quality of items leaves something to be desired it is an indication if not of the quality of the procedure then at least of that of some of its leading practitioners and thus of the fallibility of the procedure itself.

Because of the almost complete refusal of leading test-making organizations to permit verbatim publication of actual test items, I have, in my various writings on the subject, had to confine myself almost entirely to their official sample questions. Several instances are given in my book.[1]

In a more recent article[2] I exhibited and analyzed in detail four seriously defective questions taken from the most recent booklet then available[3] describing the College Entrance Examination Board's *Scholastic Aptitude Test*. Though the College Board had every opportunity, in its response to the

article,[4] to deny that the four questions were seriously defective, it did not do so. We may take it as a reasonable conclusion, therefore, that the questions were indeed seriously defective.

Since the booklet contained 127 sample questions, a psychometrist, in conversation, made the point that four out of 127 is only about three percent and thus of little consequence, a view that others may be inclined to share. Let me explain, therefore, why the four defective questions loom much larger than this simple statistic suggests.

Of the 127 sample questions, 76 pertained to verbal aptitude and the other 51 to mathematical aptitude. The four defective sample questions were chosen solely from the 76 verbal aptitude ones, and four out of 76 is approximately five percent.

Perhaps there are some multiple-choice psychometrists who can bring themselves to look with equanimity on the presence in a College Board booklet of even five percent of seriously defective verbal aptitude sample questions. But there were more than just four defective sample questions dealing with verbal aptitude. The 76 verbal aptitude questions were of only four different types. The four seriously defective sample questions that I analyzed were selected to fulfill three conditions simultaneously. First, there had to be one question of each type; second, each question had to illustrate a different sort of defect; and third, the defect had to be so sharply defined that my detailed critical analysis of it would be logically unassailable.

Is it likely that only four of the sample questions were defective, and that by the merest chance they happened to meet these three stringent criteria? Enough, then, of the argument, all too often put forward, that the number of defective questions in tests made by leading test-making organizations is negligible.

To make a strong case, I have, in my various writings, directed my main criticisms of sample questions, procedures, and the like against the College Board and Educational Testing Service because I regard them as among the very best major organizations in the field, and I say this in all sincerity. If

1 Banesh Hoffmann, *The Tyranny of Testing*. New York: Crowell-Collier, 1962; Collier Books, 1964.

2 Banesh Hoffmann "The College Boards Fail the Test," *The New York Times Magazine*, October 24, 1965, p. 52. See also "College Boards and Our Nation's Scholastic Profile," Extension of Remarks of Hon. Lee Metcalf, October 22, 1965, *The Congressional Record*, October 27, 1965.

3 *A Description of the College Board Scholastic Aptitude Test*, College Entrance Examination Board, Princeton, N.J., 1964.

4 Richard Pearson (President, College Entrance Examination Board), *The New York Times Magazine*, November 7, 1965, p. 40.

their influential booklets contain defective sample questions, do not the booklets themselves set an example of intellectual quality that contributes in its own way to that corruption of education to which I have already referred?

Nothing I say here is to be construed as implying that ETS and the College Board are inferior to analogous organizations that I have not discussed. To be fair, let me mention briefly the Selective Service pamphlet describing the draft deferment test made by Science Research Associates, now a subsidiary of IBM. The problems of draft deferment are many and profound, and the officials whose unenviable task it is to struggle with them deserve our fullest support. My remarks here are concerned solely with the technical quality of the 30 sample questions in the pamphlet. I have specified elsewhere[5] three of these questions that were defective, each in a different way, and three is 10 percent of the supply. In a situation of such national importance, one would hope that special pains would have been taken to make the sample questions impeccable. That it should be possible to take significant exception to 10 percent of them is surely unfortunate enough. Yet the situation is actually markedly worse than this, since there are more like 20 percent of such questions among the samples. One wonders how the test itself, in its various forms, compares in quality with the samples, but, if my understanding of the situation is correct, the test itself will not be released even after its use is discontinued.

I come now to my penultimate point. It concerns the reactions of psychometrists to criticisms. For brevity I shall confine myself to two incidents connected with my experiences with Educational Testing Service.

Having noticed a tendency of some psychometrists to try to overawe critics by citing statistics that were not always relevant, I devised a statistics-proof strategy to demonstrate that all was far from well in current testing. Exhibiting defective sample questions made by outstanding organizations, I challenged them to defend their own questions. In Chapters 16 and 17 of my book, I tell in full detail how ETS reacted to the challenge

in the case of two of their own sample questions in science taken from a College Board booklet.

In seeking to defend the first of these questions, ETS argued to the effect that the student who understood $E = mc^2$ ought to realize that he should ignore Einstein's formula in answering the question. Apparently ETS did not realize that, among other things, this was tantamount to an admission that the question penalized the superior student.

In seeking to defend the other question, ETS gave an invalid defense, made scientific errors, used an intendedly clinching argument that proved to be a boomerang; and, as if this were not enough, showed throughout its argument that it did not even understand what its own question was asking.

These are fully documented facts, and they have not been denied by ETS. Indeed, in a subsequent public debate an executive of ETS had the grace and the courage to admit their validity.

The point I wish to stress here is not the intellectual quality of the defenses, and I certainly am not implying that a competitor of ETS would have defended the questions more satisfactorily. No satisfactory defense was possible. The questions were manifestly defective. What I wish to stress is the fact that ETS, which has access to competent scientists, should have decided to attempt to defend the questions, and to do so in words suggesting that the questions were not in the least defective: that instead of frankly conceding that the questions were defective, it sought to brazen the matter out.

I realize how natural it is to react defensively. We all do it—even in matters of science. Certainly, in this case the reaction was neither scientific nor objective. One of its results has been to increase the logical vulnerability of ETS, and thus, because of the deservedly high standing of ETS, of multiple-choice testers in general. And when coupled with the behavior of others in connection with these and other matters, it can hardly be said to have strengthened the belief that psychometrists are scientists—despite the fact that scientists often behave unscientifically.

The second incident has to do with the penalizing of deep, subtle, creative students by multiple-choice and similar tests of convergent thinking. It is an old charge, but when I

5 Banesh Hoffmann, *The New York Times Magazine,* May 8, 1966, p. 36.

discussed it in detail with a group of ETS executives some 10 years ago they expressed doubt as to its validity, saying they would need to look into the matter experimentally.

In the 10 years since then I have repeatedly explained, among other things, how multiple-choice tests penalize depth, subtlety, and the like; and to make a strong case I have mainly used sample questions prepared by ETS. But ETS and other multiple-choice test-making organizations give the impression that they believe the charge is false. If the charge were false, the obvious strategy for ETS would have been to make experiments and prove it false forthwith. Yet there are reasons to believe from an article in *Science* by Chauncey and Hilton,[6] both of ETS, that as late as 1965 ETS had made no such experiments despite the seriousness of the charge.

I therefore pointed out in a letter to *Science*[7] that the charge that multiple-choice tests penalize depth, subtlety, and the like prevailed not only on its own merits but also by default.

If ETS had any evidence to offer against this charge of default, one would have expected it to have responded at once by presenting the evidence. But although the editor of *Science* specifically invited ETS to respond to my argument and to a criticism by another person, no official response from ETS was forthcoming. *Thus the original charge of default now itself prevails by default.*

Let me add a brief coda to this episode. An ETS study, only recently completed, of the validity of the Graduate-Record Examination Advanced Physics Test[8] showed that scores from about 625 to the top, while indicating superiority, gave so little discrimination among students with these scores that using the scores for discriminating among them might just as well be replaced by drawing lots.

My final point has to do with the behavior of ETS and the College Board in the matter of evaluating ability in English composition. It will bring me back from particular instances to my main thesis.

When, on the basis of experiment, ETS and the College Board gave up the use of essay examinations for evaluating ability in English composition, there was an outcry. To overawe the objectors, ETS and the College Board made an elaborate new experiment pitting an essay examination against both the SAT Verbal and their so-called "English Composition Test," which last involved no English composition. They found that the SAT Verbal had the highest statistical validity, the misbranded "English Composition Test" the next, and the essay test—called the General Composition Test—the lowest. They then used these validity statistics as a compelling argument for giving up essay examinations in the evaluation of ability in English composition. And by this display of pseudoscience they overawed the objectors and gained their point.

Some of you may take exception to my characterizing their procedure as pseudoscience. After all, was it not statistical and objective?

But note what happened next. Having overawed the objectors, ETS and the College Board, by their own actions, immediately repudiated their statistical argument. How? By retaining the misbranded "English Composition Test" that involved no English composition. Had they really believed in the statistical argument with which they had overawed the objectors, they would have had to give up not only the essay examination but also the misbranded "English Composition Test" and used the SAT Verbal instead—perhaps calling *it* the "English Composition Test." For had not the SAT Verbal come out best according to their statistical criterion? They have never given the SAT Verbal the name "English Composition Test," and one wonders why not. For if they were willing to call their non-essay test an "English Composition Test," then surely, according to their argument, the validity statistics should have been full scientific justification for giving that name to the SAT Verbal. If not, then the charge of misbranding stands.

I doubt that ETS and the College Board were aware of the illogic of their various actions in this matter. But the illogic does suggest that they were aware, at least subconsciously, of what I have been referring to as the fallacy of the statistical criterion.

Space does not permit a discussion of the

---

6 Henry Chauncey and Thomas H. Hilton, "Are Aptitude Tests Valid for the Highly Able?." *Science,* June 4, 1965, p. 1297.

7 Banesh Hoffmann, *Science,* July 16, 1965, p. 245.

8 Walter C. Michels, "Graduate-Record Examination Advanced Physics Test at a Predictor of Performance," *American Journal of Physics,* September, 1966, p. 362.

gradual reintroduction of essays and the illogic that has attended it. Nor of the recent ETS experiments that now show—statistically, of course—that essays are after all of value.

Let me proceed at once to the recent experiments on the grading of essays by computer,[9] these being sponsored by the College Board. The computer, of course, had no basis for judgment of its own. It had to have values fed into it by the programmer. How were these values arrived at? By scientism masquerading as objective science. From such things as the statistical analysis of samples of good prose, the experimenter obtained a plentiful yield of objective criteria: for example, the average length of sentence, the number of commas, the number of prepositions, the number of dashes, and other objective criteria too numerous to mention, each criterion having its established weighting factor.

Since a computer cannot understand, a student could bring in an essay on any subject, prepared so as to have just the right number and distribution of commas and the like. To prevent this, a list of relevant words was fed into the computer. Absence of such words would immediately reveal the deception, while the number of such words in the essay became a further criterion of merit, with its own statistical weighting.

9 Arther Daigan, "Computer Grading of English Composition," *English Journal*, January, 1966, p. 46; Ellis B. Page, "The Imminence of Grading Essays by Computer," PHI DELTA KAPPAN, January, 1966, p. 238.

When the computer produced ratings of essays that turned out to be *statistically* indistinguishable from those produced by experienced human graders, the experimenters were so delighted that they opened a bottle of champagne by way of celebration and rushed into print with arrogant pride.

That the essentials were missing was apparently of no concern. Since such crucial things as meaning, style, wit, whimsy, rhythm, emphasis, nuance, felicity of image, and the careful use of words could not be quantified, they could presumably be ignored as scientifically undefinable and thus of no interest to a true scientist.

According to the statistical criterion used by the experimenters, the computer itself could turn out gibberish that would rate higher than any man-made prose.

I have my own ideas as to the relative values of human and computer grading, and of their effects on the teaching of English composition, and on education in general. I find them far from comparable. My preference is, of course, a matter of taste, and yours may be diametrically opposite to mine. But we will surely agree that the two methods are widely dissimilar and that their effects on the identification and fostering of talent and on the whole of education would be widely different. *Yet the statistical criterion rates them as equal,* and it is in the basic fallacy of the statistical criterion that I see the major peril arising from the methodology of psychometry.

40. THE HUMAN USE OF PERSONALITY TESTS: A DISSENTING VIEW

Victor R. Lovell [1]

During the past 10 years, public resentment of personality testing has become increasingly evident (Amrine, 1965; Dailey, 1963; Gross, 1962; Hoffman, 1962; Packard, 1964; Whyte, 1956). Testimony has been given on the abuse of personality tests before the Senate Subcommittee on Constitutional Rights (1965) and the House Special Subcommittee on Invasion of Privacy of the Committee on Government Operations (1965). It seems evident that unless psychologists concerned with personality assessment voluntarily restrict their own activities in some fashion, they will soon be subject to legal restrictions. At this writing, one bill to set up such restrictions has already been introduced into the House of Representatives (Doctor, 1966).

The response of psychologists to this outcry has usually been to attribute it to public ignorance or political extremism (Amrine, 1965; Dailey, 1963; Vance, 1965). I think we have been somewhat fatuous in this matter. In my opinion, the protests we have heard, however ill informed and inarticulate they have been, are directed at misuses of psychology which are quite real and very serious, to which our vested interests have blinded us.

Fundamentally, I think the issue is one of reconciling three divergent interests: (*a*) the public's right to privacy; (*b*) the social sci-

1 I am indebted to my colleague, Norman S. Ciddan, for the benefit of numerous clarifying discussions on the problems with which this paper is concerned.

Victor R. Lovell: "The Human Use of Personality Tests: A Dissenting View"; AMERICAN PSYCHOLOGIST, 22 (1967), 383–393, Copyright 1967 by the American Psychological Association. Reprinted by permission of the American Psychological Association and the author.

entist's freedom of inquiry; and (*c*) the personnel worker's right to determine fitness for employment. Solutions, insofar as they have been proposed, have usually taken the direction of *restricting test content.* I do not think this tack can ever lead to any resolution of the basic conflicts involved.

The problem with restricting content is twofold. First, as is always the case with censorship, one does not know how to go about laying down concrete guidelines. Second, to do so will not offer adequate protection to the public, nor to the social scientist, nor to the personnel worker. Even if items dealing with sex, politics, and religion are deleted from personality inventories, the respondent's private thoughts are still likely to be probed. *Any* restriction of content is clearly an incursion on freedom of inquiry. Finally, determination of job qualifications may require the use of threatening stimuli, as, for example, when candidates for work in hospitals are given concept-formation tests involving pictures of horrible wounds.

An alternative to restricting content is to *restrict function.* Specifically, I am going to propose that certain kinds of tests should not be used in certain ways. I will lay down concrete guidelines for this proposal by arguing that certain kinds of "contracts" between assessors and respondents should be outlawed.

Basically, personality testing is used for two very different purposes, which I shall call the *personnel function* and the *client function.* I define the former as applying to situations where there is a potential conflict of interest between assessor and respondent, and the latter as applying to situations where there is not. The personnel function usually involves decisions about hiring, promotion, and termination. The client function usually involves providing services to the respondent. There are, however, important exceptions to these generalizations.

Where testing is purely for research purposes, we have the client function, except in situations where research subjects are coerced, deceived, or when their test results are not considered to be confidential, in which case we have the personnel function. The latter would include all research enterprises where participation by subjects is not voluntary. Testing serves a personnel function in all service situations where the respondent is not free to accept or reject services (as when he is committed to a mental hospital), or where he must qualify for them in some way other than by being able to pay for them (as when he is applying for welfare benefits).

THREE TEST CONTRACTS

Whether a particular assessment situation involves the client function or the personnel function becomes apparent when we examine the test contract involved. By "test contract," I mean whatever is understood between assessor and respondent. This involves some extension of the sense of "contract," since the term is usually restricted to voluntary agreements, and assessment often involves involuntary elements.

Suppose we should administer a personality inventory to a group of incoming freshmen at a college or university, and suppose the following message were to appear printed on the first inside page of the booklet which contains the test items:

To the Respondent:

We are asking you these questions because we really want to know what you think, and how you feel, and because we are convinced that it will contribute to your education in some small way for you to ask them of yourself.

The information we are asking you to give will be used in one or both of two ways. First, it may contribute to our research on the process of higher education and the character of youth in our contemporary world. Second, it may be used to help provide you with psychological services during your college career, if you should decide that you require them. It will not be used by others to make decisions about you, although it may contribute to help-

ing you make your own decisions more effectively.

If you take this inventory, the information you give us will be held in the strictest confidence. It will not be made available without your express permission (written, signed, and in our judgment uncoerced) to administrators, faculty members, parents, prospective employers, or anyone else except those on your campus whose primary obligation is to provide you with mental health or counseling services, or to do unbiased research in the social sciences.

When you take the inventory, we would like you to enter into a contract with us: *You don't try to fool us and we don't try to fool you.* The appropriate response to an item in this inventory is the one which you feel in your heart to be honest; the inappropriate one is the one which you know is not. If you do not feel that you can accept these terms, we would prefer that you did not take the inventory, for without this contract you will be wasting both your time and ours.

Since the inventory contains material which is personal and controversial, you should think carefully before deciding to take it. If you should decide not to, we shall understand and respect your decision.

If you do decide to take the inventory, we wish you a pleasant and provocative exercise in self-discovery. We hope that this experience will move you a little closer to that intimate self-knowledge which has always been one of the primary goals of higher education.

Good luck!

Signed,
(the test authors)

We shall call this message the *client contract.* Now suppose instead this message appears:

To the Respondent:

Because of the complexity of the technical considerations involved, and the limited space available here, it is not possible for us to explain to you the nature of this psychological assessment. We assure you that it is being done for sound reasons, and that nothing is being demanded of you capriciously.

The information you give us will be used in many very important ways. It will become a part of your permanent academic record. It may influence critical decisions which others will have to make about your career. It will be made available in various forms to administrators, faculty members, parents, prospective employers, and others who have a vital interest in your character and your welfare.

Make your test responses as honestly as you can. It will not be in your best interest to do otherwise. If you should try to slant your answers so as to make a more favorable impression than is justified, this will become apparent to us when we score your test, and will reflect badly upon you.

Be conscientious and be careful!

Signed,

(the test authors)

We shall call this message the *strong personnel contract*.

Finally, consider a third message:

To the Respondent:

Because of the complexity of the technical considerations involved, the limited space available here, and the uses to which the material is to be put, it is not possible for us to explain to you the nature of this psychological assessment. We assure that it is being done for sound reasons, and that nothing is being demanded of you capriciously.

The information which we will gain from this test will be used in many very important ways. It will become a part of your permanent academic record. It may influence critical decisions which others will have to make about your career. It will be made available in various forms to administrators, faculty-members, prospective employers, parents, and others who have a vital interest in your character and your welfare.

You may try to slant your test answers so as to create a favorable impression. We will take this into consideration when we score your test. Your ability to create a favorable impression is of great interest to us, for it is likely to contribute much to your success or failure in a great many life situations. If you don't want to play this game with us, you can probably get away with refusing to take this test, if you really want to push it. We will try to make it as hard as possible for you to do so, because our boss wants you tested, and we work for him, and not for you.

We have to live too!

Signed,

(the test authors)

We shall call this message the *weak personnel contract*.

TEST CONTRACTS AND TEST STANDARDIZATION

The three examples given above represent the major alternatives available to the psychologist when he administers a personality assessment program. For the sake of brevity, the research contract and the counseling con-

tract have been fused into one. It should be clear that current practice seldom involves making the nature of the situation explicit to the respondent. Typically, in the kind of situation alluded to above, the freshman class would be herded into an auditorium at some time during a crowded "orientation week," handed the test materials, and told to follow the simple instructions printed thereon. If someone should object, it is likely to be communicated to him that he is a trouble maker who has no business questioning the wisdom of professional people who obviously have only his best interests at heart.

The first point I should like to make is that, both as individuals involved in the administration of assessment programs and, I am convinced, eventually as a profession, we must choose between the alternatives suggested above, and we must make them explicit to the respondent. If we do not, we shall not be able to validate our assessment instruments in any very broad and profound fashion, because we shall not be able to maintain standard and uniform testing conditions. No matter what validation data we may have about our hypothetical personality inventory, if these data have been gathered under the client contract, we shall have difficulty making valid inferences about the meaning of test scores acquired under conditions where a personnel contract was involved. Further, if the testing actually serves a personnel function, the effect of personnel decisions will probably be a feeding back of information into the respondent population, which will alter the relationship of test variables with critical nontest variables; that is to say, people will become test wise and validity will vanish. For a discussion of the relationship between test validity and test situations, see Sarason (1950).

It has traditionally been argued that where the message making explicit the testing contract (or lack of such) is withheld, the respondent will make his own idiosyncratic interpretation of the situation, and that this interpretation, as manifested in his responses, will be indicative of broad and enduring traits of character in which the assessor is interested. While this argument is based on what is perhaps one of the most profound ideas in psychological assessment, its specific application to the *assessment contract* is naïve and wrongheaded. This is because most situations in which personality tests are administered are in fact highly structured. The respondent may be expected to infer the rules and goals of the game from the context in which it is played, even if they are not articulated by the assessors. In other words, variance due to interpretation of the test contract is probably mostly situational, rather than individual, in its determination.

If a man is applying for a job, and we give him a test, he does not need to be told that the success of his application is contingent on his responses (although present ethical standards state that he should be). He reasonably assumes that we would not do it if it were not good business, and he knows that the task at hand is to decide whether or not to hire him. If we in fact tested the job applicant for some other purpose, such as to decide where in the organization he might best be placed, we would run some danger of defeating ourselves, for our validity data would probably be based on the responses of men already placed, rather than on job applicants.

In the freshman testing situation described above, the respondent has spent a good deal of time during the past weeks providing information for various administrative records. Further, he has just spent the past year providing information to admissions officers, on the basis of which various critical decisions about his life have been made. It is unlikely to make much difference if a client contract is in fact the intention of the assessors. Even if independent psychological services exist on the campus, he will not come to the conclusion that they do, and he will infer a personnel contract.

I hold that eventually we must choose among the client contract, the strong personnel contract, and the weak personnel contract, not only for specific instruments and specific assessment programs, but also, as a profession, for all "personality tests." This is because each time any one of us administers a personality test, he is participating in the creation of a cultural institution. Which test contract is understood by the respondent depends not only upon what cues are present in the testing situation, nor upon the immediate institutional context which surrounds it, but also upon the respondent's general understanding of the legitimate functions of personality assessment in his society. If one looks

at what is said about personality tests, one gets the impression that, outside the private practice of psychology, with individual clients, the weak personnel contract is fast becoming normative, both from the point of view of the lay public, and from the point of view of professional psychologists. If we do not make the decision, it will be made for us as a result of the institutional processes in which we are involved. I am concerned lest it be already too late for a rational and considered choice to be possible.

If the reader has followed the argument thus far, three questions are likely to come to mind. First, what sort of contract with the respondent is most consistent with the ethical practice of psychology? Second, what sort of contract is most likely to lead in the long run to the valid measurement of personality? And third, what contract will allow us to offer the community the broadest range of psychological services?

In the remainder of this essay, I shall argue for a client contract on all three counts. I shall further take the view that our three questions cannot ultimately be considered independently from one another, because ethics, science, and services are all outcomes of a single activity, and this activity is one of many interdependent components of a unitary social process. One cannot do something ethically, if one cannot do it at all. We cannot use our personality tests to provide psychological services if we are unable to construct valid measures. And, as I have already tried to suggest comparing sample contracts, the validity of our tests is not independent of our ethics, because our ethics supply the social context in which our tests are administered, and in which they are validated.

TEST CONTRACTS AND ETHICS

In its public manifestos, the profession of psychology is firmly committed to political democracy, civil liberties, and the dignity of the individual. In practice, we sometimes violate these commitments, on behalf of bureaucratic or commercial interests. I do not believe that the strong personnel contract has any place in a free society, and I think that its occasional appearance is psychology's unique contribution to creeping totalitarianism in our times.

The strong personnel contract flatly denies the respondent's right to privacy. It proposes that kind of total surveillance of the individual which is characteristic of police states. Further, the strong personnel contract reeks with paternalism. It suggests total supervision as well as total surveillance. Finally, it creates the conditions for mutual suspicion and distrust among men. It invokes the possibility that deceit, if successful, may be richly rewarded, while at the same time threatening dire consequences if it is not.

The weak personnel contract might be considered ethically marginal. It is not a clear-cut invasion of privacy. It neither demands truth, nor threatens falsehood. Surveillance is more limited to that which is directly relevant, for to the degree to which the goal of the respondent's task is made clear, the test could be considered a work sample. Like the strong personnel contract, however, it is paternalistic (perhaps "maternalistic" would be more exact). It implies that those in positions of authority need not account to the public for their actions, and that their decisions must be taken on faith. Finally, the weak personnel contract, if received sufficiently often, will contribute in some small part to undermining the foundations of democratic process, for the efficacy of that process depends upon the authentic confrontation by the citizenry of each other, in order that their collective will may be determined. Since the weak personnel contract promises to reward conformity, it may discourage the articulation of loyal opposition, if it is true that what is learned in social situations is widely generalized.

The client contract protects the right to privacy, for it guarantees confidentiality, specifies the limits of confidence, and invites the respondent to decline to take the test if this is not satisfactory. It leaves him in a good position to make his decision, since it states the nature of the assessment, and indicates the possible benefits of making the choice to participate. Finally, it attempts to promote the kind of human relationships which contribute to harmonious living in a free and open community.

Although Messick (1965) suggests that, "We should be especially careful not to let it be inferred that any change in our standards for psychological assessment necessarily reflects a general admission of past guilt [p.

137]," both the strong and the weak personnel contracts are quite permissible under present APA (1963) Ethical Standards, which simply state that:

> The psychologist who asks that an individual reveal personal information in the course of interviewing, testing, or evaluation, or who allows such information to be divulged to him, does so only after making certain that the responsible person is fully aware of the purpose of the interview, testing or evaluation and of the ways in which the information may be used [Principle 7d, p. 57].

This is analogous to the legal principle which demands that the accused be informed that anything he says may be held against him, but the analogy is not carried out consistently. The accused may not decline to testify against himself. His psychological interrogator need obtain no search warrant in order to examine his psyche.

PRIVACY AND DUPLICITY

Two related ethical themes arise when the proper use of personality tests is considered: *privacy* and *duplicity*. If the assessor is bound by no contraints in his invasions of the former, then the respondent is sure to react with the latter, and the assessor must outwit him by the use of *counterduplicity*. This is a particularly messy business, because the respondent is not typically asked to testify as to objective matters of fact, but rather to the status of his attitudes, impulses, memories, emotions, and so forth. Because of this, his testimony cannot be independently corroborated. It may be examined for its internal consistency, but this is not relevant in the way that it would be, say in a legal situation, because consistency is not necessarily a property of attitudes, impulses, memories, emotions, etc.

It is sometimes suggested that this impasse may be resolved scientifically, rather than ethically. We need only investigate duplicity as a behavioral phenomenon, and when we have come to understand it, our subjects will not be able to deceive us. This line of thought springs from the notion that social science can function outside the social contract, without reference to moral concepts. All experimenters have moral commitments, however, just as all experimenters are either male or female, and I think it reasonable to expect the former to be as much involved in determining the behavior of subjects as the latter.

Once the respondent and the assessor have entered into a contract which permits them to deceive each other, it is difficult to see how any operational meaning can be given to the notion of duplicity. In order to investigate duplicity, the assessor must have some way of determining its presence or absence, but this requires that the declarations of the respondent be in some way corroborated, and we have seen that it is not clear how this is to be done. Even if the responses of the subject are recorded under conditions where it is believed that he is not aware of being observed, the authenticity of his behavior will be hard to establish, because this belief may be mistaken, and the observer is involved in a social game which leaves him no way to check up on himself.

However, even though duplicity is neither observed nor understood, administration of personality tests accompanied by a personnel contract might make it possible to validly predict some very critical events in which someone had a legitimate interest. The question of whether it is likely that this *can* be done will be taken up at a later point. The question at hand is whether it *should* be done.

Those who think it should often espouse what might be called the "hired-gun ethic." Duplicity in human relations, particularly in the presentation of one's own character to others, seems to be a common and pervasive characteristic of human society in general and personnel situations in particular. As long as this sort of thing is going to go on, the game might as well be played as well as possible by all concerned. It is not the business of professional psychologists either to rebel against the human condition, or to make policy for their employers. A similar defense is usually given by scientists and technicians involved in the design and production of war machines intended for the destruction of human property and human life.

Another kind of cold war could result. Some psychologists will make it their business to devise ever more complex and subtle ways of tricking their unwilling victims into revealing themselves. Others will offer their services as coaches to the respondent, to help him outwit the assessor. It is difficult to see how the enterprise of measuring individual differences could survive such a social holocaust, or how the individual would retain a voice in the conduct of his society. Actually, the orthodox version of the hired-gun ethic usually assumes that it is ethical for the psychologist to help the personnel worker to deceive the respondent, but not vice versa. The reasons for this bias are commercial, not ethical. So far, respondent coaching has been by nonpsychologists (Alex, 1965; Whyte, 1956).

In a nation where private enterprise is the dominant form of economic organization, it may be argued that while public agencies may be restricted, private institutions should be allowed to handle their personnel problems as they see fit, and therefore that professional psychologists who are employed by them should feel free to help them do so. A little thought should convince one that this is not so. Under our present system, hiring and firing practices are regulated by ethics and by legislation, just as working conditions are. To deny that this is as it should be would be to argue, for example, that personnel workers should be able to tap the telephone lines of job applicants, or inject them with truth serums.

ETHICS, PREJUDICE, AND PATERNALISM

It is sometimes argued that the use of personality tests in selection is equalitarian in effect, if not libertarian in method. The advent of abilities tests as selection devices contributed a great deal to the leveling of barriers to social mobility in our society. It tended to make advancement more dependent on merit, and less on privilege. It has been claimed that personality tests, if used in the same fashion, may do the same. I think it is more likely that they will have the opposite effect. The correlation between personality traits and demographic variables such as social class, caste, and religious persuasion is well known.

Suppose a personality inventory contained the following item:

I am a Negro.   (T)   (F)

As social scientists, we know that this item would be a valid predictor of all sorts of critical social outcomes in which the personnel worker has a legitimate interest, such as whether or not the respondent's conduct is likely to be criminal. However, we also know that the validity of the item would depend upon the operation of social forces the existence of which most of us deplore. Few of us would use this item if we could, because we would recognize that to do so would help perpetuate those social forces. Our prediction would be self-fulfilling, and contribute to the maintenance of barriers to social mobility. Yet it is probable that whenever we use personality tests in selection, we capitalize upon, and perpetuate, all sorts of prejudices, more subtle, less well understood, and perhaps more profound and in the very long run even more destructive than those regarding race. No matter how inclined we might be to use brute empiricism with our prediction problems, Federal law would prohibit us from using the item above. However, for the most part, the choice of what test content to use for what assessment purpose is presently left to our own discretion, as well as the use we make of such. I suggest that we should exercise discretion, before this choice is taken away from us by a justifiably resentful public.

It is often pointed out that effective selection may protect the respondent from being put in a situation where he will fail, or where he will be uncomfortable. If the information necessary to do this must be extracted from him without his consent, is it not doing him a service to extract it? The trouble with this view is that it presupposes a paternalistic view of society which seems hardly compatible with the democratic values to which we are committed. In order to afford the respondent this kind of "protection," someone else has to decide what is good for him. In some areas, it makes sense to do this. A doctor does not usually feel the need to ask permission to save a patient's life; he assumes that the patient wants to live. But in the area of physical well-being there are norms with which it can be safely assumed that almost everyone will agree. In the area of emotional well-being there are no such norms.

TEST CONTRACTS AND TEST VALIDITY

Our grandiosity in assuming that we can measure people who we can safely assume do not wish to be measured barely conceals our manifest failure, at least up to now, to measure nonintellective personality traits at all. I suspect that there is some kind of connection between the two. Would a physiologist attempt to measure basal metabolism without the cooperation of his subject? Why should we think we can do better?

The public seems well informed of the basic principles underlying the use of personality tests in personnel work, including the rather crude devices presently in existence for the detection of faking (Alex, 1965). This has been true for some time now (Whyte, 1956). I think it likely, as Whyte suggests, that the general nature of the game is understood intuitively even by unsophisticated respondents. The vast body of "hard data" in existence on dissimulation is probably irrelevant here, since almost all of it has been collected in totally artificial situations.

What is ethical is usually what is practical when one takes a broad view of things. We guarantee complete confidentiality to our clients in psychotherapy because we know that if we did not do so, they would not trust us and we would not obtain the kind of communication from them which we require in order to effectively provide this service. I believe that something of this sort applies to the relationship between validity and contract in personality testing.

What kind of test contract will tend to maximize overall validity? This, of course, is an "empirical question," but if it is approached in the hammer-and-tongs fashion which the term often implies when used by psychologists, the results could well be disastrous. If we gave our hypothetical personality inventory to three different groups of freshmen from the same class, each with a different one of our three contracts printed in the test booklet, we might then proceed to examine its validity under the three conditions, relative to various prediction problems. However, even if our consciences permitted us to conduct such an experiment, and we were able to obtain administrative approval for it, we might run some danger of precipitating a student revolt. In any case, we would create an atmosphere on the campus which would make validity data collected there subsequently somewhat difficult to interpret.

Nevertheless, let us suppose that as a profession we embark on a program of research of the sort alluded to above. I doubt that after

10 or 15 years of this sort of thing we will be much closer to resolving the issue on so-called empirical grounds than we are right now. We will have accumulated another one of those vast and diffuse bodies of literature which have become so common, of late. Even those of us working in the immediate area will not have time to read it all. Everyone who has taken a stand on the issue will find ways to produce results consistent with his position. Everyone who has not will be unable to digest the data and make up his mind.

Investigations of this kind are fruitless because they rest on an outmoded and wrong-headed notion of what validity is. They are addressed to no legitimate theoretical issue. They proliferate, not because one finding leads to others which can be reconciled with it in more general terms, but because one finding provokes the production of others which are interesting only because they can be made to appear inconsistent with it, or with each other. The proper dialectic of science is not advanced. Such research programs regard validity solely in terms of predictive power, without taking predictive scope into consideration.

To decide the issue at hand in light of the outcome of some set of particular predictive ventures would be to make the implausible assumption that there exists some general solution which would be true for all test variables, all criterion variables, all populations, and all combinations thereof. If would be to treat a methodological bias as if it were a theoretical model. Moreover, the decision would have to be based on investigations limited by the marginal level of validity characteristic of most existent personality measures.

If the empirical question be approached in a less concretistic fashion, I believe that there are good empirical grounds for choosing the client contract, in order to facilitate the development of valid procedures for personality assessment. All of our psychological theories contain propositions, well supported by empirical evidence, to the effect that when an organism is in danger, its behavior becomes less variable and less complex. Such behavior may not lend itself to the enterprise of differentiating between organisms.

Learning theory tells us that when organisms are placed on a reinforcement schedule their behavior becomes less variable. Cogni-tive theory informs us that when an organism is exposed to the threat of punishment or to induced conflict, dedifferentiation of the cognitive structure and isolation of its components is the result. Social psychology tells us that when the status of human beings is in jeopardy, their behavior will be characterized by rigid and pervasive conformity to norms which are perceived as associated with its maintenance. Psychoanalytic theory holds that the threat of ego damage evokes anxiety, and that anxiety produces repression and constriction, which prevent expression and articulation of the whole personality. All of these propositions seem to suggest that the threat and coercion involved in personnel contracts will tend to militate against the measurement of individual differences, where honesty is required of the subject.

Good psychological theory therefore, would seem to predict that under many conditions, with many variables, the effect of test administration involving personnel contracts will be to restrict the dispersion of the test variables, while at the same time increasing their inter-correlation, an effect which we would expect in general to render them less useful in the prediction of external criteria. To specify for which test variables, which criterion variables, and under exactly what conditions this will be so is the task of the theorist. Because this task is part of a process which is never complete, the issue at hand can never be summarily "settled" empirically, although it may always be further investigated, if other considerations do not dictate otherwise.

In terms of common sense, what is being suggested here is that we will obtain more information from people if we trust them and they trust us. This thesis is in good accord with the accumulated wisdom of the Judeo-Christian heritage. To hold that it will be true for all people, all situations, and all kinds of information would indeed be naïve. It is both normative and descriptive in intent, for as a prediction, it is likely to be self-fulfilling. I do not think it naïve to suggest that, for our profession, there is a presumption that it is the most viable game, both scientifically and socially.

Those who do personality research are often concerned lest if the option to refuse to take a personality test is made explicit and avilable, and is as a result often accepted, the generality of their findings will suffer. Potential respondents who decline to be tested will surely be different from those who do not, in ways that are important to us as scientists. I do not think that the truth of this can be disputed, but I think that it is often felt to have implications which it does not, namely, that opportunity for empirical inquiry is seriously diminished. Offering potential respondents the option of refusing to be tested will enable us to record and search for correlates of this behavior. An imaginative investigator who has a clear understanding of the theoretical questions and practical applications to which he has addressed himself will be able to use the data to achieve his goals. The loss involved in making the population tested more highly selected may not seem so great when we recall that most of the populations we test are already highly selected. Furthermore, we will now administer an additional "test," namely the acceptance or rejection of the assessment itself. We psychologists sometimes involve ourselves in an interesting paradox: On one hand we claim that our understanding of human nature will contribute to the "control" of human behavior, while on the other we demand that the control of human behavior be handed over to us in order that we may accomplish our ends.

A NEW ETHICAL STANDARD

It should be clear from what has already been said that I am proposing a considerable restriction of the uses to which certain kinds of mental tests may be put. The client contract is clearly appropriate to different assessment goals from those of the personnel contract. What will be the effect of this restriction on our capacity to provide psychological services? In order to discuss this question it is necessary to specify exactly what restrictions I advocate.

Up to now I have used the term "personality test." Although this more or less accords with popular usage, it is a misnomer, because all mental tests are properly speaking tests of personality. The kinds of tests I mean this discussion to refer to might best be called tests of character, virtue, psychopathology, and the like. The kinds of tests I do not mean to include under this rubric are tests of ability, aptitude, achievement, proficiency, and their

ilk, where what is assessed is a work capacity or a work sample. In the remainder of this paper, I shall refer to the former as *tests of character,* and to to the latter as *tests of capacity.*

A test of capacity is one for which there are criteria for deciding which responses are correct and which responses are incorrect, which are independent of the respondent, and of which the respondent is properly informed. By "correct responses" I mean those which will be rewarded; by "incorrect responses" those which will be punished. In testing for capacity, the respondent is told that he is to be evaluated, given an understanding of what is to constitute success and what failure, and success and failure are determined by norms which are external to him, be they subjective, as in an essay examination, or objective, as in an intelligence test. A test of character is one for which there are no criteria for deciding which responses are correct and which responses are not, or one for which the criteria of "correctness" are norms which are relative to the respondent, i.e., when the respondent is told that the "correct" answer is the "honest" one. Tests of character involve the recording of behavior under conditions where the assessor has not defined success and failure for the respondent, or under conditions where the assessor has defined success and failure for the respondent only in terms of the authenticity of self-report.

Personality inventories and projective techniques usually involve tests of character. Tests of capacity are most often concerned with ability, skills, problem solving, learning, the production of specified mechanical outputs, and so forth. But none of this is necessarily so, because the definition given above is independent of the nature of the test stimuli. A personality inventory becomes a test of capacity if the respondent is instructed to give the responses which will make a good impression on some particular class of people, and his protocol is scored for its correspondence with some reasonable determination of what responses do in fact make a good impression on this class. An intelligence test becomes a test of character if the respondent is asked not to solve problems but rather to indicate which kinds of problems he prefers and which he does not. It is still a test of character if the respondent is asked to solve problems, but his protocol is scored for his style of problem solving, rather than for the merit of his solutions. A person perception test is a test of capacity if it is scored for accuracy; if it is scored in terms of preferences for certain response categories, regardless of the appropriateness of these categories to actual persons, it is a test of character. Whether a test involves character or capacity depends upon what the respondent is told to do, and upon how response categories are defined by the assessor when he scores the test protocol.

Tests of *social stimulus value,* in which the respondent is not identical with the person assessed, fall into a third category. Letters of recommendation, ratings of others, sociometric data, and so forth, are neither tests of capacity nor tests of character with respect to the person recommended, rated, or chosen. *With respect to the respondent,* they may be either tests of capacity or of character, depending upon the nature of his contract with the assessor.

One may determine whether a test is one of character or of capacity by asking if the respondent can "fake good." The notion of representing oneself as *better than one is* is never applicable to tests of capacity, but always applicable to tests of character. The latter are motivationally labile in a way that the former are not.

A moment's reflection should reveal that this distinction is independent not only of test content, but also of the construct which is measured. If intelligence is measured by the success of problem-solving activity, as it usually is, we have a test of capacity. But if it is measured, as it occasionally is, by the tendency to claim attitudes characteristic of successful problem solvers, then we have a test of character. If flexibility is measured by some kind of self-report device, then it is measured by a test of character. But if it is measured by success in a problem-solving situation, then it is measured by a test of capacity.

If the administration of a personality inventory involves the client contract or the strong personnel contract, as given earlier, the inventory is a test of character, because the respondent is asked to give an honest self-report. The interesting thing about the weak personnel contract is that it is a mixed bag. In terms of the distinction between character and capacity it is neither fish nor fowl. The question of whether a correct response is to be defined in terms of internal or external norms is left ambiguous. The accused is properly informed that what he says may be used against him, but he does not know how. If the task assigned the respondent were solely to make a good impression, and the persons to be impressed were indicated, and the scoring of the test were based in some way on the actual attitudes of these persons towards the test items, then we would have a *pure* test of capacity; otherwise we would not.

It may be objected that the categories of character and capacity may not be mutually exclusive. The weak personnel contract may make the inventory *both* a test of character and of capacity, since it is suggested that a correct response may be defined either with reference to internal or to external norms. The nature of the situation where the categories seem to overlap is perplexing, because the distinction involves what the respondent is asked to do, and it is not clear what he is being asked to do when he is told that his responses will be evaluated in terms of potentially conflicting norms. My inclination is to argue that under such conditions, we have a test of character, rather than of capacity, because if it is not clear what the respondent has been asked to do, then he has not been asked to do anything in particular.

The distinction between tests of character and tests of capacity is similar to that made by Cronbach (1960) between *tests of typical performance* and *tests of maximal performance,* and to that made by Wallace (1966) between *response predisposition* and *response capability.* The principle difference is that the categories used here are based solely on the nature of the test instructions and the test scoring, while those used by Cronbach and Wallace have reference also to theoretical constructs.

My position is that tests of character should never be used for any kind of personnel function, whether it be selection or placement. They should be used only for unbiased research, subject to the restrictions implicit in the client function, and to provide psychological services in situations where the assessor's first professional loyalty is to the respondent. I have argued this position on ethical grounds and on scientific grounds. I shall now consider what effect its implementation might have on the marketing of psychological services.

ETHICS AND PSYCHOLOGICAL SERVICES

I should first like to reemphasize a point which has already been made. Our capacity to provide assessment services cannot be discussed independently of the validity, present and future, of our assessment procedures, nor of the ethical standards which are to be applied to these procedures. We cannot provide services with invalid instruments. It is likely that we shall not be allowed to offer services if our ethics offend the public. Bills to restrict the activity of psychological testing have been appearing in our state legislatures for some time. They appeal to a variety of political groups for a variety of reasons, and are capable of attracting widespread support.

I have tried to define the sort of assessment procedure which must be restricted as narrowly as possible. In principle, the personnel psychologist is not to be enjoined from measuring any construct, nor from using any kind of test content. Essentially, all that must be given up is the demand for a certain kind of contract with the respondent, one which I doubt that much sense can be made of anyway, either in a legalistic or a scientific way. In practice, the personnel psychologist will not be able to measure constructs involving the notions of self-report or spontaneous behavior. I doubt that this is a real limitation; I think that the logic of such constructs dictates that they cannot be measured in personnel settings anyway, because of the likelihood that spontaneous or authentic behavior may be penalized. Many writers on the subject have reached similar conclusions. Cronbach (1960), for example, says:

> Complete frankness cannot be anticipated in any situation where the subject will be rewarded or punished for his response. Some degree of reward and punishment is implicit in any institutional use of tests, such as clinical diagnosis or employee selection. Honest self-examination can be hoped for only when the tester is helping the subject solve his own problems, and even then the subject may have a goal for which he wishes the support of the counselor's authority, which biases his response [p. 454].

I would not go so far as to endorse the suspicion, suggested by the last phrase, that the notion of "honest self-examination" can have no place at all in our psychological constructs. Rather, my position is that the only way to escape from this dilemma is to make it clear in our testing contracts whether or not we intend to reward and punish, and if we do so intend, to indicate which response classes are to be rewarded and which punished, and then to try to the best of our ability to keep the contract, and that the only way to do this is to uniformly confront our potential respondents as a profession with some simple and broad ethical commitment. I think that if we do this we can become involved with constructs in which the concept of authenticity plays a part, while if we do not we shall of necessity close off many possible areas of research and service. I do not mean that we can produce interpersonal processes in which self-deception and the need to deceive others will not play a part; dynamic psychology dictates otherwise. I mean that we can only give operational value to such notions as authenticity and honest self-examination by creating situations where the integrity of interpersonal processes is protected by a particular kind of ethical structure, such as we have with regard to the processes of counseling and psychotherapy.

By restricting the activities of the personnel psychologist and in some cases those of the research psychologist, I believe we will act to protect the integrity of a variety of other psychological services, such as counseling and psychodiagnosis. These enterprises are simpler and more profound if we have the trust of our clients. Service-oriented research will also be facilitated if psychological assessors are trusted by their subjects. The counseling service might even be extended. Institutions which formerly depended only upon the personnel process to assign persons to places might employ private counseling psychologists who would report only to the candidate, and who would guarantee complete confidentiality to him. Self-selection and self-placement could then contribute to personnel decisions at the option of the candidate.

REFERENCES

Alexander, C. *How to beat personality tests.* New York: Arco, 1965.

American Psychological Association. Ethical standards of psychologists. *American Psychologist,* 1963, *18,* 56–60.

Amrine, M. The 1965 Congressional inquiry into testing: A commentary. *American Psychologist,* 1965, *20, 859–870.*

Cronbach, L. J. *Essentials of psychological testing.* (2nd ed.) New York: Harper, 1960.

Dailey, J. T. Emotional criticisms of testing. Paper read at American Educational Research Association and National Council on Measurement in Education (joint meeting), Chicago, February 1963.

Doctor, R. F. Testing: The heat is on in Congress. *California State Psychologist,* 1966, *7,* 3.

Gross, M. L. *The brain watchers.* New York: Random House, 1962.

Hoffmann, B. *The tyranny of testing.* New York: Crowell-Collier, 1962.

Messick, S. Personality measurement and the ethics of assessment. *American Psychologist,* 1965, *20,* 136–142.

Packard, V. *The naked society.* New York: McKay, 1964.

Sarason, S. B. The test-situation and the problem of prediction. *Journal of Clinical Psychology,* 1950, *6,* 387–392.

Testimony before the House Special Subcommittee on Invasion of Privacy of the Committee on Government Operations. *American Psychologist,* 1965, *20,* 955–988.

Testimony before the Senate Subcommittee on Constitutional Rights of the Committee on the Judiciary. *American Psychologist,* 1965, *20,* 888–954.

Vance, F. L. Work of the APA Committee on Psychological Assessment in relation to public concern about testing. *American Psychologist,* 1965 *20,* 873–874.

Wallace, J. An abilities conception of personality: Some implications for personality measurement. *American Psychologist,* 1966, *21,* 132–138.

Whyte, W. H. *The organization man.* New York: Simon & Schuster, 1956.

RECOMMENDED FURTHER READING

*Alexander, C.: *Personality Tests: How to Beat Them and Make Top Scores;* New York, Arco (No. 1324) 1965

Anastasi, Anne: *Psychological Testing* (3rd Ed.); New York, Macmillan 1968

Anastasi, Anne and J. P. Foley, Jr.: *Differential Psychology* (3rd Ed.); New York, Macmillan 1958

Anderson, H. H. and G. L. Anderson (eds.): *An Introduction to Projective Techniques;* Englewood Cliffs, N.J., Prentice-Hall 1951

Bloom, Benjamin and F. Peters: *The Use of Academic Prediction Scales for Counseling and Selecting College Entrants;* New York, Free Press 1961

Cronbach, Lee J.: *Essentials of Psychological Testing* (2nd Ed.); New York, Harper & Row 1960

*Gross, Martin: *The Brainwatchers;* New York, Random House 1962

*Hoffmann, Banesh: *The Tyranny of Testing;* New York, Crowell Collier 1962

*Huff, Darrell and Irving Geis: *How To Lie With Statistics;* New York, Norton 1954

Meehl, Paul: "Wanted—A Good Cookbook"; *American Psychologist, 11* (1956), 263–272

Messick, S. and D. N. Jackson (eds.): *Problems in Human Assessment;* New York, McGraw-Hill 1967

Rosenthal, R.: *Experimenter Effects in Behavioral Research;* New York, Appleton-Century-Crofts 1966

Ruebhausen, Oscar M. and Orville G. Brim, Jr.: "Privacy and Behavioral Research"; *Columbia Law Review,* 65 (1965), 1184–1211

* Paperback edition available.

Sarason, I. G.: *Personality: An Objective Approach;* New York, John Wiley 1966

Stern, G. G., M. I. Stein and B. Bloom: *Methods in Personality Assessment;* New York, Free Press 1956

"Testing and Public Policy"—special issue of the *American Psychologist,* November 1965 (Vol. 20)

Thorndike, Robert L. and E. Hagen: *Measurement and Evaluation in Psychology and Education;* New York, John Wiley 1961

Tyler, L. E.: *The Psychology of Human Differences* (3rd Ed.); New York Appleton-Century-Crofts 1965

Vernon, Philip E.: *Personality Assessment: A Critical Survey;* New York, John Wiley 1964

Painting by Jean-Paul Goude. Reproduced by permission of Esquire Magazine ©
1969 by Esquire, Inc.

PART IX

PERSONALITY AND THE SELF

Of all the words in psychology's lexicon "personality" is one of the easiest to use and one of the most difficult to understand. The word itself is derived from the Latin *persona,* which originally meant a theatrical mask, then came to mean the part or role that a person plays in life, and only later acquired something like its present meaning. Despite the underlying connotations of transience and changeability most psychologists define personality as the unique and relatively stable configuration of traits and responses that characterizes an individual in dealing with his life situation—as, that is, the individual's unique life style.

Yet, how much does such a definition tell us? Precisely because each personality is an unique creation it is also incommensurable, qualitatively different from every other. There is no personality "in general"—although psychologists may speak of "modal personality" or personality "types"—and an understanding of it can come only through the study and understanding of individuals, a task which, in contemporary American psychology, has been left largely to clinical psychologists and psychoanalysts. That and the fact that systematic study of personality originated in the treatment of the emotionally disturbed may explain why we understand disturbed (or abnormal) personalities rather better than healthy ones, why we have more theories of psychopathology than of "normal" personality development.

While personality refers to a stable configuration of traits and responses it is not therefore static and unchanging, not simply a series of characteristics that are inherent and permanent parts of the individual, like the color of his skin or the shape of his head. On the contrary, personality is never fixed but is always dynamic—a constant state of *becoming* rather than a crystallized state of *being.* In reality, an individual's "personality" is but an abstraction constructed from his actual behaviors in countless situations both important and trivial, from his ways of dealing with people and events. Because personality is an abstraction from behavior it changes along with behavior and thus, in a real sense, every individual creates and recreates his personality as he responds to ever changing internal and external environments. Any adequate theory of personality must, therefore, account equally well for change as for continuity. The extent to which the outcome of these processes is determined by genetic factors, by early life experiences, and by opportunistic behavior over which the individual has no control, as opposed to the influence of conscious choice, planning, and goal-directed striving remains a lively controversy among psychologists as it has been for centuries among philosophers—under the rubric "free will" versus "determinism." We have already referred to this dispute in our discussion of motivation.

But personality also has a history. No one is born with a personality, although every physically and mentally normal child has the potentiality for developing one. While the infant and young child may exhibit characteristic patterns of response to both internal and external stimuli, patterns which are later integrated into his personality, the latter develops only slowly, beginning about the fifth year of life. As the child matures biologically his personality becomes more differentiated, a development that proceeds through active transactions with the physical and social environments and in which socialization and learning play decisive parts. The importance of learning to the creation of human personality may explain why humans alone have personalities as well as the capacity of the individual to adapt and change his personality. Only metaphorically—by projecting distinctively human traits and motives onto their behavior—can we speak of animals having personalities, a tendency known, appropriately enough, as "personification."

Normal personality development culminates in the establishment of a stable (though not static) "self" or, to use Erik Erikson's term, an "ego-identity," a sense of "I-ness" that serves to unify and integrate the disparate and often inconsistent aspects of the total personality (the self or ego is not identical with the whole personality) around a stable core of awareness, memories and responses, of values, attitudes and goals that the individual experiences as peculiarly his own. That such integration is never total and the sense of self often precarious (as the prevalence of mental and emotional disturbances attests) is but another way of saying that personality is a becoming rather than a being, a continuous process rather than a finished product.

To unlock the riddle of personality or at least to make that riddle intellectually manageable students of human nature have, in the course of time, devised various classifications or typologies of personality (despite the logical contradiction between that enterprise and the definition of personality) as well as various theories to account for its development. While we cannot discuss all this work here we will review the broad classes into which such typologies and theories fall.

The oldest and by all odds the most popular "explanations" of personality are what we will call *descriptive typologies,* for to call them "theories" would be both pretentious and logically incorrect. Such typologies may involve classifications either of *types* or of *traits*. Type classifications date back to classical Greek times and derive originally from the belief that a man's personality is determined by the relative proportions in him of the four bodily fluids (or "humors," as a later age called them): blood, phlegm, yellow bile, and black bile. While such a classification may be useful for polemical and literary purposes (it was all the rage during the Elizabethan period; both Shakespeare and Ben Jonson freely employed it) it provides a series of descriptive labels rather than any sure knowledge or causal understanding. More modern, if not more enlightening, typologies have classified people according to their body builds (e.g., William Sheldon's *ectomorph—mesomorph—endomorph* classification) or their overall behavioral styles (e.g., Carl Jung's *extravert* and *introvert*). To the extent that any coherent theory underlies these classifications it tends toward asserting the primacy of genetic factors over cultural in the determination of personality. More seriously, few significant correlations have ever been established between any of these types and other personality or behavioral variables.

Trait classifications, such as those of Gordon Allport and Raymond Cattell, represent attempts to categorize and characterize individuals on the basis of specified personal characteristics or traits—both those common to a culture and those unique to an individual—the number of which many vary from a dozen to several hundred. The traits themselves are usually verbal names determined deductively and related to questionnaire responses, but without any validation in actual behavior. In reality, trait classifications are little more than sophisticated and differentiated versions of type classifications. While of some use descriptively a trait characterization tells us nothing about the processes through which an individual comes to exhibit his particular traits (are those processes biological or cultural?) and assumes that a trait is a permanent characteristic of the person to be displayed under all circumstances rather than a disposition which may or may not be manifested depending on the circumstances and the trait's interaction with other personality factors (e.g., other traits, drives, goals, etc.). Again, trait profiles of individuals have not correlated impressively with actual behavior although a few worthwhile results have been attained and the approach may eventually prove of some practical predictive value.

The serious theoretical approaches to the study of personality are fundamentally two: the *developmental* and the *dynamic,* approaches that differ more in interpretation and emphasis than in their underlying conceptual frameworks.

All the major developmental theories (psychoanalytic theory, learning theory, and role theory) stress the gradual growth of personality over time, the constraining—but not determining—influence of biological potentialities, and the explanation of present behavior in terms of past learning and experience. Psychoanalytic theory emphasizes the role of sexual and aggressive drives, the importance of early childhood experiences, the sequence of psychosexual stages (oral, anal, phallic, genital) and the problems and pitfalls associated with each, especially the Oedipus complex and its resolution. Learning theory asserts that other primary drives besides sex and aggression are important to personality development and stresses the building up of habits through particular experiences of learning rather than the crises of biologically determined psychosexual stages. In many respects, however, the differences between psychoanalytic and learning theories are more verbal than substantive. Role theory, on the other hand, sees the individual's personality as the sum of all the roles he plays at a given period of his life. Roles, to be sure, are learned but it is the stability and continuity of the roles one plays that give stability and continuity to personality. Personality change, according to this view, is adequately accounted for by changes in the roles an individual plays and in the shifting demands to which they subject him. In practice, role theory does not necessarily conflict with either of the other two. We will return to some of these theories when we examine their therapeutic applications in Part XI.

Dynamic theories of personality all emphasize that present behavior is the result of conflicting forces or pressures operating in the here and now and try to deal with the present constellation of forces rather than with its historical antecedents or "causes." This approach does not deny that present problems may have their sources in the past but considers the individual's current situation and future prospects of greater importance. The psychoanalytic variant of this approach points to conflicts and tensions among the id, ego, and super-ego and usually tries to strengthen the ego in its battle with the other two; learning theory points to conflicts among various drives and habits and role theory to incompatibilities and conflicts among various of the individual's roles.

Once more we note that most of these theories have been derived from the study of disturbed or malintegrated individuals, persons who have not managed satisfactorily to balance the conflicting pressures under which virtually all of us must live. No theory has yet done and perhaps none ever will do full justice to the richness and uniqueness of the individual personality; that, perhaps, is to ask more than any theory can deliver. But, given the character of existing theories, personality psychologists might well devote greater attention to the study of the healthy, self-actualizing personality and take more explicitly into account that behavior may be determined as much by future goals as by past traumas. (That future goals may themselves be chosen because of past events suggests, however, that the distinction between past and future may, in the study of personality, not always be clear.)

In our first selection, Sigmund Freud (1856–1939), the father of psychoanalysis, describes, in a selection from his last book, the basic elements of the human psychic apparatus: the *id, ego,* and *super-ego,* and the relationship that exists among them. For Freud, the development of the individual's adult personality hinges largely on how the antagonistic demands emanating from these three psychic systems are balanced and resolved as the individual matures. Freud believed that the id is never fully socialized or domesticated by the ego and the super-ego; an element of immaturity thus remains even in the most mature of personalities. While Freud's translator here uses the word "instinct" the German *Trieb* might better be rendered as "drive." Freud's tendency to treat the id and the ego as things and his attempt to localize them in particular areas of the brain is consistent with his hope that, ultimately, all psychological functions would be found to have physiological bases, a hope long since abjured by most contemporary psychoanalysts but revived by a younger generation of experimental psychologists (see Parts II and IV above for examples).

In the second selection Erich Fromm, one of the leading neo-Freudian psychoanalytic theorists, presents the model of a personality orientation he believes characteristic of modern industrial societies such as our own. Persons with the marketing orientation think of themselves primarily as commodities to be packaged as attractively as possible so as to bring the highest price on the "personality market." Fromm's analysis, which draws heavily on Karl Marx's theory of alienation, suggests that the image one projects, the image of what one *seems* to others to be is more important than what one *is* or even than what one can *do*. The reader might consider this analysis in relation both to his own behavior and to his experience of advertising, television, and the other mass media. Remember, however, that Fromm is presenting the model of a pure type of personality orientation, not describing any particular individual. The personalities of individuals who exhibit the marketing orientation are not fully characterized by that label alone and may in other respects be very different from one another. The ideas in this selection were one of the chief sources for David Riesman's portrait of the "other-directed" character type in *The Lonely Crowd*.

The late Gordon W. Allport (1897–1968) then presents a humanistic defense of the idea of the self (or the "proprium," as he calls it) in modern psychology. For Allport, the self stands for those aspects of personality that make for inward unity and coherence, that we feel to be uniquely ours. Admitting that the concept of "self" or "ego" does not sit well with the positivist (behaviorist) orientation of most American psychologists, Allport considers it necessary in order to call attention to the various "propriate" functions, functions that are not exhausted by the concepts of tension reduction and defense mechanisms. While stressing the creative, synthesizing, and striving functions of the self, a self often oriented toward the future, Allport warns against reifying it (turning it into a thing) and then using it to "explain" behavior. It is the propriate behaviors or functions themselves that need to be studied, for which the term "self" is only a convenient symbol.

Kenneth Keniston's characterization of the alienated self serves as counterpoint to Allport's theme. His portrait of alienated youth is based on several years' intensive work with a group of intellectually superior and socially advantaged Harvard undergraduates. The attitudes, feelings, and behavior patterns that Keniston describes may evoke recognition and empathy from many readers, although his conclusion that such alienated individuals have but a precarious sense of self is not likely to reassure them. The reader might consider for himself the possible relationship between these psychological patterns and contemporary radical movements, both student and non-student, with their overwhelmingly negative thrust.

In the next excerpt, Albert Camus (1913–1960), the great French novelist and essayist, portrays a different type of alienation—the total self-alienation of Meursault, an Algiers' office worker whose mother has recently died in a nursing home and who, at this point in the novel, is conducting a desultory affair with a girl named Marie. Later, at a swimming party, Meursault shoots and kills an Arab, a crime for which he is tried and eventually condemned to death. Meursault is acted upon rather than acting, an object rather than a subject of life; nothing except the present moment matters to him and even that matters little. The psychologist Nathan Leites has called Camus' novel a study of "affectlessness" although a clinican might conclude that Meursault is in a state of chronic, though not acute, depression. If Keniston's students are ideologically alienated and seek salvation through the experience of deep and genuine feeling Camus' anti-hero is furthest estranged precisely from his own feelings, which he fears more than death itself.

In the final selection of this group Abraham Maslow (1908–1970), founder of the Human Potential Movement and one of the leaders of humanistic psychology, argues for a new approach to personality that will stress the healthy, self-actualizing potentialities of every man. He argues against the traditional Western view (deriving primarily from late Judaism and Pauline Christianity) that man's nature is basically evil. Behavior that is labeled evil may be but a reaction to the frustration of the individual's inner needs, needs that are either morally neutral or positively good. People, Maslow maintains, must be true to their inner natures while society must change its views of sickness and health as well as its attitudes toward personality "problems." Maslow's views develop and extend those of Allport while his remarks regarding mental illness echo the position of Thomas Szasz (see Selection 47).

41. THE PSYCHIC APPARATUS

Sigmund Freud

...The core of our being, then, is formed by the obscure *id*, which has no direct communication with the external world and is accessible even to our own knowledge only through the medium of another agency. Within this id the organic *instincts* operate, which are themselves compounded of fusions of two primal forces (Eros and destructiveness) in varying proportions and are differentiated from one another by their relation to organs or systems of organs. The one and only urge of these instincts is towards satisfaction, which is expected to arise from certain changes in the organs with the help of objects in the external world. But immediate and unheeding satisfaction of the instincts, such as the id demands, would often lead to perilous conflicts with the external world and to extinction. The id knows no solicitude about ensuring survival and no anxiety; or it would perhaps be more correct to say that, though it can generate the sensory elements of anxiety, it cannot make use of them. The processes which are possible in and between the assumed psychical elements in the id (the *primary process*) differ widely from those which are familiar to us through conscious perception in our intellectual and emotional life; nor are they subject to the critical restrictions of logic, which repudiates some of these processes as invalid and seeks to undo them.

From AN OUTLINE OF PSYCHOANALYSIS *by Sigmund Freud, authorized translation by James Strachey in* THE STANDARD EDITION OF THE COMPLETE PSYCHOLOGICAL WORKS OF SIGMUND FREUD, *Revised and Edited by James Strachey, Vol. 23, pp. 197–202, 204–206. English translation copyright 1949,* © *1964 by James Strachey. Reprinted by permission of W. W. Norton & Co., Sigmund Freud Copyrights Ltd., and The Institute of Psychoanalysis and the Hogarth Press Ltd.*

The id, cut off from the external world, has a world of perception of its own. It detects with extraordinary acuteness certain changes in its interior, especially oscillations in the tension of its instinctual needs, and these changes become conscious as feelings in the pleasure-unpleasure series. It is hard to say, to be sure, by what means and with the help of what sensory terminal organs these perceptions come about. But it is an established fact that self-perceptions—coenaesthetic feelings and feelings of pleasure-unpleasure—govern the passage of events in the id with despotic force. The id obeys the inexorable pleasure principle. But not the id alone. It seems that the activity of the other psychical agencies too is able only to modify the pleasure principle but not to nullify it; and it remains a question of the highest theoretical importance, and one that has not yet been answered, when and how it is ever possible for the pleasure principle to be overcome. The consideration that the pleasure principle demands a reduction, at bottom the extinction perhaps, of the tensions of instinctual needs (that is, *Nirvana*) leads to the still unassessed relations between the pleasure principle and the two primal forces, Eros and the death instinct.

The other agency of the mind, which we believe we know best and in which we recognize ourselves most easily—what is known as the *ego*—has been developed out of the id's cortical layer, which, through being adapted to the reception and exclusion of stimuli, is in direct contact with the external world (*reality*). Starting from conscious perception it has subjected to its influence ever larger regions and deeper strata of the id, and, in the persistence with which it maintains its dependence on the external world, it bears the indelible stamp of its origin (as it might be

'Made in Germany'[1]). Its psychological function consists in raising the passage [of events] in the id to a higher dynamic level (perhaps by transforming freely mobile energy into bound energy, such as corresponds to the preconscious state); its constructive function consists in interpolating, between the demand made by an instinct and the action that satisfies it, the activity of thought which, after taking its bearings in the present and assessing earlier experiences, endeavours by means of experimental actions to calculate the consequences of the course of action proposed. In this way the ego comes to a decision on whether the attempt to obtain satisfaction is to be carried out or postponed or whether it may not be necessary for the demand by the instinct to be suppressed altogether as being dangerous. (Here we have the *reality principle*.) Just as the id is directed exclusively to obtaining pleasure, so the ego is governed by considerations of safety. The ego has set itself the task of self-preservation, which the id appears to neglect. It [the ego] makes use of the sensations of anxiety as a signal to give a warning of dangers that threaten its integrity. Since memory-traces can become conscious just as perceptions do, especially through their association with residues of speech, the possibility arises of a confusion which would lead to a mistaking of reality. The ego guards itself against this possibility by the institution of *reality-testing,* which is allowed to fall into abeyance in dreams on account of the conditions prevailing in the state of sleep. The ego, which seeks to maintain itself in an environment of overwhelming mechanical forces, is threatened by dangers which come in the first instance from external reality; but dangers do not threaten it from there alone. Its own id is a source of similar dangers, and that for two different reasons. In the first place, an excessive strength of instinct can damage the ego in a similar way to an excessive 'stimulus' from the external world. It is true that the former cannot destroy it; but it can destroy its characteristic dynamic organization and change the ego back into a portion of the id. In the second place, experience may have taught the ego that the satisfaction of some instinctual demand which is not in itself intolerable would involve dangers in the external world, so that an instinctual

demand of that kind itself becomes a danger. Thus the ego is fighting on two fronts: it has to defend its existence against an external world which threatens it with annihilation as well as against an internal world that makes excessive demands. It adopts the same methods of defence against both, but its defence against the internal enemy is particularly inadequate. As a result of having originally been identical with this latter enemy and of having lived with it since on the most intimate terms, it has great difficulty in escaping from the internal dangers. They persist as threats, even if they can be temporarily held down.

We have heard how the weak and immature ego of the first period of childhood is permanently damaged by the stresses put upon it in its efforts to fend off the dangers that are peculiar to that period of life. Children are protected against the dangers that threaten them from the external world by the solicitude of their parents; they pay for this security by a fear of *loss of love* which would deliver them over helpless to the dangers of the external world. This factor exerts a decisive influence on the outcome of the conflict when a boy finds himself in the situation of the Oedipus complex, in which the threat to his narcissism by the danger of castration, reinforced from primeval sources, takes possession of him. Driven by the combined operation of these two influences, the contemporary real danger and the remembered one with its phylogenetic basis, the child embarks on his attempts at defence—repressions—which are effective for the moment but nevertheless turn out to be psychologically inadequate when the later re-animation of sexual life brings a reinforcement to the instinctual demands which have been repudiated in the past. If this is so, it would have to be said from a biological standpoint that the ego comes to grief over the task of mastering the excitations of the early sexual period, at a time when its immaturity makes it incompetent to do so. It is in this lagging of ego development behind libidinal development that we see the essential precondition of neurosis; and we cannot escape the conclusion that neuroses could be avoided if the childish ego were spared this task—if, that is to say, the child's sexual life were allowed free play, as happens among many primitive peoples. It may be that the etiology of neurotic illnesses

---

1 [In English in the original.]

is more complicated than we have here described it; if so, we have at least brought out one essential part of the etiological complex. Nor should we forget the phylogenetic influences, which are represented in some way in the id in forms that we are not yet able to grasp, and which must certainly act upon the ego more powerfully in that early period than later. On the other hand, the realization dawns on us that such an early attempt at damming up the sexual instinct, so decided a partisanship by the young ego in favour of the external as opposed to the internal world, brought about by the prohibition of infantile sexuality, cannot be without its effect on the individual's later readiness for culture. The instinctual demands forced away from direct satisfaction are compelled to enter on new paths leading to substitutive satisfaction, and in the course of these *détours* they may become desexualized and their connection with their original instinctual aims may become looser. And at this point we may anticipate the thesis that many of the highly valued assets of our civilization were acquired at the cost of sexuality and by the restriction of sexual motive forces.

We have repeatedly had to insist on the fact that the ego owes its origin as well as the most important of its acquired characteristics to its relation to the real external world. We are thus prepared to assume that the ego's pathological states, in which it most approximates once again to the id, are founded on a cessation or slackening of that relation to the external world. This tallies very well with what we learn from clinical experience—namely, that the precipitating cause of the outbreak of a psychosis is either that reality has become intolerably painful or that the instincts have become extraordinarily intensified—both of which, in view of the rival claims made on the ego by the id and the external world, must lead to the same result. The problem of psychoses would be simple and perspicuous if the ego's detachment from reality could be carried through completely. But that seems to happen only rarely or perhaps never. Even in a state so far removed from the reality of the external world as one of hallucinatory confusion, one learns from patients after their recovery that at the time in some corner of their mind (as they put it) there was a normal person hidden, who, like a detached spectator, watched the hubbub of illness go past him. I do not know if we may assume that this is so in general, but I can report the same of other psychoses with a less tempestuous course. . . .

Whatever the ego does in its efforts of defence, whether it seeks to disavow a portion of the real external world or whether it seeks to reject an instinctual demand from the internal world, its success is never complete and unqualified. The outcome always lies in two contrary attitudes, of which the defeated, weaker one, no less than the other, leads to psychical complications. In conclusion, it is only necessary to point out how little of all these processes becomes known to us through our conscious perception.

We have no way of conveying knowledge of a complicated set of simultaneous events except by describing them successively; and thus it happens that all our accounts are at fault to begin with owing to one-sided simplification and must wait till they can be supplemented, built on to, and so set right.

The picture of an ego which mediates between the id and the external world, which takes over the instinctual demands of the former in order to lead them to satisfaction, which derives perceptions from the latter and uses them as memories, which, intent on its self-preservation, puts itself in defence against excessively strong claims from both sides and which, at the same time, is guided in all its decisions by the injunctions of a modified pleasure principle—this picture in fact applies to the ego only up to the end of the first period of childhood, till about the age of five. At about that time an important change has taken place. A portion of the external world has, at least partially, been abandoned as an object and has instead, by identification, been taken into the ego and thus become an integral part of the internal world. This new psychical agency continues to carry on the functions which have hitherto been performed by the people [the abandoned objects] in the external world: it observes the ego, gives it orders, judges it and threatens it with punishments, exactly like the parents whose place it has taken. We call this agency the *super-ego* and are aware of it in its judicial functions as our *conscience*. It is a remarkable thing that the super-ego often displays a severity for which no model has been provided by the real parents, and moreover that it calls the ego to account not only for its deeds but equally for its thoughts and unexecuted intentions, of which the super-ego seems to have knowledge. This reminds us that the hero of the Oedipus legend too felt guilty for his deeds and submitted himself to self-punishment, although the coercive power of the oracle should have acquitted him of guilt in our judgment and his own. The super-ego is in fact the heir to the Oedipus complex and is only established after that complex has been disposed of. For that reason its excessive severity does not follow a real model but corresponds to the strength of the defence used against the temptation of the Oedipus complex. Some suspicion of this state of things lies, no doubt, at the bottom of the assertion made by philosophers and believers that the moral sense is not instilled into men by education or acquired by them in their social life but is implanted in them from a higher source.

So long as the ego works in full harmony with the super-ego it is not easy to distinguish between their manifestations; but tensions and estrangements between them make themselves very plainly visible. The torments caused by the reproaches of conscience correspond precisely to a child's fear of loss of love, a fear the place of which has been taken by the moral agency. On the other hand, if the ego has successfully resisted a temptation to do something which would be objectionable to the super-ego, it feels raised in its self-esteem and strengthened in its pride, as though it had made some precious acquisition. In this way the super-ego continues to play the part of an external world for the ego, although it has become a portion of the internal world. Throughout later life it represents the influence of a person's childhood, of the care and education given him by his parents and of his dependence on them—a childhood which is prolonged so greatly in human beings by a family life in common. And in all this it is not only the personal qualities of these parents that is making itself felt, but also everything that had a determining effect on them themselves, the tastes and standards of the social class in which they lived and the innate dispositions and traditions of the race from which they sprang. Those who have a liking for generalizations and sharp distinctions may say that the external world, in which the individual finds himself exposed after being detached from his parents, represents the power of the present; that his id, with its inherited trends, represents the organic past; and that the super-ego, which comes to join them later, represents more than anything the cultural past, which a child has, as it were, to repeat as an after-experience during the few years of his early life. It is unlikely that such generalizations can be universally correct. Some portion of the cultural acquisitions have undoubtedly left a precipitate behind them in the id; much of what is contributed by the super-ego will awaken an echo in the id; not a few of the child's new experiences will be intensified because they are repetitions of some primeval phylogenetic experience.

'Was du ererbt von deinen Vätern hast, Erwirb es, um es zu besitzen.'[2]

Thus the super-ego takes up a kind of intermediate position between the id and the external world; it unites in itself the influences of the present and the past. In the establishment of the super-ego we have before us, as it were, an example of the way in which the present is changed into the past....

---

2 ['What thou hast inherited from thy fathers, acquire it to make it thine.' Goethe, *Faust*, Part I, Scene 1.]

42. THE MARKETING ORIENTATION

Erich Fromm

The marketing orientation developed as a dominant one only in the modern era. In order to understand its nature one must consider the economic function of the market in modern society as being not only analogous to this character orientation but as the basis and the main condition for its development in modern man.

Barter is one of the oldest economic mechanisms. The traditional local market, however, is essentially different from the market as it has developed in modern capitalism. Bartering on a local market offered an opportunity to meet for the purpose of exchanging commodities. Producers and customers became acquainted; they were relatively small groups; the demand was more or less known, so that the producer could produce for this specific demand.

The modern market[1] is no longer a meeting place but a mechanism characterized by abstract and impersonal demand. One produces for this market, not for a known circle of customers; its verdict is based on laws of supply and demand; and it determines whether the commodity can be sold and at what price. No matter what the *use value* of a pair of shoes may be, for instance, if the supply is greater than the demand, some shoes will be sentenced to economic death; they might as well not have been produced at all. The market day is the "day of judgment" as far as the *exchange value* of commodities is concerned.

The reader may object that this description

1 Cf., for the study of history and function of the modern market, K. Polanyi's *The Great Transformation* (New York: Rinehart & Company, 1944).

From MAN FOR HIMSELF *by Erich Fromm, pp. 67–78. Copyright 1947 by Erich Fromm. Reprinted by permission of Holt, Rinehart and Winston, Inc. and Routledge & Kegan Paul Ltd.*

of the market is oversimplified. The producer does try to judge the demand in advance, and under monopoly conditions even obtains a certain degree of control over it. Nevertheless, the regulatory function of the market has been, and still is, predominant enough to have a profound influence on the character formation of the urban middle class and, through the latter's social and cultural influence, on the whole population. The market concept of value, the emphasis on exchange value rather than on use value, has led to a similar concept of value with regard to people and particularly to oneself. The character orientation which is rooted in the experience of oneself as a commodity and of one's value as exchange value I call the marketing orientation.

In our time the marketing orientation has been growing rapidly, together with the development of a new market that is a phenomenon of the last decades—the "personality market." Clerks and salesmen, business executives and doctors, lawyers and artists all appear on this market. It is true that their legal status and economic positions are different: some are independent, charging for their services; others are employed, receiving salaries. But all are dependent for their material success on a personal acceptance by those who need their services or who employ them.

The principle of evaluation is the same on both the personality and the commodity market: on the one, personalities are offered for sale; on the other, commodities. Value in both cases is their exchange value, for which use value is a necessary but not a sufficient condition. It is true, our economic system could not function if people were not skilled in the particular work they have to perform and were gifted only with a pleasant personality. Even the best bedside manner and the most beautifully equipped office on Park Avenue would not make a New York doctor successful if he did not have a minimum of medical knowledge and skill. Even the most winning personality would not prevent a secretary from losing her job unless she could type reasonably fast. However, if we ask what the respective weight of skill and personality as a condition for success is, we find that only in exceptional cases is success predominantly the result of skill and of certain other human qualities like honesty, decency, and integrity. Although the proportion between skill and human qualities on the one hand and "personality" on the other hand as prerequisites for success varies, the "personality factor" always plays a decisive role. Success depends largely on how well a person sells himself on the market, how well he gets his personality across, how nice a "package" he is; whether he is "cheerful," "sound," "aggressive," "reliable," "ambitious"; furthermore what his family background is, what clubs he belongs to, and whether he knows the right people. The type of personality required depends to some degree on the special field in which a person works. A stockbroker, a salesman, a secretary, a railroad executive, a college professor, or a hotel manager must each offer different kinds of personality that, regardless of their differences, must fulfill one condition: to be in demand.

The fact that in order to have success it is not sufficient to have the skill and equipment for performing a given task but that one must be able to "put across" one's personality in competition with many others shapes the attitude toward oneself. If it were enough for the purpose of making a living to rely on what one knows and what one can do, one's self-esteem would be in proportion to one's capacities, that is, to one's use value; but since success depends largely on how one sells one's personality, one experiences oneself as a commodity or rather simultaneously as the seller *and* the commodity to be sold. A person is not concerned with his life and happiness, but with becoming salable. This feeling might be compared to that of a commodity, of handbags on a counter, for instance, could they feel and think. Each handbag would try to make itself as "attractive" as possible in order to attract customers and to look as expensive as possible in order to obtain a higher price than its rivals. The handbag sold for the highest price would feel elated, since that would mean it was the most "valuable" one; the one which was not sold would feel sad and convinced of its own worthlessness. This fate might befall a bag which, though excellent in appearance and usefulness, had the bad luck to be out of date because of a change in fashion.

Like the handbag, one has to be in fashion on the personality market, and in order to be in fashion one has to know what kind of personality is most in demand. This knowledge is transmitted in a general way throughout the whole process of education, from kindergarten to college, and implemented by the family. The knowledge acquired at this early stage is not sufficient, however; it emphasizes only certain general qualities like adaptability, ambition, and sensitivity to the changing expectations of other people. The more specific picture of the models for success one gets elsewhere. The pictorial magazines, newspapers, and newsreels* show the pictures and life stories of the successful in many variations. Pictorial advertising has a similar function. The successful executive who is pictured in a tailor's advertisement is the image of how one should look and be, if one is to draw down the "big money" on the contemporary personality market.

The most important means of transmitting the desired personality pattern to the average man is the motion picture.* The young girl tries to emulate the facial expression, coiffure, gestures of a high-priced star as the most promising way to success. The young man tries to look and be like the model he sees on the screen. While the average citizen has little contact with the life of the most successful people, his relationship with the motion-picture stars is different. It is true that he has no real contact with them either, but he can see them on the screen again and again, can write them and receive their autographed pictures. In contrast to the time when the actor was socially despised but was nevertheless the transmitter of the works of great poets to his audience, our motion-picture stars have no great works or ideas to transmit, but their function is to serve as the link an average person has with the world of the "great."

* Now, of course, we would have to add television. (Eds.)

Even if he cannot hope to become as successful as they are, he can try to emulate them; they are his saints and because of their success they embody the norms for living.

Since modern man experiences himself both as the seller and as the commodity to be sold on the market, his self-esteem depends on conditions beyond his control. If he is "successful," he is valuable; if he is not, he is worthless. The degree of insecurity which results from this orientation can hardly be overestimated. If one feels that one's own value is not constituted primarily by the human qualities one possesses, but by one's success on a competitive market with ever-changing conditions, one's self-esteem is bound to be shaky and in constant need of confirmation by others. Hence one is driven to strive relentlessly for success, and any setback is a severe threat to one's self-esteem; helplessness, insecurity, and inferiority feelings are the result. If the vicissitudes of the market are the judges of one's value, the sense of dignity and pride is destroyed.

But the problem is not only that of self-evaluation and self-esteem but of one's experience of oneself as an independent entity, of one's *identity with oneself.* As we shall see later, the mature and productive individual derives his feeling of identity from the experience of himself as the agent who is one with his powers; this feeling of self can be briefly expressed as meaning *"I am what I do."* In the marketing orientation man encounters his own powers as commodities alienated from him. He is not one with them but they are masked from him because what matters is not his self-realization in the process of using them but his success in the process of selling them. Both his powers and what they create become estranged, something different from himself, something for others to judge and to use; thus his feeling of identity becomes as shaky as his self-esteem; it is constituted by the sum total of roles one can play: *"I am as you desire me."*

Ibsen has expressed this state of selfhood in Peer Gynt: Peer Gynt tries to discover his self and he finds that he is like an onion—one layer after the other can be peeled off and there is no core to be found. Since man cannot live doubting his identity, he must, in the marketing orientation, find the conviction of identity not in reference to himself and his

powers but in the opinion of others about him. His prestige, status, success, the fact that he is known to others as being a certain person are a substitute for the genuine feeling of identity. This situation makes him utterly dependent on the way others look at him and forces him to keep up the role in which he once had become successful. If I and my powers are separated from each other then, indeed, is my self constituted by the price I fetch.

The way one experiences others is not different from the way one experiences oneself. Others are experienced as commodities like oneself; they too do not present *themselves* but their salable part. The difference between people is reduced to a merely quantitative difference of being *more or less* successful, attractive, hence valuable. This process is not different from what happens to commodities on the market. A painting and a pair of shoes can both be expressed in, and reduced to, their exchange value, their price; so many pairs of shoes are "equal" to one painting. In the same way the difference between people is reduced to a common element, their price on the market. Their individuality, that which is peculiar and unique in them, is valueless and, in fact, a ballast. The meaning which the word *peculiar* has assumed is quite expressive of this attitude. Instead of denoting the greatest achievement of man—that of having developed his individuality—it has become almost synonymous with *queer.* The word *equality* has also changed its meaning. The idea that all men are created equal implied that all men have the same fundamental right to be considered as ends in themselves and not as means. Today, equality has become equivalent to *interchangeability,* and is the very negation of individuality. Equality, instead of being the condition for the development of each man's peculiarity, means the extinction of individuality, the "selflessness" characteristic of the marketing orientation. Equality was conjunctive with difference, but it has become synonymous with "in-difference" and, indeed, indifference is what characterizes modern man's relationship to himself and to others.

These conditions necessarily color all human relationships. When the individual self is neglected, the relationships between people must of necessity become superficial, because not they themselves but interchangeable commodities are related. People are not able and cannot afford to be concerned with that which is unique and "peculiar" in each other. However, the market creates a kind of comradeship of its own. Everybody is involved in the same battle of competition, shares the same striving for success; all meet under the same conditions of the market (or at least believe they do). Everyone knows how the others feel because each is in the same boat: alone, afraid to fail, eager to please; no quarter is given or expected in this battle.

The superficial character of human relationships leads many to hope that they can find depth and intensity of feeling in individual love. But love for one person and love for one's neighbor are indivisible; in any given culture, love relationships are only a more intense expression of the relatedness to man prevalent in that culture. Hence it is an illusion to expect that the loneliness of man rooted in the marketing orientation can be cured by individual love.

Thinking as well as feeling is determined by the marketing orientation. Thinking assumes the function of grasping things quickly so as to be able to manipulate them successfully. Furthered by widespread and efficient education, this leads to a high degree of intelligence, but not of reason. For manipulative purposes, all that is necessary to know is the surface features of things, the superficial. The truth, to be uncovered by penetrating to the essence of phenomena, becomes an obsolete concept—truth not only in the prescientific sense of "absolute" truth, dogmatically maintained without reference to empirical data, but also in the sense of truth attained by man's reason applied to his observations and open to revisions. Most intelligence tests are attuned to this kind of thinking; they measure not so much the capacity for reason and understanding as the capacity for quick mental adaptation to a given situation; "mental adjustment tests" would be the adequate name for them. For this kind of thinking the application of the categories of comparison and of quantitative measurement—rather than a thorough analysis of a given phenomenon and its quality —is essential. All problems are equally "interesting" and there is little sense of the respective differences in their importance. Knowl-

edge itself becomes a commodity. Here, too, man is alienated from his own power; thinking and knowing are experienced as a tool to produce results. Knowledge of man himself, psychology, which in the great tradition of Western thought was held to be the condition for virtue, for right living, for happiness, has degenerated into an instrument to be used for better manipulation of others and oneself, in market research, in political propaganda, in advertising, and so on.

Evidently this type of thinking has a profound effect on our educational system. From grade school to graduate school, the aim of learning is to gather as much information as possible that is mainly useful for the purposes of the market. Students are supposed to learn so many things that they have hardly time and energy left to *think*. Not the interest in the subjects taught or in knowledge and insight as such, but the enhanced exchange value knowledge gives is the main incentive for wanting more and better education. We find today a tremendous enthusiasm for knowledge and education, but at the same time a skeptical or contemptuous attitude toward the allegedly impractical and useless thinking which is concerned "only" with the truth and which has no exchange value on the market.

Although I have presented the marketing orientation as one of the nonproductive orientations, it is in many ways so different that it belongs in a category of its own. The receptive, exploitative, and hoarding orientations have one thing in common: each is one form of human relatedness which, if dominant in a person, is specific of him and characterizes him. (Later on it will be shown that these four orientations do not necessarily have the negative qualities which have been described so far.) The marketing orientation, however, does not develop something which is potentially in the person (unless we make the absurd assertion that "nothing" is also part of the human equipment); its very nature is that no specific and permanent kind of relatedness is developed, but that the very changeability of attitudes is the only permanent quality of such orientation. In this orientation, those qualities are developed which can best be sold. Not one particular attitude is predominant, but the emptiness which can be filled most quickly with the desired quality. This quality, however, ceases to be one in the proper sense of the word; it is only a role, the pretense of a quality, to be readily exchanged if another one is more desirable. Thus, for instance, respectability is sometimes desirable. The salesmen in certain branches of business ought to impress the public with those qualities of reliability, soberness, and respectability which were genuine in many a businessman of the nineteenth century. Now one looks for a man who instills confidence because he *looks* as if he had these qualities; what this man sells on the personality market is his ability to look the part; what kind of person is behind that role does not matter and is nobody's concern. He himself is not interested in his honesty, but in what it gets for him on the market. The premise of the marketing orientation is emptiness, the lack of any specific quality which could not be subject to change, since any persistent trait of character might conflict some day with the requirements of the market. Some roles would not fit in with the peculiarities of the person; therefore we must do away with them —not with the roles but with the peculiarities. The marketing personality must be free, free of all individuality. . . .

43. THE SELF

Gordon W. Allport

IS THE CONCEPT OF SELF NECESSARY?

We come now to a question that is pivotal for the psychology of growth: Is the concept of *self* necessary? While there is a vast literature in philosophy devoted to this issue from the points of view of ontology, epistemology, and axiology, let us for the time being bypass such discussions. For it is entirely conceivable that a concept useful to philosophy or theology may turn out to be merely an impediment in the path of psychological progress.

Since the time of Wundt, the central objection of psychology to *self*, and also to *soul*, has been that the concept seems questionbegging. It is temptingly easy to assign func-

tions that are not fully understood to a mysterious central agency, and then to declare that "it" performs in such a way as to unify the personality and maintain its integrity. Wundt, aware of this peril, declared boldly for "a psychology without a soul." It was not that he necessarily denied philosophical or theological postulates, but that he felt psychology as science would be handicapped by the *petitio principii** implied in the concept.

* The logical fallacy of assuming in the premise of an argument that which one wishes to prove. (Eds.)

1 Until about 1890 certain American writers, including Dewey, Royce, James, continued to regard self as a necessary concept. They felt that the analytical concepts of the New Psychology lost the manifest unity of mental functioning. But for the ensuing fifty years very few American psychologists made use of it, Mary Whiton Calkins being a distinguished exception; and none employed "soul." See G. W. Allport, "The Ego in Contemporary Psychology," *Psychological Review*, 50 (1943), 451–78; reprinted in *The Nature of Personality: Selected Papers*, Cambridge, Addison-Wesley, 1950.

From BECOMING *by Gordon W. Allport, pp. 36–55 (slightly abridged). Copyright © 1955 by Yale University Press and reprinted by their permission.*

For half a century few psychologists other than Thomists have resisted Wundt's reasoning or his example.[1] Indeed we may say that for two generations psychologists have tried every conceivable way of accounting for the integration, organization, and striving of the human person without having recourse to the postulate of a self.

In very recent years the tide has turned. Perhaps without being fully aware of the historical situation, many psychologists have commenced to embrace what two decades ago would have been considered a heresy. They have reintroduced self and ego unashamedly and, as if to make up for lost time, have employed ancillary concepts such as *self-image, self-actualization, self-affirmation, phenomenal ego, ego-involvement, ego-striving,* and many other hyphenated elaborations which to experimental positivism still have a slight flavor of scientific obscenity.

We should note in passing that Freud played a leading, if unintentional role, in preserving the concept of ego from total obliteration throughout two generations of strenuous positivism. His own use of the term, to be sure, shifted. At first he spoke of assertive and aggressive ego-instincts (in a Nietzschean sense); later for Freud the ego became a rational, though passive, agency, whose duty it was to reconcile as best it could through planning or defense the conflicting pressures of the instincts, of conscience, and of the outer environment. With the core concept thus preserved, even with stringently limited meanings, it was easier for dynamically inclined psychologists, including the neo-Freudians, to enlarge the properties of the ego, making it a far more active and important agent than it was in the hands of Freud.

There still remains, however, the danger that Wundt wished to avoid, namely that the ego may be regarded as a *deus ex machina,* invoked to reassemble the dismembered parts of the throbbing psychic machine after positivism has failed to do so. The situation today seems to be that many psychologists who first fit personality to an external set of co-ordinates are dissatisfied with the result. They therefore re-invent the ego because they find no coherence among the measures yielded by positivistic analysis. But unfortunately positivism and ego-theory do not go well together.

Bergson has criticized the use of "ego" in this face-saving way by likening the process to the dilemma of an artist. An artist, he says, may wish to represent Paris—just as a psychologist may wish to represent personality. But all he can do with the limitations of his medium is to draw this and then that angle of the whole. To each sketch he applies the label "Paris," hoping somehow that the sections he has ablated will magically reconstitute the whole. Similarly in psychology we have a state of affairs where empiricists, finding that they have gone as far as possible with analytic tools and being dissatisfied with the product, resort as did their predecessors to some concept of self in order to represent, however inadequately, the coherence, unity, and purposiveness they know they have lost in their fragmentary representations.

I greatly fear that the lazy tendency to employ self or ego as a factotum to repair the ravages of positivism may do more harm than good. It is, of course, significant that so many contemporary psychologists feel forced to take this step, even though for the most part their work represents no theoretical gain over nineteenth-century usage. Positivism will continue to resent the intrusion, and will, with some justification, accuse today's resurgent self-psychologists of obscurantism.

The problem then becomes how to approach the phenomena that have led to a revival of the self-concept in a manner that will advance rather than retard scientific progress.

A possible clue to the solution, so far as psychology is concerned, lies in a statement made by Alfred Adler. "What is frequently labeled 'the ego,'" he writes, "is nothing more than the style of the individual." Lifestyle to Adler had a deep and important meaning. He is saying that if psychology could give us a full and complete account of lifestyle it would automatically include all phenomena now referred somewhat vaguely to a self or an ego. In other words, a wholly adequate psychology of growth would discover all of the activities and all of the interrelations in life, which are now either neglected or consigned to an ego that looks suspiciously like a homunculus.*

* A tiny man: In this case, a tiny man secreted within the person and who acts for him. (Eds.)

The first thing an adequate psychology of growth should do is to draw a distinction between what are matters of *importance* to the individual and what are, as Whitehead would say, merely matters of *fact* to him; that is, between what he feels to be vital and central in becoming and what belongs to the periphery of his being.

Many facets of our life-style are not ordinarily felt to have strong personal relevance. Each of us, for example, has innumerable tribal habits that mark our life-style but are nothing more than opportunistic modes of adjusting. The same holds true for many of our physiological habits. We keep to the right in traffic, obey the rules of etiquette, and make countless unconscious or semiconscious adjustments, all of which characterize our life-style but are not *propriate,* i.e., not really central to our sense of existence. Consider, for example, the English language habits that envelop our thinking and communication. Nothing could be of more pervasive influence in our lives than the store of concepts available to us in our ancestral tongue and the frames of discourse under which our social contacts proceed. And yet the use of English is ordinarily felt to be quite peripheral to the core of our existence. It would not be so if some foreign invader should forbid us to use our native language. At such a time our vocabulary and accent and our freedom to employ them would become very precious and involved with our sense of self. So it is with the myriad of social and physiological habits we have developed that are never, unless interfered with, regarded as essential to our existence as a separate being.

Personality includes these habits and skills, frames of reference, matters of fact and cultural values, that seldom or never seem warm and important. But personality includes what is warm and important also—all the regions of our life that we regard as peculiarly ours, and which for the time being I suggest we call the *proprium.* The proprium includes all aspects of personality that make for inward unity.

Psychologists who allow for the proprium use both the term "self" and "ego"—often interchangeably; and both terms are defined with varying degrees of narrowness or of comprehensiveness. Whatever name we use for

it, this sense of what is "peculiarly ours" merits close scrutiny. The principal functions and properties of the proprium need to be distinguished.

To this end William James over sixty years ago proposed a simple taxonomic scheme. There are, he maintained, two possible orders of self: an empirical self (the *Me*) and a knowing self (the *I*). Three subsidiary types comprise the empirical Me: the material self, the social self, and the spiritual self. Within this simple framework he fits his famous and subtle description of the various states of mind that are "peculiarly ours." His scheme, however, viewed in the perspective of modern psychoanalytic and experimental research, seems scarcely adequate. In particular it lacks the full psychodynamic flavor of modern thinking. With some trepidation, therefore, I offer what I hope is an improved outline for analyzing the propriate aspects of personality. Later we shall return to the question, Is the concept of *self* necessary?

THE PROPRIUM

1. BODILY SENSE

The first aspect we encounter is the bodily *me.* It seems to be composed of streams of sensations that arise within the organism— from viscera, muscles, tendons, joints, vestibular canals, and other regions of the body. The technical name for the bodily sense is *coenesthesis.* Usually this sensory stream is experienced dimly; often we are totally unaware of it. At times, however, it is well configured in consciousness in the exhilaration that accompanies physical exercise, or in moments of sensory delight or pain. The infant, apparently, does not know that such experiences are "his." But they surely form a necessary foundation for his emerging sense of self. The baby who at first cries from unlocalized discomfort will, in the course of growth, show progressive ability to identify the distress as his own.

The bodily sense remains a lifelong anchor for our self-awareness, though it never alone accounts for the entire sense of self, probably not even in the young child who has his memories, social cues, and strivings to help in the definition. Psychologists have paid a great deal of attention, however, to this particular component of self-awareness, rather more than to other equally important ingredients. One special line of investigation has been surprisingly popular: the attempt to locate self in relation to specific bodily sensations. When asked, some people will say that they *feel* the self in their right hands, or in the viscera. Most, however, seem to agree with Claparède that a center midway between the eyes, slightly behind them within the head, is the focus. It is from this cyclopean eye that we estimate what lies before and behind ourselves, to the right or left, and above and below. Here, phenomenologically speaking, is the locus of the ego. Interesting as this type of work may be, it represents little more than the discovery that various sensory elements in the coenesthetic stream or various inferences drawn from sensory experience may for certain people at certain times be especially prominent.

How very intimate (propriate) the bodily sense is can be seen by performing a little experiment in your imagination. Think first of swallowing the saliva in your mouth, or do so. Then imagine expectorating it into a tumbler and drinking it! What seemed natural and "mine" suddenly becomes disgusting and alien. Or picture yourself sucking blood from a prick in your finger; then imagine sucking blood from a bandage around your finger! What I perceive as belonging intimately to my body is warm and welcome; what I perceive as separate from my body becomes, in the twinkling of an eye, cold and foreign.

Certainly organic sensations, their localization and recognition, composing as they do the bodily *me,* are a core of becoming. But it would be a serious mistake to think, as some writers do, that they alone account for our sense of what is "peculiarly ours."

2. Self-identity

Today I remember some of my thoughts of yesterday; and tomorrow I shall remember some of my thoughts of both yesterday and today; and I am subjectively certain that they are the thoughts of the same person. In this situation, no doubt, the organic continuity of the neuromuscular system is the leading factor. Yet the process involves more than reminiscence made possible by our retentive nerves. The young infant has retentive capa-

city during the first months of life but in all probability no sense of self-identity. This sense seems to grow gradually, partly as a result of being clothed and named, and otherwise marked off from the surrounding environment. Social interaction is an important factor. It is the actions of the other to which he differentially adjusts that force upon a child the realization that he is not the other, but a being in his own right. The difficulty of developing self-identity in childhood is shown by the ease with which a child depersonalizes himself in play and in speech. Until the age of four of five we have good reason to believe that as perceived by the child personal identity is unstable. Beginning at about this age, however, it becomes the surest attest a human being has of his own existence.

3. Ego-enhancement

We come now to the most notorious property of the proprium, to its unabashed self-seeking. Scores of writers have featured this clamorous trait in human personality. It is tied to the need for survival, for it is easy to see that we are endowed by nature with the impulses of self-assertion and with the emotions of self-satisfaction and pride. Our language is laden with evidence. The commonest compound of self is *selfish,* and of ego *egoism.* Pride, humiliation, self-esteem, narcissism are such prominent factors that when we speak of ego or self we often have in mind only this aspect of personality. And yet, self-love may be prominent in our natures without necessarily being sovereign. The proprium, as we shall see, has other facets and functions.

4. Ego-extension

The three facets we have discussed— coenesthesis, self-identity, ego-enhancement— are relatively early developments in personality, characterizing the whole of the child's proprium. Their solicitations have a heavily biological quality and seem to be contained within the organism itself. But soon the process of learning brings with it a high regard for possessions, for loved objects, and later, for ideal causes and loyalties. We are speaking here of whatever objects a person calls "mine." They must at the same time be objects of *importance,* for sometimes our sense of "having" has no affective tone and hence no place in the proprium. A child, however, who identifies with his parent is definitely extending his sense of self, as he does likewise through his love for pets, dolls, or other possessions, animate or inanimate.

As we grow older we identify with groups, neighborhood, and nation as well as with possessions, clothes, home. They become matters of importance to us in a sense that other people's families, nations, or possessions are not. Later in life the process of extension may go to great lengths, through the development of loyalties and of interests focused on abstractions and on moral and religious values. Indeed, a mark of maturity seems to be the range and extent of one's feeling of self-involvement in abstract ideals.

5. RATIONAL AGENT

The ego, according to Freud, has the task of keeping the organism as a whole in touch with reality, of intermediating between unconscious impulses and the outer world. Often the rational ego can do little else than invent and employ defenses to forestall or diminish anxiety. These protective devices shape the development of personality to an extent unrealized sixty years ago. It is thanks to Freud that we understand the strategies of denial, repression, displacement, reaction formation, rationalization, and the like better than did our ancestors.

We have become so convinced of the validity of these defense mechanisms, and so impressed with their frequency of operation, that we are inclined to forget that the rational functioning of the proprium is capable also of yielding true solutions, appropriate adjustments, accurate planning, and a relatively faultless solving of the equations of life.

Many philosophers, dating as far back as Boethius in the sixth century, have seen the rational nature of personality as its most distinctive property.... It may seem odd to credit Freud, the supreme irrationalist of our age, with helping the Thomists preserve for psychology the emphasis upon the ego as the rational agent in personality, but such is the case. For whether the ego reasons or merely rationalizes, it has the property of synthesizing inner needs and outer reality. Freud and the Thomists have not let us forget this fact, and have thus made it easier for modern cognitive theories to deal with this central function of the proprium.

6. SELF-IMAGE

A propriate function of special interest today is the self-image, or as some writers call it, the phenomenal self. Present-day therapy is chiefly devoted to leading the patient to examine, correct, or expand this self-image. The image has two aspects: the way the patient regards his present abilities, status, and roles; and what he would like to become, his *aspirations* for himself. The latter aspect, which Karen Horney calls the "idealized self-image," is of especial importance in therapy. On the one hand it may be compulsive, compensatory, and unrealistic, blinding its possessor to his true situation in life. On the other hand, it may be an insightful cognitive map, closely geared to reality and defining a wholesome ambition. The ideal self-image is the imaginative aspect of the proprium, and whether accurate or distorted, attainable or unattainable, it plots a course by which much propriate movement is guided and therapeutic progress achieved.

There are, of course, many forms of becoming that require no self-image, including automatic cultural learning and our whole repertoire of opportunistic adjustments to our environment. Yet there is also much growth that takes place only with the aid of, and because of, a self-image. This image helps us bring our view of the present into line with our view of the future. Fortunately the dynamic importance of the self-image is more widely recognized in psychology today than formerly.

7. PROPRIATE STRIVING

We come now to the nature of motivation. Unfortunately we often fail to distinguish between propriate and peripheral motives. The reason is that at the rudimentary levels of becoming, which up to now have been the chief levels investigated, it *is* the impulses and drives, the immediate satisfaction and tension reduction, that are the determinants of conduct. Hence a psychology of opportunistic adjustment seems basic and adequate, especially to psychologists accustomed to working with animals. At low levels of behavior the familiar formula of drives and their conditioning appears to suffice. But as soon as the personality enters the stage of ego-extension, and develops a self-image with visions of self-perfection, we are, I think, forced to postulate motives of a different order, motives that reflect propriate striving. Within experimental psychology itself there is now plenty of evidence that conduct that is "ego involved" (propriate) differs markedly from behavior that is not.

Many psychologists disregard this evidence. They wish to maintain a single theory of motivation consistent with their presuppositions. Their preferred formula is in terms of drive and conditioned drive. Drive is viewed as a peripherally instigated activity. The resultant response is simply reactive, persisting only until the instigator is removed and the tension, created by the drive, lessened. Seeking always a parsimony of assumptions, this view therefore holds that motivation entails one and only one inherent property of the organism: a disposition to act, by instinct or by learning, in such a way that the organism will as efficiently as possible reduce the discomfort of tension. Motivation is regarded as a state of tenseness that leads us to seek equilibrium, rest, adjustment, satisfactions, or homeostasis. From this point of view personality is nothing more than our habitual modes of reducing tension. This formulation, of course, is wholly consistent with empiricism's initial presupposition that man is by nature a passive being, capable only of receiving impressions from, and responding to, external goads.

The contrary view holds that this formula, while applicable to segmental and opportunistic adjustments, falls short of representing the nature of propriate striving. It points out that the characteristic feature of such striving is its resistance to equilibrium: tension is maintained rather than reduced.

In his autobiography Roald Amundsen tells how from the age of fifteen he had one dominant passion—to become a polar explorer. The obstacles seemed insurmountable, and all through his life the temptations to reduce the tensions engendered were great. But the propriate striving persisted. While he welcomed

each success, it acted to raise his level of aspiration, to maintain an over-all commitment. Having sailed the Northwest Passage, he embarked upon the painful project that led to the discovery of the South Pole. Having discovered the South Pole, he planned for years, against extreme discouragement, to fly over the North Pole, a task he finally accomplished. But his commitment never wavered until at the end he lost his life in attempting to rescue a less gifted explorer, Nobile, from death in the Arctic. Not only did he maintain one style of life, without ceasing, but this central commitment enabled him to withstand the temptation to reduce the segmental tensions continually engendered by fatigue, hunger, ridicule, and danger.

Here we see the issue squarely. A psychology that regards motivation exclusively in terms of drives and conditioned drives is likely to stammer and grow vague when confronted by those aspects of personality—of every personality—that resemble Amundsen's propriate striving. While most of us are less distinguished than he in our achievements, we too have insatiable interests. Only in a very superficial way can these interests be dealt with in terms of tension reduction. Many writers past and present have recognized this fact and have postulated some principles of an exactly opposite order. One thinks in this connection of Spinoza's concept of conatus, or the tendency of an individual to persist, against obstacles, in his own style of being. One thinks of Goldstein's doctrine of *self-actualization,* used also by Maslow and others, or McDougall's *self-regarding* sentiment. And one thinks too of those modern Freudians who feel the need for endowing the ego not only with a rational and rationalizing ability but with a tendency to maintain its own system of productive interests, in spite of the passing solicitations of impulse and environmental instigation. Indeed the fortified ego, as described by neo-Freudians, is able to act contrary to the usual course of opportunistic, tension-reducing, adaptation.

Propriate striving distinguishes itself from other forms of motivation in that, however beset by conflicts, it makes for unification of personality. There is evidence that the lives of mental patients are marked by the proliferation of unrelated subsystems, and by the loss of more homogeneous systems of motivation. When the individual is dominated by segmental drives, by compulsions, or by the winds of circumstance, he has lost the integrity that comes only from maintaining major directions of striving. The possession of long-range goals, regarded as central to one's personal existence, distinguishes the human being from the animal, the adult from the child, and in many cases the healthy personality from the sick.

Striving, it is apparent, always has a future reference. As a matter of fact, a great many states of mind are adequately described only in terms of their futurity. Along with *striving,* we may mention *interest, tendency, disposition, expectation, planning, problem solving,* and *intention.* While not all future-directedness is phenomenally propriate, it all requires a type of psychology that transcends the prevalent tendency to explain mental states exclusively in terms of past occurrences. People, it seems, are busy leading their lives into the future, whereas psychology, for the most part, is busy tracing them into the past.

8. The Knower

Now that we have isolated these various propriate functions—all of which we regard as peculiarly ours—the question arises whether we are yet at an end. Do we not have in addition a cognizing self—a knower, that transcends all other functions of the proprium and holds them in view? In a famous passage, William James wrestles with this question, and concludes that we have not. There is, he thinks, no such thing as a substantive self distinguishable from the sum total, or stream, of experiences. Each moment of consciousness, he says, appropriates each previous moment, and the knower is thus somehow embedded in what is known. "The thoughts themselves are the thinker."

Opponents of James argue that no mere series of experiences can possibly turn themselves into an awareness of that series as a unit. Nor can "passing thoughts" possibly regard themselves as important or interesting. To whom is the series important or interesting if not to *me?* I am the ultimate monitor. The self as *knower* emerges as a final and inescapable postulate. . . .

We not only know *things,* but we know (i.e., are acquainted with) the empirical features of our own proprium. It is I who have bodily sensations, I who recognize my self-identity from day to day; I who note and reflect upon my self-assertion, self-extension, my own rationalizations, as well as upon my interests and strivings. When I thus think about my own propriate functions I am likely to perceive their essential togetherness, and feel them intimately bound in some way to the knowing function itself.

Since such knowing is, beyond any shadow of doubt, a state that is peculiarly ours, we admit it as the eighth clear function of the proprium. (In other words, as an eighth valid meaning of "self" or "ego.") But it is surely one of nature's perversities that so central a function should be so little understood by science, and should remain a perpetual bone of contention among philosophers. Many, like Kant, set this function (the "pure ego") aside as something qualitatively apart from other propriate functions (the latter being assigned to the "empirical me"). Others, like James, say that the ego *qua* knower is somehow contained within the ego *qua* known. Still others, personalistically inclined, find it necessary to postulate a single self as knower, thinker, feeler, and doer—all in one blended unit of a sort that guarantees the continuance of all becoming.

We return now to our unanswered question: Is the concept of self necessary in the psychology of personality? Our answer cannot be categorical since all depends upon the particular usage of "self" that is proposed. Certainly all legitimate phenomena that have been, and can be ascribed, to the self or ego must be admitted as data indispensable to a psychology of personal becoming. All eight functions of the "proprium" (our temporary neutral term for central interlocking operations of personality) must be admitted and included. In particular the unifying act of perceiving and knowing (of comprehending propriate states as belonging together and belonging to me) must be fully admitted.

At the same time, the danger we have several times warned against is very real: that a homunculus may creep into our discussions of personality, and be expected to solve all our problems without in reality solving any. Thus, if we ask "What determines our moral conduct?" the answer may be "The self does it." Or, if we pose the problem of choice, we say "The self chooses." Such question-begging would immeasurably weaken the scientific study of personality by providing an illegitimate regressus. There are, to be sure, ultimate problems of philosophy and of theology that psychology cannot even attempt to solve, and for the solution of such problems "self" in some restricted and technical meaning may be a necessity.

But so far as psychology is concerned our position, in brief, is this: all psychological functions commonly ascribed to a self or ego must be admitted as data in the scientific study of personality. These functions are not, however, coextensive with personality as a whole. They are rather the special aspects of personality that have to do with warmth, with unity, with a sense of personal importance. In this exposition I have called them "propriate" functions. If the reader prefers, he may call them self-functions, and in this sense self may be said to be a necessary psychological concept. What is unnecessary and inadmissible is a self (or soul) that is said to perform acts, to solve problems, to steer conduct, in a trans-psychological manner, inaccessible to psychological analysis.

Once again we refer to Adler's contention that an adequate psychology of life-style would in effect dispense with the need for a separate psychology of the ego. I believe Adler's position, though unelaborated, is essentially the same as the one here advocated. An adequate psychology would in effect *be a* psychology of the ego. It would deal fully and fairly with propriate functions. Indeed, everyone would assume that psychology was talking about self-functions, unless it was expressly stated that peripheral, opportunistic, or actuarial events were under discussion. But as matters stand today, with so much of psychology preoccupied (as was Hume) with bits and pieces of experience, or else with generalized mathematical equations, it becomes necessary for the few psychologists who are concerned with propriate functions to specify in their discourse that they are dealing with them. If the horizons of psychology were more spacious than they are I venture to suggest that theories of personality would not need the concept of self or of ego except in certain compound forms, such as *self-knowledge, self-image, ego-enhancement, ego-extension.*

44. THE ALIENATED SELF

Kenneth Keniston

THE CULT OF THE PRESENT

Some outlooks make the past their psychological center and look back nostalgically to the pleasures of lost times. Others, like the tradi-

From THE UNCOMMITTED *by Kenneth Keniston, Chapter 7. Copyright* © *1962, 1965 by Kenneth Keniston. Reprinted by permission of Harcourt Brace Jovanovich, Inc.*

tional American ethos, look primarily to the future, considering both present and past mere preparations for what is to come. Still others consciously focus on the present, which is seen as the central aspect of time and history, the rationale of behavior and the *raison d'être* of life. Each of these temporal orientations accentuates its characteristic mode of experience: a focus on the past emphasizes memory, history, conservation, and nostalgia; one on the future stresses anticipation, planning, saving, and preparation; and concern with the present almost invariably involves a focus on experience, consumption, sentience, activity, and adventure in the here and now.

Of these three orientations, it is abundantly clear that the alienated focus consciously on the present. Their philosophies emphasize the irrelevance of the past and their pessimism about the future. They reject long-range idealism in favor of the personal and situational needs of the moment; they tell us of their lack of future plans; they experience time as decline or stagnation rather than progress or growth. So, too, in their daily lives they are addicted to passionate intellectual inquiry in the service of present needs rather than to efforts to acquire skills for the future. They are detached observers of their worlds, searching for ways to intensify and heighten the present, not for the wisdom of the past or for lessons for the future. Though the present is often dull, boring, or depressing to them, they can seldom escape it by pleasant fantasies about what was or what is to come. The future is closed by their pessimism; and even their fantasies of past infantile bliss are unconscious and would be unacceptable to their conscious selves. Whatever conscious meaning their lives may have is given by immediacy, experience, the here and now.

The cult of the present can take many forms, ranging from the quest for Nirvana to drug addiction, from aesthetic appreciation to violent delinquency. But we can distinguish two possible directions in any effort to intensify the present. One is a search for adventure, active, outgoing, and vigorous, which emphasizes the role of the actor in *creating* experience, in making new and heightened experiences for himself. An adventurous approach to experience leads to an equation of self and activity, in which the individual seeks to become what he does, in which emphasis is on the process rather than on the product, in which the actor tries to find and reveal himself through his activity. In our own time, such an emphasis can be seen in forms as different as action painting and juvenile delinquency; in both cases, meaning derives from action.

The more passive form of the cult of the present is the *search for sentience,* and it is this search that characterizes the alienated. Here the self is defined not by action, but by perception; and meaning is created by heightened receptivity and openness. Experience is defined as subtlety, sensitivity, and awareness: the purpose of existence is not to alter the world so as to create new experiences, but to alter the self so as to receive new perceptions from what is already there. Whereas the adventurous seeks to change the world so that it stimulates him in new ways, the sentient seeks to change himself so that he is more open to stimulation. The experiencer thus seeks above all to refine himself as perceiver, cultivating "awareness," "openness," and "sensitivity." Along with a search for heightened perceptiveness goes a desire for heightened responsiveness—"genuine" feeling, direct passion, pure impulse, and uncensored fantasy. Some seek sentience through aesthetic sensitivity, others through continual self-examination, others by vicarious experience of the lives of others. The essential quest is the effort to perceive and feel deeply, clearly, intensely, truly.

A major component of this quest is the *search for a breakthrough.* The alienated value most those moments when the barriers to perception crumble, when the walls between themselves and the world fall away and they are "in contact" with nature, other people, or themselves. These times of breakthrough are relatively rare, for much of their lives seem to them dull, depressed, and ordinary. But when such moments come, the alienated describe them in mystical terms, emphasizing the loss of distinction between self and object, the revelation of the meaning of Everything in an apparently insignificant detail, the ineffability of the experience, the inherent difficulty in describing a moment which transcends ordinary categories of language. At other times, a breakthrough may be achieved with a person in a "moment of truth," when the two understand each other in what seems a miraculously total way. Or a breakthrough may be to the inner self, involving a feeling of inner communication and psychic wholeness which—though ephemeral—can profoundly affect the individual later.

Implicit in the search for a breakthrough is the conviction of alienated subjects that they are *constricted by conventional categories,* imprisoned by the usual ways of seeing the world, of coping with their own feelings and fantasies, of dealing with other people, even of channeling inner impulse into activity. One subject described human relations in terms of people attempting to communicate through airtight space suits; others feel that they are bound and hampered in their search for experience by the conventional categories of our culture. Their laboriously acquired educations often seem to them to have built a dark screen between themselves and the world, a distorting filter which blocks clear perception. Despite their occasional break-throughs, alienated subjects feel that they are unduly constricted in expressing their feelings; that they have lost the capacity for spontaneous appreciation of the world which they once had in childhood; that they are unduly shut off from their own fantasies and feelings. Though most observers would question these self-appraisals, they are a major motive in the continual effort of the alienated to attain more immediate contact with objects, and a further expression of their inability to tolerate any restraint or self-limitation.

For many alienated youths, the search for sentience entails still another corollary, the *desire for self-expression.* As we have seen in Inburn,* this is rarely a desire to remedy wrongs or to reform society. Instead, it grows out of their conviction that they have, for brief moments, achieved some true and more total perception of the world than have most of their fellows. For some, the desire to express this perception has led to an interest in writing, the theater, or painting. We usually see artistic efforts as attempts to communicate and, in this measure, assume they require an audience; but for the alienated, the external audience is relatively unimportant. Their crucial audience is internal: they write or act or paint for themselves, to structure, order, and confirm their own experience, more as subjective catharsis, perceptual therapy, or self-justification than as an effort to reveal to an outer audience. The desire for self-expression thus becomes a facet of their effort to enhance experience, to structure and organize

* A code name for one of the subjects of the study. (Eds.)

it in new ways that will not obscure its meaning, to order the chaos of sensation with personal form.

The meanings of the cult of the present for these young men are complex. In part, it is a response to a conscious desire to escape their pasts and avoid their futures, but it is more than this. The alienated feel hemmed in and constrained by their worlds (and, unconsciously, by their unruly fantasies and feelings); they reject the culture which shaped them; they chafe under even the ordinary categories through which most men filter experience and feeling. To some extent, they are incapable of employing these categories, for their experience has disposed them to see the world differently; but in part, their ideology dictates that they should *choose* to reject these categories. They are extraordinarily aware of the blinders of selective awareness and inattention which many men use to hide the seamier sides of their lives from themselves; and though the alienated have, in fact, blinders of their own, they are at least different and unconventional blinders.

The notion of a breakthrough also has multiple meanings. A breakthrough means an ability to slough off the restrictive categories through which most men interpret their lives to themselves; it involves a kind of experience which is above all characteristic of early childhood, when perception was in fact less structured by adult categories and blindnesses, when wisdom comes from the mouths of babes because they have yet to learn what can be noticed and said without fear of adult reprisal. Even in their intense conscious orientation to the present, these youths therefore manifest an *un*conscious desire to recapture the qualities of experience that, they vaguely recall, characterized their early lives. Ultimately they seek to regain the relatively undifferentiated and uncategorized view of the world they had as small children, and to achieve the same total understanding and fusion with another that they had with their mothers.

The cult of the present is, however, not only a theme of alienation, but is found in other forms among many young people. Indeed, among the defining characteristics of American youth culture—the special world of American adolescents and young adults—are a concentration on the present, a focus on immediate experience, an effort to achieve "genuineness," "directness," "sincerity," in perception and human relations. We see this cult in both forms—as a search for external stimulation and for internal transformation—in many of the deviant behaviors of our society: in the search for adventure among delinquent gangs, in the use of drugs to break through the gates of perception, in the "beat" quest for "kicks." And in less extreme form, a similar emphasis on the present exists in the increasing American stress on consumption rather than saving, on the "rich, full life" in the present rather than the deferred goals and future satisfactions of an earlier society. All of this suggests that the alienated are reacting to a problem which transcends the peculiarities of their individual lives, and that the cult of the present is a response to historical pressures which affect alienated and unalienated alike.

THE FRAGMENTATION OF IDENTITY

No clear positive principle or program unifies and gives coherence to the lives of the alienated. The core of their ideology is negative, a repudiation of the central values of their culture, with few clear positive values or goals. Their search for sentience is a search rather than an accomplishment; and their desire to break through the ordinary categories of perception and feeling springs negatively from opposition to the constraints of culture. Lacking positive values, the alienated experience themselves as diffused, fragmented, torn in different directions by inner and outer pulls. They find little self-definition or coherence in their intellectual interests or their social relationships, for these rarely persist beyond the impulses that inspired them. So, too, in their combination of (covert) admiration and (overt) repudiation of those who might become models for them, they reveal both a sense of inner emptiness which leads to excessive admiration and a sense of inner fragility which makes them fear submersion in an admired person. Nor do their pasts provide any clear continuities in behavior and outlook which might unify their conceptions of themselves. Once homebound

children, they have now become overt rebels against the kind of world they grew up in; inwardly and unconsciously preoccupied with their lost pasts, outwardly and consciously they live in the present alone.

Any sense of personal identity achieves much of its coherence from commitment. The object of commitment can vary—a life work, a central value, some personal talent, loyalty to a person or a group, a wife or a family, a corporation or a revolution—all can give identity to an individual; but without some positive commitment, a sense of personal wholeness is difficult to achieve. Thus, a primary obstacle to the formation of a unitary sense of self among the alienated is their judgment that *commitment is submission.* Commitment to other people entails loss of individuality, acceptance of restrictions or responsibility, accountability to others who will (deliberately or unintentionally) limit their freedom. Commitment to groups is seen as conformity, as "selling out" to group pressures. Commitment to work means accepting the unhappy requirements of the work role, the burdened life of the worker who cannot call his soul his own. Every commitment means allowing others to have a claim on one; and all claims are destructive.

The problem of identity is also a problem in the exercise of freedom; and these young men experience *freedom as a burden.* They are an amply talented group, imaginative, intelligent, skilled in language, capable, when they choose, of fulfilling the complex demands of an exacting college. Their past lives have been, if anything, overprivileged when judged in terms of the kinds of schools they attended, the physical and educational advantages they enjoyed. In principle, our society allows such youths many options, many "objective" opportunities in the form of possible values, potential life styles, available jobs, girls who might become their wives, work they might make their own. But paradoxically, is it precisely for such young men as these that the problem of freedom is greatest. With a virtually limitless number of options open to them, with no self-evidently valid criterion to choose among these options, convinced that commitments are destructive, they vacillate, envying those whose choices are fewer and whose lives seem simpler. Faced with a multitude of opportunities, they eschew them all, and dimly resent the freedom that makes them responsible for their own fates.

The result is a diffusion and fragmentation of the sense of identity, an experience of themselves as amorphous, indistinct, and disorganized, a repudiation of all commitments coupled with an overwhelming desire to emulate those who are committed, a secret yearning to give up all responsibility. Insofar as they have any clear sense of self it is almost entirely defined by what they are against, what they despise, by groups they do not want to belong to and values they consider tawdry. Such *negative self-definition* creates an enormous psychological problem, for it means that the self is defined by exclusions, estrangements, repudiations, and rejections—forces that can rarely provide unity, coherence, or a sense of direction. Only when rejection has a single narrowly defined target can it provide the basis for the identity of a rebel or the purpose of a revolutionary. But the alienated, unlike true revolutionaries, have no single target as they oppose the whole of their culture; and even a commitment to reform seems, like all commitments, dangerous. As a result, these youths know what they are not, but not what they are; and often knowing what they are not is equivalent to feeling they are nothing.

This sense of inner fragmentation has complex origins. In part it reflects conflicts between the pulls and pushes of their past lives, especially between the pull of unconscious nostalgia for the past and the push of a conscious search for experience in the present. But their systematic effort to remain receptive to experience of the world and themselves itself further undermines a sense of identity. In any society, men must have conventions about what is real and what is significant, partly in order to protect themselves from an excess of stimulation. Such conventions, to be sure, prevent total openness to experience, but at the same time they serve to ward off chaos, to make the world more comprehensible and therefore more livable, to bring order into the sense of self, daily life, and human relations. To reject these conventions without having discovered others to take their place is to invite not merely experience but inundation, deliberately to deprive oneself of the

filters and screens by which the self and universe are made manageable. For most men and women, self-definition requires repudiation or neglect of much potential experience; paradoxically, the alienated, who repudiate so much else, cannot and will not repudiate the experiences that most upset their precarious sense of selfhood.

In one obvious sense, then, these students are "maladjusted." Any young man who rejects the chief values of his fellows and of his culture, who dislikes the adulthood that most of his countrymen live, is by definition and by intent not "adjusted" to his society; and he would usually be quick to admit and take pride in this fact. Furthermore, alienated students make a point of their unrelenting honesty with themselves and often revel in their own deficiencies and problems. Their intense and sometimes morbid introspectiveness gives them a relatively extensive acquaintance with their own psychic problems, and their defiant scorn for social proprieties inclines them, if anything, to exaggerate their disabilities. Thus, in some cases, the alienated may look more disturbed than unalienated subjects with equally serious problems but less awareness of them and less inclination to discuss them.

Yet it is difficult to live without some relatively clear sense of self. For all that the alienated proclaim that their discontents are but a reflection of the human condition, this insistence often has a hollow ring, even to themselves. Beneath their repudiation of happiness as a goal, behind their insistence that the world causes their pessimism and unhappiness, under their belief that all modern men are the victims of anxiety, these young men usually harbor doubts about their own ability to cope with life, fearing or suspecting that their unhappiness is partly of their own making. They frequently avoid the very relationships and commitments which might be of greatest benefit to them; they often lose effectiveness as social critics because of the lack of selectivity of their criticisms; they take on the whole world at once and can sometimes cope with none of it effectively. Furthermore, their fantasies show not only the power of their pasts, but a more ominous inability to structure, organize, or give coherence to the present. In all these respects, they pay a heavy price for their repudiation of conventional pathways to adulthood. In part, their neuroses are determined by the often unfortunate family situations in which they grew up; in part, however, they are a direct result of their alienation, which sets them more difficult and at times impossible tasks. But whichever factor is most salient in any particular individual, these young men as college students were rarely happy or psychologically integrated.

Yet though their problems are often especially acute, the inability to achieve a clear, unified, and coherent sense of identity is not a problem of the alienated alone. On the contrary, exacerbated problems of self-definition and identity are extremely common among college students as among other young people, and men and women of all generations increasingly experience identity as a problem. This suggests that we again must explain the fragmentation of identity among these students not only in terms of individual psychology, but in terms of the social and historical pressures on young people as a group in our country.

THE FANTASY OF FUSION

In examining the lives and fantasies of these young men we have repeatedly seen the continuing force of the distant personal past on their adult lives. As a theme of fantasy, it leads to story after story in which the hero's chief aim is to recover the dead, to disinter the past, to recover the lost and buried, to find oblivion in some enveloping medium, even at the price of self-destruction. And as a theme of conscious daily life, the unconscious search for the past dictates that these young men continually yearn for more direct and immediate contact with reality, for more immediate and genuine expressions of feeling, for human relationships in which all separateness is blurred—and that, when they cannot find such experience, the world seems dull and drab beside their unconscious desires. Even in the ideologies of these students, their overwhelming regret at the loss of the past is indirectly reflected in their bitterness about life, their repudiation of those who cannot give them the kind of oblivion they yearn for,

and their pessimism about finding future felicity. Paradoxically, it is precisely because unconsciously they so regret the loss of the past that they now consciously devote themselves so intensely to the present, as if they could not bear to recall the bliss they have lost.

When, as with these young men, such a lust for bygone days is strong, it regularly has several consequences. For one, the *past is idealized*. Recall here Inburn's idyllic account of his early relationship with his mother, where he describes a kind of total unity between mother and son which could not really have existed when he recalls it. In the fantasies of others we find a similarly exaggerated dream of the blissfulness of early mother-son relationships, of the capacity of truly maternal women to provide *totally* for men, of the complete absence of distinctions between self and object. Similarly, the implicit image of ideal experience in alienated youths emphasizes a unity between the perceiver and the perceived which is virtually impossible for adults and possible only in childhood *before* a differentiated conception of self emerges.

At root, probably the most powerful unconscious motive in many of these young men is their desire to merge, to fuse with, to lose themselves in some embracing person, experience, or group. This *fantasy of mystical fusion* involves the unconscious desire to lose all selfhood in some undifferentiated state with another or with nature, to be totally embraced and to embrace totally. But this unconscious desire has its opposite in the conscious effort of these young men to retain and develop their individuality and to avoid submersion. In understanding their distrust of commitment and their inability to achieve a sense of identity, both poles of this ambivalence must be kept in mind: first, their *conscious* desire to be highly differentiated individuals and, second, their opposite *unconscious* fantasy of achieving a total fusion with people and experience that would lead to obliteration of all individuality.

Contrasted with their idealized fantasies about the past, the present inevitably seems *hollow and empty*, meaningful only insofar as it can be made to yield a breakthrough to a mode of experiencing characteristic of the past. When the alienated are depressed, as they often are, it is because most of their lives seem lacking in the excitement, vitality, and immediacy they can find only in the peak experiences and breakthroughs which come close to their dreams of their early lives. Thus, *personal time is seen as decline,* as loss and as stagnation, as a steady and ever-more-irrevocable movement away from the unconscious dream of perfect union, perfect fusion, and perfect selflessness.

And finally, the romanticized dream of the lost past in which mystical fusion was possible entails unconscious *impatience with selfhood.* A clearly delineated self is, among other things, a barrier to fusion; what most men experience as the protective boundaries of personality, the alienated unconsciously feel to be walls that impede merging with experience, nature, or other people. And indeed it is true that the capacity to merge with another presupposes in the infant an absence of self-definition, just as in adult mystical experience, merging with the universe has always been said to involve a disappearance of mundane selfhood. The inability to achieve a sense of personal identity is in part the result of the unconscious wish for fusion.

I have already traced the personal origins of the search for the lost past, locating the crucial events in the apparent victory of these youths over their fathers and their consequent inability to outgrow gradually their needs for an embracing relationship with their mothers.

But we should also recall that the loss of infantile embeddedness is a universal estrangement in human development, with which every individual and every culture must somehow come to terms. As with many other themes of alienation, this is but a heightening of a fundamental problem in all human life, a universal loss made more traumatic in these young men because of its abruptness.

Nor can this theme be separated from the broader social scene. As I will argue in a later chapter, the family constellation which underlies this search for the past, like the sharp contrast between childhood experience and the demands of adult life, are built into our society, producing in most Americans—alienated or not—a special problem about renouncing childhood and accepting adulthood. The fantasy of fusion involves a desire to find in adulthood the qualities of warmth, communion, acceptedness, dependence, and intimacy which existed in childhood; and one reason why this desire leads to alienation from adulthood is because adult life in America offers so few of these qualities. The alienated, to be sure, experience this problem especially intensely, and have been prepared to do so by a personal past that deviates from the norm of American family life. But even among those whose pasts are more typical, the same contrasts between an idealized childhood and a vaguely resented adulthood often exist in more muted form.

45. THE OUTSIDER

Albert Camus

...Just then my employer sent for me. For a moment I felt uneasy, as I expected he was going to tell me to stick to my work and not waste time chattering with friends over the phone. However, it was nothing of the kind. He wanted to discuss a project he had in view, though so far he'd come to no decision. It was to open a branch in Paris, so as to be able to deal with the big companies on the spot, without postal delays, and he wanted to know if I'd like a post there.

"You're a young man," he said, "and I'm pretty sure you'd enjoy living in Paris. And, of course, you could travel about France for some months in the year."

I told him I was quite prepared to go; but really I didn't care much one way or the other.

He then asked if a "change of life," as he called it, didn't appeal to me, and I answered that one never changed his way of life; one life was as good as another, and my present one suited me quite well.

At this he looked rather hurt, and told me that I always shilly-shallied, and that I lacked ambition—a grave defect, to his mind, when one was in business.

I returned to my work. I'd have preferred not to vex him, but I saw no reason for "changing my life." By and large it wasn't an unpleasant one. As a student I'd had plenty of ambition of the kind he meant. But, when I had to drop my studies, I very soon realized all that was pretty futile.

From THE STRANGER *by Albert Camus, translated by Stuart Gilbert, Part 1, Chapter 5. English translation copyright 1946 by Alfred A. Knopf, Inc. British edition published as* THE OUTSIDER *by Hamish Hamilton Ltd., London. Reprinted by permission of Random House, Inc. and Hamish Hamilton Ltd.*

Marie came that evening and asked me if I'd marry her. I said I didn't mind; if she was keen on it, we'd get married.

Then she asked me again if I loved her. I replied, much as before, that her question meant nothing or next to nothing—but I supposed I didn't.

"If that's how you feel," she said, "why marry me?"

I explained that it had no importance really, but, if it would give her pleasure, we could get married right away. I pointed out that, anyhow, the suggestion came from her; as for me, I'd merely said, "Yes."

Then she remarked that marriage was a serious matter.

To which I answered: "No."

She kept silent after that, staring at me in a curious way. Then she asked:

"Suppose another girl had asked you to marry her—I mean, a girl you liked in the same way as you like me—would you have said 'Yes' to her, too?"

"Naturally."

Then she said she wondered if she really loved me or not. I, of course, couldn't enlighten her as to that. And, after another silence, she murmured something about my being "a queer fellow." "And I daresay that's why I love you," she added. "But maybe that's why one day I'll come to hate you."

To which I had nothing to say, so I said nothing.

She thought for a bit, then started smiling and, taking my arm, repeated that she was in earnest; she really wanted to marry me.

"All right," I answered. "We'll get married whenever you like." I then mentioned the proposal made by my employer, and Marie said she'd love to go to Paris.

When I told her I'd lived in Paris for a while, she asked me what it was like.

"A dingy sort of town, to my mind. Masses of pigeons and dark courtyards. And the people have washed-out, white faces."

Then we went for a walk all the way across the town by the main streets. The women were goodlookers, and I asked Marie if she, too, noticed this. She said, "Yes," and that she saw what I meant. After that we said nothing for some minutes. However, as I didn't want her to leave me, I suggested we should dine together at Céleste's. She'd have loved to dine with me, she said, only she was booked up for the evening. We were near my place, and I said, *"Au revoir, then."*

She looked me in the eyes.

"Don't you want to know what I'm doing this evening?"

I did want to know, but I hadn't thought of asking her, and I guessed she was making a grievance of it. I must have looked embarrassed, for suddenly she started laughing and bent toward me, pouting her lips for a kiss.

I went by myself to Céleste's. When I had just started my dinner an odd-looking little woman came in and asked if she might sit at my table. Of course she might. She had a chubby face like a ripe apple, bright eyes, and moved in a curiously jerky way, as if she were on wires. After taking off her close-fitting jacket she sat down and started studying the bill of fare with a sort of rapt attention. Then she called Céleste and gave her order, very fast but quite distinctly; one didn't lose a word. While waiting for the hors d'oeuvre she opened her bag, took out a slip of paper and a pencil, and added up the bill in advance. Diving into her bag again, she produced a purse and took from it the exact sum, plus a small tip, and placed it on the cloth in front of her.

Just then the waiter brought the hors d'oeuvre, which she proceeded to wolf down voraciously. While waiting for the next course, she produced another pencil, this time a blue one, from her bag, and the radio magazine for the coming week, and started making ticks against almost all the items of the daily programs. There were a dozen pages in the magazine, and she continued studying them closely throughout the meal. When I'd finished mine she was still ticking off items with the same meticulous attention. Then she rose, put on her jacket again with the same abrupt, robotlike gestures, and walked briskly out of the restaurant.

Having nothing better to do, I followed her for a short distance. Keeping on the curb of the pavement, she walked straight ahead, never swerving or looking back, and it was extraordinary how fast she covered the ground, considering her smallness. In fact, the pace was too much for me, and I soon lost sight of her and turned back homeward. For a moment the "little robot" (as I thought of her) had much impressed me, but I soon forgot about her.

As I was turning in at my door I ran into old Salamano. I asked him into my room, and he informed me that his dog was definitely lost. He'd been to the pound to inquire, but it wasn't there, and the staff told him it had probably been run over. When he asked them whether it was any use inquiring about it at the police station, they said the police had more important things to attend to than keeping records of stray dogs run over in the streets. I suggested he should get another dog, but, reasonably enough, he pointed out that he'd become used to this one, and it wouldn't be the same thing.

I was seated on my bed, with my legs up, and Salamano on a chair beside the table, facing me, his hands spread on his knees. He had kept on his battered felt hat and was mumbling away behind his draggled yellowish mustache. I found him rather boring, but I had nothing to do and didn't feel sleepy. So, to keep the conversation going, I asked some questions about his dog—how long he had had it and so forth. He told me he had got it soon after his wife's death. He'd married rather late in life. When a young man, he wanted to go on the stage; during his military service he'd often played in the regimental theatricals and acted rather well, so everybody said. However, finally, he had taken a job in the railway, and he didn't regret it, as now he had a small pension. He and his wife had never hit it off very well, but they'd got used to each other, and when she died he felt lonely. One of his mates on the railway whose bitch had just had pups had offered him one, and he had taken it, as a companion. He'd had to feed it from the bottle at first. But, as a dog's life is shorter than a man's, they'd grown old together, so to speak.

"He was a cantankerous brute," Salamano said. "Now and then we had some proper set-tos, he and I. But he was a good mutt all the same."

I said he looked well bred, and that evidently pleased the old man.

"Ah, but you should have seen him before his illness!" he said. "He had a wonderful coat; in fact, that was his best point, really. I tried hard to cure him; every mortal night after he got that skin disease I rubbed an ointment in. But his real trouble was old age, and there's no curing that."

Just then I yawned, and the old man said he'd better make a move. I told him he could stay, and that I was sorry about what had happened to his dog. He thanked me, and

mentioned that my mother had been very fond of his dog. He referred to her as "your poor mother," and was afraid I must be feeling her death terribly. When I said nothing he added hastily and with a rather embarrassed air that some of the people in the street said nasty things about me because I'd sent my mother to the Home. But he, of course, knew better; he knew how devoted to my mother I had always been.

I answered—why, I still don't know—that it surprised me to learn I'd produced such a bad impression. As I couldn't afford to keep her here, it seemed the obvious thing to do, to send her to a home. "In any case," I added, "for years she'd never had a word to say to me, and I could see she was moping, with no one to talk to."

"Yes," he said, "and at a home one makes friends, anyhow." . . .

46. TOWARD A PSYCHOLOGY OF HEALTH

A. H. Maslow

There is now emerging over the horizon a new conception of human sickness and of human health, a psychology that I find so thrilling and so full of wonderful possibilities that I yield to the temptation to present it publicly even before it is checked and confirmed, and before it can be called reliable scientific knowledge.

The basic assumptions of this point of view are:

1. We have, each of us, an essential biologically

From TOWARD A PSYCHOLOGY OF BEING *by Abraham H. Maslow, pp. 3–8. Copyright* © *1962, 1968 by Litton Educational Publishing, Inc. Reprinted by permission of Van Nostrand Reinhold Company.*

based inner nature, which is to some degree "natural," intrinsic, given, and, in a certain limited sense, unchangeable, or, at least, unchanging.

2. Each person's inner nature is in part unique to himself and in part species-wide.

3. It is possible to study this inner nature scientifically and to discover what it is like (not *invent—discover*).

4. This inner nature, as much as we know of it so far, seems not to be intrinsically or primarily or necessarily evil. The basic needs (for life, for safety and security, for belongingness and affection, for respect and self respect, and for self-actualization), the basic human emotions and the basic human capacities are on their face either neutral, premoral or positively "good." Destructiveness,

sadism, cruelty, malice, etc., seem so far to be not intrinsic but rather they seem to be violent reactions *against* frustration of our intrinsic needs, emotions and capacities. Anger is *in itself* not evil, nor is fear, laziness, or even ignorance. Of course, these can and do lead to evil behavior, but they needn't. This result is not intrinsically necessary. Human nature is not nearly as bad as it has been thought to be. In fact it can be said that the possibilities of human nature have customarily been sold short.

5. Since this inner nature is good or neutral rather than bad, it is best to bring it out and to encourage it rather than to suppress it. If it is permitted to guide our life, we grow healthy, fruitful, and happy.
6. If this essential core of the person is denied or suppressed, he gets sick sometimes in obvious ways, sometimes in subtle ways, sometimes immediately, sometimes later.
7. This inner nature is not strong and overpowering and unmistakable like the instincts of animals. It is weak and delicate and subtle and easily overcome by habit, cultural pressure, and wrong attitudes toward it.
8. Even though weak, it rarely disappears in the normal person—perhaps not even in the sick person. Even though denied, it persists underground forever pressing for actualization.
9. Somehow, these conclusions must all be articulated with the necessity of discipline, deprivation, frustration, pain, and tragedy. To the extent that these experiences reveal and foster and fulfill our inner nature, to that extent they are desirable experiences. It is increasingly clear that these experiences have something to do with a sense of achievement and ego strength and therefore with the sense of healthy self-esteem and self-confidence. The person who hasn't conquered, withstood and overcome continues to feel doubtful that he *could*. This is true not only for external dangers; it holds also for the ability to control and to delay one's own impulses, and therefore to be unafraid of them.

Observe that if these assumptions are proven true, they promise a scientific ethics, a natural value system, a court of ultimate appeal for the determination of good and bad, of right and wrong. The more we learn about man's natural tendencies, the easier it will be to tell him how to be good, how to be happy, how to be fruitful, how to respect himself, how to love, how to fulfill his highest potentialities.

This amounts to automatic solution of many of the personality problems of the future. The thing to do seems to be to find out what one is *really* like inside, deep down, as a member of the human species and as a particular individual.

The study of such self-fulfilling people can teach us much about our own mistakes, our shortcomings, the proper directions in which to grow. Every age but ours has had its model, its ideal. All of these have been given up by our culture; the saint, the hero, the gentleman, the knight, the mystic. About all we have left is the well-adjusted man without problems, a very pale and doubtful substitute. Perhaps we shall soon be able to use as our guide and model the fully growing and self-fulfilling human being, the one in whom all his potentialities are coming to full development, the one whose inner nature expresses itself freely, rather than being warped, suppressed, or denied.

The serious thing for each person to recognize vividly and poignantly, each for himself, is that every falling away from species-virtue, every crime against one's own nature, every evil act, *every one without exception records itself* in our unconscious and makes us despise ourselves. Karen Horney had a good word to describe this unconscious perceiving and remembering; she said it "registers." If we do something we are ashamed of, it "registers" to our discredit, and if we do something honest or fine or good, it "registers" to our credit. The net results ultimately are either one or the other—either we respect and accept ourselves or we despise ourselves and feel contemptible, worthless, and unlovable. Theologians used to use the word *"accidie"* to describe the sin of failing to do with one's life all that one knows one could do.

This point of view in no way denies the usual Freudian picture. But it does add to it and supplement it. To oversimplify the matter somewhat, it is as if Freud supplied to us the sick half of psychology and we must now fill it out with the healthy half. Perhaps this health psychology will give us more possibility for controlling and improving our lives and for making ourselves better people. Perhaps this will be more fruitful than asking "how to get *unsick*."

How can we encourage free development?

What are the best educational conditions for it? Sexual? Economic? Political? What kind of world do we need for such people to grow in? What kind of world will such people create? Sick people are made by a sick culture; healthy people are made possible by a healthy culture. But it is just as true that sick individuals make their culture more sick and that healthy individuals make their culture more healthy. Improving individual health is one approach to making a better world. To express it in another way, encouragement of personal growth is a real possibility; cure of actual neurotic symptoms is far less possible without outside help. It it relatively easy to try deliberately to make oneself a more honest man; it is very difficult to try to cure one's own compulsions or obsessions.

The classical approach to personality problems considers them to be problems in an undesirable sense. Struggle, conflict, guilt, bad conscience, anxiety, depression, frustration, tension, shame, self-punishment, feeling of inferiority or unworthiness—they all cause psychic pain, they disturb efficiency of performance, and they are uncontrollable. They are therefore automatically regarded as sick and undesirable and they get "cured" away as soon as possible.

But all of these symptoms are found also in healthy people, or in people who are growing toward health. Supposing you *should* feel guilty and don't? Supposing you have attained a nice stabilization of forces and you *are* adjusted? Perhaps adjustment and stabilization, while good because it cuts your pain, is also bad because development toward a higher ideal ceases?

Erich Fromm, in a very important book, attacked the classical Freudian notion of a superego because this concept was entirely authoritarian and relativistic. That is to say, your superego or your conscience was supposed by Freud to be primarily the internalization of the wishes, demands, and ideals of the father and mother, whoever they happen to be. But supposing they are criminals? Then what kind of conscience do you have? Or supposing you have a rigid moralizing father who hates fun? Or a psychopath? This conscience exists—Freud was right. We do get our ideals largely from such early figures and not from Sunday School books read later in life. But there is also another element in conscience, or, if you like, another kind of conscience, which we all have either weakly or strongly. And this is the "intrinsic conscience." This is based upon the unconscious and preconscious perception of our own nature, of our own destiny, of our own capacities, of our own "call" in life. It insists that we be true to our inner nature and that we do not deny it out of weakness or for advantage or for any other reason. He who belies his talent, the born painter who sells stockings instead, the intelligent man who lives a stupid life, the man who sees the truth and keeps his mouth shut, the coward who gives up his manliness, all these people perceive in a deep way that they have done wrong to themselves and despise themselves for it. Out of this self-punishment may come only neurosis, but there may equally well come renewed courage, righteous indignation, increased self-respect, because of thereafter doing the right thing; in a word, growth and improvement can come through pain and conflict.

In essence I am deliberately rejecting our present easy distinction between sickness and health, at least as far as surface symptoms are concerned. Does sickness mean having symptoms? I maintain now that sickness might consist of not having symptoms when you should. Does health mean being symptom-free? I deny it. Which of the Nazis at Auschwitz or Dachau were healthy? Those with stricken conscience or those with a nice, clear, happy conscience? Was it possible for a profoundly human person not to feel conflict, suffering, depression, rage, etc?

In a word if you tell me you have a personality problem I am not certain until I know you better whether to say "Good!" or "I'm sorry." It depends on the reasons. And these, it seems, may be bad reasons, or they may be good reasons.

An example is the changing attitude of psychologists toward popularity, toward adjustment, even toward delinquency. Popular with whom? Perhaps it is better for a youngster to be *unpopular* with the neighboring snobs or with the local country club set. Adjusted to what? To a bad culture? To a dominating parent? What shall we think of a well-adjusted slave? A well-adjusted prisoner? Even the behavior problem boy is being looked upon with new tolerance. *Why* is he delinquent? Most often it is for sick reasons. But occasionally it is for good reasons and the boy is simply resisting exploitation, domination, neglect, contempt, and trampling upon.

Clearly what will be called personality problems depends on who is doing the calling. The slave owner? The dictator? The patriarchal father? The husband who wants his wife to remain a child? It seems quite clear that personality problems may sometimes be loud protests against the crushing of one's psychological bones, of one's true inner nature. What is sick then is *not* to protest while this crime is being committed. And I am sorry to report my impression that most people do not protest under such treatment. They take it and pay years later, in neurotic and psychosomatic symptoms of various kinds, or perhaps in some cases never become aware that they are sick, that they have missed true happiness, true fulfillment of promise,

a rich emotional life, and a serene, fruitful old age, that they have never known how wonderful it is to be creative, to react aesthetically, to find life thrilling.

The question of desirable grief and pain or the necessity for it must also be faced. Is growth and self-fulfillment possible at all without pain and grief and sorrow and turmoil? If these are to some extent necessary and unavoidable, then to what extent? If grief and pain are sometimes necessary for growth of the person, then we must learn not to protect people from them automatically as if they were always bad. Sometimes they may be good and desirable in view of the ultimate good consequences. Not allowing people to go through their pain, and protecting them from it, may turn out to be a kind of overprotection, which in turn implies a certain lack of respect for the integrity and the intrinsic nature and the future development of the individual.

RECOMMENDED FURTHER READING

*Allport, Gordon W.: *Becoming;* New Haven, Yale University Press 1955

————: *Pattern and Growth in Personality;* New York, Holt, Rinehart & Winston 1961

Ansbacher, H. and R. Ansbacher (eds.): *The Individual Psychology of Alfred Adler;* New York, Basic Books 1956

Bandura, Albert and R. Walters: *Social Learning and Personality Development;* New York, Holt, Rinehart & Winston 1963

*Brenner, Charles: *An Elementary Textbook of Psychoanalysis;* New York, International Universities Press 1955

*Brown, James A. C.: *Freud and the Post-Freudians;* Baltimore, Penguin Books 1961

*Cattell, Raymond B.: *The Scientific Analysis of Personality;* Baltimore, Penguin Books 1965

Dollard, John and Neal E. Miller: *Personality and Psychotherapy;* New York, McGraw-Hill 1950

Freud, Anna: *The Ego and the Mechanisms of Defense;* London, Hogarth Press 1937

*Freud, Sigmund: *A General Introduction to Psychoanalysis;* New York, Liveright 1920

*————: *An Outline of Psychoanalysis;* New York, Norton 1949

*Hall, Calvin S.: *A Primer of Freudian Psychology;* Cleveland, World 1954

———— and Gardner Lindzey: *Theories of Personality;* New York, John Wiley 1957

Jacobi, Jolande: *The Psychology of C. G. Jung;* London, Routledge & Kegan Paul 1942

Laing, R. D.: *Self and Others* (Revised Ed.); New York, Pantheon 1969

*Maslow, A. H.: *Toward A Psychology of Being* (2nd Ed.); New York, Van Nostrand Reinhold 1968

Munroe, Ruth L.: *Schools of Psychoanalytic Thought;* New York, Dryden (Holt, Rinehart & Winston) 1955

Mussen, Paul H., J. J. Conger and J. Kagan: *Child Development and Personality* (2nd Ed.); New York, Harper & Row 1963

Whiting, John W. M. and Irvin Child: *Child Training and Personality;* New Haven, Yale University Press 1953

Wylie, R. C.: *The Self Concept;* Lincoln, Neb., University of Nebraska Press 1961

* Paperback edition available.

Edvard Munch, *The Shriek* (1895). Collection, The Museum of Modern Art, New York.

PART X

THE BREAKDOWN OF BEHAVIOR: PROBLEMS IN LIVING

In every culture or group there prevails a range of behaviors familiar and acceptable to members of the group, behaviors they consider "reasonable" and "normal," however bizarre they may appear to those from another culture or group. This is another way of saying that "normal" behavior is determined not logically or biologically but by the standards of the particular culture or group to which an individual belongs. What is normal among Eskimos may be madness among American suburbanites. Even within a single culture standards of "normal" behavior change, slowly but inevitably, with the passage of time.

Mental or emotional "health" is thus less a matter of an individual's attaining some biological ideal of optimal functioning than of his conforming to the behavioral standards and limits obtaining at a particular moment in his culture or his more immediate social groups. The observance of such standards is usually taken as proof that an individual is mentally "healthy" or stable, while their transgression is similarly adduced as proof that he is mentally "ill." (Behavior is, of course, also judged relative to the situation in which it occurs and relative to the physical and social status of the behaving individual.) Considering the strong positivistic bias of most American psychologists and psychiatrists it is, to say the least, curious that, contrary to their usual practice, they are willing to infer from unusual or socially unacceptable behaviors the existence of "disturbed," though unobserved, mental states instead of seeing in such behaviors conceivably rational responses to stressful or unique life situations. Such a reversal suggests that even supposedly "scientific" categories are determined by cultural values and prevailing social standards. This is not to deny the reality of mental or emotional disturbances (some of which may be organic in origin) but to point to the danger of judging such disturbances by the test of conventional social or even legal standards (in England and America "insanity," for example, is primarily a legal rather than a medical or psychological category).

However one defines it, therefore, whether by the exhibiting of certain desirable traits or by the criterion of effective functioning in one's life situations (however socially "deviant" those may be) mental health is not fixed but variable, not a point but a range along a continuum extending from the most familiar, acceptable, and efficacious behaviors to the most bizarre, disapproved, and seemingly irrelevant. It was the great eighteenth-century French psychiatrist Phillippe Pinel who remarked that "the insane man is not an inexplicable monster. He is but one of ourselves, only a little more so."

Conventionally, however, psychologists group behaviors and the emotional states that presumably underlie them into three categories: normal, neurotic, and psychotic. We have already suggested how slippery a concept "normality" is. One reaction to that is to consider it a residual category, to say that all behavior that is neither neurotic nor psychotic is, therefore, "normal." Practically speaking this is often how normality *is* defined as it is often easier to identify deviations from a norm than the norm itself. Yet, even this approach creates difficulties, for example, in classifying the behavior of the mentally retarded, who may be neither neurotic, psychotic, nor normal.

Neuroses or neurotic disturbances are extremely varied and widespread. They may be characterized as heightened or exaggerated forms of normal behavior, patterns of action that do not involve loss of contact with reality (as reality is socially defined) but which do usually interfere with the individual's effective occupational, social, or sexual functioning and which, particularly in the form of anxiety, cause him considerable subjective distress. Probably everyone at sometime in his life exhibits behaviors that may justifiably be labeled neurotic, a fact that indicates how relatively uninformative the label is. Anxiety reactions, phobias, obsessive and compulsive behaviors, conversion reactions, and diffuse feelings of dissatisfaction and meaninglessness are among the most common forms of neurotic disturbance.

Psychotic behavior may be regarded, in turn, as a heightened and exaggerated form of neurotic behavior, a form that involves loss of contact with reality as that is socially defined and validated together with loss of the ability to deal effectively with either the external or one's own internal environment. Psychoses may be divided into the organic, in which a physiological cause (usually some sort of brain or central nervous system damage) is present and the functional or psychogenic, in which no organic cause can be identified. While the organic (usually senile) psychoses are found overwhelmingly among older people the functional psychoses, of which schizophrenia and manic-depressive states are the most common, are most prevalent among children and adults under the age of thirty-five. While neuroses typically afflict the upper and middle classes, the rate of psychosis, on the other hand, is three times higher among the lower and working classes than among the middle and upper socio-economic groups.

Schizophrenia is by far the most common and the most crippling of the psychoses. It may develop either slowly (*process schizophrenia*) or in sudden response to an external event (*reactive schizophrenia*) and can take various forms. Common to all varieties of the disturbance is a severing of the logical processes of thought from emotional responses, a separation that results in an apparent "split" of the individual's personality. But, in fact, many schizophrenics live in a world that is well integrated and thoroughly consistent in terms of the principles on which it is constructed, principles, however, that are usually antithetical or incomprehensible to conventional thought and experience. Twenty-five percent of all those entering mental hospitals in the United States for the first time are diagnosed as schizophrenic while half the steady American mental hospital population of approximately 750,000 is so diagnosed. The number of clinical schizophrenics not in hospitals ("ambulatory" schizophrenics) can only be guessed at, but it is probably substantial.

The cause of schizophrenia has not yet been established and it seems likely that various causes can lead to the result we call by that name. Genetic factors almost certainly operate in some cases, biochemical or physiological imbalances may be causative in others, while strictly psychological factors seem to be the prime cause in many if not most cases. Quite possibly, hereditary factors predispose an individual to schizophrenia while the actual onset of the disturbance is precipitated by a biochemical change or a severe environmental stress.

Manic-depressive psychoses, far less common than schizophrenia, are characterized by alternations of mood from buoyant, unrealistic, almost megalomaniacal optimism to overwhelming, paralyzing, even suicidal depression. Some 10 percent of initial mental hospital admissions are classified in this category. The causes of manic-depressive psychoses are even more obscure (partly because less studied) than those of schizophrenia, although some investigators believe that genetic factors play an important role.

Two other forms of behavior disturbance that do not fit neatly along the normal—neurotic—psychotic continuum need to be mentioned: Character disorders (such as psychopathic and passive-aggressive behavior) involve relatively perduring patterns of morally, socially, or even legally disapproved actions. People with such disorders refuse, in other words, to play the game of life by the generally accepted rules. The psychopath, for example, is often thoroughly charming on the surface but is totally self-centered, seeks immediate gratification regardless of the cost to others, is incapable of forming intimate personal relationships, manipulates others for his own ends, and will often, quite free from guilt, perpetrate any action so long as he feels that he can "get away with it." Such people experience little psychological distress and are often highly successful by the world's criteria—a success that is usually built, however, on the ruination of others. What distinguishes the psychopath from the neurotic is that while the latter's behavior usually causes himself the greatest distress, the former invariably makes others pay for his actions. As with neurosis, there is no sharp boundary between normal and psychopathic behavior. In all of us there is probably a little of the psychopath; the difference is one of degree, a difference that, in practice, makes all the difference.

Finally, psychosomatic disorders involve the conversion or expression of psychological conflicts in the form of physical, organic symptoms. Peptic ulcers ("executives' disease") and ulcerative colitis are conditions that are frequently psychosomatic in origin and are typically associated with high levels of environmental stress. The emotional origins of psychosomatic disturbances do not make them any less "real" than organic illnesses but the egos of many Americans seem able to accept physical symptoms and incapacities more easily than emotional conflicts and unrequited psychic needs. In terms of impaired functioning the consequences of the two types of incapacity may be little, if any, different, yet the sympathy and solicitude offered those defined as physically ill but denied the emotionally disturbed may be an important factor in the "choice" of symptoms.

In our first selection Thomas Szasz, himself a psychiatrist, attacks the very concept of "mental illness" as an illusion and suggests that what we call mental illness is actually a shorthand label for the problems in living that many people encounter. While such problems are real the labels we use to describe them are often misleading. Szasz rejects the parallelism between physical and mental disease as well as the implicit assumption that relations among human beings are inherently harmonious. The judgment that a person is mentally ill depends on deviations from norms of communication and conduct that are formulated in psychosocial, ethical, or legal terms—not biological or medical ones. The making of such judgments is thus powerfully influenced by psychiatrists' own social and ethical standards as well as by the society's political values. In the Soviet Union, for example, individuals who express unacceptable political or social opinions may be defined as mentally or organically "sick" and be confined in hospitals rather than being branded as traitors or subversives and sent to jail (see for example Valery Tarsis' autobiographical novel, *Ward 7*). Formulation of a society's norms of communication and conduct is always, at bottom, a political decision. In concluding, Szasz suggests that the belief in mental illness may serve as a convenient social rationalization, an illusion or myth whose function is to conceal the ineluctable moral conflicts that characterize all human relationships. His article makes one wonder whether a solution to the phenomenon of "mental illness" should be sought through medical and psychological research or through political action; whether the causes of emotional disturbances lie within those who are disturbed or in the very structure of human social interaction.

The selection from Fyodor Dostoyevsky's (1821–1881) short novel, *The Gambler,* delineates the conversion of an unstable, would-be intellectual into a compulsive gambler. Compulsive behavior is a type of neurosis in which the individual's will appears beyond his conscious control, his actions to be dictated by a force alien to him. When under the sway of his compulsion the individual's rational faculties are overridden by irresistible, often incomprehensible needs and desires. Gambling is only one among an infinity of possible compulsions, though by no means an uncommon one. Notice both the megalomaniac quality of the narrator's fantasies of winning—the gaining of great wealth without either hard work or sustained exercise of intelligence (the "something for nothing" complex)—and his equation of success at gambling with proof of his own masculinity. The description of the narrator's behavior at the gaming table further suggests the manic phase of a manic-depressive cycle. Dostoyevsky's notebooks and letters prove conclusively that the character of Alexei Ivanovich (the narrator) is autobiographical and that the incidents themselves are drawn from his own experiences at various German resorts.

Anton Chekhov (1860–1904), a physician as well as an author, then sketches the breakdown of a provincial teacher and scribe into paranoia (or paranoid schizophrenia), a type of psychosis characterized by delusions that one is being constantly talked about and persecuted by others, often by an organized conspiracy involving many others. Such delusions are frequently accompanied by auditory hallucinations and convictions of personal power and self-importance, beliefs which may then be used to "explain" the conspiracy. Full-blown paranoia almost always results in hospitalization and is difficult to treat successfully. People who are chronically suspicious and who exhibit in milder and occasional forms some of the beliefs and reactions characteristic of paranoia may be termed "paranoid" although nowadays that word is frequently used as little more than a derogatory or descriptive epithet. Cases of paranoia should, moreover, be sharply distinguished from cases where a person actually *is* being persecuted. Not all assertions of being persecuted are delusions.

We do not know why it is that the most powerful literary portraits of abnormal emotional states have come from the pens of nineteenth-century Russian novelists but the fact is indisputable. In the final selection of this group Count Lëv (Leo) Tolstoy (1828–1910) draws an unforgettable picture of the disintegration of a man's apparent ego identity in the face of life's ultimate crisis—death. Ivan Ilyich, to all appearances a successful, if not overly distinguished, provincial judge, finds, in the face of imminent death from an unnameable disease (probably cancer) that his whole life has had no meaning, no real worth. As death approaches Ivan despairs and regresses in terror. Physically weakened, his defenses broken through, he realizes that his death is meaningless and absurd because his life has been meaningless and absurd, because he has never lived as he knew he should have. The lies that Ivan rejects and curses from his deathbed are precisely those by which, until then, he had sustained himself. At the very end, perhaps through the gift of some mysterious grace, Ivan is enabled to accept his death and, through that, his life as well. But the gift of grace can never be counted upon and for Ivan Ilyich life ends not in integrity but in resignation. Only if life has value can death have meaning.

47. THE MYTH OF MENTAL ILLNESS

Thomas S. Szasz

My aim in this essay is to raise the question "Is there such a thing as mental illness?" and to argue that there is not. Since the notion of mental illness is extremely widely used nowadays, inquiry into the ways in which this term is employed would seem to be especially indicated. Mental illness, of course, is not literally a "thing"—or physical object—and hence it can "exist" only in the same sort of way in which other theoretical concepts exist. Yet, familiar theories are in the habit of posing, sooner or later—at least to those who come to believe in them—as "objective truths" (or "facts"). During certain historical periods, explanatory conceptions such as deities, witches, and microorganisms appeared not only as theories but as self-evident *causes* of a vast number of events. I submit that today mental illness is widely regarded in a somewhat similar fashion, that is, as the cause of innumerable diverse happenings. As an antidote to the complacent use of the notion of mental illness—whether as a self-evident phenomenon, theory, or cause—let us ask this question: What is meant when it is asserted that someone is mentally ill?

In what follows I shall describe briefly the main uses to which the concept of mental illness has been put. I shall argue that this notion has outlived whatever usefulness it might have had and that it now functions merely as a convenient myth.

MENTAL ILLNESS AS A SIGN OF BRAIN DISEASE

The notion of mental illness derives its main support from such phenomena as syphilis of the brain or delirious conditions—intoxications, for instance—in which persons are known to manifest various peculiarities or disorders of thinking and behavior. Correctly speaking, however, these are diseases of the brain, not of the mind. According to one school of thought, *all* so-called mental illness is of this type. The assumption is made that some neurological defect, perhaps a very subtle one, will ultimately be found for all the disorders of thinking and behavior. Many contemporary psychiatrists, physicians, and other scientists hold this view. This position implies that people *cannot* have troubles—expressed in what are *now called* "mental illnesses"—because of differences in personal needs, opinions, social aspirations, values, and so on. *All problems in living* are attributed to physicochemical processes which in due time will be discovered by medical research.

"Mental illnesses" are thus regarded as basically no different than all other diseases (that is, of the body). The only difference, in this view, between mental and bodily diseases is that the former, affecting the brain, manifest themselves by means of mental symptoms; whereas the latter, affecting other organ systems (for example, the skin, liver, etc.), manifest themselves by means of symptoms referable to those parts of the body. This view rests on and expresses what are, in my opinion, two fundamental errors.

In the first place, what central nervous system symptoms would correspond to a skin eruption or a fracture? It would *not* be some emotion or complex bit of behavior. Rather, it would be blindness or a paralysis of some part of the body. The crux of the matter is that a disease of the brain, analogous to a disease of the skin or bone, is a neurological defect, and not a problem in living. For example, a *defect* in a person's visual field may be satisfactorily explained by correlating it

Thomas S. Szasz: "The Myth of Mental Illness"; AMERICAN PSYCHOLOGIST, 15, 1960, 113–118. *Copyright 1960 by the American Psychological Association. Reprinted by permission of the American Psychological Association and the author.*

with certain definite lesions in the nervous system. On the other hand, a person's *belief* —whether this be a belief in Christianity, in Communism, or in the idea that his internal organs are "rotting" and that his body is, in fact, already "dead"—cannot be explained by a defect or disease of the nervous system. Explanations of this sort of occurrence—assuming that one is interested in the belief itself and does not regard it simply as a "symptom" or expression of something else that is *more interesting*—must be sought along different lines.

The second error in regarding complex psychosocial behavior, consisting of communications about ourselves and the world about us, as mere symptoms of neurological functioning is *epistemological*. In other words, it is an error pertaining not to any mistakes in observation or reasoning, as such, but rather to the way in which we organize and express our knowledge. In the present case, the error lies in making a symmetrical dualism between mental and physical (or bodily) symptoms, a dualism which is merely a haibit of speech and to which no known observations can be found to correspond. Let us see if this is so. In medical practice, when we speak of physical disturbances, we mean either signs (for example, a fever) or symptoms (for example, pain). We speak of mental symptoms, on the other hand, when we refer to a patient's *communications about himself, others, and the world about him.* He might state that he is Napoleon or that he is being persecuted by the Communists. These would be considered mental symptoms *only* if the observer believed that the patient was *not* Napoleon or that he was *not* being persecuted by the Communists. This makes it apparent that the statement that "*X* is a mental symptom" involves rendering a judgment. The judgment entails, moreover, a covert comparison or matching of the patient's ideas, concepts, or beliefs with those of the observer and the society in which they live. The notion of mental symptom is therefore inextricably tied to the *social* (including *ethical*) *context* in which it is made in much the same way as the notion of bodily symptom is tied to an *anatomical* and *genetic context* (Szasz, 1957a, 1957b).

To sum up what has been said thus far: I have tried to show that for those who regard mental symptoms as signs of brain disease, the concept of mental illness is unnecessary and misleading. For what they mean is that people so labeled suffer from diseases of the brain; and, if that is what they mean, it would seem better for the sake of clarity to say that and not something else.

MENTAL ILLNESS AS A NAME FOR PROBLEMS IN LIVING

The term "mental illness" is widely used to describe something which is very different than a disease of the brain. Many people today take it for granted that living is an arduous process. Its hardship for modern man, moreover, derives not so much from a struggle for biological survival as from the stresses and strains inherent in the social intercourse of complex human personalities. In this context, the notion of mental illness is used to identify or describe some feature of an individual's so-called personality. Mental illness—as a deformity of the personality, so to speak—is then regarded as the *cause* of the human disharmony. It is implicit in this view that social intercourse between people is regarded as something *inherently harmonious,* its disturbance being due solely to the presence of "mental illness" in many people. This is obviously fallacious reasoning, for it makes the abstraction "mental illness" into a *cause,* even though this abstraction was created in the first place to serve only as a shorthand expression for certain types of human behavior. It now becomes necessary to ask: "What kinds of behavior are regarded as indicative of mental illness, and by whom?"

The concept of illness, whether bodily or mental, implies *deviation from some clearly defined norm.* In the case of physical illness, the norm is the structural and functional integrity of the human body. Thus, although the desirability of physical health, as such, is an ethical value, what health *is* can be stated in anatomical and physiological terms. What is the norm deviation from which is regarded as mental illness? This question cannot be easily answered. But whatever this norm might be, we can be certain of only one thing: namely, that it is a norm that must be stated in terms of *psychosocial, ethical,* and *legal* concepts. For example, notions such as "excessive repression" or "acting out an unconscious impulse" illustrate the use of psychological concepts for judging (so-called) mental health and illness. The idea that chronic hostility, vengefulness, or divorce are indicative of mental illness would be illustrations of the use of ethical norms (that is, the desirability of love, kindness, and a stable marriage relationship). Finally, the widespread psychiatric opinion that only a mentally ill person would commit homicide illustrates the use of a legal concept as a norm of mental health. The norm from which deviation is measured whenever one speaks of a mental illness is a *psychosocial and ethical one*. Yet, the remedy is sought in terms of *medical* measures which—it is hoped and assumed—are free from wide differences of ethical value. The definition of the disorder and the terms in which its remedy are sought are therefore at serious odds with one another. The practical significance of this covert conflict between the alleged nature of the defect and the remedy can hardly be exaggerated.

Having identified the norms used to measure deviations in cases of mental illness, we will now turn to the question: "Who defines the norms and hence the deviation?" Two basic answers may be offered: (*a*) It may be the person himself (that is, the patient) who decides that he deviates from a norm. For example, an artist may believe that he suffers from a work inhibition; and he may implement this conclusion by seeking help *for* himself from a psychotherapist. (*b*) It may be someone other than the patient who decides that the latter is deviant (for example, relatives, physicians, legal authorities, society generally, etc.). In such a case a psychiatrist may be hired by others to do something *to* the patient in order to correct the deviation.

These considerations underscore the importance of asking the question "Whose agent is the psychiatrist?" and of giving a candid answer to it (Szasz, 1956, 1958). The psychiatrist (psychologist or nonmedical psychotherapist), it now develops, may be the agent of the patient, of the relatives, of the school, of the military services, of a business organization, of a court of law, and so forth. In speaking of the psychiatrist as the agent of these persons or organizations, it is not implied that his values concerning norms, or his ideas and aims concerning the proper nature of remedial action, need to coincide exactly with those of his employer. For example, a patient in individual psychotherapy may believe that his salvation lies in a new marriage; his psychotherapist need not share this hypothesis. As the patient's agent, however, he must abstain from bringing social or legal

force to bear on the patient which would prevent him from putting his beliefs into action. If his *contract* is with the patient, the psychiatrist (psychotherapist) may disagree with him or stop his treatment; but he cannot engage others to obstruct the patient's aspirations. Similarly, if a psychiatrist is engaged by a court to determine the sanity of a criminal, he need not fully share the legal authorities' values and intentions in regard to the criminal and the means available for dealing with him. But the psychiatrist is expressly barred from stating, for example, that it is not the criminal who is "insane" but the men who wrote the law on the basis of which the very actions that are being judged are regarded as "criminal." Such an opinion could be voiced, of course, but not in a courtroom, and not by a psychiatrist who makes it his practice to assist the court in performing its daily work.

To recapitulate: In actual contemporary social usage, the finding of a mental illness is made by establishing a deviance in behavior from certain psychosocial, ethical, or legal norms. The judgment may be made, as in medicine, by the patient, the physician (psychiatrist), or others. Remedial action, finally, tends to be sought in a therapeutic—or covertly medical—framework, thus creating a situation in which *psychosocial, ethical, and/or legal deviations* are claimed to be correctible by (so-called) *medical action.* Since medical action is designed to correct only medical deviations, it seems logically absurd to expect that it will help solve problems whose very existence had been defined and established on nonmedical grounds. I think that these considerations may be fruitfully applied to the present use of tranquilizers and, more generally, to what might be expected of drugs of whatever type in regard to the amelioration or solution of problems in human living.

THE ROLE OF ETHICS IN PSYCHIATRY

Anything that people *do*—in contrast to things that *happen* to them (Peters, 1958)—takes place in a context of value. In this broad sense, no human activity is devoid of ethical implications. When the values underlying certain activities are widely shared, those who participate in their pursuit may lose sight of them altogether. The discipline of medicine, both as a pure science (for example, research) and as a technology (for example, therapy), contains many ethical considerations and judgments. Unfortunately, these are often denied, minimized, or merely kept out of focus; for the ideal of the medical profession as well as of the people whom it serves seems to be having a system of medicine (allegedly) free of ethical value. This sentimental notion is expressed by such things as the doctor's willingness to treat and help patients irrespective of their religious or political beliefs, whether they are rich or poor, etc. While there may be some grounds for this belief—albeit it is a view that is not impressively true even in these regards—the fact remains that ethical considerations encompass a vast range of human affairs. By making the practice of medicine neutral in regard to some specific issues of value need not, and cannot, mean that it can be kept free from all such values. The practice of medicine is intimately tied to ethics; and the first thing that we must do, it seems to me, is to try to make this clear and explicit. I shall let this matter rest here, for it does not concern us specifically in this essay. Lest there be any vagueness, however, about how or where ethics and medicine meet, let me remind the reader of such issues as birth control, abortion, suicide, and euthanasia* as only a few of the major areas of current ethicomedical controversy.

Psychiatry, I submit, is very much more intimately tied to problems of ethics than is medicine. I use the word "psychiatry" here to refer to that contemporary discipline which is concerned with *problems in living* (and not with diseases of the brain, which are problems for neurology). Problems in human relations can be analyzed, interpreted, and given meaning only within given social and ethical contexts. Accordingly, it *does* make a difference—arguments to the contrary notwithstanding—what the psychiatrist's socioethical orientations happen to be; for these will influence his ideas on what is wrong with the patient, what deserves comment or interpretation, in what possible directions change might be desirable, and so forth. Even in medicine proper, these factors play a role, as for instance, in the divergent orientations which physicians, depending on their religious affiliations, have

toward such things as birth control and therapeutic abortion. Can anyone really believe that a psychotherapist's ideas concerning religious belief, slavery, or other similar issues play no role in his practical work? If they do make a difference, what are we to infer from it? Does it not seem reasonable that we ought to have different psychiatric therapies—each expressly recognized for the ethical positions which they embody—for, say, Catholics and Jews, religious persons and agnostics, democrats and communists, white supremacists and Negroes, and so on? Indeed, if we look at how psychiatry is actually practiced today (especially in the United States), we find that people do seek psychiatric help in accordance with their social status and ethical beliefs (Hollingshead & Redlich, 1958). This should really not surprise us more than being told that practicing Catholics rarely frequent birth control clinics.

The foregoing position which holds that contemporary psychotherapists deal with problems in living, rather than with mental illnesses and their cures, stands in opposition to a currently prevalent claim, according to which mental illness is just as "real" and "objective" as bodily illness. This is a confusing claim since it is never known exactly what is meant by such words as "real" and "objective." I suspect, however, that what is intended by the proponents of this view is to create the idea in the popular mind that mental illness is some sort of disease entity, like an infection or a malignancy. If this were true, one could *catch* or *get* a "mental illness," one might *have* or *harbor* it, one might *transmit* it to others, and finally one could get *rid* of it. In my opinion, there is not a shred of evidence to support this idea. To the contrary, all the evidence is the other way and supports the view that what people now call mental illnesses are for the most part *communications* expressing unacceptable ideas, often framed, moreover, in an unusual idiom. The scope of this essay allows me to do no more than mention this alternative theoretical approach to this problem (Szasz, 1957c).

This is not the place to consider in detail the similarities and differences between bodily and mental illnesses. It shall suffice for us here to emphasize only one important difference between them: namely, that whereas bodily disease refers to public, physicochem-

---

* Mercy killing. (Eds.)

ical occurrences, the notion of mental illness is used to codify relatively more private, sociopsychological happenings of which the observer (diagnostician) forms a part. In other words, the psychiatrist does not stand *apart* from what he observes, but is, in Harry Stack Sullivan's apt words, a "participant observer." This means that he is *committed* to some picture of what he considers reality—and to what he thinks society considers reality—and he observes and judges the patient's behavior in the light of these considerations. This touches on our earlier observation that the notion of mental symptom itself implies a comparison between observer and observed, psychiatrist and patient. This is so obvious that I may be charged with belaboring trivialities. Let me therefore say once more that my aim in presenting this argument was expressly to criticize and counter a prevailing contemporary tendency to deny the moral aspects of psychiatry (and psychotherapy) and to substitute for them allegedly value-free medical considerations. Psychotherapy, for example, is being widely practiced as though it entailed nothing other than restoring the patient from a state of mental sickness to one of mental health. While it is generally accepted that mental illness has something to do with man's social (or interpersonal) relations, it is paradoxically maintained that problems of values (that is, of ethics) do not arise in this process.[1] Yet, in one sense, much of psychotherapy may revolve around nothing other than the elucidation and weighing of goals and values—many of which may be mutually contradictory—and the means whereby they might best be harmonized, realized, or relinquished.

The diversity of human values and the methods by means of which they may be realized is so vast, and many of them remain so unacknowledged, that they cannot fail but lead to conflicts in human relations. Indeed, to say that human relations at all levels—

from mother to child, through husband and wife, to nation and nation—are fraught with stress, strain, and disharmony is, once again, making the obvious explicit. Yet, what may be obvious may be also poorly understood. This I think is the case here. For it seems to me that—at least in our scientific theories of behavior—we have failed to *accept* the simple fact that human relations are inherently fraught with difficulties and that to make them even relatively harmonious requires much patience and hard work. I submit that the idea of mental illness is now being put to work to obscure certain difficulties which at present may be inherent—not that they need be unmodifiable—in the social intercourse of persons. If this is true, the concept functions as a disguise; for instead of calling attention to conflicting human needs, aspirations, and values, the notion of mental illness provides an amoral and impersonal "thing" (an illness") as an explanation for *problems in living* (Szasz, 1959). We may recall in this connection that not so long ago it was devils and witches who were held responsible for men's problems in social living. The belief in mental illness, as something other than man's trouble in getting along with his fellow man, is the proper heir to the belief in demonology and witchcraft. Mental illness exists or is "real" in exactly the same sense in which witches existed or were "real."

CHOICE, RESPONSIBILITY, AND PSYCHIATRY

While I have argued that mental illnesses do not exist, I obviously did not imply that the social and psychological occurrences to which this label is currently being attached also do not exist. Like the personal and social troubles which people had in the Middle Ages, they are real enough. It is the labels we give them that concerns us and, having labelled them, what we do about them. While I cannot go into the ramified implications of this problem here, it is worth noting that a demonologic conception of problems in living gave rise to therapy along theological lines. Today, a belief in mental illness implies—nay, requires—therapy along medical or psychotherapeutic lines.

What is implied in the line of thought set forth here is something quite different. I do not intend to offer a new conception of "psy-

---

1 Freud went so far as to say that: "I consider ethics to be taken for granted. Actually I have never done a mean thing" (Jones, 1957, p. 247). This surely is a strange thing to say for someone who has studied man as a social being as closely as did Freud. I mention it here to show how the notion of "illness" (in the case of psychoanalysis, "psychopathology," or "mental illness") was used by Freud—and by most of his followers—as a means for classifying certain forms of human behavior as falling within the scope of medicine, and (by *fiat*) outside that of ethics!

chiatric illness" nor a new form of "therapy." My aim is more modest and yet also more ambitious. It is to suggest that the phenomena now called mental illnesses be looked at afresh and more simply, that they be removed from the category of illnesses, and that they be regarded as the expressions of man's struggle with the problem of *how* he should live. The last mentioned problem is obviously a vast one, its enormity reflecting not only man's inability to cope with his environment, but even more his increasing self-reflectiveness.

By problems in living, then, I refer to that truly explosive chain reaction which began with man's fall from divine grace by partaking of the fruit of the tree of knowledge. Man's awareness of himself and of the world about him seems to be a steadily expanding one, bringing in its wake an ever larger *burden of understanding* (an expression borrowed from Suzanne Langer, 1953). *This burden,* then, *is to be expected and must not be misinterpreted.* Our only *rational* means for lightening it is *more understanding,* and appropriate *action* based on such understanding. The main alternative lies in acting as though the burden were not what in fact we perceive it to be and taking refuge in an outmoded theological view of man. In the latter view, man does not fashion his life and much of his world about him, but merely lives out his fate in a world created by superior beings. This may logically lead to pleading nonresponsibility in the face of seemingly unfathomable problems and difficulties. Yet, if man fails to take increasing responsibility for his actions, individually as well as collectively, it seems unlikely that some higher power or being would assume this task and carry this burden for him. Moreover, this seems hardly the proper time in human history for obscuring the issue of man's responsibility for his actions by hiding it behind the skirt of an all-explaining conception of mental illness.

CONCLUSIONS

I have tried to show that the notion of mental illness has outlived whatever usefulness it might have had and that it now functions merely as a convenient myth. As such, it is a true heir to religious myths in general, and to the belief in witchcraft in particular; the role of all these belief-systems was to act as *social tranquilizers,* thus encouraging the hope that

mastery of certain specific problems may be achieved by means of substitutive (symbolic-magical) operations. The notion of mental illness thus serves mainly to obscure the everyday fact that life for most people is a continuous struggle, not for biological survival, but for a "place in the sun," "peace of mind," or some other human value. For man aware of himself and of the world about him, once the needs for preserving the body (and perhaps the race) are more or less satisfied, the problem arises as to what he should do with himself. Sustained adherence to the myth of mental illness allows people to avoid facing this problem, believing that mental health, conceived as the absence of mental illness, automatically insures the making of right and safe choices in one's conduct of life. But the facts are all the other way. It is the making of good choices in life that others regard, retrospectively, as good mental health!

The myth of mental illness encourages us, moreover, to believe in its logical corollary: that social intercourse would be harmonious, satisfying, and the secure basis of a "good life" were it not for the disrupting influences of mental illness or "psychopathology." The potentiality for universal human happiness, in this form at least, seems to me but another example of the I-wish-it-were-true type of fantasy. I do believe that human happiness or well-being on a hitherto unimaginably large scale, and not just for a select few, is possible. This goal could be achieved, however, only at the cost of many men, and not just a few being willing and able to tackle their personal, social, and ethical conflicts. This means having the courage and integrity to forego waging battles on false fronts, finding solutions for substitute problems—for instance, fighting the battle of stomach acid and chronic fatigue instead of facing up to a marital conflict.

Our adversaries are not demons, witches, fate, or mental illness. We have no enemy whom we can fight, exorcise, or dispel by "cure." What we do have are *problems in living*—whether these be biologic, economic, political, or sociopsychological. In this essay I was concerned only with problems belonging in the last mentioned category, and within this group mainly with those pertaining to moral values. The field to which modern psychiatry addresses itself is vast, and I made no effort to encompass it all. My argument was limited to the proposition that mental illness is a myth, whose function it is to disguise and thus render more palatable the bitter pill of moral conflicts in human relations.

REFERENCES

Hollingshead, A. B., & Redlich, F. C. *Social class and mental illness.* New York: Wiley, 1958.

Jones, E. *The life and work of Sigmund Freud.* Vol. III. New York: Basic Books, 1957.

Langer, S. K. *Philosophy in a new key.* New York: Mentor Books, 1953.

Peters, R. S. *The concept of motivation.* London: Routledge & Kegan Paul, 1958.

Szasz, T. S. Malingering: "Diagnosis" or social condemnation? *AMA Arch. Neurol. Psychiat.,* 1956, 76, 432–443.

Szasz, T. S., *Pain and pleasure: A study of bodily feelings.* New York: Basic Books, 1957. (a)

Szasz, T. S. The problem of psychiatric nosology: A contribution to a situational analysis of psychiatric operations. *Amer. J. Psychiat.,* 1957, 114, 405–413. (b)

Szasz. T. S. On the theory of psychoanalytic treatment. *Int. J. Psycho-Anal.,* 1957, 38, 166–182. (c)

Szasz, T. S. Psychiatry, ethics and the criminal law. *Columbia Law Rev.,* 1958, 58, 183–198.

Szasz, T. S. Moral conflict and psychiatry, *Yale Rev.,* 1959, in press.

48. THE GAMBLER

Fyodor Dostoyevsky

...There was a terrible crowd in the rooms. How impudent and greedy they all are! I elbowed my way into the thick of them and stood close to the croupier; then I began playing modestly and tentatively, staking two or three coins at a time. Meanwhile I watched and took note; it appeared to me that pure calculation means fairly little and has none of the importance many gamblers attach to it. They sit over bits of paper ruled into columns, note down the plays, count up, compute probabilities, do sums, finally put down their stakes and—lose exactly the same as we poor mortals playing without calculation. But on the other hand I drew one conclusion, which I think is correct: in a series of pure chances there really does exist, if not a system, at any rate a sort of sequence—which is, of course, very odd. For example, it may happen that after the twelve middle numbers, the last twelve turn up; the ball lodges in the last twelve numbers twice, say, and then passes to the first twelve. Having fallen into the first twelve it passes again to the middle twelve, falls there three or four times running, and again passes to the last twelve, and from there, again after two plays, falls once more into the first twelve, lodges there once and then again falls three times on the middle numbers, and this goes on for an hour and a half or two hours: one, three, two; one, three, two. This is very entertaining. One day, or one morning, it will happen, for example, that red and black alternate, changing every minute almost without any order, so that neither red nor black ever turns up more than two or three times in succession. The next day, or the next evening, red only will come up many times running, twenty or more, for example, and go on doing so unfailingly for a certain time, perhaps during a whole day. A great deal

From THE GAMBLER *by Fyodor Dostoyevsky, translated by Jessie Coulson. Copyright* © *1966 by Jessie Coulson. Reprinted by permission of Penguin Books, Ltd.*

of all this was explained to me by Mr. Astley,* who remained standing by the tables all the morning but did not once play himself. As for me, I was cleaned right out, and very speedily. I staked twenty friedrichs d'or on *pair* [even] straight away, and won, staked again and again won, and so on two or three more times. I think about four hundred friedrichs d'or came into my possession in some five minutes. I ought to have left at that point, but a strange sort of feeling came over me, a kind of desire to challenge fate, a longing to give it a fillip on the nose or stick out my tongue at it. I staked the permitted maximum—4,000 gulden—and lost. Then, getting excited, I pulled out all I had left, staked it in the same way, lost again, and after that left the table as if I had been stunned. I could not even grasp what had happened to me, and I did not tell Polina Alexandrova† about losing until just before dinner. I had spent the time until then wandering unsteadily about in the park. . . .

Yes, sometimes the wildest notion, the most apparently impossible idea, takes such a firm hold of the mind that at length it is taken for something realizable. . . . More than that: if the idea coincides with a strong and passionate desire, it may sometimes be accepted as something predestined, inevitable, foreordained, something that cannot but exist or happen! Perhaps there is some reason for this, some combination of presentiments, some extraordinary exertion of will-power, some self-intoxication of the imagination, or something else—I don't know: but on that evening (which I shall never forget as long as I live) something miraculous happened to me. Although it is completely capable of mathematical proof, nevertheless to this day it remains for me a miraculous happening. And why, why, was that certainty so strongly and deeply rooted in me, and from such a long time ago? I used, indeed, to think of it, I repeat, not as one event among others that might happen (and consequently might also not happen), but as something that could not possibly fail to happen!

It was a quarter past ten, and I went into the casino with a confident hope and at the same time with a wild excitement such as I had never experienced before. There were still quite a few people in the gambling saloons, although only about half as many as in the morning.

After ten o'clock at night those left round the tables are the genuine, desperate gamblers, for whom nothing exists in any health resort but roulette, who have come for nothing else, who hardly notice what is going on around them and take no interest in anything else all the season, only play from morning till night and would perhaps be ready to play all through the night as well, if it were possible. They are always annoyed at having to disperse when the roulette tables close at midnight. And when, about twelve o'clock, before closing the tables, the head croupier announces '*Les trois derniers coups, messieurs!*' ['The final three plays, gentlemen'], they are sometimes prepared to stake on those last three turns everything they have in their pockets, and actually do lose the biggest amounts of all at those times. I went to the same table where Grandmamma had sat a little earlier. It was not very crowded, so that I very soon found room to stand, close to the table. Straight in front of me the word '*Passe*' was written on the green cloth.

'*Passe*' means the whole series of numbers from nineteen to thirty-six inclusive. The first series, from one to eighteen inclusive is called *Manque,* but what did that matter to me? I did not take into account, I had not heard, what the previous winning number had been, and I began to play without inquiring, as any reasonably prudent gambler would have done. I pulled out all my twenty friedrichs d'or and put them down on the word *passe* lying before me.

'*Vingt deux!* ['Twenty-two!'] called the croupier.

I had won, and again I staked everything, both the previous stake and my winnings.

'*Trente et un!*' ['Thirty-one!'] the croupier announced. Another win! That meant I now had altogether eighty friedrichs d'or! I moved all eighty to the dozen middle numbers (which pays three to one, but the chances are two to one against), the wheel turned, and twenty-four came up. I was paid out with three rolls of fifty friedrichs d'or and ten gold coins; now I had altogether 200 friedrichs d'or, including my first stake.

Feeling as though I were delirious with fever, I moved the whole pile of money to the red—and suddenly came to my senses!

For the only time in the course of the whole evening, fear laid its icy finger on me and my arms and legs began to shake. With horror I saw and for an instant fully realized what it would mean to me to lose now! My whole life depended on that stake!

'*Rouge!*' ['Red!'] cried the croupier, and I drew a deep breath, while my whole body tingled with fire. This time I was paid out in banknotes, so that I now had 4,000 florins and eighty friedrichs d'or! (I could still keep count then.)

After that, I remember, I put 2,000 florins on the twelve middle numbers again, and lost; I staked my gold, the eighty friedrichs d'or, and lost. Possessed by frenzy, I seized the 2,000 florins I had left and staked them on the twelve first numbers—haphazard, at random, without stopping to think! There was, however, one instant's expectant pause, perhaps sensation for sensation the same as that experienced by Madame Blanchard in Paris while she was plunging to the ground from the balloon.

'*Quatre!*' ['Four!'] called the croupier. Altogether, with my first stake, I now had 6,000 florins again. I already had the air of a conqueror, I no longer feared anything, whatever it might be, and I flung down 4,000 florins on black. Eight or nine others were quick to follow my example and stake on black also. The croupiers looked at one another and exchanged a few words. People all round were talking and waiting.

Black turned up. After that I remember neither the amount nor the order of my stakes. I only recall, as if it was a dream, that I had already won, I think, about sixteen thousand florins; then I suddenly dropped 12,000 in three unlucky plays; then I pushed my last four thousand on to '*passe*' (but by now I hardly felt anything at all; I only waited, almost mechanically, without thinking)—and won again; then I won four more times in succession. I can only remember scooping up money in thousands, and I am beginning to remember also that the middle twelve numbers, to which I had become positively attached, turned up most frequently of all. There was a sort of pattern—they appeared three or four times running, without fail, then disappeared for two turns, then again appeared three or four times in succession. This remarkable regularity occurs sometimes in streaks—and this is what throws out the inveterate gamblers, always doing sums with a pencil in their hands. And what terrible jests fate sometimes plays!

I do not think more than half an hour had passed since my arrival. Suddenly the croupier informed me that I had won 30,000 florins, and as the bank would not be responsible for more than that on one occasion, the game would therefore be closed until the following morning. I picked up all my gold pieces and distributed them among my pockets, then snatched up all the notes and immediately transferred myself to the table in the other room where there was another roulette wheel; the whole crowd streamed after me; a place was cleared for me at once and I began playing again, at random and without even counting. I don't know what saved me!

Now, however, some glimmerings of reason began to appear in my mind. I clung to certain numbers and chances, but soon abandoned them and began staking again almost without knowing what I was doing. I must have been very absent-minded! I remember that the croupiers corrected my play several times. I made gross mistakes. My temples were damp with perspiration and my hands trembled. Various Poles, too, hurried up to offer their services, but I did not listen to anybody. My luck held! All at once there was loud talking and laughter all round. Everybody shouted 'Bravo, bravo!' and some even clapped their hands. Here as well I had broken the bank by winning 30,000 florins, and again the game was closed until the next day!

'Go away, go away,' a voice was whispering from my right. It was a Jew from Frankfurt; he had been standing beside me all the time and had, it appears, sometimes helped me to play.

'For God's sake go away,' whispered another voice close to my left ear. I glanced round. It was a very plainly and respectably dressed lady of about thirty, with an unhealthily pale and weary face, which yet still bore the traces of its former remarkable beauty. At that moment I was stuffing my pockets with carelessly crumpled banknotes and picking up the gold that lay on the table. Taking the last role of fifty friedrichs d'or I managed to thrust it, without being noticed, into the pale lady's hand; I terribly wanted to do this, and her thin slender little fingers,

I remember, pressed my hand warmly in sign of the liveliest gratitude. It had all happened in a moment.

When I had picked everything up I hurried over to the *trente et quarante* game. *Trente et quarante* is a game for the aristocratic public. This is not roulette, it is cards. Here the bank will pay out up to 100,000 thaler at once. The highest stake, here also, is 4,000 florins. I was completely ignorant of the game and knew hardly any way of staking except on red and black, which they have there as well. I stuck to these. Everybody in the casino crowded round. I don't remember whether the thought of Polina crossed my mind even once during all this time. I felt a kind of irresistible delight in snatching up and raking in the banknotes which grew into a pile in front of me.

It really seemed that it was fate that urged me on. At the time, as luck would have it, something had happened which is, however, fairly frequently repeated in this game. The luck clings, for example, to red, and remains there ten or fifteen times in a row. Two days earlier I had been told that the previous week red had won twenty-two times running; nobody could remember such a thing ever happening in roulette, and people were talking about it with amazement. Of course, in such a case everybody immediately stops staking on red, and after it has come up say ten successive times, hardly anybody at all risks a stake on it. But at such times no experienced player will stake on the opposite colour, black, either. Experienced players know the meaning of such 'freakish chances.' One might suppose, for example, that after red has come up sixteen times, on the seventeenth it will inevitably be black that does so. Novices rush to this conclusion in crowds, double and treble their stakes, and lose heavily.

But I, with strange perversity, deliberately went on staking on red after noticing that it had turned up seven times running. I am sure vanity was half responsible for this; I wanted to astonish the spectators by taking senseless chances and—a strange sensation!—I clearly remember that even without any promptings of vanity I really was suddenly overcome by a terrible craving for risk. Perhaps the soul passing through such a wide range of sensations is not satisfied but only exacerbated by them, and demands more and more of them, growing more and more powerful, until it

reaches final exhaustion. And I really am not lying when I say that if the rules of the game had allowed me to stake 50,000 florins at one throw I would certainly have done so. The bystanders exclaimed that this was madness, and that red had already won fourteen times!

'*Monsieur a gagné déjà cent mille florins,*' ['The gentleman has already won 100,000 florins,'] I heard somebody's voice saying close beside me.

I suddenly came to my senses. What? I had won 100,000 florins that evening! But what use was any more to me? I fell upon the bank notes, crammed them into my pockets without counting, raked together all my loose gold and all the rolls of gold coins and hurried out of the casino. Everybody laughed as I went through the rooms, looking at my torn pockets and the staggering gait caused by the weight of the gold. I think there must have been more than twenty pounds of it. A few hands were stretched out towards me; I gave away money in handfuls, just what I happened to snatch up. Near the door I was stopped by two Jews.

'You are a brave man, very brave!' they said, 'but you must leave as early as possible tomorrow morning without fail, or else you will lose everything....'

I did not listen to them. The avenue was so dark that I could not see my hands in front of my face. It was about half a verst to the hotel. I have never been afraid of thieves or robbers, even when I was small; I did not think of them even now. I don't remember, though, what I did think of on the way; it could hardly be called thinking. I only felt a sort of terrible delight in success, victory, power— I don't know how to express it. The image of Polina also passed through my mind; I remembered and fully realized that I was going to her, and that presently I should be with her, telling her, showing her...but I hardly remembered what she had said to me not long before, or why I had gone, and all the sensations I had felt only an hour and a half earlier now seemed to be relics of the distant past, ancient and half-obliterated, not to be spoken of again because now everything was starting afresh. I had already almost reached the end of the avenue when sudden terror struck at me: 'What if I am robbed and murdered now?' My panic redoubled at every step. I was almost running. Suddenly the whole hotel, with all its lighted windows, blazed out at the end of the avenue; thank God, I was at home!...

I still had about five hundred francs left myself; besides that, I have a magnificent watch worth a thousand francs, diamond cufflinks, and so on, so that I can still hold out for a fairly long time without worrying. I have deliberately settled down in this little town, to collect myself and, above all, to wait for Mr Astley. I have been told for certain that he will pass through here and will stay for twenty-four hours on business. I shall find out about everything...and then—then I shall go straight to Homburg. I shan't go to Roulettenburg, except perhaps next year. They say the omens really are always against you if you try your luck twice running at one and the same table, and there is real play in Homburg.

. . .

It is a year and eight months since I looked at these notes, and now I have only read them through by chance, when, in my grief and misery, I took it into my head to amuse myself. So it seems I stopped then at the point where I was going to Homburg. Oh, God! with what a light heart, comparatively speaking, I wrote those last lines! Or rather, not exactly with a light heart, but with what self-confidence and what unshakeable hopes! Had I even the smallest doubt of myself? And now a little more than eighteen months have passed and I am, in my own estimation, far worse than a beggar! And what is beggary? I don't care a rap for beggary! I have simply destroyed myself! There is, however, almost no point in making comparisons, and none at all in drawing morals. Nothing could be more absurd than moral conclusions at a time like this! Oh, self-satisfied people: with what smug vanity the windbags are prepared to mouth their precepts! If only they knew how well I understand the whole loathsomeness of my present situation, they would not have the heart to try to instruct me. Why, what on earth can they tell me that is new or that I don't know already? And is that the point? The point here is this—one turn of the wheel and everything can be different, and those same moralists will be the first (I am sure of it) to congratulate me with friendly facetiousness. And everybody will not turn away from

me as they do now. But I don't give a damn for any of them! What am I now. Zero. What may I be tomorrow? Tomorrow I may rise from the dead and begin to live again! I may find a man within myself, before he vanishes for good!

I really did go to Homburg that time, but ...afterwards I was in Roulettenburg again, and in Spa, and even in Baden, where I went as valet to Councillor Hintze, a scoundrel who had been my master here. Yes, I have even been a servant, for five whole months! It happened immediately after I left prison. (I was held in prison in Roulettenburg for a debt I contracted here. An unknown person bought me out—who was it? Mr Astley? Polina? I don't know, but the debt, 200 thalers in all, was paid and I was set free.) Where could I go? I went to this Hintze. He is young and frivolous, and doesn't like to exert himself, and I can speak and write three languages. I went to him at first as a sort of secretary for thirty gulden a month; but I ended as his real man-servant: it became beyond his means to keep a secretary and he reduced my wages; but I had nowhere to go, I stayed where I was—and so turned myself into a servant. I did not have enough to eat and drink in his service, but on the other hand I saved seventy gulden in five months. One evening in Baden I informed him I wished to leave; the same evening I made my way to the roulette tables. Oh, how my heart thumped! No, it was not money that was dear to me! All I wanted then was for all those Hintzes, all those hotel servants, all those fine Baden ladies to be talking about me the next day, telling my story, admiring and praising me and bowing down before my new winnings. All these were childish dreams and wishes, but...who knows, perhaps I should come across Polina too, and tell her everything, and she would see that I was above all these absurd turns of fate.... Oh, it was not money that was dear to me. I am convinced that I should have squandered it all on some new Blanche,* and driven round Paris for three weeks again behind my own pair of horses worth 16,000 francs. I know for a fact that I am no miser; I even believe I am a spendthrift, and yet with what trepidation and sinking of the heart I hear the croupier's cry of '*trente et un, rouge, impair*

---

* The mistress acquired by the narrator following his huge winnings described above. (Eds.)

et passe!' or '*quatre, noir* [black], *pair et manque!*' With what greedy eyes I look at the table scattered with louis d'or, friedrichs d'or, and thalers, the little piles of gold coins when the croupier's shovel sweeps them into heaps that sparkle like fire, and the two-foot long rolls of silver lying round the wheel. When, on my way to the gaming room, I hear from two rooms away the chink of the coins pouring out of the scoops, I am thrown into a ferment.

Oh, that was another remarkable evening, when I took my seventy gulden into the gambling saloon. I began with ten gulden and once again with *passe*. I have a prejudice in favour of *passe*. I lost. I was left with sixty gulden in silver; I thought for a moment—and chose *zéro* [zero]. I began staking five gulden at a time on *zéro*; on the third stroke, *zéro* turned up; I almost died of joy when I received 175 gulden; I had not been so pleased to win 100,000 gulden. I immediately staked a hundred gulden on red—and won; the whole 200 on red—and won; the 400 on black—and won; all 800 on *manque*—and won; including what I had before, that was 1700 gulden— and in less than five minutes! Yes, in such moments one forgets all one's previous failures. I had got this. you see, at the risk of more than life, I had dared to run the risk— and now I was a man again!

I took a hotel room, locked the door, and sat counting my money until three o'clock. Next morning I woke up no longer a servant. I decided to go to Homburg that very day: I had never been a servant, or in prison, there. Half an hour before the train left I went to gamble on two further stakes, no more, and lost 15,000 florins. All the same, I did travel to Homburg, and I have been here for a month now. . . .

I live, of course, in a constant quiver of anxiety, play for the smallest possible sums, wait for something to happen, make calculations, stand all day near the roulette table and *watch* the play, even dream of it at night, but with all that it seems to me that I have grown stiff and numb, as though I was plastered with some sort of mud. I reach that conclusion from the impression made on me by meeting Mr Astley. We had not seen each other since the time I have described, and now we met by accident; it happened like this: I was walking in the gardens and calculating that I was now almost without money, but still had fifty gulden—and besides that, I had settled my hotel bill for the cubby-hole I occupy only two days before. Thus I was left with the possibility of going back to the tables once more—if I won anything at all, I could continue to play; if I lost, I should have to become a servant again, if I could not immediately find a Russian family who were in need of a tutor. Occupied with these thoughts, I pursued my usual daily walk through the park and the wood into the next principality. Sometimes I walked like this for as much as four hours, returning to Homburg tired and hungry. I had only just emerged from the gardens into the park when I suddenly saw Mr Astley sitting on a bench. He had noticed me first and called to me. I sat down beside him. Noticing a certain stiffness in him, I at once restrained my delight, otherwise I was overjoyed to see him.

'So you *are* here! I just thought I should meet you,' he said. 'Don't bother to tell me; I know, I know everything; everything about your life for the past year and eight months is known to me.'

'Ha! So you keep track of your old friends like that!' I answered. 'It does you honour that you don't forget them. Wait a minute, though, you've given me an idea: was it you who paid for me to get out of Roulettenburg prison, where I was being kept for a debt of two hundred gulden? It was somebody unknown.'

'No, oh no; I didn't buy you out of Roulettenburg prison where you were kept for a debt of two hundred gulden, but I knew you were imprisoned for a debt of two hundred gulden.'

'Does that mean that you know who did buy me out?'

'Oh no, I can't say that I know who bought you out.'

'That's strange; I am not known to any of our Russians, and it is unlikely that Russians here would buy anybody out, it's at home in Russia that the Orthodox buy out the Orthodox. But I just thought some eccentric Englishman might have been odd enough.'

Mr Astley listened to me with some surprise. I think he had expected to find me crushed and dejected.

'I am very glad, though, to see that you have retained all your independence of spirit and even your cheerfulness,' he declared with a look of some displeasure.

'You mean you are writhing inwardly with annoyance that I am not crushed and depressed,' I said laughing.

It took him some time to understand, but when he did, he smiled.

'I like the things you say. I recognize the same old clever, enthusiastic and yet cynical friend as before in those words; only Russians can find room inside themselves for so many contradictions at the same time. People really do like seeing their best friends humiliated; a great part of friendship is based on humiliation; and this is an old truth known to all intelligent people. But in the present case, I assure you, I am genuinely glad that you are not dejected. Tell me, do you intend to give up gambling?'

'Oh, to hell with gambling! I'd throw it up at once, if only . . .'

'If only you could win back what you've lost now? I thought so; you needn't finish—I know you let that slip out, and consequently you were speaking the truth. Tell me, are you doing anything besides gambling?'

'No, nothing. . . .'

He began cross-questioning me. I was ignorant of everything, I hardly even glanced at the newspapers and I had definitely not opened a single book during all that time.

'You've become insensible,' he remarked. 'You've not only renounced life, your own interests and those of society, your duty as a man and a citizen, your friends (and you did have them, all the same)—you've not only renounced every aim whatever in life, except winning at roulette—you have even renounced your memories. I remember you at a passionate and intense period in your life; but I am sure you have forgotten all the best influences of that time; your dreams, your most urgent present desires, go no further than *pair et impair, rouge, noir,* the middle dozen numbers, and so on, I'm convinced of it!'

'Stop, Mr Astley, please, please don't remind me,' I cried, stung and almost angry; 'let me tell you I've forgotten nothing at all; I've only driven it all out of my head, even my memories, for the time being, until I have radically altered my circumstances; then . . . then, you will see, I shall rise from the dead!'

'You will still be here ten years from now,'

he said. 'I am willing to bet I'll remind you of it on this very seat, if I'm still alive. . . .'

No, he's wrong! If I was harsh and stupid about Polina and de Grieux,* he was harsh and stupid about Russians. I am not talking about myself. However . . . however, for the time being all that is beside the point: it's all words, words, words, and what we want is deeds! The main thing now is Switzerland! Tomorrow, then—oh, if it were only possible to leave tomorrow! To be restored to life, to rise again. I must show them. . . . Let Polina know that I can still be a man. I need only . . . but now it is too late, but tomorrow. . . . Oh, I have a presentiment, and it cannot be otherwise! I have fifteen louis d'or now, and I was beginning with fifteen gulden! If I begin carefully . . . and surely I can't, I really can't be such a child! Surely I can understand that I am done for! But why can't I rise again? Yes! I have only to be prudent and patient for once in my life—and that's all! I have only to stand firm once, and I can change the whole course of my destiny in an hour! The chief thing is strength of will. I need only remember the incident of this sort seven months ago at Roulettenburg, before my final ruin. Oh, it was a remarkable case of determination: I had lost everything then, everything. . . . As I was going out of the casino I looked—and there in my waistcoat-pocket was one surviving gulden. 'Ah, so I shall be able to have dinner!' I thought, but when I had walked about a hundred paces I changed my mind and went back. I staked that gulden on *manque* (that time it was *manque*), and there really is something special in the feeling when, alone, in a strange country, far away from home and friends and not knowing what you will eat that day, you stake your last gulden, your very, very last! I won, and twenty minutes later I left the casino with 170 gulden in my pocket. That is a fact! You see what one's last gulden may sometimes mean! And what if I had lost courage then, if I had not dared to decide!

Tomorrow, tomorrow it will all come to an end!

---

* Polina's lover. (Eds.)

49. WARD NO. 6

Anton Chekhov

...Some twelve or fifteen years ago there lived in his own house in the main street of the town a certain official by the name of Gromov, a steady well-to-do man. He had two sons: Sergei and Ivan. Sergei, after completing three years of study at the University, contracted galloping consumption and died, and this death was the beginning of a series of disasters which overtook the Gromov family. A week after Sergei's funeral the old man was sued for forgery and embezzlement, and died soon after in the prison hospital of typhus. His house and property were sold at auction, and Ivan Dmitrich and his mother were left without any means of support.

While his father was alive Ivan Dmitrich lived in Petersburg, studying at the University, and receiving 60 or 70 rubles from home every month, so that he had never known want, but now he was forced to make drastic changes in his way of life. He had to work from morning till night, giving lessons for trifling payment, copying documents, and even so he went hungry, for he sent all he earned to his mother. Ivan Dmitrich was not fit for this sort of life; he lost heart, fell ill, left the University and went home. Here, in the small town, he got work as a teacher in the district school through influential friends, but finding he was unable to get on with his colleagues or win the sympathy of the pupils, he soon gave up the post. His mother died. He was without a job for about six months, living on bread and water, and then took the post of bailiff. This last post he held till discharged for reasons of health.

He had never, even in his student days, appeared robust. He was always pale and thin, subject to colds, eating little and sleeping badly. A single glass of wine made him giddy and hysterical. He was drawn to his fellow-mortals, but owing to his irritable and suspicious disposition, there was no one with whom he was on intimate terms, no one he could call a friend. He invariably referred to the townsmen with contempt, declaring that their gross ignorance and drowsy animal existence made him sick. His voice was shrill, and he spoke loudly and passionately, always either in wrathful indignation or in ecstasy and amazement, and always sincerely. Whatever you spoke to him about, he would manage to turn the conversation to his favourite subject: the atmosphere in our town is stifling, life is dull, society devoid of higher interests, dragging out a dreary, meaningless existence only enlivened by violence, coarse debauchery and hypocrisy; knaves are well-fed and well-clad while honest folk live from hand to mouth; schools, a progressive local newspaper, a theatre, public lectures and the co-operation of all the intellectual forces, is what is needed; society must be made aware of all this, be made to see how shocking it is. In judging his fellow-men he laid the paint on thick, but his pallette held only black and white, it admitted of no fine shades; according to him, mankind consisted of honest people and knaves, there was no intermediate category. Of women and love he spoke with ardent enthusiasm, though he had never been in love.

Despite his censoriousness and nervous irritability he was liked in our town, and behind his back referred to affectionately as Vanya. His delicacy, his readiness to oblige, his high principles and moral integrity combined with his shabby coat, sickly appearance and the afflictions which had befallen his family, all tended to create a warm, friendly feeling for him, tinged with melancholy; then he was

From "Ward No. 6" by Anton P. Chekhov in SHORT NOVELS AND STORIES *by A. P. Chekhov, translated by Ivy Litvinov; Moscow, Foreign Languages Publishing House (n.d.), pp. 156–162.*

well-educated and well-read, his fellow-citizens said there was nothing he did not know, and he was regarded by everyone as a kind of walking encyclopaedia.

He was a great reader. He would sit in the club by the hour, tugging nervously at his small beard and turning over the pages of magazines and books; and his face showed that he was not so much reading as devouring their contents, hardly giving himself time to turn them over in his mind. Reading had evidently become a morbid habit with him, for he fell upon everything that came his way with equal avidity, even though it was nothing more interesting than last year's papers and almanacs. At home he always read lying down.

.　.　.

One autumn morning Ivan Dmitrich, his coat-collar turned up, plodded through the slush of side-streets and backyards on his way to hand a writ of execution to some citizen. He was in his usual morning mood, which was bad. In one of the side-streets he met two manacled men, under an armed convoy of four. Ivan Dmitrich was used to such meetings which invariably roused in him feelings of pity and embarrassment, but this time he was strangely and unaccountably affected. For some reason it suddenly came into his head that there was nothing to prevent him from being manacled himself and led like these prisoners through the muddy streets to the prison. On his way home from delivering the writ, he met a police inspector of his acquaintance near the post-office; the latter, after exchanging greetings with him, accompanied him for a few paces, and somehow this struck Gromov as suspicious. When he got home, the thought of the prisoners and the soldiers with their rifles haunted him all day, and a strange mental disquietude prevented him from reading, and concentrating on his thoughts. He did not light his lamp in the evening, and could not sleep for thinking of how he, too, might be arrested, manacled and thrown into prison. He knew he was guilty of no crime, and could guarantee that he would never murder, commit arson, or steal; but was it not possible to commit a crime as it were accidentally, without meaning to? Besides, were there not such things as fraud or even miscarriage of justice? Does not the popular saying: "nobody is safe from the

poor-house or the prison" reflect the experience of ages? And in the present state of legal proceedings what could be more likely than a miscarriage of justice? Such people as judges, police authorities and doctors, who regard human suffering in a strictly official light, become in the course of time and from habit so callous that they cannot, even if they wanted to, treat their clients in any but a formal way; in this respect there is no difference between them and the peasant slaughtering sheep and calves in his backyard, perfectly oblivious to the blood. And once this formal, callous attitude has been established, only one thing is needed to make a judge deprive an innocent person of his rights and sentence him to hard labour—time. Just the time necessary for the observation of the few formalities for which the judge receives his salary, and all will be over. And then you may seek justice and protection in the small dirty town two hundred versts* away from the nearest railway station! And is it not absurd to think of justice when every act of oppression is regarded by society as rational and expedient, and every act of clemency, such as an acquittal, is greeted with an outburst of unsatisfied revengeful feelings?

The next morning Ivan Dmitrich rose from his bed in a state of abject terror, with cold sweat breaking out on his brow, and the conviction that he might be arrested any minute. Since the oppressive thoughts of the day before would not leave him, he told himself that there must be some real ground for them. After all, they could not have entered his mind without some good reason. A policeman passed his window at a leisurely pace: what could that mean? Two men stopped opposite his house and stood silent. Why were they silent?

Days and nights of anguish ensued for Ivan Dmitrich. He thought everyone who passed his windows or entered his yard was a spy or a detective. The district police inspector was in the habit of driving along the street in his carriage and pair every day at noon; he drove from his country estate to the police office, but to Ivan Dmitrich it seemed he was driving too fast, and that there was a significant look on his face; he was probably hastening to announce that there was a dangerous

---

* A verst is a unit of distance equal to about two-thirds of a mile. (Eds.)

criminal living in the town. Every time the door-bell rang, or there was a knock at the gate, Ivan Dmitrich started; he felt uneasy if his landlady had a visitor he had not seen before; when he met a policeman or a gen-darme he smiled and whistled a tune to appear at ease. He lay awake all night for fear of being arrested, but snored loudly and sighed drowsily to make the landlady think he was asleep; for if he did not sleep, would not it mean he had something on his conscience— and what a clue that would be! Facts and common sense assured him that his fears were absurd and morbid, that there was nothing terrible in arrest or imprisonment if one took a broad view of things—so long as one's con-science was clear; but the saner and more logical his reasoning, the greater, the acuter became his restlessness. He was like the her-mit who tried to clear himself a spot in the jungle, but found that the trees and bushes grew all the denser under the axe. Realizing the futility of it, Ivan Dmitrich at last gave up reason, and surrendered himself to terror and despair.

He began to seek solitude and shun society. His work, which he had always detested, had now become quite intolerable to him. He was afraid someone might play him a dirty trick, slip a bribe into his pocket without his notic-ing, and then expose him, that he would let some error which would be tantamount to forgery creep into the official papers or that he would lose money which did not belong to him. It was quite remarkable how ingeni-ous and versatile his mind had become, now that he daily invented a thousand reasons why he should tremble for his honour and freedom. On the other hand, his interest in the outside world and in reading was weakening, his memory had deteriorated considerably.

In the spring, after the snow had melted, the corpses of an old woman and a little boy, both in a state of decomposition, and bearing the signs of death by violence, were found in the gully outside the cemetery. The whole town talked of nothing but these corpses and the unknown murderers. To prevent people

from thinking he was the murderer, Ivan Dmitrich walked about the streets with a smile on his face and when he met his acquain-tances, he would assure them, paling and flushing by turns, that there was no crime so base as that of killing the weak and defence-less. But he soon got tired of perpetual dis-sembling and decided that the best thing for a man in his position to do would be to hide in the cellar. He spent a day, the night follow-ing, and another day in the cellar, got chilled to the bone and sneaked back to his own room like a thief as soon as it was dark. He stood still in the middle of the room till daybreak, listening. Just before daybreak some stove-makers came to the landlady. Ivan Dmitrich was perfectly aware that they had come to repair the kitchen stove, but fear whispered to him they were policemen dis-guised as stove-makers. He crept quietly out of the house, without stopping to put on his hat and coat, and rushed panic-stricken into the street. Dogs ran after him barking, a man shouted behind him, the wind whistled in his ears, and it seemed to Ivan Dmitrich that all the violence in the world had accumulated behind his back and was chasing him.

He was stopped and brought home, and his landlady sent for the doctor. Doctor Andrei Yefimich, of whom there will be more to say hereafter, prescribed cold compresses and laurel drops, shook his head sadly and went away, telling the landlady he would not come any more, it was no good trying to prevent people from going mad. Since he had no money to live on and to pay for medical treat-ment, Ivan Dmitrich was sent to the hospital, where they found a place for him in the ward for venereal patients. He did not sleep at night, was irritable, and disturbed the other patients, and soon, on the orders of Andrei Yefimich, he was transferred to Ward No. 6.

In a year nobody in the town remembered Ivan Dmitrich, and his books, which his landlady dumped into a sleigh under the roof of a lean-to, were all taken by the neighbour-ing boys. . . .

50. THE DEATH OF IVAN ILYICH

Lëv Tolstoy

...Suddenly he felt the old familiar gnawing pain—quiet, serious, insistent. And the same bad taste in his mouth. His heart sank, he felt dizzy. "My god, my god!" he muttered. "Again, again, and it will never stop." And suddenly he saw things in an entirely different light. "The caecum.* Kidneys," he said to himself. "It isn't a matter of caecum and kidneys, it is a matter of life...and death. Yes, once there was life, and now it is passing away, passing away, and there is nothing I can do to stop it. Why should I deceive myself? Is it not clear to everyone except me that I am dying, that it is merely a question of weeks, days, even hours? There was light, now there is darkness. I was here, I am going there. Where?" He broke out in a cold sweat and he had difficulty in breathing. He could hear nothing but the beating of his heart.

"I will no longer exist. What will exist? Nothing. Where will I be when I cease to exist? Is this really death? Oh, I don't want to die!" He jumped up to light the candle, he felt for it with trembling hands, he dropped the candle and candlestick on the floor, and fell back on the pillow again. "What does it matter? It's all the same," he said to himself as he stared into the darkness with wide open eyes. "Death. Yes, death. And they don't know it and don't want to know it, and have no pity. They are playing." (He heard the distant trilling of a woman's voice and the piano accompaniment coming through the closed

* The pouch at the beginning of the large intestine. (Eds.)

From "The Death of Ivan Ilyich" in SHORT STORIES *by Lëv Tolstoy, translated by Margaret Wettlin. Published by the Foreign Languages Publishing House, Moscow (n.d.)*

door.) "It's all the same to them now, but soon they will die too. The fools. I shall go first, then they; it will come to them, too. Now they are rejoicing, the beasts." His resentment fairly choked him. He was horribly, unspeakably miserable. It was inconceivable that everyone, always, should be doomed to this horror. He raised himself.

"Something is wrong; I must calm myself and think it through from the beginning." And he began to think. "The beginning of my illness. I struck my side, but I was just the same then, and the following day; it only ached a little, but then it got worse, and then I started going to see doctors, and then I felt downcast, depressed, and then more doctors; and all the while I was moving closer and closer to the edge of the precipice. My strength gave out. Closer and closer. And here I am a wreck, no life in my eyes. Death. And I still think about my caecum. I think of mending my intestines, and all the time it is death. But is it, really?" And again he was seized by terror; he gasped, bent down, felt for the matches, and knocked his elbow against the bedside table. It was in the way and it hurt him and he became angry with it and struck it a second time harder and knocked it over. In desperation, gasping for breath, he fell on his back and waited for death to come that very moment.

The guests were going home. Praskovya Fyodorovna,* who was seeing them off, heard the table fall and came into the room.

"What's the matter?"

"Nothing. I accidentally knocked it over."

She went out and came back with a candle. He lay there with his eyes fixed on her, breath-

* Ivan's wife. (Eds.)

ing loudly and quickly, like a man who had a long run.

"What is it, *Jean*?"*

"N-nothing. I knocked it...over." ("Why should I tell her? She won't understand," he thought.)

And she did not understand. She picked up the table, lighted the candle, and hurried away. She had to see her guests off.

When she came back he was still lying on his back staring at the ceiling.

"What is it, are you worse?"

"Yes."

She shook her head and sat down.

"I'm wondering, *Jean,* if we shouldn't send for Leshchetitsky?"

Sending for the celebrity meant spending a lot of money again. He gave a sardonic smile and said no. She sat down for a little while, then went over to him and kissed him on the forehead.

He hated her with his whole heart when she kissed him, and it cost him a great effort to keep from pushing her away.

"Good-night. God willing, you'll fall asleep."

"Yes."

.   .   .

Ivan Ilyich saw that he was dying, and he was in a constant state of despair. In his heart of hearts he knew he was dying, and it was not simply that he could not get used to the idea; he could not grasp it, could not possibly grasp it.

All his life he had regarded the syllogism he had learned while studying Kiesewetter's *Logics*: "Caius is a man, men are mortal, and therefore Caius is mortal," as being true only in respect to Caius, not to himself. Caius was a man, a man in the abstract sense, and so the syllogism applied to him; but Ivan Ilyich was not Caius, and not a man in the abstract sense; he had always been quite, quite different from all other men. He had been little Vanya to his mamá and papá, to his brothers Mitya and Volodya, to the coachman and the nursemaid and to his toys, and to Katya; Vanya, who had lived through all the joys and sorrows and ecstasies of childhood, boyhood, and youth. Had Caius ever known the

* French for "Ivan." Educated Russians of the upper classes during the late eighteenth and nineteenth centuries often spoke French among themselves, believing it a more elegant language than Russian. (Eds.)

leathery smell of a football that Vanya had loved so dearly? Had Caius ever kissed his mother's hand with such feeling, or so loved the rustle of her silk skirts? Had Caius ever made a row over the buns at school? Or ever been so in love? Or presided so brilliantly over a court session?

Caius was indeed mortal, and it was only right and proper that he should die, but he, Vanya, Ivan Ilyich, with all his thoughts and feelings—it was quite a different matter with him. And it could not be right and proper that he should die. The thought was too horrifying.

That was what he felt.

"If I were doomed to die like Caius I would have known of it, some inner voice would have told me. But I have never been aware of anything of the sort; I have always known, and so have all of my friends, that I was not of the same stuff as Caius. And now, lo and behold!" he said to himself. "But it cannot be. It cannot be. It cannot be, and yet it is. How is it possible? How is one to understand it?"

He could not understand it and tried to drive the thought away as being false, misleading, and unwholesome, and he tried to evoke true, wholesome thoughts to take its place. But the thought was more than a thought, it was reality itself, and it kept coming back and confronting him.

One by one he summoned up other thoughts to take its place in the hope of finding support in them. He tried to recover a former way of thinking that had protected him from thoughts of death. But, strange as it may seem, the things that had once screened, hidden, obliterated the consciousness of death, were now unable to do so. Ivan Ilyich spent most of his time of late trying to recover a former way of thinking that had screened death from him. He would, for instance, say to himself, "I must lose myself in work; after all, that was once my whole life." And he would go to court, driving all his doubts out of his mind. He would enter into conversation with his friends, and take his seat among them as he always had, casting a vague and ponderous glance over the people gathered in the court-room as he sat down, grasping the arms of his oaken chair with his thin hands, bending towards his neighbour, shifting the papers about, whispering, then suddenly straightening up and raising his eyes to pronounce the well-known words with which proceedings were opened. But in the very middle of a court sitting that pain in his side, irrespective of the stage proceedings had reached, would begin its gnawing proceedings. Ivan Ilyich would pay it brief attention, then try to drive it out of his mind, but it went right on with its work, and came and stood facing him, staring him straight in the eye, and he was confounded, and the light went out of his eyes, and once more he asked himself, "Is *It* the only truth?" And his colleagues and subordinates saw with surprise and grief that he, who had always been such a brilliant and subtle judge, was getting muddled and making mistakes. He would give a toss of his head and try to pull himself together and somehow carry proceedings through to the end, and return home, sadly aware that legal proceedings could no longer hide from him that which he wished to hide; that no legal proceedings could enable him to escape from *It*. . . .

Ivan Ilyich suffered most of all from the lie—the lie adopted by everyone for some reason, which said that he was only ill and not dying, and that everything would be all right if he just kept quiet and did what the doctors told him to. He knew perfectly well that no matter what was done, nothing would change except that his sufferings would increase and he would die. He was tortured by this lie, tortured by no one's wanting to acknowledge the lie, by his knowing the truth and everyone else's knowing the truth, and yet pressing this lie upon him because of the horror of his position, forcing him to become a party to the lie. This lie, the lie forced upon him on the eve of his death, the lie degrading the solemn, awesome act of his dying to the level of their social calls, portières, and oysters for supper, was an unspeakable torture to Ivan Ilyich. And, strangely enough, time and again when they went through the forms with him, he came within a hair's breadth of shouting out, "Stop your lying! You know and I know that I am about to die. You might at least stop lying!" But he never had the courage to do it. He could see that the dread, the fearsome act of his dying had been degraded by those about him to the level of a chance unpleasantness, a sort of breach of etiquette (they behaved towards him as they might to a man who gave off a foul odour on entering a drawing-room), a violation of that "decorum" to which he had been a bondslave all his life. He saw that no one felt sorry for him because no one cared to understand his position. The only person who understood and who felt sorry for him was Gerasim.* And for that reason the only person Ivan Ilyich cared to be with was Gerasim. He was quite content when Gerasim sat with him sometimes the whole night through, holding his feet and refusing to go to bed. . .

Next to the lie and all it entailed, the most painful thing for Ivan Ilyich was that no one felt sorry for him as he would have liked them to. There were moments when, after long suffering, the thing he most wanted, even though he was ashamed to admit it, was to be fondled pityingly, like a sick child. He wanted to be patted, kissed, cried over, as sick children are kissed and comforted. He knew that he was an important member of the law court and that his beard was turning grey and that therefore such a thing was impossible. But that was what he wanted. There was something approaching this in his relations with Gerasim, and that was why he found comfort in Gerasim. Ivan Ilyich wanted to cry, wanted to be petted and wept over, but here comes Shebek to see him, his colleague Shebek, also a member of the law court, and instead of crying and seeking comfort, Ivan Ilyich puts on a grave, profound look and, from sheer inertia, gives his opinion of the importance of the decisions of the Court of Appeal and stubbornly defends it.

Nothing did so much to poison the last days of Ivan Ilyich as this lie within him and all around him. . . .

His daughter came in all dressed up, with much of her young body naked, making a show of it, while his body was causing him such torture. She was strong and healthy, evidently very much in love, and annoyed that his illness and suffering and death should cast a shadow upon her happiness.

Fyodor Petrovich† came in wearing evening clothes and with his hair curled *à la Capoul*,‡ his long, sinewy neck encircled by a stiff white

---

* One of Ivan's household servants. (Eds.)
† Ivan's daughter's fiancé. (Eds.)
‡ A fashionable style of the times. (Eds.)

collar, his chest covered by an expanse of white shirt-front, his strong calves sheathed in narrow black trousers, one hand encased in a white glove, the other holding an opera hat.

Behind him Ivan Ilyich's son, the schoolboy, slipped in unnoticed, all decked out in a new uniform, poor chap, and with gloves on his hands and those dreadful dark circles under his eyes that Ivan Ilyich knew the meaning of.

He had always felt sorry for his son. And now there was something dreadful for him in the boy's frightened, pitying glance. Ivan Ilyich felt that Vasya was the only one besides Gerasim who understood and pitied him.

They all sat down and asked him again how he felt. A pause. Liza asked her mother about the opera-glasses. This brought on a little tiff between mother and daughter as to which of them had mislaid them. Very unpleasant.

Fyodor Petrovich asked Ivan Ilyich if he had ever seen Sarah Bernhardt. At first Ivan Ilyich did not understand the question, then he said:

"No. Have you?"

"Yes. In *Adrienne Lecouvreur*."*

Praskovya Fyodorovna said that she was particularly enchanting in something-or-other. The daughter objected. There began a discussion of the charm and naturalness of her acting, in which they said the same things that are always said on the subject.

In the middle of the conversation Fyodor Petrovich glanced at Ivan Ilyich and stopped talking. The others also glanced at him and stopped talking. Ivan Ilyich was staring in front of him with glittering eyes, unable to hide his resentment. Something had to be done, but nothing could be done. The silence had to be broken, but nobody dared to break it. They all began to fear that something might expose the lie that was being supported for decency's sake, and things would suddenly be seen in their true light. Liza was the first to pluck up courage. She broke the silence. She did it with the intention of hiding what everyone was feeling, but instead she gave it utterance.

"Well, *if we are going*, we must go," she

* A popular romantic tragedy written in 1849 by Eugène Scribe (1791–1861) and Ernest Legouvé. (Eds.)

said, glancing at her watch, which had been a present from her father, and smiling significantly but scarcely perceptibly at her young man about something that only they two were aware of. Then she got up with a rustle of silk.

They all got up, said good-bye, and went away.

Ivan Ilyich fancied he felt better when they were gone: at least the lie was gone, too —it had departed with them.

But the pain remained. The same old pain, the same old fear that made nothing harder, nothing easier. And it kept growing worse.

Again the time dragged on, minute by minute, hour by hour, just the same, without end, yet with the horror of the certain end growing upon him.

"Yes, send up Gerasim," he said in reply to Pyotr's question.

.   .   .

It was late when his wife returned. She tiptoed into the room but he heard her. He opened his eyes and quickly closed them again. She wanted to send Gerasim out and sit beside him herself, but he opened his eyes and said:

"No, go away."

"Are you suffering very much?"

"It doesn't matter."

"Take some opium."

He consented and drank it. She went out.

Until three in the morning he was in a semi-conscious state of torture. He fancied they were torturing him by trying to push him into a narrow black sack, and that they kept pushing him in deeper and deeper but could not push him to the bottom. And this dreadful business was causing him suffering. He was afraid, yet he wanted to get into the sack, and he simultaneously resisted and tried to get in. Suddenly he broke loose and fell and woke up. Gerasim was still sitting on the foot of the bed, drowsing quietly, patiently. And Ivan Ilyich was lying with his emaciated stockinged feet on the lad's shoulders. The candle was still burning behind the shade, and the pain was still with him.

"Go to bed, Gerasim," he whispered.

"That's all right, sir. I shall stay a while."

"No, go away."

He lowered his legs and turned over on his

side with his hand under his cheek and began to pity himself. He waited until Gerasim had gone into the next room, and then, letting himself go, cried like a baby. He cried because of his helplessness, because of his dreadful loneliness, because of the heartlessness of people and of God, and because of the absence of God.

"Why hast Thou done all this? Why didst Thou bring me into the world? What, oh what have I done that Thou shouldst torture me so?"

He did not expect an answer, and he cried because there was not and could not be any answer. The pain began again, but he did not stir, did not call anyone. He merely said to himself, "Very well, hit me again, Harder! But what for? What have I ever done to thee?"

Then he grew quiet and not only stopped crying, but stopped breathing as well and was all attention: he seemed to be listening not to the speaking voice, but to the voice of his soul, to the stream of thought flowing through him.

"What do you want?" was the first concept sufficiently lucid to be expressed in words. "What do you want? What do you want?" he repeated to himself. "Not to suffer. To live," he replied.

And once more he was all attention, such strained attention that even his pain could not distract him.

"Live? Live how?" asked the voice of his soul.

"Live as I lived before; a good, pleasant life."

"And was your life so good and pleasant before?" asked the voice. And he began to go over in his mind the best moments of his pleasant life. But, strange as it may seem, all the best moments of his pleasant life no longer seemed to be what he had considered them. All, except the earliest memories of his childhood. In his childhood there had been something really pleasant, something worth living for, if it could have been brought back again. But the person who had experienced this pleasantness was no more. He seemed to be calling up memories of someone else.

As soon as his memories involved the person who turned out to be the present Ivan Ilyich, all that had once seemed joyful dissolved

under his fixed attention and turned into something worthless and even disgusting.

The further away he went from his childhood and the closer he came to the present, the more worthless and dubious became his joy. This began with the school of jurisprudence. He had known things that were genuinely good there: he had known gaiety, friendship, and hope. But these good things grew more rare as he reached the higher classes. Later, during his first years of service as secretary to the governor, he had again known some good things; most of them had been connected with being in love. Then his life had grown complicated and the good things had decreased. Later on there was even less of the good, and the further he went, the less there was.

His marriage—such a chance marriage, and the disillusionment, and the odour of his wife's breath, and the sensuality, and the pretence! And that lifeless profession of his, and the worry over money—year after year, one year, two, ten, twenty, without any change. And the longer it lasted, the more lifeless everything became. "As if I had been going steadily downhill, while I fancied I was going uphill. Yes, that is how it was. In the opinion of my fellows I was going uphill, but only to the extent that life itself was crumbling away under my feet. And now here I am, dying.

"What is happening? Why? Incredible. Incredible that my life should have been so disgusting and meaningless. But even if it was so disgusting and meaningless, why must I die, and die in such agony? Something must be wrong.

"Perhaps I did not live as I ought to have?" was an idea that came into his mind. "But it cannot be that I did not live as I ought to have, for I did everything as it ought to have been done," he said to himself, and instantly drove away this one answer to the whole problem of life and death, considering it utterly impossible.

"What do you want now? To live? To live how?"

"As if you were in court, and the usher was crying out, 'The Judge is coming!' The Judge is coming, the Judge is coming!" he repeated to himself. "Here he is, the Judge. But I am not to blame!" he cried out indignantly. "What am I to blame for?" And he stopped crying, and, turning his face to the wall, went on thinking of the same thing over and over: "Why, for what reason, must I go through all this horror?"

But think as he might, he could find no answer. And whenever the thought occurred to him (as it often did) that all of this was because he had not lived as he ought to have, he instantly drove away so preposterous a thought by recalling how correctly he had lived.

Two more weeks went by. Ivan Ilyich no longer got up off the sofa. He lay on the sofa because he did not want to lie in bed. And as he lay there, mostly with his face to the wall, he suffered all alone the same inexplicable suffering, and pondered all alone the same inexplicable questions: "What is it? Can it really be death?" And the inner voice answered, "Yes, it really is." "But why this suffering?" And the inner voice answered, "For no reason at all." That was as far as it went —nothing but this. . . .

The mere remembrance of what he had been three months earlier and what he was now, the remembrance of how steadily he had been going downhill, was sufficient to destroy all possibility of hope.

During the last days of the solitude in which he lived, lying on the sofa with his face to the wall, of his solitude in the midst of the populous town, among all his many friends and relatives, a solitude that could not possibly have been more complete at the bottom of the sea or in the bowels of the earth—during the last days of that dreadful solitude Ivan Ilyich lived only in the past. One by one pictures of bygone days passed through his mind. They always began with something from the immediate past and went back to times more remote, to his childhood, and lingered there. If he recalled the plum jam he had been offered in the morning, he was sure to recall the sticky, wrinkled French prunes of his childhood, their peculiar taste, and the strong flow of saliva caused by the sucking of their stones, and this memory of a taste brought a whole train of recollections of that time in its wake: nursemaids, his brother, his toys. "I mustn't think of them. . .it is too painful," Ivan Ilyich said to himself, and switched his thoughts to the present. The button on the back of the sofa and the fold in the morocco. "Morocco is expensive and does not wear well; I quar-

relled with my wife over it. That time when we ripped papá's brief-case the morocco was different, and so was the row we had, and we were punished for it and mamá brought us pastries." And again his thoughts centred on his childhood, and again he found them painful and tried to drive them away by thinking of something else.

And simultaneously with this train of memories, others pressed themselves upon him —memories of how his illness had begun and developed. And he felt that the further back he went into the past, the more vital his life had been. There had been more goodness in his life earlier, and more vitality. The one merged with the other. "Just as my sufferings are growing worse and worse, so my whole life has grown worse and worse," he thought. There was only one bright spot, and that was back at the very beginning of life. After that things grew blacker and blacker, faster and faster. "In inverse ratio to the square of the distance separating me from death," thought Ivan Ilyich. And the metaphor of a stone falling with increasing velocity flashed into his mind. Life, a series of increasing sufferings, is falling faster and faster towards its goal, which is unspeakable suffering. "I am falling. . . ." He started, shuddered, tried to resist; but he now knew there could be no resisting. And again, weary from contemplating, but unable to turn his eyes away from that which rose up in front of them, he stared at the back of the sofa and waited—waited for that fearful fall, the final shock, the destruction. "There is no resisting," he said to himself. "If I could only understand why it should be so!" But that, too, was impossible. "It might make some sense if I had not lived as I ought to have. But such an admission is impossible," he said to himself, remembering all the correctness, the decorum, the propriety of his life. "I cannot admit such a thing," he said to himself, drawing his lips apart as if someone could see his smile and be deceived by it. "There is no sense to it. Agony. Death. Why?"

Another fortnight passed in this way. During that time the event he and his wife had hoped for occurred. Petrishchev made a formal proposal. It happened in the evening. The next morning Praskovya Fyodorovna came to her husband's room, going over in her mind how she would announce the proposal to him, but during the night Ivan Ilyich had undergone a change for the worse. Praskovya Fyodorovna found him on the same sofa, but in a different position. He was lying on his face, groaning and staring before him with a fixed gaze.

She began to speak to him about his medicine. He turned his eyes upon her. She did not finish what she was saying, so great was the hatred of her—the hatred of her—that she read in his eyes.

"For God's sake, let me die in peace," he said.

She made as if to go out, but at that moment their daughter came in and went over to say good-morning to him. He looked at her just as he had looked at his wife, and when she asked him how he felt he answered dryly that they would soon be rid of him. Both of them were silent, sat down for a moment, then went out. . . .

The doctor said his physical suffering must be dreadful, and so it was; but more dreadful than his physical suffering was his moral suffering; in this lay his real torment.

His moral suffering came from having, that night, gazed at the sleepy, good-humoured, broad face of Gerasim and thought: "What if all my life, all my mature life, really has not been what it ought to have been?"

He was struck by the thought that what had formerly seemed to him utterly impossible (that his life had been spent not as it ought to have been) might be true. He was struck by the thought that those scarcely perceptible impulses to struggle against what people in high position considered good, scarcely perceptible impulses which he had always suppressed, might be the real thing, and all the rest might be aside from the real thing. His official duties, his manner of living, his family, his social and professional interests—all of these might be aside from the real thing. He attempted a defence of these things, but suddenly he became aware of the worthlessness of what he was defending. There was nothing to defend.

"If that is the case," he said to himself, "and I am taking leave of life with the realization that I have squandered all that was given to me, and that it is too late to do anything about it—what then?" He lay on his face and began reviewing his life from an entirely different point of view.

When, in the morning, he saw first the footman, then his wife, then his daughter, and at last the doctor, their every movement, their every word, confirmed the dreadful truth revealed to him in the night. In them he saw himself, saw all that had formed his life, and saw clearly that all of this was aside from the real thing, that it was all a dreadful and enormous deception hiding the truths of life and death. This realization increased his physical sufferings, multiplied them tenfold. He moaned and tossed and clutched at his clothes. His clothes seemed to be squeezing him, suffocating him, and he hated them.

He was given a big dose of opium that made him forget, but at dinner-time it all began again. He drove everyone out and lay tossing on the bed.

His wife came to him and said:

"*Jean,* dear, do this for me." (For me?) "It cannot do you any harm and it often helps. It doesn't mean anything. And even well people sometimes—"

He looked at her wide-eyed.

"What? Take the sacrament? Why? I don't want to. And yet. . . ."

She began to cry.

"Won't you, dear? I'll send for our priest, he is such a good man."

"Very well. Excellent," he said.

When the priest came and had heard his confession, the heart of Ivan Ilyich was softened, he seemed to be relieved of his doubts, and this brought him relief from his sufferings, and for a moment he had hope. Again he began to think of his caecum and the possibility of curing it. There were tears in his eyes as he took the sacrament.

When they laid him down again after the sacrament he felt better for a moment, and he was filled once more with the hope of recovery.

He thought of the operation the doctor had suggested performing. "I want to live, to live," he said to himself. His wife came in to congratulate him; she said the usual things, and then added:

"You really do feel better, don't you?"

"Yes," he said without looking at her.

Her dress, her figure, the expression of her face, the sound of her voice—everything said to him: "Aside from the real thing. Everything that has been and still is your life is a lie and a deception hiding the reality of life and death from you." And the minute this thought came to him, hatred rose within him; and with the hatred, agonizing physical suffering; and with the suffering, the realization of his imminent and inevitable end. New sensations put in an appearance: something inside of him began to twist and snap and choke the breath out of him.

The expression of his face when he pronounced that "yes" was terrible. And having pronounced it, looking her straight in the eye, he flung himself down on his face with a swiftness incredible in anyone as weak as he was, and shrieked:

"Go away! Go away! Leave me alone!"

From that moment there began three days of such terrible and uninterrupted shrieking that even two rooms away one could not hear it without shuddering. The moment he had replied to his wife's question he had understood that all was over, that there was no hope, that the end, the very end, was at hand, that all his doubts remained doubts and would never be answered.

"Ah! Ah! Ah!" he shrieked in different tones. He had begun by shouting, "I don't wa-a-nt to!" and had gone on shouting that "Ah!"

Throughout those three days, which for him were timeless, he struggled in that black sack that some invisible and irresistible force was pushing him into. He struggled as one who is condemned to death and knows there is no hope of escape, struggles in the arms of the executioner. And he realized that with every minute, despite the desperateness of his struggle, he was coming closer and closer to that which terrified him. He felt that his torture was caused by his being pushed into that black hole, but even more by his being unable to crawl into it himself. He was prevented from crawling into it by the belief that his life had been a good one. This defence of the life he had lived was the hindrance that kept him from moving ahead, and it caused him more torture than anything else.

Suddenly some force struck him in the chest and the side and cut off his breath; he plunged straight into the hole, and there, at the end of the hole, he found a glimmer of light. He had the sensation he had once experienced while riding in a railway carriage, when he had thought he was moving forward and was actually moving backward and suddenly became aware of the true direction.

"Yes, it is all aside from the real thing," he said to himself. "But that is all right. I can still make it the real thing. But what *is* the real thing?" he asked himself, and suddenly grew quiet.

This took place at the end of the third day, an hour before his death. Just then his son crept into his room and up to his bed. The dying man was still screaming wildly and throwing his arms about. One hand fell on the head of his son. The boy seized it, pressed it to his lips, and began to cry. It was just at this moment that Ivan Ilyich plunged into the hole and saw the light, and it was revealed to him that his life had not been what it ought to have been, but he could still mend matters. "What is the real thing?" he asked himself, and grew quiet, listening. It was then he realized that someone was kissing his hand. He opened his eyes and looked at his son. He was filled with pity for him. His wife came in. He glanced at her. She stood looking at him with her mouth hanging open, with the tears unwiped on her nose and cheeks, with an expression of despair on her face. He filled with pity for her.

"I am torturing them," he thought. "They feel sorry for me, but things will be better for them when I am gone." He wanted to tell them this, but lacked the strength. "But what is the use of speaking? I must do something," he thought. He turned to his wife and indicated his son with his eyes.

"Take him away," he said. "Poor boy...and you...." He wanted to add, "Forgive," and it came out, "Forget," but he had not the strength to correct himself; he merely gave a little wave of his hand, knowing that the one who was to understand would understand.

And presently it became clear to him that all he had been tortured by and been unable to throw off, was now falling away of itself, falling away on two sides, ten sides, all sides at once. He felt sorry for them, he must do something to ease their pain. He must relieve them and himself of this suffering. "How good and how simple!" he thought. "And the pain?" he asked himself. "How am I to dispose of it? Here, where are you, pain?"

He felt for the pain.

"Ah, here it is. What of it? Let it be."

"And death? Where is death?"

He searched for his accustomed terror of

death and could not find it. Where was death? What was death? There was no fear because there was no death.

There was light instead of death.

"So that is it!" he suddenly said out loud. "What happiness!"

All of this took place in an instant, but the significance of that instant was lasting. For those present his death agony continued for another two hours. Something rattled in his throat; his emaciated body twitched. But gradually the wheezing and the rattling ceased.

"All is over," someone said.

He heard these words and repeated them in his soul.

"Death is over," he said to himself. "There is no more death."

He drew in a deep breath, broke off in the middle of it, stretched out his limbs, and died.

RECOMMENDED FURTHER READING

*Anonymous: *Autobiography of a Schizophrenic Girl* (trans. by Grace Rubin-Rabson); New York, Grune & Stratton 1951

Ariete, Silvano (ed.): *American Handbook of Psychiatry* (2 Vols.); New York, Basic Books 1959

*Braginsky, B. M., D. Braginsky, *et al.*: *Methods of Madness: The Mental Hospital as a Last Resort;* New York, Holt, Rinehart & Winston 1969

Coleman, J. C.: *Abnormal Psychology in Modern Life* (3rd Ed.); Glenview, Ill., Scott, Foresman 1964

Goldhamer, H. and A. W. Marshall: *Psychosis and Civilization;* New York, Free Press 1953

*Green, Hannah: *I Never Promised You A Rose Garden;* New York, Holt, Rinehart & Winston 1964

Hollingshead, August B. and Frederick C. Redlich: *Social Class and Mental Illness: A Community Study;* New York, John Wiley 1958

*Laing, R. D., *The Divided Self;* London, Tavistock 1959

Langner, Thomas S. and S. T. Michael: *Life Stress and Mental Health: The Midtown Manhattan Study,* Vol. 2; New York, Free Press (Macmillan) 1963

*London, Perry and David Rosenhan (eds.): *Foundations of Abnormal Psychology;* New York, Holt, Rinehart & Winston 1968

*Pfeiffer, C. C., *et al.*: *Schizophrenias: Yours and Mine;* New York, Pyramid Publications 1969

Redlich, Frederick C. and D. X. Freedman: *The Theory and Practice of Psychiatry;* New York, Basic Books 1966

Srole, Leo, *et al.*: *Mental Health in the Metropolis: The Midtown Manhattan Study,* Vol. 1; New York, McGraw-Hill 1962

*Stone, Alan A. and Sue Smart Stone (eds.): *The Abnormal Personality Through Literature;* Englewood Cliffs, N.J., Prentice-Hall 1966

Szasz, Thomas S.: *The Myth of Mental Illness;* New York, Harper & Row 1961
————: *The Manufacture of Madness;* New York, Harper & Row 1970

*Thigpen, Corbett H. and Hervey M. Cleckley: *The Three Faces of Eve;* New York, McGraw-Hill 1957

Ullmann, Leonard P. and Leonard Krasner: *The Psychological Study of Abnormal Behavior;* Englewood Cliffs, N.J., Prentice-Hall 1969

*Ward, Mary Jane: *The Snake Pit;* New York, Random House 1946

* Paperback edition available.

Philip Curtis, *The Meeting*. Property of the Lewis and Lenore Ruskin Collection.

PART XI

TO MAKE MEN WHOLE AGAIN: THE TASK OF THERAPY

Whether one believes that "mental illness" is a disease analogous to physical illness or accepts Thomas Szasz's contention that it is a psychiatric label affixed to socially unacceptable behaviors that are themselves indicative of "problems in living" there can be no disputing the immense personal and social costs of emotional disturbances or the imperative need to alleviate the suffering those disturbances cause. There are today three times as many Americans in mental hospitals (some 750,000) as in prisons and survey studies variously estimate the proportion of the population suffering from significant emotional disturbances at between 10 and 80 percent, depending on how they define "significant emotional disturbances."

In treating emotional disturbances two major strategies dominate contemporary therapeutic practice: the organic (or somatic) and the psychotherapeutic. While, in theory, these two strategies are not mutually exclusive, and while both aim to alter the disturbed person's behavior, in practice the former tends to be used with those labeled "psychotic" (e.g., schizophrenics and manic-depressives) and the latter with those labeled "neurotic."

Organic treatments, whether or not they are based on the assumption that the causes of emotional disturbances are physiological in nature, are all *symptomatic* treatments. They attempt, in other words, to relieve the symptoms of the disturbance by bringing about some change in the functioning of the patient's body either through the use of drugs (tranquilizers or energizers), electric or chemically induced shock, or neurosurgical procedures (e.g., lobotomy or leucotomy). Sometimes organic treatment (especially drugs) is used to make a psychotic patient amenable to some form of psychotherapy, but more often it constitutes the total treatment offered him. Organic therapies are the preferred strategy in large and crowded state hospitals where shortages of funds and trained personnel make psychotherapy impractical if not impossible.

Organic treatment is usually administered under the direction of a *psychiatrist,* who is, by definition, an M.D. While such treatment is often effective over the short run the patients "cured" by organic therapies show high rates of relapse and we cannot be sure that the rate of "cure" is any higher with such treatment than it would be without any treatment at all (so-called "spontaneous remission"). In the case of drug therapies sustained improvement depends on continued and often indefinite use of the relevant drugs, the side effects of which are always bothersome, often unpredictable, and sometimes harmful.

Psychotherapy or, more accurately, the psychotherapies try to bring about desired change in the patient's behavior through processes of new or re-learning, an outcome that depends on the effects of communication (both verbal and nonverbal) either between the patient and his therapist (in individual psychotherapy) or among the patient, a group of other patients, and the therapist or therapists (in group psychotherapy). While some forms of psychotherapy try to lead the patient toward emotional and intellectual insight into his problems and their roots, others, notably "behavior therapy," concentrate on changing the person's maladaptive behavior (habits or symptoms) without attempting to induce insight or understanding (although they do not reject these in principle).

The goals of all the psychotherapies are to help the emotionally troubled individual modify his behavior so as to derive more satisfaction from his life, to increase the effectiveness of his functioning as a person, and to handle more constructively the inevitable "problems in living" that all men encounter. Although drugs are sometimes used as an adjunct to psychotherapy the core of the process is emotionally meaningful communication between patient or patients and therapist. In traditional psychotherapy that communication is almost exclusively verbal in character but, since the late 1950s, psychologists have developed new forms of therapy that involve all the sense modalities and that encourage the direct expression of feelings and reactions between patient and therapist by nonverbal as well as verbal means. While some psychiatrists practice psychotherapy its most prominent practitioners are psychoanalysts (most of whom are also psychiatrists, though a few are "lay" or non-M.D. analysts), clinical and social psychologists holding Ph.D.'s, psychiatric social workers, and a smattering of sociologists, anthropologists, and theologians.

The oldest, best known, and by far the most influential form of psychotherapy is *psychoanalysis,* a technique of treatment developed by Sigmund Freud (1856–1939) in Vienna around the turn of the century. A sizeable library of books has been written about psychoanalysis as a therapy, as a systematic theory of human behavior, and as a philosophy of life; here, by way of background, we will review some of the basic techniques of psychoanalytic therapy, if only because virtually every other form of psychotherapy can be understood as either an elaboration on, a revision of, or a rejection of psychoanalytic principles and techniques.

Psychoanalysis is a form of treatment that, unlike most others, aims not only at the removal of symptoms but at a fundamental restructuring of the patient's personality through an in-depth exploration of its underlying dynamics and a "working through" of fundamental impulses and conflicts that are believed to originate in the patient's early childhood. Because of its radical aim psychoanalysis is a long and inordinately costly procedure, typically involving forty-five or fifty minute interviews between analyst and patient (or analysand) four or five times a week for anywhere from three to seven or more years. (Curiously, Freud's own analyses rarely if ever lasted more than one year and often took six months or less.) Usually the patient lies on a couch while the analyst sits in a chair behind him, screened from his view. Some analysts, however, face the patient across a desk or table. The analyst is typically non-directive, non-evaluative, and totally accepting of the patient. He tends to ask questions and give diffuse encouragement rather than make statements or answer questions.

Basic to the technique of psychoanalysis is the use of "free association," which involves the patient's speaking any thoughts or fragments of words and images that pass through his mind without in any way modifying or censoring them. To do this is far more difficult than it sounds precisely because so much of our cultural learning teaches us *not* to say what we really feel and shows us that if we do speak our minds freely we will be punished, directly or indirectly, for our indiscretion. (Recall the parable of "The Emperor's New Clothes," for example.)

A second constitutive technique of psychoanalysis is dream interpretation, a technique based on Freud's finding that dreams are often disguised, highly compressed, symbolic representations of repressed impulses and wishes, impulses and wishes that the patient cannot openly admit into consciousness. Dreams are thus a window onto the unconscious, providing clues to those aspects of an individual's life history and personality that have been deliberately repressed from consciousness or are beyond the power of verbal recall. In the course of free association and dream interpretation hitherto unconscious memories, impulses, and conflicts are made conscious and can thus be dealt with in a rational, mature way. At other times the analyst may offer interpretations that clarify the patient's unconscious resistances to the process of therapy itself or that lead him toward recognizing his own underlying motives and personality dynamics.

Because of the close relationship that arises between patient and analyst, the former usually develops what is called a "transference" (or "transference neurosis") in which the analyst becomes a kind of screen onto which the patient transfers or projects the feelings, both positive and negative, he once had toward his parents and other emotionally significant people in his life. The patient then acts out these feelings *vis-à-vis* the analyst. This re-enactment or catharsis of earlier, often unresolved, childhood feelings allows the patient and the analyst to examine them rationally, to understand their roots, and to "work through" the conflicts they present to a more satisfactory resolution.

This three-fold process of catharsis, insight, and working through is crucial to the ultimate success and termination of the psychoanalytic process. That process should not, however, be thought of as a continuous, smooth upward curve of improvement from beginning to end. The progress of a psychoanalysis is rarely either smooth or continuous and, because of the patient's resistances or the analyst's lack of skill, sometimes stalls on dead center for months or even years. Nor is the end result of even a successful analysis a problem-free existence but rather the patient's greater and more realistic acceptance of himself, the development of more effective ways of coping with his life situation, and a sense of reconciliation with what he cannot change, with life in all its manifold contradictions. Many analytic patients abandon treatment along the way either in despair or disgust, while others continue interminably without experiencing much if any improvement. Such results sometimes occur because the analyst's personality fits ill with that of the patient, sometimes because the patient should never have entered analysis in the first place.

For perhaps the greatest paradox of psychoanalysis is that it demands not only a high level of verbal facility (communication other than verbal between patient and analyst is frowned on in theory and is virtually impossible in practice) and motivation from its patients, but it demands that they be relatively healthy to begin with. Precisely because of the emotional buffeting to which analysis subjects the patient it is suitable only for those with initially strong egos. Yet, the most frequent problem encountered among those labeled "neurotic" is a lack of ego strength! From this all too brief account of psychoanalytic therapy it may be apparent why so many people—psychotherapists and patients alike—have found it a less than ideal treatment for the vast majority of the emotionally disturbed and have sought other therapeutic approaches that demand less of the patient's time and money, that are more suitable for those with weaker egos, and that allow fuller and more spontaneous emotional *interaction* between patient and therapist.

Standing at the opposite pole from psychoanalysis are the various treatment strategies collectively referred to as "behavior therapy," a development pioneered by Joseph Wolpe, a Philadelphia psychologist, in the late 1950s. Behavior therapists base their treatment largely on the foundation of learning theory, particularly on B. F. Skinner's work in operant conditioning and behavior "shaping." (See Part IV.) They are less interested in discovering the deep, often unconscious, roots and symbolic meanings of the patient's actions and feelings than in changing those behaviors that cause him anxiety and unhappiness and that make his relationships with others ungratifying. From this perspective neurotic symptoms appear less the visible results of profound inner conflicts than maladaptive habits which were once learned (perhaps at a time when they *were* adaptive or even essential for survival) and which, for various reasons, have persisted. If such a maladaptive habit was once learned it can, so the behavior therapist reasons, be unlearned or "extinguished" and replaced by a more socially adaptive and personally gratifying one. Behavior therapy thus concentrates on changing the patient's overt behavior, a change which will then, in its view, produce changes in the individual's feelings and self-perception. (This view is diametrically opposite to that held by traditional psychoanalysis.) The conception of man that underlies behavior therapy is thus thoroughly positivistic and is rooted intellectually in the work of John Locke and the British empiricists who followed his lead.

Behavior therapists employ diverse techniques few of which bear any resemblance to those used by psychoanalysts although some of them may be used in association with more traditional types of individual and group psychotherapy. At times, however, the behavior therapist may adopt a role that differs little in quality from that of an expert technician trying to repair a complex mechanism, a role that may well suit the personal needs of some therapists and patients. More specifically, the techniques of behavior therapy include: "systematic desensitization" (totally relaxing the patient, then, step by step, reducing the anxiety associated with the image of particular objects or actions until it is entirely overcome); "aversive conditioning" (rendering behavior that used to bring the patient neurotic or unhealthy "rewards" unrewarding so that he is led to abandon it); "stimulus satiation" (a type of aversive conditioning in which the patient is literally surfeited with what he appears to want until he begins to find it uncomfortable and undesirable, after which he often gives it up); the manipulation of both real and symbolic rewards; and the use of pain (typically electric shocks) either in the process of aversive conditioning or to overcome the patient's resistance to behavior which will prove gratifying but which overwhelming anxiety inhibits him from undertaking in the absence of such a prod.

In its short history behavior therapy has recorded some remarkable cures especially in the treatment of circumscribed conditions such as phobias, fears, and focussed anxieties, but it has also proved effective in treating some schizophrenics and autistic children. It has been less dramatically successful in treating diffuse anxiety states, character neuroses, and the complex of conditions underlying alcoholism and homosexuality. Yet, even in such cases its record is respectable and, contrary to the expectation of most psychoanalysts, patients treated by behavior therapy have rarely developed substitute symptoms to replace those extinguished by the treatment. In virtually all cases behavior therapy has two marked advantages over psychoanalysis and analytically oriented psychotherapy: It is a far less time-consuming and consequently less expensive form of treatment and its effectiveness is relatively easily evaluated (by the degree to which the patient's behavior has actually changed).

While there are those who repose an almost religious faith in behavior therapy (as others do in psychoanalysis) and claim that eventually it will revolutionize both the treatment of the emotionally disturbed and man's view of himself, most observers are more cautious in their estimates. Certainly behavior therapy is a promising set of techniques for the treatment of various neurotic and psychotic conditions; it is unlikely, however, to prove a panacea, as its more unrestrained apostles claim. As with many other medical and psychological therapies which, when first introduced, seemed to promise wonders behavior therapy may lose its magic as its novelty fades and as both therapists and patients lose their sovereign confidence in its efficacy. Granting this reservation, however, it seems likely that, over time, the techniques of behavior therapy will have a considerable impact not only on the treatment of the emotionally disturbed but also on education, penology and even politics.

Of *all* the psychotherapies, however, we are entitled to ask: "How effective are they?" Were mental illness in fact comparable to physical illness it would be easy enough to establish the effectiveness of a particular therapy (which may account for some of the hope that all emotional disturbances *will* eventually be found to have physiological or biochemical causes) but to the extent that emotional disturbances are the result of problems in living no therapy can effect a complete "cure" because the *problems* in living can be eliminated only with living itself. From the latter point of view therapy can, at best, as we suggested above, improve the patient's ability to deal constructively with his problems, teach him to accept himself and gain greater gratification from his life, and reconcile him to those aspects of his situation that he cannot change.

Even relative to these more limited aims how do we measure the effectiveness of psychotherapy? What constitutes a patient's "improvement?" Who judges whether or not he has "improved"—the patient, the therapist, or some disinterested third party? Even if everyone admits that the patient has improved, did he do so because of the therapy or would he have improved spontaneously without it? Was it the *therapy* or the *therapist* that wrought the improvement? These questions arise with regard to every type of therapy but they become especially acute when we attempt to compare the effectiveness of two or more different treatment procedures. The use of matched control or comparison groups is difficult if not impossible and even if we could arrange for them, variables associated with the personalities of both therapists and patients would doubtless have an important effect on the final outcome. Precisely because of the intimate relationship that arises between patient and therapist in the course of psychotherapy the "fit" between the therapist's personality and that of the patient is probably the single most important factor affecting the outcome of treatment. Paradoxically, however, this factor is one of the least studied and one of the most difficult to control or manipulate. Given the usual haphazard ways of bringing patients and therapists together it seems a matter of pure chance when a patient finds a therapist with whom he can work effectively.

In view of the shortage of qualified therapists in America the next development in psychotherapy will almost certainly be therapy by computer. In truth, computer simulation of psychotherapy is already a reality (it has been tried at Stanford University) and programs exist that make it possible for a computer to conduct a satisfactory initial psychiatric interview. As more sophisticated programs are written, including those that allow the computer to alter its original program and reprogram itself (i.e., to "learn"), actual computer treatment of patients may become possible. Whether patients will find relating to a computer a satisfactory substitute for a human therapist is open to serious doubt but the use of computers may at least make it possible to test some of the theoretical assertions regarding therapeutic procedures by controlling those variables associated with the personality of the therapist. To the degree that the therapist's personality is his strongest therapeutic weapon computers are, however, unlikely to supplant human beings in the practice of psychotherapy unless we find a way to program "personality" into computers.

Finally, we would point to the ethical and political implications of all psychotherapies. Any strategy, regardless of its aim or justification, that is able to "change" behavior can also be used to "control" behavior. As psychotherapists develop more effective means of modifying behavior the possibilities of controlling it more effectively will grow apace. (See Selections 6 and 64.) Who is to decide—and according to what criteria—what constitutes "desirable" behavior or "good social adjustment?" Whose values and interests will determine the direction and extent of approved behavioral change? Is the therapist to be the agent of the social establishment, of some elite sub-group within the society, or of the patient and his own values? Behavior therapy, especially, summons forth the specter of "therapists" using psychological techniques of behavior modification to promote conformity to political and social values imposed by a dominant establishment, a scientifically sophisticated benevolent totalitarianism that will condition people to love to do what they are made to do. Such a prospect may seem fanciful and even absurd now but then, at the dawn of the twentieth century, space flight seemed equally fanciful and absurd. If knowledge is not itself power it can easily enough be co-opted to the service of power.

For Ronald Laing, in our first selection, the relationship between patient and therapist is crucial to the success of any psychotherapy. His characterization of that relationship as an attempt by two persons—two centers of experience—to recover the wholeness of being human through an authentic relationship in the here-and-now contrasts sharply with behavior therapy's implicit view of the therapist as someone who does something to or for the patient, who removes his inhibitions or maladaptive habits as a surgeon might remove his inflamed appendix or an incipient cancer. Laing rejects all theories of psychotherapy that depersonalize the individual, either by concentrating almost entirely on intra-psychic "events," (as classical Freudians tend to), by divorcing the individual's behavior from his experience, or by treating one individual's behavior and experience in isolation from that of others. He criticizes behavior therapy because he sees in it a tendency for the therapist to manipulate and control the patient rather than to meet the latter's humanness with his own. Laing's chapter forms an eloquent plea for wholeness and authenticity in human relationships, a goal which the patient can attain only through the experience of authenticity and wholeness on the part of the therapist. This is perhaps the most important learning that takes place in the course of psychotherapy and it suggests why the therapist's own personality, not the theory to which he subscribes, is the most powerful weapon in his arsenal.

Ernest Havemann's article examines some of the newer therapies, both individual and group, that can be considered alternatives to psychoanalysis. Among those he discusses are behavior therapy, reality therapy, client-centered therapy, T-groups, encounter groups, and therapy groups without professional therapists. As Havemann himself notes these techniques are only a sample of the broad spectrum of therapies now being offered the therapy-hungry American public. Among the promising alternatives he does not discuss is *family therapy,* which is being used increasingly in the treatment of schizophrenics. This is a form of group therapy in which the group is the patient and his immediate family. Given the role that family interactions probably play in the etiology of schizophrenia this type of therapy tries to help family members to express and clarify their feelings toward one another, to develop greater empathy for each other, and to devise more satisfying and effective ways of *inter*-relating.

The vogue among Americans for group forms of therapy has by now reached the proportions of a fad, if not a mania, perhaps because they promise a degree of emotional freedom and intimacy, together with the sense of belonging, denied most of us in our jobs and our usual social relationships. The major problem, as Havemann points out, is that of adapting the emotional freedom and frankness learned in the permissiveness of the group setting to the far less permissive settings in which we live most of our lives.

In the final selection Nicholas Hobbs of the George Peabody College for Teachers discusses mental health's "third revolution"—the burgeoning community mental health movement. The essence of this movement, spurred by the Federal Community Mental Health Centers Act of 1963, is the application, for the first time, of public health concepts and strategies—such as prevention, early detection, and universal provision of necessary services—to the field of mental health. Given the steadily increasing shortage of qualified mental health specialists relative to the equally steadily increasing demand for their services, Hobbs contends that the reigning model of mental health treatment—the one-to-one relationship of therapist to patient (or client)— is frankly inadequate in practice and very likely indefensible in theory. (Needless to say, not all psychotherapists and psychiatrists would agree.)

After discussing how socioeconomic variables affect the nature and extent of treatment offered those requiring mental health services, the author examines some of the practical, professional, political, and ethical implications of this third revolution for members of the mental health professions. Following a plea for genuine innovation (as opposed to mere "change") in the organization and delivery of mental health services, Hobbs concludes by discussing his own experimental program for the treatment of disturbed children, a program that has won national attention. If Hobbs's speech solves no problems and provides no pat answers it at least highlights the present-day challenges to the mental health professions, challenges that are likely to confront us for the remainder of this century, if not beyond.

51. THE PSYCHOTHERAPEUTIC EXPERIENCE [1]

R. D. Laing

In the last twenty years, psychotherapy has developed both in theory and in practice in complex ways. And yet, through all this tangled complexity and sometimes confusion, it is impossible, in the words of Pasternak, "not to fall ultimately, as into a heresy, into unheard-of simplicity."

In the practice of psychotherapy, the very diversities of method have made the essential simplicity more clear.

The irreducible elements of psychotherapy are a therapist, a patient, and a regular and reliable time and place. But given these, it is not so easy for two people to meet. We all live on the hope that authentic meeting between human beings can still occur. Psychotherapy consists in the paring away of all that stands between us, the props, masks, roles, lies, defenses, anxieties, projections and introjections, in short, all the carryovers from the past, transference and countertransference, that we use by habit and collusion, wittingly or unwittingly, as our currency for relationships. It is this currency, these very media, that recreate and intensify the conditions of alienation that originally occasioned them.

The distinctive contribution of psychoanalysis has been to bring to light these importations, carryovers, compulsive repetitions. The tendency now among psychoanalysts and psychotherapists is to focus not only on transference, not only on what has happened before, but on what has never happened before, on what is new. Thus, in practice, the use of interpretations to reveal the past, or even to reveal the past-in-the-present, may be used as only one tactic and, in theory, there are efforts to understand better and to find words for the *non*-transference elements in psychotherapy.

The therapist may allow himself to act spontaneously and unpredictably. He may set out actively to disrupt old patterns of experience and behavior. He may actively reinforce new ones. One hears now of therapists giving orders, laughing, shouting, crying, even getting up from that sacred chair. Zen, with its emphasis on illumination achieved through the sudden and unexpected, is a growing influence. Of course such techniques in the hands of a man who has not unremitting concern and respect for the patient could be disastrous. Although some general principles of these developments can be laid down, their practice is still, and indeed must always be, for the man who has both quite exceptional authority and the capacity to improvise.

I shall not enumerate all the many practical varieties of psychotherapy, long and short, brief, intensive, experiential, directive and nondirective, those that utilize the consciousness-expanding drugs or other adjuvants, and those that use, as it were, nothing but persons. I wish rather to consider in more detail the critical function of theory.

These lines of growth that seem to expand centrifugally in all directions have intensified the need for a strong, firm primary theory that can draw each practice and theory into relation to the central concerns of all forms of psychotherapy. In the last chapter* I outlined some of the fundamental requirements of such a theory. Namely, that we need concepts which both indicate the interaction and interexperience of two persons, and help us to understand the relation between each person's own experience and his own behavior, within the context of the relationship between them.

---

1 From the point of view of the psychotherapist.

* See Selection 3. (Eds.)

And we must in turn be able to conceive of this relationship within the relevant contextual social *systems*. Most fundamentally, a critical theory must be able to place all theories and practices within the scope of a total vision of the ontological structure of being human.

What help are the prevailing theories of psychotherapy to us? Here it would be misleading to delineate too sharply one school of thought from another. Within the mainstream of orthodox psychoanalysis and even between the different theories of object relationships in the United Kingdom—Fairbairn, Winnicott, Melanie Klein, Bion—there are differences of more than emphasis; similarly within the existential school or tradition—Binswanger, Boss, Caruso, Frankl. Every theoretical idiom could be found to play some part in the thinking of at least some members of any school. At worst there are the most extraordinary theoretical mixes of learning theory, ethology, system theory, communications analysis, information theory, transactional analysis, interpersonal relations, object relations, games theory, and so on.

Freud's development of metapsychology changed the theoretical context we now work in. To understand with sympathy the positive value of metapsychology, we have to consider the intellectual climate in which it was first developed. Others have pointed out that it drew its impetus from the attempt to see man as an object of natural scientific investigation, and thus to win acceptance for psychoanalysis as a serious and respectable enterprise. I do not think such a shield is now necessary; or even, that it ever was. And the price paid when one thinks in metapsychological terms is high.

The metapsychology of Freud, Federn, Rapaport, Hartman, Kris, has no constructs for any social system generated by more than one person at a time. Within its own framework it has no concepts of social collectivities of experience shared or unshared between persons. This theory has no category of "you," as there is in the work of Feuerbach, Buber, Parsons. It has no way of expressing the meeting of an "I" with "an other," and the impact of one person on another. It has no concept of "me" except as objectified as "the ego." The ego is one part of a mental apparatus. Internal objects are other parts of this system. Another ego is part of a different system or structure. How two mental apparatuses or psychic structures or systems, each with its own constellation of internal objects, can relate to each other remains unexamined. Within the constructs the theory offers, it is possibly inconceivable. Projection and introjection do not in themselves bridge the gap *between* persons.

Few now find central the issues of conscious and unconscious as conceived by the early psychoanalysts—as two reified systems, both split from the totality of the person, both composed of some sort of psychic stuff, and both exclusively *intra*personal.

It is the relation *between persons* that is central in theory and in practice. Persons are related to one another through their experience and through their behavior. Theories can be seen in terms of the emphasis they put on *experience* or on *behavior,* and in terms of their ability to articulate the relationship between experience and behavior.

The different schools of psychoanalysis and depth psychology have at least recognized the crucial relevance of each person's experience to his or her behavior, but they have left unclarified what *is* experience, and this is particularly evident with respect to "the unconscious."

Some theories are more concerned with the interactions or transactions between people, without too much reference to the experience of the agents. Just as any theory that focuses on *experience* and neglects behavior can become very misleading, so theories that focus on behavior to the neglect of experience become unbalanced.

In the idiom of games theory, people have a repertoire of games based on particular sets of learned interactions. Others may play games that mesh sufficiently to allow a variety of more or less stereotyped dramas to be enacted. The games have rules, some public, some secret. Some people play games that break the rules of games that others play. Some play undeclared games, so rendering their moves ambiguous or downright unintelligible, except to the expert in such secret and unusual games. Such people, prospective neurotics or psychotics, may have to undergo the ceremonial of a psychiatric consultation, leading to diagnosis, prognosis, prescription. Treatment would consist in pointing out to them the unsatisfactory nature of the games they play and perhaps teaching new games. A person reacts by despair more to loss of the *game* than to sheer "object-loss," that is, to the loss of his partner or partners as real persons. The maintenance of the game rather than the identity of players is all-important.

One advantage of this idiom is that it relates persons together. The failure to see the behavior of one person in relation to the behavior of the other has led to much confusion. In a sequence of an interaction between p and o, $p_1 \rightarrow o_1 \rightarrow p_2 \rightarrow o_2 \rightarrow p_3 \rightarrow o_3$, etc., p's contribution, p_1, p_2, to p_3, is taken out of context and direct links are made between $p_1 \rightarrow p_2 \rightarrow p_3$. This artificially derived sequence is then studied as an isolated entity or process and attempts may be made to "explain" it (find the "etiology") in terms of genetic-constitutional factors or intrapsychic pathology.

Object-relations theory attempts to achieve, as Guntrip has argued, a synthesis between the intra- and interpresonal. Its concepts of internal and external objects, of closed and open systems, go some way. Yet it is still objects, not persons, that are in question. Objects are the what, not the whereby, of experience. The brain is itself an object of experience. We still require a phenomenology of experience including so-called unconscious experience, of experience related to behavior, of person related to person, without splitting, denial, depersonalization and reification, all fruitless attempts to explain the whole by the part.

Transaction, systems, games, can occur and can be played in and between electronic systems. What is specifically personal or human? A personal relationship is not only transactional, it is transexperiential and herein is its specific human quality. Transaction alone without experience lacks specific personal connotations. Endocrine and reticuloendothelial systems transact. They are not persons. The great danger of thinking about man by means of analogy is that the analogy comes to be put forward as a homology.*

Why do almost all theories about depersonalization, reification, splitting, denial, tend themselves to exhibit the symptoms they attempt to describe? We are left with transactions, but where is the individual? the individual, but where is the other? patterns of behavior, but where is the experience? information and communication, but where are the

pathos and sympathy, the passion and compassion?

Behavior therapy is the most extreme example of such schizoid theory and practice that proposes to think and act purely in terms of the other without reference to the self of the therapist or the patient, in terms of behavior without experience, in terms of objects rather than persons. It is inevitably therefore a technique of nonmeeting, of manipulation and control.

Psychotherapy must remain *an obstinate attempt of two people to recover the wholeness of being human through the relationship between them.*

Any technique concerned with the other without the self, with behavior to the exclusion of experience, with the relationship to the neglect of the persons in relation, with the individuals to the exclusion of their relationship, and most of all, with an object-to-be-changed rather than a person-to-be-accepted, simply perpetuates the disease it purports to cure.

And any *theory* not founded on the nature of being human is a lie and a betrayal of man. An inhuman theory will inevitably lead to inhuman consequences—if the therapist is consistent. Fortunately, many therapists have the gift of inconsistency. This, however endearing, cannot be regarded as ideal.

We are not concerned with the interaction of two objects, nor with their transactions within a dyadic system; we are not concerned with the communication patterns within a system comprising two computer-like subsystems that receive and process input and emit outgoing signals. Our concern is with two origins of experience in relation.

Behavior can conceal or disclose experience. I devoted a book, *The Divided Self*,[2] to describing some versions of the split between experience and behavior. And both experience and behavior are themselves fragmented in myriad different ways. This is so even when enormous efforts are made to apply a veneer of consistency over the cracks.

I suggest the reason for this confusion lies in the meaning of Heidegger's phrase, *the Dreadful has already happened.*

Psychotherapists are specialists in human relations. But the Dreadful has already hap-

---

* A correspondence of structure and derivation from a common origin. (Eds.)

2 London: Tavistock Publications, 1960; Penguin Books, 1965.

pened. It has happened to us all. The therapists, too, are in a world in which the inner is already split from the outer. The inner does not become outer, and the outer become inner, just by the rediscovery of the "inner" world. That is only the beginning. As a whole, we are a generation of men so estranged from the inner world that many are arguing that it does not exist; and that even if it does exist, it does not matter. Even if it has some significance, it is not the hard stuff of science, and if it is not, then let's make it hard. Let it be measured and counted. Quantify the heart's agony and ecstasy in a world in which, when the inner world is first discovered, we are liable to find ourselves bereft and derelict. For without the inner the outer loses its meaning, and without the outer the inner loses its substance.

We must know about relations and communications. But these disturbed and disturbing patterns of communication reflect the disarray of personal worlds of experience whose repression, denial, splitting, introjection, projection, etc.—whose general desecration and profanation—our civilization is based upon.

When our personal worlds are rediscovered and allowed to reconstitute themselves, we first discover a shambles. Bodies half-dead; genitals dissociated from heart; heart severed from head; head dissociated from genitals. Without inner unity, with just enough sense of continuity to clutch at identity—the current idolatry. Torn—body, mind and spirit—by inner contradictions, pulled in different directions. Man cut off from his own mind, cut off equally from his own body—a half-crazed creature in a mad world.

When the Dreadful has already happened, we can hardly expect otherwise than that the Thing will echo externally the destruction already wrought internally.

We are all implicated in this state of affairs of alienation. This context is decisive for the whole practice of psychotherapy.

The psychotherapeutic relationship is therefore a re-search. A search, constantly reasserted and reconstituted, for what we have all lost and whose loss some can perhaps endure a little more easily than others, as some people can stand lack of oxygen better than others, and *this re-search is validated by the shared experience of experience regained in and through the therapeutic relationship in the here and now.*

True, in the enterprise of psychotherapy there are regularities, even institutional structures, pervading the sequence, rhythm and tempo of the therapeutic situation viewed as process, and these can and should be studied with scientific objectivity. But the really decisive moments in psychotherapy, as every patient or therapist who has ever experienced them knows, are unpredictable, unique, unforgettable, always unrepeatable and often indescribable. Does this mean that psychotherapy must be a pseudo-esoteric cult? No.

We must continue to struggle through our confusion, to insist on being human.

Existence is a flame which constantly melts and recasts our theories. Existential thinking offers no security, no home for the homeless. It addresses no one except you and me. It finds its validation when, across the gulf of our idioms and styles, our mistakes, errings and perversities, we find in the other's communication an experience of relationship established, lost, destroyed or regained. We hope to share the experience of a relationship, but the only honest beginning, or even end, may be to share the experience of its absence.

52. ALTERNATIVES TO ANALYSIS

Ernest Havemann

John Blank, at the age of 33, was in many respects a model husband and father. He was also, as it happened, a confirmed, habitual, compulsive transvestite. He had started before he was 12 to dress up in his mother's or his sister's clothes whenever they were away from the house. By the age of puberty, he was hooked.

Service in the Army forced him to give up the habit for a while—a barracks being hardly the place to practice transvestitism. It was a miserable period for John Blank. By the time he got out of the Army and back to a secret wardrobe of women's clothing, he had developed a full-fledged ulcer.

Civilian life and marriage, though they calmed his ulcer, did nothing else to change him. He found, indeed, that he could not have sexual relations with his wife unless he dressed up first. Every now and then, he had an irresistible urge to spend an evening in public in a dress, nylon stockings, high-heeled shoes and a woman's wig.

As he neared his mid-30s, John Blank was almost as unhappy as he had been in the Army. He worried about being arrested some night and losing his job. He wondered how long his wife would put up with him. Above all, he worried about the fact that his son was getting to the age where the boy would surely discover his secret. In addition to being addicted to the strange wardrobe, he was now also addicted to sedatives, which he gulped constantly to soothe his jangling nerves.

In desperation, John Blank sought help from a new kind of treatment, totally different from psychoanalysis in theory and prac-

tice: behavior therapy. The treatment prescribed for him was extremely simple. He did not lie on a couch and try to produce free associations about the childhood origins of his compulsion; indeed, he hardly talked to the therapist at all except to explain his problem. On each visit to the therapist's office, he merely undressed, put on a dressing gown and went behind a screen, where his favorite outfit of women's clothing was laid out on a chair. On signal from the therapist, he took off the gown and began dressing in this clothing. At some point, at times soon after he had started, at other times when he was nearly finished, he was rudely interrupted by a jolt of electricity delivered through a grid on the floor. He then, as instructed by the therapist, began to remove the clothes. The shock—or sometimes just the sound of a buzzer—was repeated at intervals, until he had them all off.

At each session in the therapist's office, this process was repeated five times. John Blank never knew when the electric shock would hit him, whether to expect the shock or just the buzzer nor how many times shock or buzzer would be repeated while he pulled off the clothes. After 80 visits to the office, he had had his fill of this kind of nerve-racking waiting for the blow to strike—and the therapist figured he had also lost his taste for women's clothing.

The treatment proved to be a striking success. When the therapist looked him up six months later, John Blank reported that he had not once gone back to his secret wardrobe. He felt better than he had felt in years; his worries were vanishing and he was tapering off his use of sedatives.

. . .

Behavior therapy, which produced such remarkable results for John Blank, is one of many forms of patching, refurbishing and expanding the human psyche that have begun to flourish as the influence of psychoanalysis has waned. By the careful count of one observer of the psychotherapeutic scene, there are now no fewer than 200 different schools of thought, most of them very new, on how to make Americans less neurotic, more normal, more "fulfilled" than they have been in the past.

The new schools of thought cover a broad and baffling range, from the commonsensical to the exotic. At one extreme is the growing number of psychiatrists who believe that mental disturbances are caused by faulty brain chemistry and can best be treated with the new personality-control drugs. Near this end of the scale is behavior therapy, a product of the psychology laboratory. At the opposite end are numerous methods that have no scientific basis at all, such as the mystical tenets of yoga and Zen Buddhism.

Some methods are still based, like psychoanalysis, on a one-to-one meeting of therapist and patient. But the great move today is toward groups—all kinds of groups made up of young and old, men and women, single and married, rich and poor, black and white, sometimes led by professional therapists and sometimes meeting on their own, seeking in various ways to help one another get over their hangups. The most publicized branch of the group movement is Esalen Institute, high on a cliff above the Pacific Ocean, where, on almost any day of the year, 20 or 30 people at once can be found running across the magnificent California landscape, singing, shouting, dancing, looking into one another's eyes and otherwise engaging in a mass effort to help their inner feelings bubble to the surface.

There are not only 200 different approaches but roughly 10,000 specific techniques, most of them developed for use in groups. At any given moment of the day, most or all of these techniques are being practiced somewhere. Groups of ordinarily staid businessmen work as if their lives depended on it to build playhouses of index cards; a college professor and an unemployed chorus girl sit back to back on the floor and try to "communicate" with their shoulder muscles; a plump California housewife and an ascetic clergyman stand barefoot on a bed sheet, trying to tune their senses to the feel of the grass beneath; a man who earns $100,000 per year breaks down and weeps in front of a dozen strangers because nobody likes him; another group of strangers, men and women, shed their clothes and plunge naked into a swimming pool with a therapist who believes that nudity frees the emotions. All this varied activity goes on not only by day but often through the night; one of the most popular new approaches is the "group marathon," which continues for 24 hours without interruption or sleep, leaving its members weary and groggy but somehow exhilarated.

The new brands of therapy and the new group encounters have been sampled by hundreds of thousands more Americans than ever have had any personal experience with psychoanalysis. For one thing, they are far more available. There are more psychiatrists and clinical psychologists using various new methods and techniques of therapy than there ever were analysts in the U.S. As for the groups, these are springing up everywhere; they have even been conducted by television, with everybody within the station's broadcasting range welcome to tune in and take part. For another thing, the new methods are far cheaper. Even the new one-to-one therapy is much less expensive than psychoanalysis, if only because it is faster; the 80-session treatment of John Blank, though far above average for behavior therapy, was still much shorter than the three to five or more years usually required in psychoanalysis. Groups are cheaper yet. It costs nothing at all to organize your own group and as little as $50 to attend a group or marathon led by a professional. You can spend a weekend at Esalen, the holy of holies of the group movement, for as little as $65, including room and board.

Psychoanalysis has never promised its patients very much—only that if they were willing to work long enough and hard enough on the couch, and then the rest of their lives on their own, they might be able to conquer their most crippling conflicts. Most of the new schools of thought, by contrast, have a kind of evangelical optimism and fervor. One of the Esalen psychologists, William C. Schutz, has written a book on Esalen's methods and goals; he calls it *Joy* and his subtitle is "Expanding Human Awareness." Other terms popular among spokesmen for the new schools are mind expansion, self-realization, self-fulfillment, bodily awareness, personal growth and ecstasy. Spurred on by these slogans and, evidently, by pleasurable experiences in group encounters, quite a few Americans have turned into a new kind of fanatic; they are not alcohol addicts, not heroin addicts but group addicts, eagerly tracking down every new group encounter and rushing to every one that they can possibly attend.

Americans, of course, have had many previous infatuations—in recent years, bowling, astrology, the hula hoop, isometric exercises, jogging, health foods and the drinking man's diet. Are the new alternatives to psychoanalysis also fads, or are they the way of the future? Since the new methods vary so widely from the fact-conscious products of the psychology laboratory to the hashish-inspired visions of Oriental mystics, from the commonplace to the far-out, there is probably no single answer. An examination of some of the most prominent of the new methods, however, will offer some clues.

Behavior therapy, the newest treatment method with a truly scientific basis, is in large part the creation of Joseph Wolpe, a psychiatrist who teaches at Philadelphia's Temple University School of Medicine. Dr. Wolpe was originally a follower of Freud, but changed his mind after studying the learning theories that have been developed by psychologists; he was particularly influenced by the evidence that behavior that is in some way rewarded tends to be repeated, while behavior that is not rewarded or is punished tends to be abandoned. To Dr. Wolpe, a neurotic symptom such as John Blank's transvestitism, far from representing an unconscious conflict, as maintained by Freud, is, in fact, "just a bad habit." It was acquired through some unfortunate quirk of learning and is in some way rewarding to the patient—but it can be eliminated or modified by taking away its reward value.

Dr. Wolpe spends no time at all discussing a patient's childhood or trying to probe into the patient's unconscious mind. Instead, he and his followers make a direct frontal attack on the current problem. John Blank, for example was treated by associating the wearing of women's clothing with the punishment of electric shock, rather than the reward of whatever kind of pleasurable feelings it previously produced. Similarly, Dr. Wolpe has

successfully treated a homosexual by strapping an electrode on the man's calf and showing him pictures of naked men and women. When a man appeared, the electrode produced a shock; when a woman appeared, the electricity went off.

Most people who visit a psychotherapist, however, do not have a simple "bad habit" such as transvestitism or homosexuality. They are more likely to be troubled by anxiety—for example, by a fear of entering an elevator, going to social events, meeting the opposite sex or talking to the boss. For such patients, Dr. Wolpe has developed a method that he calls "desensitization." One of his patients was a 52-year-old housewife terrified by thoughts of death. She had feelings of anxiety every time she saw an ambulance or a hospital, much stronger feelings when she drove past a cemetery and intense fear when she thought of her first husband dead in his coffin. Dr. Wolpe treated her by having her relax completely, then asking her to think about the sight of an ambulance but to stop thinking about it if she began to feel at all anxious. Step by step, he led her to remain relaxed while thinking about all the things that had previously frightened her. By the end of the treatment, she had been fully "desensitized" —the sights and thoughts once associated with anxiety were now associated, instead, with feelings of relaxation.

Recently, the school of behavior therapy has been given a new dimension through an experiment conducted by Albert Bandura a psychologist noted for his studies of the learning process. Dr. Bandura, who teaches at Stanford University, advertised in the local paper for people who were disturbed by a fear of snakes. To his surprise, since Stanford is in the San Francisco metropolitan area and hardly infested with snakes, nearly 100 people responded. To his further surprise, about a third of the volunteers turned out to have diagnosed themselves incorrectly; when actually confronted with a snake, they were not afraid at all (a fact that has led Dr. Bandura to suspect that perhaps many people only *think* they are neurotic).

From the volunteers, Dr. Bandura finally selected 48 people, both men and women, young and old, who were genuinely terrified of snakes. Among them: a plumber who was afraid to work outdoors, a real-estate salesman who could never bring himself to show a house in which there was a pet snake and two members of the Peace Corps who were frightened by the very thought of being assigned to jungle country. From the Freudian viewpoint, all of them would have been considered victims of deep-seated sexual conflicts, for a snake is the most obvious kind of phallic symbol. Dr. Bandura, however, chose to regard them as the victims of something quite different—namely, a pure-and-simple fear of snakes.

To one third of the volunteers Dr. Bandura applied the Wolpe desensitization technique. Another third were turned into their own therapists: they were shown how to relax completely (by first tensing and then slackening all the muscles of the body) and asked to watch a moving picture of children and adults approaching and finally playing with snakes, as shown by a projector that the patient himself could stop and turn back if the pictures became disturbing. The remaining third watched through a window while one of Dr. Bandura's colleagues, in the next room, approached a snake, touched it and, after a time, let it crawl around his neck. Once these patients had got up their courage, they were invited in to imitate this procedure.

All the volunteers lost some of their fear of snakes—the third group most quickly and completely of all. Within an average of two hours, indeed, many members of the third group were playing with snakes the way they might play with a puppy. The two other groups, switched to the method of watching through the window, quickly reached the same level of almost complete fearlessness.

The significance of Dr. Bandura's experiment is its indication that at least one kind of neurotic fear can be conquered through the simple process of imitating another person. To psychologists, imitation is one of the most effective forms of learning; babies learn to speak in large part by imitating the sounds their parents make; older children learn to write by imitating the strokes the teacher makes on the blackboard; all of us learn to dial a telephone, play baseball and drive an automobile through imitation. Dr. Bandura's new experiment seems to indicate that people can learn how to be normal instead of neurotic in the same fashion—a finding that may open up an entirely new frontier in psychotherapy.

Another new kind of treatment, called reality therapy, developed by Los Angeles psychiatrist William Glasser, is of special interest, because it appears to produce good results even though it is the exact opposite of psychoanalysis in every respect. The psychoanalyst speaks of mental illness; Dr. Glasser believes that there is no such thing. The psychoanalyst searches for the origins of the patient's problem; Dr. Glasser believes that there is no point in dealing with past events because these events are over and done with and cannot be changed. The psychoanalyst tries to remain as neutral and anonymous toward the patient as possible; Dr. Glasser tries to establish a strong, intimate personal relationship. The psychoanalyst looks for the patient's unconscious conflicts and motivations; Dr. Glasser holds that these matters, though perhaps interesting, have nothing to do with helping the patient. The psychoanalyst avoids making any moral judgments of the patient; Dr. Glasser makes the patient face up to the question of whether his behavior is right or wrong, not necessarily in the ultimate moral sense but in terms of social realities and his own desires. ("If a patient says he's thief and is willing to accept the consequences of being a thief, that's all right," says Dr. Glasser. "I don't judge it, but it's basic to reality therapy for him to judge it.") Finally, the psychoanalyst avoids giving advice, on the theory that the patient should find his own way of living; Dr. Glasser tries to help the patient plan better ways of fulfilling his needs.

The basic problem of all people who require therapy, in Dr. Glasser's view, is that they are "irresponsible." They have never learned, or have forgotten, how to accept the world as it is, take responsibility for their own lives, get along in society and meet their needs while respecting the needs of others. Dr. Glasser worked for many years with the inmates of a California school for delinquent girls; possibly as a result, there is a very down-to-earth and even hard-boiled quality in his thinking. He rejects as "psychiatric garbage" the long sad stories of unhappy childhoods with which patients often attempt to justify their present inadequacies. "A lot of people," he states, "are looking for excuses. Reality therapy says the hell with the excuses; let's get on with the business of improving our lives."

As a therapist, however, Dr. Glasser radiates a good deal of warmth, and he is regarded with much affection by his former patients, including some of the once toughest of the delinquent girls. His therapy proceeds in three steps. First, he attempts to establish what he calls "involvement" with the patient —so that the patient, who in all probability has been feeling friendless, realizes that he is genuinely eager to help. Next, while preserving this close relationship, he begins to ask the patient to examine his behavior for signs that it might be irresponsible and unrealistic. Finally, he tries to help the patient find more responsible and realistic ways of behaving. Throughout this process, he talks almost entirely about behavior, seldom about the patient's motives or feelings. Once the patient can be taught to behave more responsibly even in one small area of his life, Dr. Glasser maintains, this often sets up a chain reaction in which better behavior leads to better attitudes, which lead in turn, to more forms of better behavior.

Compared with psychoanalytical theory, reality therapy is the height of simplicity; indeed, Dr. Glasser says he could teach any bright young trainee all he needs to know about the theory in a day. Applying it to patients, however, is another matter. As Dr. Glasser puts it, "Psychoanalysis is difficult to learn but easy to practice; reality therapy is easy to learn but difficult to practice." The psychoanalyst mostly listens. The reality therapist engages in an active, close and often exhausting dialogue. He must establish a genuine friendship with patients who may resist it, feel a genuine sympathy with their sufferings, yet be tough enough never to let his sympathy divert him from getting along with the hard task of improvement.

Of all the new schools of thought that constitute today's alternatives to psychoanalysis, reality therapy is at the farthest extreme of the plain-spoken, the nonmystical—and the modest. Far from promising joy or ecstasy, Dr. Glasser warns his patients that reality therapy is not even primarily directed toward making them happy. In his opinion, people can find happiness only for themselves; therapy can only give them a reasonable chance at finding it. In his book *Reality Therapy,* he describes a woman patient, a divorcee, who was given to promiscuous and unhappy love affairs, emotional outbursts and fits of depression; since treatment, she has abandoned her frantic "scrambling for love" and has learned to control her emotions and is depressed less

often. She also has found a better job and moved from a shabby furnished room to an apartment. However she is still a divorcee with few friends, living in a strange city and without much income. Dr. Glasser says bluntly, "No one would describe her as happy, because she hasn't that much to be happy about, but she is no longer painfully unhappy."

.   .   .

Dr. Glasser is by no means the only member of the new breed of psychotherapists to conclude that the key to successful treatment is a warm, close human relationship between therapist and patient. The same idea has been adopted by many other therapists, including some whose theories are otherwise quite different. It is, indeed, a sort of common denominator that runs through most of today's nonanalytical office therapy. It is also the basic principle behind the various kinds of group activities that have sprung up outside the office setting.

The man responsible for popularizing the idea of the intimate therapist-patient relationship is Carl Rogers, a psychologist who founded what is known as client-centered therapy. This is not one of the newest methods; in fact, it goes back to the early 1940s. But it has been one of the most widely used and influential; and Dr. Rogers, who has now turned his attention from individual treatment to groups, continues to be among the most respected of today's innovators.

Client-centered therapy is based on Dr. Rogers' view of the human personality, which is quite different from the psychoanalytical or any other theory of personality that preceded it. Dr. Rogers believes that each person has a self-image—that is, a picture of himself as having many polarized characteristics, such as brave-cowardly, friendly-unfriendly, aggressive-submissive, ambitious-lazy, and so on. Ideally, the self-image is built up out of clear and honest observation of one's experiences, behavior, thoughts and feelings. In the maladjusted person, however, there are many disturbing conflicts between the self-image and the actual facts; it is these conflicts that explain why he is neurotic.

A simple example of conflict would be this: A man who has an image of himself as completely honest cashes a check at his bank one day, is overpaid ten dollars by the teller and knowingly walks off with the money. He is now caught up in a psychological crisis. One way of meeting it is to face the facts, see clearly that he has committed a dishonest act and admit to himself that, although he is generally a very honest person, he is not above an occasional slip. This is the healthy course; it keeps his image of himself in line with reality. On the other hand, the man may be so afraid of condemnation by society or by his own conscience that he cannot bear to own up to the truth. He may try to deny that he stole the ten dollars by telling himself that he kept the money to avoid embarrassing the teller. Or he may try to justify his action by telling himself that the teller had tried to cheat him in the past. In this case, he tries to maintain a self-image of total and unbending honesty that is simply not in accord with reality.

The well-adjusted person, says Dr. Rogers, is one whose self-image is realistic and flexible, changing constantly to take honest account of new experiences. The maladjusted person has a self-image so rigid that he cannot bear to accept any unpleasant truths; he must set up more and more defenses against reality, resulting in more and more tension and anxiety.

The basic technique of client-centered therapy is to provide an atmosphere of great warmth and empathetic understanding in which the patient feels free to begin exploring his true thoughts and feelings and to discover and remedy the conflicts. In Dr. Rogers' many years of treating individual patients, he attempted at all times to be a sensitive and understanding friend to the patient, displaying complete acceptance of all aspects of the patient's personality. As the patient began to feel freer to discuss what he considered to be his faults, Dr. Rogers never acted surprised and never criticized; he was totally permissive toward even the cruelest expressions of hostility or the strangest sexual fantasies. As he has said, his aim was to offer constant assurance that he regarded the patient "as a person of unconditional self-worth; of value, no matter what his condition, his behavior or his feelings." Given this kind of unqualified support, the patient gradually came to acknowledge his true thoughts and feelings, learned for the first time what he was really like and began to revise his self-image in line with reality. As with the rest of the treatment, its conclusion was also permissive; Dr. Rogers let the patient himself decide when it was successful and could end.

To many people who hear about client centered therapy for the first time, it sounds downright dangerous. If everybody were encouraged to be completely himself, it seems only natural to ask, how could society survive the sudden appearance of hordes of self-seeking, brawling, murderous, lustful, rapacious brutes? A psychoanalyst would certainly worry, for according to Freud, the human psyche has a dark and evil side; one of man's basic instinctual drives, constantly struggling for expression, is the blind urge to annihilate anyone who dares try to keep him from getting his own way in all matters, large and small. Dr. Rogers' therapy, however, is based on the optimistic assumption that all human beings, if only they have the chance, will grow in the direction of social cooperation. "The individual has a very strong drive toward wholesome self-actualization," he says. "What we have to do is give him a climate in which this can thrive."

. . .

Providing a climate in which the human psyche can thrive is also the general purpose of the various kinds of encounter groups that have come to dominate, in sheer numbers, at least, the American psychotherapeutic scene. The group movement has expanded rapidly in the past few years; new Esalen-type centers have opened in all parts of the nation; the professionals who are experienced at conducting groups receive more invitations, from all kinds of people in all kinds of cities and towns, than they can possibly accept. Yet, though it seems to have sprung up almost overnight, the movement actually began more than 20 years ago and struggled along inconspicuously for a long time before achieving sudden popularity.

The strange thing about the group is that nobody invented it; its birth was strictly an accident. The event took place at a conference held in Connecticut in 1946, on the training of community leaders. Among the professors and Government officials present was the late, highly regarded social psychologist Kurt Lewin, a tireless student of group dynamics (the processes through which groups are formed, go about their business and succeed or fail). With him, Dr. Lewin had brought four members of his research staff—not to participate in the conference but to study it by recording their observations of how individual delegates and their committees behaved and reacted to one another. Somebody suggested that the findings of the four researchers, if presented in the evening when there was no other conference activity, might be a valuable form of feedback that would help the people at the conference judge their own effectiveness and work together more smoothly and efficiently. The first evening, only a few people showed up; these few were so excited by the feedback that the word quickly spread and next evening, everybody was there. After that, the original purpose of the conference was almost forgotten, as the delegates became absorbed in such questions as how each of them looked to the others, how they succeeded or failed at communicating their ideas and how committee decisions were influenced by the interplay of personalities (what a psychologist might call the "interpersonal relationships") among committee members.

The unexpected turn taken by the Connecticut conference seemed to prove that people are fascinated by their behavior in groups —also that, if they are helped to understand their behavior, they tend to become open, more honest, more aware of their own feelings and more spontaneous. Hot on the trail of something new in human experience, some of the conference leaders quickly set up a nonprofit institute called the National Training Laboratories to refine the techniques of group self-studies and promote their widespread use.

N.T.L. describes itself as being in the business of encouraging social change through sensitivity training—that is, the attempt to teach people to become more aware of their own feelings and motives and the feelings and motives of others, and thus to become more perceptive, open-minded, understanding and creative members of the organizations to which they belong. (N.T.L.'s first groups were for psychologists and other educators; it since has expanded into group training for corporation executives, administrators and teachers in public school systems and universities and community leaders.) Its method is the T group, the T standing for training.

In a typical T group, 12 to 14 business executives meet with a professional leader from N.T.L. The leader announces that the group will gather at certain specified times—say, for six hours a day over a five-day period—to try to learn about the forces that influence the behavior of individuals and groups; the learning will come from the members' own behavior, reactions and feelings; there are no rules of procedure and the group is free to go about the task in any way it sees fit; the leader will try to help the members learn from their experiences in the group but will make no attempt to direct or influence their activities.

To most businessmen, used to attending meetings with a formal agenda and conventions with a formal program, the T-group leader's announcement is a surprising and even frightening introduction to a whole new world in which the ordinary rules of conduct are suspended; there are no lines of authority and each individual must make his own way without benefit of guidelines or corporate title. What usually results, after an initial confusion and hesitation, is a remarkably frank group discussion in which individual members feel perfectly free to reveal their own deepest problems and their opinions of one another, whether affectionate or hostile. Given the candid atmosphere of the group and the honest feedback on how their behavior appears to others, the members often become aware of feelings, fears, guilts, desires and frustrations they had previously concealed even from themselves. Abraham Maslow, a past president of the American Psychological Association who has conducted T groups, says, "It's very hard to believe in sober minutes that a dozen utter strangers will suddenly let all their defenses clatter to the floor like old shoes—but I've seen it happen."

. . .

Out of the T group have risen the other kinds of shoulder rubbing and psyche baring, usually called encounter groups, that take place at Esalen and other centers and under the direction of individual leaders throughout the country. Whereas the members of T groups usually have a good deal in common in their working-day lives, the members of encounter groups usually do not; they get together haphazardly from all walks of life. What takes place, however, is quite similar to the activity of the T group. Members of encounter groups tend to let down their defenses, reveal their self-doubts and tell each other frankly what they like and do not like about one another. There are occasional flare-ups of hostility and moments of deep affection. There is a good deal of laughter—also, to a greater extent than in T groups, a good deal of weeping.

Why are people so willing—even eager—to bare their souls to strangers? Dr. Rogers says it is a sign of the times, something that could never have happened at an earlier stage of history. "When a man is scrambling very hard to get his three meals a day," says Dr. Rogers "he doesn't have time to feel alienated from his fellow human beings. Now that we have the affluent society, we do have the time and we realize that we are alone and lonely, lacking deep contacts with others. We begin to say, 'I wish there were someone I could talk to honestly; I wish someone cared about me.'" Charles Seashore, a psychologist with N.T.L., says "There's a kind of immaturity and thwarted growth in all of us. As human beings, we have all kinds of potentialities—to be warm or standoffish, loving or hostile, open or suspicious, enthusiastic or constrained, adventuresome or cautious, emotional or reserved. But our society rewards some of these traits and discourages others, and most of us wind up as adults with just one or two stereotyped responses that we display automatically to all the hundreds of different situations in which we find ourselves. The popularity of groups rests on the fact that most of us feel deprived; probably 85 to 95 percent of us feel that we're not as close to people as we'd like to be, or that we're not as open and honest about our feelings, or that we have an anxiety over submitting to or exercising authority, or that our lives are too boxed in and narrowly predictable from day to day. Since the group encourages intimacy, honesty and adventure, it's a great experience even if its effects are only temporary."

Is the group a form of therapy? Dr. Maslow says no: "Although I'm very impressed with groups, I don't think they can help with serious problems—only minor hangups. A neurosis just won't fade away at a T group or a weekend marathon." The N.T.L. staff is careful to call its aim not therapy but "personal learning and personal growth." Dr. Seashore points out that he himself once experienced what he considered a therapeutic breakthrough in a T group—but that it occurred in the 139th group he attended or

conducted, a figure hardly likely to be reached by nonprofessionals.

Dr. Rogers, on the other hand, has no doubt that the group is a form of therapy and a highly effective form, at that; he has come to believe that 20 hours in a group are more effective than 20 hours of one-to-one treatment. The secret of the group, he thinks, is that "it gives people permission to be helpful to one another"—a privilege that is not generally available in society and that is grasped eagerly and often with great skill, resulting in very much the same kind of support offered in client-centered therapy. In one way, says Dr. Rogers, the group is superior to client-centered therapy as he practiced it in the past; this is the fact that members of the group freely express their negative as well as their positive feelings toward one another. Thus, each person in the group is at times deeply liked and supported for his good qualities and, at other times, confronted with harsh criticism of the bad, a push-pull process that seems to speed awareness of the true self. If Dr. Rogers returned to one-to-one practice, he says, he would be very free to give his patients constant feedback on his inner reactions to them, pro or con.

．　．　．

Whether the encounter group should properly be called therapy or just a form of education, it certainly does *something* for people. At the Western Behavioral Sciences Institute, psychologists gathered interviews from 1000 people who had taken part in groups; these people agreed almost unanimously that they had greatly enjoyed the experience and had been profoundly influenced; typical comments were, "It was the most important thing that ever happened to me" and "It changed my whole life." What, exactly, about the group had produced this effect? As the psychologists had expected, the one thing mentioned most frequently was some particularly dramatic example of deep exchange of understanding and emotion between two or more members of the group—sometimes an incident in which they themselves had taken part, sometimes an incident that they had merely observed (another example, perhaps, of Dr. Bandura's learning through imitation). To the psychologists' surprise, however, these outstanding incidents did not necessarily involve the therapist who led the group; in fact, the therapist was responsible for no more of them than anybody else. To psychologist Richard Farson this suggested a strange possibility: To the extent that the encounter group is therapeutic, is it a form of therapy that requires no therapist? In other words, can a group succeed without a professional leader?

Dr. Farson's idea of experimenting with leaderless groups was opposed by every therapist he knew. Without professional guidance, he was warned, members of the group would quickly be at one another's throats. Nonetheless, he went ahead, though with extreme caution. The first leaderless group was watched anxiously by two professional therapists behind a one-way see-through mirror, ready to intervene quickly if the group got stalled or out of hand. As it turned out, the two observers were unneeded. In fact, every time the group seemed on the verge of serious trouble, the two therapists were amazed to see some completely untrained member step in and do exactly what they themselves would have done. With this reassurance, Dr. Farson then set up a full-scale experiment comparing leaderless groups with groups led by professional therapists. It developed that the leaderless groups, even when composed of people who had never before taken part in an encounter, behaved very much like the led groups; their members got right down to business, avoided excess hostility and did a good job of helping one another. To Dr. Farson, the experiment suggests a startling answer to the problem of how the nation can possibly train enough therapists for all the people who need help. "It may turn out," he says, "that our greatest resource for solving human problems is the very people who have the problems."

One immediate result of Dr. Farson's experiment has been a do-it-yourself kit for nonprofessionals eager to organize their own groups. The kit was created largely by a young psychologist named Betty Berzon, a former associate of Dr. Farson at the Western Behavioral Sciences Institute; it is a set of tape recordings, each running about an hour and a half, designed to be played by a group that will hold eight meetings. For each session, the voice on the tape suggests various activities that have been found helpful in groups. For example, all members but one are asked to form a tight circle, into which the missing member then tries to break. Or the members are asked to write down, anonymously, some secret of which they are ashamed; the slips are shuffled and handed out; each member, in turn, then reads the paper he has drawn and discusses how it might feel to have such a secret. Following each suggestion, the tape goes silent, to give the group time to carry out the instructions; then the voice returns with something new. The recordings are called Encountertapes and are manufactured by the Human Development Institute of Atlanta, a subsidiary of Bell & Howell (an indication that the group movement has grown big enough to interest the multimillion-dollar corporation world).

"What we've done," says Miss Berzon, "is package the group experience and make it available to schools, churches and industries. This takes it out of the esoteric centers like Esalen and right into the mainstream of everyday life." Miss Berzon was one of the several thousand people marooned for three days at New York's Kennedy Airport by an unexpected snowstorm last winter. Listening to the incessant bulletins over the airport loudspeakers, and watching her frustrated fellow travelers grow increasingly bored and glassy-eyed, she kept grieving at the lost opportunity for playing her Encountertapes over the speakers and turning an ordeal into a delightful mass initiation into the marvels of the encounter group. She can never pass a tall office building without thinking of it as a place where a public-address system and a single set of Encountertapes could bring the group experience to many thousands of people at a time.

Even enthusiasts such as Miss Berzon, however, concede that the group has one serious defect for which no remedy is as yet apparent. It is one thing to confess your secrets, pour out your angers and break into tears among a few people gathered expressly in behalf of this kind of free and frank communication; it is quite another thing to do so at home or in the office. Says Miss Berzon, "Once you've had this taste of honey—once you've had the opportunity to really relate in depth to other people—it's hard to go back to the cocktail-party kind of superficiality. But everyday life isn't like the group. And your family, your boss and your friends probably have a vested interest in keeping you just as you've always been. So the effect tends to get dissipated when you go home." Says Dr. Farson, "People *feel* they're changed by the group, but no matter how you observe them, test them or question their families and friends, you don't find any significant changes in their actual behavior. The reason is that what happens in the group is something that a person can't make happen anywhere else."

Trying to transfer the atmosphere of the group into real life can, in fact, be downright dangerous. One businessman who attended a T group reports, "I learned that I had been making myself miserable by bottling up my hostilities and being overpolite to everybody, so I decided to change all that. Three days later, I realized that I was losing my customers, my employees and my wife—and I changed back in a hurry." Dr. Glasser, who is skeptical of encounter groups, says, "They're based on a false premise. Until all people are open and honest at all times, it's unrealistic to think that you can be—without getting hurt."

In one way or another, most leaders of the group movement are now grappling with this problem. Many of them believe that the solution is to expand the movement, through Encountertapes and the establishment of hundreds of new Esalens, until millions of Americans have had group training of one kind or another; these millions will then reshape society into a sort of single big, happy, uninhibited, affectionate, turned-on encounter group. But as one skeptical psychologist has said, "There are a lot of religious overtones to the movement; these people are like the early Christians, who thought that all of society's problems would vanish as soon as everybody became a Christian."

Others are making a more direct attempt to bring the group and everyday life closer together. The National Training Laboratories, for example, has made some significant changes in the way it organizes its T groups. One N. T. L. psychologist says, "We used to be willing to take just one person from a business organization; we'd get him all revved up and then send him back to office colleagues and a job that hadn't changed a bit. Now we try to get at least two men from the firm, so that they can support each other after they go back. And what we really like is to have many people from the same company and work with the management to open up the lines of communication and creativity; we're trying to change the climate of the big organizations, such as corporations and universities, in which people are embedded." Dr. Farson has been thinking about what he calls "social architecture," a possible new science of the future. "If you want to help people transcend themselves," he says. "you've got to rearrange the social situations in which they constantly find themselves—the job, family, school and church." Thus, the attempt to heal and bolster the human psyche, having already expanded from couch to group, seems likely to expand further into all kinds of social situations. What started as Freud's first modest efforts to help a few hysterical patients has indeed come a long way.

SOME OTHER ALTERNATIVES TO PSYCHOANALYSIS

IN ADDITION TO THE TYPES OF PSYCHOTHERAPY DISCUSSED IN THE TEXT, THERE IS A WIDE VARIETY OF OTHER METHODS AVAILABLE

(NOTE: Some forms of psychotherapy use the Freudian technique of having the patient free associate while in a relaxed position, usually on a couch, but reject Freud's theories of the structure of the mind and the causes of personality disorders. Others retain the Freudian theory but use different methods of therapy; still others have abandoned both the theory and the practice of psychoanalysis. These brief and necessarily simplified descriptions emphasize the ways, theoretical or practical, in which various psychotherapies most sharply depart from classical psychoanalysis.)

Chemotherapy concentrates on chemical imbalances in the nervous system that may be the causes or the results of mental disorders and attempts to treat these disorders with drugs such as tranquilizers and psychedelics. Chemotherapy may be used as an aid to other kinds of psychotherapy, and is often effective in dealing with severe psychoses.

Directive psychotherapy assumes that the patient is not in a condition to work through his own problems or to establish therapeutic goals, and the therapist undertakes these responsibilities. The therapist uses any technique that seems indicated and tries to base his plan of action on all available scientific knowledge.

Existential therapy is based on the existentialist philosophical belief that each individual has to choose his values and decide the meaning of his life. The therapist attempts to achieve an authentic, spontaneous relationship with the patient to help him discover his free will and make his choices.

Experiential therapy is a system in which therapist and patient jointly enter the patient's fantasy world, often acting out fantasies together. The resulting emotional experiences aim at re-educating the patient on the deepest level of his psyche.

General semantics postulates that neurotic behavior results from unrealistic use of words, especially the error of identifying the word with the object for which it stands. The therapist tries to teach the patient to use language more accurately and realistically in thinking and communicating, thereby achieving a more effective orientation.

Gestalt therapy focuses on the patient's difficulty in forming meaningful, organized "wholes" (referred to by the German word *Gestalt*) out of experiences that have left him with unresolved problems. Through encounters between therapist and patient, usually in the presence of a group, the therapy seeks to restore the individual's fragmented integrity of thinking, feeling and acting so that he can regain contact with reality and resume personality growth.

Horneyan psychology was developed by Karen Horney, who believed that neurosis springs from basic anxiety acquired in childhood. Horneyan therapy aims to overthrow the idealized self-image the patient is trying to live up to, making him face his actual self and release his potential for healthy personality development.

Hypnotherapy uses hypnosis to increase the patient's suggestibility and to lift repressions, to remove neurotic symptoms when they prevent progress in therapy or to persuade the patient to adopt more constructive general attitudes.

Interpersonal psychology locates the causes of personality disorders in the relations between the individual and society rather than in purely internal psychological developments and aims at improving interpersonal attitudes and relations.

Learning-theory therapy treats mental disorders as self-defeating behavior patterns that the individual has learned to rely on when he feels anxiety. The therapist applies all available scientifically discovered principles of learning to make the patient unlearn these patterns and to countercondition him against the attitudes that produced them.

Orgonomy is based on the theory of Wilhelm Reich that there is a specific energy—called orgone—that accounts for life. Reichian therapy combines psychoanalysis with manipulation of the patient's body in order to remove muscular armor—muscular attitudes an individual develops to block emotions and organ sensations.

Psychodrama is a form of improvised play-acting of certain roles and dramatic incidents resembling those situations that produce problems for the patient in his daily life. The purpose is to provide the patient with both theoretical insight and corrective emotional experience. This acting out is often conducted before an audience.

Rational-emotive therapy, developed by Albert Ellis, asserts that emotional disturbance arises when individuals mentally reiterate unrealistic, illogical, self-defeating thoughts. The therapist identifies these thoughts, argues against them and persuades the patient to undertake actions that will disprove the undesirable beliefs and, hence, strip them of their power.

Transactional analysis postulates that all interpersonal communications spring from specific ego states called Parent, Adult and Child. The therapist attempts to identify the ego state producing each communication from the patient with the aim of discovering the plan the individual has unconsciously chosen for his life and of replacing it, if necessary, with a more realistic and constructive one. Transactional analysts prefer to work with groups.

53. MENTAL HEALTH'S THIRD REVOLUTION

Nicholas Hobbs

The exciting thing for me about this session on movement and resistance to change in the mental health professions is the assumption that professional people have a responsibility for the management of innovation. The implication is that the mature profession does not simply respond to the needs of society but claims a role in determining what society should need and how social institutions, as well as individual professional careers, can be shaped to the service of an emerging social order. The responsible professional person becomes the architect of social change.

AN OVERVIEW

I see a two-phase process: the invention phase and the engineering phase. The invention phase is what we are about in this session; the engineering phase invokes, among other things, the development of new training programs and the building of new institutions. I propose to talk about the third mental health revolution, the inventions it requires and their implications for training programs.

The first mental health revolution may be identified with the names of Philippe Pinel in France, William Tuke in England, and Benjamin Rush and Dorothea Lynde Dix in America. It was based on the heretical notion that the insane are people and should be treated with kindness and dignity. Though 170 years old, this revolution has, unhappily, not yet been consummated. Its ideals may not yet be taken for granted and must therefore

From the AMERICAN JOURNAL OF ORTHOPSY-CHIATRY, 34 *(1964),* 822–833. *Copyright* © *1964 by the American Orthopsychiatric Association, Inc., Reprinted by permission of the* American Journal of Orthopsychiatry *and the author.*

be given a major emphasis in training programs at all levels. You will recall that the central thesis of *Action for Mental Health,* its story line, is that the mentally ill do not get adequate care because they are unconsciously rejected by family, neighbor and professional alike. I regard this as an oversimplification, but the fact that there are still practices to support the argument of the Joint Commission's report may remind us that the work of Pinel is not yet done.

The second revolution was born in Vienna —its charismatic leader, Sigmund Freud. Its agents were the wearers of Freud's ring and other disciples who carried his ideas, making a few adjustments of their own, throughout the Western world. Freud was a giant, a companion of Darwin, Marx and Einstein in shaping our culture, our beliefs about man. It is impossible not to include Freud in a training program today, for if his ideas were to be omitted from the syllabus they would be brought in, as the clothes they wear, by every participant who has been exposed to novels, plays, poetry, television, the jokes of the day and even to *Infant and Child Care,* the most popular publication of the United States Government Printing Office.

Revolutions generally tend to excess and Freud's is no exception. A counterrevolution is required to restore balance and common sense. Freud has led us to a preoccupation with the intrapsychic life of man. No, I think "obsession" is a better word to suggest the passionate commitment we have to the world inside a man's skull, to the unconscious, the phenomenal, the stuff that dreams are made of. Everyone must become a therapist, probing the argument of insidious intent, stalking ragged claws scuttling over the bottoms of silent seas. The psychiatrist forgets Adolph Meyer and can no longer give a physical examination. The psychologist lays down his diagnostic tools, forgets research and gets behind a desk to listen. The social worker goes inside and waits for the patient to come. The preacher takes to his study and the teacher to the case conference. The most thoroughly trained person of all, the psychiatrist who has completed psychoanalytic training, becomes a monument of Veblenian inutility, able to treat maybe a hundred patients in his entire professional career. We owe a tremendous debt to Freud, as a son to a wise and insightful father, but to use our heritage we must break with him and discover our own, authentic idiom. The pendulum is already swinging back, and I am here trying to give it a little push.

The third mental health revolution, the one we are now challenged to further, is not readily identified with the name of a person but is evident in the common theme that runs through many seemingly disparate innovations of the last 15 years.

The therapeutic community, the open hospital, the increased interest in children, the growth of social psychiatry, the broadened base of professional responsibility for mental health programs, the search for new sources of manpower, the quickened concern for the mentally retarded, the proposed comprehensive community mental health centers, these developments are evidences of a deep-running change, indicative of this: *The concepts of public health have finally penetrated the field of mental health.* Up to the last decade the mental health effort was developed on a clinical model; now we are committing ourselves to a new and more promising public health model and are seeking specific ways to make it work in practice.

Mental health used to mean its opposite, mental disease; now it means not just health but human well-being. The revolution of our time is manifested not only in changed practices but more consequentially in changing assumptions about the basic character of mental disorders and of mental health. A great stride forward was made when aberrant behavior was recognized not as madness, lunacy or possession by a devil but as an illness to be treated like other illnesses; a perhaps even greater stride forward may result from the growing recognition that mental illness is not

the private organic misery of an individual but a social, ethical and moral problem, a responsibility of the total community.

By an accident of history the problem of mental retardation is being brought into prominence, with a clear demand that the mental health professions no longer shirk their responsibility for the mentally handicapped individual. Thus the scope of the mental health field is broadening at the same time that its basic character is undergoing change. Mental retardation is also being redefined to recognize the preponderant involvement of social and educational influences in the over-all problem.

It is a paradox that the care of the mentally ill has always been largely a public responsibility but that the concepts of public health, of early detection, of prophylaxis and prevention, of adequate treatment of all regardless of wealth or social position, have never had much influence. Toward the end of the Eighteenth Century, the *maisons de santé* in Paris did give humane treatment to the insane, but these facilities were expensive and thus not available to the great masses of the afflicted. In America moral and humane treatment was established in a few of the better early institutions, such as the Friends Asylum in Philadelphia, but the indigent insane continued to be neglected, to be housed in overcrowded and filthy quarters, to be bound in camisoles and forgotten. The chains that Pinel had struck off were simply turned to leather. It was in the interest of the indigent insane that Dorothea Dix launched her crusade. Of course, the situation today is much better, but the dominant theme of advantage for the well-to-do and relative neglect for those without substantial means remains depressingly evident. In June 1963, The National Institute of Labor Education presented a report, "Issues in the New National Mental Health Program Relating to Labor and Low Income Groups," in which the following observations are central to the argument: "While in principle the state hospital is available to the community at large, in practice its population is overwhelmingly drawn from lower income groups. To bring about a reduction in state mental hospital populations, therefore, requires that treatment and rehabilitation services be created in the community which can effectively reach lower socioeconomic groups.... To a larger extent, the orientation and treatment methods of existing community facilities have been based on services to middle and upper class individuals. They have neither attracted blue collar workers nor found them to be suitable clients when and if they presented themselves for help."

Two contemporary books seem to me to present in boldest relief the character of the public health, mental health problem today. One is by Hollingshead and Redlich and the other is by George Albee.

The former, *Social Class and Mental Illness,* is often quoted but not for its main point, a point so startling and so revealing of the character of much of our current mental health effort that one suspects its neglect can only be due to professional embarrassment and consequent repression of the disturbing facts. Hollingshead and Redlich studied all persons receiving psychiatric treatment in New Haven, Connecticut, during a specific period, to find out what determined the kind of treatment they received. One would normally make the simple-minded assumption that diagnosis would determine treatment, that what was done for a patient would be based on what was the matter with him. The investigators found no relationship between diagnosis and treatment. They studied other variables such as age and sex, and found these unrelated to treatment. The one variable related to type of treatment received was the socioeconomic status of the patient. If he were from the lowest socioeconomic group, he received some kind of mechanical, inexpensive and quick therapy such as electric shock. If he were from a high socioeconomic group, he received extended, expensive, talking-type psychotherapy. If the patient were not only affluent but also a member of an old, prestigious family, so situated in life that he bestowed honor on his helper, he received extended talking-type psychotherapy, but at a discount. The relationship between socioeconomic status and type of treatment received was not manifested in private practice alone but was also evident in the treatment provided by clinics and other public supported agencies. Thus all the mental health professions are involved.

The second pivotal book is George Albee's. I regard his monograph *Mental Health Manpower Trends,* prepared for the Joint Commission on Mental Illness and Health, as a most important and instructive book for the shaping of a national mental health program as well as for the development of curricula for the training of psychiatrists, psychologists, social workers and other mental health specialists. The book requires, it seems to me, a fundamental shift in strategy in providing mental health services to the people of this nation.

Albee's main thesis can be stated simply: The prospective supply of people for training in the mental health professions is limited, demands for services will continue to grow more rapidly than the population of the country, and there will not be in the forseeable future enough mental health personnel to meet demands for service.

It is widely and I think erroneously assumed that the personnel shortages so much with us everywhere are a local and a temporary phenomenon. We assume that it is a matter of waiting a year or so for the training programs to catch up. Albee's point is that they will not catch up. We can't solve the problem in the way we are trying to solve it.

Keep these two disturbing books in mind and then consider: (1) the geographical distribution of psychiatrists and (2) the growth of private practice in clinical psychology. Most psychiatrists are concentrated in urban centers in proportions much higher than the relative concentration of population. Over 50 per cent of the psychiatrists trained under NIMH grants go into private practice. Mental health services flow in the direction of money and sophistication. The most vigorous development in clinical psychology today is the extension of private practice, following the model of psychiatry, which has followed the model of the private practice of medicine. Psychologists in private practice are a major power in the American Psychological Association. Several universities are working toward the establishment of professional schools for the training of psychological practitioners.

Now there is nothing wrong with the private practice of psychiatry or psychology except that it does not provide a sound base for the development of a national mental health program. The one-to-one relationship, the fifty-minute hour, are a dead-end, except perhaps for the two participants or as a source of new knowledge. This mode of offering service consumes far too much manpower for the benefit of a far too limited segment of society. We must find a more efficient way of deploying our limited resources of mental health manpower.

These two books, more than any I know, tell us what the third mental health revolution must accomplish. We must find new ways of deploying our resources of manpower and of knowledge to the end that effective mental health services, for prevention, for diagnosis, for treatment, for rehabilitation, can be made available to all of the people. Furthermore, we now have two other books that provide us with guidelines to action. They are *Action for Mental Health*, the report of the Joint Commission on Mental Illness and Health, and *National Action to Combat Mental Retardation*, the report of the President's Panel on Mental Retardation.

IMPLICATIONS FOR TRAINING PROGRAMS

To prescribe the content of professional curricula is hazardous at all times and downright foolhardy in a time of revolution. The most useful and productive thing to do is to keep up a lively debate on educational objectives for mental health professions and to leave it to local initiative, to the faculties of graduate and professional schools and to directors of inservice training programs, to determine what to teach and how to teach it. As a contribution to the debate on goals, I would identify nine objectives that should guide the development of educational programs for social work, nursing, psychiatry, medicine in general, clinical psychology and the various adjunctive disciplines.

1. The changing conception of the nature of mental illness and mental retardation will require that the mental health specialist be a person of broad scientific and humanistic education, a person prepared to help make decisions not only about the welfare of an individual but also about the kind of society that must be developed to nurture the greatest human fulfillment.

I am, frankly, gravely concerned about the proposed comprehensive community mental health centers. Here is a bold and imaginative proposal that may fail because top-level mental health personnel may not be prepared to discharge the responsibilities of a comprehensive community mental health program. When the great state hospitals were built across this country in the Nineteenth Century, someone must have thought them the last word, the best way to care for the mentally ill. There is a chance that the new mental health centers will be nothing more than a product of the general urbanization of America, a movement from country to city. Twenty years from now, people may moan not over bricks and mortar but over glass and steel; there is a real danger that we shall succeed in changing only the location and the architecture of the state hospital. If the new centers turn inward toward the hospital, they too will be monuments to failure. If they turn outward to the community, as some of the testimony before the Congress said they should, who among us will know what to do? Psychiatrists, social workers, nurses and psychologists have been trained primarily as clinicians, as intrapsychic diagnosticians, as listeners with the third ear; we are clinicians, not public health, mental health experts. Who among us knows enough about schools, courts, churches, welfare programs, recreation, effects of automation, cultural deprivation, population mobility, delinquency, family life, city planning and human ecology in general to presume to serve on the staff of a community mental health center? The first training program we should plan should be for ourselves. We have nothing more urgent to do.

2. The concept of the responsibility of the doctor for patient, case worker for client, so appropriately honored in traditional educational programs for the physician, social worker and clinical psychologist, must be reconceptualized to define the responsibilities of these specialists as workers with other professionals who can contribute to the development of social institutions that promote effective functioning in people.

The psychiatrist might have limited himself to the treatment of the hospitalized psychotic or the acutely debilitated neurotic, leaving lesser problems of adjustment to teachers, clergymen and counselors of various types. With respect to the mentally retarded he might have limited himself to those so handicapped as to require institutionalization, defining the rest as slow learners and thus the responsibility not of medicine but of education. Psychiatry has, wisely I think, chosen not to take this constricted course but to concern itself with a broad spectrum of problems that are also the historical concerns of other professional groups. Most of the mental health effort, as we now define it, overlaps substantially with the domains of education, religion, welfare, correction and even recreation, communication, architecture and city planning. There is nothing in most mental health training programs to provide either content or method for dealing collaboratively with other professional groups to solve the problems legitimately defined as both mental health and something else. Indeed, there is much in the education of the doctor, the psychologist and the social worker that actually militates against effective collaboration in these areas of overlapping concern. For example, the honorable concept of the physician's responsibility for his patient, so carefully and appropriately nurtured in medical training, gets extended unconsciously to relationships with other professional people and becomes an issue not of responsibility but of hegemony. What the physician sees as being responsible, his colleague sees as being arrogant. The physician always seems surprised and hurt by this incongruity in role perception, this seemingly unwarranted misunderstanding of his intent. The more thorough his clinical training, the less well prepared he may be for public health responsibilities. Somehow, without sacrifice of clinical competence, the psychiatrist must be trained to meet role requirements of truly cooperative enterprises involving a variety of professional people. Is there anywhere an approved residency program in psychiatry that explicitly trains for this concept of professional responsibility?

Clinical psychology is equally vulnerable to charges of incompetence in collaborative skills. Its arrogance is not that of responsibility but of detachment, a product perhaps of professional timidity and defensiveness, coupled with the platitudinous allegation that we need more research before we can contribute to social action programs. Perhaps only the social worker, before the advent of the sit-behind-the-desk-and-do-therapy era, is prepared for public health, mental health responsibilities.

3. The mental health specialist must be trained in ways to multiply his effectiveness by working through other less extensively and expensively trained people. The one-to-one model of much current practice does not provide a sound basis for a public health, mental health program.

The most promising approach to this problem at the present time is to use the extensively trained, expensive, and scarce mental health specialists to guide the work of other carefully selected persons with limited training. Such manpower is available, even in abundance, and its effective use depends on the ingenuity of the mental health specialist and his willingness to extend himself by working through other people. I would cite the work of Margaret Rioch in training carefully selected housewives to do psychotherapy under supervision; the use of college student volunteers in mental hospitals, and our Project Re-ED in Tennessee and North Carolina in which carefully selected teachers are working with disturbed children with the support of mental health and educational specialists. The place to start is in the universities, medical schools, residency centers and in-service training programs. The challenge to the mental health specialist in training should be, after establishing his own basic clinical competence, to work out ways in which he can multiply his effectiveness, say by a factor of six, by discovering means of working through other people.

4. Current developments will require that mental health training programs be revised to give attention to mental retardation commensurate with the degree of responsibility that the mental health professions have already assumed for the retarded. Since mental retardation is a much broader problem than it is usually considered to be in those few medical, social work and psychological training programs that have given it attention, the inclusion of mental retardation in these curricula will require a substantial extension of their conceptual underpinnings. Slums are more consequential than galactosemia* or phenylketonuria.†

I surmise that few things could so radically

---

* An hereditary disorder of carbohydrate metabolism, characterized by vomiting, diarrhoea, malnutrition, etc., in early infancy. (Eds.)

† An inherited metabolic abnormality usually first characterized by symptoms of mental retardation in infancy. (Eds.)

alter the character of education in medicine, psychiatry, psychology and social work as a serious commitment to doing something about the problem of mental retardation. The health professions have laid claim to much of the problem; at least three of the institutes of the National Institutes of Health are involved; a substantial portion of every state's mental health program is devoted to the retarded. Yet in most training programs it receives peripheral attention.

For one thing, mental retardation is not a disease entity. It is a host of conditions manifested in impaired intellectual and social competence. It is due to chromosomal aberrations, intrauterine trauma, prematurity, metabolic disorders, accidents, cultural deprivation, inadequate opportunities to learn and acute emotional disturbances. Mental retardation is widely regarded as a hopeless condition; yet it is hard to think of a human affliction as amenable to productive intervention. But again, a radical reconceptualization of the problem is required. When it is in our interest to make the problem of mental retardation loom large, we cite the figure of 5,400,000 retarded in the country. Yet the major emphasis of most of our programs is on the 400,000 who have some apparent physical anomaly, to the neglect of the 5,000,000 who are primarily a challenge to the adequacy of our social institutions. We are more intrigued by galactosemia than challenged by slums and poor schools. We presume to claim the finest medical care in the world but stand eleventh among nations in infant mortality, evidence of widespread inadequate prenatal care that also produces prematurity and much mental retardation. Assumption of responsibility for the retarded will require that our major professional groups make as their cause equal access to medical services and educational opportunity for all people without regard to means or social status.

5. Curriculum constructors in social work, psychiatry and psychology must come to terms with the issue of the relationship between science and practice. Are the scientist and the practitioner to be one or are their functions separable? Just at the time when psychologists seem ready to back off a bit from their insistence that the two functions should go together, there is an opposite trend developing in medical education. The issue is absolutely basic and must be clearly resolved before the content of training programs can be discerned.

6. The main source of nourishment for the mental health professions has been clinical practice leavened and limited by research. The shift toward a public health emphasis in mental health programs will require that the mental health specialist work through social institutions. He must acquire an appreciation of how disparate groups of people organize to achieve common goals and he must know how to encourage this process. He will need to be adept at institution building, at social invention, at the ordering of individual and community resources in the interest of mental health. I have found instructive a study by Harlan Cleveland of the successful Foreign Service Officer, who is in a position very much like that of the public health, mental health officer. He is confronted with a tremendous problem, his resources are limited, his staff is inadequate and he is expected to make a difference in the lives of a substantial number of people. Cleveland found that the highly effective Foreign Service Officer had, among other attributes, a strong institutional sense, a sense of the ways in which social groups invent institutions to serve their ends and a notion of how this process can be furthered in the interest of his concerns. It seems to me that the public health, mental health specialist must develop a comparable sensitivity and skill.

7. An increased public health emphasis in mental health programs will accentuate the need for prevention and thus lead to a greater emphasis in professional training on problems of children, on childhood disorders and early indications of later difficulties and, especially, on normal patterns of development.

I would urge that we invest approximately 25 per cent of our resources to mount a holding action against the mental health problems of the adult, devoting the major portion, at least 75 per cent, of our resources to the mental health problems of children. This is the only way to make substantial changes in the mental health of our adult population a generation from now. I have made this suggestion on a number of occasions and no one ever takes exception to the substance of the argument. But, alas, children are unprofitable clients and, furthermore, they don't vote, so I expect they will continue to be neglected unless the public health challenge grips the mental health professions.

8. The new curricula should paradoxically reinstate an age-old study, that of morals and ethics, not professional ethics but classical ethics. There are two reasons for this. First, the therapeutic relationship, whether between two people or in a broader social effort, is at heart an ethical enterprise, with respect to both method and outcome. Second, we face the awesome prospect of becoming efficient in our efforts to influence human behavior. With increasing effectiveness we must become increasingly concerned with the consequences of our work. We cannot responsibly remain satisfied with vague definitions of what we mean by mental health.

9. Educational programs for mental health specialists should anticipate an increasing obsolescence rate for knowledge and build habits of continuing scholarship and independent study. The more productive we are in mental health research, the more ingenious in the development of new social institutions, the more quickly will training programs become obsolete. The mental health specialist must be a continuing learner; training for independent learning must be a major commitment of mental health educational programs. National conferences are pleasant but they can only suggest new directions for study. Learning is ultimately a lonely enterprise.

From these nine considerations, these nine objectives for the training of mental health workers, there is instruction perhaps for the improvement of training programs, but there is a more insistent challenge that we reexamine the total structure of our mental health program to test its adequacy to get done the tremendous task that confronts us.

I thus come to a potentially distressing point. There is a possibility that the improvement of training is not our problem at all. I see little profit, from a public health viewpoint, in the following:

To train better and better psychotherapists to treat fewer and fewer people.

To improve the training of nurses to take care of increasing numbers of hospitalized old people who are no longer ill.

To hone to a fine edge the group work skills of an attendant who must watch more than 80 mentally retarded adults in a cyclone fence compound.

To improve the skills of the obstetrician in providing prenatal care to the poor in big cities when his contact with the mother is limited to 30 minutes before the arrival of the baby.

To train for exquisite precision in diagnosis when differentiated treatments are not available for differential diagnoses.

And so on for the social worker, the recreational worker, the occupational therapist, the community volunteer.

I come back to the possibility that we may not be able to solve the problem the way we are trying to do it, no matter how adequate our training. We must pay attention to the organizational structures for providing services, to the more effective deployment of our limited resources of highly trained people, to invention of new patterns for the provision of mental health services. These new patterns of organization may then have more influence on training than any other single consideration. Indeed perhaps a major goal of all inservice training programs today should be to train for the invention of new and more efficient forms for providing service, and then for skill in the diffusion of innovation.

A CASE STUDY IN INNOVATION

I should like, in conclusion, to present a case study in social innovation, to illustrate the thesis that it will be of no moment simply to train ourselves to do better what we are already doing. There must be invention of new forms for the provision of mental health services, forms that will treat realistically the problems of cost, of limited resources of highly trained talent, and of the necessity of extending mental health services to all of the people and not to a privileged few. Actually I might cite many new inventions, for the necessity of building public health concepts into mental health programs has already commanded attention and stimulated innovation, but I shall limit myself to one example simply because I know it well and can describe it fairly. I refer to our Project Re-ED, which is a compressed way of saying "a project for the Re-education of Emotionally Disturbed Children."

Project Re-ED was deliberately planned to meet a pressing social need that had been identified some eight years ago by a study of mental health resources in the South conducted by the Southern Regional Education Board. That study revealed an acute shortage in the region of specialized services for emotionally disturbed children. There were a few hospital units but most children in trouble were placed in detention homes, in institutions for the retarded, on wards with psychotic adults, or were left at home to fester there, occasionally seen by an itinerant teacher. The specialized services of all 16 states would not meet the requirements of the least populous state. While the situation has improved in recent years the problem remains acute. Furthermore, it is nationwide. The problem promises to be chronic, for we aspire to apply the clinical model to all disturbed children, and this simply can't be done because of limitations on the supply of personnel—even if it were desirable, which I question. We must turn to a public health, mental health model if we are to make any substantial headway at all. Re-ED is one such approach; there could of course be many others.

Two residential schools for emotionally disturbed children have been established, one in Nashville, Tennessee, the other in Durham, North Carolina. Each school will serve 40 children between the ages of six and 12, who are too disturbed or disturbing to be retained in a public school and who come from families that are too disrupted for the child to benefit from day care. The schools are staffed entirely by carefully selected young college graduates who have skills in teaching, recreation, camping, physical education, crafts and so on. They have been given nine months of specialized training for their work, and are called Teacher-Counselors. There is one social worker to mobilize community resources in the interest of the child and his family and one liaison teacher to co-ordinate a Re-ED school with the child's regular school. The Teacher-Counselors are backed by consultants: psychiatrists, psychologists, social workers, pediatricians and curriculum specialists. This is a sketch of the basic plan.

Now let us look at some of the principles that guide the program and warrant, I believe, the use of Re-ED as an example of a deliberate turning away from a clinical model toward a public health, mental health model for the provision of services to emotionally disturbed children.

1. The program draws on a source of manpower that is in reasonably good supply and does not compromise on the quality of the person who works with the child 24 hours a day.

2. Re-ED is basically a plan by which highly trained mental health specialists can multiply their effectiveness by working through other less well-trained people. If we could get most mental health specialists thinking along these lines, and then if we could invent the institutions to support them, the mental health personnel problem might be solved.

3. Re-ED concentrates on children from six to 12, hoping to prevent more serious later difficulties by early intervention. This is the mental health analog to the public health strategy of early case finding.

4. The program in Re-ED is organized around ecological rather than intrapsychic concepts. The task is not to "cure" the child (a clinical goal) but to get into reasonably functioning order the circumscribed social system of which the child is an essential part (a public health goal). The effort is to get the child, the family, the school, the neighborhood and the community just above threshold with respect to the requirements of each with respect to the other. When it is judged that the system has reached a level of functioning so that the probability of its successful operation exceeds the probability of failure, the child is returned home. A little improvement in all components or a dramatic improvement in any one component may make the system operational for the child. With this concept, it makes sense to plan for an average length of stay for a child in a Re-ED school of from four to six months.

5. A public health effort must have a public-vocabulary. All of the theory of Re-ED, the objectives of the program and the processes by which these objectives are furthered, have been put into a simple vocabulary using English words as English words are commonly used.

6. A public health effort must be economically feasible. We think Re-ED is. The existing clinical model for the residential care of disturbed children costs from $25 to $80 a day, with an average of around $50. We think that Re-ED schools can be operated for around $12 to $15 per day. More important than the daily cost is the cost per child re-

turned to his family and school as described above.

I describe Project Re-ED not as a solution to the problem of the emotionally disturbed child. It obviously is not that. An array of services will be required—as in any good public health program—to do the job, including hospitals and better public school programs for the disturbed child. I see it, rather, as one social invention that can make a difference. For an effective public health, mental health program in America, we need similar innovations in a number of fields: in the prevention of mental retardation due to inadequate prenatal care and to acute cultural deprivation; in the care of the chronic schizophrenic, the alcoholic, the drug addict; in programs to arrest deterioration in the aged and for the care of hospitalized oldsters who are no longer ill. By such innovations the concept of public health can come to the field of mental health.

RECOMMENDED FURTHER READING

Bandura, Albert: *Principles of Behavior Modification;* New York, Holt, Rinehart & Winston 1969

*Berne, Eric: *Games People Play;* New York, Grove Press 1964

Deutsch, Albert: *The Mentally Ill in America: A History of Their Care and Treatment from Colonial Times* (2nd ed.); New York, Columbia University Press 1949

Ford, D. N. and H. B. Urban: *Systems of Psychotherapy;* New York, John Wiley 1963

*Harper, R. A.: *Psychoanalysis and Psychotherapy: 36 Systems;* Englewood Cliffs, N.J., Prentice-Hall 1959

Haley, Jay: *Strategies of Psychotherapy;* New York, Grune & Stratton 1963

*Kubie, Lawrence S.: *Practical and Theoretical Aspects of Psychoanalysis;* New York, International Universities Press 1950

*Laing, R. D.: *The Politics of Experience;* New York, Pantheon 1967

London, Perry: *The Modes and Morals of Psychotherapy;* New York, Holt, Rinehart & Winston 1964

*Luchins, Abraham S.: *Group Therapy: A Guide;* New York, Random House 1964

Mabry, J. H. *et al.: *Control of Human Behavior;* Glenview, Ill., Scott, Foresman 1966

Menninger, Karl: *Theory of Psychoanalytic Technique;* New York, Basic Books 1958

Rogers, Carl R.: *On Becoming A Person: A Therapist's View of Psychotherapy;* Boston, Houghton Mifflin 1961

*Rosen, George: *Madness in Society;* New York, Harper & Row 1968

*Schofield, William: *Psychotherapy: The Purchase of Friendship;* Englewood Cliffs, N. J., Prentice-Hall 1964

*Schutz, William C.: *Joy: Expanding Human Awareness;* New York, Grove Press 1967

Shepard, Martin and Marjorie Lee: *Games Analysts Play;* New York, Putnam's 1970

Watts, Alan: *Psychotherapy East and West;* New York, Pantheon 1961

Wolpe, Joseph, A. Salter and L. J. Reyna (eds.): *The Conditioning Therapies;* New York, Holt, Rinehart & Winston 1964

---

* Paperback edition available.

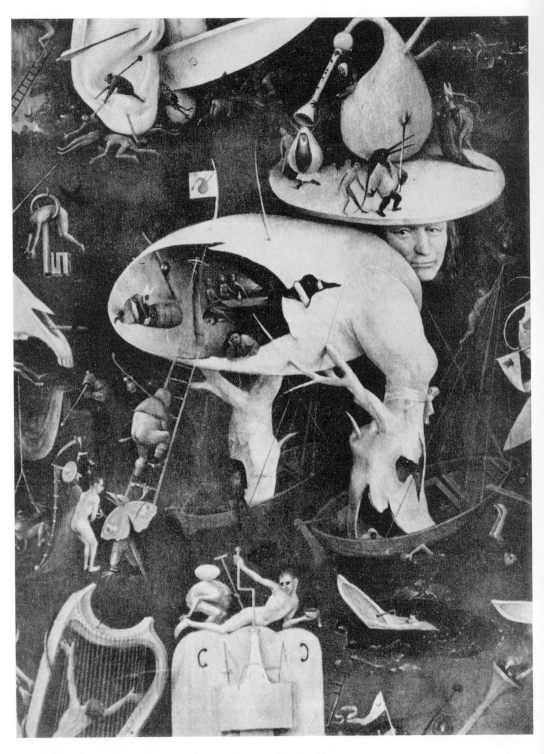

Hieronymus Bosch, *The Garden of Delights: Hell* (detail),
Museo del Prado, Madrid.

PART XII

DRUGS AND DRUG USE:
DAMNATION OR SALVATION?

A pharmacologist defines a drug as "any chemical which is introduced into a living organism and which leads to physiological effects...which can be detected by objective means."[1] By this definition use of drugs is probably as old as human life itself and has characterized every civilization of which we have knowledge. For most of human history drugs were, of necessity, natural substances, but as science has grown sophisticated chemists have not only synthesized most of the natural drugs in the laboratory but have created literally thousands of new ones never encountered in nature. The range of potential drugs open to human use and abuse is thus vastly greater today than ever before and seems to be increasing geometrically. Of these thousands of substances only a small percentage is, at any given time, of more than passing interest to psychology or to society at large.

In contemporary America, where everyone uses *some* drugs, it is absurd to oppose the label "drug users" to the label "non-drug users." We should rather ask who uses particular drugs, when, and why; what effects that use has on the individual and on society; and what (and why) are the attitudes of those who do not use a given drug toward those who do? In the illumination cast by such more refined questions it appears that the "problem" of drug use or abuse (the two are often equated) is less a physiological or psychological than a political and social one. At a particular moment in its history every society is characterized by an array of drugs the use of which is legally and socially approved (or, at least, accepted) and by a second array whose use is proscribed, denounced, and, when discovered, punished. In consequence the "problem" of drugs is almost always defined by the use of legally and socially *disapproved* substances. For the psychologist this problem often reduces to the practical one of understanding the reasons for the use of such substances together with treating the untoward consequences of such use, in cases where users are defined as "disturbed" or "sick" rather than as criminals. (Experimental psychologists are, of course, also interested

---

1 C. R. B. Joyce in Brian M. Foss (editor): *New Horizons in Psychology*; Harmondsworth, England, Penguin Books, 1966, p. 272.

in the effects of various drugs on consciousness, perception, emotion, learning, and performance. See Selection 24, for example.)

Quantitatively speaking, the most dangerous drugs used in contemporary America are unquestionably ethyl alcohol, nicotine, and the numberless brands of tranquilizers, all of which are legally and socially accepted, are, we might say, "respectable" drugs. Both alcohol and nicotine are physiologically addictive in the strict sense that the body develops a tolerance for them (meaning that ever larger amounts are needed to attain a given effect) and that characteristic physiological symptoms (withdrawal symptoms) develop when their use is abruptly discontinued. Estimates place the number of chronic alcoholics in the United States at between 6 and ? *million* while the annual number of deaths from lung cancer (of which cigarette smoking is a primary cause—it is a contributing cause of several other serious diseases) now exceeds 50,000. Yet the consumption of liquor and tobacco, because both are legally and socially accepted, are not considered aspects of the drug problem by society's leaders nor, apparently, is the indiscriminate ingestion of trillions of tranquilizers with its inevitable annoying and often deleterious side effects.

But even illegal drugs cannot be treated as though there were no distinctions among them. Partly for historical reasons and partly for physiological ones illegal drug use has at least two distinct aspects, although these are often jumbled together in political and journalistic discussions: narcotics use narrowly defined and the use of non-narcotic drugs, notably the psychedelics and amphetamines.

We have already defined narcotics as those drugs which are, with continued use, physiologically addicting. Major substances falling within this category are opium and its derivatives (e.g., morphine and codein), heroin (a morphine derivative) and the barbiturates. Prior to 1914 these drugs (the barbiturates excepted) were easily and legally available to the general public at pharmacies (i.e., "*drug* stores") and their use entailed no legal and little, if any, social stigma. For these reasons no one knows exactly how many narcotics' addicts there were prior to 1914 but it seems probable that the number was greater than today (out of a population half the size) and that a large percentage—perhaps the majority—were respectable middle-class people, many of them women. The passage of the Harrison Act in 1914, only six years before Prohibition took effect, confined the dispensing of narcotics to physicians and surrounded that dispensing with such ambiguous restrictions as to discourage almost entirely their prescription.

Over time the effect of that law and the manner of its enforcement was to reduce the total number of addicts, to drive those who remained into a despised, outcast subculture, to criminalize the use of narcotics, and to alter the social characteristics of those who, for whatever reason, turned to narcotics' use.

Current estimates place the number of hard-core narcotics' addicts in America at between 100,000 and 250,000 (not to be confused with the number of people who, at some time or other, have experimented with a narcotic drug without becoming addicted to it), most of whom are concentrated in a few large metropolitan areas, especially New York. Nowadays, addicts are usually males under forty years of age and are drawn disproportionately from the ranks of the lowest socioeconomic groups, especially those groups, such as blacks, Puerto Ricans, and Mexicans, who are denied equal participation in American life. While many addicts are characterized by "passive-dependent" personalities the resort to narcotics use among the socially despised and disadvantaged is probably, in large part, a reaction to their social position and to the despondency that it fosters. Heroin and other narcotics, such as alcohol, offer the promise of temporary escape from an otherwise hopeless situation.

To the extent that narcotics' addiction is an actual rather than a verbal social problem it is so less because of the addiction itself (which is not illegal) than because of the criminal activities to which addicts are driven in order to obtain the money to support their exceedingly expensive habit. The social-psychological "problem" of narcotics use is, therefore, largely a product of the very legislation that restricted the legal availability of narcotic drugs, a pattern that was repeated with marijuana following the passage of the Marijuana Tax Act in 1937.

If narcotics' use represents the "old" drug problem, the "new" one, on which our selections will concentrate, arises from the increasing use of non-narcotic substances (sometimes called "soft" drugs)—many of them quite new—which, in general, can be characterized either as psychedelic (consciousness expanding) or as euphoriants (pleasure giving)—or both. Among the most widely used of these are marijuana and hashish (both derived from the female *Cannabis sativa* plant and, in sufficient strength, mildly psychedelic), the amphetamines (including methedrine or "speed"), LSD (lysergic acid diethylamide), mescaline (peyote), psilocybin, THC (tetrahydrocannabinol or synthetic marijuana), DMT (dimethyltriptamine), DET (diethyltriptamine) PCP (phencyclidine or "angel dust") and STP.

While some of these drugs are very ancient (the earliest extant mention of Cannabis or Indian hemp dates back to the pharmacopoeia of the Chinese Emperor Shen Nung, written sometime around 2737 B.C.) more are relatively recent products of the pharmaceutical laboratories (LSD was first synthesized by Albert Hofmann in Basel, Switzerland in 1943, psilocybin in the early 1950s, THC, DMT, DET not until the 1960s). While none of these drugs is physiologically addicting, individuals may and often do develop a strong psychological dependence on them, a situation that has been characterized as "psychological addiction." While we yet know little regarding the long-term physiological and psychological effects of many of these drugs it is already clear that official political and social attitudes toward their use have been shaped less by scientific skepticism or justified caution than by often irrational fears of the unfamiliar and by emotional reactions to the label "narcotic" that has been indiscriminately and thoughtlessly affixed to them, especially by law enforcement agents and careless journalists. The passions aroused by such labeling have often been further fanned by politicians, by representatives of self-interested law enforcement agencies, and even perhaps by the liquor and cigarette industries, groups which have a vested interest in maintaining the illegal status of drugs that might compete with their own.

Regarding the physiological effects of these drugs there is considerable historical, cultural, and scientific evidence that the user of marijuana or hashish runs considerably less physical risk than the heavy cigarette smoker or the inveterate liquor drinker. That both marijuana and hashish have been used in the Far East for over 4,500 years without any conspicuous physiological ill effects strongly supports such a contention. Moreover, no causal link between marijuana or hashish use and personal violence has ever been demonstrated (something that can hardly be said of alcohol), an assertion that holds for the use of narcotics as well (the narcotic addict becomes violent when he does *not* have his drug and often in order to get it, not when he is "on" it). The more powerful psychedelic drugs, such as LSD, are far more unpredictable but, as we will see below, their effects depend importantly on the expectations of the user and the setting in which he takes them. In addition, individual personality predispositions seem to affect reactions to the stronger psychedelics more than to the milder ones. Perhaps the most serious charge leveled against LSD is that its use may damage the individual's chromosomal structure, the carriers of his genetic code, and thus may produce deformed or defective offspring among users of the drug. This finding was reported by a team of researchers in 1967 but remains in dispute. Approximately half the subsequent studies (not all of them comparable to the original) reported in the scientific literature have confirmed, in general, the original report while the other half have contradicted it. Obviously, both more and more careful research is required before any final verdict can be rendered on this charge, as on most of the positive claims made by their champions on behalf of LSD and the other psychedelics. Equally obviously, indiscriminate or excessive use of such drugs, especially by individuals with unstable or depressive personalities, can be extremely dangerous.

The second critical difference between the new drug problem and the old is not only that the psychedelics are far more widely used than narcotics but that they are used, not by the members of a small, proscribed, and despised subculture, but by many of the most respectable and advantaged members of society, perhaps alienated from the latter but certainly not disadvantaged or rejected by it. The use of such drugs by college students and college-age individuals, especially the more intelligent and sensitive ones, is especially frequent but its use by older businessmen, professionals, artists, and even clergymen is by no means rare. We do not yet know the number of regular or occasional users of marijuana or the stronger psychedelics but most "guesstimates" place the number of occasional users at several million. It also seems probable, although we cannot prove it, that the mass media, by dramatizing the use and the effects of psychedelic drugs, have helped to spread not only knowledge of but also demand for them.

Drug use as a psychological and social problem (defining the latter as an unacceptable state of affairs which the society or some organized group within it acts to change) exists, therefore, not primarily because of a dramatic increase in the use of drugs as such but, in the first place, because of legal and social attitudes toward certain drugs and their use and, in the second place, because of a shift among certain highly visible and articulate groups from the use of acceptable to the use of unacceptable drugs. American society's harsh and uncomprehending reaction to that shift reminds us of the disastrous attempt during the 1920s to enforce Prohibition on an increasingly resistant public. The current "drug problem" is therefore at least as much that of those who do not use the currently unacceptable drugs as it is that of those who do. Any time a society outlaws the use of a particular substance it automatically creates a class of criminals or deviants encompassing those who do use the substance, as happened in the case of alcohol users from 1919 to the repeal of Prohibition in 1933, with narcotics' users after 1914 and with marijuana users after 1937.

It might be comforting could we believe that, as new drugs are introduced and their use gradually assimilated into the culture, public attitudes toward them would follow a kind of "natural history" that moves gradually from fear coupled with attempts at suppression through growing social, if not necessarily legal, toleration (both as effect and further cause of the drug's use), to full legal and social acceptance. In a long-gone day both tobacco and alcohol were condemned and reviled as diabolic, unhealthy, and morally corrupting to individuals and society. Despite attempts to suppress them or to restrict their use public demand finally won acceptance for both, notwithstanding the patently destructive effects of excessive alcohol consumption to health and life itself.

Yet, both the Harrison Act and Prohibition were enacted in an access of misplaced moralism long after opiates and alcohol both had seemed secure in public acceptance. The effect of such legislative enactment was to transform what might have remained the personal psychological problem of their users into major social problems. A potentially more convincing explanation for the repressive American attitude toward drugs, especially toward the psychedelics, would point out that no society can permit the very principles and values by which it lives to be undermined and would further point to the traditional anti-hedonistic moralism of American culture, its implacable, religiously grounded hostility to pleasure as an end in itself. Drugs that sustain or restore a man's capacity to work or that aid him to function "normally" may be countenanced (if not necessarily approved) but those that have no other purpose than to give pleasure and insight (a "good trip") and whose effects often suggest that "normal" social functioning may in fact be little more than the quintessence of folly, meaninglessness, and neurosis pose a threat to society that cannot go unmet. It is from this point of view that the new drug use poses a disconcerting challenge to the conscience, the complacency, and the social structure of contemporary America.

In our first selection Leslie Farber, a psychoanalyst, characterizes our entire society as addicted—addicted to addiction. We live in what he chooses to call the "Age of the Disordered Will" and we try, through the use of many drugs, to bridge the gulf between our will and the aims of our willing. For most Americans drugs have become the answer to their "problems in living," the path to a spurious sense of integrity and wholeness. While Farber admits that drugs do sometimes allow us to function more effectively he concludes that we pay a price in the deadening of our imaginative and critical faculties, that drugs accentuate our usual behavioral traits rather than allowing the emergence of new ones. Drugs, in other words, make us more what we already are.

In the next selection Kenneth Keniston presents a social-psychological analysis of the use of psychedelic drugs (he refers to them as "hallucinogenic") among contemporary college students. After estimating the number and distribution of student users Keniston presents a typology of users, whom he calls "tasters," "seekers," and "heads." He then proceeds to delineate the modal personality patterns of the latter two groups. Rather than viewing drug use with alarm or dismay Keniston sees it as part of a general pattern of experimentation, of a quest for meaning on the part of intelligent, sensitive young people. He sees the hippie subculture as a rest and rehabilitation area, a counter-culture in which alienated youth can search for meaning and examine its personal experience while withdrawing from the demands of the larger society. Most hippies, Keniston notes, reemerge after a year or two and reenter the mainstream of society. At the same time he sees this withdrawal and its associated drug use both as a response to a definite constellation of social forces and as a negation by many young people of any belief in the possibility of meaningful involvement with society's established institutions. Drug use may thus be an ominous portent for the future of American society; at the least it should compel us to ask whether its causes lie in the idiosyncrasies or weaknesses of individual personalities or in the very structure of our society, in its failure to provide worthwhile causes to which young people can commit their loyalties and energies.

Timothy Leary has for some time been the leading spirit and intellectual mentor of the psychedelic movement. He begins his article on a familiar theme: the distinction between behavior and consiousness (or subjective experience), between subject and object. For Leary, behavior, including psychiatry and psychology, is a series of learned games (we might also call them cultural stereotypes) that are played according to determinate, discoverable rules. Because most people are unaware of the game character of reality they mistake the rules of their particular games for the "natural" and inescapable "laws" of human behavior. For Leary it is visionary experience that alone permits us to move beyond mere game-playing, to see the reality of our previous games and to develop new and more appropriate ones. Once this insight has been won, once consciousness has been altered, behavior can change rapidly and dramatically. The most efficient means to this change of consciousness is, in Leary's view, the use of consciousness expanding (psychedelic) drugs. Yet, Leary candidly admits that even the consciousness expanding experience is a game and he concludes that what society needs is good games rather than no games at all. That change itself would be a revolutionary transformation. (The alert reader may note that Leary's game model of behavior and his model of behavior change can both be restated in terms of Skinnerian learning theory and behavior therapy. If you would care to try such a restatement ask yourself what, if anything, is lost in the translation.)

In the final selection Sanford Unger discusses the psychological and physiological effects of the three most popular consciousness expanding drugs (compare Harry Asher's account in Selection 24) and concludes that the effects of all three are virtually equivalent. While he admits that individual personality differences can influence the effect of drug use Unger emphasizes the expectations of the user and the context in which he takes the drug as overriding personality factors and largely determining the kind of experience the user will have, especially with LSD. (Under the rubric "set and setting" Leary and Richard Alpert have emphasized the same factors.) When LSD is used in connection with psychotherapy the attitudes and expectations of the therapist can be decisive in determining the patient's experience with the drug. Unger then reviews some of the therapeutic uses of LSD, especially its dramatic successes in the treatment of alcoholism. It would be more than a little ironic if such a politically unacceptable drug as LSD were to prove successful in overcoming the destructive effects of such a politically favored drug as alcohol. Yet, of such ironies is history often made. Regrettably, Unger's concluding plea for more research and openmindedness in this entire area has gone largely unheeded.

54. OURS IS THE ADDICTED SOCIETY

Leslie H. Farber

This has been called the "Age of Anxiety." Considering the attention given the subject by psychology, theology, literature, and the pharmaceutical industry, not to mention the testimony from our own lives, we could fairly well conclude that there is more anxiety today, and, moreover, that there is definitely more anxiety about anxiety now than there has been in previous epochs of history. Nevertheless, I would hesitate to characterize this as an "Age of Anxiety," just as I would be loath to call this an "Age of Affluence," "Coronary Disease," "Mental Health," "Dieting," "Conformity," or "Sexual Freedom," my reason being that none of these labels, whatever fact or truth they may involve, goes to the heart of the matter.

Much as I dislike this game of labels, my preference would be to call this the "Age of the Disordered Will." It takes only a glance to see a few of the myriad varieties of willing what cannot be willed that enslave us: We will to sleep, will to read fast, will to have simultaneous orgasm, will to be creative and spontaneous, will to enjoy our old age, and, most urgently, will to will.

If anxiety is more prominent in our time, such anxiety is the product of our particular modern disability of will. To this disability, rather than to anxiety, I would attribute the ever-increasing dependence on drugs affecting all levels of our society. While drugs do offer relief from anxiety, their more important task is to offer the illusion of healing the split between the will and its refractory object. The resulting feeling of wholeness may not be a responsible one, but at least within that wholeness—no matter how perverse the

drugged state may appear to an outsider—there seems to be, briefly and subjectively, a responsible and vigorous will. This is the reason, I believe, that the addictive possibilities of our age are so enormous.

Let me be more specific about the addictive consequence of this disability of will which, in varying degree, affects us all. Increasingly, I believe we are addicted to addiction. This is to say that, with few exceptions, we subscribe to the premise—whether implicit or explicit—that this life cannot be lived without drugs. And those who would repudiate this unpleasant premise by living without drugs are still more or less captive to it, in that so much of their consciousness must be given over to withstanding the chemical temptations that beset them. Withstanding is a lesser evil than yielding, but it is no escape from the issue of addiction, so that I would have to characterize the predicament as one of being addicted to not being addicted. I do not mean to suggest that we choose one course or the other, but rather that both the premise and its negative variation exist in all of us. Even the most debilitated heroin addict retains his pride in the few items to which he has not become addicted.

Not many years ago, we had best remind ourselves, the problem of addiction seemed confined to a few chemicals—narcotics, alcohol and, perhaps, barbiturates—and it was then possible to make fairly clear distinctions between addiction and habituation, based mainly on the presence or absence of physiological withdrawal symptoms. However, today, even the well-publicized and allegedly extreme agonies of heroin withdrawal have been disputed by the Lazaruses who came back. Recently, a member of Synanon expressed to a reporter his disagreement with the fictional clichés which have acquired the status of scientific fact, remarking: "Kicking the habit is easy. It's not like that Frank Sinatra movie, crawling all over the walls. Sure, it's tough for a couple of days, but it's more like getting over a bad cold."

Fearing this view might be as extravagant in one direction as Nelson Algren's violent imaginings were in another, I checked with a friend who had been a staff member at Lexington.* He thought the "bad-cold" analogy an accurate one, and added: "We had far more trouble with withdrawal symptoms in barbiturate users."

Our appropriation of the drug-user's vocabulary for our own purposes shows the extent to which the problem of addiction has invaded our daily existence. When our absorption with not only a chemical but a person, an activity, an ideology seems to have more weight than is warranted, we say we are "hooked," meaning either that we wish we could be cured of our vice or else that we value the passion contained in our infatuation.

If someone or something excites us pleasurably, we say he or it "turns us on," but if our response is indifference or boredom, we are "turned off." Our extension of these terms for our own purposes is, to some degree, a fashionable reaction to the notoriety drugs have earned in the mass media. However, my own belief is that we resort to the junkie vocabulary because it expresses a metaphysical or addictive shift in our existence that the older vocabulary did not quite account for—at least in ordinary usage.

Even if we try to restrict ourselves to drugtaking, statistics about the extent and degree of addiction are hard to come by. Certainly we are no longer surprised to learn of the growing proportion of college students who resort to such drugs as marijuana, amphetamines, barbiturates, LSD, tranquilizers. One expert is quoted in *The New York Times* to the effect that about 40 per cent of the students at the University of California use drugs from time to time. This figure falls somewhat short of Timothy Leary's immoderate proclamation: "Today, in the molecular age, the issue is not what books you read or which symbols you use, but which chemicals are part of your life and your growth."

Numerical estimates notwithstanding, on the theory that convicts tend to riot for those

privileges society deems essential, such as humane treatment, recreation, adequate food, civil rights, I am more persuaded by this news release:

> "WALPOLE, Mass., Aug. 13 (AP)—Inmates rioted outside a medication dispensary at the Massachusetts State Prison in an attempt to steal drugs late last night, injuring nine guards.... Two guards were stabbed and five others beaten as the inmates pushed their way into the 'pill' room, yelling, thrashing and literally gobbling down as many pills as they could at one time...State Police Cpl. James Dunne, who led the squad equipped with 12-gauge shotguns, gas masks and crash helmets, said about 18 of the inmates were reeling 'on Cloud Nine' when he arrived..."

And from industry, where access to drugs is sufficiently relaxed not to require riots, I offer this item:

> "LOS ANGELES, Oct. 9 (Los Angeles Times)— Use of illegal drugs in industry, especially among production-line workers, is so common that to arrest everybody who sold or used them would mean some plants would have to hire whole new shifts of employes, according to a police narcotics specialist. The drugs most commonly used are amphetamine sulfate compounds and barbiturate derivatives, which keep workers awake, or put them to sleep..."

Since it is forbidden to peddle or "push" most drugs, including whisky, on television, Madison Avenue has responded to the double dilemma of addiction by advertising aspirin as though it were *the* drug for every tribulation we must undergo. On television we are shown scenes in which mothers snap at their children, employers lose their tempers with employes. With only an awkward swipe at the questionable ethics of permitting this poor old headache remedy to carry such a heavy burden, advertisers show these embattled and suffering creatures putting one hand to their heads while a kindly neighbor advises them that this new aspirin combination is the perfect cure for "tension." The happy scenes following their use of the drug are deliberate efforts to imitate the style in which the pharmaceutical companies persuade physicians of the virtues of their products.

Most touching are aspirin commercials in which an aging movie star, long past his prime and no longer regularly employed, sits thoughtfully in his well-appointed study, telling the television audience that movie-making is a

---

* The United States Public Health Service hospital for drug addicts at Lexington, Kentucky. (Eds.)

hectic and demanding affair. To avoid tension and headache, intrinsic to such activity, he has always resorted to this particular remedy.

Although probably unintentional, such a commercial goes to the heart of addiction, for we must contemplate the pathos of this formerly glamorous creature whose powers have so dwindled that he is reduced to doing headache commercials in which, fooling no one, he pretends nothing has changed. As he holds his bottle of pills to the audience, he seems to say life is really impossible without these pills. But we know, and he knows, that aspirin is not enough; for the vast restitution he demands of life, more powerful drugs are needed.

Should he seek them, he will not have to resort to any illicit drug traffic. He will have no trouble finding a physician who will pre-scribe amphetamines or psychic energizers to brighten his mood as he waits for calls from his agent. And if the phone refuses to ring, one or several of the many tranquilizers can be prescribed so that he can endure the wait-ing. Whatever insomnia may have originally been his lot will now be painfully exacerbated by his drug-taking so that other sedatives, fortified often by alcohol, will insure his sleep-ing. As he moves from one drug to another, mixing and testing the chemicals he believes his state requires and countering their dis-agreeable effects with still other chemicals, from time to time the sheer immodest scope of his undertaking will strike him; he has be-come a deranged chemist, his only laboratory his own poor body.

No matter how haggard that body becomes, he must unfortunately depend on it for fresh chemical inspiration. And, if everything else fails, there is LSD for instant revelation, if not wisdom, about the pretentious games that have brought him to this impasse, allowing him the death and rebirth that are now ac-cepted pieties of the LSD mystique.

While it is true that the medical profession and the pharmaceutical industry together are the largest and most powerful group of pushers for the new drugs, I see no conspiracy on their part to make addicts of us all. It has long been common knowledge that physicians are the most devoted users of the drugs they prescribe, unlike the more disreputable pushers whose livelihood depends on abstaining from the drugs they peddle. The men who devise and merchandise these pills and the physicians who dispense them are, by and large, decent human beings who share the same disability of will that afflicts everyone.

Believing, as we do, that we should be able to will ourselves to be calm, cheerful, thin, industrious, creative—and, moreover, to have a good night's sleep—they simply provide the products to collaborate in such willing. If the satisfactions turn out to be short-lived and spurious and if their cost in terms of emo-tion, intellect and physical health is disagree-able, these scientists are ready to concoct new drugs to counter this discomfort. In other words, they offer us always new chances—virtually to the point of extinction—to will away the unhappiness that comes from willing ourselves to be happy.

Recently, Dr. Carroll L. Witten, president-elect of the American Academy of General Practice, was quoted in the press as being in agreement with a report issued this year by the United Nations Commission on Narcotics which expressed concern over "the alarming rise in the sale of barbiturates, tranquilizers and amphetamines."

The report suggested further that the "ex-plosive expansion of the use of drugs...was most likely a result of their being used less as medication than as agents for producing sleep, a sense of happiness and relaxation." Dr. Witten declared:

> "I believe these drugs are not only used wrong-ly, to excess and without adequate indication, but that in many cases their indiscriminate use has led to dependency, habituation and addic-tion, with all of the consequent results thereof."

Dr. Witten said he was referring specifically to the non-narcotic drugs used as "psychic energizers, stimulators, activators, deactiva-tors, depressants, alleviators, levelers, eleva-tors or in whatever imaginative category one might place them. One must note with a great deal of alarm," he declared, "that the vast majority of cases first obtained their drugs through the prescription of a physician."

If willing what cannot be willed has led us to being addicted to addiction, it would seem that our addictive appetite will always be more than a match for the ever-mounting number of chemicals that are fashioned to gratify that appetite. And even if we eliminate actual drugs from our consideration, the addictive possibilities are endless: cigarettes, chocolate, detective and spy stories, football on television, psychoanalysis—to mention only a few of my own excesses, which I would unhesitatingly characterize as addictive. Everyone, I am convinced, has his own list, as well as another more prideful list of those objects and activities whose addictive claims he has successfully withstood.

If the term is not to be altogether meaningless, some distinction must now be made between one addiction and another. Concretely, when it comes to putting myself to sleep, how shall I distinguish between detective stories and sleeping pills? Or between watching football on TV and enduring my Sunday with tranquilizers? Or completing a tedious chore on amphetamines and procrastinating as usual?

The first generalization I would make about these sets of alternatives is that in an immediate sense drugs are clearly more effective. Detective stories, for me at least, are not entirely reliable as sedatives. If the story is so poor as to outrage or challenge my diminished sensibilities, I am in trouble, whereas I can always take another sleeping pill.

Watching even an exciting, well-played football game on TV, I cannot entirely obliterate from my awareness the perception that there are other ways in which I could more profitably spend my time. And if the game is inept and boring and still I do not turn the set off, my view of my condition is grim indeed. On the other hand, with tranquilizers, I could achieve a state of not unpleasant relaxation, unruffled by the sort of nagging self-concern which interrupts my absorption with even a good football game.

It is the last set of alternatives that will prove the most troublesome. If I have a group of evaluations of psychoanalytic candidates to write, I am inclined to put it off. The reasons and/or rationalizations for my procrastination will be various: I don't feel well; such reports are too tedious to be endured; I resent the bureaucratic rule requiring these reports; I am reluctant to set myself up as a judge of the performance of these young men; I am convinced I am not equal to the imaginative discriminations that would do these human beings justice.

With a dose of amphetamine, however, my self-concern, with its associated fatigue and hesitations and doubts, will vanish, so that in a singleminded way I shall vigorously engage my task. Within a few hours all the evaluations will be completed. Like a schoolboy who has at the last minute finished his term paper, I shall feel relieved and virtuous to have at long last done what my organization demands of me.

Reading over my reports after I have recovered from the drug, I may be chagrined to note a breathless, assertive and yet self-indulgent quality to my writing that did not trouble me at the time. But I can counter my dissatisfaction by assuring myself these deficiencies matter very little, since I have done all that was asked of me. It was my own sin of pride that initially led me to regard my task as such an intricate and demanding responsibility. Besides, I will tell myself, wasn't it a choice between doing nothing and doing something, however imperfectly?

Thus will my mood of accomplishment prevail, helping me to disown my self-criticism and perhaps persuading me, since I won't have to read these reports again, that I had indeed been discriminating in preparing them. And my earlier doubts as to whether these evaluations should have been written at all can be postponed for another time.

The sensation of being a going, if unquestioning, member of society should not be slighted, because it is hard to come by these days. Nevertheless, we must concede that while the drugs in these sets of alternatives may be more effective, their effectiveness is largely dependent on the chemical deadening of important imaginative and critical capacities, whose privileges are admittedly problematic. Practically every drug invented, from opium to LSD, has had its champions in both science and the arts who insisted that their particular brew was not only not reductive but was actually heightening of human potentiality.

The objective evidence for their claims, however, has always been depressing, and of the same order as my own reports, whether it be the music played under marijuana or heroin, the pictures painted and the poetry composed under LSD, the deadlines met by means of amphetamines, or even—perhaps especially—the perceptions and insights granted by drugs.

At this point, the question must be raised: aren't other addictions—nondrug addictions—also reductive? The answer has to be a qualified affirmative. The friend watching me glued for hours to the television set, isolated from all intelligible life, impervious to the claims of my children who have waited all week to have a few moments with me, has to find my human condition bizarre, to say the least.

Far more seriously incapacitating, of course, are those nondrug addictions that involve ideas and habits of thought. Those who over the years develop an addiction to shopworn ideologies—religious, scientific, political, esthetic, psychological—in a sense forfeit, in willful dedication, the very capacities of spirit and intellect that might set them free.

Nevertheless, there is a difference between drugs and no drugs. While disdain and denial of these capacities will cause them to shrivel and grow ever more paralyzed as years go by, there remains the possibility of a response, however minimal at first, to some human claim. Chemical deadening, on the other hand, if pursued, will, by its very nature, render such capacities eventually heedless to any call.

But to return to my evaluations of those psychoanalytic candidates—my will, with the help of amphetamine, has had its undiscriminating way in my reports, without the reflective give-and-take between me and my writing that could be called dialogic, causing this enterprise to resemble other headstrong monologic sprees in which the speaker is deaf and blind to those about him at the same time that he is convinced of a singular openness and freedom and mutuality to the exchange.

The nonuser has a dispiriting effect on groups enthusiastically consolidated by such convictions, so that they would prefer him to find his own sober companions. And his response to them will be marked by his discouraged observation that, despite the cries of mutual congratulation, all he can hear are colliding monologues, breathlessly composed so that each participant gives in to his own worst headstrong and literal-minded inclinations.

The person who ordinarily must guard against his habit of vast abstraction now becomes even more abstract in his theoretical pronouncements. The person top-heavy with esthetic sensibility becomes even more indulgent to that side of himself, abdicating his ability to temper such estheticism with moral and psychological discriminations.

The most blatant examples of the literal-minded aspect of the drugged state come from the public writings on LSD, but it is by no means restricted to this particular drug. Under LSD, it would seem one is at the mercy of any fancy that strikes him, much like the hypnotic subject responding to the commands of the hypnotist. Should he note that his hand is ugly, that hand becomes literally swollen and grotesque. Should the thought strike him that he is alone in the world, he will quickly and literally find himself as one small mortal in the midst of an endless desolate landscape. In each instance, what properly should be no more than a beginning metaphor has been exalted, at the behest of the will, into physical reality. Similarly, the death undergone with LSD can be regarded as more deathly than death itself. In a section, jarringly titled "Running Smack Into Your Essence," of "LSD: The Acid Test," published in *Ramparts,* one evangelist, Donavan Bess, wrote:

"The psychedelic death is especially lonely— lonelier, perhaps, than for the soldier who physically dies in a Vietnamese field hospital. He at least has the comfort of cuddling up in the image of his mother. Under LSD you have no such bourgeois comfort; you have no familial figure at all. You die grown up. If you can hang onto that, afterward, you can offer society some adult values. You came to this point in a rite of passage as explicit, as terrible and as meaningful as those rites used in aboriginal Australia."

In considering the addictive state which may result from drugs, narcotic and non-narcotic, I must of course neglect the specific effects each drug has or purports to have on the central nervous system. An unfortunate consequence of such neglect will be to give the false impression that my own addiction to nonaddiction has led me to advocate an impossibly ascetic life, requiring abstention from all chemical assistance, come what may. Let me quickly insist that all the drugs I have mentioned may be taken in nonaddictive ways for reasons that are appropriate to the effects of the particular drug. This is to say, there are times when prolonged sleeplessness can and should be interrupted by sedatives, just as there are painful occasions when morphine is the only answer. Even amphetamines may allow the completion of a low-level chore.

The difficulty, however, here, as indicated earlier, is that the mood of accomplishment may persuade us to disregard the quality, or lack of quality, of our performance, not to mention the disagreeable side-effects, so that we turn to the drug in situations that require more of our wits and equanimity than amphetamines will allow. Perhaps a greater danger, as the use of amphetamines becomes more widespread, is that the deadlines asked of us are increasingly determined by the amphetamine intoxications of those who ask. (Another illustration of the manner in which the drugged state influences social values is suggested by aspirin commercials referred to in this article. The writers of these advertisements seem to be selling not only aspirin but also their conviction—possibly arrived at through their own experience with tranquilizers —that our ordinary difficulties, since they are only subjective and therefore not worth contending with, are best erased with drugs. Thus, an advertisement for meprobamate, addressed to physicians, shows a picture of an overwrought mother with a child, the caption reading: "Her kind of pressures last all day ...shouldn't her tranquilizer?")

For the sake of completeness, alcohol and marijuana are two drugs whose object is explicitly pleasure, and which may be used nonaddictively. However, too much has been made recently by the younger generation of the nonaddictive properties of marijuana simply because its physical effects are less dramatic than those of alcohol and other drugs. More dramatic is its effect upon relations: the pleasures of monologue, experienced as dialogue under the drug, persist as a habit of tolerance for such illusion—which in a sense is the very issue of addiction.

Let us consider briefly the addictive course —from initial pleasure to ultimate disaster— that will result from prolonged and excessive use of any of the drugs I have mentioned, singly or in combination.

The first subjective experience of wholeness and the pleasure accompanying it will acquire its intensity partly through contrast with the discomfort which preceded the use of the drug and partly through the manner a particular drug answers a particular person's need at a particular time. Thus, users are labeled according to their preferences as "Up-Heads" or "Speed-Heads," "Down-Heads," "Acid-Heads," "Pot-Heads," "Lushes," "Junkies."

With further sophistication and availability, and the cooperation of the medical profession,

drug-users already are specializing less and availing themselves more of other products and mixtures of products. But the initial feeling of well-being is difficult to duplicate precisely, regardless of the ingenuity of the user. As the drug and the state associated with it begin to wear off, the user returns to a world which has lost none of its oppressiveness and with which, in the midst of the drug hangover, he feels less able to cope.

The distance between himself and the wholeness he sought has grown somewhat, so that he is now vulnerable to the beginning belief that the relief the drug afforded is an extraordinary sort of transcendence which his usual life with others cannot provide, except in the occasional unpredictable and surprising manner in which such moments arise. In other words, he has been burned by the demonic and addictive notion that he need not wait on life for the transcendence he seeks, that he may invoke it whenever he so decrees or wills by returning to the drug or drugs which first allowed him this remarkable feeling.

With this seeming triumph of his will, he will be more impatient of the often frustrating give-and-take of life without drugs, willfully demanding his well-being of those about him and thereby suffering even more the penalties of such willing. In a sense he insists futilely that life now be his drug.

Needless to say, his mounting impatience will be inimical to the exercise or development of such qualities as imagination, judgment, humor, tact. And should he glimpse, however dimly, his impoverishment, he may wish to believe these qualities at least can return with drugs, disowning the evidence accumulating to the contrary. However, without these qualities he is more and more confined to the exigencies of the moment, for he can no longer really remember his drug experience in the past nor can he imagine what may follow. As his intolerance for life without drugs increases, his competence for such life diminishes, so that with every return to the drug he is, in the spirit of Heraclitus, a different and lesser person who attempts to cross the same stream twice.

What seemed the feeling of transcendence at the beginning has long since been abandoned as his drug goal in favor merely of getting from one moment to the next, in favor of mindlessly and minimally staying alive.

What began with his will to decree well-being for himself without having to wait on life now culminates in almost a paralysis of will for every trivial action, even getting dressed or feeding himself. It is as though all the taken-for-granted stream of activity had disintegrated into a swarm of tiny yet insurmountable enterprises for his will, every one seeming to require further drugs for its accomplishment.

As a result of the bombardment of his body by such large dosages of drugs, his physical debilitation grows extreme. Yet even this bodily exhaustion and derangement offers a last resort to the will which is now unequal to practically every small movement in his world. Unlike other depleting illnesses that mysteriously overtake us, this one has been induced by himself and seems to be within his control. That is, he may try to assuage his agonies with more chemicals or he can withdraw the noxious agent so that his body can slowly recover its strength.

All other dramas in which his will has been involved have given way now to the one small immediate drama of whether he shall live or die to this world. It is a far cry from the transcendence he sought originally, but every addict knows the drama of his failing body is the last plot his will must confront. Unlike the proponents of LSD, he is beyond metaphysical conceits about the meaning of dying to this world, nor will he glamorize recovery, to whatever degree it may occur, as spiritual rebirth.

Nietzsche, I believe, was not as interested in theological argument about the disappearance of the divine will in our lives as he was in the consequences of its disappearance. Today, the evidence is in. Out of disbelief we have impudently assumed that all of life is now subject to our own will. And the disasters that have come from willing what cannot be willed have not at all brought us to some modesty about our presumptions. Instead, we have turned to chemicals, which seem to enhance our willful strivings. It was only a question of time before man, in his desperation, would locate divinity in drugs and on that artificial rock build his church.

55. *HEADS AND SEEKERS:*

Drugs on Campus, Counter-Cultures and American Society

Kenneth Keniston

...The term "drug" covers a multitude of substances that affect human physiology and functioning. Virtually every American is a routine user of prescribed and unprescribed

From THE AMERICAN SCHOLAR, *Vol. 38, No. 1, Winter 1968–69, pp. 99–112 (slightly abridged). Copyright © 1968 by the United Chapters of Phi Beta Kappa. Reprinted by permission of the publishers and the author.*

psychoactive drugs like aspirin, alcohol, sleeping pills or stimulants whose primary intended effect is to alter mood, feeling, or psychological states. Indeed, at the present time, more than seventy percent of all prescriptions written in the United States are for psychoactive compounds—for example, tranquilizers, painkillers and antidepressants. If we include—as we must—ethyl alcohol, caffeine and nicotine among drugs, then the American who has never "used" drugs is a statistical freak.

Although drug use itself is not novel in American society, what is novel is the student use of new types of drugs for the sole purpose of altering mood and state of consciousness. Most student drug use involves the hallucinogens—a family of nonaddictive drugs that includes not only marihuana (cannabis) but other hallucinogenic, psychedelic or psychotomimetic drugs like LSD, DMT, STP, psilocybin and mescaline (peyote). Some of these drugs have been widely used since the beginning of recorded history, others are recent discoveries; what is new, then, is their use by a growing segment of American college youth. To be sure, most definitions of "drug abuse" lump together distinct individuals for whom drug use and experimentation have very different meanings. But for a start, let us accept the prevailing definition of "drug user" as anyone who has *ever* tried any one of the hallucinogens, and examine the pattern of use that results from accepting this definition.

Student drug use, defined as use of the hallucinogens, is rapidly increasing. But the widely publicized estimates that one in seven, one in four, or one in two of the seven million college students in America can be considered a "drug abuser" are vastly exaggerated. Even at those few colleges where drug use is most prevalent, surveys arrive at estimates of between five and seventy-five percent of the student body who have "ever used" any of the hallucinogens. These studies, furthermore, tend to have been conducted at select colleges like California at Berkeley, Wisconsin at Madison, Michigan at Ann Arbor, Harvard, Stanford, Yale, Cal. Tech, Princeton, Antioch, Swarthmore, Wesleyan (Connecticut), Goddard and Reed. Approximately three percent of American college students attend these institutions. Among the remaining ninety-seven percent, it already seems clear that drug use is far rarer, and in many instances nonexistent. A recent Gallup Poll arrives at an estimate of five to six percent of college youth who have "ever tried" any hallucinogenic drug. Thus, while student drug use constitutes an important phenomenon, it probably touches directly less than one in ten of the young Americans who attend institutions of higher education.

The public impression of astronomically high rates of drug use in American college youth stems in part from the great visibility of the colleges where drug use is most common. Students of college cultures have found it useful to categorize colleges according to the relative presence or absence of what they term an "intellectual climate." The correlation between "intellectual climate" and rates of drug use is very close. That is, the highest rates are found at small, progressive, liberal arts colleges with a nonvocational orientation, a high faculty-student ratio, high student intellectual caliber as measured by College Boards, close student-faculty relationships, and a great value placed on the academic independence, intellectual interests, and personal freedom of students. At perhaps a dozen or so such colleges, it seems likely that the proportion of students who have ever tried marihuana or some other hallucinogen exceeds fifty percent. But there are more than twenty-two hundred other colleges in the country.

Farther down the list, with regard to both intellectual climate and drug use, are the private university colleges, like Harvard, Stanford, Yale and Chicago, and the major state universities, like Michigan, Wisconsin and California, with a tradition (at least within their Colleges of Arts and Sciences) of intellectual excellence and academic freedom. Included on this list, as well, should be the major technological institutions like Cal. Tech and M.I.T., notable for the extremely high ability of students they recruit. At such colleges, student drug use rates of between ten and fifty percent will be found at present.[1] Still farther down on the list are other state universities with a lesser reputation for academic excellence and intellectual or personal freedom. Here one thinks of colleges like Ohio State and the University of Oregon. At such institutions rates of drug use probably vary between five and twenty percent. At the bottom of the list in terms of both student drug use and intellectual climate are those colleges that together enroll the majority of American students—upgraded state teachers colleges, junior colleges, community colleges, normal schools, the smaller religious and denominational colleges, and most Catholic col-

1 Regional differences are also important: drug use is higher on the West Coast than on the East Coast. Also, proximity to a metropolitan center probably increases drug use, other things being equal.

leges and universities. On such campuses, student drug use rarely exceeds five percent. These are the colleges most notable for their vocational and practical orientation, the absence of serious student intellectual interests, and the presence of strong anti-intellectual student subcultures centered around technical training and/or social activities like sports and fraternities.

Nor are drug users randomly distributed *within* any one institution. At large universities that include a number of separate "schools," drug use is concentrated in the College of Arts and Sciences, the Graduate School, and in the Schools of Drama, Music, Art and Architecture. Rates of drug use are notably lower in such schools as Business Administration, Engineering, Agronomy and Education. Furthermore, within any school or faculty, drug users are most likely to be found in the most intellectual, humanistic and "introspective" fields (for example, music, literature, drama, the arts and psychology); they are likely to be less common in practical, applied, extroverted and "harder" areas like engineering or economics. Indeed, there is evidence from one liberal arts college that students who use drugs are characterized by *higher* grades than those who do not. The demographic evidence suggests a strong relationship between intellectuality and drug use within the college population.

These inferences, however, are open to two different interpretations. On the one hand, we might conclude that colleges with an "intellectual climate" recruit students with special personal characteristics that make them more prone to experiment with drugs. The institution, according to this view, merely acts as a magnet for young men and women who are likely to smoke pot no matter where they go to college. On the other hand, it could be argued that the climate and culture of some colleges actively push students toward drug use regardless of their personal characteristics. If a student attends a college where "everyone" is using drugs, he is more likely to do so himself. Similarly, certain college pressures (for example, relentless pressure for grades) or certain administrative practices (for example, respect for student autonomy) may also increase the likelihood of student drug use. In practice, both these interpretations seem correct: some colleges attract large numbers of potential drug users and then expose them

to a climate in which using drugs becomes even more probable. To understand this interaction, we must consider types of drug users, motivations for drug use, and some of the pressures on college students today.

TASTERS, SEEKERS AND HEADS

A "drug abuser" is often defined as anyone who has ever experimented with any of the hallucinogens—who has ever inhaled marihuana, ever ingested any other hallucinogenic drug, or, in some instances, ever taken a barbiturate to get to sleep or an amphetamine (Benzedrine, Dexedrine) before an examination. If we limit ourselves to the hallucinogens, however, we usually find that up to half of the students listed as "users" turn out to have "used" drugs no more than three times, and to have no plans to continue. To call such students drug "abusers" or even "users" is misleading. It is like applying the epithet "alcoholic" or "drinker" to the college girl who once tasted a sip of beer but didn't like it, or labeling as a "smoker" the adult who at the age of twelve smoked a cigarette behind the barn but was sick and never smoked again. Probably the single largest group called "drug abusers" are in reality *tasters*. Such individuals have no place in a discussion of why students use drugs, since these particular students no longer use them.

If we eliminate the tasters from the ranks of student drug users, we are left with a contingent of probably less than five percent of the college population. These students have used drugs (usually marihuana) a number of times, and they tell us that they "plan" to continue their experimentation. But even within this group of continuing users there are important distinctions to be made. The largest single group of actual drug users are students who have used drugs a relatively small number of times (for example, have smoked pot less than fifteen times) and who do not use them regularly (for example, not every weekend). Such a pattern of use generally indicates that, despite willingness to continue drug experimentation, the individual has in no way organized his life around it. For these occasional users, drug use is generally a part of a more general pattern of experimentation and search for relevance both within and without the college experience—it is one aspect of a more encompassing effort to find meaning in life. Such students can be termed *seekers*, in that they seek in drug use some way of intensifying experience, expanding awareness, breaking out of deadness and flatness, or overcoming depression.

Finally, there is a relatively small but highly visible group of students who have made drug use a central focus of college life. Such students use drugs often and "regularly" —for example, every weekend—and they often experiment with a variety of different drugs. For such young men and women, drug use is not just an intermittent assist in the pursuit of meaning, but a part of a more general "turned-on" ideology, and a membership card to one of the collegiate versions of the hippie subculture. Such students are generally called *heads* (pot-heads or acid-heads) by their contemporaries; and they are by far the most knowledgeable about the effects, side effects, interactions and meanings of the drugs available to students today.

But even among heads, drug use does not invariably constitute the deeply psychopathological and self-destructive phenomenon it is sometimes said invariably to be. Many such students have sufficient strength of character (and perhaps of physiology) to endure regular experimentation with marihuana (and even with more powerful hallucinogens or amphetamines) without suffering any enduring personal disorganization. Many students who use marihuana routinely do *not* experience the ominous personal deterioration, the "bad trips" or the loss of motivation that is sometimes thought to accompany even casual drug experimentation. To be sure, one of the intended effects of drug use is to produce a *transient* alteration of experience and consciousness; and to those who view this alteration from the outside, it may appear deplorable. Yet a majority of students who have used the hallucinogens report that the experience was enlightening, enjoyable or meaningful. Most students who use marihuana regularly, and many of those who use the more powerful hallucinogens, never appear in clinics or consulting rooms (much less psychiatric hospitals). They "recover" from the drug experience, not obviously the worse for the wear, sometimes proclaiming loudly that they have gained a profound and valuable (if usually ineffable) insight into their own natures or that of the world. Judged by such criteria of mental health as the ability to work, to love

and to play, such individuals do not seem especially less "mentally healthy" than before their drug experiences.

A smaller but highly publicized group of "heads," however, suffers serious ill effects from even single experiences with the hallucinogens. Students with serious preexisting psychopathology are most vulnerable. And these same students seem most likely to experiment with drugs under conditions that even experienced drug users consider adverse —intense depression, personal isolation and unpleasant surroundings. In extremely rare instances, marihuana can produce panic states or transient psychotic reactions, and similar reactions to LSD have been reported more often. Perhaps more important than the highly dramatic but usually reversible drug psychosis is the danger of lapsing into some relatively enduring form of personal disorganization— most commonly, a life-style that involves a virtually total and apparently self-destructive immersion in a drug-using "hippie" subculture.

Yet even here, short-term changes and long-range effects need to be distinguished. There are clearly some individuals who "regress" into a drug-using subculture for a period of months and even years, but who eventually reemerge into a productive relationship with their fellow man and with society itself. "Dropping out" into the hippie world seems to be defined, for growing numbers of students, as a way of testing psychological and social limits as a preparation for returning to the world of action and commitment. To be sure, most Americans would argue that there are better ways of testing the relationship of self to society than by entering the hippie subculture for two years. But our evaluation of the "ominous" implications of student drug use must be tempered by an awareness that many of those who "drop out" into the drug-using world eventually slide back into the mainstream. One of the disadvantages of the opprobrium that attends drug use is that labeling drug users "felons" or irredeemable "addicts" may in fact make it virtually impossible for them to return to a productive role in society.

THE QUESTION OF MOTIVES

Drug use is no different from any other form of human behavior, in that a great variety of distinct motives can cooperate to produce it. The particular weight of each of these motives and the way they are combined differs in each individual. Furthermore, drug use is affected not only by motives and forces *within* the individual, but by what is happening *outside* of him in his interpersonal environment, and in the wider social and political world. Thus, any effort to delineate "types" of motivations that enter into drug use is bound to be an oversimplification. For example, there are many individuals who share common characteristics with drug users but who do not use drugs because drugs are not available on their particular campus. Similarly, there are individuals who have little in common with other drug users, but who nonetheless use drugs.

With these important qualifications, at least two of the more common patterns of motivation in student drug users can be defined. Consider first the "seekers." Occasional but continuing drug users are rarely part of the hippie subculture, but such students do tend to have certain common characteristics. They are generally better-than-average students; they are intellectual and antivocational in their approach to their educations; and they are likely to be uncertain as to their future career plans. Sociologically, they tend to come from upper-middle-class professional and business families. Psychologically, such students are usually intense, introspective and genuinely involved in their academic work, from which they hope to find "solutions" to the problems of life and society. (Often, however, they are disappointed in this hope.) As individuals, they usually have a great capacity for hard work. They are rarely "lazy" or indolent; and, when called upon, they can be orderly, regular and highly organized. They also find it relatively easy to separate ideas from feelings, a fact that helps explain their high grades. They are strongly opposed to the war in Southeast Asia, do not express anger readily, and are often extremely idealistic.

But despite considerable academic success and the prospects of a good graduate school (possibly with a Woodrow Wilson Fellowship thrown in), such students are less seekers after grades or professional expertise than seekers after truth. They are extremely open to the contradictory crosscurrents of American culture; they read widely, be it in the theater of the absurd, modern existentialist literature, or the writings of the New Left. They are not in any systematic way "alienated" from American society, but they have not really made their minds up whether it is worth joining, either. Often, their own life-styles and the exertions required to do well in a demanding college make such students feel "out of touch" with themselves. Although to an outside observer they usually appear more thoughtful and "in touch" than their classmates in the School of Engineering or Business Administration, they do not consider themselves to be sentient at all. On the contrary, they are continually struggling to experience the world more intensely, to make themselves capable of greater intimacy and love, to find some "rock bottom" from which they can sally forth to social and interpersonal commitments. Such students characteristically make enormously high demands upon themselves, upon experience and upon life; contrasted with these demands, their current experience is often barren, flat and dull.

Marihuana and the more powerful hallucinogens fit very neatly with the search for experience for such students. On the one hand, they promise a new kind of experience to a young man or woman who is highly experimental. On the other hand, they promise intensity, heightened sentience, intensified artistic perceptiveness, and perhaps even self-understanding. Self-understanding is, of course, a prime goal for such individuals; for they are far more inclined to blame themselves than others for the inadequacies of thier lives, and they often deliberately seek through self-analysis to change their personalities.

In students of this type, beginning or increasing drug use is often associated with feelings of flatness, boredom, stagnation and depression. It is surprising how often drug users mention a major loss, depression, or feeling of emptiness in the period preceding intensified drug use. The loss may be a break-up with a girl friend, the realization that one's parents are even more fallible than one had previously known, the blow to intellectual self-esteem that almost invariably accompanies the first midterm grades in the freshman year at a selective college, or the growing sense of confusion and purposelessness that follows abandoning previously cherished vocational goals or religious values. Under such circumstances, if there is pot around, the likelihood of trying it (and continuing to use it) is increased.

The "head" is in many respects different from the "seeker." Drug use occupies a more central place in the head's life and is almost always accompanied by disengagement from ordinary social expectations, by intense and often morbid self-exploration, and by a "turned-on" ideology profoundly hostile to the careerist, materialistic and success-oriented goals of middle-class American society. Almost invariably, then, the head is a member of a drug-using subculture, in which he finds an identity that enables him to drop temporarily out of the Establishment America from which he comes and toward which he was headed. For most young men and women, of course, membership in the hippie subculture lasts a summer, a term, a year, or possibly longer, but is followed by a gradual reentry into the System. One student of drug-using college dropouts estimates that they stay in the hippie world an average of a year and a half. After this, most return to their families in the suburbs (average parental income: $15,000 a year) and usually to the highly academic colleges from which they dropped out. Only those with unmistakable artistic talent and those with major psychiatric problems (or both) are likely to remain longer.

Unlike most seekers, heads are genuinely alienated from American society. Their defining characteristic is their generalized rejection of prevalent American values, which they criticize largely on cultural and humanistic grounds. American society is trashy, cheap and commercial; it "dehumanizes" its members; its values of success, materialism, monetary accomplishment and achievement undercut more important spiritual values. Such students rarely stay involved for long in the political and social causes that agitate many of their activist classmates. For alienated students, the basic societal problem is not so much political as aesthetic. Rejecting middle-class values, heads repudiate as well those conventional values and rules that deem experimentation with drugs illicit. For heads, the goal is to find a way out of the "air-conditioned nightmare" of American society. What matters is the interior world, and, in the exploration of that world, drugs play a major role.

A second characteristic of many heads is a more or less intense feeling of estrangement from their own experience. Such students are highly aware of the masks, facades and defenses people erect to protect themselves; they are critical of the social "games"and "role-playing" they see around them. They object to these games not only in others, but even more strongly in themselves. As a result, they feel compelled to root out any "defense" that might prevent awareness of inner life; self-deception, lack of self-awareness or "phoniness" are cardinal sins. They have, moreover, a conscious ethic of love, expressed in a continual struggle for "meaningful relationships" —direct, honest and open encounters with others. This ethic is sincerely felt, but it is often difficult for the alienated to achieve in practice. Thus, perhaps the deepest guilts in such individuals spring from their internal impediments to genuineness, directness and open communication with others. As one student said, "For me, sin equals hang-up."

Despite their efforts to make contact with their "real selves" and to have "meaningful relationships" with others, alienated students often feel unusually separated from both self and others. They experience themselves as separated from others by a gray opaque filter, by invisible screens and curtains, by protective shells and crusts that prevent them from the fullness of experience. They recriminate themselves for their lack of expressiveness, spontaneity and contact. One such student described human relations as being like people trying to touch each other through airtight space suits. Another talked of a wax that was poured over his experience, preventing him from rapport with the world. Possessed of an unusually strong desire for intense experience, but also unusually full of feelings of estrangement, such students find drugs that promise to heighten experience a tempting way out of the shell.

A third frequent characteristic of alienated students is a fantasy of fusion and merger, which contrasts sharply with their current feelings of estrangement. Many have a semiconscious concept of almost mystical union with nature, with their own inner lives, or with other people—of communication that requires no words, of the kind of oneness with nature, people, or the world that has always characterized intense religious experience. For a student with unusual impatience with the boundaries that separate the self from the not-self, the powerful hallucinogens are especially attractive, for they can profoundly alter the boundaries of body and self. This change in boundaries is by no means always pleasant, and one of the most common sources of panic during drug experiences is the feeling of being "trapped" in an isolated, barricaded subjectivity. But at other times, the hallucinogens *do* produce feelings of being in unusually direct contact, even fusion, with others.

On several grounds, then, the alienated student is strongly attracted by drugs and by the hippie world. Arguments against drug use based on traditional American values carry little weight for him; on the contrary, he takes great pleasure in violating these "middle-class" norms. His feelings of estrangement from his own experience lead him to attempt to break through the boundaries, shells, walls, filters and barriers that separate him from the world. And his fantasy of fusion disposes him to seek out chemical instruments to increase his "oneness" with others. For a student who is young, alienated and anticonventional, drug use is primarily a way of searching for meaning via the chemical intensification of personal experience.

In a broader developmental context, too, immersion in the drug-using hippie subculture is generally a part of a phase of disengagement from American society. Confronted with a society whose rules and values he profoundly distrusts, the head seeks in the counter-culture of hippiedom a respite, a moratorium, or an escape from pressures and demands he does not want to confront. Yet merely to note the important element of withdrawal in the hippie's use of drugs may be to ignore the more important developmental meaning of drug use for the hippie. However ill-advised society may consider his choice of methods, the hippie is often unconsciously searching for a way to engage himself with himself and with others. And however "regressive" or "self-destructive" it may appear to some for a young man to "drop out" of American society, the hippie subculture often proves a rest-and-recovery area, or even a staging area, from which unusually sensitive, talented and/or disturbed individuals take stock of themselves, explore their inner lives and their relationships with a small group of other people, and sometimes *return* to the established society. It seems likely that most hippies will follow this path.

There are, however, a few heads for whom drug use is both a symptom of and a trigger for serious psychopathology. In some cases,

drug use clearly accelerates a downhill course upon which the individual is already embarked; in other cases, an overwhelmingly bad trip may topple a student whose previous equilibrium was fragile. Thus, drug use may really be a contributing factor to a picture of psychopathology. Indeed, some of those who are most compulsively drawn to chronic drug use are the same people who can least tolerate it. Already confused and precarious, they are unable to bear the induced alterations of consciousness produced by the hallucinogens, and may move steadily or suddenly downhill. . . .

THE EXPERIENTIAL COUNTER-CULTURE

The "better" American colleges rarely attempt to provide students with neatly packaged answers to their existential questions. To be sure, the most demanding colleges make systematic efforts to provoke undergraduates to challenge previous beliefs and to abandon unexamined dogmas. But they expect students to arrive at individual solutions to the riddles of life, all the while occupying themselves with getting good grades and getting ahead in the academic world. The college's message is often highly paradoxical: "Ruthlessly discard previous convictions and values; don't look to us for answers; most of your questions are sophomoric, in any case."

To the most sophisticated undergraduates, the traditional avenues to significance seem irrelevant, exhausted, insincere or superficial. Traditional religious faith and the great political ideologies arouse relatively little interest among today's determinedly anti-ideological undergraduates. Nor does success within the "American way of life" constitute an answer to life's riddles for most students. There was a day when the quest for campus popularity seemed to many undergraduates but a reflection of a broader life philosophy of making friends, influencing people, and developing social skills. But today, "popularity" has become a dirty word. Nor does "getting ahead in the world" provide an answer for intellectual students, most of whom start out already ahead in the world—the children of well-educated and well-situated middle-class parents. For these students, the old American dream of giving one's children "a better chance" makes little sense: they find it pointless to struggle for greater affluence when they already have more than enough. They are more worried about how to live with what they already have.

As the traditional avenues to meaning have dried up, and as academic performance itself seems increasingly irrelevant to the major existential concerns of students, a new informal student subculture has begun to emerge. Although not opposed to the life of the mind, this subculture is antiacademic. Although students who participate in it are publicly headed for professional careers, they privately focus on experience in the present rather than on long-range goals. Theirs is an informal *experiential counter-culture,* which complements the formal culture of the academically-oriented college. Central to this counter-culture is a focus on the present—on today, on the here and now. At one level, intellectual college students are required to defer enjoyment for a distant future in their academic and preprofessional work. But, informally, they emphasize immediate pleasure and experience. While society at large expects from them a reverence for the traditions of the past and a respect for traditional institutions, they stress in their own subcultures activity and receptivity in the present. Such future-oriented qualities as control, planning, waiting, saving and postponing are little honored in the student subculture; nor are past-oriented qualities like revering, recalling, remembering and respecting much emphasized. In contrast, the experiential subculture stresses genuineness, adventure, spontaneity, sentience and experimentation. Since the past is seen as irrelevant (or "exhausted") and since the future seems profoundly uncertain, the real meaning of life must be found within present experience—even as one worries about the Graduate Record Examinations.

The experiential counter-culture has many variants, at least some of which are visible on almost every major American campus. One variant is what is sometimes called "student existentialism." At the more sophisticated campuses, this outlook is manifest in an intense interest in existential writers, in the theater of the absurd, and in philosophers and psychologists who stress "existential" concepts. But even at less sophisticated colleges, a similar focus is apparent in student emphasis on simple human commitments as contrasted with absolute values, in a "situation ethic"

that questions the possibility of long-range value commitments, and by a pervasively high estimation of sincerity, authenticity and directness. Student existentialism is humanistic rather than religious, and its most immediate goals are love, immediacy, empathy, "encounter" with one's fellow man. Thus, in the counter-culture, what matters most is interpersonal honesty, "really being yourself" and a special kind of open and disinterested genuineness. What is most unacceptable is fraudulence, exploitation, "role-playing," artificiality, hypocrisy and "playing games."

Along with the focus on the present and on "existential" values goes a very great tolerance for experimentation. Youth is increasingly defined (by youth itself) as a time for exploration, trial and error, and deliberate efforts to enlarge, change or expand personality. Experimentation in the interest of deliberate self-change is seen as essential to pursuit of meaning. Convinced that meaning is not found but created, members of the counter-culture consider their own personalities the prime vehicles for the creation of significance. Since significance emerges from the self, it is only by transforming the self that significance can be achieved. In a kind of deliberate, self-conscious and intentional identity-formation, apparently unconnected activities and experiences find their rationale. Self-exploration, psychotherapy, sexual experimentation, travel, "encounter groups," a reverence for nature, and "sensitivity training" are tools in the pursuit of meaning—along with drug use.

The high rates of drug use at the more intellectual and academically demanding colleges are therefore not to be explained solely by the presence at such colleges of students of the same psychological type—although this fact is important. In addition, the more intellectual colleges tend to impose upon students an unusually strong set of pressures for academic and intellectual performance: they require high cognitive ability, a preprofessional orientation, and a postponement of immediate gratifications without offering much in return by way of fun or answers to life's riddles. In such an environment, students have spontaneously created a counter-culture, which, while not explicitly opposed to academic pursuits, complements them with a focus on the present, on "existential" values, on personal experimentation, and on deliberate self-transformation as a way of creating meaning. Participation in this counterculture provides a powerful support for efforts to explore oneself, to intensify relationships with other people, to change the quality and content of consciousness. It provides a sanctioning context for drug use as one of the pathways of changing the self so as to create meaning in the world.

DRUGS AS A COMMENTARY ON SOCIETY

It is widely feared that student drug use is a commentary upon American society; words like degeneracy, addiction, thrill-seeking and irresponsibility are eventually introduced into most popular discussions of student drug use. So, too, student drug use is said to be related to the excessive permissiveness of parents, to the laxness of adult standards, to breaches in law enforcement, to disrespect for law and order, and to an impending breakdown of our social fabric.

Although these particular interpretations of the social implications of drug use are incorrect, drug use *is* importantly influenced by social, political and historical factors. Those students who lust after significance or reject the prevalent values of American society are in fact reacting to and within a societal context. The sense of being locked-off and enclosed in an impermeable shell is related not only to individual psychological states like depression, but to broader cultural phenomena. And the fact that a considerable number of the most able students have become convinced that significance and relevant experience are largely to be found within their own skulls is indirectly related to their perception of the other possibilities for fulfillment in the social and political world. In a variety of ways, then, student drug use is a commentary on American society, although a different kind of commentary than most discussions of youthful "thrill-seeking" would lead us to believe.

To single out a small number of social changes as especially relevant to understanding student drug use is to make a highly arbitrary decision. A variety of factors, including rapid social change, the unprecedented possibilities for total destruction in the modern world, the prevalence of violence both domestic and international, the high degree of specialization and bureaucratization of Ameri-

can life, and a host of others are relevant to creating the context of values and expectations within which drug use has become increasingly legitimate. But of all the factors that could be discussed, three seem particularly relevant: first, the effect of modern communications and transportation in producing an overwhelming inundation of experience, which I will term *stimulus flooding;* second, the effect of *automatic affluence* in changing the values and outlooks of the young; third, the importance of recent social and historical events in producing a kind of *social and political disenchantment* that leads many students to seek salvation through withdrawal and inner life rather than through engagement and societal involvement.

STIMULUS FLOODING AND PSYCHOLOGICAL NUMBING

Every society subjects its members to pressures and demands that they simply take for granted. Such pressures are woven into the fabric of social existence, are assumed to be a natural part of life, and become the object of automatic accommodation. These accommodations are rarely examined, yet they may profoundly alter the quality of human experience. Such is the case with the quantity, variety and intensity of external stimulation, imagery and excitation to which most Americans are subjected. As Robert J. Lifton has pointed out, modern man in advanced societies is subjected to a flood of unpredictable stimulation of the most varied kinds; by newspapers, television, radio and rapid travel, he continually exposes himself to novel and unanticipatable experience. This stimulus inundation, in turn, produces a self-protective reaction which, following Lifton, we can term psychic numbing.

Most individuals in most societies have at some point in their lives had the experience of being so overcome by external stimulation and internal feelings that they gradually find themselves growing numb and unfeeling. Medical students commonly report that after their first, often intense reactions to the cadaver, they simply "stop feeling anything" with regard to the object of their dissection. And we have all had the experience of listening to so much good music, seeing so many fine paintings, being so overwhelmed by excellent cooking that we find ourselves simply unable to respond further. Similarly, at moments of extreme psychic pain and anguish, most individuals "go numb," no longer perceiving the full implications of a catastrophic situation or no longer experiencing the full range of their own feelings. This lowered responsiveness, this psychological numbing, seems causally related to the variety, persistence and intensity of stimulation and emotion. . . .

This psychological numbing operates at a great variety of levels for modern man. Our experience, from childhood onward, with the constantly flickering images and sounds of television, films, radio, newspapers, paperbacks, neon signs, advertisements and sound trucks numbs us to the sights and sounds of our civilization. Our continual exposure to a vast variety of ideologies, value systems, philosophies, political creeds, superstitions, religions and faiths numbs us to the unique claims to validity and the special spiritual and intellectual values of each one: we move among values and ideologies as in a two-dimensional landscape. Similarly, the availability to us in novels, films, television, theater and opera of moments of high passion, tragedy, joy, exaltation and sadness often ends by numbing us to our own feelings and the feelings of others.

Modern men thus confront the difficult problem of keeping "stimulation" from without to a manageable level, while also protecting themselves against being overwhelmed by their own inner responses to the stimuli from the outer world. Defenses or barriers against both external and internal stimulation are, of course, essential in order for us to preserve our intactness and integrity as personalities. From earliest childhood, children develop thresholds of responsiveness and barriers against stimulation in order to protect themselves against being overwhelmed by inner or outer excitement. Similarly, in adulthood, comparable barriers, thresholds and defenses are necessary, especially when we find ourselves in situations of intense stimulation.

A problem arises, however, if the barriers we erect to protect ourselves from the clamors of the inner and outer world prove harder and less permeable than we had originally wanted. In at least a minority of Americans, the normal capacity to defend oneself against undue stimulation and inner excitation is exaggerated and automatized, so that it not only protects, but walls off the individual from inner and outer experience. In such individuals, there develops an acute sense of being trapped in their own shells, unable to break through their defenses to make "contact" with experience or with other people, a sense of being excessively armored, separated from their own activities as by an invisible screen, estranged from their own feelings and from potentially emotion-arousing experiences in the world. Most of us have had some inkling of this feeling of inner deadness and outer flatness, especially in times of great fatigue, letdown, or depression. The world seems cold and two-dimensional; food and life have lost their savor; our activities are merely "going through the motions," our experiences lack vividness, three-dimensionality, and intensity. Above all, we feel trapped or shut up in our own subjectivity.

The continual flooding of stimulation to which modern men are subjected is thus related not only to the psychological conditions and institutional pressures that help create the feelings of numbness, but, indirectly, to the nature of perception and experience in an advanced technological society. One problem every modern American faces is how to avoid becoming entrapped in the protective shell he must construct to defend himself against being overwhelmed by stimulation. And the use of drugs, especially in the context of the experiential counter-culture, becomes more attractive to youth precisely because the drugs preferred by students often have the effect of dissipating, blurring, or breaking down the boundaries of individual selfhood and personality.

AUTOMATIC AFFLUENCE

No society in world history has ever provided its citizens with the automatic abundance that our society provides to a majority of Americans. In over ten years of interviewing students from middle-class and upper-middle-class backgrounds, I have yet to find one who was worried about finding a job, and have met relatively few who were worried about finding a *good* job. Whatever their levels of aspiration, today's advantaged youth rarely think in terms of getting ahead in the world, acquiring increasing status, or struggling to "succeed." These goals, both relevant and important to their parents (products of the 1920's and the Great Depression), are largely irrelevant to today's youth. Like youth in every era, they turn from the successes of the past to the problems of the present and future. Thus, paradoxically, although they live in a society more affluent than any before it, they are far more outraged at poverty, injustice, inequality, exploitation and cruelty than were their parents, who lived in a more impoverished society. Indeed, one of the central demands of today's politically active youth is that everyone have the benefits which they themselves have always taken for granted.

One of the undeniable benefits of affluence is that it brings increased opportunities for enjoyment and leisure, and destroys the need to devote oneself to a life of unrelenting toil in order to prosper. Affluence permits a deemphasis of hard work, self-control and renunciation, and makes possible the development of new cultures of leisure. As work, success and achievement decline in relative importance, new values are beginning to replace them, and new patterns of consumption are beginning already to reflect these new values. As "getting ahead in the world" no longer suffices to define the meaning of life, today's advantaged students turn increasingly to explore *other* meanings of life.

Two rather different alternatives have so far been tried. The first is the solution of the political activist, who remains primarily concerned with the fact that his own affluence and freedom have not been extended to all. Within America, his concern is with the poor, the deprived, the excluded and the disadvantaged. Abroad, he focuses on the many failures of American foreign policy, failures that in his eyes involve a catastrophic gap between the values of a democratic society and the foreign policies that purportedly implement them. The activist would have us support rather than oppose movements of national liberation, and use our affluence not in military engagements but in programs of assistance to the developing nations. The activist is most likely to accept the traditional values of American society, especially those emphasizing justice, equality, opportunity and freedom, and to insist that these values be more thoroughly practiced.

The second response to the question, "What lies beyond affluence?," while not incompatible with the first, looks in a different area for an answer. This second response turns to a more fundamental critique of the premises and assumptions upon which technological America has been based. Instead of equality, it champions diversity; instead of pressing for the extension of affluence, it questions the meaning of affluence. Associated with a long tradition of romantic criticism of industrial and postindustrial society, this response points to the price of affluence—dehumanization, professionalization, bureaucracy, a loss of power over society, the absence of a sense of small scale, and the erosion of traditional community. For the romantic critic of American society, fulfillment and personal wholeness are more important than abundance and achievement. The life of the affluent middle class in America is seen as empty, spiritually impoverished, driven and neurotic; the vaguely defined alternative involves expressiveness, self-knowledge, involvement with the small group of others, the fulfillment of nonmaterial artistic, spiritual and psychological needs. "Self-actualization" is the goal; "let each man do his thing" is the motto.

Automatic affluence, then, inevitably means that many of those who experience abundance as routine, attempt to create goals beyond affluence. These goals may involve a reform of the world so as to extend affluence to all, or a critique of the technological assumptions upon which affluence itself was based. Insofar as the individual's main effort is to extend affluence, he is relatively immune to the appeals of the experiential, drug-using world, for his energies are oriented toward changing the world rather than himself. But insofar as his primary focus is antitechnological—upon self-fulfillment, personal change, and spiritual or humanistic fulfillment—this focus is highly consistent with the use of drugs. For drug use among college students is closely related to the effort to change oneself, to become more creative, to be more expressive, more emotionally open and more genuinely in contact with the world. And the use of drugs is associated with a questioning or rejection of the traditional success ethic of American life, and with a search for new styles of living more oriented to leisure, to intimate personal relationships, and to spiritual expression. Thus, affluence indirectly produces a mood among some of its recipients that makes them receptive to drug use and other forms of personal experimentation.

SOCIO-POLITICAL DISENCHANTMENT

In juxtaposing two answers to the quest for meaning beyond abundance, I have implied a certain tension between them. It is not accidental that full-time and committed political activists are rarely intensive drug users; it is also important that the full-time denizens of the drug-using hippie subculture are rarely capable of sustained political activity. Sustained engagement in an effort to change the world is rarely compatible with the kind of self-absorption and inwardness that results from intensive and regular drug use; conversely, however strongly the committed drug user may feel about the inequities of American society, his primary efforts are usually directed toward self-change, rather than changing the world around him. Although some individuals alternate at different times in their lives between activism and alienation, it is very difficult to be an active social reformer and a "head" at the same time.

This argument suggests that disenchantment with the possibilities of meaningful social action is related to the development of an outlook conducive to drug use. To trace student drug use directly to such factors as racial injustices or the war in Vietnam would, of course, be a major over-simplification. But disenchantment with meaningful and honorable political activity creates a general climate of opinion that *is*, in turn, favorable to drug use. Specifically, the change in student attitudes toward political life and social reform since the assassination of President Kennedy seems importantly connected to the rise of drug use.

The influence of Kennedy upon the attitudes of youth is often exaggerated or stated in an oversimplified way. Many of the young, of course, disliked Kennedy, as did many of their parents. Furthermore, most of those who admired Kennedy personally had no intention whatsoever of entering public life. Kennedy's impact on the attitudes of youth was indirect: he and the group around him symbolized the conviction that it was possible for young, idealistic and intelligent men and women to enter the political world and to "make a difference." Such Kennedy ventures as the Peace Corps further provided an outlet—and more importantly a symbol—for the idealistic energies of activist youth. Although Kennedy

himself in fact rarely listened to the advice of students, such symbolic Kennedy acts as pots of coffee for peace marchers in front of the White House indicated at least an awareness of the opinion of the dedicated young.

The image of political life conveyed by the Johnson Administration, especially from 1966 to late 1968, was vastly different. Not only have older views of politics as a form of horse trading, "compromising," and "wheeling and dealing" been reinstated, but large numbers of American college students have come to associate political involvement with gross immorality and even with genocide. In this context, such revelations as that of covert C.I.A. funding of liberal student organizations like the National Students Association have the effect of convincing many intelligent and idealistic youth that politics—and, by extension, efforts to work to change the System from within—are dishonorable or pointless occupations.

The demise of the Civil Rights Movement and the collapse of the War on Poverty have also helped change the climate of opinion about political reform. In the early 1960s, the Civil Rights Movement was the chief catalyst for the rising tide of student political involvement. Sit-ins, Freedom Rides, the work of S.N.C.C. and other groups in the Deep South helped convince students that their efforts at social change would be honored, recognized and responded to by the society at large. Students in the early 1960s saw themselves not so much in opposition to the policies of the nation as in the vanguard of those policies; and the passage of major Civil Rights legislation in 1964, followed by the promise of a major "War on Poverty," gave support to this conviction. Thus there arose a hope that "American society would crash through" in remedying its own inequities. This hope had a widespread impact, not only upon that small minority of students who were actively involved in civil rights work, but upon others who were indirectly encouraged to plan careers of responsible social involvement.

But the events of subsequent years have altered this initial hope. The "white backlash" has made legislators extremely reluctant to assist the Negro revolution. The war in Vietnam drained funds away from domestic programs just when federal assistance was needed most. The student Civil Rights Movement for its part discovered that legal reforms exposed more clearly the depths of the problem of black Americans, and pointed toward more far-reaching psychological, social and economic changes that were more difficult to legislate from Washington. The War on Poverty collapsed into a small skirmish. Equally important, the rising militancy of black radicals has pushed white students out of organizations like S.N.C.C. and CORE with the demand, "Go home and organize your own people." Lacking national support, and "rejected" by their former black allies, white activists have increasingly despaired of working within the System, have become more radical, and are talking more militantly about "changing the System."

The changing image of political involvement has had two effects. On the one hand, it has contributed to the "radicalization" of those individuals who have remained activists: especially now among such students, disaffection with the established system is at a high that has not been reached in this country since the 1930's. But equally important, the revitalized image of the political process as dishonest, reprehensible, immoral and unresponsive to both the ideals of America and the rights of the deprived has created a climate in which it is more and more possible to argue that salvation—if it can be found at all—must be found within the self or the counter-community, rather than within the wider society. Given this belief, the individual in search of meaningful engagement with the world must either create new political institutions (as stressed by the rhetoric of the New Left), or else abandon political struggle altogether in a search for meaning within small groups of other disaffected people. It is in these latter groups that drug use is most common. If the world outside is corrupt, dehumanized, violent and immoral, the world within—the almost infinitely malleable world of perception, sensation, communication and consciousness—seems more controllable, more immediate, less corrupting, and ofttimes more pleasant. To be sure, there is a price to be paid for exclusive involvement in the interior world, but, for many young Americans, there simply seems to be no alternative.

Political and historical events do not have a direct, one-to-one relationship with drug use: the war in Vietnam does not *cause* students to smoke marihuana or experiment with LSD. But the political climate of the past few years has created a negative view of the possibility of meaningful involvement within the established institutions of the society, at the same time that it has convinced many students that society is in desperate need of reform. This climate of opinion in turn contributes to the assumption that if meaning, excitement and dignity are to be found in the world, they must be found within one's own cranium. Drug use can indeed be a kind of cop-out, not from perversity or laziness, but simply because there seems to be no other alternative. Student drug use is indeed a commentary upon American society, but it is above all an indirect criticism of our society's inability to offer the young exciting, honorable and effective ways of using their intelligence and idealism to reform our society.

56. HOW TO CHANGE BEHAVIOR

Timothy Leary

It is my plan to talk to you tonight about methods of effecting change—change in man's behavior and change in man's consciousness.

Behavior and consciousness. Please note the paired distinction. Behavior and consciousness. Up until recently I considered myself a behavioral scientist and limited the scope of my work to overt and measurable behavior. In so doing I was quite in the *Zeitgeist* of modern psychology, studing the subject matter which our American predecessors defined some fifty years ago, behavior, routinely following the ground rules they laid down, scrupulously avoiding that which is most important to the subject—his consciousness, concentrating instead, on what is most important to we who seek to observe, measure, manipulate, control and predict—the subject's overt behavior.

This decision to turn our backs on consciousness is, of course, typically Western and very much in tune with the experimental, objective bent of Western science. Professor Huston Smith of the Massachusetts Institute of Technology has pointed out some basic differences between the Western approach and the philosophies of China and India, differences which have some importance for the applied psychologist concerned with behavior change. Professor Smith reminds us that our Western culture has stressed measurement and control of objects; whereas China has historically emphasized the rules of the social encounter; and Indian philosophy the development and expansion of human consciousness. Tonight I speak to you from a point midway between

From TOWARDS INTERNATIONAL BEHAVIOR APPROPRIATE TO A NUCLEAR AGE: PSYCHOLOGY AND INTERNATIONAL AFFAIRS *edited by Charles E. Osgood (Proceedings of the XIV International Congress of Applied Psychology, Vol. 1), pp. 109–132. Copyright* © *1962 by Ejnar Munksgaard Ltd., Copenhagen. Reprinted by permission of Munksgaard and the author.*

the Western and Eastern hemispheres of the cortex presenting a theory and method which is Chinese in that behavior is seen as an intricate social game; Indian in its recognition of consciousness and the need to develop a more cosmic awareness, and finally Western in its concern to do good measurably well.

I plan to present, first, some thoughts on behavior change, then some new conceptions of consciousness and its alteration, and finally some data from recent research in these areas.

BEHAVIOR AND ITS CHANGE

Except for reflexes and instinctual reactions and random muscular movements (which fall into the province of physiology) all behavior is learned.

Behavior is therefore artifactual and culturally determined. Behavior sequences might usefully be considered as game sequences.

The use of the word "game" in this sweeping context is likely to be misunderstood. The listener may think I refer to "play" as opposed to the stern, real-life, serious activities of man. But as you shall see I consider the latter as "game."

At this point you are asking for and you deserve a definition. What do I mean by game? A game is a learned cultural sequence characterized by six factors:

1. *Roles:* The game assigns roles to the human beings involved.
2. *Rules:* A game sets up a set of rules which hold only during the game sequence.
3. *Goals:* Every game has its goals or purpose. The goals of baseball are to score more runs than the opponents. The goals of the game of psychology are more complex and less explicit but they exist.
4. *Rituals:* Each game has its conventional behavior pattern not related to the goals or

rules but yet quite necessary to comfort and continuance.

5. *Language:* Each game has its jargon. Unrelated to the rules and goals and yet necessary to learn and use.

6. *Values:* Each game has its standards of excellence or goodness.

Baseball and basketball have clearly definable roles, rules, rituals, goals, languages and values. Psychology, religion, politics are games, too, learned cultural sequences with clearly definable roles, rules, rituals, goals, jargons, values. They are less explicitly formulated than the so-called sports and therein, dear friends, lies the pity. For this simple reason millions have died and we may die tomorrow.

The behavior which psychiatrists label as disease entities can be considered as games, too. Dr. Thomas Szasz, the distinguished psychoanalyst-philosopher, in his book, *The Myth of Mental Illness,* suggests that "hysteria" is the name we give to a certain doctor-patient game involving deceitful helplessness. The "bluff" in poker is a similar deceitful but perfectly legitimate game device. Psychiatry according to this model is behavior-change game.

Far from being frivolous, many so-called "play games" are superior in their behavioral science and in their behavior-change techniques to the "not-called games," such as psychiatry and psychology.

In terms of epistemology and scientific method employed, the "game" of American baseball is superior to any of the socalled behavioral sciences. Baseball officials have classified and they reliably record molecular behavior sequences (the strike, the hit, the double play, etc.). Their compiled records are converted into indices most relevant for summarizing and predicting behavior (RBI, runs batted in; ERA, earned run average, etc.). Baseball employs well-trained raters to judge those rare events which are not obviously and easily coded. Their raters are called umpires.

When we move from behavior science to behavior-change we see that baseball experts have devised another remarkable set of techniques for bringing about the results which they and their subjects look for. Coaching. Baseball men understand the necessity for sharing time and space with their learners, for setting up role models, for feedback of relevant information to the learner, for endless practice of the desired behavior. And most important of all, baseball scientists understand the basic, cosmic lesson of percentage: that the greatest player gets on the average one hit in three tries, the winning team loses at least one game in three, that no team can lead the league every year, neither Rome, nor Athens, nor London, nor Moscow, nor Washington. Those who wish to measure, summarize, predict, and change human behavior could do worse than model themselves after this so-called "game."

All behavior involves learned games. But only that rare Westerner we call "mystic" or who has had a visionary experience of some sort sees clearly the game structure of behavior. Most of the rest of us spend our time struggling with roles and rules and goals and concepts of games which are implicit and confusedly not seen as games, trying to apply the roles and rules and rituals of one game to other games.

Worst of all is the not knowing that it is a game. Baseball is a clean and successful game because it is seen as a game. You can shift positions. You know the game is limited in space and in time. You renew your contract. You can quit, start a new game.

Culturally, stability is maintained by keeping the members of any cultural group from seeing that the roles, rules, goals, rituals, language, and values are game structures. The family game is treated by most cultures as far more than a game, with its implicit contracts, limited in time and space. The nationality game. It is treason not to play. The racial game. The religious game. And that most treacherous and tragic game of all, the game of individuality, the ego game. The Timothy Leary game. Ridiculous how we confuse this game, overplay it. Our own mystics and the Eastern philosophers have been warning us about this danger for centuries.

Cultural institutions encourage the delusion that the games of life are inevitable givens involving natural laws of behavior. These fixed delusions tend to rigidify behavior patterns. This rigidity, as Professor Osgood pointed out in his significant opening address of the Copenhagen Congress, now threatens the very survival of the human species itself.

So now we come to behavior change. The currently popular method of behavior change is called psychotherapy. A medical game. A curing of the psyche. Psychotherapy interprets confusion and inefficiency in game playing as illness. We call it sickness and attempt to cure it employing the medical game. Consider the football player who doesn't know the rules. Perhaps he picks up the ball and runs off the field. He is punished for not playing the game correctly. He feels badly. Shall we pronounce him sick and call the doctor?

The failure to understand the game nature of behavior leads to confusion and eventually to helplessness. Helplessness. Let's look at this word for a moment. It's a big concept in understanding science, technology, rehabilitation and, for that matter, the working of the mind itself.

The basic aim of physical science is to reduce human helplessness in the face of the physical environment. Physical science has other goals, of course: to understand, explain, control, measure, predict. But certainly these are means rather than ends. Why explain? Why predict? To lessen fearful ignorance. The technologies which have grown up around the physical sciences, engineering, medicine, also take as their goal the reducing of human helplessness.

Do they not stem from the same survival motive? And the social technologies—psychiatry, social work, applied psychology—is not their goal the reduction of confusion and the increase in human freedom?

Judged by these criteria the game of Western science has not been a glorious success. Our helplessness in the face of physical disease has certainly diminished. Our control over natural forces has given us a sense of mastery. We live longer and healthier lives. Good.

We have created a game model—the subject-object model—which allows us on the one hand to dominate "object" but which has created a world full of human objects. Most of what we do in the name of science results in more and greater human helplessness.

The science game creates wonder drugs whose action is not understood by the user. And worse yet we turn over these drugs to those who play the doctor game, the medical game—whose roles, rules, rituals, language, goals and values place the patient into a passive object status.

The science game, the healing game, the knowledge game are magnificent human structures. They are our proudest game accomplishments. But they are great only as long as they are seen as game. When they go beyond

this point the trouble begins—claims to a non-game reality status: the emergence of experts, professionals, priests, status-favored authorities; claims to power and control and priority. Look at the A.E.C. Look at the A.M.A. And watch out! At this point you will find that games which began with the goal of decreasing human helplessness end up increasing it.

Human beings inhabiting those areas of the globe which the geographic game calls East are, for the most part, well aware of the foregoing issues. It's hard for Westerners to back away, and see the artifactual game structures. We are so close to our games. We have been born into them. And we are born into a philosophic system which glorifies hierarchical expertise on the one hand and helplessness on the other: monotheism, the Judaic-Christian tradition. Monotheism, that game started by a few persecuted outcasts (game losers) in the Mid-Eastern desert: the subject game; the false quality game; the manipulating, predicting, controlling game. Monotheism breeding helplessness.

Now, let's apply this general discussion of helplessness and the behavior game to the issue of behavior change. In spite of our apparent executive control over nature we have had small success in developing behavior change games. Indeed most of our attempts to change behavior increase human helplessness, lessen human freedom and thereby exaggerate the problem we set out to solve. Our behavior change games invariably set up structures which give more power to the few and less power to the many, invidious role models: doctor-patient; professor-student; inequitable rules involving secrecy and control; the one-upmanship language we call jargon.

When people come to us and ask us to change their behavior, why can't we do it? Why can't we teach them to see the game structure of human society? The problem seems simple enough. Why can't we find out what games they are caught up in? Find out what games they want to commit themselves to? Make them explicit? Help them discover the rules of the game, the role, the rituals, the goals, the concepts? Expose them to models of successful game playing; encourage them to practice; feed back objective appraisals of their performance; care for them and their game struggles? How do you care for them? You share time and space with them. Nothing else can substitute. We have little else to offer. If we don't, they'll learn the games of those who do share time and space. If they're prisoners, then who will teach them behavior games? Who shares the most time and space with prisoners? That's right, the other prisoners, older criminals and younger criminals. So who influences behavior in what direction? And who shares the most amount of time and space with prisoners? That's right, the prison guards who, in most American prisons, teach them how to play the role of robber in the game of "cops and robbers." And we professional middle-class experts? How much time and space do we share with the prisoners? An hour a week on the medical ward?

O.K. It sounds simple enough, doesn't it? Just show people that their social identity and their entire cultural commitment is a game. They aren't aware of it, Sure, just tell them.

Yes, you smile when I say this. It's not quite that easy, is it? Here's the rub. Few people, a very few people (and we Westerners call them mystics) are willing and able to admit that the game is a game. Most of our people become upset and even angry when the game is identified—the game of "I-and-all-I-stand-for."

At this point when you hear the word "mystic" you may be uneasily wondering if you are going to be subjected to a vague metaphysical discourse on general principles. Perhaps you will be surprised to hear me suggest the hypothesis that the most effective approach to the "practical" games of life is that of applied mysticism. Identify the game structure of the event. Make sure that you do not apply the rules and concepts of other games to this situation. Move directly to solve the problem avoiding abstractions and irrelevant rituals. A mystic Martian or a person from a different culture might be an excellent consultant for a behavioral problem. They might be able to cut through irrelevant game rules to what is most relevant to survival and peace of mind.

How can we make the point? How can we learn the lesson? How can we Westerners come to see that our own consciousness is infinitely greater than our little egos and the ego games into which we are so blindly caught up? That the universe within our skulls is infinitely more than the flimsy game world which our words and minds create?

Put in a sentence—the task is to see that

the mind is a tiny fragment of the brain-body complex. It is the game-playing fragment—a useful and entertaining tool but quite irrelevant to survival, and indeed usually antagonistic to well-being.

The process of getting beyond the game structure, beyond the subject-object commitments, the dualities—this process is called the mystic experience. The visionary experience is the nongame, metagame experience. Change in behavior can occur with dramatic spontaneity once the game structure of behavior is seen. The visionary experience is the key to behavior change.

CONSCIOUSNESS AND ITS CHANGE

How do we obtain the visionary state?

There are many methods for expanding consciousness beyond the game limits. Mr. Aldous Huxley this afternoon presented a scholarly history of some classic and modern methods. Margaret Mead, the American anthropologist, has suggested several cross-cultural methods. Have a psychotic episode. (This is to say, just stop playing the social game for a while and they'll call you insane, but you may learn the great lesson.) Or expose yourself to some great trauma that shatters the gamesmanship out of you. Birth by ordeal is a well-documented phenomenon. The concentration camp experience has done this for some of our wisest men. Physical traumas can do it. Electric shock. Extreme fatigue. Live in another and very different culture for a year where your roles and rituals and language just don't mean a thing. Or separate yourself from the game pressure by institutional withdrawal. Live for a while in a monastic cell. Or marry a Russian. Sensory deprivation does it. Sensory deprivation cuts through the game.

Certain forms of sensory stimulation alter consciousness beyond games. The sexual orgasm is certainly the most frequent and natural, although so brief and so built into interpersonal courtship games that it has lost much of its mystical meaning in the West. We have recently learned from W. Grey Walters and William Burroughs about photostimulation as a means of consciousness alteration. Concentrated attention to a stroboscope or flicker apparatus can produce visionary experiences.

The most efficient way to cut through the

game structure of Western life is the use of drugs, consciousness-expanding drugs. From here on I shall use the abbreviation CE to refer to consciousness-expanding substances, such as LSD, mescaline, psilocybin.

Now the reaction of the Western world to consciousness-expanding drugs is extremely interesting. We tend to apply our familiar game roles, rituals, goals, rules, concepts to the nongame experience produced by these substances. Those of you who have not had the shattering exposure to such old and worshipped plants as peyote and the sacred mushroom and cannabis or such startling newcomers as psilocybin[1] and lysergic acid will wonder at this point about the nature of these experiences. What do these substances do? The neuro-physiological answer—the answer from outside—to this question is not yet ready. The answer from the inside (from the awareness of the subject) can be cast in countless metaphors. Let's try a physiological analogy. Let's assume that the cortex, the seat of consciousness, is a millionfold network of neurones, a fantastic computing machine. Cultural learning has imposed a few, pitifully small programs on the cortex. These programs may activate perhaps one tenth or one one-hundredth of the potential neural connections. All the learned games of life can be seen as programs which select, censor, alert and thus drastically limit the available cortical response (Mr. Aldous Huxley's reducing valves).

The CE (i.e., consciousness-expanding) drugs unplug these narrow programs. They unplug the ego, the game machinery, and the mind (that cluster of game concepts). And with the ego and mind unplugged, what is left? Not the "id"; no dark, evil impulses. These alleged negative "forces" are, of course, part of the game, being simply antirules. What is left is something that Western culture knows little about: the open brain, the uncensored cortex—alert and open to a broad sweep. Huxley and Dr. Barron have told you in their own words what is left, and there is no need to add my lumbering prose.

1 Psilocybin is a synthetic of the active ingredients of the sacred mushroom of Mexico. The divinitory mushroom was introduced to the Western culture by Professor Roger Heim of Paris and R. Gordon Wasson of New York and synthesized by Dr. A. Hofmann of the Sandoz Laboratory in Basel, Switzerland, who is also known through his work on lysergic acid. We are grateful to Sandoz, Inc., for providing the research materials used in these studies.

There is need, however, to ask another question. Why is this ecstatic, brain-opening experience so strange and horrid to Western culture? Why have our ancestors and our colleagues tended to ignore and even to oppose the visionary experience? Mr. R. Gordon Wasson, banker, mycologist,* anthropologist, gentleman-scholar turned mystic, has traced the persecution of the divine and divinitory mushroom back through the millennia. Why the irrational fear so often aroused by research on CE drugs even to this day? Perhaps because our Western world is committed to overplaying the objective, external behavior game.

In particular we overvalue the mind—that flimsy collection of learned words and verbal connections; the mind, that system of paranoid delusions with the learned self as center. And we eschew the nonmind, nongame intuitive insight outlook which is the key to the religious experience, to the love experience.

We seem to oppose any process which puts the game of here and now onto the long evolutionary timetable. This is a natural opposition and a healthy one. It is the greatest game of "the game" versus the "nongame." Behavior versus consciousness. The universal brain-body versus the cultural mind. The ego versus the species. A dialogue old and holy, like the dialogue of sea against land.

But this old game should be made explicit if it is to be fun. Unfortunately, the West has no concepts for thinking and talking about this basic dialogue. There is no ritual for mystical experience, for the mindless vision. What should provoke intense and cheerful competition too often evokes suspicion, anger, and impatience. What can be holy and intensely educational in the action of CE drugs on the cortex finds no ritual for application. This is to me one of the greatest challenges of our times.

The nongame visionary experiences are, I submit, the key to behavior change—drug-induced *satori*.† In three hours under the right circumstances the cortex can be cleared. The games that frustrate and torment can be seen in the cosmic dimension. But the West has no ritual, no game to handle the CE drug experience. In the absence of relevant rituals

* A person who studies fungi, especially mushrooms. (Eds.)

† A term borrowed from Japanese Zen Buddhism, meaning a sudden flash of illumination or insight. (Eds.)

we can only impose our familiar games, the politics of the nervous system, the mind controlling the brain. Physicians seek to impose their game of control and prescription. The bohemians naturally strive to impose their games of back-alley secrecy. The police, the third member of the happy, symbiotic drug triangle, naturally move in to control and prosecute.

Clearly we need new rituals, new goals, new rules, new concepts to apply and use these precious substances for man's welfare, to give the brain back to the species.

A group of investigators in the United States and Europe are now at work building up new games for the visionary experience, trying to develop new roles, rules, rituals, concepts and values. While these will, of course, vary from group to group the goal remains constant: expansion of consciousness, freedom of brain from the mind,, freedom of the cortex from those centers—reticular (?), diencephalic (?), prefrontal (?)—which control, alert, censor and select what the cortex attends to. The work has hardly begun. This much is clear. The theory of the new game will be simple and basic. Space and time will be among the few variables required. Human equality will be a central principle, for the mystic experience tells us that the game differences between men are infinitely small compared with the age-old species similarities.

In our research endeavors we have developed eleven egalitarian principles based on the game nature of the human contract: equality in determining role, rule, ritual, goal, language, commitment; equality in the explicit contractual definition of the real, the good, the true, the logical; equality of the right to speak and to have access to relevant information. Any contract between men should be explicit about any temporary suspension of these equalities.

This past year at the Center for Research in Personality, Harvard University, two research projects have attempted to put these egalitarian principles into operation. The first of these is a naturalistic study of drug-induced visions and the games which Americans impose on these new experiences. The second is a systematic study of the effects of consciousness-expanding drugs in a rehabilitation program. I hope that a description of these

two projects will illustrate and clarify the preceding discussion.[2]

A NATURALISTIC STUDY OF PSILOCYBIN

The purpose of this study was to determine the effects of psilocybin when administered in a naturalistic, supportive setting, to observe the rituals and language imposed by Americans on an experience quite alien to their culture. One hundred and sixty-seven subjects were given the mushrooms, 43 female and 124 male. Of these, 26 were internationally distinguished intellectuals, scholars, artists; 10 were medical doctors, 73 were professional intellectuals, 21 nonprofessional normals; 27 were drug addicts (psychological or physical), and 10 were inmates in a state prison.

The eleven principles for the human contract led to the following operations:

1. Participants alternated roles of observer and subject, i.e., the researchers took the drug with the subjects. The humanizing effect of this procedure cannot be overestimated. Among other things the subject-object issue is clearly settled.
2. Participants were given all available information about the drug. An atmosphere of mystery and secret experimentation was avoided.
3. Participants were given control of their own dosage. A maximum dosage was determined by the research team and this maximum number of tablets was given to the subject

2 The Director of the Center for Research in Personality, Prof. David C. McClelland, has provided these two projects with advice, support, and has labored to interpret our work to the nonvisionary world. All American psychologists are indebted to Professor Henry A. Murray for his pioneer explorations into the human condition. From his neighborly presence, friendly interest and deep understanding of man's potentialities we have benefited. Dr. Frank Barron and Dr. Richard Alpert have been coinvestigators in the mushroom research. Dr. W. Madison Presnell has lent psychiatric experience, administrative enthusiasm and clinical wisdom. George Litwin, James Ciarlo, Gunther Weil, Ralph Metzner, Ralph Schwizgebel and Jonathan Shay have played important roles in charting the new realms of consciousness. Edward Travers, John Moinski, James Maloney, Frank Rafferty, Rodney Harrington, Henry Kinney, and Donald Levine have made significant contributions to the Concord project. Mr. George Litwin and his staff have taken responsibility for the computer analysis of the questionaire data. Mrs. Pearl Chan, research administrator, has made things run.

and he was free to dose himself at the rate and amount desired.

4. A comfortable, homelike environment was employed. The sterile impersonality of the laboratory was avoided.

5. Subjects were allowed to bring a relative or friend. No subject took the drug in a group where he was a stranger.

Three sets of data were obtained: questionnaires covering the reactions; written reports and tape recordings; observations by the research team.

While the results of this study are too extensive to summarize at this point, a few major conclusions can be stated: The psilocybin experience is pleasant and educational; seventy-three percent of our subjects reported the experience as "very pleasant" or ecstatic; ninety-five percent thought the experience had changed their lives for the better.

Three out of four subjects reported happy and insightful reactions. When we recall that the drug was given only once under informal circumstances, with no attempt to be therapeutic or problem-oriented, these data stimulate thoughts about the healing-educational possibilities of psilocybin. But how do these changes come about?

The most common reaction reported is the sudden perception of the effect of abstractions, rituals, learned-game routines—ecstatic pleasure at being temporarily freed from these limitations, a game-free honesty. Set and suggestive contexts account for ninety-nine percent of the specific response to the drug. Thus, you cannot sensibly talk about the effects of psilocybin. It's always the set and suggestive context triggered off by the drug. A fascinating tension between these two factors—set and context—inevitably develops. If both are positive and holy then a shatteringly sacred experience results. If both are negative then a hellish encounter ensues. There is, of course, the tendency for people to impose their familiar games on to the psilocybin experience. The more rigidly committed to the game, the stronger this tendency. If the drug-giving person is secure, flexible, supportive, then the experience is almost guaranteed to be pleasant and therapeutic. Intensely deep communication occurs. Deep insights of a personal, social, and philosophic nature take place.

THE USE OF PSILOCYBIN IN A REHABILITATION PROGRAM

For many people one or two psilocybin experiences can accomplish the goals of a long and successful psychotherapy, a deep understanding and game-free collaboration between participants plus insight. But what then? People vary tremendously in their readiness to move forward from this point. Many of the 167 subjects in our naturalistic study were able to exploit the close, honest relationship and the insight. They were already involved in rewarding games to which they could return with renewed vision and energy.

But many of our subjects came through the psilocybin experience with the knowledge that they were involved in nonrewarding games, caught in routines which they disliked. Some realized that they had no games they wanted to play. The "therapeutic" effect of the experience did not last for these subjects. Expanded consciousness narrowed back. They were left with pleasant memories of their visionary journey and nothing more.

After insight comes the deeper question as to the meaning of life: What games to play? Behavior change must follow change in consciousness.

Our research group is now committed to a series of investigations which seek to develop methods of perpetuating the positive effects of the psilocybin experience, methods for helping the subject select and learn new games which give meaning to life.

The first of these projects concerned itself with the rehabilitation of inmates in a state prison. In helping prisoners we have of course found that the prisoners have rehabilitated us —changed our notions about crime, punishment, taught us about their games, made us see the limitations of our middle-class conceptions, expanded our consciousness and given deeper meaning to our lives.

Ten volunteer prisoners. A maximum security prison. The recidivism rate is eighty percent. Eight of the ten would be expected back in prison a year after release. In baseball terms, eighty percent is the error percentage our team attempted to lower.

After three orientation meetings with the prisoners, the drug was given. I was the first one to take the drug in that bare hospital room behind barred windows. Three inmates joined me. Two psychologists and the other inmates served as observers—taking the drug three hours later. The psilocybin session was followed by three discussions, then another drug session, then more discussions. At this point the inmates had taken the drug an average of four times. There had been not one moment of friction or tension in some forty hours of egoless interaction. Pre-post testing has demonstrated marked changes on both objective and projective instruments: dramatic decreases in hostility, cynicism, depression, schizoid ideation; definite increases in optimism, planfulness, flexibility, tolerance, sociability.

The group has become a workshop for planning future games. Some prisoners are being trained to take over the functions of research assistants. They are performing the tasks of a vocational guidance clinic—preparing occupational brochures for inmates about to be released, making plans to act as rehabilitation workers after their release, for organizing a halfway house for ex-convicts. Other prisoners are using their time to prepare for the games to which they will return—the family game, their old job.

The psilocybin experience made these men aware of the stereotyped games in which they had been involved, the game of "cops and robbers," the game of being a tough guy, the game of outwitting the law, the game of resentful cynicism. "My whole life came tumbling down and I was sitting happily in the rubble." But insight is the beginning, and the more demanding task is to help these men choose new games, help them learn the rules, the concepts, the rituals of the new game—practical, collaborative reality education. Of course, this phase of our work requires help from others. But the helpers get helped. The businessmen who help our inmates get jobs are invited into a new and exciting game which gives more meaning to their lives.

Our work progresses slowly and against strong opposition. Our new game of allowing criminals to take over responsibility and authority and prestige as experts on "crime and rehabilitation" brings us into game competition with the professional middle class. Anger and anxiety is aroused. Society has always produced and needed a criminal class. When criminals drop their roles and begin to play a different game, incredulous panic can ensue. Can society play its game without some men acting the part of criminals? If criminals are no longer criminals, where do the rest of us stand? The game of rehabilitator and client (i.e., a professional and a criminal) is being threatened. People are upset when their games are changed.

But our new game has begun. The game statistic for measuring success is clearcut. Eighty percent of convicts return to prison. Next season will reveal how well we have played our game.

SUMMARY

Let me summarize. We have been concerned with change in behavior and change in consciousness. It is considerably easier to change behavior if you understand the learned-game nature of behavior. This sort of insight can be brought about by the administration of consciousness-expanding drugs, of which psilocybin is the most effective. But insight must be followed by behavior change. In the rehabilitation game" we have been developing, the role of the helper is threefold. He provides a serious, supportive context for the CE experience, sets up an atmosphere in which insight can quickly occur. He then joins with the subject in an all-out collaborative process of selecting and mastering new games. He keeps accurate records of his activities and those of his subjects so that the success of his game performance can be objectively appraised by his fellow men.

A final word of clarification: Those of us who talk and write about the games of life are invariably misunderstood. We are seen as frivolous, or cynical anarchists tearing down the social structure. This is an unfortunate misapprehension. Actually, only those who see culture as a game, only those who take this evolutionary point of view can appreciate and treasure the exquisitely complex magnificence of what human beings do and have done. To see it all as "serious, taken-for-granted reality" is to miss the point, is to derogate with bland passivity the greatness of the games we learn.

Those of us who play the game of "applied mysticism" respect and support good gamesmanship. You pick out your game. You learn the rules, rituals, concepts. You play fairly and cleanly. You don't confuse your games with other games. You do not impose your game rituals on others' games. You win today's game with humility. You lose tomorrow's game with dignity. Anger and anxiety are irrelevant because you see your small game in the context of the great evolutionary game which no one can win and no one can lose.

57. MESCALINE, LSD, PSILOCYBIN AND PERSONALITY CHANGE *

Sanford M. Unger

...our normal waking consciousness...is but one special type of consciousness, whilst all about it, parted from it by the filmiest of screens, there lie potential forms of consciousness entirely different.... No account of the universe in its totality can be final which leaves these...disregarded. How to regard them is the question—for they are so discontinuous with ordinary consciousness.—William James.

In recent years, how to regard the "forms of consciousness entirely different" induced by mescaline, LSD-25, and psilocybin has posed a seemingly perplexing issue. For articulate self-experimenters from Mitchell to Huxley, mescaline has provided many-splendored visual experiences, or a life-enlarging sojourn in "the Antipodes of the mind." For Stocking, it may be recalled, mescaline produced controlled schizophrenia—a thesis which earned the Bronze Medal of the Royal Medico-Psychological Association and apparently inaugurated, in conjunction with the advent of LSD-25, a period of concerted chemical activity in the exploration and experimental induction of "model psychoses." In counterpoint, this same so-called "psychotomimetic"† LSD has increasingly found use as a purposeful intervention or "adjuvant" in psychotherapy. The recently arrived "magic mushroom," psilocybin, has been similarly equivocal—"psychotogenic" for some, "mysticomimetic" for others. The present paper will review the literature on drug experience—paying particular attention to the effects of *extradrug* variables, for the realization of the extent of their potential influence has only recently crystallized, and promises to reduce some of the abundant disorder in this area.

The phenomenon of drug-associated rapid personality or behavior change will be discussed in some detail. For example, a number of different alcoholic treatment facilities, especially in Canada, have reported, for many of their patients, complete abstinence after a single LSD session. More generally, neurotic ailments over the full range have been described as practically evaporating. Given this picture, and the present state and practice of the therapeutic art, it is not surprising to find at least one psychiatrist envisioning "...mass therapy: institutions in which every patient with a neurosis could get LSD treatment and work out his problems largely by himself." James would have been much attracted by the "spectacular and almost unbelievable results"

* Grateful acknowledgment is made of the substantial contributions of Miss Judith C. Marshall and the assistance of Mrs. Linda B. J. P. Moncure in the preparation of this paper.

Sanford M. Unger: "Mescaline, LSD, Psilocybin, and Personality Change"; PSYCHIATRY, 26, 1963, 111–125 (Abridged, references omitted). Reprinted with the permission of the author.

† Literally, imitating or simulating a psychosis. (Eds.)

reported on the modern drug scene; and, in fact, their resemblance to the "instantaneous transformations" attendant on "mystical" religious coversions—which he discussed so eloquently—may well be more than superficial and seems worthy of attention.

THE EQUIVALENT ACTION OF MESCALINE, LSD-25, AND PSILOCYBIN

Since the evidence and testimony accumulated over the years on the separate drugs will be treated interchangeably, this raises a preliminary point of some importance. Although the conclusion was delayed by both dissimilarities in their chemical structure and differing modes of introduction to the scientific community, it is now rather commonly adjudged that the subjective effects of mescaline, LSD-25, and psilocybin are similar, equivalent, or indistinguishable. Both Isbell and Abramson have administered LSD and psilocybin in the same study; Wolbach and his co-workers have administered all three. All have found that their subjects were unable to distinguish between the drugs.

The reported equivalence in subjective reactions seems quite consistent—or at least not inconsistent—with present pharmacodynamic knowledge. Studies of radioactively tagged mescaline and LSD indicate that the compounds largely disappear from the brain in relatively short order—in fact, at about the same time that the first "mental phenomena" make their appearance. Hence, it has been tentatively suggested that the characteristic effects, which persist for a relatively long period, are to be attributed not to the action of the drug itself but to some as yet unidentified aspect of the chain of events *triggered* by drug administration. Isbell, observing the "remarkably similar" reactions to LSD and psilocybin, hypothesized "some common biochemical or physiological mechanism" to be responsible for the effects—that is, that the various compounds share a final common path. The most direct support for this inference of biological identity in ultimate mechanism of action has come from cross-tolerance studies wherein subjects rendered tolerant to one drug—that is, nonreactive after repeated administrations—have then been challenged by a different drug. Present indica-tions are that cross-tolerance among the drugs does in fact develop.

This is not intended to suggest that a drug experience is invariable among subjects—quite the contrary has been the case. In fact, experiences even for the same subject differ from one session to the next. But when relevant extradrug variables are controlled, the within-drug variance is apparently coextensive with between-drug variance, and is attributable to ubiquitous personality differences; in other words, while a range of reactions is reported to *all* of the drugs, there is no reaction distinctively associated with any particular drug. Extradrug variables, which have been uncontrolled and largely unrecognized until recently, are apparently responsible for much of the variance erroneously attributed to specific drug action.

INVARIANT DRUG REACTIONS

By common consent, the drug experience is paranormal—that is, beyond or outside the range of the normal, the everyday. Exclamations of "indescribable" recurrently appear in the literature. However, whenever descriptions are essayed, there is relative unanimity about certain features. These, it may be said, are attributable to the drug administration, per se, independent of the personality of the subject, the setting, or the experimenter's or subject's expectations. A sampling from the literature of subjective reports and testimony may communicate, or at least transmit the flavor of, these invariant reactions.

First, and perhaps most easily conveyed, is the characteristic of the drug experience called by Ellis a "saturnalia" or "orgy" of vision. Subsequent authors have been only slightly more restrained: ...

There is a great intensification of light; this intensification is experienced both when the eyes are closed and when they are open. ... With this intensification of light there goes a tremendous intensification of color, and this holds good of the outer world as well as of the inner world. (Aldous Huxley)

When I closed my eyes...I experienced fantastic images of an extraordinary plasticity. These were associated with an intense kaleidoscopic play of colors. (Albert Hofmann) ...

A second invariant set of drug reactions, more difficult to characterize or communicate, has been called, variously, depersonalization, dissociation, levitation, derealization, abnormal detachment, body image distortion or alteration, and the like:

> There is an awareness of an abnormal distance between the self and what happens in its consciousness; on the other hand, the experience of an abnormal fusion of subject and object. (E. Guttman and W. S. Maclay)
>
> My ideas of space were strange beyond description. I could see myself from head to foot as well as the sofa on which I was lying. About me was nothingness, absolutely empty space. I was floating on a solitary island in the ether. No part of my body was subject to the laws of gravitation. (K. Beringer)...

Regardless of whatever else a drug experience may be reported to include, alterations in visual experience and in experience of self, as detailed above, may be predicted with considerable confidence.

In connection with the so-called dissociation phenomenon—and in view of the connotations of the "psychotomimetic" and "intoxicant" labels—it may be well to emphasize that drug experiences, at least for most nonpsychotic subjects, do not seem to approximate delirium....

The nondelirious condition of normal volunteers, at least with low to moderate drug dosage, has been objectively attested by their ability to perform psychological tests. The most exhaustive series of investigations along this line has been carried out for LSD by Abramson and his associates. Generally, although not consistently, subjects show slight decrements in performance—at least some of which may well be attributable to an altered state of attention-motivation-affect. However, the test setting itself seems to contaminate the drug experience; Savage, among others, has noted "a less profound effect when subjects are kept busy doing psychological tests...."

Another and final set of seemingly invariant reactions concerns the retrospective impressiveness of the drug experience. The succession of testimonials to this effect is a striking and salient feature of the history of research with these compounds:

> In some individuals, the "ivresse divine" is rather an "ivresse diabolique."* But in either

case...one looks "beyond the horizon" of the normal world and this "beyond" is often so impressive or even shocking that its after-effects linger for years in one's memory. (Heinrich Kluver)

> The experience of the intoxication, as Beringer also observed, makes a particularly deep impression.... The personality is touched to its core and is led into provinces of psychic life otherwise unexplored; light is shed on boundaries otherwise dark and unrevealed and in this some aid may be given to *Existenzerhellung* (illumination of existence). (Guttman and Maclay)
>
> ...
>
> ...the whole experience is (and is as) a profound piece of knowledge. It is an indelible experience; it is forever known. I have known myself in a way I doubt would have ever occurred except as it did. (Philip B. Smith)

THE "PSYCHOTOMIMETIC" LABEL

After the above renditions, a querulous reader may be concerned about the appellation "psychotomimetic drugs." So are many contemporary researchers and therapists, too numerous to mention. Holliday has provided a trenchant analysis of "how the semantics in the field of psychopharmacology became so confused and generally misleading"; here, only a few points will be noted.

Early mescaline investigators clearly tempered their comparisons between the mescal-induced state and the hallucinations and dissociations of endogenous psychosis. As far back as 1930, it was found that when chronic schizophrenics suffering from persistent hallucinations were given mescal, they distinguished the mescal phenomena, remarked on their appearance, and usually blamed them on the same persecutors who had molested them before. Kluver, though he foresaw and extensively discussed the "model" values of mescal, persisted in calling it "the divine plant." It was apparently difficult to consider a sacramental substance—"the comfort, healer, and guide of us poor Indians...the great teacher" —as unequivocally psychotomimetic.

With LSD, a laboratory-born drug having no history to contend with, the situation changed. The adventurous Hofmann, on that fateful day in 1943, started his self-experiment with 250 micrograms* of LSD, thinking,

---

* "Divine drunkenness"; ... "devilish drunkenness." (Eds.)

* A microgram or gamma equals 1 *one-millionth* of a gram. (Eds.)

as he put it, that such a small amount would probably be harmless. His response to this quite large dose—in terms of present-day experimental standards—was as follows:

> I noted with dismay that my environment was undergoing progressive change. Everything seemed strange and I had the greatest difficulty in expressing myself. My visual fields wavered and everything appeared deformed as in a faulty mirror. I was overcome by a fear that I was going crazy, the worst part of it being that I was clearly aware of my condition. The mind and power of observation were apparently unimpaired.

Hofmann went on to list, as his most marked symptoms, visual disturbances, motor restlessness alternating with paralysis, and a suffocating sensation, and added: "Occasionally I felt as if I were outside my body. My 'ego' seemed suspended in space. . . ."

Stoll, who in 1947 reported experimental confirmation of Hofmann's experience, is widely reputed to have warned informally of a case of suicide as the aftermath of an experimental trial. The most common accounts thereafter had a psychotic female subject committing suicide two weeks after the administration; or, in another version, a subject committing suicide after the drug had been administered without her knowledge. At any rate, this story, though itself never appearing in print, is referred to in one form or another in nearly all of the early work with LSD; it apparently influenced experimenter attitudes for a number of years.

For many and varied reasons, too involved to trace here, the initial formulation of the "model psychosis" properties of LSD engendered enormous investigative enthusiasm. In this climate, latent reservations on the score of psychotomimesis tended to go unvoiced. In the more recent, postenthusiasm era, however, reservations have been more or less vigorously expressed—for example:

> There are considerable differences between LSD-induced and schizophrenic symptoms. The characteristic autism and dissociation of schizophrenia are absent with LSD. Perceptual disturbances due to LSD differ from those due to schizophrenia and, as a rule, are not true hallucinations. Finally, disturbances of consciousness following LSD do not resemble those occurring in schizophrenia. (B. Manzini and A. Saraval)

Many alternatives to the "psychotomimetic" characterization of "hallucinogenic" agents have recently been proposed. In 1957, Osmond offered, among others, "psychelytic" (mind-releasing) and "psychedelic" (mind-manifesting). Other investigators have proposed consciousness-expanding, transcendental, emotionalgenic, mysticomimetic, and so forth. It becomes ever more apparent, though, that old labels never die.

VARIABLE DRUG REACTIONS AND EXTRADRUG VARIABLES

It may probably be stated as a pharmacopoeial commonplace that the effects of a drug administration of any kind are likely to be compounded by factors other than specific pharmacologic action. Often this is attributed to "personality," to individual differences. However, though there have been as yet very few controlled investigations in the case of the drugs considered here, it has become abundantly clear from the *systematic* variability reported in subject and patient reactions—in both the affective and ideational dimensions of drug experience—that factors other than "personality" are also at issue.

Affective reactions attendant on a drug administration have varied, according to reports, all the way from hyperphoric ecstasy to unutterable terror—though *not* with all investigators. The opinion leader Hoch, through a decade of observations, consistently maintained:

> LSD and mescaline disorganize the psychic integration of the individual...
> ...mescaline and LSD are essentially anxiety-producing drugs. . . .

The following interchange was recorded at the 1959 conference on the use of LSD in psychotherapy held under the auspices of the Josiah Macy, Jr. Foundation:

> *Hoch:* Actually, in my experience, no patient asks for it [LSD] again.
> *Katzenelbogen:* I can say the same.
> *Denber:* I have used mescaline in the office . . .and the experience was such that patients said, "Once is enough." The same thing happened in the hospital. I asked the patients there if, voluntarily, they would like to take this again. Over 200 times the answer has been "No."

Subsequently, Malitz also stated:

> None of our normal volunteers wanted to take it [LSD] again.

In contrast, DeShon and his co-workers reported the results of the first LSD study done with normal subjects in this country as follows:

> ...anxiety was infrequent, transient, and never marked.... All subjects were willing to repeat the test.

The experience of other investigators has been similar:

> During the past four years we have administered the drug [LSD] hundreds of times to nonpsychotics in doses up to 225 micrograms. ... Those who have participated in these groups are nearly always definitely benefited by their experiences. Almost invariably they wish to return and to participate in new experiments. (Harold Abramson)

> ...few patients discontinue treatment, in fact, enthusiasm and eagerness to continue are among the features of LSD patients. (R. A. Sandison)

The rapidly expanding use of LSD in psychotherapeutic contexts has provided highly revealing clues to the patterning of extradrug variability. Busch and Johnson were the first to report administering LSD to neurotic patients whose therapy had "stalled" and whose prognosis was "dim." The result was "a reliving of repressed traumatic episodes of childhood," with "profound" influence on the course of therapy. Sandison and his colleagues also found that LSD "produces an upsurge of unconscious material into consciousness," and that "repressed memories are relived with remarkable clarity"—with therapeutically beneficial consequences.

Since these early reports, whenever psychoanalytically oriented therapists have employed LSD, practically without exception the patient relives childhood memories. The interesting point is that this phenomenon has practically *never* been noted in the experimental literature!

Jungian therapists, on the other hand, have repeatedly found that their patients have "transcendental" experiences—a state beyond conflict—often with rapid and dramatic therapeutic results. As a matter of fact, in an amusing and somewhat bemused account, Hartman has described his LSD-using group comprised of two Freudians and two Jungians, in which the patients of the former report childhood memories, while those of the latter have "transcendental" experiences. In addition, for Jungian patients, the transcendental state is associated with "spectacular" therapeutic results, while for Freudians, should such a state "accidentally" occur, no such spectacular consequence is observed.

While not from a therapeutic setting, the reports which have emanated from Harvard are noteworthy on the score of ideational content. Under psilocybin, Harvard subjects do not relive their childhood experiences, but grapple with age-old paradoxes:

> ...the problem of the one and the many, unity and variety, determinism and freedom; mechanism and vitalism; good and evil; time and eternity; the plenum and the void; moral absolutism and moral relativism; monotheism and polytheism and atheism. These are the basic problems of human existence.... We need not wonder that the Indians called the mushroom sacred and gave it a name which means "the flesh of the god." (Frank Barron)

Without multiplying or belaboring divergences further, it should be apparent that affective reactions and ideational content may be *systematically* variable dimensions of drug experience; in addition, the possible therapeutic uses or consequences, however these are conceived, seem clearly variable. Once these "facts" are arrayed, in Baconian fashion, they nearly speak for themselves. At the Josiah Macy conference, the emerging consensus was perhaps best expressed by Savage:

> This meeting is most valuable because it allows us to see all at once results ranging from the nihilistic conclusions of some to the evangelical ones of others. Because the results are so much influenced by the personality, aims, and expectations of the therapist, and by the setting, only such a meeting as this could provide us with such a variety of personalities and settings. It seems clear, first of all, that where there is no therapeutic intent, there is no therapeutic result.... I think we can also say that where the atmosphere is fear-ridden and skeptical, the results are generally not good. ...This is all of tremendous significance, for few drugs are so dependent on the milieu and

require such careful attention to it as LSD does. . . .

More specifically, anxiety in the therapist or experimenter about administering the drug, about "inducing psychosis," seems likely to render the experience anxiety-ridden for the subject. Abramson has flatly declared: "The response of the subject. . . will depend markedly upon the attitude of the therapist. . . . In particular, if the therapist is not anxious about the use of the drug, anxiety in the patient will be much decreased." . . . Huxley had intimated this before it became clarified in the psychiatric literature:

. . . the reasonably healthy person knows in advance that, so far as he is concerned, mescaline is completely innocuous. . . . Fortified by this knowledge, he embarks upon the experience without fear—in other words, without any disposition to convert an unprecedentedly strange and other than human experience into something appalling, something actually diabolical.

That the positive or negative character of the experience can be systematically directed, overriding even personality factors, seems now to have been fairly conclusively demonstrated. With "adequate" preparation—that is, with the specific intent of rendering drug experiences "positive"—approximately 90 percent of the subjects or patients, in each of the two most recent studies, reported at least a "pleasant" or "rewarding" session, and nearly as many called it "an experience of great beauty" or something equally superlative.

In content, as in affect, subjects apparently respond to the implicit or explicit suggestion or expectation of the therapist or experimenter. The Harvard subjects were prepared for their metaphysical binges, it may be noted, with such assigned readings as the "Idols of the Cave" parable in Plato's *Republic* and passages from *The Tibetan Book of the Dead*. The preparation of psychotherapy patients hardly needs specification.

Finally, what may be said about therapeutic implications?—given the fact that the compounds under discussion may induce a powerful paranormal experience whose affective and ideational content can be guided. Only perhaps that the extent to which the experience can serve as a useful adjunct to traditional interview therapies, or vice versa, or even as a

"compleat therapie" would seem to depend on the particular practitioner of the art—his conceptions of therapeutic gains and consequences, his philosophy and enthusiasm, and his orientation toward "placebo" or "faith" cures. Schmiege has summarized the current state of affairs as follows:

Those using LSD in multiple doses as an adjunct to psychotherapy feel that it is so useful because of its ability to do the following: (1) It helps the patient to remember and abreact both recent and childhood traumatic experiences. (2) It increases the transference reaction while enabling the patient to discuss it more easily. (3) It activates the patient's unconscious so as to bring forth fantasies and emotional phenomena which may be handled by the therapist as dreams. (4) It intensifies the patient's affectivity so that excessive intellectualization is less likely to occur. (5) It allows the patient to better see his customary defenses and sometimes allows him to alter them. Because of these effects, therapists feel that psychotherapy progresses at a faster rate. Of course this poses the age old problem of what is the essence of psychotherapy. . . .

RAPID PERSONALITY CHANGE

An increasing number of subjects, patients, experimenters, and psychiatrists—spontaneously or with priming—have declared their drug experiences to be transcendental, mystical, cosmic, visionary, revelatory, and the like. There seems to be difficulty in finding the right name for the experience, even among the professional so-called "mystics":

There is no really satisfactory name for this type of experience. To call it mystical is to confuse it with visions of another world, or of god and angels. To call it spiritual or metaphysical is to suggest that it is not also extremely concrete and physical, while the term "cosmic consciousness" itself has the unpoetic flavor of occultist jargon. But from all historical times and cultures we have reports of this same unmistakable sensation emerging, as a rule, quite suddenly and unexpectedly and from no clearly understood cause. (Alan Watts)

Whatever this type of experience is called, however, a growing body of "expert" testimony apparently confirms the possibility of its induction by drugs. Watts, the dean of current Western Zen scholars, has recently described "cosmic consciousness," courtesy of

LSD, in exquisite detail. Seminary students and professors in the Boston area are said to have definitely concluded that their contact with psilocybin was "mystico-religious" (as to whether or not it was "Christian," however, they are still in doubt)....

Nearly invariably, whenever dramatic personality change has been noted following the use of these drugs, it has been associated with this kind of experience—that is, one called transcendental or visionary—with the particular name the experience is given seemingly most dependent upon whether the investigator focuses on affect or content....

DRUG-ASSOCIATED PERSONALITY CHANGE: A "NEW CONCEPT" IN PSYCHOTHERAPY

It is an intriguing historical accident that, on the one hand, anthropological studies of the Native American Church (Peyotism) consistently record the peyote-associated reformation of alcoholic and generally reprobate characters, and, on the other hand, LSD has been increasingly utilized in the treatment of the white man's "fire-water" ills. LSD was first systematically administered to non-Indian alcoholics in order to explore a putative similarity between the so-called model psychosis and delirium tremens. Two independent undertakings along this line, one in the U.S. and one in Canada, resulted in highly unexpected and sudden "cures."

Investigators in Saskatchewan pursued this serendipitous result aggressively. The outcome, with lately-evolved refinements in technique, has been an explicitly formulated "new concept" in psychotherapy. The following narrative, pieced together from Hoffer's statements at the Macy LSD conference, describes the conditions under which the rapid change phenomenon seems first to have occurred in sizeable numbers:

> ...we have what we call the "businessman's special," for very busy people, the weekend treatment.... They come in because the police or Alcoholics Anonymous or others bring them in. They come in on day *one*. They know they are going to take a treatment, but they know nothing about what it is. We take a psychiatric history to establish a diagnosis. That is on day *one*. On day *two*, they have the LSD. On day *three*, they are discharged.
> Our objective [in using 200–400 gamma

doses] is to give each patient a particular LSD experience.

> The results are that 50 per cent of these people are changed [that is, they stop drinking or are much improved].... As a general rule ...those who have not had the transcendental experience are not changed; they continue to drink. However, the large proportion of those who have had it are changed.

The only other investigators to report a "weekend treatment" are Ball and Armstrong. They describe a small series of "sex perverts," at least two of whom had had, over a number of years, "a variety of forms of psychotherapy, including psychoanalysis... [resulting in] no improvement whatever." The large-dose LSD experience, however, is said to have had "remarkable, long-lasting remedial effects."

MacLean and his co-workers in British Columbia, Canada, have reported on a series which included 61 alcoholics and 33 neurotics (personality trait distu.bance and anxiety reaction neurosis). Each patient was carefully and intensively prepared for the 400–1500 gamma, "psychedelic LSD-day"—which was jointly conducted by a psychiatrist, a psychologist, a psychiatric nurse, and a music therapist. Their follow-up data (median follow-up was for 9 months) were interpreted to yield a "much improved" or "improved" rating for over 90 percent of the neurotics and 60 percent of the alcoholics, with just under 50 percent of the alcoholics found at follow-up to have remained "totally dry." The results of this single LSD session with the alcoholic cases seem most impressive, in view of the picture provided:

> These were considered to be difficult cases; 59 had experienced typical delirium tremens; 36 had tried Alcoholics Anonymous and were considered to have failed in that program. The average period of uncontrolled drinking was 14.36 years. The average number of admissions to hospital for alcoholism during the preceding 3 years was 8.07.

Since Hoffer's account, procedures in Saskatchewan have apparently been modified to incorporate considerable "psychotherapy"—as an adjunct to, and preparation for, the LSD experience. In a recent report, Jensen has described a greatly expanded treatment method and its results:

The treatment program includes three weekly A.A. meetings. The patients are strongly encouraged, but not forced, to attend. There are also 2 hours of group psychotherapy, in the course of which those who are not already familiar with the A.A. program are indoctrinated mainly by the other patients' discussion. ...Because of the fairly short time available, the group therapy is superficial in nature and primarily educational.

Toward the end of hospitalization (which averaged 2 months), the patients were given an LSD experience. They routinely received 200 gamma of the drug....

Of 58 patients who experienced the full program, including LSD, and were followed up for 6 to 18 months, 34 had remained totally abstinent since discharge or had been abstinent following a short experimental bout immediately after discharge; 7 were considered improved, i.e., were drinking definitely less than before; 13 were unimproved; and 4 broke contact.

Of 35 patients who received group therapy without LSD, 4 were abstinent, 4 were improved, 9 were unimproved and 18 were lost to follow-up.

Of 45 controls, consisting of patients admitted to the hospital during the same period who received individual treatment by other psychiatrists, 7 were abstinent, 3 improved, 12 unimproved, and 23 lost to follow-up.

Among the reservations that might be expressed about Jensen's study, two are outstanding. First, there is some ambiguity about the assignment of patients to the different treatment conditions—it does not seem to have been entirely random. Second, Jensen's assumption that patients who broke or refused follow-up contact with the hospital staff are safely categorized, for statistical purposes, as "treatment failures" would seem somewhat overweening. At any rate, on his count, the difference in percentages of patients "abstinent or improved" between the "full program-LSD" group (41 out of 58, or 71 percent) and the "individual psychotherapy" group (10 out of 45, or 22 percent) was highly statistically significant.

The present "official policy" of the Saskatchewan Department of Public Health may be of interest. A recently issued document, which reviews the results of four such follow-up studies as Jensen's, concludes with the directive that the single, large-dose LSD treatment of alcoholism is to be considered "no longer as experimental," but rather, "to be used where indicated."

There seem to have been only two efforts in the U.S. to explicitly and systematically follow the Canadian model. In quite different contexts, both are reported as at least "doing well." Leary and his co-workers at Harvard, over the last two years, have conducted a research and treatment program at Massachusetts Correctional Institution, Concord, "designed to test the effects of consciousness-expanding drugs on prisoner rehabilitation." This undertaking, which emphasizes the crucial importance of drug-induced "far-reaching insight experiences"—prepared for, supported, and reinforced by group therapy sessions—has resulted in a recidivism rate considerably reduced from actuarial expectation. The number of posttreatment cases on which this evaluation is based, however, is only 26. The program is ongoing.

In a much more familiar setting, a group of workers on the West Coast has been treating the full range of garden-variety neuroses. The patients are intensively prepared over a two- to three-week period for a large-dosage, "transcendental" drug session. The stated intent is to induce a "single overwhelming experience...so profound and impressive that ...the months and years that follow become a continuing growth process." Thus far, in over 100 treated cases, at least "marked improvement" in the condition for which treatment was sought has been reported in about 80 percent—after one so-called overwhelming experience.

It is a commonplace that new psychiatric treatments seem to effect remarkable cures—at least for a short time and in the hands of their originators. In raising the spectre of the powerful placebo effect,* it need hardly be pointed out that the results reviewed above should be regarded with healthy skepticism. On the other hand, they are more than merely trifling. . . .

---

* An effect caused not by the physiological action of a substance but by faith in its efficacy, even though it be chemically inert. (Eds.)

RECOMMENDED FURTHER READING

*Alpert, Richard, S. Cohen and L. Schiller: *LSD;* New York, New American Library 1966

Andrews, George and Simon Vinkenoog (eds.): *The Book of Grass: An Anthology on Indian Hemp;* London, Peter Owen 1967

Barron, Frank, Murray E. Jarvik and Sterling Bunnell, Jr.: "The Hallucinogenic Drugs"; *Scientific American,* April 1964

Blum, Richard, *et al.: Utopiates: The Use and Users of LSD-25;* New York, Atherton 1964

De Bold, Richard and Russell Leaf (eds.): *LSD, Man and Society;* Middletown, Conn., Wesleyan University Press 1967

*Goode, Erich (ed.): *Marijuana;* New York, Atherton 1969

————: *The Marijuana Smokers;* New York, Basic Books 1970

Leary, Timothy: *High Priest;* New York, New American Library-World 1967

————: *The Politics of Ecstasy;* New York, Putnam's 1968

*Masters, R. E. L. and J. Houston: *The Varieties of Psychedelic Experience;* New York, Holt, Rinehart & Winston 1966

*Nowlis, Helen H.: *Drugs on the College Campus;* Garden City, N.Y., Doubleday Anchor 1969

*Polsky, Ned: *Hustlers, Beats and Others;* Chicago, Aldine 1967

*Solomon, David (ed.): *LSD: The Consciousness Expanding Drug;* New York, Putnam's-Berkley 1964

*———— (ed.): *The Marijuana Papers;* Indianapolis, Ind., Bobbs-Merrill 1966

Uhr, L. and J. G. Miller (eds.): *Drugs and Behavior;* New York, John Wiley 1960

Weil, T., N. E. Zinberg and J. Nelsen: "Clinical and Psychological Effects of Marijuana in Man"; *Science, 162* (1968), 1234–1242

* Paperback edition available.

George Tooker, *The Subway* (1950). Collection of the Whitney Museum of American Art, New York.

PART XIII

PSYCHOLOGY IN
THE WIDER WORLD

Social psychology is often treated, even by some psychologists, as though it were a side issue, a kind of intellectual no-man's land indeterminately situated between the territories of "real" psychology and sociology. In reality, as we suggested in the Preface and as many of the preceding selections should have made clear, most aspects of psychology (the physiological perhaps excepted) can only be understood adequately by reference to a context of relationships, experiences, and influences that is, in every sense, social. This is as true for normal as for disturbed behaviors, for processes of perception as for those of development, motivation, and communication. Man, as Aristotle held, is a "social animal" who *becomes human* only in and through a context of social relationships. Accurately speaking, therefore, most of psychology is social psychology.

As they use the phrase "social psychology," however, psychologists typically refer either to the behavior of groups as such or to the study of an individual's behavior (physical or verbal) as it is affected by the real or presumed presence and behavior of others or by the immediately preceding behavior of others. In both cases the point of view is interactive rather than developmental (see the introduction to Part I) although, again in reality, it is virtually impossible to understand an individual's behavior solely as the result of immediate situational factors without some regard for what past learning and experience he brings to that situation. That different people behave very differently in response to the same situational pressures indicates that the latter are rarely if ever the sole determinants of behavior.

Among those problems or problem areas to which social psychologists have, over the years, devoted considerable attention are: the structure and behavior of groups and crowds ("collective behavior"), the development of social roles and norms within groups as they go about their tasks, the effects of differing leadership "climates" or styles (e.g., "authoritarian," "democratic," and "laissez-faire") on group performance and efficiency, the creation and reduction of intergroup tensions, the phenomena of prejudice and discrimination, and the effects of group membership and group pressures on the individual's perceptions, attitudes, and opinions. Other researchers have investigated the conditions and limits of compliant (obedient) and non-compliant behavior, the social factors that foster personal and group violence, the formation and change of attitudes and opinions[1] through the use of various techniques and under conditions of inducement, of persuasion, and of coercion (i.e., "brainwashing"), the social correlates of political preference and voting choice, and the tendency of individuals to create at least a seeming consistency among their various attitudes and between their attitudes and their overt behavior (cognitive "balance," "congruity," or "consonance").

Obviously, we can neither present nor review all this work; we mention it both to show the range of interests embraced by the rubric "social psychology" and to indicate that the latter is an area in which the concerns and techniques of psychologists meet and overlap those of sociologists, political scientists, economists, and even historians. That some of these interrelationships have barely begun to be explored seems less a result of the intrinsic difficulty of the problems than of the way in which American academic life arbitrarily compartmentalizes the study of an indivisible social reality. The selections in this concluding section represent not only significant work in the field of social psychology as we have characterized it but attempts to use the findings of psychology to illuminate, if not to solve, important social problems.

Conformity: its extent, its causes, and its consequences, is one of the most talked about features of the contemporary American social scene. Granted that some degree of conformity is necessary for social life to proceed at all, recent discussions and polemics have suggested that the degree of conformity now prevailing in American society far exceeds that indispensable minimum. Avoiding for the moment the value-laden question "conformity to what?" (since conformity must always be *to* something), we can concede that the problem of avoiding unnecessary conformity is particularly critical for any society committed to the values of democracy, diversity, and the encouragement of individuality. We will not discuss here the degree to which American society is truly committed to those values. We can, however, assert that the vitality and adaptability of a society depends, in large measure, on the ability of at least some of its members to resist the stultifying, stereotyping effects of traditional patterns of thought and action, to resist pressures toward a fashionable consensus, whatever the content of that consensus may be.

From a large body of research findings we know that when an individual becomes a member of a group, especially one to which he is strongly motivated to belong and whose standards he accepts as his own (i.e., a "reference group") his own attitudes, opinions, and social perceptions tend to conform more closely than before to the group's norms; he tends to perceive other members of the group as more like himself than may, in fact, be so.

The classic experiments of Solomon Asch (now at the Institute for Advanced Study in Princeton) reported in our first selection show that the expression of majority opinion within a group will cause many individuals to

1 We define an attitude as a favorable or unfavorable orientation, sometimes conscious and sometimes not, toward an object, person, idea, or situation coupled with a readiness to act in a particular manner toward that object, person, idea or situation. An opinion may be defined as a verbalized or verbalizable attitude, involving an expectation or prediction of some action either by oneself or another.

distort their judgment of a straightforward visual perception even when the group is a temporary one of little long-range significance to its members. In Asch's experiment the mere expression of the majority's opinion, without any attempt on their part to persuade or coerce the naïve subject caused one-third of the latter to report a judgment that patently contradicted the evidence of their senses (members of a control group showed virtually no errors in judgment). Whether or not the conforming individuals subjectively believed the judgment they reported they went along with the majority and acted *as if* the clearly erroneous perception were true. Depending on whether one is an optimist or a pessimist one may say either that *only* one-third or that *fully* one-third of the subjects knuckled under to the informal group pressure. Further research has shown that the more ambiguous the situation or stimulus to be judged, the greater the tendency of naïve subjects (regardless of their intelligence or training) to go along with the majority consensus. As ambiguity is typical of actual social situations the relevance of these findings to real life is obvious and may suggest how the media of mass communication can often mold so-called "public opinion."

Asch's findings further indicate that Americans (even college students) are far less independent than they might wish to believe. Yet, two beacons of hope shine forth through the general gloom of these findings: the wide range of individual differences in degree of conformity and the effect that even a single ally can have in increasing the independence of even the most compliant subjects. The latter finding alerts us to the importance of providing social and institutional supports for non-conformity and to the crucial role that so-called "deviant" subcultures may sometimes play in nurturing independent thought and upholding alternative interpretations of reality, interpretations that, at a later day, may themselves become fashionable and even "self-evident."

If Asch's work reveals that people, under informal social pressures, will *say* things that contradict the evidence of their senses the work of Stanley Milgram, as reported by Philip Meyer in our second selection, shows that under formal social pressures people will often *do* things that contravene their beliefs and principles, provided they do not have to assume personal responsibility for their actions. This state, which Milgram calls one of "agency" (as opposed to "autonomy," in which the individual has control over and assumes responsibility for what he does) can be epitomized by the words: "What can I do? I'm only following orders." In a state of agency the individual abdicates personal moral responsibility and allows some superior authority that he perceives as legitimate to define his situation for him and to prescribe his action therein. The scandalous degree of obedience shown by most of Milgram's experimental subjects is considerably greater than the degree of conformity exhibited by Asch's and raises questions of what conditions lead to the perception of authority and its orders as legitimate and what the limits of even legitimate authority may be. How, in other words, can people be made to *disobey*, to assert their own consciences against the orders of authority; and at what point *should* they do so? Such conflicts between two kinds of authority, between two "rights" is the essence of tragedy, as the German philosopher, Hegel, long ago realized. While they are among the burning social and moral issues of this hour they have been perennial issues for concerned, reflective men in every age: it was the same conflict that Sokrates faced after his trial in fourth century B.C. Athens and that was referred to by whoever said that "resistance to tyranny is obedience to God."

Milgram's work suggests that many Americans are or can easily be induced to be highly obedient (although, once again, individual differences are significant), that tyranny and totalitarianism—perhaps under the label "Americanism"—can indeed happen here. Regrettably, the catchy title of Meyer's article tends only to mislead the reader: the question is not whether you or I might have executed a stranger at Hitler's command (many "good" Germans did, some of them on a mass scale) but whether you or I, despite our knowledge of the Hitler era, might do so tomorrow at Richard Nixon's command, or our boss's or teacher's, or Stanley Milgram's or, for that matter, at the behest of an anonymous but authoritative seeming stranger or even of a faceless "they." The ethical issues raised by Milgram's research techniques themselves pale to insignificance beside the importance of the moral and social issues to which his findings point.

In the third selection, the late J. C. Flugel, a British psychoanalyst, discusses the personality characteristics that differentiate tolerant (unprejudiced) from intolerant (prejudiced) individuals. Among other factors Flugel notes that the intolerant have a greater propensity to stereotyped thinking: the tendency to perceive and react to people not as differentiated beings but as members of a class or group to which certain characteristics (favorable or unfavorable) are imputed. These characteristics are then automatically ascribed to all individuals who belong to the group. (See also Selection 22). The intolerant also exhibit a greater tendency to see the world in sharp "either...or" dichotomies (e.g., "good" versus "evil" or "black" versus "white") and to overlook the many possible intermediate positions between the extremes.

Yet, despite the real personality differences between the tolerant and the intolerant, it would be misleading and grossly oversimple were we to "explain" all prejudice and intolerance solely as the result of personality variables or of differing childhood experiences. Many other forces such as ignorance, cultural traditions, the need to feel superior to others, and the conscious actions of political and economic interest groups help to create and sustain intolerance and to support patterns of economic and social discrimination even in the absence of personal prejudice. Moreover, attitudes of intolerance do not necessarily find expression in over action; such expression may be inhibited by cultural factors, by situational counter-pressures, or by sheer lack of opportunity. One of the greatest challenges to attitude and opinion research is to relate the verbal expression of attitudes and opinions to the overt acts of those who hold the attitudes and express the opinions, for we know that a wide gap often exists between people's verbal and their non-verbal behavior. Part of this discrepancy may be explained by situational factors and by differences in the absolute intensity with which attitudes are held, the latter a factor virtually impossible to measure with present survey research techniques.

Lillian Smith is a novelist (a Southern novelist at that) not a psychologist and her article is based on personal experience and reflection rather than on laboratory or even field research. Yet, unquestionably, it is a penetrating psycho-social analysis of the roots of racism in the American South—and the American Everywhere. Miss Smith sees the sources of racism as much in historical and sociological factors as in the personality dynamics of whites, yet, over time, the splitting of society into black and white castes came to be paralleled by a split in the psyches of whites, a phenomenon that has given rise to many of the classical mechanisms of defense discussed by psychoanalysts. Although Miss Smith does not employ psychoanalytic terminology it would not be difficult to translate her figurative imagery into that more clinical idiom. The "ghosts" of which she writes, for example, are the deeply buried impulses, fears, and guilts that some people must, at all cost, repress from awareness.

For Miss Smith the ideology of white superiority is a drug that relieves the feeling of powerlessness that afflicts so many in the modern world, while the response to the breakdown of the racial caste system may be likened to the withdrawal symptoms experienced by a narcotics' addict. She concludes that a change in racist patterns of behavior can result only from changes within individuals, changes that "poetry" alone can effect, by creating new myths that will heal old wounds and reconcile ancient hatreds.

As a final exercise the reader might ask how well Dr. Flugel's analysis of intolerance and the prejudiced personality fits with Miss Smith's account of the dynamics of white racism. As Freud, Jung, and many other pioneers of psychoanalysis well knew psychological truth can be expressed as cogently in the language of the poet as in that of the scientist.

Next, Hans Toch of the State University of New York at Albany, examines the personality and situational configurations that encourage the resort to violence. He believes that the conjunction of a violence-prone individual— usually characterized by personal insecurities and a power-centered model of human relationships—and a violence-provoking incident almost invariably leads to violent acts. Once experienced, however, violence can become a habit-forming game, an habitual mode of relating to others that individuals will almost consciously pursue for its various gratifications. Toch then discusses subcultures of violence that perpetuate themselves and are characterized by norms that demand violent behavior of their members. He concludes with some reflections on the interrelations between personal and collective violence. Remembering that overt violence is but one form of aggression, the reader might nonetheless ask whether the selections dealing with aggression in Part VII cast any light on Toch's discussion. While the author believes that the personalities of those who glory in violence must be re-socialized (perhaps by means of behavior therapy?) for life in a civilized community, the incidence of violence might also be reduced by forestalling violence-provoking incidents or by devising techniques that will effectively disrupt the sequence by which such incidents lead on to violent outcomes.

Continuing with the theme of violence, Morton Deutsch of Columbia University denies the inevitability of that international collective violence called "war" and calls for the creation of functional alternatives to it. (Once again, the selections on aggression in Part VII are relevant to this discussion.) Deutsch believes that nuclear war would not even be a satisfying way of expressing aggression because of the lack of direct physical contact between aggressor and victim and the consequent psychological distancing of the actor from the results of his actions. He then discusses those misperceptions in the conduct of international relations that could lead to war, how they are perpetuated and how they may be corrected. According to Deutsch, if we are to build a world in which genuine peace is possible we must create an atmosphere of mutual trust among nations to replace the present climate of mutual suspicion; each nation must work not for narrow "national" security but for "mutual" security; each side must accept the legitimacy of the other's political and social system and have a stake in its success rather than its failure. World politics, in other words, is not a zero-sum game in which what one player wins the others must necessarily lose. Deutsch points out how a strong third force in world affairs—whether it be the UN or a neutralist bloc of nations—would add stability to the present international system. He then offers a set of rules for international negotiations, rules drawn from the experience of labor-management relations. Many of Deutsch's analyses and prescriptions seem as valid for the conduct of inter*group* (racial and ethnic) as for inter*national* relations, but for all their sophistication and insight they seem to have been completely ignored by those who might put them into practice. Perhaps the President of the United States should have a behavioral science advisor in addition to one representing the natural sciences.

In the penultimate selection the American Friends Service Committee examines the psychological effects of the draft (a social institution) on the draftee, his family, and the structure and values of American society as a whole. The problem itself is one worthy of serious study—especially for college-age students—but the conclusions of the report should not be accepted uncritically even by those who oppose the draft. The arguments that life in the armed forces encourages authoritarian personality traits and types, that it emphasizes unquestioning obedience rather than rational persuasion, that it exalts the group over the individual, that it destroys the finer human sensibilities, that, in essence, it tends to subvert those very values the armed forces ostensibly exist to defend are not new, and though plausible, have never been adequately substantiated by systematic research. Plausibility as such is no guarantee of truth. The selection itself has a frankly rhetorical and polemical purpose, as might be anticipated from an organization that advocates pacifism. At the same time the authors, either deliberately or inadvertently, confuse several distinct issues: They identify and thus confound the effects of being drafted with the effects of military service as such and they further identify the effects of combat experience with those of non-combatant service. The effects of military service (combat or non-combatant) are presumably the same for individuals regardless of whether they are drafted or volunteer for induction and are distinct from the effects of being drafted or of living subject to conscription. We have included this selection not because we are convinced by its reasoning or because we are opposed to the draft but because it raises important questions and points to ways in which they might be fruitfully investigated.

In the final selection of the book Leonard Krasner, one of the leading exponents of behavior therapy, courageously confronts the dilemma to which we pointed in Part XI: the ethical and political issues raised by the growing ability of psychologists to control human behavior. Krasner affirms his belief that behavior is controllable and points to two basic models of such control: "social reinforcement," in which the behavior of one person and the structure of the situation are used to modify the behavior of another; and coercive change, in which drugs, physical devices or gross manipulations of the physical and social environment are used to attain the same goal. Krasner's chief concern is with social reinforcement, ultimately a more powerful and dangerous technique because more subtle and often imperceptible to the person whose behavior is being manipulated.

For Krasner, the psychotherapeutic relationship is the paradigm of behavior change through social reinforcement, a fact which many therapists have long resisted admitting. But once we recognize all forms of psychotherapy (not only behavior therapy or behavior modification therapy) as attempts to, in some way, change the patient's behavior, we need to ask who determines the values and goals to be realized through therapy and what role the therapist's own values, attitudes, and even prejudices play in the process. Though Krasner does not answer those questions it is to his credit that he asks them—directly and unequivocally. He asserts the need to be concerned with the ethical problems of behavior control *before* the techniques of control have been perfected (a point that echoes the Brechers' forebodings in Selection 6) and suggests that our awareness of how behavior can be controlled is the best defense against the unscrupulous or socially irresponsible use of such techniques.

Above all, Krasner feels, we must have full and frank discussion of the ethical issues involved in behavior control and a closer scrutiny of the goals, values, and attitudes of those—psychologists, psychotherapists, psychiatrists, psychoanalysts, and even teachers—who, consciously or not, use the techniques that psychology has developed. It is at this point that the social and political implications of psychology loom the most momentous, that the usual distinction between science and politics becomes no longer tenable. Should the reader of this article be left with a sense of disquiet and unease we will be well content. The call to social responsibility sounds not for psychologists alone.

58. EFFECTS OF GROUP PRESSURE UPON THE MODIFICATION AND DISTORTION OF JUDGMENTS

S. E. Asch

We shall here describe in summary form the conception and first findings of a program of investigation into the conditions of independence and submission to group pressure.[1]

Our immediate object was to study the social and personal conditions that induce individuals to resist or to yield to group pressures when the latter are perceived to be *contrary to fact*. The issues which this problem raises are of obvious consequence for society; it can be of decisive importance whether or not a group will, under certain conditions, submit to existing pressures. Equally direct are the consequences for individuals and our understanding of them, since it is a decisive fact about a person whether he possesses the freedom to act independently, or whether he characteristically submits to group pressures.

The problem under investigation requires the direct observation of certain basic processes in the interaction between individuals,

and between individuals and groups. To clarify these seems necessary if we are to make fundamental advances in the understanding of the formation and reorganization of attitudes, of the functioning of public opinion, and of the operation of propaganda. Today we do not possess an adequate theory of these central psycho-social processes. Empirical investigation has been predominantly controlled by general propositions concerning group influence which have as a rule been assumed but not tested. With few exceptions investigation has relied upon descriptive formulations concerning the operation of suggestion and prestige, the inadequacy of which is becoming increasingly obvious, and upon schematic applications of stimulus-response theory.

Basic to the current approach has been the axiom that group pressures characteristically induce psychological changes *arbitrarily*, in far-reaching disregard of the material properties of the given conditions. This mode of thinking has almost exclusively stressed the slavish submission of individuals to group forces, has neglected to inquire into their possibilities for independence and for productive relations with the human environment, and has virtually denied the capacity of men under certain conditions to rise above group passion and prejudice. It was our aim to contribute to a clarification of these questions, important both for theory and for their human implications, by means of direct observation of the effects of groups upon the decisions and evaluations of individuals.

1 The earlier experiments out of which the present work developed and the theoretical issues which prompted it are discussed in S. E. Asch, *Social Psychology* (Englewood Cliffs, N.J.: Prentice-Hall, Inc., 1952), Ch. 16.

THE EXPERIMENT AND FIRST RESULTS

To this end we developed an experimental technique which has served as the basis for the present series of studies. We employed the procedure of placing an individual in a relation of radical conflict with all the other members of a group, of measuring its effect upon him in quantitative terms, and of describing its psychological consequences. A group of eight individuals was instructed to judge a series of simple, clearly structured perceptual relations—to match the length of a given line with one of three unequal lines. Each member of the group announced his judgments publicly. In the midst of this monotonous "test" one individual found himself suddenly contradicted by the entire group, and this contradiction was repeated again and again in the course of the experiment. The group in question had, with the exception of one member, previously met with the experimenter and received instructions to respond at certain points with wrong—and unanimous—judgments. The errors of the majority were large (ranging between ½″ and 1¾″) and of an order not encountered under control conditions. The outstanding person—the critical subject—whom we had placed in the position of a *minority of one* in the midst of a *unanimous majority*—was the object of investigation. He faced, possibly for the first time in his life, a situation in which a group unanimously contradicted the evidence of his senses.

This procedure was the starting point of the investigation and the point of departure for the study of further problems. Its main features were the following: (1) The critical subject was submitted to two contradictory and irreconcilable forces—the evidence of his own experience of a clearly perceived relation, and the unanimous evidence of a group of equals. (2) Both forces were part of the immediate situation; the majority was concretely present, surrounding the subject physically. (3) The critical subject, who was requested together with all others to state his judgments publicly, was obliged to declare himself and to take a definite stand *vis-à-vis* the group. (4) The situation possessed a self-contained character. The critical subject could not avoid or evade the dilemma by reference to conditions external to the experimental situation. (It may be mentioned at this point that the forces generated by the given conditions acted so quickly upon the critical subjects that instances of suspicion were infrequent.)

The technique employed permitted a simple quantitative measure of the "majority effect" in terms of the frequency of errors in the direction of the distorted estimates of the majority. At the same time we were concerned to obtain evidence of the ways in which the subjects perceived the group, to establish whether they became doubtful, whether they were tempted to join the majority. Most important, it was our object to establish the grounds of the subject's independence or yielding—whether, for example, the yielding subject was aware of the effect of the majority upon him, whether he abandoned his judgment deliberately or compulsively. To this end we constructed a comprehensive set of questions which served as the basis of an individual interview immediately following the experimental period. Toward the conclusion of the interview each subject was informed fully of the purpose of the experiment, of his role and of that of the majority. The reactions to the disclosure of the purpose of the experiment became in fact an integral part of the procedure. The information derived from the interview became an indispensable source of evidence and insight into the psychological structure of the experimental situation, and in particular, of the nature of the individual differences. It should be added that it is not justified or advisable to allow the subject to leave without giving him a full explanation of the experimental conditions. The experimenter has a responsibility to the subject to clarify his doubts and to state the reasons for placing him in the experimental situation. When this is done most subjects react with interest, and some express gratification at having lived through a striking situation which has some bearing on them personally and on wider human issues.

Both the members of the majority and the critical subjects were male college students. We shall report the results for a total of fifty critical subjects in this experiment. In Table 1 we summarize the successive comparison trials and the majority estimates. The reader

TABLE 1
Lengths of Standard and Comparison Lines

TRIAL	LENGTH OF STANDARD LINE (IN INCHES)	COMPARISON LINES (IN INCHES)			CORRECT RESPONSE	GROUP RESPONSE	MAJORITY ERROR (IN INCHES)
		1	2	3			
1	10	8¾	10	8	2	2	—
2	2	2	1	1½	1	1	—
3	3	3¾	4¼	3	3	1*	+¾
4	5	5	4	6½	1	2*	−1.0
5	4	3	5	4	3	3	—
6	3	3¾	4¼	3	3	2*	+1¼
7	8	6¼	8	6¾	2	3*	−1¼
8	5	5	4	6½	1	3*	+1½
9	8	6¼	8	6¾	2	1*	−1¾
10	10	8¾	10	8	2	2	—
11	2	2	1	1½	1	1	—
12	3	3¾	4¼	3	3	1*	+¾
13	5	5	4	6½	1	2*	−1.0
14	4	3	5	4	3	3	—
15	3	3¾	4¼	3	3	2*	+1¼
16	8	6¼	8	6¾	2	3*	−1¼
17	5	5	4	6½	1	3*	+1½
18	8	6¼	8	6¾	2	1*	−1¾

* Starred figures designate the erroneous estimates by the majority.

will note that on certain trials the majority responded correctly; these were the "neutral" trials. There were twelve critical trials on which the majority responded incorrectly.

The quantitative results are clear and unambiguous.

1. There was a marked movement toward the majority. One third of all the estimates in the critical group were errors identical with or in the direction of the distorted estimates of the majority. The significance of this finding becomes clear in the light of the virtual absence of errors in the control group, the members of which recorded their estimates in writing. The relevant data of the critical and control groups are summarized in Table 2.

2. At the same time the effect of the majority was far from complete. The preponderance of estimates in the critical group (68 percent) was correct despite the pressure of the majority.

3. We found evidence of extreme individual differences. There were in the critical group subjects who remained independent without exception, and there were those who went nearly all the time with the majority. (The maximum possible number of errors was 12, while the actual range of errors was 0–11.) One fourth of the critical subjects was completely independent; at the other extreme, one third of the group displaced the estimates toward the majority in one half or more of the trials.

The differences between the critical subjects in their reactions to the given conditions were equally striking. There were subjects who remained completely confident throughout. At the other extreme were those who became disoriented, doubt-ridden, and experienced a powerful impulse not to appear different from the majority.

For purposes of illustration we include a brief description of one independent and one yielding subject.

INDEPENDENT

After a few trials he appeared puzzled, hesitant. He announced all disagreeing answers in the form of "Three, sir; two, sir"; not so with the unanimous answers on the neutral trials. At Trial 4 he answered immediately after the first member of the group, shook his head, blinked, and whispered to his neighbor:

TABLE 2

Distribution of Errors in Experimental and Control Groups

NUMBER OF CRITICAL ERRORS	CRITICAL GROUP* (N = 50)	CONTROL GROUP (N = 37)
	F	F
0	13	35
1	4	1
2	5	1
3	6	
4	3	
5	4	
6	1	
7	2	
8	5	
9	3	
10	3	
11	1	
12	0	
Total	50	37
Mean	3.84	0.08

* All errors in the critical group were in the direction of the majority estimates.

"Can't help it, that's one." His later answers came in a whispered voice, accompanied by a deprecating smile. At one point he grinned embarrassedly, and whispered explosively to his neighbor: "I always disagree—darn it!" During the questioning, this subject's constant refrain was: "I called them as I saw them, sir." He insisted that his estimates were right without, however, committing himself as to whether the others were wrong remarking that "that's the way I see them and that's the way they see them." If he had to make a practical decision under similar circumstances, he declared, "I would follow my own view, though part of my reason would tell me that I might be wrong." Immediately following the experiment the majority engaged this subject in a brief discussion. When they pressed him to say whether the entire group was wrong and he alone right, he turned upon them defiantly, exclaiming: "You're *probably* right, but you *may* be wrong!" To the disclosure of the experiment this subject reacted with the statement that he felt "exultant and relieved," adding, "I do not deny that at times I had the feeling: 'to heck with it, I'll go along with the rest.'"

YIELDING

This subject went with the majority in 11 out of 12 trials. He appeared nervous and somewhat confused, but he did not attempt to evade discussion; on the contrary, he was helpful and tried to answer to the best of his ability. He opened the discussion with the statement: "If I'd been first I probably would have responded differently"; this was his way of stating that he had adopted the majority estimates. The primary factor in his case was loss of confidence. He perceived the majority as a decided group, acting without hesitation: "If they had been doubtful I probably would have changed, but they answered with such confidence." Certain of his errors, he explained, were due to the doubtful nature of the comparisons; in such instances he went with the majority. When the object of the experiment was explained, the subject volunteered: "I suspected about the middle—but tried to push it out of my mind." It is of interest that his suspicion did not restore his confidence or diminish the power of the majority. Equally striking is his report that he assumed the experiment to involve an "illusion" to which the others, but not he, were subject. This assumption too did not help to free him; on the contrary, he acted as if his divergence from the majority was a sign of defect. The principal impression this subject produced was of one so caught up by immediate difficulties that he lost clear reasons for his actions, and could make no reasonable decisions.

A FIRST ANALYSIS OF INDIVIDUAL DIFFERENCES

On the basis of the interview data described earlier, we undertook to differentiate and describe the major forms of reaction to the experimental situation, which we shall now briefly summarize.

Among the *independent* subjects we distinguished the following main categories:

(1) Independence based on *confidence* in one's perception and experience. The most striking characteristic of these subjects is the vigor with which they withstand the group opposition. Though they are sensitive to the group, and experience the conflict, they show a resilience in coping with it, which is expressed in their continuing reliance

on their perception and the effectiveness with which they shake off the oppressive group opposition.

(2) Quite different are those subjects who are independent and *withdrawn*. These do not react in a spontaneously emotional way, but rather on the basis of explicit principles concerning the necessity of being an individual.

(3) A third group of independent subjects manifests considerable tension and doubt, but adhere to their judgment on the basis of a felt necessity to deal adequately with the task.

The following were the main categories of reaction among the *yielding* subjects, or those who went with the majority during one half or more of the trials.

(1) *Distortion of perception* under the stress of group pressure. In this category belong a very few subjects who yield completely, but are not aware that their estimates have been displaced or distorted by the majority. These subjects report that they came to perceive the majority estimates as correct.

(2) *Distortion of judgment.* Most submitting subjects belong in this category. The factor of greatest importance in this group is a decision the subjects reach that their perceptions are inaccurate, and that those of the majority are correct. These subjects suffer from primary doubt and lack of confidence; on this basis they feel a strong tendency to join the majority.

(3) *Distortion of action.* The subjects in this group do not suffer a modification of perception nor do they conclude that they are wrong. They yield because of an overmastering need not to appear different from or inferior to others, because of an inability to tolerate the appearance of defectiveness in the eyes of the group. These subjects suppress their observations and voice the majority position with awareness of what they are doing.

The results are sufficient to establish that independence and yielding are not psychologically homogeneous, that submission to group pressure and freedom from pressure can be the result of different psychological conditions. It should also be noted that the categories described above, being based exclusively on the subjects' reactions to the experimental conditions, are descriptive, not presuming to explain why a given individual responded in one way rather than another. The further exploration of the basis for the individual differences is a separate task.

EXPERIMENTAL VARIATIONS

The results described are clearly a joint function of two broadly different sets of conditions. They are determined first by the particular character of the relation between social evidence and one's own experience. Second, the presence of pronounced individual differences points to the important role of personal factors, or factors connected with the individual's character structure. We reasoned that there are group conditions which would produce independence in all subjects, and that there probably are group conditions which would induce intensified yielding in many, though not in all. Secondly, we deemed it reasonable to assume that behavior under the experimental social pressure is significantly related to certain characteristics of the individual. The present account will be limited to the effect of the surrounding conditions upon independence and submission. To this end we followed the procedure of experimental variation, systematically altering the quality of social evidence by means of systematic variation of the group conditions and of the task.

THE EFFECT OF NONUNANIMOUS MAJORITIES

Evidence obtained from the basic experiment suggested that the condition of being exposed *alone* to the opposition of a "compact majority" may have played a decisive role in determining the course and strength of the effects observed. Accordingly we undertook to investigate in a series of successive variations the effects of *nonunanimous* majorities. The technical problem of altering the uniformity of a majority is, in terms of our procedure, relatively simple. In most instances we merely directed one or more members of the instructed group to deviate from the majority in prescribed ways. It is obvious that we cannot hope to compare the performance of the same individual in two situations on the assumption that they remain independent of one another; at best we can investigate the effect of an earlier upon a later experimental condition. The comparison of different experimental situations therefore requires the use of different but comparable groups of critical subjects. This is the procedure we have followed. In the variations to be described we have maintained the conditions of the basic experiment (e.g., the sex of the subjects, the size of the majority, the content of the task, and so on) save for the specific factor that was varied. The following were some of the variations studied:

1. The Presence of a "True Partner." (*a*) In the midst of the majority were *two* naïve, critical subjects. The subjects were separated spatially, being seated in the fourth and eighth positions, respectively. Each therefore heard his judgments confirmed by one other person (provided the other person remained independent), one prior to, the other after announcing his own judgment. In addition, each experienced a break in the unanimity of the majority. There were six pairs of critical subjects. (*b*) In a further variation the "partner" to the critical subject was a member of the group who has been instructed to respond correctly throughout. This procedure permits the exact control of the partner's responses. The partner was always seated in the fourth position; he therefore announced his estimates in each case before the critical subject.

The results clearly demonstrate that a disturbance of the unanimity of the majority markedly increased the independence of the critical subjects. The frequency of promajority errors dropped to 10.4 percent of the total number of estimates in variation (*a*), and to 5.5 percent in variation (*b*). These results are to be compared with the frequency of yielding to the unanimous majorities in the basic experiment, which was 32 percent of the total number of estimates. It is clear that the presence in the field of *one other* individual who responded correctly was sufficient to deplete the power of the majority, and in some cases to destroy it. This finding is all the more striking in the light of other variations which demonstrate the effect of even small minorities provided they are unanimous. Indeed, we have been able to show that a unanimous majority of 3 is, under the given conditions, far more effective than a majority of 8 containing 1 dissenter. That critical subjects will

under these conditions free themselves of a majority of 7 and join forces with one other person in the minority is, we believe, a result significant for theory. It points to a fundamental psychological difference between the condition of being alone and having a minimum of human support. It further demonstrates that the effects obtained are not the result of a summation of influences proceeding from each member of the group; it is necessary to conceive the results as being relationally determined.

2. Withdrawal of a "true Partner." What will be the effect of providing the critical subject with a partner who responds correctly and then withdrawing him? The critical subject started with a partner who responded correctly. The partner was a member of the majority who had been instructed to respond correctly and to "desert" to the majority in the middle of the experiment. This procedure permits the observation of the same subject in the course of the transition from one condition to another. The withdrawal of the partner produced a powerful and unexpected result. We had assumed that the critical subject, having gone through the experience of opposing the majority with a minimum of support, would maintain his independence when alone. Contrary to this expectation, we found that the experience of having had and then lost a partner restored the majority effect to its full force, the proportion of errors rising to 28.5 percent of all judgments, in contrast to the preceding level of 5.5 percent. Further experimentation is needed to establish whether the critical subjects were responding to the sheer fact of being alone, or to the fact that the partner abandoned them.

3. Late Arrival of a "True Partner." The critical subject started as a minority of 1 in the midst of a unanimous majority. Toward the conclusion of the experiment one member of the majority "broke" away and began announcing correct estimates. This procedure, which reverses the order of conditions of the preceding experiment, permits the observation of the transition from being alone to being a member of a pair against a majority. It is obvious that those critical subjects who were independent when alone would con-

TABLE 3

Errors of Critical Subjects with Unanimous Majorities of Different Size

SIZE OF MAJORITY	CONTROL	1	2	3	4	8	10–15
N	37	10	15	10	10	50	12
Mean number of errors	0.08	0.33	1.53	4.0	4.20	3.84	3.75
Range of errors	0–2	0–1	0–5	1–12	0–11	0–11	0–10

tinue to be so when joined by a partner. The variation is therefore of significance primarily for those subjects who yielded during the first phase of the experiment. The appearance of the late partner exerts a freeing effect, reducing the level of yielding to 8.7 percent. Those who had previously yielded also became markedly more independent, but not completely so, continuing to yield more than previously independent subjects. The reports of the subjects do not cast much light on the factors responsible for the result. It is our impression that some subjects, having once committed themselves to yielding, find it difficult to change their direction completely. To do so is tantamount to a public admission that they had not acted rightly. They therefore follow to an extent the precarious course they had chosen in order to maintain an outward semblance of consistency and conviction.

4. The Presence of a "Compromise Partner." The majority was consistently extremist, always matching the standard with the most unequal line. One instructed subject (who, as in the other variations, preceded the critical subject) also responded incorrectly, but his estimates were always intermediate between the truth and the majority position. The critical subject therefore faced an extremist majority whose unanimity was broken by one more moderately erring person. Under these conditions the frequency of errors was reduced but not significantly. However, the lack of unanimity determined in a strikingly consistent way the *direction* of the errors. The preponderance of the errors, 75.7 percent of the total, was moderate, whereas in a parallel experiment in which the majority was unanimously extremist (i.e., with the "compromise" partner excluded), the incidence of moderate errors was 42 percent of the total. As might be expected, in a unanimously moderate majority, the errors of the critical subjects were without exception moderate.

THE ROLE OF MAJORITY SIZE

To gain further understanding of the majority effect, we varied the size of the majority in several different variations. The majorities, which were in each case unanimous, consisted of 2, 3, 4, 8, and 10–15 persons, respectively. In addition, we studied the limiting case in which the critical subject was opposed by one instructed subject. Table 3 contains the mean and the range of errors under each condition.

With the opposition reduced to 1, the majority effect all but disappeared. When the opposition proceeded from a group of 2, it produced a measurable though small distortion, the errors being 12.8 percent of the total number of estimates. The effect appeared in full force with a majority of 3. Larger majorities did not produce effects greater than a majority of 3.

The effect of a majority is often silent, revealing little of its operation to the subject, and often hiding it from the experimenter. To examine the range of effects it is capable of inducing, decisive variations of conditions are necessary. An indication of one effect is furnished by the following variation in which the conditions of the basic experiment were simply reversed. Here the majority, consisting of a group of 16, was naïve; in the midst of it we placed a single individual who responded wrongly according to instructions. Under these conditions the members of the naïve majority reacted to the lone dissenter with amusement. Contagious laughter spread through the group at the droll minority of 1. Of significance is the fact that the members lacked awareness that they drew their strength from the majority, and that their reactions would change radically if they faced the dissenter individually. These observations demonstrate the role of social support as a source of power and stability, in contrast to the preceding investigations which stressed the effects of social opposition. Both aspects must be explicitly considered in a unified formulation of the effects of group conditions on the formation and change of judgments.

THE ROLE OF THE STIMULUS-SITUATION

It is obviously not possible to divorce the quality and course of the group forces which act upon the individual from the specific stimulus-conditions. Of necessity the structure of the situation molds the group forces and determines their direction as well as their strength. Indeed, this was the reason that we took pains in the investigations described above to center the issue between the individual and the group around an elementary matter of fact. And there can be no doubt that the resulting reactions were directly a function of the contradiction between the observed relations and the majority position. These general considerations are sufficient to establish the need to vary the stimulus-conditions and to observe their effect on the resulting group forces.

Accordingly we have studied the effect of increasing and decreasing the discrepancy between the correct relation and the position of the majority, going beyond the basic experiment which contained discrepancies of a relatively moderate order. Our technique permits the easy variation of this factor, since we can vary at will the deviation of the majority from the correct relation. At this point we can only summarize the trend of the results which is entirely clear. The degree of independence increases with the distance of the majority from correctness. However, even glaring discrepancies (of the order of 3–6″) did not produce independence in all. While independence increases with the magnitude of contradiction, a certain proportion of individuals continues to yield under extreme conditions.

We have also varied systematically the structural clarity of the task, employing judgments based on mental standards. In agreement with other investigators, we find that the majority effect grows stronger as the situation diminishes in clarity. Concurrently, however, the disturbance of the subjects and the conflict-quality of the situation decrease markedly. We consider it of significance that the majority achieves its most pronounced effect when it acts most painlessly....

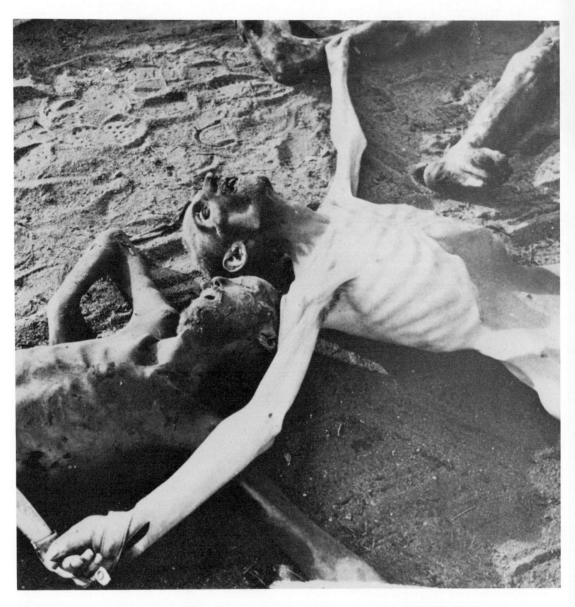

Photo taken at Belsen Concentration Camp, Germany, 1945. *Wide World Photos.*

59. IF HITLER ASKED YOU TO ELECTROCUTE A STRANGER, WOULD YOU?

Philip Meyer

In the beginning, Stanley Milgram was worried about the Nazi problem. He doesn't worry much about the Nazis anymore. He worries about you and me, and, perhaps, himself a little bit too.

Stanley Milgram is a social psychologist, and when he began his career at Yale University in 1960 he had a plan to prove, scientifically, that Germans are different. The Germans-are-different hypothesis has been used by historians, such as William L. Shirer, to explain the systematic destruction of the Jews by the Third Reich. One madman could decide to destroy the Jews and even create a master plan for getting it done. But to implement it on the scale that Hitler did meant that thousands of other people had to go along with the scheme and help to do the work. The Shirer thesis, which Milgram set out to test, is that Germans have a basic character flaw which explains the whole thing, and this flaw is a readiness to obey authority without question, no matter what outrageous acts the authority commands.

The appealing thing about this theory is that it makes those of us who are not Germans feel better about the whole business. Obviously, you and I are not Hitler, and it seems equally obvious that we would never do Hitler's dirty work for him. But now, because of Stanley Milgram, we are compelled to wonder. Milgram developed a laboratory experiment which provided a systematic way to measure obedience. His plan was to try it out in New Haven on Americans and then go to Germany and try it out on Germans.

He was strongly motivated by scientific curiosity, but there was also some moral content in his decision to pursue this line of research, which was, in turn, colored by his own Jewish background. If he could show that Germans are more obedient than Americans, he could then vary the conditions of the experiment and try to find out just what it is that makes some people more obedient than others. With this understanding, the world might, conceivably, be just a little bit better.

But he never took his experiment to Germany. He never took it any farther than Bridgeport. The first finding, also the most unexpected and disturbing finding, was that we Americans are an obedient people: not blindly obedient, and not blissfully obedient, just obedient. "I found so much obedience," says Milgram softly, a little sadly, "I hardly saw the need for taking the experiment to Germany."

There is something of the theatre director in Milgram, and his technique, which he learned from one of the old masters in experimental psychology, Solomon Asch, is to stage a play with every line rehearsed, every prop carefully selected, and everybody an actor except one person. That one person is the subject of the experiment. The subject, of course, does not know he is in a play. He thinks he is in real life. The value of this technique is that the experimenter, as though he were God, can change a prop here, vary a line there, and see how the subject responds. Milgram eventually had to change a lot of the script just to get people to stop obeying. They were obeying so much, the experiment wasn't working—it was like trying to measure oven temperature with a freezer thermometer.

457

The experiment worked like this: If you were an innocent subject in Milgram's melodrama, you read an ad in the newspaper or received one in the mail asking for volunteers for an educational experiment. The job would take about an hour and pay $4.50. So you make an appointment and go to an old Romanesque stone structure on High Street with the imposing name of The Yale Interaction Laboratory. It looks something like a broadcasting studio. Inside, you meet a young, crew-cut man in a laboratory coat who says he is Jack Williams, the experimenter. There is another citizen, fiftyish, Irish face, an accountant, a little overweight, and very mild and harmless-looking. This other citizen seems nervous and plays with his hat while the two of you sit in chairs side by side and are told that the $4.50 checks are yours no matter what happens. Then you listen to Jack Williams explain the experiment.

It is about learning, says Jack Williams in a quiet, knowledgeable way. Science does not know much about the conditions under which people learn and this experiment is to find out about negative reinforcement. Negative reinforcement is getting punished when you do something wrong, as opposed to positive reinforcement which is getting rewarded when you do something right. The negative reinforcement in this case is electric shock. You notice a book on the table, titled, *The Teaching-Learning Process,* and you assume that this has something to do with the experiment.

Then Jack Williams takes two pieces of paper, puts them in a hat, and shakes them up. One piece of paper is supposed to say, "Teacher" and the other, "Learner." Draw one and you will see which you will be. The mild-looking accountant draws one, holds it close to his vest like a poker player, looks at it, and says, "Learner." You look at yours. It says, "Teacher." You do not know that the drawing is rigged, and both slips say "Teacher." The experimenter beckons to the mild-mannered "learner."

"Want to step right in here and have a seat, please?" he says. "You can leave your coat on the back of that chair...roll up your right sleeve, please. Now what I want to do is strap down your arms to avoid excessive movement on your part during the experiment. This electrode is connected to the shock generator in the next room.

"And the electrode paste," he says, squeezing some stuff out of a plastic bottle and putting it on the man's arm, "is to provide a good contact and to avoid a blister or burn. Are there any questions now before we go into the next room?"

You don't have any, but the strapped-in "learner" does.

"I do think I should say this," says the learner. "About two years ago, I was at the veterans' hospital...they detected a heart condition. Nothing serious, but as long as I'm having these shocks, how strong are they —how dangerous are they?"

Williams, the experimenter, shakes his head casually. "Oh, no," he says. "Although they may be painful, they're not dangerous. Anything else?"

Nothing else. And so you play the game. The game is for you to read a series of word pairs: for example, blue-girl, nice-day, fat-neck. When you finish the list, you read just the first word in each pair and then a multiple-choice list of four other words, including the second word of the pair. The learner, from his remote, strapped-in position, pushes one of four switches to indicate which of the four answers he thinks is the right one. If he gets it right, nothing happens and you go on to the next one. If he gets it wrong, you push a switch that buzzes and gives him an electric shock. And then you go to the next word. You start with 15 volts and increase the number of volts by 15 for each wrong answer. The control board goes from 15 volts on one end to 450 volts on the other. So that you know what you are doing, you get a test shock yourself, at 45 volts. It hurts. To further keep you aware of what you are doing to that man in there, the board has verbal descriptions of the shock levels, ranging from "Slight Shock" at the left-hand side, through "Intense Shock" in the middle, to "Danger: Severe Shock" toward the far right. Finally, at the very end, under 435- and 450-volt switches, there are three ambiguous X's. If, at any point, you hesitate, Mr. Williams calmly tells you to go on. If you still hesitate, he tells you again.

Except for some terrifying details, which will be explained in a moment, this is the experiment. The object is to find the shock level at which you disobey the experimenter and refuse to pull the switch.

When Stanley Milgram first wrote this script, he took it to fourteen Yale psychology majors and asked them what they thought would happen. He put it this way: Out of one hundred persons in the teacher's predicament, how would their break-off points be distributed along the 15-to-450-volt scale? They thought a few would break off very early, most would quit someplace in the middle and a few would go all the way to the end. The highest estimate of the number out of one hundred who would go all the way to the end was three. Milgram then informally polled some of his fellow scholars in the psychology department. They agreed that very few would go to the end. Milgram thought so too.

"I'll tell you quite frankly," he says, "before I began this experiment, before any shock generator was built, I thought that most people would break off at 'Strong Shock' or 'Very Strong Shock.' You would get only a very, very small proportion of people going out to the end of the shock generator, and they would constitute a pathological fringe."

In his pilot experiments, Milgram used Yale students as subjects. Each of them pushed the shock switches, one by one, all the way to the end of the board.

So he rewrote the script to include some protests from the learner. At first, they were mild, gentlemanly, Yalie protests, but, "it didn't seem to have as much effect as I thought it would or should," Milgram recalls. "So we had more violent protestation on the part of the person getting the shock. All of the time, of course, what we were trying to do was not to create a macabre situation, but simply to generate disobedience. And that was one of the first findings. This was not only a technical deficiency of the experiment, that we didn't get disobedience. It really was the first finding: that obedience would be much greater than we had assumed it would be and disobedience would be much more difficult than we had assumed."

As it turned out, the situation did become rather macabre. The only meaningful way to generate disobedience was to have the victim protest with great anguish, noise, and vehemence. The protests were tape-recorded so that all the teachers ordinarily would hear the same sounds and nuances, and they started with a grunt at 75 volts, proceeded through a "Hey, that really hurts," at 125 volts, got desperate with, "I can't stand the pain, don't do that," at 180 volts, reached complaints of heart trouble at 195, an agonized scream at 285, a refusal to answer at 315, and only heartrending, ominous silence after that.

Still, sixty-five percent of the subjects, twenty- to fifty-year-old American males,

everyday, ordinary people, like you and me, obediently kept pushing those levers in the belief that they were shocking the mild-mannered learner, whose name was Mr. Wallace, and who was chosen for the role because of his innocent appearance, all the way up to 450 volts.

Milgram was now getting enough disobedience so that he had something he could measure. The next step was to vary the circumstances to see what would encourage or discourage obedience. There seemed very little left in the way of discouragement. The victim was already screaming at the top of his lungs and feigning a heart attack. So whatever new impediment to obedience reached the brain of the subject had to travel by some route other than the ear. Milgram thought of one.

He put the learner in the same room with the teacher. He stopped strapping the learner's hand down. He rewrote the script so that at 150 volts the learner took his hand off the shock plate and declared that he wanted out of the experiment. He rewrote the script some more so that the experimenter then told the teacher to grasp the learner's hand and physically force it down on the plate to give Mr. Wallace his unwanted electric shock.

"I had the feeling that very few people would go on at that point, if any," Milgram says. "I thought that would be the limit of obedience that you would find in the laboratory."

It wasn't.

Although seven years have now gone by, Milgram still remembers the first person to walk into the laboratory in the newly rewritten script. He was a construction worker, a very short man. "He was so small," says Milgram, "that when he sat on the chair in front of the shock generator, his feet didn't reach the floor. When the experimenter told him to push the victim's hand down and give the shock, he turned to the experimenter, and he turned to the victim, his elbow went up, he fell down on the hand of the victim, his feet kind of tugged to one side, and he said, 'Like this, boss?' Zzumph!"

The experiment was played out to its bitter end. Milgram tried it with forty different subjects. And thirty percent of them obeyed the experimenter and kept on obeying.

"The protests of the victim were strong and vehement, he was screaming his guts out, he refused to participate, and you had to physically struggle with him in order to get his hand down on the shock generator," Milgram remembers. But twelve out of forty did it.

Milgram took his experiment out of New Haven. Not to Germany, just twenty miles down the road to Bridgeport. Maybe, he reasoned, the people obeyed because of the prestigious setting of Yale University. If they couldn't trust a center of learning that had been there for two centuries, whom could they trust? So he moved the experiment to an untrustworthy setting.

The new setting was a suite of three rooms in a run-down office building in Bridgeport. The only identification was a sign with a fictitious name: "Research Associates of Bridgeport." Questions about professional connections got only vague answers about "research for industry."

Obedience was less in Bridgeport. Forty-eight percent of the subjects stayed for the maximum shock, compared to sixty-five percent at Yale. But this was enough to prove that far more than Yale's prestige was behind the obedient behavior.

For more than seven years now, Stanley Milgram has been trying to figure out what makes ordinary American citizens so obedient. The most obvious answer—that people are mean, nasty, brutish and sadistic—won't do. The subjects who gave the shocks to Mr. Wallace to the end of the board did not enjoy it. They groaned, protested, fidgeted, argued, and in some cases, were seized by fits of nervous, agitated giggling.

"They even try to get out of it," says Milgram, "but they are somehow engaged in something from which they cannot liberate themselves. They are locked into a structure, and they do not have the skills or inner resources to disengage themselves."

Milgram, because he mistakenly had assumed that he would have trouble getting people to obey the orders to shock Mr. Wallace, went to a lot of trouble to create a realistic situation.

There was crew-cut Jack Williams and his grey laboratory coat. Not white, which might denote a medical technician, but ambiguously authoritative grey. Then there was the book on the table, and the other appurtenances of the laboratory which emitted the silent message that things were being performed here in the name of science, and were therefore great and good.

But the nicest touch of all was the shock generator. When Milgram started out, he had only a $300 grant from the Higgins Fund of Yale University. Later he got more ample support from the National Science Foundation, but in the beginning he had to create this authentic-looking machine with very scarce resources except for his own imagination. So he went to New York and roamed around the electronic shops until he found some little black switches at Lafayette Radio for a dollar apiece. He bought thirty of them. The generator was a metal box, about the size of a small footlocker, and he drilled the thirty holes for the thirty switches himself in a Yale machine shop. But the fine detail was left to professional industrial engravers. So he ended up with a splendid looking control panel dominated by the row of switches, each labeled with its voltage, and each having its own red light that flashed on when the switch was pulled. Other things happened when a switch was pushed. Besides the zzumphing noise, a blue light labeled "voltage energizer" went on, and a needle on a dial labeled "voltage" flicked from left to right. Relays inside the box clicked. Finally, in the upper left-hand corner of the control panel was this inscription, engraved in precise block letters:

Shock Generator Type ZLB
Dyson Instrument Company
Waltrum, Mass.
Output: 15 Volts—450 Volts

One day a man from the Lehigh Valley Electronics Company of Pennsylvania was passing through the laboratory, and he stopped to admire the shock generator.

"This is a very fine shock generator," he said. "But who is this Dyson Instrument Company?" Milgram felt proud at that, since Dyson Instrument Company existed only in the recesses of his imagination.

When you consider the seeming authenticity of the situation, you can appreciate the agony some of the subjects went through. It was pure conflict. As Milgram explains to his students, "When a parent says, 'Don't strike old ladies,' you are learning two things: the content, and also, to obey authority. This experiment creates conflicts between the two elements."

Here is a partial transcription from one of the experiments. The naïve "teacher" is a heavyset, worried-looking man with prematurely grey hair. He is wearing a polo shirt. He is very polite. He has just pushed the 180-volt lever. A hidden camera is recording the performance.

LEARNER (*who from the teacher's point of view is heard but not seen, an offstage voice*): Ow, I can't stand the pain. Don't do that. . . .

TEACHER (*pivoting around in his chair and shaking his head*): I can't stand it. I'm not going to kill that man in there. You hear him hollering?

EXPERIMENTER: As I told you before, the shocks may be painful, but—

TEACHER: But he's hollering. He can't stand it. What's going to happen to him?

EXPERIMENTER (*his voice is patient, matter-of-fact*): The experiment requires that you continue, Teacher.

TEACHER: Aaah, but, unh, I'm not going to get that man sick in there. . .know what I mean?

EXPERIMENTER: Whether the learner likes it or not, we must go on, through all the word pairs.

TEACHER: I refuse to take the responsibility. He's in there hollering!

EXPERIMENTER: It's absolutely essential that you continue, Teacher.

TEACHER (*indicating the unused questions*): There's too many left here, I mean, Geez, if he gets them wrong, there's too many of them left. I mean who's going to take the responsibility if anything happens to that gentleman?

EXPERIMENTER: I'm responsible for anything that happens to him. Continue please.

TEACHER: All right. (*Consults list of words.*) The next one's "Slow—walk, truck, dance, music." Answer, please. (*A buzzing sound indicates the learner has signaled his answer.*) Wrong. A hundred and ninety-five volts. "Dance." (*Zzumph!*)

LEARNER: Let me out of here. My heart's bothering me! (*Teacher looks at experimenter.*)

EXPERIMENTER: Continue, please.

LEARNER (*screaming*): Let me out of here, you have no right to keep me here. Let me out of here, let me out, my heart's bothering me, let me out! (*Teacher shakes head, pats the table nervously.*)

TEACHER: You see, he's hollering. Hear that? Gee, I don't know.

EXPERIMENTER: The experiment requires. . . .

TEACHER (*interrupting*): I know it does, sir, but I mean—hunh! He don't know what

he's getting in for. He's up to 195 volts! (*Experiment continues, through 210 volts, 225 volts, 240 volts, 255 volts, 270 volts, delivered to the man in the electric chair, at which point the teacher, with evident relief, runs out of word-pair questions.*)

EXPERIMENTER: You'll have to go back to the beginning of that page and go through them again until he's learned them all correctly.

TEACHER: Aw, no. I'm not going to kill that man. You mean I've got to keep going up with the scale. No sir. He's hollering in there. I'm not going to give him 450 volts.

EXPERIMENTER: The experiment requires that you go on.

TEACHER: I know it does, but that man is hollering in there, sir.

EXPERIMENTER (*same matter-of-fact tone*): As I said before, although the shocks may be painful. . . .

TEACHER (*interrupting*): Awwww. He—he —he's yelling in there.

EXPERIMENTER: Start with "Blue," please, at the top of the page. Continue, please, Teacher. Just go ahead.

TEACHER (*concentrating intently on list of words in front of him, as if to shut everything else out*): "Blue—boy, girl, grass, hat." (*Buzz indicates answer.*) Correct. "Night—day, sky, job, chair. Buzz*)* Wrong. The answer is "day." Two hundred and eighty-five volts. (*Zzumph!*)

LEARNER: Ohhhuhhoohhh!

EXPERIMENTER: Continue, please.

TEACHER: "Fat—man, lady, tub, neck." Answer, please. (*Buzz*) Wrong. The answer is "neck." Three hundred volts. (*Zzumph!*)

LEARNER: Ohh. I absolutely refuse to answer any more. (*Shouting urgently, now*) Let me out of here. You can't hold me here. Get me out. Get—me—out—of—here.

EXPERIMENTER: Continue. The next word is "Green," please.

TEACHER: "Green—grass, hat, ink, apple." (*Nothing happens. No answering buzz. Just gloomy silence.*)

TEACHER: I don't think he is going to answer.

EXPERIMENTER: If the learner doesn't answer in a reasonable time, about four or five seconds, consider the answer wrong. And follow the same procedures you have been doing for wrong answers. Say "Wrong," tell him the number of volts, give him the punishment, read him the correct answer. Continue, please.

TEACHER: "Green—grass, hat, ink, apple." Answer, please. (*More silence. Teacher just sits there.*)

EXPERIMENTER: Go on with the procedure, please, Teacher.

TEACHER: Three hundred and fifteen volts. The answer is "ink." (*Zzumph!*)

LEARNER: Ohh. Ooohh.

TEACHER (*relieved to hear response*): Next one....

LEARNER: I absolutely refuse to answer.

TEACHER: You got to. You get a shock if you don't answer. (*Experiment continues with learner refusing to answer, and, finally, failing even to grunt or groan. At 375 volts, the teacher stands up. Has he had enough? Will he break off the experiment? Will he disobey?*)

TEACHER: I think something's happened to that fellow in there. I don't get no answer. He was hollering at less voltage. Can't you check in and see if he's all right, please?

EXPERIMENTER (*same detached calm*): Not once we've started. Please continue, Teacher.

TEACHER (*sits down, sighs deeply*): "Cool —day, shade, water, paint." Answer, please. Are you all right in there? Are you all right?

EXPERIMENTER: Please continue, Teacher. Continue, please. (*Teacher pushes lever. Zzumph!*)

TEACHER (*swiveling around in his chair*): Something's happened to that man in there. (*Swiveling back*) Next one. "Low—dollar, necklace, moon, paint." (*Turning around again*) Something's happened to that man in there. You better check in on him, sir. He won't answer or nothing.

EXPERIMENTER: Continue. Go on, please.

TEACHER: You accept all responsibility.

EXPERIMENTER: The responsibility is mine. Correct. Please go on. (*Teacher returns to his list, starts running through words as rapidly as he can read them, works through to 450 volts.*)

TEACHER: That's that.

EXPERIMENTER: Continue using the last switch on the board, please. The four-fifty switch for each wrong answer. Continue, please.

TEACHER: But I don't get no anything!

EXPERIMENTER: Please continue. The next word is "White."

TEACHER: Don't you think you should look in on him, please.

EXPERIMENTER: Not once we've started the experiment.

TEACHER: But what if something has happened to the man?

EXPERIMENTER: The experiment requires that you continue. Go on, please.

TEACHER: Don't the man's health mean anything?

EXPERIMENTER: Whether the learner likes it or not....

TEACHER: What if he's dead in there? (*Gestures toward the room with the electric chair.*) I mean, he told me he can't stand the shock, sir. I don't mean to be rude, but I think you should look in on him. All you have to do is look in the door. I don't get no answer, no noise. Something might have happened to the gentleman in there, sir.

EXPERIMENTER: We must continue. Go on, please.

TEACHER: You mean keep giving him what? Four hundred fifty volts, what he's got now?

EXPERIMENTER: That's correct. Continue. The next word is "White."

TEACHER (*now at a furious pace*): "White —cloud, horse, rock, house." Answer, please. The answer is "horse." Four hundred and fifty volts. (*Zzumph!*) Next word, "Bag—paint, music, clown, girl." The answer is "paint." Four hundred and fifty volts. (*Zzumph!*) Next word is "Short—sentence, movie....

EXPERIMENTER: Excuse me, Teacher. We'll have to discontinue the experiment.

(*Enter Milgram from camera's left. He has been watching from behind one-way glass.*)

MILGRAM: I'd like to ask you a few questions. (*Slowly, patiently he dehoaxes the teacher, telling him that the shocks and screams were not real.*)

TEACHER: You mean he wasn't getting nothing? Well, I'm glad to hear that. I was getting upset there. I was getting ready to walk out.

(*Finally, to make sure there are no hard feelings, friendly, harmless Mr. Wallace comes out in coat and tie. Gives jovial greeting. Friendly reconciliation takes place. Experiment ends.*)

© Stanley Milgram 1965.

Subjects in the experiment were not asked to give the 450-volt shock more than three times. By that time, it seemed evident that they would go on indefinitely. "No one," says Milgram, "who got within five shocks of the end ever broke off. By that point, he had resolved the conflict."

Why do so many people resolve the conflict in favor of obedience?

Milgram's theory assumes that people behave in two different operating modes as different as ice and water. He does not rely on Freud or sex or toilet-training hang-ups for this theory. All he says is that ordinarily we operate in a state of autonomy, which means we pretty much have and assert control over what we do. But in certain circumstances, we operate under what Milgram calls a state of agency (after *agent*, n...one who acts for or in the place of another by authority from him; a substitute: a deputy.—*Webster's Collegiate Dictionary*). A state of agency, to Milgram, is nothing more than a frame of mind.

"There's nothing bad about it, there's nothing good about it," he says. "It's a natural circumstance of living with other people....I think of a state of agency as a real transformation of a person; if a person has different properties when he's in that state, just as water can turn to ice under certain conditions of temperature, a person can move to the state of mind that I call agency...the critical thing is that you see yourself as the instrument of the execution of another person's wishes. You do not see yourself as acting on your own. And there's a real transformation, a real change of properties of the person."

To achieve this change, you have to be in a situation where there seems to be a ruling authority whose commands are relevant to some legitimate purpose; the authority's power is not unlimited.

But situations can be and have been structured to make people do unusual things, and not just in Milgram's laboratory. The reason, says Milgram, is that no action, in and of itself, contains meaning.

"The meaning always depends on your definition of the situation. Take an action like killing another person. It sounds bad.

"But then we say the other person was about to destroy a hundred children, and the only way to stop him was to kill him. Well, that sounds good.

"Or, you take destroying your own life. It sounds very bad. Yet, in the Second World War, thousands of persons thought it was a good thing to destroy your own life. It was set

in the proper context. You sipped some saki from a whistling cup, recited a few haiku. You said, 'May my death be as clean and as quick as the shattering of crystal.' And it almost seemed like a good, noble thing to do, to crash your kamikaze plane into an aircraft carrier. But the main thing was, the definition of what a kamikaze pilot was doing had been determined by the relevant authority. Now, once you are in a state of agency, you allow the authority to determine, to define what the situation is. The meaning of your action is altered."

So, for most subjects in Milgram's laboratory experiments, the act of giving Mr. Wallace his painful shock was necessary, even though unpleasant, and besides they were doing it on behalf of somebody else and it was for science. There was still strain and conflict, of course. Most people resolved it by grimly sticking to their task and obeying. But some broke out. Milgram tried varying the conditions of the experiment to see what would help break people out of their state of agency.

"The results, as seen and felt in the laboratory," he has written, "are disturbing. They raise the possibility that human nature, or more specifically the kind of character produced in American democratic society, cannot be counted on to insulate its citizens from brutality and inhumane treatment at the direction of malevolent authority. A substantial proportion of people do what they are told to do, irrespective of the content of the act and without limitations of conscience, so long as they perceive that the command comes from a legitimate authority. If, in this study, an anonymous experimenter can successfully command adults to subdue a fifty-year-old man and force on him painful electric shocks against his protest, one can only wonder what government, with its vastly greater authority and prestige, can command of its subjects."

This is a nice statement, but it falls short of summing up the full meaning of Milgram's work. It leaves some questions still unanswered.

The first question is this: Should we really be surprised and alarmed that people obey? Wouldn't it be even more alarming if they all refused to obey? Without obedience to a relevant ruling authority there could not be a civil society. And without a civil society, as

Thomas Hobbes pointed out in the seventeenth century, we would live in a condition of war, "of every man against every other man," and life would be "solitary, poor, nasty, brutish and short."

In the middle of one of Stanley Milgram's lectures at C.U.N.Y.* recently, some miniskirted undergraduates started whispering and giggling in the back of the room. He told them to cut it out. Since he was the relevant authority in that time and that place, they obeyed, and most people in the room were glad that they obeyed.

This was not, of course, a conflict situation. Nothing in the coeds' social upbringing made it a matter of conscience for them to whisper and giggle. But a case can be made that in a conflict situation it is all the more important to obey. Take the case of war, for example. Would we really want a situation in which every participant in a war, direct or indirect —from front-line soldiers to the people who sell coffee and cigarettes to employees at the Concertina barbed-wire factory in Kansas— stops and consults his conscience before each action. It is asking for an awful lot of mental strain and anguish from an awful lot of people. The value of having civil order is that one can do his duty, or whatever interests him, or whatever seems to benefit him at the moment, and leave the agonizing to others. When Francis Gary Powers was being tried by a Soviet military tribunal after his U-2 spy plane was shot down, the presiding judge asked if he had thought about the possibility that his flight might have provoked a war. Powers replied with Hobbesian clarity: "The people who sent me should think of these things. My job was to carry out orders. I do not think it was my responsibility to make such decisions."

It was not his responsibility. And it is quite possible that if everyone felt responsible for each of the ultimate consequences of his own tiny contributions to complex chains of events, then society simply would not work. Milgram, fully conscious of the moral and social implications of his research, believes that people should feel responsible for their actions. If someone else had invented the experiment, and if he had been the naïve subject, he feels certain that he would have been among the disobedient minority.

"There is no very good solution to this,"

* The City University of New York. (Eds.)

he admits, thoughtfully. "To simply and categorically say that you won't obey authority may resolve your personal conflict, but it creates more problems for society which may be more serious in the long run. But I have no doubt that to disobey is the proper thing to do in this [the laboratory] situation. It is the only reasonable value judgment to make."

The conflict between the need to obey the relevant ruling authority and the need to follow your conscience becomes sharpest if you insist on living by an ethical system based on a rigid code—a code that seeks to answer all questions in advance of their being raised. Code ethics cannot solve the obedience problem. Stanley Milgram seems to be a situation ethicist, and situation ethics does offer a way out: When you feel conflict, you examine the situation and then make a choice among the competing evils. You may act with a presumption in favor of obedience, but reserve the possibility that you will disobey whenever obedience demands a flagrant and outrageous affront to conscience. This, by the way, is the philosophical position of many who resist the draft. In World War II, they would have fought. Vietnam is a different, an outrageously different, situation.

Life can be difficult for the situation ethicist, because he does not see the world in straight lines, while the social system too often assumes such a God-given, squared-off structure. If your moral code includes an injunction against all war, you may be deferred as a conscientious objector. If you merely oppose this particular war, you may not be deferred. Stanley Milgram has his problems, too. He believes that in the laboratory situation, he would not have shocked Mr. Wallace. His professional critics reply that in his real-life situation he has done the equivalent. He has placed innocent and naïve subjects under great emotional strain and pressure in selfish obedience to his quest for knowledge. When you raise this issue with Milgram, he has an answer ready. There is, he explains patiently, a critical difference between his naïve subjects and the man in the electric chair. The man in the electric chair (in the mind of the naïve subject) is helpless, strapped in. But the naïve subject is free to go at any time.

Immediately after he offers this distinction, Milgram anticipates the objection.

"It's quite true," he says, "that this is almost a philosophic position, because we have learned that some people are psychologically incapable of disengaging themselves. But that doesn't relieve them of the moral responsibility."

The parallel is exquisite. "The tension problem was unexpected," says Milgram in his defense. But he went on anyway. The naïve subjects didn't expect the screaming protests from the strapped-in learner. But they went on.

"I had to make a judgment," says Milgram. "I had to ask myself, was this harming the person or not? My judgment is that it was not. Even in the extreme cases, I wouldn't say that permanent damage results."

Sound familiar? "The shocks may be painful," the experimenter kept saying, "but they're not dangerous."

After the series of experiments was completed, Milgram sent a report of the results to his subjects and a questionnaire, asking whether they were glad or sorry to have been in the experiment. Eighty-three and seven-tenths percent said they were glad and only 1.3 percent were sorry; 15 percent were neither sorry nor glad. However, Milgram could not be sure at the time of the experiment that only 1.3 percent would be sorry.

Kurt Vonnegut, Jr., put one paragraph in the preface to *Mother Night,* in 1966, which pretty much says it for the people with their fingers on the shock-generator switches, for you and me, and maybe even for Milgram. "If I'd been born in Germany," Vonnegut said. "I suppose I would have *been* a Nazi, bopping Jews and gypsies and Poles around, leaving boots sticking out of snowbanks, warming myself with my sweetly virtuous insides. So it goes."

Just so. One thing that happened to Milgram back in New Haven during the days of the experiment was that he kept running into people he'd watched from behind the one-way glass. It gave him a funny feeling, seeing those people going about their everyday business in New Haven and knowing what they would do to Mr. Wallace if ordered to. Now that his research results are in and you've thought about it, you can get this funny feeling too. You don't need a one-way glass. A glance in your own mirror may serve just as well.

60. THE PSYCHOLOGY OF TOLERATION

J. C. Flugel

When people think about tolerance or toleration, it is most often with religious, racial, political, or moral questions in mind. I would like to invite you to consider this subject from a slightly different angle—that of psychology. What is tolerance considered as a state of mind? I think it would be generally accepted that in the first place tolerance lies somewhere between love and approval on the

one hand, hate and disapproval on the other. We do not have to tolerate a person we love, or a cause to which we are devoted; but we may have to exercise tolerance towards the presence or behaviour of a person who irritates us, or in listening to the advocacy of a cause which we think wrong. Tolerance is indeed in some ways nearer to hate than to love. But it implies that the natural and immediate reaction to hate is held in check. What is our immediate reaction to a person we dislike? It is to say: 'Clear out!' while to someone advocating a cause we disapprove we should say 'Shut up!'

HEARING THE OTHER SIDE

But in the attitude of tolerance such reactions are, as the psychologist would say, inhibited. This means, in effect, that we are willing to suspend judgment for a while and, in the words of St. Augustine, 'hear the other side.' And if we are willing to listen to what the other fellow has to say, this implies that, after all, there may be something in it; what he says may not be mere wickedness or nonsense, and we ourselves may not have a monopoly of what is right and true.

This attitude is a very important one in science. No scientist pretends that he possesses 'the whole truth and nothing but the truth'; there is always something to be added to his knowledge or modified in his beliefs. The bigot, on the other hand, feels that he alone is right and that anyone who ventures to differ from him is wallowing in heresy and error—error so pernicious that it obviously needs to be suppressed. Bigotry thus inevitably leads to intolerance, while open-mindedness is intimately associated with toleration—and with liberty. As an American judge once put it, 'The spirit of liberty is the spirit that is not too sure that it is right.' Intolerance, on the other hand, is closely connected with prejudice, being a judgement formed without due knowledge and consideration of the facts.

I have mentioned prejudice because it is a subject which has much engaged the attention of psychologists in recent years (especially in America) and they have carried out a number of investigations, the results of which cast a good deal of light upon the nature and mental make-up of those who display tolerance or intolerance. A consideration of some of these studies will take us a little beyond the superficial and more or less common-sense approach with which I have been dealing so far.

Most of these investigations had their origin in the study of what psychologists have come to call 'attitudes,' especially the attitudes of the members of one race or nation towards those of another. For instance the subjects of an experiment were presented with a list of attributes, such as 'industrious,' 'artistic,' 'religious,' 'lazy,' 'cruel,' etc., and were asked to say which of these attributes were applicable to a list of certain races or nations. In other cases, the races or nations had to be put in order of personal preference, or the subjects had to say how far they would allow members of these races to various degrees of social intimacy, to visit their own country, to reside in it, to become members of their own professions, to join their own clubs or to intermarry with their own near relatives. These studies revealed the existence of so-called 'stereotypes,' more or less rigid, exaggerated, and emotionally toned beliefs, for the most part based on very insufficient knowledge—sometimes indeed on no knowledge at all; in fact, in one investigation catch questions were included on non-existent races, such as 'Daneirians,' 'Pyrenians' and 'Wallonians,' and many subjects gaily attributed good or bad qualities to these, based on nothing better than dim and confused associations. These 'stereotypes,' in fact, were for the most part just striking examples of racial and national prejudice.

In some more recent investigations psychologists have picked out those who display unusually great or unusually little prejudice of this sort, and have studied more intensively the mental background of the two sorts of people. Starting with childhood, it was found that the prejudiced and intolerant had grown up in a home atmosphere of greater harshness, discipline, and fear—one in which authority played a more important role than love. On the other hand, those who in later life showed less prejudice and greater tolerance felt that fundamentally they were accepted, and that if they were punished it was some particular act rather than they themselves as persons that had met with disapproval. They thus had less deep irrational anxiety and a greater sense of security—and this security indeed seems to emerge as the first basic factor in the tolerant attitude, whether in the individual or in social groups.

The tolerant and the intolerant individuals showed a further interesting difference, one which reveals itself in a contrast between two levels of the mind. At a more superficial level the tolerant people were ready to criticize their parents, though at a deeper level they still loved and respected them, in spite of the fact they could recognise their failings. The intolerant on the other hand would stoutly maintain that they liked their parents, and were loath to say anything against them, though deeper psychological probing showed the presence of jealousy, suspicion, and hostility at more unconscious levels. All children both love and hate their parents; they all display what psychologists call 'ambivalence' towards them. But in the tolerant the conflict was more at the surface, whereas in the intolerant the hostility had been repressed.

It is interesting to note that much the same kind of difference was brought out in other experiments in which groups of young people were deliberately conducted on authoritarian or democratic lines respectively. The members of the democratic groups, who participated in the government, could more openly criticise their leaders (though without necessarily disrespecting them), but the members of the authoritarian groups, who had simply to obey their leaders' orders, had more suppressed aggression—aggression which tended, moreover, to find an outlet in hostility towards others, especially towards other groups. It is as though aggression will out, must find expression somewhere; and it may find what seems to be a relatively harmless outlet at a superficial level within our own group, or it may find a more harmful and dangerous one towards innocent victims, strangers or external groups.

If we allow ourselves to generalise from these experiments, we can say that democratic government, whether in the home or in the larger group, is associated with tolerance, whereas authoritarianism breeds suppressed aggression and intolerance. The political implications of this are obvious enough, though we must be careful in applying conclusions drawn from small and relatively simple groups to the much more complicated conditions operative in great nations.

IMPORTANCE OF INNER SECURITY

As far as our present knowledge goes, then, the basic conditions of toleration are to be found in these two interconnected factors: a certain fundamental inner security on the one hand, and on the other an ability to express some degree of criticism and aggression at a relatively superficial level—often towards people whom at bottom we still love and respect. But several other aspects of this fundamental condition have been made out—aspects which are all, to some extent, interrelated with one another and with what I have called the two basic factors.

In the first place, we may notice among the intolerant a greater tendency towards what the psychoanalysts call 'splitting', or what one eminent American psychologist prefers to call

by the more erudite name of 'dichotomisation.' This means that the good and bad aspects of the parent or other authoritarian figure are, as it were, separated and attributed to different persons. This has long been recognised as one of the means which the mind employs for getting rid of the uncomfortable tension caused by the ambivalent attitude, the coexistence of love and hate towards the same person. In some degree it is a common human tendency, as exemplified in the contrast between *le bon Dieu* and the Devil, or, as in certain fairy stories, between the wicked stepmother and the fairy godmother. When generalized, this splitting process tends to make one see everything in terms of white or black. It has been found, for instance, that the intolerant type of person is likely to disagree with such propositions as are contained in the doggerel rhyme:

There is so much good in the worst of us,
So much bad in the best of us,
That it scarcely behoves any of us
To talk about the rest of us.

The tendency to split the good and bad in this way, helpful as it may be as a refuge from intolerable tensions, inevitably does violence to psychological fact; the rhyme I have just quoted comes much nearer to the facts of human life than does the whitewashing and denigrating of the 'splitter.' It is therefore not surprising that the tolerant are better psychologists than the intolerant. This applies both to self-knowledge and to the understanding of others. Several researches show that the tolerant have a greater knowledge of their own deficiencies and limitations, can tolerate their own shortcomings as well as those of other people; while at the same time they can sum up another's character in a short interview more accurately than the intolerant can do.

They may, however, sometimes show less tolerance to themselves than they do to others; in fact the danger which threatens those who are externally tolerant is that they may judge themselves too harshly and fall victims to feeling of guilt and inferiority; whereas the corresponding danger of the externally intolerant is that they do not consciously admit their own faults, but only too often attribute them to others. This process of projection, as it is called, the inclination to blame others for what are at bottom our own deficiences or faults, is responsible for the tendency to find scapegoats—a sinister tendency—which has played a long and terrible role in human history.

Another characteristic of the intolerant is that they tend to lean more heavily on authority. This is true both of the more intangible values of opinion and convention, and of actual institutions in which authority is embodied, such as the state with its legal sanctions. The tolerant, though they may by no means be less moral, are more flexible in their morality; they are more ready to exercise their own judgment as to what is right or wrong in any particular instance, whereas the intolerant are apt to lay more stress on the letter of the law. The tolerant are more capable of laughing at themselves and at the things and persons they love; and it appears that they can do this because of their greater sense of inner security, which is not seriously threatened even if they do admit that they themselves, their parents, their country, and their customs may in certain ways be a little ridiculous. They do not need the law of *lèse majesté** or the inner attitude which corresponds to it.

This sense of security can, of course, apply to nations and institutions as well as individuals; and in the light of this we can appreciate an incident which was credibly reported to me in my youth. A foreigner, an ardent admirer of Britain, who had recently come to this country, was horrified to hear a tub orator at a street corner shouting 'Down with the Queen, down with the Royal Family!' He hurried off to fetch a policeman, who, when he saw the speaker, said 'Why, bless your soul! Old Bill Bloggs has talked here of a Saturday night last twenty years or more!' Bill Bloggs had, in fact, become an institu-

* High treason. (Eds.)

tion, and Queen Victoria at the zenith of British power was felt by all to be so securely seated on her throne that Bloggs could be safely left to express his anti-royalist sentiments to all who cared to listen to him.

I have tried to put before you a few of the findings of recent psychological research regarding this question of tolerance. If they seem to you almost suspiciously favourable to what we might call the democratic way of life, I would ask you to bear in mind three things. A good many of the experiments I have described are based on the selection of the top and bottom twenty-five per cent as regards tolerance, and they give too clear-cut a picture when we try to apply it to any random sample of the population as a whole; at least fifty per cent of us fall in between the extremes—we are, as it were, lukewarm both in our tolerance and in our intolerance. Secondly, I have said nothing, or next to nothing, about the possible dangers of toleration, which in the past history of humanity have sometimes placed the tolerant at the mercy of their more bigoted and fanatical neighbours. In the third place, psychology is a relatively new science, and too much faith must not be placed on the results from methods which are still often crude as compared with those at the disposal of the physical sciences.

Nevertheless, the mere adoption of the psychological point of view to social problems, apart from the results obtained, can, I believe, be of great significance in dealing with the anxiety, suspicion, and aggression which create so much havoc in our human relations. When those who hold strong views start to think in psychological terms, they begin to acquire both some interest in, and some respect for, what goes on in their own minds and in those of other people, and this itself is a first step in diminishing intolerance.

61. THE MOB AND THE GHOST

Lillian Smith

I do not remember when I first heard the word segregation, but I knew its meaning from babyhood. I learned it the hard way, for I was separated from people I loved by death. These were my first lessons in segregation. Other lessons came quickly. I learned of the segregation that cuts one off from knowledge. There were things I wanted to know which no one would tell me; questions no one would answer. What is death? I needed to know but no one could explain it. I asked about time and eternity; I wanted to know when eternity ended. People told me to go play dolls; and my Sunday school teacher said if I asked about eternity again she would not let me come to her class.

Eight years old: hugging great questions which burned as they touched me. But all children want to know what cannot be known, what words cannot say. Science was just creeping into our town; new doubts were blowing even in that small place. But I dared not say them aloud. I doubted God, yet at the same time I feared Him. This was another ambiguity I was learning to live with. How could part of me question the existence of God and another part be aware of His presence? I kept worrying the idea of time and eternity as a kitten plays with a ball of yarn—getting myself more and more entangled in it. I laughed at the absurd whenever I saw it, as all children do; but my spine ached with the burden of silence as I asked: *Where did I come from? Where am I going? Who am I besides a name?* And no one answered.

Then came another question, more and more often, that concerned me every day: the question about race and its ritual of segregation.

From the PROGRESSIVE MAGAZINE, *December 1962. Copyright © 1962 by the* Progressive Magazine *and reprinted by its permission.*

My first concern with it was because it affected *me,* not because it affected Negroes. I just did not like to be segregated. I wanted to be free to ask questions, free to seek answers, free to learn about the mysteries of birth, death, the human body and soul; free to question God, free to love Him, free to run away from Him and deny Him; I wanted also—a want closer to my consciousness—to choose my own friends. I did not like being restricted to members of the white race. Some of the most interesting and daring and skillful youngsters in town were my colored friends to whom I secretly attached myself. This hurt: the secrecy hurt, the fact that they were not welcomed on our street. I wanted the people I loved to come through the front door. I was taught to love freedom, to love the dignity of men, to consider other people's comfort and rights, to respect the human being, to believe in Christian brotherhood, to admit mistakes, and to speak the honest word. My family taught me these things; and yet, there was always the quiet, gentle, back door treatment of the dark people we loved. Love without dignity: the thought chilled me.

I was also taught to go to church, to listen carefully and to believe what the preachers said. Of course, those questions curled up in my head shot like rockets through the discrepancies in this intertwining mesh of family lessons and church lessons and street lessons and school lessons. Everything contradicting everything else, and I knew it. But gradually I "adjusted" better; I grew the third skin which all white Southerners finally grow, and it shut off the quick pain, the sudden glimpse of horror, the ever-pressing whispers of conscience. I got used to my colored friends living in shacks on the edge of town while I lived in a big, fine house on the "best" street. I got used to playing with them on my way home from school but never inviting them to my house. I got used to seeing an all-white congregation in our church, although I asked questions before I grew silent. I got used to being split apart inside, conscience segregated from reality, body segregated from heart, mind separated from the knowledge it craved.

My earth was trembling—not only out near Big Swamp but in the bigger swamp of my interior life. And yet, there were rich experiences, fine glimpses of knowledge and art and poetry; there was love, there was compassion. But beneath it all were not only the unchangeable uncertainties on which the human condition is based, but another uncertainty that *need not be.* It was this that hurt me, this knowledge that racial separation does not belong in the category of the archetypal and unchangeable separations: birth, death, a universe which we can never know save in small fragments, a God whose existence we can never prove, a *why was I born?* which even a man's vocation does not answer in full. This separation was different; it could be *changed.*

And yet, others seemed to accept it as unchangeable. Their families told them they were members of the white race and that was enough for anybody to be; their demagogues told them this superiority gave them the right to treat Negroes like things and animals and they need not listen when their conscience did not agree. They became solid with certainty; hard, undifferentiated in their mystique of whiteness. Faces took on a bleak surety which frightened me as a child more than even the ghosts I could not name. I would run to the security of a home where such racial hate talk never took place, though my family were long-time Southerners; where no man was considered less than a human being; where dignity was acted out by my parents in their relationships with their children. And because of this retreat, this peaceful cloister, I never accepted "the Southern way of life." I knew someday it could be changed; and so my loyalties never became too tied up with "the South." I love the South not for its sins but because it is home, where my memories hover; I love its climate, its strange and beautiful jungles, swamps, beaches, forests, hills, mountains; I love the softness of voice; I still cherish the easy kindnesses, even though I know that many of these "kind" people have cared little about Negroes' rights or welfare.

The small acts of grace can sometimes blind you to the large cruelties. For the cruelties keep distance. Most white Southerners have never seen a lynching, have never seen a Negro wounded or whipped, have never heard a dark scream of pain, never come close to the awful humiliation which colored women endured for so long from many white men; have never visited a Negro school; have never asked what happens to Negroes when they get sick; never looked hard at a starving face or a crippled mind; never whispered the sorrow and shame of a love without esteem. Most knew these terrors only remotely, never letting them creep into consciousness. They thought of them, often, as "exaggerations"—or lies. They blamed the worst of them on "outsiders" even though the outsiders might live on their street. And until recently, they pulled the silence tight around their hearts and made like they felt nothing. The third skin has had its uses even for the best of us in the South (as well as in Germany); and yes, let me say it: in those Northern cities where few of the privileged have ever visited *their* dark ghettos. The wound is unhealed in all of us, but we cover it with sweet-smelling salve and pretend the stench comes from somewhere else. Each of us in our own way has to struggle to step back a few inches and look, really look, at our home town and its cruelties and blindnesses and pitiful, tragic lies.

I have never been sure that racial segregation has hurt the Negro more than the white. I am not certain that physical lynching of the few is worse than the spiritual lynching of many white children by their own parents and school and church. There is a spiritual lynching of black children, too; different, but perhaps no more terrible than that of the white children. What segregation has actually done is to destroy spiritually and mentally millions of its children of both races. Arrogance, or shame—which do you prefer that your child feel? A mind deadened to knowledge, or a body shut out of a decent school? An indifference to the suffering of others, or suffering itself? The choice is hard to make for all these things will dehumanize the child.

Neither Negroes nor whites have fully realized that segregation is a two-edged sword, that it cuts both ways and cuts to kill. If this could once be seen clearly, if white people could for one hour stare at the faces around them, could peer even for one minute into the hollow souls they work with and play with, they could not say, "It must come slowly; a little token sanity, yes, but not too much sanity, not too much compassion, not too much fairness—just a moderate amount." To hear thoughtful men speak of postponing decency, postponing excellence, postponing the return of rights they have stolen from Negroes and from their own children, leaves me gasping in astonishment. How can our people be so blind?

We need someone to blame. We cannot bear our anguish if we know it springs from our own hearts. We look around; some name our own U.S. Supreme Court as the mortal enemy; others blame "the North" or the National Association for the Advancement of Colored People or the Communists. But besides ourselves, we can blame the immediate trouble today only on the demagogues (the racist politicians) and the ghosts which the demagogues whistle back—those old guilts and memories, the consciences we killed but which never died, the children we maimed, the souls we destroyed. Now they are sent forth as maenads* by the demagogues to cut the head off of every Orphic† truth, to whip and lash every one who dares to disagree, to speak what is right, to measure and examine reality.

And we let them. The churches let them, the preachers let them, the businessmen let them, the unions let them. All? No. There has been a small minority of mute dissenters since the Civil War; there has been a small minority of soft speakers since 1925; there have been more and more who have spoken and written clearly, persuasively, in recent decades, but the maenads torment them: tongues lash, houses are burned or dynamited, friends shun, critics destroy not only books but status, reviewers sneer (not only in the South but in the North, too), saying, "This writer is angry; he is excited; too disturbed." I say in reply, "How under God's heaven could a sane, observant, sensitive human being be less than disturbed over a region that has sacrificed its children to a white Moloch?‡ How could a deeply religious person feel anything but anguish at the springing up of idolatries not

only in this South of ours but throughout the country and the world? How can we, with gentlemanly decorum, accept for one minute the philosophical implications of 'gradualism' and the caution of racial 'moderates'?"

And yet, many do. Many others are so glazed over, so frozen by fear, so toughened by this third skin of ours that they obey the demagogues and run from the ghosts, or chase them, as ordered. Otherwise, how could we have had Little Rock? Or those jeering women persecuting children in New Orleans? Or those students mobbing one lone girl at the University of Georgia? Or those deaths at Oxford, Mississippi? And worst of all, the dreadful silence of the good, the respectable, the prominent: the collapse of the poet in each of us.

I was close to the mob at Athens, Georgia; not in the town but close enough to watch it build (even a year before it exploded). It was not surprising to many Georgians when a mob of two thousand students (helped by the Klan) attacked one girl. But the point that few have seen is that the mob was not attacking a real girl named Charlayne Hunter but a symbol, a ghost into which they had stuffed noisome memories, guilts, and words from the white supremacy ritual. They had never met Charlayne Hunter, would not have recognized her on the streets, yet their rage was tremendous and uncontrolled. They felt they must kill Something, Something that had haunted them a long time, Something that kept them split and torn and confused.

When we see this kind of thing happening, when we see a governor of a state act like a mad fool, when we watch students go berserk as if they were in psychotic flight, when we see responsible men of a community turn dumb and mute as if they were cowed animals, when suddenly crowds of people begin to lie, to blame on mythic outsiders what they themselves brought to pass—when such outbursts occur, we can be sure we are not dealing with reasonable problems such as poverty or a one-party political system or the memories of a war fought a century ago which no living man knows anything about from personal experience, or an outmoded peonage system of sharecropping. Although all have their effect and all exacerbate the situation, the cause for such turmoil is not on rational levels of men's thinking.

We shall more likely find the answer in lower depths of personality, lower—and higher.

---

* Frenzied or raging women; in Greek mythology, followers of Dionysios. (Eds.)

† From Orpheus, the supreme poet celebrated in later Greek mythology. (Eds.)

‡ In the Old Testament, a god of the Phoenicians to whom children were sacrificed by burning. (Eds.)

A look at the charismatic power of the demagogue should warn any observer that depths, not surfaces, are being stirred. Ghosts are on the loose and one somehow knows it. Ghosts are, of course, breathing symbols; they are symbols with a half-life; they are memories that cannot end their story and in restlessness keep haunting men's minds with unfinished business; they are guilts that have never asked forgiveness. Above all else, they are powerful, for they can turn men into things and things into men. How could Hitler have killed millions of Jews had not the Nordic ghosts helped him turn them into things? But—and this we need to remember—the ghosts could not have done the bloody, grisly business alone. They had to have a witch doctor to free them—for ordinarily ghosts are segregated—and then direct them to do their work. The demagogue understands this; so he uses incantation and hypnotic gestures to loosen the ghosts from the mythic level of men's minds where they ordinarily stay. In the South he repeats words that are close to men's bodies, words that have taken on symbolic meanings: *blood, white, black, menace, mixing, mingling, white, black,* and with these words he creates, actually makes, a new situation that does not exist in terms of facts but exists, nevertheless; and men, listening, react to this mythic situation as though it were literally real.

The racists dehumanize the man, Negro, into the thing, Negro. On this mythic level where the reason's categories and logical processes are never found, it is easy to ask why the Negro (now a fetish, a symbol) should have human rights. Why should a *thing* be protected by the Supreme Court and the Department of Justice? There are people who actually cannot grasp the fact that a Negro is not an object but a human being.

The demagogue knows he can force people into this primitive state by the skilled use of the ghosts and by the freeing of demonic impulses from the restrictive covenants of conscience. The demagogue, speaking with the authority of a priest, tells the crowd they are justified in doing anything in the name of white supremacy. They believe him. And because of the release he gives them, they give him obedience.

In this slave condition, reason won't work. For decades, demagogues have fattened on this powerful bit of knowledge. Reason cannot undo magic tricks once they have been performed. Only physical force can control the external violence; and only the poetic truth can subdue the inner turmoil. The poet, therefore, is the demagogue's mortal enemy—for he and he alone can overcome the evil state of men's minds. The poet can do this not only because he, too, uses ghosts—"the good ghosts"—but because he has power over the poetic, truth-seeking levels of the mythic mind. This is why the silence of the poet in all of us is so dread a thing when the mob begins to merge. This is the moment when only truth can kill the lie, when only love can weaken hate: reason cannot do it, nor common sense, nor logic; but poetic truth spoken to people with compassion and beauty has the strange power to arouse their good feelings and desires.

The mythic mind is, above all else, highly creative: it can create lies and demons and mobs and riots; but it can also create art and poetry by careful addition of heart and intelligence and the proper use of symbols and ghosts. What the demagogues do is to change gold into straw; what the poets do is to change straw into gold; their purpose is different, their grasp of knowledge is different, their procedures are different, but they use the same magic. They both know the power of metaphor; they both know how to change a person into a thing or a thing into a person; they both understand that "holy" can be the holiness of devils or the holiness of God. A demagogue by his tricks melts a thousand people into a mob. A poet by his "tricks" builds bridges among those people, separating them a little so they can feel their own edge, yet drawing them closer by the new relationship to truth he gives them. Can you not see that "rational man" with his logic and his scrupulously collected facts does not have much chance with the people in crisis who are chasing ghosts, who are acting symbolically? Reason must do its work *before the crisis comes.*

Mobs and demagogues, riots and hate slogans, are also symptoms of a collective illness. The South is suffering from such a malaise. The illness is by no means limited to the South or to our country. It comes not primarily from racism (racism is a symptom, not the disease itself); it comes from two centuries of Western man's misunderstanding of science and over-esteem of proof and from his unnecessary subjection to the machine he created. Combined, these have caused him to misinterpret religion, have pushed him toward the facts of the laboratory and away from the truth found in poetry. And now, most men no longer believe that there is something bigger than a man, that spiritual laws exist which no one can disregard without destroying himself.

This is the heart of the matter. To understand the compulsive fury of people caught in racial stress, we must understand not only the mechanisms they use but their emptiness; and to understand the emptiness we must understand their basic, often unverbalized, rejection of God and the terrible hunger that is a consequence of this rejection. No wonder men in a bi-racial situation have seized upon color (their own) and made of it a fetish. They need and must have something to worship. What now—if God is dead? Who will be our new God? Who will be our new priests?

The ignorant, the culturally stunted, and a small but noisy group of psychotics are the demagogue's natural audience. The strain of living in both a spiritual vacuum and a scientific world which is totally beyond their comprehension is eased by this frank regression to more primitive ways. They love the demagogue's ghost stories; the threat of "the Negro" is more titillating than terrifying; it helps them forget the atom bomb; they feel by casting a vote or taking part in a riot they can "do something about the Negro," but they can't do anything about those missile bases. Substituting a spurious menace for a real one and promising security plays a big part in the demagogue's success. These deprived people were once pitiable, but with the vote, with jobs, with spending power, they grow dangerous; dangerous because a large group of them are addicts who for years have given themselves kicks with the drug, white supremacy; and they will not give up their "white powder" without a nasty struggle.

Of all our Southern sins—and we have plenty—the persistent, blind ignoring of the needs of our poor and ignorant whites is perhaps the worst; our culture has fed them lies—not folk wisdom; our power structure, instead of giving jobs, gave them for decades a false and ridiculous sense of superiority, teaching them that excellence lay simply in possessing a white skin. These people heard nothing about dignity, human growth, relationships; they heard nothing of the myths and poetry by which Western man has become great. You can know the wisdom of the poets without reading poetry if other men will speak of this wisdom, but the uncultivated white Southerner, for eighty years, has heard nothing except lies about white superiority, skin color, mongrelization.

Now, suddenly, they are told to obey the law. What law, they ask in astonishment—for they had been told they could break any law that protected a Negro; that no one could have civil rights in this country unless his skin was white. Now they are told to obey: to obey not because the laws are good and right but because they are The Law. This is supposed to be a clever way out, a face-saver for politicians and the power structure and for certain editors who have exclaimed editorially for years that nobody but a fool would question segregation. Now, the new slogan is, "Even though we despise the Supreme Court's decision, we must obey."

It is not the truth but a half-lie, and we shall suffer from it. The ignorant white can take the truth, if the truth is spoken in kindness. I know face-saving is sometimes expedient—I did not live in China for three years without learning this—but in a time of deep stress and spiritual turmoil, to try to settle for a half-lie is dangerous. People must change their ways and their values, but to do so without breaking to pieces physically and spiritually they must *change inside*. They must fill the hollowness with the full Orphic truth; only in this way can they master their ordeal as men. And now, our leaders are once more offering them only face-saving subterfuges.

One could weep. Like the old Greek warriors one could lift one's face to the sky and weep. When the sharecroppers in Arkansas were thrown out in snow and ice by the plantation owners, an old Negro prayed, "Break their hearts, O God; give them tears." I heard him pray and ever since it has haunted me with its pathos and its truth.

Things are changing, but much too slowly; the "old forms are breaking," and we are beginning to "feel the new things"—but much too slowly. Our leaders have not yet faced the truth that we, too, must hurt, we must suffer with the poor white and the Negro, not only to be redeemed from our past but to find the wisdom to create our future.

We must say with Aeschylus: "Cry sorrow—and let the good prevail."

62. THE ANATOMY OF VIOLENCE

Hans Toch

We have suggested that two types of orientation are especially likely to produce violence: one of these is that of the person who sees other people as tools designed to serve his needs; the second is that of the individual who feels vulnerable to manipulation. These two perspectives, when we examine them more closely, become faces of the same coin: both rest on the premise that human relationships are power-centered, one-way affairs; both involve efforts at self-assertion with a desperate, feverish quality that suggests self-doubt.

Of course, this description does not fit all cases. Some of the rep defenders, for instance, initially respond to a draft, instead of promoting their own reputation; some self-defenders react to a human jungle in which they are unfairly asked to survive; pressure removing sometimes represents little more than feeblemindedness. But even in these instances, experiences with violent encounters teach the person to respond overeagerly, suspending the dictates of equity, ignoring the norm of reciprocity, and asserting personal autonomy at the expense of others. Such, it appears, is the nature of the violence-prone game.

The violence-provoking incident typically consists of several stages: first there is the classification of the other person as an object or a threat; second, there is some action based on this classification; third, the other person may act—if he has the chance—to protect his integrity. At this juncture, the violent incident reaches its point of no return. The initial stance of the violence-prone person makes violence probable; his first moves increase the probability of violence; the reaction of

Reprinted from Hans Toch, VIOLENT MEN *(Chicago: Aldine Publishing Company, 1969); copyright © 1969 by Hans Toch. Reprinted by permission of the publisher and the author.*

the victim converts probability into certainty.

The extent to which violent incidents are predetermined depends on how aggressive the aggressor feels. If his violence-propensity is substantial, he may insist on conflict; if his requirements are modest, the victim may be left with pacifying moves. For instance, a mildly scared individual can be reassured; a person who feels somewhat inadequate can be satisfied with flattery or a show of humor. But if the aggressor's ego demands blood, the victim may find himself pursued remorselessly, no matter what he says or does....

The probability of violence in violence-provoking incidents is tied to the extent to which the aggressor indulges in preclassification or selective perception. For instance, many of the participants in our police incidents scan human contacts assiduously for the possibility of threatening implications. They do so with varying degrees of intensity and with differing abilities to "spot" suggestive information. The actions of other people are eventually classified as either non-challenging (safe) or as challenging (requiring action). Because of the dreaded consequences of error, the scales are far from evenly weighed: with greater or lesser distortion, potentially harmless encounters become transmuted into "unprovoked" onslaughts by "vicious" bullies. And at this point, the time-worn formula of the weak ego prescribes an aggressive confrontation. If this confrontation consists of direct aggression, it ends the incident; when it does not, the other person must somehow cope with the affront to which he has been subjected. His response is likely to lead to violence, because it usually feeds into the hypothesis that provides the aggressor's rationale for offensiveness.

For several reasons, the probability of violence in personal encounters increases with each new act of aggression. Violence is habit-forming. Aggressors discover that they can satisfy new and unsuspected needs by becoming aggressive. They also learn to view themselves as participants in violent games. Most importantly, they start seeing elements of past violent encounters as they approach fresh situations and begin to respond routinely. They seek and find consistency of self at the expense of their victims. . . .

Although the logic of violence may emerge from the practice of violence, it probably originates most frequently in interpersonal relationships early in life. Thus, manipulative efforts mark the failure of socialization somewhere between unbridled infancy and the assumption of social responsibility. Self-assertiveness or defensiveness suggest that one's upbringing has been deficient in stability and emotional support, thus making it difficult for positive self-perceptions to develop. In both instances, brittle egos spend their adult years in belated efforts to buttress themselves at the expense of other people, and these efforts become productive of violence.

Of course, a brittle ego is a relative contruction; some situations can shatter selves of steel, while others cater to the lowest levels of maturity. The young police officer out on his first beat faces all kinds of problems with which he is unprepared to cope. And what of the "fish"—our Sam, for instance—entering the prison yard for his first time, expecting to be terrorized into a state of emasculated slavery? And what of the fact that both the young officer and the young fish have learned that they are entering a world in which power is the only voice that carries, and in which attention to the feelings of others is a dangerous weakness?

Situations promotive of violent reactions undoubtedly exist; individuals are faced with human relations problems of almost insoluble complexity and serious personal import. These problems awaken fear and a sense of inadequacy; violence-prone solutions advocated by persons who are presumed to be experienced and sophisticated are persuasive. It would almost follow that these solutions would be adopted.

It would *almost* follow, that is, except for the circumstance that these solutions involve violations of the integrity and the aspirations of other people, and that this circumstance can be plainly inferred. It is obvious that the mythology of violence-proneness at minimum requires the short-circuiting of rules of procedure, or calls for precipitous aggressive action with little inquiry into its justification. And it is because violence is primitive that the most successfully socialized persons among those exposed to a potentially explosive situation will resist premature acceptance of the violent formula of survival.

The willingness to adopt the violence-prone mythology of survival distinguishes the members of our sample from other inmates or police officers or slum children or unhappily married men. It distinguishes them as persons with a starting capital of insecurity or ego-centricity available for investment in violence-promoting premises.

Unfortunately, as the game of violence unfolds in our interviews, it appears to be insidious in its cumulative character. Once a person discovers that the ego can be buttressed at the expense of others, the discovery seems to be recurrently applied. The routine, moreover, gains from both success and failure; its stability rests on the fact that it feeds on personal insecurity, rather than on the reactions of victims and the sanctions of authority. The task of re-educating the violence-prone person is thus one of considerable magnitude and a challenge worthy of the best the social sciences and helping professions can offer.

THE SUBCULTURE OF VIOLENCE

We have made much of the role of violence-prone premises or assumptions in the creation of violent incidents. We have seen that persons who tend to interpret situations as threatening, or goading, or challenging, or overpowering can turn harmless encounters into duels, purges, struggles for survival, or violent escapes.

To be sure, the propensity satisfies personal needs; it resolves doubts about self-importance, it brings social prominence and respect, and it preserves a consumer role in personal relations. But these ends can be achieved in other ways—sometimes with considerably less risk or consequence.

Violence-prone premises tie neatly into immature personality patterns, but the connection is not inevitable. Some use violence as a crutch, and others do not; some use violence as a weapon, and others do not. The question is, what accounts for the difference? Where do violence-prone assumptions have their origin—where are they learned? One explanation would be that violent alternatives may be accidentally discovered and that, once violence has been exercised, the experience transfers to successive encounters. But this explanation is too related to chance. It seems easier to assume that in some segments of our society violence-prone premises are widely accepted and that they are available for adoption by susceptible individuals.

This type of explanation has been advanced by Marvin Wolfgang, and has been expanded in Wolfgang and Ferracuti's treatise *The Subculture of Violence*.[1] The basis for the idea is a statistical one: it rests on the finding that some groups are more prone to use violence to solve their problems than are other people. For instance, Italy has several localities in which it is customary to retaliate against private affronts, and in some parts of Mexico citizens are apt to settle their disputes with physical combat. In the United States, young men who have grown up in Negro ghettos have learned to be dispensers (and victims) of violence.

Such situations can be labeled "subcultures of violence" because they imply a code which prescribes violent conduct and which is passed on—through word and deed—from one generation to the next. Why is violence thus taught and why is it learned? In some cases, the reason is sociopsychological. American and Mexican slums, for instance, contain many homes in which the mother is of considerably more consequence that the father, who may be rarely in evidence. In such homes, the masculine role may not seem imposing, and growing boys may feel compelled to evolve physical means of demonstrating their manhood. Violence here becomes one of the facets or vehicles of the well-known *machismo* syndrome. In other subcultures, emphasis on violence can originate in transformed social customs or group relationships. Family feuds and tribal rivalries, for instance, can give rise to a tradition of retaliation, as in parts of Italy. Frontier justice can be transformed into a system for privately punishing presumed offenders. And nonviolent career lines may often be unavailable.

Whatever the origins of the subculture of violence, it exists in the form of values, beliefs, and attitudes held by its members. These may relate to all manner of situations, and may prescribe appropriate conduct for them. Violence is one such form of conduct, and it is permissively viewed. That such a doctrine is prevalent does not mean, of course, that every person residing in a given geographical area will be equally subjected to it, nor that everyone exposed to these assumptions will adopt them. Violence-proneness is restricted to the select minority within the subculture who have fully assimilated its violence-prone teachings and who live by them.

For these select persons, a wide range of situations would be defined as justifying aggressive responses. Violence-prone people do not merely espouse violence as a doctrine or philosophy, but they tend to see the world in violent terms and respond to it accordingly. In the words of Wolfgang and Ferracuti, "variations in the surrounding world... [would] have a greater chance of being perceived and reacted upon...as menacing, aggressive stimuli which call for immediate defense and counter-aggression."[2] In the American Negro ghetto, for example, "a male is usually expected to defend the name and honor of his mother, the virtue of womanhood...and to accept no derogation about his race (even from a member of his own race), his age, or his masculinity. Quick resort to physical combat as a measure of daring, courage, or defense of status appears to be a cultural expression..."[3]

Members of the subculture of violence perceive themselves as aggressive; they see opportunities for violence in the world around them, and they play stereotyped violence-prone games. An example of stereotyped violence is the procedure known as "playing the dozens," which is popular in the slums and in prisons. "The dozens" is a form of verbal interaction designed to test one's own equanimity, to produce rage in one's opponent, and to build up a rationale for physical violence. Ralph Berdie describes one form of this interaction as follows:

> One of the tormenters will make a mildly insulting statement, perhaps about the mother

1 M. Wolfgang and F. Ferracuti, *The Subculture of Violence: Toward an Integrated Theory of Criminology* (London: Tavistock, 1967).

2 *Ibid.*, p. 157.
3 M. Wolfgang, *Patterns in Criminal Homicide* (Philadelphia: University of Pennsylvania Press, 1958), p. 188.

of the subject, "I saw your mother out with a man last night." Then he may follow this up with "She was as drunk as a bat." The subject, in turn, will then make an insulting statement about the tormenter or some member of the tormenter's family. This exchange of insults continues, encouraged by the approval and shouts of the observers, and the insults become progressively nastier and more pornographic, until they eventually include every member of the participants' families and every act of animal and man.... Finally, one of the participants, usually the subject, who has actually been combating the group pressure of the observers, reaches his threshold and takes a swing at the tormenter, pulls out a knife or picks up an object to use as a club. That is the sign for the tormenter, and sometimes some of the observers, to go into action, and usually the subject ends up with the most physical injuries....[4]

The subculture of violence thus prescribes certain rules for the exercise of violence and also equips its members with motives, attitudes, and perceptions which produce the games in which these rules apply.

Fannin and Clinard, who studied the self-images of lower-class and middle-class delinquents, report that it is usual for the lowerclass boys to see themselves as tough, powerful, fierce, and fearless. It is also usual, according to them, for these boys to want to become even tougher, harder and more violent than they are. The boys further feel that their prestige depends on advertised ability and willingness to fight, on physical superiority over others, and on general fearlessness. The interesting point is that the delinquent boys do not uniformly live up to the prescription, nor do they have similar conceptions of their own activities....

Personality can intersect with group norms in one of several ways. For one, personal needs will dictate how well subcultural teachings are assimilated. Ultimately, it is the individual who decides whether violence is to be eagerly adopted, casually rehearsed, or totally ignored. And given the rewards of violence, weak egos are apt to best assimilate violence-prone lessons. Moreover, neighborhood definitions can leave considerable latitude for excitability thresholds, for preferences in roles, for variations in physical tactic, and for individual styles of response. Cultural definitions can

4 R. F. Berdie, Playing the Dozens, *Journal of Abnormal and Social Psychology* (1947), 42: 120–21, p. 120.

reflect all manner of personal sensitivities and can accommodate every stage of maturity in interpersonal dealings. Thus, subcultural prescriptions for violence may not specify whether insults should be sought out or reacted to, whether aggression should take physical or verbal forms, whether the individual should lead or follow in matters of aggression. Whereas the subculture of violence promotes violence, it does not prescribe the violent encounters of individual members. The nature of the person's violent acts can therefore reflect both the spirit of the times and the unique contribution of his individual needs.

This is especially the case with persons who take to the "violence" in the subculture of violence with more alacrity and enthusiasm than their neighbors. It is these individuals, who meet the norm "thou shalt be violent" much more than halfway, who best personify the sociopsychological model of subculturally induced violence. For it is these persons whose needs are most felicitously responded to by the license to destroy which they feel is furnished them. And ultimately, these persons carry violence to such an extreme that even their subcultural coreligionaries may classify them as violence-prone....

SOCIAL VIOLENCE AND PERSONAL VIOLENCE

In our discussion so far, we have only been able to hint at the relationship between collective violence and personal violence. At first glance, the two types of violence differ. Whereas the violent person approaches his encounters as a solitary agent, the rioter becomes mobilized as a member of a group; whereas the violent person has affinity for aggressive action, the rioter is a product of history; whereas the violent person provokes violence, the rioter seems to respond to a situation created to provoke him. The appropriate kind of analysis differs: while in personal violence we expect to find consistency within the individual, in collective violence we assume that people respond uniformly to a sequence of frustrating experiences.

But these divergences are less sharp after we examine the motivating patterns in riots. For one, we see that violent incidents must come into being to provide a focus for grievances. In the genesis of such incidents, individuals with violence-prone personalities play roles similar to those which they play in their other encounters.

We have seen that in a riot the man in the street can gain benefits usually reserved to the Violent Man. He can gain these benefits by availing himself of ready-made opportunities, which make violence possible for him. Riots contain provisions for the replication (in miniature) of several of our violent types. A person may become a rioter to promote his self-image, or to defend his status, or to remove pressure, or to release pent-up feelings. And the quality of riot participation is probably to some measure dependent on such preferred modes of adjustment, or on favored styles of relating to others.

On the other hand, the motives and perceptual content of a riot are restricted, compared to the rich tapestry of free lance violence. Most rioters are self-defined revolutionaries; many of them see rioting as vengeance; almost all are inspired by the fellowship of their comrades; and in all instances, they have a mythical, collective conception of the Enemy. We have also seen that in the development of riot motivation, economic grievances and social disappointments are prominent in the awareness of rioters.

Riots gain uniformity from the fact that they are institutionalized: The Ghost of Riots Past hovers like a friendly specter over each new outbreak; it provides historical sanction, and it furnishes vivid images of how and why to proceed. This kind of advance prescription reduces the room for individual initiative.

This does not mean that personality cannot express itself in riots. There is occasion for the display of personal style, and opportunity for the satisfaction of personal needs. Riot participation can be lighthearted or grim; it can be angry or playful; it can be fearful or calm. And the riot situation can be viewed in many different ways: rioting may thus be an act of revenge for some, and an emotional discharge, or an act of rebellion for others. Violence may serve as a vehicle to personal identity, or as a means to power or material gain. A riot can be many things to many people; some of its meanings may run deep or may extend far back into time.

In this sense, riots are less psychologically confining than are some other forms of collective violence, such as war. In battle, violence is committed because the individual's military vocation demands it. The soldier is instructed to follow destructive routines (such as shooting at moving targets or pressing a button that operates equipment to release a projectile), and he largely complies because he has learned to do so, because he respects his superiors, and because he accepts his role as defined for him. Typically, he gains no satisfaction from violence beyond those of efficiently discharging his obligations and of participating in the collective destruction of a consensually defined enemy.

There are soldiers, to be sure, who seek out blood and gore beyond the call of duty and who gain considerable reward from the administration of death and destruction. There are those who volunteer for elite killer units that operate behind enemy lines and engage in assassinations or sabotage; there are others who prize assignments as snipers or scouts; and there are figures of heroic stature with a penchant for singlehandedly launching offensive operations in defiance of sensible odds. It is within the ranks of soldiers such as these that we find our violence-prone persons, those driven by the desire for physical action, those who seek a new identity or a bolstered image in the eyes of themselves and others. And it is these individuals—praiseworthy though they may be from the viewpoint of the military—who must be monitored and eventually resocialized for membership in the civilized community. . . .

63. PSYCHOLOGICAL ALTERNATIVES TO WAR

Morton Deutsch

I shall assume the truth of the following propositions:

1. A large-scale nuclear war would achieve a result that no sane man could desire.

2. When a small war occurs, there is a risk that it may turn into a large war; this risk would be considerably enhanced by the use of nuclear weapons. In the course of many small wars, the probability of a great war would become almost a certainty.

3. The knowledge and capacity to make nuclear and other weapons of mass destruction cannot be destroyed; they will exist as long as mankind exists.

4. Any war in which a nuclear power is faced with the possibility of major defeat or a despairing outcome is likely to turn into a large-scale nuclear war even if nuclear disarmament had previously occurred.

5. A hostile peace will not long endure. From these propositions it follows that, if mankind is to avoid utter disaster, we must see to it that irrational men are not in a position to initiate nuclear war, we must find alternatives to war for resolving international conflicts and we must develop the conditions which will lead conflicting nations to select one or another of these alternatives rather than resort to war.

My discussion in this paper centers primarily on the question of: How do we take the hostility out of the hostile peace? This question proliferates into other, related questions: How do we prevent the misperceptions and misunderstandings in international relations which foster and perpetuate hostility? How do we move from a delicately balanced peace of mutual terror to a sturdy peace of mutual trust? How do we move in the direction of a world community in which law, institutions, obligations, and simple human decencies will enable mankind to enjoy a more amiable life? These are the central questions which must be answered if the world is to avoid disaster. The world will never again be in a position where it cannot destroy itself.

It is well for me to emphasize that opposition to war as a means of conflict resolution does *not* connote an opposition to controversy among nations. Controversy is as desirable as it is inevitable. It prevents stagnation, it is the medium through which problems can be aired and solutions arrived at; it is the heart of social change. Our objective is not to create a world in which controversy is suppressed but rather a world in which controversy is civilized; in which it is lively rather than deadly.

I do not pretend to have answers to the difficult questions I have raised. I raise them because I have something relevant to say and because I believe it is important to confront the fundamental questions. Too often we are distracted from them by short-run urgencies. You may well ask what can a psychologist say that is relevant? A wide reading, however, of acknowledged authorities in the study of war and international relations has convinced me that the dominant conceptions of international relations are psychological in nature. Such psychological concepts as "perception," "intention," "value," "hostility," "confidence,"

Morton Deutsch: "Psychological Alternatives to War"; THE JOURNAL OF SOCIAL ISSUES, 18, *1962, 97– 119. Copyright 1962 by the Society for the Psychological Study of Social Issues; reprinted by its permission and that of the author.*

"trust," and "suspicion" recur repeatedly in discussions of war and peace.[1]

I wish to make it clear that what I have to say in this paper is *not* based upon well-established, scientifically verified, psychological knowledge. As psychologists, we have only meager, fragmentary knowledge of how to prevent or overcome distortions in social perceptions, of how to move from a situation of mutual suspicion to a situation of mutual trust, of how to establish cooperative relationships despite intense competitive orientations, of how to prevent bargaining deadlocks. I take it for granted that we need more and better research before we may claim to speak authoritatively on these matters. However, my intent here is not to outline the research which is needed but rather to discuss these urgent matters as wisely as I can. In so doing, I shall necessarily go beyond the facts to draw upon the insights and orientations which I have developed in a research career devoted to the understanding of the conditions affecting cooperation and in a psychoanalytic practice devoted to helping people overcome their self-defeating attitudes and their interpersonal distortions. The proposals which I make in this paper flow from these personal insights and orientations. They are, I believe, consistent with the meager knowledge that we have; but it is apparent that much more research-grounded knowledge is necessary if we are ever to get beyond the stage of "informed hunches." Although my "informed hunches" are offered with personal conviction, I hope that you will understand that my research continues and that I do not plan to leave these hunches untested.

IS WAR INEVITABLE?

Is it possible that war is inevitable, that the psychological nature of man is such that war

1 Perhaps there has been too much psychologizing about these matters; there are, after all, critical differences between persons and nations. Not the least of these is the fact that in a deadly quarrel between people it is the quarrelers who are most apt to be killed while, in a deadly quarrel among nations, the decision-makers are rarely the ones who have the highest probability of dying. Be that as it may, I shall assume that there is some merit in viewing nations, like persons, as behaving units in an environment and to conceive of international relations in terms somewhat analagous to those of interpersonal relations.

is an indispensable outlet for his destructive urges? True, there have been wars throughout human history and men have found outlets for psychological drives of all kinds in war—sadistic, masochistic, creative, heroic, altruistic, adventurous, etc. Yet, as Jerome Frank ...has pointed out, the historical prevalence of a behavior pattern is not proof of its inevitability. Human sacrifice in religious rites, slavery, sorcery, certain forms of child labor, etc., have largely disappeared in modern, industrialized nations although such practices have existed throughout human history.

William James, in his classic paper, "The Moral Equivalent of War" (1911), recognized that war and the military spirit produced certain virtues which are necessary to the survival of any society. However, he went on to point out that militarism and war is not the only means for achieving the virtues of self-discipline and social cohesiveness, that it is possible to find alternative means for achieving the same psychological ends. (It is of interest to note that James's suggestion for a moral equivalent to war was a "Peace Corps" of youth enlisted in an army against *Nature*.) The view that alternative means for satisfying psychological motives can always be found is, of course, a basic concept in modern psychology. Egon Brunswick went so far as to elevate "vicarious functioning" (*i.e.,* the equivalence and mutual intersubstitutability of different behaviors in relation to goal achievement) to the defining criterion of the subject matter of psychology.

Man's make-up may always contain the psychological characteristics which have found an outlet in militarism and war. There is no reason, however, to doubt that these characteristics can find satisfactory outlets in peaceful pursuits. Aggressiveness, adventurousness, idealism, and bravery will take a peaceful or destructive outlet depending upon the social, cultural, and political conditioning of the individual and upon the behavioral possibilities which exist within his social environment. Some may assert that war provides a more natural, spontaneous, or direct outlet for hostility and aggressiveness than any peaceful alternatives. Such an assertion is based upon a fundamental misconception of war: war is a highly complex, organized social activity in which personal outlets for aggression and hostility are primarily vicarious, symbolic, in-

direct, and infrequent for most of the participants. This is especially true for the highly
mechanized warfare of modern times which
largely eliminates the direct physical contact
between the aggressor and his victim.[2] Moreover, it is evident that no matter what his
psychological make-up an individual, *per se,*
cannot make war. War-making requires the
existence of complex social institutions necessary to organize and maintain a "war machine." This is not to say that a war machine
cannot be activated by the decision of strategically placed individuals. Obviously, one of
the great dangers of our era is that a small
group of men have the power to create a
nuclear holocaust. Even a strategically placed
individual can only activate a war machine
if it exists; the mass of people, not being
strategically placed, cannot directly activate
a war no matter what their psychological
predispositions are. It is relevant to note here
that research by T. Abel indicates that warlike
attitudes in the populace tend to follow rather
than precede the outbreak of war.

The impersonal character of modern war,
as Erich Fromm has pointed out, makes it
difficult for an individual to comprehend fully
the meaning of his actions as he kills. It is
easier for most people to kill faceless symbols
of human beings at a distance, than to kill
people with one's bare hands. Thus, if the
airmen of our Strategic Air Command were
suddenly ordered to fly to the Soviet Union
or China (or if Soviet airmen were ordered
to fly to the United States) to drop nuclear
weapons, most of them would comply. They
would, I assume, be distressed by the thought,
but they would comply. Would they comply
if the killings were personal—if they had to
burn, mutilate, or suffocate the victims one
by one? The psychological danger of modern
impersonal war is not that it is a good outlet
for aggression but rather, to the contrary, that
it does not permit the button-pusher to appreciate fully the destructive nature of his ac-

2 War is vastly overrated as an outlet for direct aggressiveness; it does not compare with the directness of
reckless automobile driving, a boxing match, or a football game. War is defined to be such a good outlet *only*
because of our cultural conditioning: the military toys
children are given to play with, the identification of
heroism and bravery with war in so many novels, TV
dramas, and films that we all are exposed to; the definition of patriotism in military terms in so many of our
public ceremonials and holidays, etc.

tions. Were he to do so, his destructive actions
might be inhibited rather than encouraged.

MISPERCEPTIONS WHICH LEAD TO WAR

Neither war nor peace is psychologically
inevitable. Exaggeration of the inevitability
of war contributes to a self-fulfilling prophecy:
it makes war more likely. Exaggeration of the
inevitability of peace does not stimulate the
intense effort necessary to create the conditions for a durable peace: a stable peace has
to be invented and constructed. There is nothing inevitable about it.

A fundamental theorem of the psychological
and social sciences is that man's behavior is
determined by the world he perceives. Perception is not, however, always veridical to the
world which is being perceived. There are a
number of reasons why perceptions may be
distorted. I would like to consider with you
five common causes of misperception, to
illustrate the operation of each in international relations, and to indicate how these
misperceptions can be counteracted or prevented.

1. *The perception of any act is determined
both by our perception of the act itself and
by our perception of the context in which the
act occurs.* Thus, the statement "You did that
extremely well" will be perceived rather differently if a captain is saying it to a private than
if a private is saying it to a captain. A common source of distorted social perception
results from misconceptions or false perceptions of context. The contexts of socials acts
are often not immediately given in perception
and often they are not obvious. When the
context is not obvious, we tend to assume a
familiar context—*i.e.,* the context which is
most likely in terms of our own experience.
Since both the present situations and past experiences of the actor and the perceiver may
be rather different, it is not surprising that
they will supply different contexts and interpret the same act quite differently. Misunderstandings of this sort, of course, are very
likely when the actor and the perceiver come
from rather different cultural backgrounds and
they are not fully aware of these differences.
The stock conversation of returning tourists
consists of amusing or embarrassing anecdotes
based upon misunderstandings of this sort.

Urie Bronfenbrenner's first-hand observations lead him to conclude that the Soviets and Americans have a similar view of one another; each says more or less the same things about the other. For example, each states: *"They* are the aggressors"; *"their* government exploits and deludes the people"; "the mass of *their* people is not really sympathetic to the regime"; *"they* cannot be trusted"; *"their* policy verges on madness"; etc.

It is my contention that mutual distortions such as those described above arise, in part, because of an inadequate understanding of the other's context. Take, for instance, the Soviet Union's reluctance to conclude any disarmament agreement which contains adequate provisions for international inspection and control. We view this as a device to prevent an agreement or to subvert any agreement on disarmament which might be worked out. However, as Joseph Nogee has pointed out in his monograph on "The Diplomacy of Disarmament": "Under present circumstances, any international control group reflecting the realities of political power would inevitably include a majority of non-Communist nations. Decisions involving actual and potential interests vital to the USSR would have to be made continuously by a control board, the majority of whose members would represent social and economic systems the USSR considers inherently hostile. Any conflicts would ultimately have to be resolved by representatives of governments, and it is assumed that on all major decisions the capitalist nations would vote as a bloc.... Thus, for the Soviet Union, representation on a control board along the lines proposed by the West would be inherently inequitable...."

I may assert that one can subjectively test the creditability of the Soviet position by imagining our own reactions if the Soviet bloc could consistently outvote us at the UN or on an international disarmament control board. Under such conditions, in the present world situation, would we conclude an agreement which did not give us the security of a veto? I doubt it. Similarly, one can test the creditability of the American position by imagining that the Soviet Union had experienced a Pearl Harbor in a recent war and that it had no open access to information concerning the military preparations of the United States. Under such circumstances, in the present world situation, would it be less concerned about inspection and control than we are? I doubt it. . . .

How can we prevent and overcome distortions and misunderstandings of this sort? Obviously, more communication, a great increase in interchanges of scholars, artists, politicians, tourists, and the like might be helpful. However, I think we should take cognizance of the findings of the vast body of research on intergroup contact: casual contact of limited duration is more likely to support deeply rooted distortions than remove them. To have any important effect, contact must be prolonged, functional, and intimate.

I suggest that the most important principle to follow in international communication on issues where there is controversy is one suggested by Anatol Rapoport.... He advocates that each side be required to state the position of the other side to the other side's complete satisfaction before either side advocates its own position. Certainly the procedure would not eliminate all conflict, but it would eliminate those conflicts based upon misunderstanding. It forces one to place the other's action in a context which is acceptable to the other and, as a consequence, prevents one from arbitrarily rejecting the other's position as unreasonable or badly motivated. This is the strategy followed by the good psychotherapist. By communicating to the patient his full understanding of the patient's behavior and by demonstrating the appropriateness of the patient's assumptions to the patient's behavior and past experiences, he creates the conditions under which the current validity of the patient's assumptions can be examined. The attempt to challenge or change the patient's behavior without mutual understanding of its assumptions usually produces only a defensive adherence to the challenged behavior.

2. Our perceptions of the external world are often determined indirectly by the information we receive from others rather than by our direct experiences. Human communication, like perception itself, is always selective. The perception of an event is usually less detailed, more abstract, and less complex than the event which is perceived; the communication about an event is also likely to be less detailed and less complex than its perception. The more human links there are in the communication of information about any event, the more simplified and distorted will be the representation of the event. Distortion in communication tends to take characteristic form: on the one hand, there is a tendency to accentuate the unusual, bizarre, controversial, deviant, violent, and unexpected; on the other hand, there is a tendency for communicators who are communicating to their superiors to communicate only that information which fits in with the preconceptions of their superiors.

If we examine our sources of information about international affairs, we see that they are particularly vulnerable to distorting influences. There are only a small number of American reporters in any country; they do not necessarily work independently of one another. They are under subtle pressure to report items which will catch the reader's interest and conform to their publisher's viewpoint. In a period of hostility between nations, these conditions are not conducive to getting a clear understanding of how events are perceived by the other side or a clear understanding of the other's frame of reference.

I suggest that we should recognize the dangers inherent in not perceiving the other side's point of view regularly. Recognizing these dangers, shouldn't we offer to make arrangements with the Soviet Union whereby we would each be enabled to present our own point of view over the other's radio and TV and in their leading newspapers? Suppose the Soviet leaders are afraid to participate on a reciprocating basis, should we make the offer anyway? My answer is in the form of a question: Do we have anything to lose by understanding their viewpoint as well as we can; wouldn't "truth squads" adequately protect us from deliberate attempts to mislead us?

3. *Our perceptions of the world are often very much influenced by the need to conform to and agree with the perceptions of other people.* Thus, in some communities it would be difficult for an individual to survive if he perceived Negroes as his social equals or if he perceived Communist China as having legitimate grievances against the United States. If he acted upon his perceptions, he would be ostracized socially; if he conformed to the perceptions of other people without changing his own perceptions, so that they were similar to those prevalent in his community, he might feel little self-respect.

It is my impression that most social and political scientists, most specialists in inter-national relations, most intellectuals who have thought about it, and many of our political leaders personally favor the admission of Communist China into the UN and favor our taking the initiative in attempting to normalize our relations with Communist China. Yet, conformity pressures keep silent most of us who favor such a change in policy. The strength of these conformity pressures in the United States on this issue is so great that it is difficult to think of Communist China or to talk about it in any terms except those which connote absolute, incorrigible evil. I believe this is an extremely dangerous situation, because without a fundamental change in United States-Chinese relations the world may be blown up shortly after China has acquired a stockpile of hydrogen bombs; this may take less than a decade.

How can we break through the veil of conformity and its distorting influences? Asch's insightful studies of conformity pressures point the way. His studies reveal that when the monolithic social front of conformity is broken by even one dissenter, other potential dissenters feel freer to break with the majority. The lesson is clear: those who dissent must express their opinions so that they are heard by others. If they do so, they may find more agreement than they anticipate.

4. *A considerable body of psychological research indicates that an individual attempts to perceive his environment in such a way that it is consistent with his self-perception.* If an individual feels afraid, he tends to perceive his world as frightening; if he feels hostile, he is likely to see it as frustrating or unjust; if he feels weak and vulnerable, he is apt to see it as exploitative and powerful; if he is torn by self-doubt and self-conflict, he will tend to see it as at odds with him. Not only does an individual tend to see the external world in such a way as to justify his feelings and beliefs but also so as to justify his behavior. If an individual is a heavy smoker, he is apt to perceive cigarette smoking as less injurious to health than a nonsmoker; if he drives a car and injures a pedestrian, he is likely to blame the pedestrian; if he invests in something (*e.g.,* a munitions industry), he will attempt to justify and protect his investment. Moreover, there is much evidence that an individual tends to perceive the different parts of his world as consistent with one another. Thus, if somebody likes you, you expect him

to dislike someone who dislikes you. If somebody disagrees with you, you are likely to expect him to agree with some one who disagrees with you.

The danger of the pressure for consistency is that it often leads to an oversimplified black-white view of the world. Take, for instance, the notions that since the interests of the United States and the Soviet Union are opposed in some respects, we must be opposed to or suspicious of anything that the Communists favor and must regard any nation that desires friendly relations with the Soviet Union as opposed to the United States. If the Soviet Union is against colonialism in Africa, must we be for it? If nations in Latin America wish to establish friendly, commercial relations with the Communist nations, must we feel threatened? If Canada helps Communist China by exporting food to it, must we suspect its loyalty to us? Are nations which are not for us necessarily for the Communists? The notions expressed in affirmative answers to these questions are consistent with the view that the conflict between the United States and the Soviet Union can only be ended by total defeat for one or the other. But is it not possible that the conflict can be resolved so that both sides are better off than they are now? Recognition of this latter possibility may suggest that what benefits the Soviet Union does not necessarily harm us, and that nations with amicable relations with both the United States and the Soviet Union may be an important asset in resolving the cold war before it turns into a hot one.

The pressure for self-consistency often leads to rigid, inflexible positions because it may be difficult to change a position that one has committed oneself to publicly without fear of loss of face. To some extent, I believe this is our situation *vis-à-vis* the admission of Communist China to the United Nations and with regard to our policies toward Cuba. We are frozen into positions which are unresponsive to changing circumstances because a change in our positions would seem to us to be admission of mistaken judgment which could lead to a loss of face.

What can we do to avoid the "consistency of little minds" and rigidities of false pride? These dangers to accurate perception are most likely when an individual feels under threat, when his self-esteem is at stake. I think in such circumstances it is prudent to seek the advice and counsel of trusted friends who are not so emotionally involved in the issues. Thus, I think it would be wise to consult with such nations as Brazil, France, and Great Britain on our policy toward Cuba and Communist China precisely because they do not have as deep an involvement with these countries as we do. Similarly, consultation with more or less neutral nations such as India, Sweden, Austria, and Nigeria might prevent us from developing an oversimplified view of the nature of our relations with the Soviet Union.

5. Ichheiser has described a mechanism, similar to that of projection, which leads to misunderstandings in human relations: the *mote-beam mechanism*. It consists in perceiving certain characteristics in others which we do not perceive in ourselves. Thus, the characteristics are perceived as though they were peculiar traits of the others and, hence, the differences between the others and ourselves are accentuated. Since the traits we are unable or unwilling to recognize in others are usually traits we consider to be undesirable, the mote-beam mechanism results in a view of the other as peculiarly shameful or evil. Thus, although many of us who live here in the North easily recognize the shameful racial discrimination and segregation in the South, we avoid a clear awareness of the pervasive racial discrimination in our own communities.

Similarly, in international relations it is easy to recognize the lack of political liberties in the Soviet Union, their domination of the nations in Eastern Europe, their obstructiveness in the United Nations, etc., but it is difficult for us to recognize similar defects in the United States: *e.g.,* the disenfranchisement of most Negro voters in many states, our domination of Latin America, our unfair treatment of the American Indian, our stubbornness in the UN in pretending that the representative from Taiwan is the representative of Mainland China. Since the mote-beam mechanism, obviously, works on both sides, there is a tendency for each side to view the other as peculiarly immoral and for the views to mirror one another.

What can be done to make the mote-beam mechanism ineffective? The proposals I have made to counteract the effects of the other type of perceptual distortions are all relevant here. In addition, I would suggest that the mote-beam mechanism breeds on a moral-evaluative approach to behavior, on a readiness to condemn defects rather than to understand the circumstances which produced them. Psychoanalytic work suggests that the capacity to understand rather than to condemn is largely determined by the individual's sense of self-esteem, by his ability to cope with the external problems confronting him, and by his sense of resoluteness in overcoming his own defects. By analogy, I would suggest that we in the United States will have less need to overlook our own shortcomings or to be fascinated with the defects of others to the extent that we have a thriving society which is resolutely overcoming its own problems of racial prejudice, economic stagnation, and lack of dedication to common public purposes.

While distortions in perception are very common for the reasons I have outlined above, it is also true that, in many instances, everyday experience provides a corrective to the distortions. When reality is sufficiently compelling and when the contact with reality occurs with sufficient frequency, the distortions will be challenged and may yield. However, there are circumstances which tend to perpetuate and rigidify distortions. Let me briefly describe three major reasons for the perpetuation of distortions:

1. *A major psychological investment has been made in the distortion.* As a consequence, the individual may anticipate that giving up the investment will require drastic personal reorganization which might result in personal instability and the loss of social face and might precipitate unknown dangers. Anyone who has done psychoanalytic therapy with neurotic patients knows that no matter how costly and painful it is, a distorted but familiar mode of adjustment is hard to give up until the patient has sufficient self-confidence or confidence in his analyst to venture into unfamiliar terrain.

With regard to international relations, I think we have to consider that a disarmed world, a world without external tensions to justify internal political policies, a world without violence as a means of bringing about changes in the status quo would be an unfamiliar world: a world in which some would feel that their vested interests might be destroyed. For example, I am sure that many military men, scientists, industrialists, workers, and investors fear a disarmed world because they anticipate that their skills and knowledge will become obsolete, or they will lose social status, or they will lose financially. These fears have to be dealt with constructively or else they may produce defensive adherence to the views which justify a hostile, armed world. I suggest that we must carefully plan to anticipate the psychological difficulties in the transition to a peaceful, disarmed world. As a basic strategy to overcome some of these difficulties, I would recommend that we consider a policy of *overcompensating* those who might be adversely affected by the change: we want to change the nature of their psychological investment from an investment in military pursuits to one in peaceful pursuits.

2. *Certain distorted perceptions perpetuate themselves because they lead the individual to avoid contact or meaningful communication with the object or person being perceived.* This is especially true when the distortions lead to aversion or hostility toward the object being perceived. For example, for reasons which go back to my childhood and about which I am not clear, I have a strong aversion to coffee, becoming nauseated at the thought of drinking it. As a consequence, I avoid coffee and my aversion is perpetuated. Newcomb has described a similar process of *autistic hostility* in interpersonal relations in which a hostile impulse may give rise to barriers to communication behind which a persistent attitude is protected. Similarly, in international relations, hostile attitudes between the United States and Communist China produce barriers to communication which eliminate the possibility of a change in attitudes. Here, the best antidote would seem to be communication which followed the rules of procedure suggested by Anatol Rapoport.

3. Merton, in his classic paper on *"The Self-fulfilling Prophecy,"* has pointed out that distortions are often perpetuated because they may evoke new behavior which makes the originally *false* conception come true. The specious validity of the self-fulfilling prophecy perpetuates a reign of error. The prophet will cite the actual course of events as proof that he was right from the very beginning. The dynamics of the self-fulfilling prophecy help to explain individual pathology—*e.g.,* the anxious student who, afraid he might fail, worries so much that he cannot study, with the consequence that he does fail. It also contributes to our understanding of social pathology—*e.g.,* how prejudice and discrimination against

the Negro keeps him in a position which seems to justify the prejudice and discrimination. So, too, in international relations. If the representatives of East and West believe that war is likely and either side attempts to increase its military security vis-à-vis the other, the other side's response will justify the initial move. The dynamics of an arms race has the inherent quality of a *"folie à deux,"** wherein the self-fulfilling prophecies mutually reinforce one another.

PSYCHOLOGICAL ALTERNATIVES TO WAR

In the preceding section, I have attempted to indicate some of the sources of misperception in international relations and some of the conditions which tend to perpetuate the distortions or make them come true. Our present international situation suggests that the distortions have come true. The East and the West are in an arms race and in the throes of an ideological conflict in which each side, in reality, threatens and feels threatened by the other. How can we reverse this hostile spiral which is likely to result in mutual annihilation?

As I present some specific proposals, I will indicate the psychological assumptions underlying them: assumptions which come from theoretical and experimental research I have been doing on interpersonal trust and suspicion and interpersonal bargaining.

1. *There are social situations which do not allow the possibility of "rational" behavior so long as the conditions for mutual trust do not exist.* Let me illustrate with a two-person game that I have used in my experimental work on trust and suspicion. In this game, each player has to choose between pressing a red button and a green button: if both players press the red button each loses $1.00; if both players press the green button, each wins $1.00; if Player A presses the green button and Player B presses the red button, A loses $2.00 and B gains $2.00; and if Player B presses the green button and Player A presses the red button, B loses $2.00 and A gains $2.00. A superficial rational calculation of self-interest would lead each player to press his red button since he either wins as much as he can or loses as little as he can this way. But, if both players

* "Mutual madness." (Eds.)

consider only their self-interest and press their red buttons, each of them will lose. Players oriented toward defeating the other player or toward their self-interest only, when matched with similarly oriented players, do in fact choose the red button and do end up losing consistently.

I believe our current international situation is in some respects similar to the game I have described. A characteristic symptom of such "nonrational situations" is that any attempt on the part of any individual or nation to increase its own welfare or security (without regard to the security or welfare of the others) is self-defeating. In such situations the only way that an individual or nation can avoid being trapped in a mutually reinforcing, self-defeating cycle is to attempt to change the situation so that a basis of mutual trust can develop.

Comprehension of the basic nature of the situation we are in suggests that *mutual security* rather than national security should be our objective. The basic military axiom for both the East and West should be that *military actions should only be taken which increase the military security of both sides; military actions which give a military superiority to one side or the other should be avoided.* The military forces of both sides should be viewed as having the *common* primary aim of preventing either side (one's own or the other) from starting a deliberate or accidental war. Awareness of this common aim could be implemented by regular meetings of military leaders from East and West; the establishment of a continuing joint technical group of experts to work together to formulate disarmament and inspection plans; the establishment of mixed military units on each other's territory, etc. The key point we must recognize is that if military inferiority is dangerous, so is military "superiority"; it is dangerous for either side to feel *tempted* or *frightened* into military action.

2. *Our research indicates that mutual trust is most likely to occur when people are positively oriented to each other's welfare—i.e., when each has a stake in the other's doing well rather than poorly.* Unfortunately, the East and West, at present, appear to have a greater stake in each other's defects and difficulties than in each other's welfare. Thus, the Communists gloat over our racial problems and our unemployment and we do like-

wise over their agricultural failures and their lack of political liberties.

We should, I believe, do everything possible to reverse this unfortunate state of affairs. First of all, we might start by accepting each other's existence as *legitimate* and by rejecting the view that the existence of the other, *per se,* is a threat to our existence. As Talcott Parsons...has pointed out, there is considerable merit in viewing the ideological battle between East and West in the world community as somewhat akin to our own two-party system at the national level. An ideological conflict presupposes a common frame of reference in terms of which the ideological differences make sense. The ideologies of East and West do share many values in common: technological advance, economic development, universal education, encouragement of science, cultural progress, health advances, peace, national autonomy, etc. We must accept the possibility that one side or the other will obtain an advantage on particular issues when there is a conflict about the procedures for attaining these objectives. But this is not catastrophic unless each side views the conflict as an all-or-none conflict of survival.

To establish a basis for mutual trust we, of course, have to go beyond the recognition of each other's legitimacy to a relationship which promotes cooperative bonds. This would be facilitated by recognition of the profound human similarities which link all mankind together. The human situation no longer makes it feasible to view the world in terms of "we" or "they"; in the modern era, our destinies are linked objectively; the realistic attitude is "we" *and* "they." More specifically, I think our situation would be improved rather than worsened if the people in the various Communist nations had a high standard of living, were well educated, and were reaping the fruits of the scientific revolution. Similarly, I think we would be better off rather than worse off if the political leaders of the Communist nations felt they were able to provide their citizenry with sufficient current gratifications and signs of progress to have their support; and if they were sufficiently confident of their own society not to fear intensive contacts with different points of view.

The implication of the above calls for a fundamental reorientation of our foreign policy toward the Communist nations. We must initiate cooperative trade policies, cooperative research programs, cooperative cultural exchanges, cooperative loan programs, cooperative agricultural programs, etc., and we must not be concerned if, at first, they appear to benefit more than we. We are, after all, more affluent than the Communist nations. Our objective should be simply to promote the values of economic well-being, educational attainment, scientific and industrial development which we share in common and which we believe are necessary to a stable, peaceful world. Let me emphasize here that I think this is especially important to do in our relations with Communist China. (It amazes me constantly that so little public attention is given to the extraordinary dangers involved in allowing our current relations with Communist China to continue in their present form.) The Communist nations (especially China) are likely to be suspicious of our motives, may even rebuff our initial attempts to establish cooperative relationships, and will undoubtedly not feel grateful for any assistance they may receive. These reactions are all to be expected because of the present context of international relations. Our policy of cooperation must be a *sustained* policy of *massive reconciliation* which does not reciprocate hostility and which always leaves open the possibility of mutual cooperation despite prior rebuff. In my view, we must sustain a cooperative initiative until it succeeds; in the long run, the alternative to mutual cooperation is mutual doom.

My rationale here is very simple. We have no realistic alternative but to coexist with the Soviet Union and Communist China. Coexistence among nations will be considerably less dangerous if we each recognize that poverty, illiteracy, economic difficulties, internal strain and crisis in a nation are likely to produce reckless, belligerent international policies rather than peaceful ones. After all, the delinquents and criminals in our local communities rarely come from those segments of our populace that are successfully dealing with their own internal problems or that are well integrated into and accepted by the broader community.

3. To induce a cooperative orientation in another and to develop adherence to a set of rules or social norms for regulating interaction and for resolving disputes, it is necessary: (a) to demonstrate that one's own orientation to the other is cooperative; (b) to articulate fair rules which do not system- atically disadvantage the other; (c) to demon- strate one's adherence to these rules; (d) to demonstrate to the other that he has more to gain (or less to lose) in the short and long run by adherence to the rules than by viola- tion of them; and (e) to recognize that mis- understandings and disputes about compliance will inevitably occur and hence are not neces- sarily tokens of bad faith.

The importance of a cooperative orienta- tion to the development of mutual trust has been discussed above; it is reiterated here to emphasize the significance of a cooperative orientation in the development of any work- able system of rules to regulate international relations. In discussion and negotiations con- cerning arms control and disarmament, there has been much emphasis on developing rules and procedures for inspection and control which do not rely upon cooperative orienta- tions; surveillance of the other's actions is to replace trust in the other's intent. I think it is reasonable to assert that no social order can exist for long without a minimum basis in mutual trust; surveillance cannot do the trick by itself. This is not to deny the necessity of surveillance to buttress trust, to enable one's trustworthiness to be confirmed and one's suspicions to be rejected. However, I would question the view which seems to characterize our approach to arms control negotiations: namely, the less trust, the more surveillance. A more reasonable view might state that when there is little trust the only kinds of agree- ments which are feasible are ones which allow for simple, uncomplicated but highly reliable techniques of surveillance. Lack of trust be- tween equals, paradoxically, calls for but also limits surveillance when the negotiations are not part of an effective community.

How can the formulation of fair rules be facilitated? A suggestion by Bertrand Rus- sell...is pertinent here. He proposes the formation of a conciliation committee com- posed of the best minds from the East and West, with some of the leading thinkers from neutral nations also included. Such a com- mittee, meeting together in quiet, unpublicized deliberation, might be given the responsibility of formulating rules which would be acceptable to both sides. The hope is that, with suf- ficient time, intelligent men of good will whose perspectives reach beyond the cold war

may be able to formulate rules that are fair to all mankind.

Fair rules for certain matters, of course, do already exist. Some of these rules are written in the Charter of the United Na- tions, some in the decisions of the Inter- national Court of Justice at the Hague, some in the legal traditions which have governed various aspects of international relations through the centuries (*e.g.,* the international postal system, international trade, "freedom of the seas," ambassadorial rights). As Arthur Larson...has pointed out, there is much need for legal research to make the existing body of international rules accessible and up-to-date and to establish a legal machinery which is also accessible and adapted to settling the kinds of disputes that today's world produces. In addition, there is a need to induce ac- ceptance of the body of law and legal machin- ery by the persons affected.

4. *Mutual trust can occur even under cir- cumstances where the parties involved are un- concerned with each other's welfare providing their relations to an outside, third party are such that this trust in him can substitute for their trust in one another.* This indirect or mediated trust is, of course, a most common form of trust in interpersonal relations. Since we exist in a community in which various types of third parties—the law, the police, public opinion, mutual friends, etc.—can be mobilized to buttress an agreement, we can afford to be trusting even with a stranger in most circumstances. Unfortunately, in a bipolar world community, which does not con- tain powerful "third parties," it is difficult to substitute mediated trust for direct trust.

There are two policy implications of this fact which I would like to stress. The first is the importance of encouraging the develop- ment of several strong, neutral groups of nations and the development of a strong, neutral United Nations that might mediate in conflicts between East and West. We have, of course, to be aware of the dangers of a *tertius gaudens,** in which a third party would attempt to play East and West off against one another to its own advantage. However, what I am suggesting is not a third bloc but rather a group of diverse, independent nations with criss-crossing interests that have the common

_____
* A third person, especially one who profits from a quarrel between others. (Eds.)

objective of developing and maintaining an orderly world. In a neutral United Nations, with a large group of independent voters, we would sometimes find ourselves on the losing side. But can we afford a United Nations in which the other side has little chance of ever winning a dispute with us?

The second implication follows from the realization that strong, responsible, independent nations and a strong, neutral United Nations do not yet exist and will take time to develop. Where no strong external community exists, it is important to recognize that bargaining—*i.e.,* the attempt to find a mutually satisfactory agreement in circumstances where there is a conflict of interest—cannot afford to be guided by a Machiavellian or "outwitting the other" attitude. Where no external community exists to compel agreement, the critical problem in bargaining is to establish sufficient community between the bargainers that a mutually satisfactory agreement becomes possible: the question of who obtains the minor advantages or disadvantages in a negotiation is trivial in comparison to the question of whether an agreement can be reached which leaves both parties better off than a lack of agreement. I stress this point because some political scientists and economists, misled by the fact that bargaining within a strong community can often fruitfully be conducted with a Machiavellian attitude, unwittingly assume that the same would be true where no real community exists.

In concluding this section, let me quote from a monograph on the *Causes of Industrial Peace* (National Planning Association, 1953, p. 92) which lists the conditions that have led to peaceful settlement of disputes under collective bargaining:

1. There is full acceptance by management of the collective bargaining process and of unionism as an institution. The company considers a strong union an asset to management.

2. The union fully accepts private ownership and operation of the industry; it recognizes that the welfare of its members depends upon the successful operation of the business.

3. The union is strong, responsible, and democratic.

4. The company stays out of the union's internal affairs; it does not seek to alienate the workers' allegiance to their union.

5. Mutual trust and confidence exist between the parties. There have been no serious ideological incompatibilities.

6. Neither party to bargaining has adopted a legalistic approach to the solution of problems in the relationship.

7. Negotiations are "problem-centered"—more time is spent on day-to-day problems than on defining abstract principles.

8. There is widespread union-management consultation and highly developed information-sharing.

9. Grievances are settled promptly, in the local plant whenever possible. There is flexibility and informality within the procedure.

This is in accord with our discussion of the basic conditions for world peace: namely, the necessity of developing attitudes which consciously stress mutual acceptance, mutual welfare, mutual strength, mutual interest, and mutual trust and the necessity of developing approaches to disputes which consistently emphasize full communication, willingness to negotiate, and the specific issues in dispute rather than the ideological frame of reference of the parties in dispute.

64. THE PSYCHOLOGICAL
EFFECTS OF THE DRAFT

American Friends Service Committee

Any attempt to assess the psychological effects of conscription is complicated by this question: How does one differentiate between the effect of the draft and the effect of the armed forces and war? It is impossible to examine the psychological effects of compulsory service without a context, and the context must, of course, be that of the military establishment. As we shall attempt to show, conscription has profound effects upon the individual, upon his family, and upon society.

THE EFFECTS ON THE INDIVIDUAL

The draft usurps the individual's opportunity to choose his own future and assigns that right to government officials. This is a serious enough deprivation for the individual, but the folly of it is magnified when we reflect that the institution of conscription casts aside voluntary choice in favor of an extremely inefficient system that unquestionably mismatches a high percentage of individuals.

Certain people are eminently more suited than others to life in the armed forces. The authoritarian personality as identified by Adorno *et al.* combines the traits of conventionalism and conformity with a submissive, uncritical deference to superiors, a tendency to overassertion toward underlings, and a punitive, rejecting attitude toward those who violate conventional values; he opposes the subjective, the imaginative, and the tender-minded. His thinking is superstitious, stereotyped, and rigid; he exaggerates assertion of

strength and toughness; he has a generalized hostility and a relative lack of personal regard for others. The authoritarian personality has a tendency to attribute evil intent and actions to other groups, particularly minorities; he shows an exaggerated interest in and vigilance against sexual activity on the part of others, coupled with unconscious self-doubts about sexual adequacy.[1]

Whether an authoritarian personality can be determined with certainty by psychological testing is a matter of some professional difference of opinion; however, clinical observation does seem to identify individuals who combine many, if not all, of these personality traits. People with these traits fit quite well in the armed forces. The draft, however, instead of allowing authoritarian persons, by their own decision, to choose the military where they will fit and be psychologically comfortable while others choose civilian life, forces all types of draftees into the military milieu, a setting that welcomes the confirmed authoritarians, seduces the latent authoritarians, and makes the large remainder miserable.

A major evil of the draft is that it takes certain decisions out of the hands of individuals and places men in military life where they must submit to being continually manipulated. As Adorno *et al.* pointed out, for our democratic way of life to flourish "there must be an increase in people's capacity to see themselves and to be themselves. This cannot be achieved by the manipulation of people however well grounded in modern psychology

1 T. W. Adorno *et al., The Authoritarian Personality* (New York: Harper & Bros., 1950).

the devices of manipulation might be. . . ."[2] An example of the kind of manipulation indulged in by the armed forces is the manner in which recruitment literature plays upon the need of men, particularly with authoritarian personality tendencies, to assure themselves of their masculinity. The following are excerpts from "The Mark of a Man," a recruiting pamphlet for the army (italics ours throughout):

An "action guy" can't just wait for things to happen—he makes them happen. Routine plugging along just isn't for him. He's *too much of a man* for that. His mind and muscles thrive on the challenge of action! *If you are this kind of man you can prove it to the world* in a way that really counts...as a modern combat soldier.

A countdown on the launching pad is an experience no *real man* can forget.

You'll meet *regular men* who really know the score and you'll proudly wear the *Mark of a Man* as one of the action guys of the combat arms.[3]

The appeal of the armed forces recruiters to the masculinity theme is psychologically effective in getting men to sign up. Concern about masculinity also plays a role during training. In a group of navy frogmen trainees studied psychologically, the 25 per cent who successfully completed the grueling training showed evidence of fear of women and doubts about their own sexual adequacy. The author of the report comments ". . .it is quite possible that their unconscious motivation to complete the course was based on a need to prove their masculinity coupled with a fear of involvement with women."[4] These men were also less successful than their fellow trainees in coping with anxiety by verbal expression; they were "action men" in the words of the recruiting pamphlet cited. These characteristics have also been found in a disproportionately large number of paratroopers, among whom some observers have reported a high incidence of acting out socially destructive behavior apparently related to efforts to prove masculinity.

The recruiting approach, by appealing to masculinity, not only exploits a psychological

need but also strengthens the popular fallacy that the armed forces will "make a man of him," a fallacy that is subscribed to by many law enforcement officials and parents dealing with disturbed youth. The advent of nuclear weapons and advanced military technology, however, has rendered this concept even more ridiculous. The amount of positive character formation involved in releasing napalm or bombs on a distant civilian population must be minimal, while the carrying out of a task without moral commitment or even against personal conviction is psychologically destructive of a man as an independent rational being.

The following is a description without apology by military psychiatrists of the basic training of an airman:

Basic training is designed to orient individuals to a new way of life and to establish new identities for them. Adaptation to and development of a sense of identification with the military are the goals of basic training. To accomplish this the basic trainee initially experiences an increasing depreciation of self-esteem as a result of his inadequacy to achieve the standards of basic training. However, in the attempt to adapt to the psychical and psychological stresses, he begins to reconstitute his scale of values by fusing some of his old values with a newly acquired set. A critical element in the introduction of this orientation . . .is the. . .leadership of the training instructors, which clearly raises the suggestibility of the airmen and encourages them to accept a new viewpoint. . . . Earlier training in the postponement of gratification, in the toleration of negative feelings of hostility, fear and anxiety and in the acceptance of authority (arbitrary) is critical for preparing individuals to adjust to the stress of basic training.[5]

Depreciation of self-esteem, reduction to a state of relatively helpless suggestibility, and then rescue by identification with military superiors, and reliance on early training in the acceptance of arbitrary authority are all parts of a carefully engineered process in basic military training; but these negative factors in the development of a socially responsible human being are essential for military life.

Another description of the process of basic military training follows:

2 *Ibid.*

3 "The Mark of a Man." U.S. Government Printing Office, 1963: 690248.

4 D. W. Heyder and H. S. Wambach, "Sexuality and Affect in Frogmen," *Arch. General Psychiatry,* September 1964, Vol. 11, No. 3, pp. 286–289.

5 A. Kiev and M. B. Giffen, "Some Observations on Airmen Who Break Down During Basic Training," *American Journal of Psychiatry,* August 1965, Vol. 122, No. 2, pp. 184–188.

The basic training period was, therefore, not one of gradual inculcation of the Army mores but one of intensive shock treatment. The new recruit, a lone individual, is helplessly insecure in the bewildering newness and complexity of his environment. Also he is a man; he must show that he is tough enough to "take it." . . . With personal insecurity on the one hand and the motivation to "see it through" on the other he is malleable to the discipline, which consists of a fatiguing physical ordeal and continued repetition of acts until they become semi-automatic, in an atmosphere dominated by fear. . . .[6]

Some of the elements of this process bear remarkable resemblance to the techniques of "brain washing" as reported from prisoner-of-war camps. The fact that our military is willing to exploit the psychological helplessness of the new soldier in this manner is an indictment, not only of the draft, but of the entire war system.

If one selects such military training for oneself, the personality characteristics, overt or latent, which have led one to accept it may also assist one to endure it and to adapt it to one's psychological needs; it is quite another thing to undergo this same military training under compulsion. Though the draftee may endure the training, its psychological effect upon him may be quite destructive. In fact, as Dubin states,

> The very nature of military administration and command is predicated on the implicit assumption that the rank and file of soldiers will be either indifferent or non-job oriented. Accordingly we find of all forms of administration the military is the most mechanical, the most highly structured, and most impersonal and indifferent to personal variability.[7]

Once drafted, and totally submerged in military ways and having lost his identity as a civilian, the draftee may be relatively free from conflict and uncertainties but this freedom is accompanied by a greater narrowness or perhaps rigidity of identity and a greater dependence upon external definition and support. This mold, while it may make for relative absence of discomfort, cramps personality growth and expansion.

There are other negative effects of "service" with the armed forces on the part of the men who are acting against their will. The conscript in peacetime, for example, often fails to experience the stabilizing influence of close interpersonal relationships with his peers in that he avoids full commitment to friends in the armed forces because of probable transfer or rotation of assignment.

The sense of inexorability of the draft aggravates feelings of personal helplessness and undermines the young person's sense of his own responsibility to society. Often, for example, behavioral excesses are occasioned by a feeling that "If they are going to 'get me' soon anyway, why should I place strict curbs on my behavior now?" At the same time the uncertainty of the timing of the draft call prevents taking the usual defensive measures against feelings of insecurity, such as planning, building, and saving.

Depression is a prominent psychiatric problem in peacetime overseas troops. An army psychiatrist states, "An important determinant in these reactions was the feeling of being passively forced into an intolerable situation which they felt helpless to alter."[8]

Conscription is part of a whole system that subordinates the individual to the group. Even army psychiatrists are forced to accept and condone this because it is pragmatically necessary: "Success in therapy is largely determined by the degree with which the psychiatrist identifies with the needs of the combat group, as opposed to his participation with the desires of the individual."[9] Worse than this, conscription prostitutes all the finer traits of man—duty, loyalty, sense of responsibility, etc.—placing them in the service of an unworthy cause—aggression against his fellow men. This is a severe contradiction which requires us to live with many fictions in order to maintain reason. Such fictions include the idea that our enemy is not really "people," that God is on our side, etc.

How much personality change is possible in

---

6 S. A. Stouffer *et al., The American Soldier: Adjustment During Army Life,* Vol. 1, Studies in Social Psychology in World War II (Princeton, N.J.: Princeton University Press, 1949).

7 R. Dubin, *The World of Work: Industrial Society and Human Relations* (Englewood Cliffs, N.J.: Prentice-Hall, 1958), p. 259.

8 R. F. Yazmajian, "Depression in Peacetime Overseas Troops," *Psychiatric Quarterly,* Vol. 38, 1964, pp. 504–511.

9 A. J. Glass "Psychotherapy in the Combat Zone," *American Journal of Psychiatry,* April 1954, Vol. 110, No. 10, pp. 725–731.

late adolescence and early adulthood, i.e., the years when men are drafted? It has been argued that the armed forces do not make young men any more or less military or aggressive or authoritarian than they were destined to be anyway because their personalities were already largely formed by the time they were six or so. Sanford points out that the individual between the ages of seventeen and twenty-two does have the potential for change in at least five different ways: stabilizing of the ego identity, deepening of interests, freedom in personal relations, humanizing of values, and general development and strengthening of the ego.[10]

Conscription interferes seriously with all of these modes of growth. For example, stabilizing of ego identity requires "being placed in social roles that require new responses, having to make decisions concerning what roles one is going to take, learning from experience that some roles are suited and others not suited to one's interests and needs." The draftee is hardly in a position to profit from such circumstances. He is given little opportunity to develop freedom in personal relationships, since he is required to relate to his peers and others according to a very limited, inflexible series of authoritarian patterns. Sensitive values are discounted in a dehumanized milieu which encourages the authoritarian, punitive portions of his conscience at the expense of its more generous aspects. His opportunities to grow by successful decision-making are few since most decisions are made for him.

Although one need not fear that the military can create authoritarian personalities out of the men who are least oriented in that direction, the military does furnish a setting in which latent authoritarian traits are reinforced and in which humaneness, imagination, tolerance, and human brotherhood are discouraged. The armed forces give opportunity for some to achieve a kind of success and recognition in an authoritarian setting. Especially vulnerable are great numbers of the culturally deprived young men who before entering the military have had little chance for success and recognition. Therefore, those who find any success and satisfaction in military life are likely to incorporate within their personalities some of the authoritarian atmosphere that attended that success.

In summary, not only does the draft interfere with positive personality growth, it tends to foster the development of authoritarian personality traits.

Studies made by the army's Mental Health Consultation Services and by the U.S. Disciplinary Barracks have shown that among the "problem group" of soldiers (stockade prisoners, disciplinary barracks prisoners, AWOL's) there is a disproportionately higher percentage of Regular Army men as opposed to draftees. Military medical studies also suggest that there may be a slightly higher incidence of psychiatric disorder among men who enlisted (RA). However, it is also the impression of military psychiatrists that among the group identified as excellent soldiers there is also a disproportionately higher percentage of Regular Army men. This seems to say that while the armed forces attract some marginally adjusted individuals, many of them have or develop traits, even some psychopathic traits, that make them proficient fighters (as in the case of the frogmen and paratroopers). In fact, Marshall says

> Company by company we found in our work that there were men who had been consistently bad actors in the training period, marked by faults of laziness, unruliness and disorderliness, who just as consistently became lions on the battlefield, with all of the virtues of sustained aggressiveness, warm obedience and thoughtfully planned action.[11]

The draftees tend to be those who comply with the authoritarian system without causing it trouble.

The basic injury to personality caused by military conscription is the injury caused by militarism. Conscription seems to compound the evil, but similar damage is done to personality by military life whether it is entered by voluntary enlistment or by conscription.

THE EFFECTS ON THE FAMILY

Much less is written and understood about the effect of military conscription on the

10 R. N. Sanford, *Self and Society* (New York: Atherton Press, 1966), p. 274ff.

11 S. L. A. Marshall, *Men Against Fire* (New York: William Morrow, 1961). See Chapter V, "Fire as the Cure." [Quotations from *Men Against Fire* are reprinted here by permission of the publisher. Copyright, 1947, by S. L. A. Marshall.]

family than one might expect. This seems to be related to the fact that less is known about the effect of the father-child relationship than about the mother-child relationship. The main reasons for this may be that: (1) mothers are more involved and perhaps more concerned than are fathers with child-rearing, and (2) mothers are more available for inteview. Ackerman states:

> The psychological implications of military service are many, for the military takes over some of the protective and educational functions of parents in preparing young males for adulthood. At the same time it may create certain conflicts in the adolescent, divided allegiance between parental authority and the authority of the military, conflict between standards of the family and the standards of the peer group in the military unit, which may involve a temporary renunciation of personal responsibility for sexual aggression and for violence. There may also arise conflict over the necessity for automatic and uncritical obedience to superior officers and the surrender of individual responsibility to the dictates of the military ...it is certain, however, that changes in the character of the adolescent male result from this societally imposed period of transition. ...Eventually the adolescent returns from the military to his civilian community and feels the full impact of the conflict of values that dominate it, all too often ill prepared to deal with its problems.
>
> The feminine half of the adolescent comunity, although not directly involved in compulsory military service, reacts to its influence on the males. If the serviceman, feeling the urge to live while he can, fast and furiously, indulges himself totally in the appetites of the body, the girl responds. If as soon as he gets by the hurdle of the military he turns cautious and seeks out a safe niche in the community, a steady job, a home, a car, she responds. She too is out to get what she can, particularly the security of marriage, home, and a respected place in the community. But today's young woman cannot easily trust herself to the man. He may be gone tomorrow.[12]

Except for physicians and dentists fathers have not been drafted since World War II, but many draftees have become husbands and fathers while in the armed forces. These men affect the emotional health of their children in at least two ways: first by their relationship

with the mother, and second with the child himself. Bartemeier summarizes the effect via the mother as follows:

> While it is true that a woman's attitude toward pregnancy, childbirth and motherhood has been definitely molded and determined by her relationship with her own parents and siblings, it is equally true that her emotional needs in her relationship with her husband are of major importance for her sense of well-being. How adequately or inadequately his relationship with her satisfies these needs determines very importantly how well or poorly she functions as a mother to their children.
>
> To give consistently to her child the love he needs, a woman needs the consistent love of her husband and the certainty of his love for their child...she may not be aware of any [of her] antagonistic feelings, but the infant may sense them through her tenseness, through her lack of customary gentleness, through awkward movements which are frightening to an infant, or through the cessation of her breast milk.[13]

We might add that not only does the young mother need to know that her husband loves her and that he loves their child; both mother and child need his actual presence.

Young families face many insecurities because of the draft. Research would be in order concerning the effect of the draft on the age at which young people marry, but in any case it is probably safe to say that the draft does produce some young and hasty marriages founded on shaky motivation and anxiety about immediate separation or separation at a frighteningly uncertain time. The young man who is draft eligible faces the frustration of having his occupational choice limited since employers are unwilling to hire him for the better-paying job. There is also anxiety and conflict among young married students over the demands of family life and the necessity of maintaining grades high enough to avoid being drafted. Once drafted, "hostility which is suppressed by the draftee rather than expressed to officers or NCO's because of possible consequences is often released to his wife, much to her surprise and chagrin."[14]

While many of these destructive psychologi-

12 N. W. Ackerman, *The Psychodynamics of Family Life* (New York: Basic Books, 1958), pp. 213ff.

13 L. Bartemeier, "The Contribution of the Father to the Mental Health of the Family," *American Journal of Psychiatry,* October 1953, Vol. 110, No. 4, p. 277–280.

14 E. S. Uyeki, "Draftee Behavior in the Cold-War Army," *Social Problems,* Vol. 8, 1960, pp. 151–158.

cal effects on the family are the result of the military system itself, the added anxiety of the uncertainty of the draft adds a further dimension to the disruption of family life and therefore of the personalities and emotional health of the next generation. It is our children who must have the chance to work the miracle. It is they who must carve out a world that has meaning and value; we deny them the chance if we damage the family matrix for their growth.

THE EFFECTS ON SOCIETY

All the psychological effects on the individual and his family, as members of society, have their inevitable influence on society itself. It is especially damaging to a society when its officials engage in the immorality of manipulating personalities and thereby set the interests of the state over and against the needs of the individual.

Men have a natural aversion to killing men. As S. L. A. Marshall, a military historian, has pointed out: "The fear of aggression has been expressed to him so strongly and absorbed by him so deeply and pervadingly—practically with his mother's milk—that it is part of the normal man's emotional makeup. This is his great handicap when he enters combat. It stays his trigger finger...." Marshall's World War II studies showed that on the average, even in a heavy engagement, fewer than 25 per cent of the riflemen in actual front-line combat fired their weapons at all. "The best showing that could be made by the most spirited and aggressive companies was that one man in four had made at least some use of his fire power."

To the field commander this is an intolerable state of affairs, one that leads even a relatively humane military observer like Marshall to write:

The fundamental problem is how to build up fire volume and develop more willing firers. One cannot deny that looseness of fire at times creates a certain hazard for troops. But this problem must be viewed in proportion; we cannot afford to miss the forest for the sake of a few trees. Though it is hard on the nerves at the time, so far as the end result is concerned it is better by far to have a company of green, trigger-happy soldiers than a company that lacks the will to use its weapons.[15]

As Marshall also states, it seems reasonable to believe that

If resistance to the idea of firing can be overcome for a period, it can be defeated permanently. Once the plunge is made, the water seems less forbidding. As with every other duty in life, it is made easier by virtue of the fact that a man may say to hismelf: "I have done it once, I can do it again."

But what happens when the army succeeds in overcoming man's natural aversion to killing? Marshall cites the following incident from an actual June 1944 battle in Normandy:

At the foot of the hill an enemy machine gun opened fire on the patrol but the bullets went high. The men broke and "ran like dogs." Millsaps (their Lieutenant) and a sergeant beat them back with physical violence. After they were again collected, Millsaps lost almost an hour, alternately bullying and pleading with them before they would go forward.

At last they charged the enemy, closing within hand-grappling distance. The slaughter began with grenade, bayonet and bullet. Some of the patrol were killed and some wounded. But all now acted as if oblivious to danger. The slaughter once started could not be stopped, Millsaps tried to regain control but his men paid no heed. Having slaughtered every German in sight they ran on into the barns of the French farmhouses where they killed the hogs, cows and sheep. The orgy ended when the last beast was dead.[16]

In February 1967, a young American soldier returned from Vietnam was tried and acquitted after shooting to death his wife and another man in a rage. He had told police, "It was just like in Vietnam—everything went red."

What connection exists between these two incidents and the effect of the draft on society is uncertain. Certainly both episodes are unusual, but no matter what the incidence of crimes of violence among veterans is, it seems logical that that incidence must be increased by the draft because the draft increases the total number of men trained to overcome their natural aversion to killing.

It is interesting that the panel of thirty-two physicians, psychologists, and nationally known psychiatrists, convened by Governor John

15 Marshall, *op. cit.*, pp. 78, 82.

16 *Ibid.*, p. 183.

Connally to make a report on the "Texas sniper," murderer of sixteen people, recommended that a massive, nation-wide study be made to determine whether there is a growing tendency toward violence in the U.S. Dr. Dana L. Farnsworth, director of health service at Harvard University and spokesman for the group, said, "I am concerned in that it appears there is an increasing tendency toward violence. We would like to know what the reasons are."[17] Significantly, the committee suggested that combat-trained soldiers should be given training to de-emphasize violence before they are returned to civilian life.

Disturbing phenomena in addition to crimes of violence also seem to increase as veterans return, according to Waller:

> Military experience also weakens the taboos which protect property and hedge about sexual indulgence...veterans are frequently restless and highly mobile, and thus they tend to drift away from the local communities which would either hold them in line or make allowances for their behavior. For these reasons many veterans become criminals....
>
> Even in the most favorable cases, however, it seems probable that the veteran's anger does not disappear altogether. Instead, the residues of resentment are redirected into different channels, usually into channels of class, race, and religious antagonism. Whomever a man would naturally hate, he hates a little more because he has been a soldier.[18]

Waller gives as an example the Ku Klux Klan which was founded in 1865 by Civil War veterans and which still has a strong appeal to veterans who have absorbed the authoritarianism of the military system.

One serious effect of the draft on society is that it creates a class of veterans who did not have the benefit of stable models for independent adulthood during a critical phase of development. This is especially true as the draft tends to focus on the nineteen-year-old:

> Especially will the strain of transition be marked in those younger men who entered the army at age 18 or 19; they were still adolescents when inducted. They have come of age within the army and have no remembered experience of adulthood in civilian society. From a paternalistic school system, they have come straight into the paternalism of the army, substituting one cloister for another. Lacking the earlier experience of adjustment in adulthood, they will have fewer memories to give them bearing in the quest for stability.[19]

Society desperately needs persons with a sense of responsibility, but the armed forces produce in the soldier the habit of thinking of himself as the dependent cog in a gigantic mechanism. "The average soldier diminishes as a self-directing person and becomes more and more an entity governed by exterior compulsions. Personal irresponsibility becomes in mounting degree the theme of his social existence."[20]

Last, conscription, or the acquisition of military manpower, is like the stockpiling of military material, possession of which is a strong psychological impetus toward its use in war. The use of men and weapons is seen then as justification for their possession, particularly if they are expensive. Justification may require the maintenance of an atmosphere of fear and suspicion by the support of the "bogey man" fantasy, for example, of an 'international conspiracy.'

Since the psychological effects of military conscription upon the individual, the family, and society are highly negative, it seems appropriate to ask why the draft, despite its evils, receives so much support from so many and why there are so few, relatively speaking, who succeed in resisting it. Representative Thomas B. Curtis, Missouri, points to the persistence of the old attitude: "If I had to serve in the Army, then everybody else should have to also."[21] He points out that this attitude is "not in tune with technological and demographic changes that have reduced the need for raw manpower while making more of it available." However, proponents of the draft, he says, are intent on realizing their own past experience in the younger generation. The World War II "days of heroics and sacrifice are fondly remembered and the horrors and follies of those experiences are erased by time."

The Group for the Advancement of Psy-

---

17 *New York Times*, September 9, 1966.

18 W. Waller, *The Veteran Comes Back* (New York: Dryden Press, 1944).

19 R. A. Nisbet, "The Coming Problem of Assimilation," *American Journal of Sociology*, Vol. L, No. 4, January 1945, pp. 261ff.

20 *Ibid.*

21 T. B. Curtis, "Conscription and Commitment," *Playboy*, February 1967, pp. 89ff.

chiatry, a group of prominent psychiatrists, suggests that

> As the individual feels more alienated in mass society, he finds it more and more difficult to place himself in opposition to the huge pressures of the Organization. Fear of losing occupational security or of attacks on one's integrity, loyalty, or family are more than people can bear. As a defense against such fears and conflicts, one feels great relief in joining the party, the organization, or the club, and in becoming only an inconspicuous particle in the larger scheme.[22]

Erich Fromm sees this problem as an escape from freedom: "The frightened individual seeks for somebody or something to tie himself to; he cannot bear to be his own individual self any longer, and he tries frantically to get rid of it and to feel security again by the elimination of this burden; the self."[23]

The draft places the young man who seeks to oppose it in a serious psychological squeeze. He must be strong enough to withstand not only his own internal doubts, if any, about his course of action, but also the probability of direct public censure. Society does, in fact, deal sternly with some of those who refuse to register for the draft. For example, a study of draft resisters in prison during World War II showed that despite their excellent previous records, the members of one of the religious groups (Jehovah's Witnesses) were meted out comparatively severe sentences, the median being 4.4. years.[24] This was almost two years higher than the median sentence imposed on psychopathic prisoners or confirmed criminals.

Any institution that persists despite obsolescence must have some psychological support as well as its more material justification. Why have so many submitted to the draft? Perhaps because of the reasons already outlined. Perhaps because they desire an "escape from freedom" into the security of a life where the burden of making decisions has been removed. Perhaps because of its appeal to "manliness," although clearly it requires far more courage to refuse. Perhaps because the military system represents control of and at the same time a legitimatized channeling of the expression of aggression.

The psychological costs of the draft to individuals, families, and society itself are so great that, if we persist in the draft as our way of protecting our present way of life, we will destroy from within what we are attempting to protect. It seems essential that society, for the protection of its future, abandon conscription. Society desperately needs a generation of men of good will, men as free as possible of prejudice and aggression. The draft is systematically destroying our hope for such a generation.

22 Group for the Advancement of Psychiatry, *Psychiatric Aspects of the Prevention of Nuclear War*, GAP Report No. 57, 1954, p. 253.

23 E. Fromm, *Escape from Freedom* (New York: Rinehart, 1941).

24 M. J. Pescor, "A Study of Selective Service Law Violators," *American Journal of Psychiatry*, March 1949, Vol. 163 pp. 642–652.

65. BEHAVIOR CONTROL
AND SOCIAL RESPONSIBILITY [1]

Leonard Krasner

In recent years, research in psychotherapy has increasingly focused on investigations which could be interpreted as being part of a broad psychology of behavior control (Bandura, 1961; Frank, 1961; Kanfer, 1961; Krasner, 1958, 1961; Salzinger, 1959; Skinner, 1953). The essential element of behavior control studies is the influence, persuasion, and manipulation of human behavior. Two broad categories of controlling techniques have been utilized. The first can be termed the "social reinforcement" process, namely, those techniques which utilize the behavior of the examiner and structure of the interview situation as a means of influencing behavior. These include studies of psychotherapy, hypnosis, operant conditioning, attitude influence, placebos, and brainwashing. A second category of influence techniques involves the use of physical devices or drugs, such as tranquillizers, brain stimulation, sensory deprivation, or teaching machines. Both categories of investigation have in common the development of techniques for enhancing the effectiveness of the control or manipulation of individual behavior. Many investigators in this field have been

1 Portions of this paper wer presented at the annual meeting of the Western Psychological Association, Seattle, Washington, June, 1961. The preparation of this paper was facilitated by support, in part, from Research Grant M-2458 from the National Institute of Mental Health, Public Health Service.

influenced by Skinnerian behaviorism with its emphasis on environmental control and shaping of behavior (Skinner, 1953). Although there is as yet no direct evidence on this point, it is hypothesized that the social reinforcement type of influence is more effective than physical devices because the subject is less likely to be aware of them and thus is more likely to respond to them.

It is in the field of psychotherapy that the issues of the *moral and ethical implications* of behavior control first arose as a relevant problem. Psychotherapy involves the direct application of the finding of behavior control (Krasner, 1961). A professionally trained individual uses a variety of techniques to change, modify, or direct the behavior of another person. It differs from brainwashing in the implied assent given by the patient to this manipulation This view of the therapist as a manipulator of behavior is one that arouses considerable opposition from many therapists who deny that they are actively involved in controlling behavior. This is perhaps best expressed by Rogers, both in his debate with Skinner (Rogers & Skinner, 1956) and in his article on "Persons or Science" (1955). In this latter paper, he goes into the dangers of control and deplores the tendency toward social control implicit in the results of the kinds of studies discussed in this paper. His attitude is that therapy is a process which is "intensely personal, highly subjective in its inwardness, and dependent entirely on the relationship of two individuals, each of whom is an experiencing media." Rogers contends that:

Therapists recognize—usually intuitively—that any advance in therapy, any fresh knowledge of it, any significant new hypothesis in regard to it, must come from the experience of the therapists and clients, and can never come from science.

He feels that there is a danger in science which may lead toward manipulation of people, and cites as examples of this the attempts to apply laws of learning to control people through advertisements and propaganda. Skinner's *Walden Two* (1948) is cited as a psychologist's picture of paradise:

A paradise of manipulation in which the extent to which one can be a person is greatly reduced unless one can be a member of the ruling council.

This point of view can be best summarized as Rogers does, as follows:

What I will do with the knowledge gained through scientific method—whether I will use it to understand, enhance, enrich, or use it to control, manipulate, and destroy—is a matter of subjective choices depending upon the values which have personal meaning for me.

Yet in another paper (Rogers & Skinner, 1956) even Rogers is willing to concede that:

In client-centered therapy, we are deeply engaged in the prediction and influencing of behavior, or even the control of behavior. As therapists, we institute certain attitudinal conditions, and the client has relatively little voice in the establishment of these conditions. We predict that if these conditions are instituted, certain behavioral consequences will ensue in the client.

The "anti-control" view is also well presented in a series of papers by Jourard (1959, 1961). He contends that manipulation will have harmful effects both on the patient and on the therapist. Jourard (1959) contends that:

"Behavioristic" approaches to counseling and psychotherapy, while rightly acknowledging a man's susceptibility to manipulation by another, ignore the possibly deleterious impact of such manipulation on the whole man and, moreover, on the would-be manipulator himself—whereas the essential factor in the psychotherapeutic situation is a loving, honest and spontaneous relationship between the therapist and the patient.

In contrast, a "behavioristic" viewpoint might argue that apparent spontaneity on the therapist's part may very well be the most effective means of manipulating behavior. The therapist is an individual programed by his training into a fairly effective behavior control machine. Most likely the machine is most effective when it least appears like a machine.

Despite the views of Rogers and of other therapists, the evidence seems quite strong that psychotherapy as a social reinforcement process is part of a broader psychology of behavior control in which the therapist is actively influencing the behavior, attitudinal and value system of the patient (Krasner, 1961). Further, recent research has begun to put the therapist back into the therapy situation insofar as studying his personality and other personal attributes, including his value system. Marmor (1961) points out that psychoanalysis, as well as other types of psychotherapy, involves the communication of the therapist's implicit values and behavioral characteristics. Marmor's conviction is that:

Whether or not the analyst is *consciously* "tempted to act as a teacher, model, and ideal" to his patients, he *inevitably* does so to a greater or lesser extent; and this is a central aspect of the psychoanalytic process.

One of the reasons for denial on the part of therapists that they control behavior, or that they even desire to do so, is that such control would raise many moral, ethical, and legal problems, which the therapist is not prepared to handle. Thus, therapists are put in the paradoxical position of saying to the patient, "we will change your behavior, but we do not really want to change your behavior." Generally, science fiction is more willing to come to grips with some of the basic issues involved than is the professional therapist (Vandenberg, 1956).

Yet, we cannot avoid facing the issue of values. In fact, psychology is in the process of having a strong revival of interest in values. Recognition of the need for concern with the *ethics* or *moral values* of the therapist is implicit in an increasing number of articles (May, 1953; Papanek, 1958; Patterson, 1958; Rotter, 1961; Watson, 1958; Whitehorn, 1959). For example, May (1953) points out that the progress of psychoanalysis in the last decade can be judged by the increasing recognition that it is an illusion for the analyst to suppose that he can avoid value judgments. He feels that this recognition is explicit in the writings of Fromm and Horney and implicit in the works of Fromm-Reichman, Kubie, Alexander, and French. May cites a statement of J. McV. Hunt, who says "...I have reluctantly come to the conclusion that the scientist cannot avoid the value assumptions merely by deciding to do so." Hunt concludes, and May agrees, that values do belong to the subject material of science and must be taken into account in devising measuring instruments of behavioral or situational change. The study of Rosenthal (1955) on changes in "moral values" following psychotherapy is an illustration. Patients who are rated as "improved" changed significantly in their performance on a value test in the direction of values held by their therapists in sex, aggression, and authority, whereas unimproved patients tended to become less like their therapists in these values.

Lowe (1959) points out some of the ethical dilemmas involved insofar as the therapist is concerned, with possible conflicts over four sets of values. After reviewing value systems in four different categories, called naturalism, culturism, humanism, theism, Lowe concludes that "there is no single professional standard to which the psychologist's values can conform." The dilemma for the psychologist, as he sees it, is that if *one* set of values is to become absolute, psychology would cease to be a science and would become a social movement. However, he feels that psychologists cannot, on the other hand, do research without intending it to serve a particular value orientation. His suggestion is that value orientations be dealt with as objectively as possible, and that each area in psychology become more fully aware of the implications of its efforts. Further, since value orientations are in such conflict that at this point they are unresolvable, each therapist must understand his own values and those of others.

There have been infrequent attempts to measure attitudes of therapists, but most of these have been in terms of attitudes to therapy rather than attitudes to the broader implications of their social role (Shaffer, 1953). There have certainly been investigations of personality variables of the therapist, or psychologist, or psychiatrist (Holt & Lubor-

sky, 1958; Kelley & Fiske, 1951), but these have been generally oriented towards traditional personality variables rather than value attitudes. Shaffer (1953), for example, found in his analysis of objective versus intuitive psychologists, that the differences are not in terms of personality but in terms of attitudes toward role. Skinner (Rogers & Skinner, 1956), who was among the first to call attention to the ethical problems inherent in a psychology of behavior control, has pointed out that an important reinforcement for the therapist himself is his success in manipulating human behavior.

While the issue of behavior control first arose in regard to psychotherapy, it is now far broader and covers other areas such as operant conditioning, teaching machines, hypnosis, sensory deprivation, subliminal stimulation, and similar studies. There is considerable public interest, concern, and misunderstanding about the range and power of psychological findings.

How does a "psychology of behavior control" differ from the science of psychology? The differences are subtle, but important. A science of psychology seeks to determine the lawful relationships in behavior. The orientation of a "psychology of behavior control" is that these lawful relationships are to be used to deliberately influence, control, or change behavior. This implies a manipulator or controller, and with it an ethical and value system of the controller. As we learn more about human behavior it is increasingly obvious that it is controllable by various techniques. Does this mean that we, as psychologists, researchers, or even therapists, *at this point* could modify somebody's behavior in any way we wanted? The answer is no, primarily because research into the techniques of control thus far is at the elementary stage. Science moves at a very rapid pace, however, and now is the time to concern ourselves with this problem before basic knowledge about the techniques overwhelms us.

The obvious analogy is with the atomic physicists, who have been very concerned about the application of their scientific findings. Of course, many of the comments from the physical scientists have come *since* the dropping of the first atom bomb. The concern of the psychologist must come before the techniques of behavior control are fully developed. *Public* concern is more readily discernible at this point as shown by popular articles (Brecher & Brecher, 1961) and the cries of indignation some years back when subliminal stimulation was a going fad.

Carl Rogers has recently been quoted as saying that:

> To hope that the power which is being made available by the behavioral sciences will be exercised by the scientists, or by a benevolent group, seems to me to be a hope little supported by either recent or distant history. It seems far more likely that behavioral scientists, holding their present attitudes, will be in the position of the German rocket scientists specializing in guided missiles. . . . If behavioral scientists are concerned solely with advancing their science, it seems most probable that they will serve the purpose of whatever group has the power (Brecher & Brecher, 1961).

This rather pessimistic quotation is from a popular article in a recent issue of *Harper's* magazine. The authors cite this and other research, particularly the work of Olds on brain stimulation, as evidence for deep concern about the role of the behavioral scientist. In what is perhaps an overdramatization of the situation, yet one which may legitimately express lay concern, they conclude that:

> New methods of controlling behavior now emerging from the laboratory may soon add an awe-inspiring power to enslave us all with our own engineered consent.

Oppenheimer (1956), in comparing the responsibility of the physicist with that of the psychologist, makes the cogent point that:

> The psychologist can hardly do anything without realizing that for him the acquisition of knowledge opens up the most terrifying prospects of controlling what people do and how they think and how they behave and how they feel.

We can approach the problem of social responsibility by asking three basic questions:

1. Is human behavior controllable? Overwhelming experimental evidence in fields of motivation, conditioning, and personality development indicates that this is true.
2. If so, is it desirable or wise for psychologists to continue research in these fields? Psychologists have no choice but to continue their research. The findings can be used just

as meaningfully to help man as to hinder him. Further, methods of counter control can be developed. The danger is *not* in the research findings but in their potential misuse.

3. What safeguards can be incorporated into this type of research? The answer to this is the crux of the psychologist's dilemma. First, a code of ethics such as that of the APA is a good first step, but certainly not enough. An ethical code merely says that the psychologist will not deliberately misuse his findings. It does not go into the more basic question of the psychologist or behavior controller's value system. If we see him as one who is in a position to change or modify others' behavior, this implies a value decision as to what is "good behavior," what is "mental health," and what is desirable adjustment. To deny control is to do a disservice and, in effect, to hide one's head in the sand like the proverbial ostrich. The fact that the behavior controllers are professional individuals is no guarantee that behavior control will not be misused. We have only to turn to the role of German physicians in medical atrocities as evidence of misuse by a supposedly professional group.

Berg (1954) goes into one aspect of the ethical and value problem in discussing principles that should guide the use of human subjects in psychological research. His concern with the problem is an outgrowth of the "barbarous medical experiments" performed on human subjects by Nazi physicians in the name of science. These German physicians were not mere tools, but were leaders in their profession. Berg suggests that future researchers using human subjects adhere to the principles of "consent," "confidence," and "standard procedure." He cites the basic principles governing permissible government experiments laid down at the Nuremberg trials. These are relevant for future discussion of the kinds of behavior permissible, or not permissible, to behavior controllers.

Basically, they are similar to the principles that Roe (1959) pointed out, namely, that *awareness* is a major ingredient in defense against manipulation. Roe makes pertinent comments in stressing the need for man to be aware of himself and the world around him:

> Awareness of our own needs and attitudes is our most effective instrument for maintaining our own integrity and control over our own reactions.

Roe contends that the psychologist's role in changing society should be an active one. She cites a talk by Halpern who reported a survey which showed that an overwhelming number of our young psychologists were interested only in the practice of therapy. Halpern is quoted as follows:

> It seems to me that there is something a bit amiss with a group of scientists who are so overwhelmingly service oriented and who, recognizing that life adjustment has been increasingly complex and difficult, offer to cure the ills resulting from the present state of affairs, but do little or nothing to help society learn how best to meet their interpersonal, emotional and social problems so that the present seemingly all-pervasive disturbances may be avoided.

A somewhat similar view is expressed by Cattell (1948), who also calls for research into ethical values and feels that moral laws can be derived from psychological and physiological investigation of living matter. He does not accept the viewpoint, which he attributes to a majority of psychologists and most laymen, that ethical values lie outside the realm of science. Creegan (1958) also concerns himself with the need for scientific investigation of ethical problems. In comparing the responsibility of the psychologist with that of the atomic physicist he points out that:

> Psychology does not produce nuclear warheads, nor does it produce the apocalyptic birds which may take them to a selected target, but psychology is concerned with human decisions. ...The greatest power in the world is the power of rational decision. Atomic physics deals with the release of great forces, but answers to ethical questions may be the decisive ones for the future of humanity.

Creegan further goes into questions of whether force and hidden persuasion ought to be used for a good cause. Once we have committed ourselves on economic, social, and religious problems, how should we go about implementing our ideas? How does the psychologist define "the good life?" Does the psychologist constitute an ethical elite? Creegan points out that at present it is the physicist who communicates with the public about moral problems, rather than the psychologist. Muller (1958) also feels that values are a legitimate

source of scientific investigation. He disagrees with those who say that man's values are determined by a higher authority outside of himself or those who say that values are a private matter. But Muller is a biologist, not a psychologist.

The attacks on psychological investigators of behavior control are often quite unfair. For example, Krutch (1954) is highly critical of the implications of Skinner's *Walden Two* because of a fear that social control will pass into the hands of experimentalists who are not concerned with moral issues. Yet it is often these experimenters who are most concerned with value problems and who are in a position to approach on an objective basis the whole question of moral and value issues.

We would suggest two major steps be taken at this point. The first is to develop techniques of approaching experimentally the basic problem of social and ethical issues involved in behavior control. One initial approach would be to investigate the attitudes and fantasies of experimenters and therapists toward their own role as behavior controllers in studies in which the effectiveness of their influence can be readily tested. As an example, in our laboratory we are presently devising ways of measuring attitudes toward mental health, "the good life," and applications of science. Fantasy behavior will be elicited in response to special stimuli and reports of role perception and role reaction will be obtained from therapists and from experimenters in psychotherapy, verbal conditioning, and other behavior controlling experiments. The attitude measures will be associated with behavioral ratings of these "controllers" and subject responsivity to them. These studies are undertaken within a framework of investigating the variables that go into resisting influence situations.

A second major step in dealing with this problem is communication between the general public and the research investigators. In this field, particularly, researchers must keep in contact with each other. Any kind of research which is kept secret, such as work in sensory deprivation, is to be deplored. Furthermore, it is the psychologist-researcher who should undertake the task of contact with the public rather than leaving it to sensationalists and popularizers.

In summary, behavior control represents a relatively new, important, and very useful development in psychological research. It also may be horribly misused unless the psychologist is constantly alert to what is taking place in society and unless he is active in investigating and controlling the social uses of behavior control.

REFERENCES

Bandura, A. Psychotherapy as a learning process. *Psychol. Bull.,* 1961, 58, 143–159.

Berg, I. A. The use of human subjects in psychological research. *Amer. Psychologist,* 1954, 9, 108–111.

Brecher, Ruth, & Brecher, E. The happiest creatures on earth? *Harper's,* 1961, 222, 85–90.

Cattell, R. B. Ethics and the social sciences. *Amer. Psychologist,* 1948, 3, 193–198.

Creegan, R. F. Concerning professional ethics. *Amer. Psychologist,* 1958, 13, 272–275.

Frank, J. D. *Persuasion and healing: a comparative study of psychotherapy* (Baltimore: Johns Hopkins Press, 1961).

Holt, R. R., & Luborsky, L. *Personality patterns of psychiatrists.* New York: Basic Books, 1958.

Jourard, S. I-thou relationship versus manipulation in counseling and psychotherapy. *J. Indiv. Psychol.,* 1959, 15, 174–179.

Jourard, S. On the problem of reinforcement by the psychotherapist of healthy behavior in the patient. In F. J. Shaw (Ed.), *Behavioristic approaches to counseling and psychotherapy: A Southeastern Psychological Association symposium.* University: Univ. Alabama Press, 1961.

Kanfer, F. H. Comments on learning in psychotherapy. *Psychol. Rep.,* 1961, 9, 681–699.

Kelly, E. L., & Fiske, D. W. *The prediction of performance in clinical psychology.* Ann Arbor: Univer. Michigan Press, 1951.

Krasner, L. Studies of the conditioning of verbal behavior. *Psychol. Bull.,* 1958, 55, 148–170.

Krasner, L. The therapist as a social reinforcement machine. Paper presented to second Conference on Research in Psychotherapy, Chapel Hill: University of North Carolina, May 1961.

Krutch, J. W. *The measure of man.* Indianapolis, Ind.: Bobbs, Merrill, 1954.

Lowe, C. M. Value orientations: An ethical dilemma. *Amer. Psychologist,* 1959, 14, 687–693.

Marmor, J. Psychoanalytic therapy as an educational process: Common denominators in the therapeutic approaches of different psychoanalytic "schools." Paper presented to the Academy of Psychoanalysis, Chicago, May 1961.

May, R. Historical and philosophical presuppositions for understanding therapy. In O. H. Mowrer (Ed.) *Psychotherapy theory and research.* New York: Ronald Press, 1953.

Muller, H. J. Human values in relation to evolution. *Science,* 1958, 127, 625–629.

Oppenheimer, J. R. Analogy in science. *Amer. Psychologist.* 1956, 11, 127–135

Papanek, H. Ethical values in psychotherapy. *J. Indiv. Psychol.,* 1958, 14, 160–166.

Patterson, C. H. The place of values in counseling and psychotherapy. *J. Counsel. Psychol.,* 1958, 5, 216–223.

Roe, Anne. Man's forgotten weapon. *Amer. Psychologist,* 1959, 14, 261–266.

Rogers, C. R. Persons or science: A philosophical question. *Amer. Psychologist,* 1955, 10, 267–278.

Rogers, C. R., & Skinner, B. F. Some issues concerning the control of human behavior: A symposium. *Science,* 1956, 124, 1057–1066.

Rosenthal, D. Changes in some moral values following psychotherapy. *J. Consult. Psychol.,* 1955, 19, 431–436.

Rotter, J. B. Psychotherapy. *Annu. Rev. Psychol.,* 1961, 11, 318–414

Salzinger, K. Experimental manipulation of verbal behavior: A review. *J. Gen. Psychol.,* 1959, 61, 65–94.

Shaffer, L. F. Of whose reality I cannot doubt. *Amer. Psychologist,* 1953, 8, 608–623.

Skinner, B. F. *Walden two.* New York: Macmillan, 1948.

Skinner, B. F. *Science and human behavior.* New York: Macmillan, 1953.

Vandenberg, S. G. Great expectations or the future of psychology (as seen in science fiction). *Amer. Psychologist,* 1956, 11, 339–342.

Watson, G. Moral issues in psychotherapy. *Amer. Psychologist,* 1958, 13, 574–576.

Whitehorn, J. C. Goals of psychotherapy. In E. A. Rubinstein & M. B. Parloff (Eds.) *Research in psychotherapy.* Washington, D.C.: American Psychological Association, 1959.

RECOMMENDED FURTHER READING

Allport, Gordon W.: *The Nature of Prejudice;* Reading, Mass., Addison-Wesley 1954

―――― and Leo Postman: *The Psychology of Rumor;* New York, Holt Rinehart & Winston 1947

Bennis, Warren, *et al.* (eds.): *Interpersonal Dynamics;* Homewood, Ill., Dorsey Press 1964

Berg, I. A. and B. M. Bass (eds.): *Conformity and Deviation;* New York, Harper & Row 1961

Berkowitz, Leonard: "The Effects of Observing Violence"; *Scientific American,* February 1964

Biderman, A. D. and H. Zimmer (eds.): *The Manipulation of Human Behavior;* New York, John Wiley 1961

*Brown, James A. C.: *Techniques of Persuasion;* Baltimore, Penguin Books 1963

Brown, Roger: *Social Psychology;* New York, Macmillan 1965

*Bruner, Jerome S.: "The Control of Human Behavior" in his *On Knowing;* Cambridge, Mass., Harvard University Press 1962

Cohen, A. R.: *Attitude Change and Social Influence;* New York, Basic Books 1964

Fraiberg, Selma: "The Science of Thought Control"; *Commentary,* May 1962

Greenwald, A. G. (ed.): *Psychological Foundations of Attitudes;* New York, Academic Press 1968

*Hoffer, Eric: *The True Believer;* New York, Harper 1951

Janis, Irving L. and Carl I. Hovland (eds.): *Personality and Persuasibility;* New Haven, Yale University Press 1969

Kelman, Herbert (ed.): *International Behavior: A Social Psychological Analysis;* New York, Holt, Rinehart & Winston 1965

*Kozol, Jonathan: *Death At An Early Age: The Destruction of the Hearts and Minds of Negro Children in the Boston Public Schools;* Boston, Houghton Mifflin 1967

*Le Bon, Gustave: *The Crowd: A Study in the Popular Mind;* London, Ernest Benn 1952 (first published 1896)

Lifton, Robert Jay: *Thought Reform and the Psychology of Totalism;* New York, Norton 1961

Lindzey, Gardner and Eliot Aronson (eds.): *Handbook of Social Psychology* (Revised Ed.); Reading, Mass., Addison-Wesley 1967

London, Perry: *Behavior Control;* New York, Harper & Row 1969

*Mackay, Charles: *Memoirs of Extraordinary Popular Delusions and the Madness of Crowds;* London, Richard Bentley 1841

Osgood, Charles E.: *An Alternative to War or Surrender;* Urbana, Ill., University of Illinois Press 1962

Pettigrew, Thomas: *A Profile of the Negro American;* Princeton, N.J., Van Nostrand Reinhold 1964

*Rudé, George: *The Crowd in History: A Study of Popular Disturbances in France and England 1730–1848;* New York, John Wiley 1964

Schein, Edgar: "The Chinese Indoctrination Program for Prisoners of War: A Study of Attempted Brainwashing"; *Psychiatry, 19* (1956), 149–172

————, I. Schneier and C. H. Barker: *Coercive Persuasion;* New York, Norton 1961

Skinner, B. F.: "Freedom and Control of Men"; *American Scholar, 25* (1955–56), 45–65

Smelser, Neil J.: *The Theory of Collective Behavior;* New York, Free Press 1962

Steiner, I. D. and M. Fishbein (eds.): *Current Studies in Social Psychology;* New York, Holt, Rinehart & Winston 1965

* Paperback edition available.